EUROPEAN CONSUMER ACCESS TO JUSTICE REVISITED

European Consumer Access to Justice Revisited takes into account both procedural and substantive law questions in order to give the term 'access to justice' an enhanced meaning. Specifically, it analyses developments and recent trends in EU consumer law and aims to evaluate their potential for increasing consumer confidence in the cross-border market. Via a critical assessment of the advantages and disadvantages of the means initiated at the EU level, the author highlights possible detriments to the cross-border business-to-consumer (B2C) market. To remedy this, he introduces an alternative method of creating a legal framework that facilitates B2C transactions in the EU – 'access to justice 2.0'.

STEFAN WRBKA is Associate Professor for European and Comparative Private Law at Kyushu University, Fukuoka, Japan. His principal field of academic research concerns various aspects of consumer protection law, with a focus on developments within the European Union.

EUROPEAN CONSUMER ACCESS TO JUSTICE REVISITED

STEFAN WRBKA

CAMBRIDGE
UNIVERSITY PRESS

CAMBRIDGE
UNIVERSITY PRESS

University Printing House, Cambridge CB2 8BS, United Kingdom

Cambridge University Press is part of the University of Cambridge.

It furthers the University's mission by disseminating knowledge in the pursuit of education, learning and research at the highest international levels of excellence.

www.cambridge.org
Information on this title: www.cambridge.org/9781107072374

© Cambridge University Press 2015

First published 2015

Printed in the United Kingdom by Clays, St Ives plc

A catalogue record for this publication is available from the British Library

Library of Congress Cataloguing in Publication data
Wrbka, Stefan, 1976– author.
European consumer access to justice revisited / Stefan Wrbka.
pages   cm
Includes bibliographical references and index.
ISBN 978-1-107-07237-4 (hardback)
1. Consumer protection–Law and legislation–European Union countries.
2. Due process of law–European Union countries.   3. Legal services–European Union countries.   I. Title.
KJE6577.W73 2014
343.2407′1–dc23
2014032250

ISBN 978-1-107-07237-4 Hardback

Rie, Lisa and Leo

CONTENTS

List of tables   xii
Preface   xiii
Acknowledgments   xv
Abbreviations   xvii

PART I   Setting the scene: access to justice 2.0   1

1 At the very outset   3

2 Access to justice 2.0: breaking it into pieces   5

Access   5

Justice   5
   Non-valuing justice   6
   Value-oriented justice   6
     Hans Kelsen   8
     Aristotle   10
     John Rawls   13
     Value-oriented justice – key observations for further
       arguments   16

Access to justice   18
   Taken literally   18
   Access to justice in the course of time   19
   The more recent traditional discussion at the EU level   25

2.0   27

Access to justice 2.0   27

PART II   Procedural law – the traditional pillar of access
to justice 2.0   31

3 A brief outline of developments at the pan-EU level   33

4   **Prime examples**   40

The Injunctions Directive (1998/2009)   40

The Legal Aid Directive (2003)   53

The Regulation on Consumer Protection Cooperation (2004)   60

The Small Claims Regulation (2007)   71

Alternative Dispute Resolution (2008/2013)   83
Initial ADR trends at the EU level and the 2008 Mediation Directive   83
The ADR Directive (2013)   90
The ODR Regulation (2013)   97

5   **Compensatory collective redress – the next step?**   102

The road towards the Green Paper on Consumer Collective Redress   102

From the Green Paper on Consumer Collective Redress to the Commission's Collective Redress Recommendation   109

Multilayer interests   118
Multilayer interests – a definition   118
Multilayer interests in the debate on collective redress   121

Scattered damages v. mass damages   124

The answer(s)   132
General remarks   132
Scattered damages   133
Mass damages   140
Further questions   143

6   **Where do we go from here?**   150

PART III   Substantive law – complementing access to justice 2.0   153

7   **Widening the scope of the value-oriented justice discussion**   155

8   **Substantive consumer law making over time**   162

9 Recent trends and developments   169

The Directive on Consumer Rights   169
Background and genesis   169
A brief overview of the CRD   178

The consumer acquis beyond the CRD and towards
the CESL   186

10 The Common European Sales Law   190

The genesis of the proposal on a Common European Sales
Law or: the long and winding road   190

The CESL Regulation Proposal in a nutshell   208

A brief analysis of the CESL Regulation Proposal   215
Recalling the assumptions of the Commission   215
First assumption: simplification of the legal environment for
traders, reduction of business costs and lower final prices for
consumers   217
Second assumption: the CESL will lead to improved certainty for
consumers   221
Third assumption: the CESL is clearly needed   225
Fourth assumption: the CESL will be a bilaterally voluntary,
secondary regime   229
Fifth assumption: the CESL will guarantee a high(er) standard of
consumer protection without exception   234
Sixth assumption: the CESL will necessarily solve the 'problems'
caused by Rome I   237
First Scenario: the parties do not agree on any
applicable law   243
Second Scenario: the parties agree on the law of the trader's
home Member State without reference to its CESL   243
Third Scenario: the parties agree on the law of the consumer's
home Member State without reference to its CESL   244
Fourth Scenario: the parties agree on the law of
the consumer's home Member State and its CESL   244
Fifth Scenario: the parties agree on the law of the trader's home
Member State and its CESL   245
Sixth Scenario: the parties agree on the CESL without reference
to either Member State's legislative regime   252
Summarising the true consequences of the contractual choice of
the applicable law in cross-border B2C transactions   252

The Common European Sales Law after the CESL
    Regulation Proposal   255

11 Summarising comments on the defragmentation of
    substantive consumer laws in the context of the CRD
    and the CESL   263

PART IV   Consumer access to justice 2.0 – a
    multidimensional framework   265

12 From the current state of consumer law to consumer
    access to justice 2.0   267

Recapitulating the rationale behind the Commission's
    efforts to regulate cross-border B2C trade   267

Recapitulating the situation with respect to procedural EU
    (consumer) laws   269

Recapitulating the situation with respect to substantive EU
    (consumer) laws   274

Taking a more comprehensive approach for the sake of
    consumer access to justice   276

13 The justice debate and consumer legislation   280

Expressions of justice   280

Social justice and consumer access to justice 2.0   281

Individual well-being, consumer confidence, access to
    justice 2.0 and EU consumer law making   283

14 (Responses to) counter-arguments to third-party
    intervention   284

Paternalism v. liberalism   284

Attempts to answer the concerns towards third-party
    intervention in consumer issues   286
    What needs to be answered   286
    Soft paternalism as an attempt to mediate between hard
        paternalism and classical liberalism   286
    Justice-related thoughts on mandatory law   288
    The need for alternative third-party intervention in B2C
        issues   291

Reconciling social justice and market stimulation   295

15 Consumer empowerment 296

A definition of consumer empowerment and general
thoughts on how to achieve it 296

Consumer empowerment in the context of access to justice
2.0 – applying an enhanced regime of consumer
empowerment 301

Consumer empowerment as an attempt to facilitate B2C
transactions 301

The facilitating intermediaries approach 302

General thoughts on ECC-Net as a prime example for
a facilitating intermediary in cross-border B2C
trade 302

ECC-Net: current activities 303

ECC-Net: current status 306

The 2011 ECC-Net evaluation report on how to improve the
impact of ECC-Net 309

Thoughts on the future of ECC-Net 312

The Enterprise Europe Network (EEN) 317

The legislative approach 319

The procedural law pillar 319

The substantive law pillar 323

16 Lessons to be drawn 333

Bibliography 335
Name index 386
Subject index 389

TABLES

1 Comparison of scattered damages and mass damages 130
2 Comparison of the 'old' v. 'new' approach in substantive EU law making 168
3 Consequences of the contractual choices of the applicable law in cross-border B2C contracts according to the Commission 242
4 Comparison of the consequences of the contractual choices of the applicable law in cross-border B2C contracts according to the Commission and in reality 253
5 Selected prominent flaws of the tools discussed in Part II of this book 271
6 Number of personnel (in FTEs) per ECC in 2009 and 2013 308

PREFACE

'Access to justice' is a term that embodies a concept purporting to an ideal situation. Like happiness or satisfaction, access to justice is something that most people are looking for but that nobody can really explain. At least, there is no standardised way to describe it. What is meant by 'justice' and what by 'access to justice'?

In a legal context, access to justice traditionally refers to ideas closely interlinked with legal aid tools, or more generally speaking, to mechanisms that aim to empower the 'underprivileged' to access the judicial system. Other procedural mechanisms, such as collective redress or alternative dispute resolution tools, are also commonly found in this context and take into consideration additional obstacles to accessing courts and other dispute resolution institutions. This is especially true in the field of consumer law where various issues that can impact on whether individuals pursue their claims are particularly strong. These issues include a lack of legal information, a lack of confidence in dispute resolution, the financial risks of losing a case (in cases where the loser-pays principle applies) or low amounts in dispute. Contemporary EU policy-making aims to remove some of these obstacles.

More recently, however, discussions on how to better benefit consumers via substantive law have given fresh impetus to the access to justice debate, which is shifting from a discussion on justice understood as the judicial system towards a broader value-oriented understanding of justice. Thus, parameters such as substantive 'fairness' and 'equality' are more strongly infiltrating current debates. The question in this regard is whether legislative trends at the EU level ensure that consumer interests are properly considered in the law-making process.

In addition, both recent procedural and substantive law trends transcend the mere legal discussion. They also raise political, social and economic issues and relate to questions such as the 'correct' balancing of interests between weaker private actors and bigger players, the possible threat of sacrificing consumer interests for the sake of primarily satisfying those of traders in easy market access and the quest to raise consumer confidence in the internal market. The literature (thus far) is divided about the best possible means to answer these questions.

The purpose of this book is to add value to the discussion by providing new food for thought. The idea for this stems from the practical experience I have collected during my time working in law firms and the private sector before joining academia. Having seen how law works in practice, and not only on paper, has surely enhanced my research because it has allowed me to better understand the actual issues faced by traders and consumers when trying to transact with each other. The book aims to facilitate the quest for the most appropriate future of EU consumer law by examining EU consumer protection from a different angle. The key to this approach is a refined understanding of consumer access to justice. This revised concept takes procedural and substantive consumer law matters comprehensively into consideration and analyses both from a broader justice perspective that ranges from the judicial system itself to moral expressions of justice (such as satisfaction or fairness) without neglecting the traders' wish to reach the widest audience possible. The ultimate goal of the analysis is to introduce a multidimensional framework for EU consumer protection that synergises different solutions that (as a total package) could hopefully maximise both consumer satisfaction and the potential of the internal market.

Although the book tries to be as up to date as possible, I should note that the legislation and legislative developments analysed within are those as of June 2014. As far as later trends are concerned, I truly hope that this book will be read in time to implement the key ideas I introduce in the following chapters.

ACKNOWLEDGMENTS

During the research and writing process, I have received invaluable feedback from many people who helped to bring this project to fruition. First and foremost I would like to thank my dear colleague Mark Fenwick for the extensive exchange of opinion and his critical comments on my various arguments given in this book. This has helped me to scrutinise my own argumentation and to refine it in more detail. Several other people and institutions have also contributed to the realisation of this project. I would like to thank them here (in no particular order): Professor Geraint Howells and Professor Sebastien Borghetti for their feedback on the issue of transaction costs and final product prices; Professor Jürgen Basedow for his feedback on the situation in the newer EU Member States with respect to consumer contract law; Professor Monika Hinteregger whose encouragement provided me with motivation throughout this project; Professor Kunihiro Nakata for whetting my appetite for consumer law more than a decade ago; Beate Pirker-Hörmann from the Austrian Federal Ministry of Social Security, Generations and Consumer Protection for providing me with insights into national policy-making with respect to collective actions and consumer contract law; the European Consumers' Organisation (BEUC) for feedback on the latest trends in consumer law policy-making from the perspective of consumer interest groups at the EU level; the European Consumer Centres Network (ECC-Net) and the local European Consumer Centres (ECCs) for providing me with first-hand information and data related to their work; the Enterprise Europe Network (EEN) for information about third-party assistance for traders provided within its framework in cross-border trade; and both the Japan Society for the Promotion of Science (JSPS) and the European Union Institute in Japan, Kyushu (EUIJ-Kyushu) for providing me with generous funding to carry out the underlying research.

Special thanks go also to Cambridge University Press, especially to Kim Hughes, who has accompanied and supported this book project from a very early stage. I would also like to thank the anonymous referees from Cambridge University Press, who trusted in this project from day one and, with their constructive feedback, added important new perspectives. Also Katie Stallard should not be left unmentioned. I would like to thank her for support in linguistic matters.

Last but not least I would also like to thank my family for their understanding and patience with me throughout the whole process.

I truly hope that this book will contribute to further discussions and developments of EU consumer law and consumer access to justice.

ABBREVIATIONS

ABGB	*Allgemeines Bürgerliches Gesetzbuch* (Austrian Civil Code)
ADR	alternative dispute resolution
ADR Directive	Directive on alternative dispute resolution for consumer disputes
AK	*Arbeiterkammer*
ALI	American Law Institute
B2B	business-to-business
B2C	business-to-consumer
BEUC	*Bureau Européen des Unions de Consommateurs* (European Consumers' Organisation)
BGB	*Bürgerliches Gesetzbuch* (German Civil Code)
BGH	*Bundesgerichtshof* (The Federal Court of Justice of Germany)
C2B	consumer-to-business
CESL	Common European Sales Law
CFR	Common Frame of Reference
CISG	United Nations Convention on the International Sale of Goods
CJEU	Court of Justice of the European Union
CoPECL	Joint Network on European Private Law
CPC Network	Regulation on Consumer Protection Cooperation Network
CPC Regulation	Regulation on Consumer Protection Cooperation
CPC System	Regulation on Consumer Protection Cooperation System
CPEC	Consumer Policy Evaluation Consortium
CRD	Directive on Consumer Rights
CSD	Consumer Sales Directive
CTM	Community Trade Mark
DCFR	Draft Common Frame of Reference
DG COMP	Directorate-General for Competition
DG ENTR	Directorate-General for Enterprise and Industry
DG IPOL	Directorate-General for Internal Policies
DG JUST	Directorate-General for Justice
DG SANCO	Directorate-General for Health and Consumers
EC	European Community
ECC	European Consumer Centre

ECC-Net	European Consumer Centres Network
ECHR	European Convention on Human Rights
ECON	Economic and Monetary Affairs Committee
ECU	European Currency Unit
EEC	European Economic Community
EEJ-Net	Network for the extra-judicial settlement of consumer disputes
EEN	Enterprise Europe Network
EGBGB	*Einführungsgesetz zum Bürgerlichen Gesetzbuch* (German Introductory Act to the Civil Code)
EJN	European Judicial Network in Civil and Commercial Matters
ELI	European Law Institute
EMOTA	European Multi-channel and Online Trade Association
ESCP	European Small Claims Procedure
EU	European Union
EUIJ-Kyushu	European Union Institute in Japan, Kyushu
EUR	Euro
FRA	European Union Agency for Fundamental Rights
FTE	full-time equivalent
GWB	*Gesetz gegen Wettbewerbsbeschränkungen* (German Act Against Restraints of Competition)
IMCO	Internal Market and Consumer Protection Committee
JSPS	Japan Society for the Promotion of Science
JURI	Legal Affairs Committee
KapMuG	*Kapitalanleger-Musterverfahrensgesetz* (German Capital Markets Model Case Act)
KSchG	*Konsumentenschutzgesetz* (Austrian Consumer Protection Act)
MEP	Member of the European Parliament
ODR	online dispute resolution
ODR Regulation	Regulation on online dispute resolution for consumer disputes
OFT	Office of Fair Trading
OI	optional instrument
OJ	Official Journal of the European Union
PLD	Product Liability Directive
SE	*Societas Europaea*
SGECC	Study Group on a European Civil Code
SIN	Standard Information Notice
SMEs	small and medium-sized enterprises
TFEU	Treaty on the Functioning of the European Union
UCPD	Unfair Commercial Practices Directive
UCTD	Unfair Contract Terms Directive
UNIDROIT	International Institute for the Unification of Private Law
UWG	*Gesetz gegen den unlauteren Wettbewerb* (German Act Against Unfair Competition)
VKI	*Verein für Konsumenteninformation*

PART I

Setting the scene: access to justice 2.0

And, if it is true that effective, not merely formal, equality before the law is the basic ideal of our epoch, the access-to-justice approach can only lead to a judicial product of far greater 'beauty' – or better quality – than that we now have.[1]

(Mauro Cappelletti, 1927–2004, and Bryant Garth, 1949–)

---

[1] M. Cappelletti and B. Garth, 'Access to Justice: the Worldwide Movement to Make Rights More Effective – A General Report' in M. Cappelletti and B. Garth (eds.), *Access to Justice – A World Survey, Book 1* (Alphen aan den Rijn: Slijthoff and Noordhoff, 1978), p. 124.

1

At the very outset

Teaching someone a foreign language and teaching a child to speak require the ability to explain terminology in a plain, simple and intelligible language. Writing a law book, in the present case a book about access to justice in the context of European consumer law, cannot, of course, be directly compared to teaching a language. Nevertheless, the situation more or less resembles language teaching, especially if the book is to be understood not only by legal scholars specialising in the particular field at hand, but by a broader audience. Even if one wanted to address only the first group, writing a book on the somewhat vague term 'access to justice' would clearly benefit from a precise definition. The problem with this, however, is that there is not just one legitimate definition of access to justice. While it can be assumed that the meaning of 'access' is easy to understand, the term 'justice' can be interpreted in different ways; it has been a prominent object of academic writing, not only in legal academia and in recent times, but also in various other fields and for hundreds of years, as will be seen in the course of this book.

To make matters even more complicated, combining both terms, 'access' and 'justice', leads to a number of further questions of how to define the result. 'Access to justice' reveals some additional and controversial issues, especially in light of recent developments in the field of European consumer law, which is why this book was written. It will define and discuss the issues at hand and offer additional food for thought. At the same time, the analysis in this book tries to provide the reader with an alternative definition of consumer access to justice by taking stronger account of more recent developments. For the sake of simplicity, I decided to refer to this concept as 'access to justice 2.0'. The key question in this context is whether the chosen path leads in the 'right' direction for consumers in Europe or, to put it differently, whether the recent trends provide consumers with the proper procedural *and* substantive rights to effectively protect their interests.

To avoid a leap in the dark, I should first clarify the meaning of access to justice in the present context. This will also answer the question that the attentive reader would certainly have: what does 'access to justice 2.0' mean? To answer this, it makes sense to take a brief look at the components of the term: access, justice, access to justice and 2.0. This will allow the construction of a legal framework, or at least offer some parameters to analyse current trends in the field of European consumer law from the perspective of the consumers' benefit.

Access to justice 2.0: breaking it into pieces

Access

The first component of 'access to justice 2.0', access, might cause the fewest difficulties. It can be generally understood as the chance or means to reach or accomplish something. The *Oxford English Dictionary*, for example, defines access as '[t]he action of going or coming to or into; coming into the presence of, or into contact with; approach, entrance'.[1]

Access thus stands for some kind of gateway or movement, leading from one point to another or from an actual state to a different one, from the viewpoint of the acceding person (hopefully) to a desired condition. One can also say that access, if granted, enables a person to enter a certain condition.

Justice

Unlike access, the term justice can have several different meanings. It is clearly beyond the scope of this analysis to go into too much detail, but taking a slightly closer look will make it easier to understand the argumentation in later chapters.

For the purpose of the current discussion, one can basically distinguish between two divergent definitions. Several non-English languages clearly draw a linguistic line between the two definitions. English, however, uses the word justice for two, not necessarily always intertwined concepts: one rather technical definition free from value judgements, which for the sake of simplicity I will refer to as 'non-valuing justice' in the context of this book, and a definition that is more morally inclined or with added values, which I shall call 'value-oriented justice'. Although differing in meaning, both definitions have their own *raison d'être* when discussing access to justice.

---

[1] J. A. Simpson and E. S. C. Weiner (eds.), *The Oxford English Dictionary* (2nd edn, Oxford University Press, 1991), p. 72.

Non-valuing justice

The non-valuing justice concept can be seen as a synonym for the court system, its proceedings and judges, who play the leading role in solving disputes brought to court. The *Oxford English Dictionary* refers to this meaning as the '[j]udicial administration of law'[2] when referring to dispute resolution proceedings or as the 'administrator of justice'[3] as an equivalent for professional judges and other members of the judicature.

In this sense, one can understand the term justice as standing for the judicial apparatus, its main decision-making actors or court proceedings. Non-valuing justice does not take any value judgement into consideration, but rather refers to the judicial system in a more technical way.

Value-oriented justice

Justice can, however, also have a more philosophical or interdisciplinary meaning. If one understands it in this way, then justice can be described as fairness, equality or moral correctness. The *Oxford English Dictionary* further uses terms such as 'uprightness, equity'[4] or '[t]he quality of being (morally) just or righteous'[5] as synonyms for this second understanding of justice. To distinguish it from non-valuing justice, it might be helpful to refer to it as 'value-oriented justice' to differentiate it from a plain, basically non-valuing definition of justice.

One might be tempted to argue that value-oriented justice resembles what others call 'substantive justice'.[6] Value-oriented justice in the context of this book, however, goes beyond this concept and also includes certain

---

[2] *Ibid.*, p. 326.   [3] *Ibid.*   [4] *Ibid.*   [5] *Ibid.*

[6] Allan Horwitz and Michael Wasserman define substantive justice as a concept 'to decide particular cases on their individual merits or to refer to substantive goals' (A. Horwitz and M. Wasserman, 'Formal Rationality, Substantive Justice, and Discrimination', *Law and Human Behavior*, 4 (1980), 103, 104). Michael Quinn links substantive justice to 'the reasons which ground the rules' which, under the concept of formal justice, require a 'consistent application' (M. Quinn, *Justice and Egalitarianism: Formal and Substantive Equality in Some Recent Theories of Justice* (New York: Garland, 1991), p. 6). For further definitions and comments see, for example, David Lewis Schaefer's analysis of substantive justice in D. L. Schaefer, 'Procedural Versus Substantive Justice: Rawls and Nozick', *Social Philosophy and Policy*, 24 (2007), 164–86; Rawls's reference to substantive justice in J. Rawls, *A Theory of Justice* (Cambridge, MA: Harvard University Press, 1971), pp. 58–60. For a purely legal context see, for example, Wojciech Sadurski's definition of substantive justice as 'the justice of outcome [of a legal process]' (W. Sadurski, 'Social Justice and Legal Justice' in H.-W. Micklitz (ed.), *The Many Concepts of Social Justice in European Private Law* (Cheltenham: Edward Elgar, 2011), p. 73).

ideas of formal justice, such as applying legal rules equally in comparable cases.[7] Thus, for the later argumentation, it might make more sense to draw the distinguishing line in accordance with English dictionaries at the point where they differentiate between the mere technical apparatus of the judiciary on the one hand and a more value-centred system on the other. As will be shown later, this might better suit the more comprehensive justice debate in this book.

In the literature, one can also find other ways to refer to 'value-oriented justice'. In their comparative study of European access to justice concepts, Eva Storskrubb and Jaques Ziller, for example, call it 'Justice with a capital J ... expressed in German as *Gerechtigkeit* rather than *Justiz*'.[8] Although

---

[7] Agnes Heller refers to formal justice (or what she calls 'static justice') as follows: '[T]he norms and rules which constitute a human cluster, should be applied consistently and continuously to each and every member of that cluster. Members of the same cluster are constituted as equals ... while members who belong to different and interrelated clusters are constituted as unequals' (A. Heller, 'Rights, Modernity, Democracy', *Cardozo Law Review*, 11 (1990), 1377, 1385. For some of her more detailed argumentation see A. Heller, *Beyond Justice* (Oxford: Basil Blackwell, 1987), pp. 1–47). John Rawls defines formal justice as the 'impartial and consistent administration of laws and institutions, whatever their substantive principles [are]' (Rawls, *Theory of Justice*, p. 58). In a legal–political context, this kind of justice can further be referred to as the 'equality of the citizens before the law' (K. Popper, *The Open Society & Its Enemies* (1st single-volume edn, Princeton University Press, 2013), p. 88). Craig L. Carr refers to formal justice as the 'equal treatment' of subjects and argues that the concept 'is ... reducible to the unbiased, impartial, and consistent adherence to rule or principle' (C. L. Carr, 'The Concept of Formal Justice', *Philosophical Studies*, 39 (1981), 211, 222 and 223). As I will explain in the following, determining 'equality' definitely requires some kind of value judgement. Nevertheless, formal justice must be distinguished from substantive justice. The latter goes beyond the equal application of rules and also touches upon questions of material 'fairness' or 'justness'. David Lyons comments on the difference between these two concepts by defining formal justice as 'identif[ying] conformity to law not with justice overall [note: this refers to 'substantive justice'] but with justice in the administration of the law, and thus with justice in the conduct of public officials' (D. Lyons, 'On Formal Justice', *Cornell Law Review*, 58 (1973), 833, 836). John Rawls succinctly explains that '[t]reating similar cases similarly [note: this refers to formal justice] is not a sufficient guarantee of substantive justice' (Rawls, *Theory of Justice*, p. 59). Rawls adds that 'the strength of the claims of formal justice, of obedience to system, clearly depend upon the substantive justice of institutions and the possibilities of their reform' (*ibid.*). For a description of the interplay between formal justice, the equal application of procedural rights, the rule of law and substantive justice see T. Campbell in P. Cane and J. Conaghan (eds.), *The New Oxford Companion to Law* (Oxford University Press, 2008), p. 660, where it is explained that formal justice understood as a 'narrow conception of the rule of law ... does not require any judgment as to the justice of the rules themselves ..., but strong feelings of resentment are aroused when an authorized rule is not applied in the same manner to all persons who are similarly situated. Moreover, formal justice may be necessary for the attainment of substantive justice'.

[8] E. Storskrubb and J. Ziller, 'Access to Justice in European Comparative Law' in F. Francioni (ed.), *Access to Justice as a Human Right* (Oxford University Press, 2007), p. 188.

law, at least to some extent, does undeniably function as a tool to guarantee certain values,[9] or, as Roger Cotterrell puts it, 'promotes justice',[10] value-oriented justice goes beyond mere legal concepts and also touches upon sociological, political or philosophical ideas.

In all objectivity, value-oriented justice cannot be defined in a standardised way. It does make sense though, to briefly look at some influential commentators in the long-established debate on value-oriented justice. The selection is, undeniably, not exhaustive and cannot do 'justice' to all influential commentators – it would clearly go beyond the purpose and scope of this book to do so. Nevertheless, the short excursion will hopefully make it easier to understand some of the underlying ideas of the concept of value-oriented justice as used in this book.

Hans Kelsen

Admittedly, Hans Kelsen, especially with his *Pure Theory of Law*,[11] cannot be regarded as a true advocate of value-oriented justice.[12] However, he does not deny the fact that the concept of value-oriented justice is heavily debated when he, on a different occasion, vividly comments that '[n]o other question has been discussed so passionately; no other question has caused so much precious blood and so many bitter tears to be shed; no other question has been the object of so much intensive thinking by the most illustrious thinkers from Plato to Kant'.[13]

Kelsen also rightly realises that it is very difficult, maybe even impossible, to come forward with a one-size-fits-all definition of justice. In his quest to find an answer to the question of what (value-oriented) justice is, Kelsen comes to the following conclusion:

> I started … with the question as to what is justice. Now, at … [the] end I am quite aware that I have not answered it. My only excuse is that in

---

[9] With respect to European contract law the Study Group on Social Justice in European Private Law comments that 'any system of contract law expresses a set of values, which strives to be coherent, and which is regarded as fundamental to the political morality of each country' (Study Group on Social Justice in European Private Law, 'Social Justice in European Contract Law: a Manifesto', *European Law Journal*, 10 (2004), 653, 656). For a more general discussion on the interplay between law and equality and law and morality and values in general see S. Jørgensen, *On Justice and Law* (Aarhus University Press, 1996), pp. 96–8 and 103–5; S. Ratnapala, *Jurisprudence* (2nd edn, Cambridge University Press, 2013).

[10] R. Cotterrell, *The Sociology of Law: An Introduction* (London: Butterworths, 1984), p. 73.

[11] H. Kelsen, *Reine Rechtslehre* (Leipzig: Franz Deuticke, 1934).

[12] See D. Miller, *Social Justice* (Oxford University Press, 1976), p. 17.

[13] H. Kelsen, 'What Is Justice?' in H. Kelsen (ed.), *What Is Justice? Collected Essays* (Berkeley, CA: University of California Press, 1957), p. 1.

this respect I am in the best of company. It would have been more than presumptuous to make the reader believe that I could succeed where the most illustrious thinkers have failed. And, indeed, I do not know, and I cannot say what justice is, the absolute justice for which mankind is longing. I must acquiesce in a relative justice and I can only say what justice is to me. ... [J]ustice, to me, is that social order under whose protection the search for truth can prosper. 'My' justice, then, is the justice of freedom, the justice of peace, the justice of democracy – the justice of tolerance.[14]

As can be seen from this statement, Kelsen differentiates between two forms of justice, absolute and relative justice, and claims that only the second type can exist. With respect to the first, Kelsen argues that justice can neither mean absolute happiness[15] nor absolute equality, understood as the postulate according to which the legal order should, in any event, treat every person in exactly the same way,[16] nor can it stand for a state of absolute justness.[17] In answer to two philosophical schools of thought – he refers to them as 'metaphysical-religious' and '(pseudo)rationalistic'[18] – Kelsen explains that solving the question of what justice is requires a value judgement. However, as values cannot be absolute in the sense of being shared by every single individual living on this planet, justice cannot be defined in an absolute way.[19] Thus, both the metaphysical-religious approach, based on transcendentally existing absolute values, and its (pseudo)rationalistic counterpart, trying to explain justice with the help of rational thinking, must fail, as they, according to Kelsen, would presuppose that absolute values exist.

Still, Kelsen admits that certain *relative* values can be found in every society. General or societal values are the outcome of a certain kind of trade-off between conflicting individual values and interests. They lead to relative justice, a concept that results from majority decisions and that could be used to achieve and secure a stable society. Understood in such a way, justice is a flexible system, which might lead to different results depending on the cultural or geographical background, and one that can change from one generation to the next or even within the same generation, if the outer parameters are altered.

---

[14] *Ibid.*, p. 24.
[15] '[I]t is ... inevitable that the happiness of one individual will, at some time, be directly in conflict with that of another' (*ibid.*, p. 2).
[16] However, this, according to Kelsen, does not mean that it is at the legislator's discretion to introduce or maintain a law that (without any good reason) differentiates between two individuals (see *ibid.*, pp. 14–16).
[17] *Ibid.*, pp. 7–11.   [18] *Ibid.*, p. 11.   [19] *Ibid.*

Aristotle

In his analysis, Kelsen comments on some of the most influential early value-oriented justice advocates. Plato with his concept of ideas is a paramount example of a representative of the metaphysical-religious school. Aristotle, one of Plato's students and an advocate of the (pseudo)rationalistic school, might however be regarded as being even more influential, or at least more often referred to and studied in the field of value-oriented justice.

In Book V of the *Nicomachean Ethics*, Aristotle outlines his understanding of value-oriented justice. According to Aristotle, (general) justice is an expression of moral virtue, and the one who follows the law is considered as being just.[20] In the second chapter of Book V, Aristotle introduces a more specific form of justice: particular justice.[21] Particular justice stands primarily for equality[22] and can further be subdivided into two forms: distributive justice on the one hand and corrective on the other.[23]

To a certain extent, both distributive justice and corrective justice deal with the 'right balance' of rights, duties and goods between two parties. Aristotle explains both with mathematic formulas, which – in his opinion – lead to a logical and correct allocation by the state. Simply put and in a more generalised way, one could say that distributive justice deals with dispute avoidance by preventing inequality from occurring. Corrective justice on the other hand can be seen as a mechanism to solve a dispute between two individuals caused by some wrongdoing, which can result from either a voluntary or involuntary transactional relationship.[24]

This is not the place to go into further detail about Aristotle's description of value-oriented justice. Nevertheless, it should be registered that Aristotle (like Kelsen) does not claim that it can be described in a standardised way, as he uses different definitions for different scenarios.

---

[20] Book V, chapter 1 of Aristotle's *Nicomachean Ethics*; for details see D. Ross, *The Nicomachean Ethics of Aristotle* (Oxford University Press, 1954), p. 107; F. H. Eterovich, *Aristotle's Nicomachean Ethics: Commentary and Analysis* (Washington D.C.: University of America, 1980), p. 90.

[21] Eterovich, *Aristotle's Nicomachean Ethics*, p. 92.

[22] Ross, *Nicomachean Ethics*, p. 109.

[23] Aristotle refers to these two groups in chapter 3 (distributive justice) and chapter 4 (corrective justice) of Book V.

[24] Some commentators identify a third form of particular justice in Aristotle's concept of proportionality introduced in chapter 5 of Book V of the *Nicomachean Ethics*. David Ross refers to this concept as reciprocity. Unlike distributive justice (which aims at the equal allocation of rights, duties and goods among the public in general) and corrective justice (which deals with the rectification of a result of some unlawful activity),

Although each approach would – in his opinion – lead to only one correct result, Aristotle has to differentiate between different layers of value-
oriented justice. Thus, even according to Aristotle's argumentation, one
must realise that value-oriented justice cannot lead to an absolute, uniform definition of justice.

Aristotle's analysis of justice, especially his work on the two theories
of distributive and corrective justice, has been influential on many later
commentators on value-oriented justice. Some focus on distributive justice, others on corrective justice, and again others compare and develop
both concepts further.

Samuel Fleischacker represents the first category. According to
Fleischacker, Aristotle does not use the concept of distributive justice to
determine the fair allocation of goods, but rather (only) the equal allocation of *political* rights and duties.[25] Fleischacker claims that the concept
of distributive justice as understood by most authors today, i.e., as encompassing the equal, public allocation of goods between people to benefit
the poor, was only developed in the eighteenth century.[26] He argues that
leading philosophers of that time, especially Adam Smith and Immanuel
Kant, declared distributive justice as going beyond covering only political rights and duties, as it includes material aspects as well. Either way,
Fleischacker confirms that the concept of distributive justice nowadays
comprises both political *and* proprietary rights and obligations, as well

reciprocity instead refers to the mathematically correct exchange of rights, duties and
goods between *two individuals before* a dispute can arise. It addresses neither the public
doctrine of equal distribution among citizens in general (distributive justice) nor inter-
party dispute avoidance/solution mechanisms (corrective justice). Both Ross and Francis
Eterovich discuss reciprocity in the context of business transactions. They claim that
the proportionality concept explains how to determine an equal exchange of goods or
services between two private parties (and place their arguments around the idea that
the overall value given by one contractual party to the other shall equal the value of the
good or service that the other party gets in return). Ross and Eterovich give the example
of an architect and a shoemaker who trade shoes for a house. In their interpretation the
concept of reciprocity is needed to correctly calculate the number of shoes that have to be
given by the shoemaker in return for the house (see Eterovich, *Aristotle's Nicomachean
Ethics*, pp. 98–9 and Ross, *Nicomachean Ethics*, pp. 118–20). The mathematically correct
determination shall satisfy both parties' expectations and needs and, as a consequence,
it is deemed to ensure broader social peace, as '[r]eciprocity is necessary if the State is
to be held together, for it is held together by the exchange of [goods and] services, and
people will not exchange [goods and] services unless they get as good as they give' (Ross,
Nicomachean Ethics, p. xiii).

25 S. Fleischacker, *A Short History of Distributive Justice* (Cambridge, MA: Harvard
University Press, 2004), p. 5.
26 *Ibid.*, chapters 1 and 2.

as their allocation between individuals. It necessarily embodies a balancing of interests and requires a value judgement to determine the 'correct' distribution.

Ernest J. Weinrib deals with corrective justice in several of his works.[27] In a more recent publication, succinctly titled *Corrective Justice*, he describes it as 'the relational structure of reasoning in private law',[28] distinguishing it from distributive justice, which is instead based on public law ideas of the administrative allocation of rights and duties.[29] Analysing the meaning of corrective justice as a private law concept, Weinrib takes the view that it has to be understood in a broader sense rather than just implying the mathematically correct rectification of an imbalanced situation between two parties caused by a wrongful act. It is undeniably true that it refers to the ideas of compensation or legal remedies. However, corrective justice further expresses the 'reasons that would justify'[30] the rectification. In other words, corrective justice also rests on certain substantive values.

Izhak England belongs to the third category of post-Aristotle value-oriented justice commentators. With his historical overview of both corrective and distributive justice, he draws a line from Aristotle's concepts to today's society.[31] Focusing on common law countries, he argues that there has been a gradual shift from the original, philosophical understanding of value-oriented justice as an expression of moral virtue in the sense of equality, towards the legal conception of justice, 'relat[ing] justice to law'.[32] In the same vein as Weinrib, he explains that the classical division into distributive and corrective justice[33] had for a long time been used independently by public law (distributive justice) and private law scholars (corrective justice).[34] According to England, some recent trends, however, take a more holistic understanding. Notions of distributive justice on the

---

[27] See, for example, E. J. Weinrib, *The Idea of Private Law* (Oxford University Press, 1995); E. J. Weinrib, *Corrective Justice* (Oxford University Press, 2012).

[28] Weinrib, *Corrective Justice*, p. 2.

[29] Weinrib adds that corrective justice and distributive justice can sometimes overlap. He explains this by claiming as follows: '[A] given slice of social life, such as workplace injuries or automobile accidents can be coherently treated under either form of justice' (*ibid.*, p. 6).

[30] *Ibid.*, p. 337.

[31] I. England, *Corrective & Distributive Justice: From Aristotle to Modern Times* (Oxford University Press, 2009).

[32] *Ibid.*, pp. 177 and 213.

[33] England uses also the term 'commutative justice' when referring to corrective justice.

[34] England, *Corrective & Distributive Justice*, p. 177.

one hand and corrective justice on the other merge into a broader, comprehensive concept of value-oriented justice.[35] This is also true with respect to non-common law societies and – to a certain, yet still rather limited, extent – the current situation at the EU level. Ideas of corrective justice also have an impact on policy-making regarding procedural devices, for example by asking which procedural tool is the most suitable for solving existing disputes about substantive private law issues. Distributive justice, on the other hand, also pervades debates led in the field of private law. A good example of the latter is the discussion found in the context of European contract law and its distributive effects. The Study Group on Social Justice in European Private Law (the Social Justice Study Group), for example, defines the ideal interplay between fairness, contract law and private autonomy as an expression of a 'scheme of distributive justice'.[36] They further explain the relationship as follows: '[a]lthough freedom is a fundamental value and supports private autonomy in contract law, it must be balanced against other values ... such as respect for equality, diversity, social inclusion, access to services of general economic interest, a high level of environmental protection and consumer protection, and fair and just working conditions'.[37] The traditional boundaries between Aristotle's concepts of justice thus become blurred. At the same time, one can note that his concepts, as a total package, continue to influence modern policy-making in any legal field.

John Rawls

Discussing (value-oriented) justice further benefits from mentioning one of the most influential philosophical thinkers of the more recent past, John Rawls. More than forty years ago Rawls defined value-oriented justice in his epic work *A Theory of Justice*.[38] Unlike Aristotle and some of the commentators influenced by the distributive and corrective justice models, Rawls does not place the main focus on equality; at least it is neither the only nor the most important factor in his argumentation. Rawls

---

[35] *Ibid.*, pp. 212–13.
[36] Study Group on Social Justice in European Private Law, 'Social Justice in European Contract Law', 664.
[37] *Ibid.*, 667. For a detailed analysis of European contract law (including consumer contract law) from a distributive justice perspective see, e.g., S. Arnold, *Vertrag und Verteilung* (Tübingen: Mohr Siebeck, 2014).
[38] A collection of Rawls's papers that influenced his justice concept can be found in S. Freeman (ed.), *John Rawls – Collected Papers* (Cambridge, MA: Harvard University Press, 1999).

instead starts with the question of what *fairness* means. In his opinion fairness is an important parameter on which a sound society should be built.[39] This ideal state is reached via a social contract that is concluded by people who accept certain just values in a position he describes as the 'original position'.[40] He explains the interplay between justice (understood as fairness), society and the original position as follows:

> [T]he guiding idea is that the principles of justice for the basic structure of society are the object of the original agreement. They are the principles that free and rational persons concerned to further their own interests would accept in an initial position of equality as defining the fundamental terms of their association. These principles are to regulate all further agreements; they specify the kinds of social cooperation that can be entered into and the forms of government that can be established. This way of regarding the principles of justice I shall call justice as fairness.[41]

The original, 'purely hypothetical'[42] position is reflected in Rawls's well-known veil of ignorance, a condition one could also call empty consciousness. In such a situation, individuals do not possess any knowledge about their own social position. Rawls refers to this as a condition in which 'no one knows his place in society, his class position or social status; nor does he know his fortune in the distribution of natural assets and abilities, his intelligence and strength, and the like'.[43] Out of this state, each individual is said to draw an uninfluenced conclusion driven by rational self-interest. It is only in this state of an absence of extraneous influence that people can identify principles on which justice, i.e., fairness, is built.

According to Rawls, one would arrive at two justice principles: one relates to basic liberties and the other to inequalities in terms of social and economic status. The first principle, taking priority over the second, states that '[e]ach person is to have an equal right to the most extensive total system of equal basic liberties compatible with a similar system of liberty for all'.[44] As Samuel Freeman comments, these liberties are 'basic', because they are considered as being more important for reaching the ideal state

---

[39] *The Oxford Companion to Philosophy* refers to this as 'the hope for social institutions that do not confer morally arbitrary lifelong advantages on some persons at the expense of others' (T. Honderich (ed.), *The Oxford Companion to Philosophy* (2nd edn, Oxford University Press, 2005), p. 786).

[40] For details on Rawls's original position see Rawls, *Theory of Justice*, pp. 118–92.

[41] *Ibid.*, p. 11.   [42] *Ibid.*, p. 120.

[43] *Ibid.*, p. 137.   [44] *Ibid.*, p. 302.

of justice than other liberties.[45] To guarantee freedom and equality for all, the basic liberties need to be respected. Rawls defines their concept in chapter 4 of his *A Theory of Justice*, and although they cannot be equated with constitutional human rights ideas, there is a certain overlap. Rawls's category of basic liberties comprises the liberties of conscience and freedom of thought and association, liberties regarding the freedom of the person, political liberties and the rule of law.

Rawls's first principle of justice is followed by another intrinsic dimension of justice, his second, hierarchically lower-ranked justice principle. According to the second principle '[s]ocial and economic inequalities are to be arranged so that they are both: (a) to the greatest benefit of the least advantaged, consistent with the just savings principle, and (b) attached to offices and positions open to all under conditions of fair equality of opportunity'.[46] In this second principle, Rawls presents his concept of a fair distribution of goods and rights. One can also say that this second principle explains how he understands distributive justice.[47] The first subcategory, i.e., what he defines under (a), covers differences in goods.[48] Rawls does not ask for an equal distribution of wealth and income in the sense of allocating identical amounts to each individual. Instead he claims that dealing with societal inequalities should lead to the best possible gain for the least advantaged members of society without infringing the basic liberties of others, i.e., without infringing the first justice principle.[49] This understanding is supported by the second pillar of the second principle (sub principle (b)), according to which each member of society should be treated in a similar way to any other individual with the same skills and abilities.[50]

---

[45] For detailed comments on Rawls's first justice principle see S. Freeman, *Rawls* (Abingdon: Routledge, 2007), pp. 44–59; T. Pogge, *John Rawls: His Life and Theory of Justice* (Oxford University Press, 2007), pp. 82–105.

[46] Rawls, *Theory of Justice*, p. 302.

[47] See Freeman, *Rawls*, pp. 86–140, where Samuel Freeman extensively comments on Rawls's distributive justice ideas.

[48] For more details on this 'difference principle' see, for example, P. van Parijs, 'Difference Principle' in S. Freeman (ed.), *The Cambridge Companion to Rawls* (Cambridge University Press, 2003), pp. 200–40.

[49] *The Cambridge Dictionary of Philosophy* defines the interplay between the two justice principles as follows: 'This [second] principle is to be consistent with the "priority" of the first principle, which requires that equal basic liberties cannot be traded for other benefits ... [A] basic liberty can be limited only for the sake of maintaining other basic liberties' (R. Audi (ed.), *The Cambridge Dictionary of Philosophy* (2nd edn, Cambridge University Press), pp. 774–5).

[50] For a more detailed overview of Rawls's second justice principle see, for example, Pogge, *John Rawls*, pp. 106–34.

Rawls's complex conception of justice as fairness has been the subject of both enormous support and heavy criticism. One point of criticism should be noted in this context: the interplay between liberties, equality and the distribution of goods and rights. On subsequent occasions,[51] Rawls clarified his argument in response to the claim that he wanted to introduce a universally applicable and absolute concept of justice.[52] He explained that with his model of justice and fairness, he did not intend to define 'universal truth, or … the essential nature and identity of persons'.[53] Rawls defines his justice model rather as 'political, not metaphysical',[54] directed at policy makers to balance interests and to determine the features of modern constitutional democracy. By applying his fairness concept, he believes that modern societies could reach a state of stability, an important consequence of fairness and justice.[55]

Value-oriented justice – key observations for further arguments

What was hopefully garnered from my brief excursion was that value-oriented justice is not as easy to define as what I termed non-valuing justice. In the more than two millennia that value-oriented justice has been debated, a standardised definition still has not been found. However, with all due respect to everyone who has sought to find a standardised definition, one has to question whether such a definition is even possible or ultimately so desirable. Is value-oriented justice not an ever-evolving and flexible concept to be used differently in a variety of scenarios? This does not mean, though, that it is not worthwhile asking what value-oriented justice is. However, the answer can only be found in and for a particular legal, political, economic and spatiotemporal context.

For the later argumentation in this book there are several things that can be concluded from the matters discussed in the pages above. First, value-oriented justice can be determined by several parameters. Most prominently, value-oriented justice can (to a certain extent) be circumscribed with the help of fairness and equality. Both play an important role in every endeavour to define the term. Societal stability, as was shown in the cases

---

[51] See, for example, J. Rawls, 'Justice as Fairness: Political not Metaphysical', *Philosophy & Public Affairs*, 14 (1985), 223–51; J. Rawls, *Political Liberalism* (New York: Columbia University Press, 1993). For comments on Rawls's complementary definition of the justice concept see, for example, A. Sen, *The Idea of Justice* (London: Penguin, 2010), p. 55, in particular, and Amartya Sen's further references and critique in that book.

[52] R. Wacks, *Philosophy of Law – A Very Short Introduction* (Oxford University Press, 2006), pp. 73–4.

[53] Rawls, 'Justice as Fairness', 223.

[54] *Ibid.*   [55] *Ibid.*, 250–1.

of Rawls, Aristotle and Kelsen,[56] can be added. It should be noted, however, that other factors, such as an effective judicial system, satisfaction or happiness, can also be an expression or consequence of justice.

Second, none of these parameters can be understood in an absolute, perfect or pure way. Value-oriented justice is characterised by its relativity. The realisation of value-oriented justice is ultimately linked to policymaking.[57] Determining value-oriented justice requires an act of balancing interests, which might lead to varied results in different scenarios depending on factors such as time, space or region or the particular academic field.

Third, and in the same vein as Kelsen who claimed that '[j]ustice is primarily a possible, but not a necessary, quality of social order regulating mutual relations of men',[58] it is true that justice is both possible but not absolutely necessary. However, this does not mean that value-oriented justice is not worth striving for. On the contrary, it is and should be an important determinant for policy-making in every modern society, as will be shown in this book with the example of consumer law in the EU.

Fourth, and putting it into a more legal context, value-oriented justice can pervade different areas of law. It is the 'right' interplay between these different legal fields that is crucial for ensuring value-oriented justice in today's society.

Fifth, procedural laws address non-valuing justice (the judicial system – or generally put, dispute resolution – understood in a technical way) from the perspective of value-oriented justice. By doing so, procedural laws (as will be shown briefly) function as the starting point for debates on access to justice. They touch upon questions of finding ways to make courts generally accessible or finding the most suitable procedural device by discussing various different means to enforce individuals' rights. This, as explained earlier, goes beyond what can be described as formal justice, or in other words, beyond the equal application of procedural law norms by the judiciary. It also deals with questions of fairness or justness, i.e., substantive justice arguments, as in various cases the availability of procedural devices is limited to certain types of material disputes.[59]

---

[56] See Kelsen's conclusion in Kelsen, 'What Is Justice?', p. 24, where he states that 'justice, to me, is that social order under whose protection the search for truth can prosper. "My" justice, then, is the justice of freedom, the justice of peace, the justice of democracy – the justice of tolerance'.

[57] Rawls, 'Justice as Fairness', 223.   [58] Kelsen, 'What Is Justice?', p. 1.

[59] For an explanation of formal and substantive justice see notes 6 and 7 above. For a differentiation between different types of material disputes as a determinant of the availability of concrete procedural devices see the examples in Part II below.

Sixth, substantive laws (like procedural laws) are characterised by value considerations. Interests that are sometimes incongruent have to be reconciled in attempts to find the best possible content-related solution. In the following sections, I will try to show how these observations fit into the debate on access to justice.

Access to justice

Taken literally

When trying to define the English term access to justice, one inevitably faces a problem. As seen in the previous chapter, English belongs to that group of languages where justice has an ambiguous meaning. It can stand for the non-valuing side of the judicial system (non-valuing justice) as well as for value-oriented justice embodying a concept with certain values added. One can therefore ask what in particular should be accessible or reachable. The court system?[60] A state of 'fairness', 'equality' or any other state that can be described with value-oriented justice?[61] Or both? Similar problems of definition can also be found in French. Here too, 'justice' as in *l'accès à la justice*,[62] can have the same two meanings as in English.

Other languages, however, draw a clearer line, putting the focus on the more traditional understanding of access to justice. German is a

[60] For other examples that associate the concept of access to justice to discussions on the judicial system and rights enforcement see M. Gramatikov *et al.*, *A Handbook for Measuring the Costs and Quality of Access to Justice* (Apeldoorn: Maklu, 2010) (broadened by ADR mechanisms); C. E. F. Rickett and T. G. W. Telfer (eds.), *International Perspectives on Consumers' Access to Justice* (Cambridge University Press, 2003); D. L. Rhode, *Access to Justice* (Oxford University Press, 2004); R. Moorhead and P. Pleasence (eds.), *After Universalism: Re-engineering Access to Justice* (Oxford: Blackwell, 2003); R. Cranston, *How Law Works: The Machinery and Impact of Civil Justice* (Oxford University Press, 2006), pp. 35–82.

[61] See, for example, Hans-W. Micklitz's broader analysis of justice in the context of access to justice in H.-W. Micklitz, 'Privatisation of Access to Justice and Soft Law – Lessons from the European Community?' in T. Wilhelmsson and S. Hurri (eds.), *From Dissonance to Sense: Welfare State Expectations, Privatisation and Private Law* (Aldershot: Ashgate, 1999), pp. 505–48, where he links it to both non-valuing and value-oriented justice. For a broad discussion of EU consumer law from the perspective of human rights and value-oriented justice see I. Benöhr, *EU Consumer Law and Human Rights* (Oxford University Press, 2013).

[62] See, for example, the French title of the Aarhus Convention, a prime example of an international treaty dealing with access to justice: 'la convention d'Aarhus sur l'accès à l'information, la participation du public au processus décisionnel et *l'accès à la justice* en matière d'environnement' (emphasis added).

prominent example. Here, 'access to justice' is traditionally translated as *Zugang zum Recht*[63] or *Zugang zu den Gerichten*[64]. *Gerechtigkeit,* the German translation of value-oriented justice, is usually not found in this context.[65] Japanese is another example of a language with a clear distinction. The Japanese translation of access to justice, 司法へのアクセス (*shihō he no akusesu*), takes the same approach as its German counterpart. It is the judicial system itself (司法; *shihō*) and not value-oriented justice (正義; *seigi*) that (primarily) should be made accessible.

The *Oxford English Dictionary* this time fails to provide a definition. As seen in the following, the term access to justice has, however, been widely discussed, especially in legal literature. *Black's Law Dictionary* provides a good traditional definition as a starting point for further observations. It defines access to justice as '[t]he ability within a society to use courts and other legal institutions effectively to protect one's rights and pursue claims'.[66] Let me now briefly examine how this concept has evolved over the years.

Access to justice in the course of time

When a group of legal scholars under the leadership of Mauro Cappelletti launched the so-called Florence Access-to-Justice Project (the Florence Project) in the early 1970s, the value-oriented justice debate had just reached a new level. In 1971, Rawls had published his *A Theory of Justice,* which sounded the bell for a new, comprehensive round in the debate, especially in the United States and among contemporary philosophical thinkers. On the other side of the Atlantic, Cappelletti and his colleagues focused on something that at first glance appeared somewhat related to Rawls's theory: access to justice. The Florence Project, however, did not aim at primarily dealing with the core issues of (value-oriented) justice

---

[63] See, for example, ec.europa.eu/justice/civil/access-justice/index_de.htm.

[64] See, for example, the German title of the Aarhus Convention: 'Übereinkommen über den Zugang zu Informationen, die Öffentlichkeitsbeteiligung an Entscheidungsverfahren und den *Zugang zu Gerichten* in Umweltangelegenheiten' (emphasis added).

[65] Exceptions prove the rule and can usually be found in the area of legal theory. See K. T. Do, 'Idee der Gerechtigkeit und öffentlicher Vernunftgebrauch in einer demokratischen Gesellschaft', *Rechtstheorie,* 43 (2012), 241, 242; J. Wallacher, 'Ethische Perspektiven einer entwicklungsgerechten Weltwirtschaft', *Zeitschrift für Wirtschafts- und Unternehmensethik,* 4 (2003), 307, 315; R. Weiskopf, 'Management, Organisation und die Gespenster der Gerechtigkeit' in G. Schreyögg and P. Conrad (eds.), *Managementforschung 14. Gerechtigkeit und Management* (Wiesbaden: Gabler, 2004), pp. 211–51.

[66] B. A. Garner (ed.), *Black's Law Dictionary* (9th edn, St. Paul, MN: Thomson Reuters, 2009), p. 16.

on a broad basis; at least it did not start with the assumption that law was lacking morality. Cappelletti and his colleagues took a more traditional, narrower approach and started at a different point: the accessibility of the legal system and how it could be improved.[67]

The Florence Project is best known for having set a new standard by categorising access to justice into three stages. Cappelletti and Bryant Garth call them 'waves'. The three waves illustrate the shift in the over-all meaning of the access to justice concept, from a narrower theory to a more comprehensive value-oriented concept.[68]

The starting point is the argument that the judicial system is not gen-erally accessible, as many people cannot afford to go to court.[69] The first access to justice wave thus covers cases where the poor lack financial resources. It was first believed that access to justice could be improved by lowering the financial burden and risks, which are immanent in seeking help from the courts. Launching legal proceedings was considered too expensive by this approach.

Traditionally, legal scholars have ascribed the (alleged) shortcomings of the judicial system to these barriers. Although it marks the oldest of Cappelletti and Garth's three access to justice waves, the discussion of how to improve legal aid for those in need still continues. The issue is also deeply enshrined in several constitutional frameworks. In 2007, Francesco Francioni presented the outcome of an academic workshop on access to justice, which linked the topic to human rights. In his introduc-tory remarks he argues that 'access to justice can be used to describe the legal aid for the needy, in the absence of which judicial remedies would be available only to those who dispose of the financial resources necessary

---

[67] See Cappelletti and Garth, 'Access to Justice', p. 6: 'The words "access to justice" are admittedly not easily defined, but they serve to focus on two basic purposes of the legal system – the system by which people may vindicate their rights and/or resolve their dis-putes under the general auspices of the state. First, the system must be equally accessible to all, and second, it must lead to results that are individually and socially just. Our focus here will be primarily on the first component, access, but we will necessarily bear in mind the second.'

[68] For a summary of the three waves see already S. Wrbka et al., 'Access to Justice and Collective Actions: "Florence" and beyond' in S. Wrbka et al. (eds.), Collective Actions: Enhancing Access to Justice and Reconciling Multilayer Interests? (Cambridge University Press, 2012), pp. 3–8.

[69] For examples that focus on this aspect see I. van den Meene and B. van Rooij, Access to Justice and Legal Empowerment: Making the Poor Central in Legal Development Co-operation (Leiden University Press, 2008); D. Leipold, 'Limiting Costs for Better Access to Justice – The German Experience' in A. A. S. Zuckerman and R. Cranston (eds.), Essays on 'Access to Justice' (Oxford: Clarendon Press, 1995), pp. 265–78.

to meet the, often prohibitive, cost of lawyers and the administration of justice'.[70] Francioni goes on to explain that the call for ensuring access to justice is a core postulation of international human rights instruments.

As far as the EU and its Member States are concerned, the pertinent (international) statements can most notably be found in Articles 6 ('right to a fair trial') and 13 ('right to an effective remedy') of the 1950 European Convention on Human Rights (ECHR), and in Article 47 (on both the right to an effective remedy and to a fair trial) of the 2000 Charter of Fundamental Rights of the European Union.[71] Article 47(3) of the Charter of Fundamental Rights of the European Union expressly covers the first access to justice wave claim, stating that '[l]egal aid shall be made available to those who lack sufficient resources in so far as such aid is necessary to ensure effective access to justice'.[72]

National constitutions of some Member States use similar expressions and ask their legislator to enact adequate laws. Article 18(2) of the Dutch Constitution, for example, states that '[r]ules concerning the granting of legal aid to persons of limited means shall be laid down by Act of Parliament'. In a similar vein, Article 24(3) of the Italian Constitution proclaims that '[t]he poor are entitled by law to proper means for action or defence in all courts'.[73] Not all Member States' constitutions contain such express wording, but in many cases they at least enshrine the right to 'one's natural judge'.[74] Either way, while the constitutions of Member States usually include some reference to access to the judicial system, be it explicitly or not, concrete rules follow in ordinary laws. Such rules contain more substantive requests directed at the state, e.g., asking for the provision of legal aid to those who cannot afford to finance court proceedings.[75] Without any doubt, the concept of effective access to justice as a 'new social right'[76] has progressed over the years and now plays an

---

[70] F. Francioni, 'The Rights of Access to Justice under Customary International Law' in F. Francioni (ed.), *Access to Justice as a Human Right* (Oxford University Press, 2007), p. 1.

[71] Charter of Fundamental Rights of the European Union, OJ 2000 No. C364/1.

[72] For a more detailed commentary of the interplay between European human rights tools and access to justice see Storskrubb and Ziller, 'Access to Justice in European Comparative Law', pp. 177–203.

[73] Comparable constitutional provisions can also be found outside the EU (see, for example, Article 32 Constitution of Japan: 'No person shall be denied the right of access to the courts' (translation mine)).

[74] For more information see, e.g., Storskrubb and Ziller, 'Access to Justice in European Comparative Law', pp. 180–1.

[75] Legal aid can be provided by various means such as by granting free lawyers' support, offering free interpretation services or installing open-court days.

[76] Cappelletti and Garth, 'Access to Justice', p. 49.

important role as a key feature of 'the welfare state ideal',[77] an issue that I will discuss in more detail later in this book.

The discussion of providing legal aid, however, is neither limited to human rights doctrines nor to laws enacted to comply with them at a national level. At the pan-EU level, one of course has to mention the Legal Aid Directive,[78] which deals with cross-border issues. At a more international level, one should especially mention various academic working groups, such as the International Academy of Comparative Law[79] and other international initiatives, such as the United Nations Guidelines for Consumer Protection[80] and the Principles of Transnational Civil Procedure,[81] created by the American Law Institute (ALI) in cooperation with the International Institute for the Unification of Private Law (UNIDROIT). It must be noted too that several legal scholars commenting on legal aid issues[82] show that financial issues related to court proceedings are – despite all efforts – still a concern, both for those who would like to make use of the judicial system and for policy makers who have identified problems related to acceding courts.

However, financial issues are not the only reason people refrain from going to court. Several additional factors need to be considered when

[77] Storskrubb and Ziller, 'Access to Justice in European Comparative Law', p. 179.
[78] For details see 'The Legal Aid Directive' in Chapter 4 below.
[79] U. Mattei, 'Access to Justice. A Renewed Global Issue?', *Electronic Journal of Comparative Law*, 11.3 (2007), available at www.ejcl.org/113/article113-14.pdf. See also the national reports on cost and fee allocation in civil procedure prepared for the 18th World Congress of the International Academy of Comparative Law in Washington D.C., 21–31 July 2010, available at www-personal.umich.edu/~purzel/national_reports.
[80] See UN General Assembly resolution, A/Res/39/248, 16 April 1985, para. 28, where it says that '[g]overnments should establish or maintain ... measures to enable consumers ... to obtain redress through formal and informal procedures that are expeditious, fair, inexpensive and accessible. Such procedures should take particular account of the needs of low-income consumers'.
[81] American Law Institute/UNIDROIT, *Principles of Transnational Civil Procedure* (Cambridge University Press, 1995).
[82] Deborah Rhode explains that 'about four-fifths of the civil legal needs of the poor, and two- to three-fifths of the needs of middle-income individuals, remain unmet [in the United States]' (Rhode, *Access to Justice*, p. 3). Later in that book she suggests that '[t]hose who need but cannot realistically afford lawyers should have the opportunities for government-subsidized services' (*ibid.*, p. 185), indicating that limited financial resources of individuals still pose a major threat to the guarantee of access to justice. For further discussions of financial obstacles to access to justice see T. Goriely, 'The Government's Legal Aid Reforms' in Zuckerman and Cranston (eds.), *Essays on 'Access to Justice'* (Oxford: Clarendon Press, 1995), pp. 346–69; C. Hodges *et al.* (eds.), *The Costs and Funding of Civil Litigation: A Comparative Perspective* (Oxford: Hart, 2010); and the references in note 69 above.

discussing why individuals do not make greater use of the judicial system. As pointed out by Cappelletti and Garth, a prime example is the lack of requisite legal information and knowledge to launch a proceeding.[83] Another non-financial impediment, which goes hand-in-hand with the need to raise legal awareness, is identified by Marc Galanter. He distinguishes between 'repeat-player litigants' and 'one-shot litigants'.[84] The first group is already court experienced and thus enjoys a practical advantage over the second group, whose members have not yet set foot in a courtroom. In Galanter's opinion, one-shot litigants will only very rarely file a suit, whereas repeat players would be more willing to go to court again. Because of their court experience, repeat players can prepare claims more easily and spread litigation costs or minimise the financial risk of losing cases more effectively. As will be seen later, depending on the amount at stake and the 'importance' of the matter for the respective potential plaintiff, additional factors also come into play, such as psychological barriers if the amount at stake is either too low ('not worth the effort') or too high ('risk of losing the case' is too high in cases where the loser-pays principle applies), or motivational issues ('going to court would take too much time').

Cappelletti and Garth's second access to justice wave covers some of these primarily non-financial issues. Whereas the legal aid wave mainly aims to remove obstacles to launching proceedings between two individual parties, the second wave goes beyond that to cover what the Florence Project calls 'diffuse interests'. Diffuse interests, as defined by Cappelletti and Garth, refer to cases where 'collective or fragmented interests, such as those in clean air or consumer protection'[85] are concerned, with 'the basic problem ... that either no one has a right to remedy the infringement of a collective interest or the stake of any one individual in remedying the infringement is too small to induce him or her to seek enforcement action'.[86] Consumers might encounter similar goods- and services-related problems. In other words, consumers might incur the same or very similar damages. This can happen both in one and the same country and, regardless of national borders, in an international setting. Mechanisms developed in the first access to justice wave, i.e., legal aid instruments,

---

[83] Cappelletti and Garth, 'Access to Justice', pp. 15–17.
[84] M. Galanter, 'Why the "Haves" Come out Ahead: Speculations on the Limits of Legal Change', *Law and Society Review*, 9 (1974), 95–160; M. Galanter, 'Afterword: Explaining Litigation', *Law and Society Review*, 9 (1974), 347–68.
[85] Cappelletti and Garth, 'Access to Justice', p. 18.
[86] *Ibid.*

are of only limited value in this respect, as the enforcement of collective rights and interests cannot be fully guaranteed merely by equipping
the poor or others who need financial backing with legal support tools.
Collective redress mechanisms try to also tackle non-financial court
access impediments. However, compared with the mechanisms covered
by the first access to justice wave, national tools in Europe are in many
cases still in development. For example, approximately forty years after
Cappelletti and Garth first identified collective interests as being insufficiently protected by law, only slightly more than half of the EU Member
States have provided for a collective redress mechanism for monetary
claims. The situation at the pan-EU level lags even further behind. At the
time of writing this book, EU policy makers have not yet been able to
design a legal instrument that obliges Member States to introduce compensatory collective redress mechanisms.[87]

It was soon realised, however, that stabilising the financial situation of
individual plaintiffs and simplifying the proceedings for enforcing collective rights, though being of undeniable importance for improving procedural access to justice, is not a panacea; it is not enough to facilitate
more or less traditional court proceedings. Thus, the third access to justice wave goes one step further. While the first wave focuses on the poor
and how they (individually) could be supported in their pursuit of rights
enforcement, and the second wave deals with diffuse interests, i.e., collective interests, by discussing collective redress mechanisms, the third
wave takes a more holistic approach and broadens the value-oriented
justice discussion. By doing so, the Florence Project has gradually shifted
its attention to certain aspects that can be more closely linked to substantive justice, as it discusses the merits and demerits of the judicial system
as a whole and evaluates the advantages and disadvantages of different,
occasionally innovative, mechanisms to find a fair,[88] suitable and satisfying solution.

Cappelletti and Garth refer to the third wave as 'the "access-to-justice approach" because of its overall scope; its method is not to abandon
the techniques of the first two waves of reform, but rather to treat those
reforms as but several of a number of possibilities for improving access'.[89]
Unlike in the case of compensatory collective redress mechanisms dealing with collective interests, the EU has, as will be shown in more detail

---

[87] For details see Chapter 5 below.
[88] See, for example, Cappelletti and Garth, 'Access to Justice', pp. 61 and 64, where the
authors write about ways to '[e]ncourag[e] fair settlements'.
[89] *Ibid.*, p. 49.

later in this book,[90] reacted in this respect with binding instruments already. In this context, one can, for example, identify tools dealing with claims of a comparatively low value, harmonised for cross-border cases at a pan-EU level via the Small Claims Regulation,[91] or attempts to ease the burden of ordinary courts by implementing alternative dispute resolution mechanisms (ADR) and online dispute resolution (ODR).[92]

Cappelletti and Garth also briefly touch upon one different obstacle that is of importance in the context of my analysis, but which is usually not, at least not prominently, covered in the traditional access to justice debate (which focuses on rights enforcement issues). They also locate access to justice-related problems in the corpus of *substantive* law, arguing that simplifying substantive law rules could possibly benefit those who are affected by them. Cappelletti and Garth conclude 'that there remain large sectors where simplification is both desirable and attainable'.[93] I will come back to this issue at a later stage in more detail.[94]

The more recent traditional discussion at the EU level

What started as a discussion of how to empower the poor in terms of easing the financial burden of bringing individual cases to the courts, later turned into a more general debate on the most effective ways to settle disputes. This debate cannot be detached from the respective case at stake. Different scenarios ask for different solutions. Finding the best possible solution requires a weighing of pros and cons and a balancing of involved interests. The access to justice debate has continuously expanded the discussion, taking a broader account of value-oriented justice ideas.

Nevertheless, purely financial issues and the question of how to provide individuals with legal aid still remain on the agenda. One of the more recent EU-driven projects, a study on the current status of access to justice in Europe led by the European Union Agency for Fundamental Rights (FRA), for example, deals with this issue and once more places it within the context of human rights arguments. The FRA, which evaluates various mechanisms in the context of anti-discrimination law, confirms that the term access to justice cannot be defined in a uniform way. In taking a

---

[90] See Part II below.
[91] For details see 'The Small Claims Regulation (2007)' in Chapter 4 below.
[92] For details see 'The ADR Directive (2013)' and 'The ODR Regulation (2013)' in Chapter 4 below.
[93] Cappelletti and Garth, 'Access to Justice', p. 118.
[94] See Part III below.

closer look at various international human rights instruments it comes to the conclusion that access to justice comprises five pillars: '1. the right to effective access to a dispute resolution body; 2. the right to fair proceedings; 3. the right to timely resolution of disputes; 4. the right to adequate redress; 5. the principles of efficiency and effectiveness'.[95] These five pillars led the FRA to argue that the term access to justice can be used to express one or more of the following, depending on the context: effective remedies, redress, access to courts, judicial protection, fair trial and due process.[96] The FRA closely links these keywords to the financial needs of affected citizens and argues that legal aid is the primary tool used to enhance access to justice.

The procedural side of access to justice at a more comprehensive level has been at the centre of various EU policy-making initiatives. The 1998 Vienna Action Plan, which asked to identify 'the rules on civil procedure having cross-border implications which are urgent to approximate for the purpose of facilitating access to justice for the citizens of Europe and examine the elaboration of additional measures accordingly to improve compatibility of civil procedures'[97] or several sessions of the European Council ranging from Tampere in 1999 to Stockholm in 2009 exemplify this approach.[98] In the first decade of the new millennium several procedural tools were adopted in accordance with these calls.[99] The Stockholm Programme with its policy guidelines for 2010 to 2014 asked the European Commission (Commission) to further intensify its quest for improving access to justice.[100] First results in response to that have already followed. As I will explain later in more detail, the Commission's plans for an ADR

---

[95] European Union Agency for Fundamental Rights, 'Access to Justice in Europe: An Overview of Challenges and Opportunities', report, (2010), p. 14, available at fra.europa. eu/sites/default/files/fra_uploads/1520-report-access-to-justice_EN.pdf.

[96] *Ibid.*, p. 16.

[97] Action Plan of the Council and the Commission on how best to implement the provisions of the Treaty of Amsterdam on an area of freedom, security and justice, 3 December 1998, OJ 1999 No. C19/1, 41(d).

[98] For some general details on the 1999 Tampere and the 2004 Hague Programmes see E. Storskrubb, *Civil Procedure and EU Law: A Policy Area Uncovered* (Oxford University Press, 2008), pp. 65–70.

[99] For some examples that are of importance in the area of consumer law see Part II below.

[100] A timetable for these undertakings can be found in the Annex of the Stockholm Programme Action Plan (see Communication from the Commission to the European Parliament, the Council, the European Economic and Social Committee and the Committee of the Regions – Delivering an area of freedom, security and justice for Europe's citizens – Action Plan Implementing the Stockholm Programme, 20 April 2010, COM(2010) 171 final, pp. 23–4 ('[p]roviding easier access to justice')).

Directive and ODR Regulation were realised in 2013 and also very recently the discussion in the area of compensatory redress has come to some (at least) temporary result.[101]

2.0

The term '2.0' is not defined in any leading English dictionary, but it could simply be translated as 'fresh', 'advanced', 'updated' or 'new version'. It usually refers to something that refines already existing things or concepts. By using 2.0, one could further claim that a new product, service or idea is enhanced, better or more suitable for its user.

Access to justice 2.0

Each of the access to justice analyses carried out in the past has had its own *raison d'être*. It would be wrong to argue that discussing access to justice does not make sense. On the contrary, various studies indicate that the issue is still not resolved.[102] However, approaches in the past usually did not focus (primarily) on consumer issues and even if they did, they exclusively dealt with procedural questions related to accessing the judicial system.[103] The argumentation in the field of consumer law was therefore quite one-dimensional (if existing at all). There has been a gradual shift in the debate towards discussing value-oriented justice matters more comprehensively within the field of procedural law. But the related discussions had, for a long time, still not addressed substantive law issues, at least not under the pillar of access to justice.

Recently, however, the Commission began to broaden the discussion by also attributing the effects of consumer satisfaction as one expression of value-oriented justice in the context of consumer law, not only to procedural law, but also to substantive law rules. This trend can also be linked to one of the above-shown findings of the FRA, namely that access to justice is also characterised by 'efficiency and effectiveness'.[104] The expression 'consumer satisfaction' is no longer inextricably linked with procedural

---

[101] See 'From the Green Paper on Consumer Collective Redress to the Commission's Collective Redress Recommendation' in Chapter 5 below.
[102] See the studies referred to in Parts II and III below.
[103] See the procedural devices discussed in Part II below.
[104] See European Union Agency for Fundamental Rights, 'Access to Justice in Europe', p. 14 and the section 'Value-oriented justice – key observations for further arguments' above.

law issues. Efficiency and effectiveness can also be ascribed to substantive rights. The Commission has started to realise that consumer satisfaction also requires efficient, effective, or in other words, fair and just *substantive* rights. Various and more recent academic contributions on private law issues adopt a similar view.[105] Consumers thus should also be able to enjoy 'access' to suitable substantive rights, since a functional procedural system of rights enforcement alone cannot guarantee consumer satisfaction. Some of the latest relevant developments at the EU level include the partial revision of the consumer acquis by the Directive on Consumer Rights (Consumer Rights Directive, CRD)[106] or the likely introduction of a pan-EU sales law, the Common European Sales Law (CESL).[107] These examples show that the Commission, at least on paper, has intensified its use of consumer interest arguments in its increasing efforts to enhance the internal market.[108]

It might, however, be feared that most procedural law scholars and policy makers will continue to focus only on the procedural side of access to justice, i.e., on procedural law issues, and that private law scholars and policy makers, on the other hand, will concentrate only on their domain, i.e., substantive law. Of course, both approaches are helpful, but one should not disregard their respective counterpart. Trying to solve existing procedural law issues could benefit the affected consumers even more if one would also take substantive law issues into consideration and vice versa; or in other words, even the 'best' procedural law rules will not satisfy consumers and enhance the internal market if the substantive law body contains 'bad' rules. At the same time 'good' or even 'perfect' substantive law rules will never be of any help if they are not safeguarded by

---

[105] See, for example, H.-W. Micklitz (ed.), *The Many Concepts of Social Justice in European Private Law* (Cheltenham: Edward Elgar, 2011); Study Group on Social Justice in European Private Law, 'Social Justice in European Contract Law' and further references discussed and/or listed in Chapter 7 below. For a general comment on the interplay between fairness and European contract law see, e.g., S. Arnold, 'Zum Verhältnis von Rechtsphilosophie, Rechtstheorie und europäischem Vertragsrecht' in S. Arnold (ed.), *Grundlagen eines europäischen Vertragsrechts* (Munich: Sellier, 2014), p. 17.

[106] For details see 'The Directive on Consumer Rights' in Chapter 9 below.

[107] For details see Chapter 10 below.

[108] See, e.g., Explanatory Memorandum accompanying the Proposal for a Regulation of the European Parliament and of the Council on a Common European Sales Law, 11 October 2011, COM(2011) 635 final (CESL Regulation Proposal), p. 4, where the Commission claims that '[t]he overall objective of the proposal is to improve the establishment and the functioning of the internal market by facilitating the expansion of cross-border trade for business and cross-border purchases for consumers'.

proper procedural rules, or as Geraint Howells and Stephen Weatherill put it: 'Consumer rights are only as effective as their enforcement'.[109] Hence, what is needed is a more holistic approach towards access to justice. With their three waves of access to justice, Cappelletti and Garth have gradually taken the discussion from one level to the next, moving towards a comprehensive value-oriented justice system, but they did so by mainly focusing on procedural law issues. However, as they both indicate in their research and as some of the more recent European trends to be discussed later in this book show, the time has come to talk about access to justice in a multidimensional way. This requires that the issue be approached from various angles – procedural as well as substantive law issues reflecting different ideas of value-oriented justice have to be taken into consideration. In other words, access to justice in the context of European consumer law should progress to the next stage, a stage that could be called 'access to justice 2.0'.

The concept of access to justice 2.0 adds new perspectives to the access to justice debate and embodies a concept that combines both procedural law and substantive law issues. It tries to provide an answer to the question of how to protect consumers' needs and interests in the best possible way in practice, not only on paper. In this respect, it is important to make sure that one does not lose track of the factors that are of importance for consumers. The access to justice 2.0 concept should introduce a relatively fast, uncomplicated, consumer-satisfying (and economy-boosting), easy-to-understand and easy-to-use mechanism for enforcing well-considered and fair substantive consumer rights. This enhanced, broader understanding of access to justice will also help reconcile policy-making in

---

[109] G. Howells and S. Weatherill, *Consumer Protection Law* (2nd edn, Aldershot: Ashgate, 2005), p. 660. In a similar vein are Anthony Ogus's observation that '[d]evising "better regulation" without sufficient attention to the enforcement dimension is unsatisfactory' (A. Ogus, 'Better Regulation – Better Enforcement' in S. Weatherill (ed.), *Better Regulation* (Oxford: Hart, 2007), p. 121) and Micklitz's analysis that a sound system of European consumer protection asks for taking account of both procedural and substantive law issues. With regard to the more recent trends (which, as will be shown in Part III below, focus rather on the substantive law side) he worries that losing track of a more comprehensive approach would lead to a 'step back into an academic world, where substance remains distinct from procedure' (H.-W. Micklitz, 'Enforcement and Compliance: Editorial Introduction' in R. Brownsword *et al.* (eds.), *The Foundations of European Private Law* (Oxford: Hart, 2011), p. 415). For a similar critique see I. Tzankova and M. Gramatikov, 'A Critical Note on Two EU principles: A Proceduralist View on the Draft Common Frame of Reference (DCFR)' in *ibid.*, pp. 421–35; H.-W. Micklitz, 'A 'Certain' Future for the Optional Instrument' in R. Schulze and J. Stuyck (eds.), *Towards a European Contract Law* (Munich: Sellier, 2011), pp. 181–93.

the field of consumer law with the practical consequences of subsequent laws. By taking a broader approach, one might also better understand the potential shortcomings of the existing system and envisage future steps, which could eventually facilitate the search for a suitable and effective consumer-protective mechanism and thus put European consumer law on the right track.[110]

---

[110] It should be noted that – not least because of readability considerations – the explanations with respect to substantive law will primarily focus on selected issues related to contract law (and to a large extent to cross-border issues in the context of the debate on the enhancement of the internal market). This does not mean that other substantive law issues fall outside the scope of access to justice 2.0. However, it would go beyond the scope of this book to cover every single aspect of (European) consumer law. Instead, some selected core issues will be discussed to introduce the concept of access to justice 2.0. Nevertheless, the key points of the argumentation can (in principle) *mutatis mutandis* be applied to substantive consumer laws not directly covered by this book.

PART II

Procedural law – the traditional pillar of access to justice 2.0

the three dimensions of justice – truth, time and cost[1]
(Adrian Zuckerman, 1944–)

---

[1] A. A. S. Zuckerman, 'Justice in Crisis: Comparative Dimensions of Civil Procedure' in A. A. S. Zuckerman (ed.), *Civil Justice in Crisis, Comparative Perspectives of Civil Procedure* (Oxford University Press, 1999), p. 47.

3

A brief outline of developments at the pan-EU level

As shown in Part I of this book, the traditional concept of access to justice is based on procedural law issues and its scope has been gradually expanded to include broader questions of value-oriented justice.[1] The discussions initially focused more or less exclusively on the financial feasibility of filing a case. The contemporary European debate in the field of procedural consumer law, however, does not only deal with questions regarding the affordability of launching legal proceedings. It goes beyond the first access to justice wave of the Florence Project and covers also the two other stages identified by Cappelletti and his colleagues: safeguarding collective interests and enhancing means of individual dispute resolution.

In the field of procedural consumer law, the starting point is the general assumption that consumer rights lack enforcement in Europe, at both the national and pan-EU levels.[2] Although access to justice, understood here as access to the judicial system, is not directly denied, consumers often refrain from taking further action for several reasons. These include certain legal obstacles as well as other factors such as financial concerns or psychological disincentives. The Commission has thus increased its efforts to introduce additional consumer redress mechanisms and enhance those already in existence.

The debate in this regard dates back to the 1970s.[3] It was during this time that one of the predecessors of the EU, the European Economic

---

[1] For comments on this development in the context of consumer law from an international perspective see the contributions in Rickett and Telfer (eds.), *International Perspectives on Consumers' Access to Justice*. Charles Rickett and Thomas Telfer explain that 'consumer law is fundamental to an understanding of the dimensions of a just, fair and efficient … justice system' (C. E. F. Rickett and T. G. W. Telfer, 'Consumers' Access to Justice: An Introduction' in *ibid.*, p. 13). Iain Ramsay adds that one must differentiate between a 'narrow and a broad concept of access to justice' that refer to various stages of the access to justice movement (I. Ramsay, 'Consumer Redress and Access to Justice' in *ibid.*, p. 19).
[2] See the following chapters for details.
[3] For general comments on EU consumer law, its development and policy-making see S. Weatherill, *EU Consumer Law and Policy* (2nd edn, Cheltenham: Edward Elgar, 2013);

Community (EEC), started to make express reference to consumer issues. Two of the first relevant policy papers were the 1975 Council Resolution on a preliminary programme of the EEC for a consumer protection and information policy[4] and the annexed Preliminary Programme of the EEC for a consumer protection and information policy (1975 Preliminary Programme).[5] The latter identified five 'basic rights', of which one directly referred to procedural issues: the 'right of redress'.[6] The 1975 Preliminary Programme went on to state that 'these rights should be given greater substance by action under specific Community policies'.[7] With regard to redress rights, the Commission was asked to study and evaluate various existing redress mechanisms and, if deemed necessary, to come forward with proposals for improving the situation in the EU.[8]

The 1980s and early 1990s were characterised by the enactment of the first consumer protection directives to regulate specific fields of interests. Although some of them contained certain procedural rules,[9] most directives enacted during that period primarily focused on *non*-procedural aspects. However, where they did contain procedural rules, the rules were

---

I. Ramsay, *Consumer Law and Policy* (3rd edn, Oxford: Hart, 2012), pp. 1–126; N. Reich and H.-W. Micklitz, *Europäisches Verbraucherrecht* (4th edn, Baden-Baden: Nomos, 2003); S. Weatherill, 'Consumer Policy' in P. Craig and G. de Búrca (eds.), *The Evolution of EU Law* (2nd edn: Oxford University Press, 2011), pp. 837–76; H.-W. Micklitz and S. Weatherill, 'Consumer Policy in the European Community: Before and after Maastricht', *Journal of Consumer Policy*, 16 (1993), 285–321; P. Nebbia and T. Ashkam, *EU Consumer Law* (Oxford University Press, 2004); B. Lurger and S. Augenhofer, *Österreichisches und Europäisches Konsumentenschutzrecht* (2nd edn, Vienna: Springer, 2008), pp. 34–40 and 45–217; N. Reich et al. (eds.), *European Consumer Law* (2nd edn, Cambridge: Intersentia, 2014), pp. 1–65; the contributions in N. Reich and G. Woodroffe (eds.), *European Consumer Policy after Maastricht* (Dordrecht: Kluwer Academic, 2010).

4 Council Resolution on a preliminary programme of the European Economic Community for a consumer protection and information policy, 14 April 1975, OJ 1975 No. C92/1.

5 Preliminary programme of the European Economic Community for a consumer protection and information policy, 25 April 1975, OJ 1975 No. C092/2.

6 *Ibid.*, para. 3. The other four basic rights listed there are the right to protection of health and safety, to protection of economic interests, to information and education and the right of representation/the right to be heard, e.g., via public consultation processes.

7 *Ibid.*, para. 4.   8 *Ibid.*, paras. 33–4.

9 See, for example, Article 4 Misleading Advertising Directive (Council Directive 84/450/EEC relating to the approximation of the laws, regulations and administrative provisions of the Member States concerning misleading advertising, 10 September 1984, OJ 1984 No. L250/17); Article 12 Medicinal Products Advertising Directive (Council Directive 92/28/EEC on the advertising of medicinal products for human use, 31 March 1992, OJ 1992 No. L113/13); Article 7 Unfair Contract Terms Directive (see 'The Directive on Consumer Rights' in Chapter 9 below for details on the directive); Article 11 Distance Selling Directive (see 'The Directive on Consumer Rights' in Chapter 9 below for details).

only applicable in that specific sector, within the scope of the respective directive.

It was nearly two decades after the 1975 Preliminary Programme's appeal for a comprehensive answer that the Commission finally presented something more concrete with regard to comprehensive procedural law issues. In the mid-1990s, two important policy papers were published: the 1993 Green Paper on the access of consumers to justice and the settlement of consumer disputes in the single market (1993 Consumer Access to Justice Green Paper)[10] and the 1996 follow-up Action Plan on consumer access to justice and the settlement of consumer disputes in the internal market (1996 Action Plan).[11] Focusing mainly on cross-border issues, both came to the conclusion that a multidimensional procedural approach should be taken. Introducing only one kind of mechanism might have solved some issues, but it was acknowledged that consumer disputes can adopt various forms and therefore warrant several different redress devices. At that time, however, the only procedural European tools used in consumer disputes were the aforementioned sectoral mechanisms of some older directives. The 1993 Consumer Access to Justice Green Paper and the 1996 Action Plan both emphasised the need for the introduction of additional and more far-reaching tools.[12]

The contemporary debate intensified in 2003 when shortly after a pan-EU survey on cross-border business-to-consumer (B2C) trade had provided evidence for the existence of consumer distrust in the cross-border B2C market,[13] the Directorate-General for Health and Consumers (DG SANCO) asked for further detailed research related to consumer complaints in general. The result of this, the 2004 Eurobarometer study on European Union citizens and access to justice[14] (2004 Access to Justice Survey) revealed several shortcomings in consumer rights enforcement.

[10] Green Paper on access of consumers to justice and the settlement of consumer disputes in the single market, 16 November 1993, COM(93) 576 final.

[11] Action Plan on consumer access to justice and the settlement of consumer disputes in the internal market, 14 February 1996, COM(96) 13 final.

[12] See the 'proposed initiatives' in *ibid.*, pp. 13–19 or the 'themes for discussion' in the 1993 Consumer Access to Justice Green Paper, pp. 77–85.

[13] European Opinion Research Group and EOS Gallup Europe, 'Public Opinion in Europe: Views on Business-to-consumer Cross-border Trade', Standard Eurobarometer 57.2 / Flash Eurobarometer 128, (2002), available at ec.europa.eu/public_opinion/archives/ebs/ebs_175_fl128_en.pdf.

[14] European Opinion Research Group, 'European Union Citizens and Access to Justice', Special Eurobarometer 195, (2004), available at www.medsos.gr/medsos/images/stories/PDF/eurobarometer_11-04_en.pdf. Several other 'official' European Union surveys and studies followed and confirmed the research results (see, for example, TNS Opinion & Social,

First and foremost, it was shown that consumers generally do not complain (47 per cent)[15] or do so very rarely (30 per cent)[16] if they encounter a problem with a good or service. The survey also explained that only a minority (13 per cent) of those who actually complained brought the case to court if they could not reach an amicable solution.[17] Furthermore, approximately two-thirds of the consumers who participated in the 2004 Access to Justice Survey claimed that they would generally be willing to go to court but that several factors prevented them from taking further action. The most cited reasons for this included financial issues and issues related to the length or presumed complexity of legal proceedings.[18] At the same time, interesting supplementary data were presented that influenced further actions in European consumer policy-making: (1) the majority of consumers who had already heard about the existence of ADR bodies would be willing to resort to them;[19] (2) the availability of collective redress mechanisms would encourage consumers to bring their cases to courts;[20] and (3) the vast majority of consumers were not aware of the Network for the extra-judicial settlement of consumer disputes (EEJ-Net: a pan-EU body established to enhance cross-border ADR tools), with 92 per cent having never heard of EEJ-Net.[21]

As will be shown in more detail in later chapters, the first two issues strongly influenced the policy-making of the Commission in the fields of ADR/ODR and compensatory collective redress tools. In response to the third issue of consumers' general unawareness of the existence of EEJ-Net and the need to facilitate and coordinate further consumer assistance by specialised agencies, EEJ-Net and the Euroguichet Network, a network focusing on general consumer information, were merged in 2005, creating

---

'Consumer Protection in the Internal Market', Special Eurobarometer 252, (2006), available at ec.europa.eu/public_opinion/archives/ebs/ebs252_en.pdf (2006 Consumer Protection Eurobarometer Study); The Gallup Organization Hungary, 'Attitudes towards Cross-border Sales and Consumer Protection', Flash Eurobarometer 282, (2010), available at ec.europa. eu/public_opinion/flash/fl_282_en.pdf).

[15] European Opinion Research Group, 'European Union Citizens and Access to Justice', p. 9.

[16] Ibid.

[17] Ibid., p. 26. The accompanying executive summary explains that consumers did so by either consulting 'a solicitor who brought the matter to court' or by bringing 'the matter to court [by] themselves' (European Opinion Research Group, 'European Union Citizens and Access to Justice – Executive Summary', summary accompanying Special Eurobarometer 195, (2004), p. 11 (on file with the author)).

[18] European Opinion Research Group, 'European Union Citizens and Access to Justice', p. 32.

[19] Ibid., p. 15.   [20] Ibid., p. 36.   [21] Ibid., p. 66.

the European Consumer Centres Network (ECC-Net). It was hoped that such a move would reorganise and unify consumer support at the EU level. I will revisit also ECC-Net and its activities later in this book. The deliberations in the field of redress mechanisms have led to the introduction of new consumer protection tools at the EU level, such as the 1998 Injunctions Directive[22] (repealed by the 2009 Injunctions Directive[23]), the 2004 Regulation on Consumer Protection Cooperation,[24] the 2007 Small Claims Regulation[25] and tools to enhance alternative dispute resolution – the ADR Directive and ODR Regulation are the most recent examples.[26] The Commission furthermore opened the public discussion on the possibility of a mandatory introduction of a compensatory collective redress mechanism in 2007 with the EU Consumer Policy Strategy 2007–2013[27] and the Leuven 'brainstorming event on collective [consumer] redress' later that year.[28] Both led to a more concrete step in 2008 when the Commission published its Green Paper on Consumer Collective Redress[29] and to further, heavy debates among stakeholder groups (I will explain this later in more detail). The debate on consumer collective redress also reaffirmed the Commission's long-term goal. According to the Commission, the ultimate purpose of effective procedural access to justice is to enhance the internal market. Serving consumer interests in the sense of simplifying their rights enforcement would, in

---

[22] See 'The Injunctions Directive (1998/2009)' in Chapter 4 below for details.

[23] See *ibid.* for details.

[24] See 'The Regulation on Consumer Protection Cooperation (2004)' in Chapter 4 below for details.

[25] The European Consumer Complaint Form is included in the Communication from the Commission on the out-of-court settlement of consumer disputes, 30 March 1998, COM(1998) 198 final.

[26] See 'Alternative Dispute Resolution (2008/2013)' (in particular 'The ADR Directive (2013)' and 'The ODR Regulation (2013)) in Chapter 4 below for details.

[27] Communication from the Commission to the Council, the European Parliament and the European Economic and Social Committee – EU Consumer Policy Strategy 2007–2013 – Empowering consumers, enhancing their welfare, effectively protecting them, 13 March 2007, COM(2007) 99 final (EU Consumer Policy Strategy 2007–2013). The 2007 Consumer Policy Strategy Paper considered the existing redress mechanisms as being one of '[t]he obstacles to a fully-fledged retail internal market' (*ibid.*, p. 5). It also emphasised the importance of considering 'action on collective redress mechanisms for consumers both for infringements of consumer protection rules and for breaches of EU anti-trust rules in line with its 2005 Green Paper on private damages actions' (*ibid.*, p. 11).

[28] See 'The Road towards the Green Paper on Consumer Collective Redress' in Chapter 5 below for details.

[29] See 'From the Green Paper on Consumer Collective Redress to the Commission's Collective Redress Recommendation' in Chapter 5 below for details.

the eyes of the Commission, also eventually benefit the business sector.[30] While this argument sounds convincing, a practical problem lies in the fact that the Commission often seems to lose sight of the necessity to improve consumer trust in the market. As will be discussed later, most of the mechanisms introduced thus far, when looked at closely, appear to be ill-conceived. Thus, it remains doubtful whether the Commission is really interested in meeting and satisfying the need to properly protect consumers' actual interests. I will also come back to this issue later in this book.

With the introduction of the aforementioned instruments and plans to introduce complementary procedural tools, the Commission responded to various procedural peculiarities, and although these are not restricted to the field of consumer law, they are undeniably of particular importance in this area. The traditional form of dispute solving, i.e., litigation between two individual parties, does not work in every case. It is obvious that not every consumer complaint reaches the courts when left unanswered. I have already briefly identified several reasons why consumers do not go to court, such as a rational disinterest in pursuing their claims because of the low individual amount at stake (that would not make it 'worth' suing), or the general risk of losing the case if one has to bear the court costs and attorney fees. A potential lack of time, motivation or legal knowledge are further impediments. Moreover, not every consumer who is frustrated by a defective good or imperfect service even complains. This passivity is even more common in a cross-border context, where additional practical problems such as language differences or difficulties in meeting the other party in person are encountered. Thus, it was only a matter of time before the Commission decided to react.

When taking a closer look at the introduced or often discussed complementary ways of dispute settlement, one can distinguish between various forms of rights enforcement tools. They extend from rights enforcement by private individuals to that by private bodies or public authorities; from devices for individual plaintiffs to collective mechanisms; from mechanisms that can be used in a preventive manner, i.e., before a dispute arises

---

[30] For examples see Article 1(1) Injunctions Directive; Recital 7 Small Claims Regulation; Green Paper on Consumer Collective Redress, paragraph 1. For a critical comment on the argument that enhancing international litigation raises consumer confidence in cross-border shopping see G. Wagner, 'Kollektiver Rechtsschutz – Regelungsbedarf bei Massen- und Streuschäden' in M. Casper *et al.* (eds.), *Auf dem Weg zu einer europäischen Sammelklage?* (Munich: Sellier European Law Publishers, 2009), pp. 44–6.

to ensure that traders[31] comply with the law – for example, by way of public approval for pharmaceutical products – to instruments that offer injunctive relief or compensatory tools when something has gone wrong; and from litigative to non-litigative means.

One can also observe a further feature: the linking of the development of procedural laws to a more comprehensive understanding of access to justice as outlined in Part I of this book. One can see that all these efforts, especially when examined as a whole, go beyond attempts to simply 'open' the courts. As Adrian Zuckerman observed shortly after the introduction of the Injunctions Directive, 'the function of the courts is not only to decide cases according to the law and the facts, but also to ensure that the limited resources of the system of civil justice are justly distributed between all those seeking justice'.[32] It is thus not only a question of enabling potential plaintiffs to file a claim by providing them with legal aid or granting them standing, it is also important that the judicial system itself and the availability of procedural devices are fair and efficient not only on paper, but also in practice. Even the best resources can only be of help if, to quote Zuckerman again, they 'are justly distributed'.[33] This requires that the best possible or best workable solutions are found for each individual case by evaluating the possible positive and negative consequences of the respective tool for consumers. In the following section, I will look at how some selected, prominent examples serve (or do not serve) these requirements in the field of consumer law.

---

[31] In the context of this book, the terms 'trader' and 'business' will be used interchangeably.
[32] Zuckerman, 'Justice in Crisis', p. 51.   [33] *Ibid.*

4

Prime examples

The Injunctions Directive (1998/2009)

The 1998 Directive on injunctions for the protection of consumer interests[1] (1998 Injunctions Directive, or when referring to both the 1998 Injunctions Directive and its successor, the 2009 Injunctions Directive, the Injunctions Directive) was one of the first instruments to deal with procedural consumer issues at the EU level. Unlike earlier approaches,[2] its scope of application is not limited to just one field of consumer law. Instead, the Injunctions Directive takes a more holistic approach in its applicability to several different directives.[3] Although it does not fit neatly in the consumer redress scheme in its literal meaning – the Injunctions Directive does not deal with questions of compensating consumers – it is worth mentioning the 1998 Injunctions Directive in the context of consumer access to justice, as it was the first directive to take a more comprehensive approach.

The Injunctions Directive reflects a more traditional view on protecting consumer rights. In the mid-1990s, it was believed that consumer interests were best protected using injunctions to fight business non-compliance with substantive law rules. Christopher Hodges, for example, comments on this as follows: 'The phenomenon [of European consumer redress] started with mechanisms to protect general consumer interests, often as an adjunct to enforcement of the new national consumer protection legislation. The available remedies would typically be limited to orders related to the defendant's conduct, such as injunctive relief, rather than monetary claims.'[4] In other words, the Commission was convinced

---

[1] Directive 98/27/EC of the European Parliament and of the Council on injunctions for the protection of consumers' interests, 19 May 1998, OJ 1998 No. L166/51.
[2] See the examples in Chapter 3, note 9 above.
[3] The respective directives are listed in Annex I Injunctions Directive.
[4] C. Hodges, *The Reform of Class and Representative Actions in European Legal Systems – A New Framework for Collective Redress in Europe* (Oxford: Hart, 2008), p. 6.

that special actions were needed to stop unlawful business practices that could potentially affect a large number of consumers. This was considered the key to improving consumer trust, and it was generally believed that this in turn would prove to be beneficial to enhance the internal market, the ultimate goal of the Commission.[5]

The Commission decided to craft a new pan-EU tool, the 1998 Injunctions Directive, to address collective consumer interests in trader compliance to certain consumer directives at both domestic and cross-border (or intra-community[6]) levels. Article 3 1998 Injunctions Directive asked Member States to designate suitable bodies, 'qualified entities', to represent collective consumer interests in injunction proceedings against traders who do not comply with the consumer directives (as transposed into the national laws of the Member States) listed in the Annex of the directive.

When evaluating possible mechanisms, the Commission learnt that those Member States that had already introduced injunction tools employed different approaches. Some Member States relied on enforcement by public authorities, others on rights enforcement by private bodies to protect consumer interests. A one-size-fits-all approach was therefore not considered the best possible solution if one wanted to rely on the expertise and experience of bodies already engaged in injunction proceedings at the national level. Under the Injunctions Directive, Member States are thus free to choose between public authorities and private bodies, or both. All qualified entities are to be listed in the Official Journal of the European Union (OJ) with updates every six months.[7] Article 2 1998 Injunctions Directive lists the possible actions that qualified entities could take. Article 7 clarifies that the directive is designed as a minimum harmonisation directive; Member States are thus given the means to introduce or maintain rules that go beyond the minimum standard of Article 2.

A key provision for cross-border cases is found in Article 4 1998 Injunctions Directive, which deals with 'intra-community infringements', understood as cases in which a trader from Member State A causes an infringement of consumer interests in Member State B. In such

---

[5] See, for example, Recital 4 1998 Injunctions Directive, where the Commission states that unlawful business practices 'can disrupt the smooth functioning of the internal market' and Recital 5 where the Commission claims that 'those difficulties are likely to diminish consumer confidence in the internal market'.

[6] See the heading of Article 4 1998 Injunctions Directive.

[7] Article 4(3) 1998 Injunctions Directive.

a case, qualified entities from Member State B should be given the chance to launch injunction proceedings in Member State A. I will return to this issue shortly in the following analysis of the actual relevance of the 1998 Injunctions Directive.

As will be shown in greater detail in Part III of this book, the Commission set the path for evaluating the transposition of eight consumer directives into national law with its Communication on European contract law[8] (2001 Contract Law Communication), the Action Plan for a more coherent European contract law[9] (2003 Contract Law Action Plan) and the Communication on European contract law and the revision of the acquis[10] (2004 Acquis Communication). The 1998 Injunctions Directive was one of the eight directives. The evaluation study report, the EC Consumer Law Compendium (Consumer Law Compendium),[11] revealed several shortcomings and peculiarities of the 1998 Injunctions Directive and its national transposition.

Regarding the installation of qualified entities under Article 3 1998 Injunctions Directive, data have shown that numbers widely diverged throughout the EU. Germany, Greece and the UK (if one counts the 204 weights and measures authorities separately and not as forming a single qualified entity)[12] headed the list with dozens of listed entities.[13] At the other end of the spectrum, however, several Member States had not yet made extensive use of the listing, and Malta had not even listed a single

---

[8] Communication from the Commission to the Council and the European Parliament on European Contract Law, 11 July 2001, COM(2001) 398 final. For some comments on this communication see D. Staudenmayer, 'The Commission Communication on European Contract Law and Its Follow-Up' in S. Grundmann and J. Stuyck (eds.), *An Academic Green Paper on European Private Law* (The Hague: Kluwer Law International, 2002), pp. 37–55.

[9] Communication from the Commission to the European Parliament and the Council – A more coherent European contract law – An action plan, 12 February 2003, COM(2003) 68 final. For critical comments on the 2003 Contract Law Action Plan see M. Kenny, 'The 2003 Action Plan on European Contract Law: Is the Commission Running Wild?', *European Law Review*, 28 (2003), 538–50.

[10] Communication from the Commission to the European Parliament and the Council – European Contract Law and the revision of the acquis: the way forward, 11 October 2004, COM(2004) 651 final.

[11] The study results are available both online at www.eu-consumer-law.org/ and as a hardcopy (H. Schulte-Nölke *et al.* (eds.), *EC Consumer Law Compendium: The Consumer Acquis and Its Transposition in the Member States* (Munich: Sellier, 2008)).

[12] On this issue see Schulte-Nölke *et al.* (eds.), *EC Consumer Law Compendium*, p. 399 and the (respectively) current list of qualified entities.

[13] Schulte-Nölke *et al.* (eds.), *EC Consumer Law Compendium*, pp. 398–9.

entity by 2006.[14] However, this does not necessarily mean that Member States with a comparatively low number of qualified entities did not make use of injunctions in the consumer field. Belgium, which had registered only two entities by 2006,[15] as well as Hungary and Sweden with only one registered entity each by 2006,[16] were among those Member States where injunction proceedings were found to be relatively popular.[17] Thus, a larger number of listed qualified entities did not necessarily guarantee the filing of more injunction suits. The central question was (and still is) whether listed entities possess(ed) enough financial power, personnel and expertise to launch proceedings.

Another interesting aspect revealed by the Consumer Law Compendium is the fact that the intra-community infringement procedure of Article 4 1998 Injunctions Directive, the central provision that allows for cross-border injunctions by listed entities, principally failed to show the desired effects. By the time the Consumer Law Compendium was published, only one cross-border case decided by the courts had been reported, a fact that prompted Christian Twigg-Flesner, the Consumer Law Compendium's rapporteur with respect to the 1998 Injunctions Directive, to comment that '[t]he evidence to date shows that the cross-border procedure is not being utilised'.[18] In the case at hand, the British Office of Fair Trading (OFT) sued Duchesne, a Belgian company, in a misleading marketing mailings case in a Belgian court.[19] Duchesne, engaging in distance-selling activities, approached consumers in various Member States, including the UK, by sending catalogues that allegedly gave the misleading impression that the recipients had won prizes. The OFT based its arguments on English substantive law and argued that Duchesne's promotion activities infringed several provisions of the 1991 Trade Practices Act and the 1988 Control of Misleading Advertising Regulations, claiming that Duchesne's activities had misled English consumers. While standing was not an issue, Duchesne tried to argue that its activities were governed by Belgium's business-friendlier substantive law and not the English equivalent. Passing the first ever cross-border European B2C judgment under

---

[14] *Ibid.*, p. 398.   [15] *Ibid.*   [16] *Ibid.*
[17] See J. Stuyck *et al.*, 'An Analysis and Evaluation of Alternative Means of Consumer Redress other than Redress through Ordinary Judicial Proceedings', report, University of Leuven, (2007), p. 346, available at www.eurofinas.org/uploads/documents/policies/OTHER%20POLICY%20ISSUES/comparative_report_en.pdf.
[18] Schulte-Nölke *et al.* (eds.), *EC Consumer Law Compendium*, p. 406.
[19] *Office of Fair Trading* v. *D Duchesne SA*, Cour d'Appel Bruxelles, 8 December 2005.

the 1998 Injunctions Directive,[20] both the court of first instance in 2004 and the appellate court in 2005 ruled in favour of the OFT.

Shortly after the publication of the Consumer Law Compendium, a second cross-border case reached the courts, again on the initiative of the OFT. In a case very similar to Duchesne, the OFT sued a Dutch distance-selling company, Best Sales, in the Netherlands.[21] The OFT argued that Best Sales had illegally approached British consumers promoting its products with the help of misleading prize-winner notifications. The Dutch court decided similarly to the Belgian courts and ordered Best Sales to stop its illegal promotional activities.[22]

In late 2008, the Commission issued its own first report on the application of the 1998 Injunctions Directive (2008 Injunctions Directive report).[23] From a consumer perspective, the findings were again disappointing. On the positive side, it was noted that every Member State had introduced injunction proceedings and that '[t]he field of application of the injunction procedure has widened over time',[24] at least at the national level. And although only two Article 4 cross-border cases had been decided at that time, Duchesne and Best Sales, the report also stressed the positive impact of the 1998 Injunctions Directive on the internal market. The OFT was able to beneficially use the Duchesne judgment, in particular, in negotiations with several other wrongdoers and secure binding undertakings from them, clearly showing a certain dissuasive effect on opportunistic traders.[25] Thus, according to the Commission, the cross-border

---

[20] Micklitz reports on a pre-1998 Injunctions Directive case launched by the German Verbraucherschutzverein in cooperation with the French Union Fédérale des Consommateurs (UFC Que Choisir) and the European Consumers' Organisation (BEUC) against 'Direct Shopping', a distance-shopping business operating from Germany (see H.-W. Micklitz, 'Cross-Border Consumer Conflicts – A French-German Experience', *Journal of Consumer Policy*, 16 (1993), 411–34).

[21] Rb Breda, 9 July 2008 (2009) 2 TvC 66–71, *Office of Fair Trading* v. *Best Sales BV*.

[22] See www.oft.gov.uk/shared_oft/press_release_attachments/bestsalesjudgment.pdf for a translation of the full decision into English and the accompanying press release of OFT at www.oft.gov.uk/news-and-updates/press/2008/86-08#.UT651Tdu0f4 for a summary.

[23] Report from the Commission concerning the application of Directive 98/27/EC of the European Parliament and of the Council on injunctions for the protection of consumers' interests, 18 November 2008, COM(2008) 756 final (2008 Injunctions Directive report).

[24] *Ibid.*, para. 4.

[25] See the cross-border examples of *OFT* v. *D.C. Direct Communications Venk BV* (2005) and *OFT* v. *Fitanova BV* (2005) in IBF International Consulting, 'Study on the Application of Directive 2009/22/EC on Injunctions for the Protection of Consumers' Interests (former Directive 98/27/EC)', report for DG SANCO, (2011), pp. 160–1 (on file with the author); *OFT* v. *William Pince Publishers* (2005) in OECD, 'Report on the Implementation of the 2003 OECD Guidelines for Protecting Consumers from Fraudulent and Deceptive

mechanism as introduced under Article 4 1998 Injunctions Directive was basically welcomed from a deterrence perspective.

However, there is no light without darkness. Despite the fact that the 1998 Injunctions Directive showed positive effects at the national level, i.e., Member States that had no injunction mechanisms in place prior to the adoption of the 1998 Injunctions Directive installed injunction tools on a broad basis,[26] the Commission could not hide its disappointment regarding cross-border cases. Two Article 4 cases decided by the courts within ten years was clearly not what the Commission had hoped for.

The 2008 Injunctions Directive report identified three main obstacles to the proper functioning of the cross-border mechanism: costs, procedure-related issues such as the length and complexity of injunction proceedings and – in several Member States – the limited impact of cessation rulings.[27]

As far as the first issue, the financial risk, is concerned, the situation does not largely differ from more traditional dispute-solving tools. The loser-pays principle is still the predominantly applied cost scheme in the EU.[28] In an international context, however, the problem is magnified, as it can be assumed that additional costs, such as translation costs or increased preparation costs resulting from the need to research the applicable legal regime or competent jurisdiction, might have to be taken into consideration.

The complexity and length of proceedings also takes a special position in cross-border cases. The 2007 Leuven report, a study conducted by the Study Centre for Consumer Law at the University of Leuven, showed that the overall length of injunction proceedings differed widely between Member States, ranging from a few months to several years.[29] A number

Commercial Practices across Borders', report, (2006), p. 47, available at www.oecd.org/internet/consumer/37125909.pdf.

[26] See IBF International Consulting, 'Study on the Application of Directive 2009/22/EC', p. 15.

[27] 2008 Injunctions Directive report, paras. 17–27. On the first two issues see, in addition, *ibid.*, para. 32, where the report explains that 'the mechanism created by the Directive to allow qualified entities of one Member State to act in another Member State has clearly not been as successful as was hoped. The main obstacle, which explains why so few injunctions have been sought to stop intra-Community infringements, is the lack of resources in the light of the financial risks borne by any eligible qualified entity, but also in the light of the expertise required to deal with the different procedures in the various Member States.'

[28] See, e.g., Hodges *et al.* (eds.), *The Costs and Funding of Civil Litigation* for details, in particular pp. 114–131 (Table 1) for an overview.

[29] Stuyck *et al.*, 'An Analysis and Evaluation of Alternative Means of Consumer Redress', p. 324.

of reasons could explain this considerable difference. For example, the general workload of courts in some Member States might be heavier than in others. Producing evidence might take longer than it would in purely domestic cases. A more technical reason, however, may be the fact that the complexity of injunction proceedings differs among Member States because the 1998 Injunctions Directive failed to introduce a standardised procedure.

With its 2008 Injunctions Directive report, the Commission also identified a different but nevertheless significant problem: the issue of the limited impact of cessation orders in many Member States. The Commission noted that, despite some notable exceptions, injunctions issued by the competent court in the majority of the Member States would not show any *erga omnes* effects, i.e., the effects of a cessation order would be limited to the particular case at hand and would not affect similar actions by the same trader in the future.[30] Further limitations can exist with respect to the territorial impact of cessation orders. The report explains that in several instances the effects of cessation orders might further be limited to the territory of a certain Member State. This basically means that traders could continue with their illegal practices, operating from another Member State or with respect to consumers in a different Member State.[31]

The 2008 Injunctions Directive report further provided another important explanation with respect to the low number of cross-border injunctions sought under the 1998 Injunctions Directive. It stated that many qualified entities might be limited in their actions not only because of a lack of sufficient financial resources, 'but also in the light of the expertise required to deal with the different procedures in the various Member States'.[32] The comment made in the 2008 Injunctions Directive report is justified because the Injunctions Directive does not ask Member States to guarantee that the qualified entities show a sufficient level of expertise to cope with these issues. Hence, one factor that is missing in this context is clear instructions directed at the Member States to facilitate cross-border activities with the help of properly educated, trained or experienced personnel in the qualified entities.

The 2008 Injunctions Directive report also briefly mentioned a potentially important complementary instrument: the 2004 Consumer

---

[30] 2008 Injunctions Directive report, paras. 25–6, which mention for example injunctions with respect to unfair contract terms in Austria, Germany, Hungary, Poland or Slovenia, which allow for certain *erga omnes* effects.

[31] *Ibid.*, para. 27.   [32] *Ibid.*, para. 32.

Protection Cooperation Regulation (CPC Regulation). The CPC Regulation, which I will discuss in more detail later,[33] was designed to enhance cross-border cooperation between 'competent authorities'. The term competent authorities as defined by Article 3(c) CPC Regulation refers to 'any *public* authority established either at national, regional or local level with specific responsibilities to enforce the laws that protect consumers' interests' (emphasis added). Article 8 CPC Regulation allows for 'requests for enforcement measures' by a competent authority from one Member State to a competent authority in another Member State. This makes sense in cases where a competent authority believes the best way to ensure a trader's legal compliance is to become active in the trader's home country but does not want to sue abroad. Pursuant to Article 8(1), the 'requested authority shall ... take all necessary enforcement measures to bring about the cessation or prohibition of the intra-Community infringement without delay'.[34] The 2008 Injunctions Directive report expresses the view that the CPC Regulation could solve, or at least mitigate, some of the obstacles in cross-border scenarios if the case was to be solved in the trader's home country. Without a doubt, the authorities in the trader's country have more experience with actions in that country than foreign authorities.[35] In addition, relying on Article 8 CPC Regulation enforcement requests can also decrease the overall costs of ensuring a trader's compliance.[36]

Shortly after the publication of the 2008 Injunctions Directive report, the 2009 Injunctions Directive was adopted.[37] In line with the Commission's conclusion of the 2008 Injunctions Directive report that 'it is not the time to propose any amendments to, or the repeal of, the Directive but that, on the contrary, [the Commission] should continue to examine the application of the Directive', the 2009 Injunctions Directive did not introduce any

---

[33] See 'The Regulation on Consumer Protection Cooperation (2004)' below.
[34] The term 'intra-Community infringement' is defined by Article 3(b) CPC Regulation as 'any act or omission contrary to the laws that protect consumers' interests, as defined in (a), that harms, or is likely to harm, the collective interests of consumers residing in a Member State or Member States other than the Member State where the act or omission originated or took place; or where the responsible seller or supplier is established; or where evidence or assets pertaining to the act or omission are to be found'.
[35] 2008 Injunctions Directive report, pp. 8–9.
[36] 2012 Injunctions Directive report, p. 7.
[37] Directive 2009/22/EC of the European Parliament and of the Council on injunctions for the protection of consumers' interests, 23 April 2009, OJ 2009 No. L 110/30. (It should be noted once again that the term 'Injunctions Directive' is used in this book when referring to both the 1998 Injunctions Directive and its successor, the 2009 Injunctions Directive.)

innovation. Rather it clarified the actual situation in 2009, as over time, the scope of the 1998 Injunctions Directive (as expressed in its Annex) was extended to several new consumer directives, which all together were (re)listed in Annex I 2009 Injunctions Directive.

However, the discussions of whether the scope and contents of the Injunctions Directive should be changed did not abate. On the contrary, several of the obstacles identified by the Consumer Law Compendium and the 2008 Injunctions Directive report were confirmed in 2012 when the Commission issued another report on the application of the Injunctions Directive (2012 Injunctions Directive report).[38] The 2012 Injunctions Directive report also commented on issues that were not prominently covered by the previous Injunctions Directive report.

One of these issues is linked to Article 7 Injunctions Directive, which allows for 'wider actions', which basically means that Member States are allowed to introduce or maintain stricter provisions. Taking the later shift in EU consumer law policy-making towards an increased use of maximum harmonisation into consideration,[39] it must – from a consumer perspective – be a relief that the 2009 Injunctions Directive retained the traditional, minimum harmonisation solution taken by the 1998 Injunctions Directive. This allowed Member States with more stringent regimes to go or stay beyond the standard of the Injunctions Directive.[40] In the 2012 Injunctions Directive report, the Commission admitted that '[t]he extension [i.e., the fact that several Member States go beyond the Injunctions Directive standard] is positive for consumers'.[41]

The findings of the 2012 Injunctions Directive report prove that the extent of the use of injunction tools varies from one Member State to the other, a fact that has prompted some stakeholders to ask for greater harmonisation.[42] In this context, however, harmonisation does not relate to the maximum versus minimum harmonisation debate, which I will touch upon several times later in this book. Instead, it refers to the lack of actual rules and guidelines on how injunction proceedings should be procedurally designed and how injunctions should be used. What the Injunctions

---

[38] Report from the Commission to the European Parliament and the Council Concerning the application of Directive 2009/22/EC of the European Parliament and of the Council on injunctions for the protection of consumers' interest Brussels, 6 November 2012, COM(2012) 635 final (2012 Injunctions Directive report).

[39] See Part III below for details. The terms maximum harmonisation and full harmonisation are used interchangeably in this book.

[40] For practical examples see Schulte-Nölke *et al.* (eds.), *EC Consumer Law Compendium*, pp. 384.

[41] 2012 Injunctions Directive report, p. 5.   [42] *Ibid.*, p. 15.

Directive does is instruct Member States to introduce mechanisms under which qualified entities can seek injunction actions as defined in Article 2 Injunctions Directive. It does not, however, introduce clear minimum rules regarding the procedural side of those cessation order procedures. Harmonisation, as requested by some stakeholders in the course of the evaluation underlying the 2012 Injunctions Directive report, is thus understood as a criticism of the absence of more concrete standards and specifications and not as a call to put an end to the minimum harmonisation approach of Article 7. If the Commission wants, it could precisely define the mechanism and (in addition) of course broaden the scope by adding further fields to the Injunctions Directive, as was suggested by several stakeholders in the context of the 2012 Injunctions Directive report.[43] However, the primary critique with respect to harmonisation related to a lack of precise minimum standards for cessation procedures. The Commission comments on the need to reach a certain standard as follows: 'In any event, it would be appropriate for those provisions that are particularly useful for improving the effectiveness of injunctions used in some Member States to be introduced into the others.'[44]

On a positive note, the 2012 Injunctions Directive report revealed that the number of qualified entities had risen further. By March 2012, more than 300 national bodies had been registered and even Malta, who had no listed entities in 2006, had introduced 4 by 2012.[45] Although this trend should be welcomed, at the same time one should note that most of the reported injunction cases were launched by qualified entities with a comparatively strong financial background and above-average legal knowledge and experience, while most of the other qualified entities remained passive.

Another basically positive aspect identified by the 2012 Injunctions Directive report was that the number of cross-border injunctions had generally risen compared with those in the previous report. Whereas the 2008 Injunctions Directive report mentioned only two cross-border injunctions, the 2012 Injunctions Directive report listed approximately

---

[43] See *ibid.*, where it is shown that some stakeholders asked for the inclusion of privacy or personal data protection-related aspects.

[44] *Ibid.*

[45] *Ibid.*, p. 5. The 204 UK weights and measures authorities are not counted separately here. For details see Commission communication concerning Article 4(3) of Directive 2009/22/EC of the European Parliament and of the Council on injunctions for the protection of consumers' interests, which codifies Directive 98/27/EC, concerning the entities qualified to bring an action under Article 2 of this Directive, OJ 2012 No. C97/1, 35.

seventy.[46] While the two first ever cross-border cessation orders under the Injunctions Directive framework were initiated by the British OFT,[47] the 2012 Injunctions Directive revealed that other qualified entities in other Member States had caught up: the Federation of German Consumer Organisations, for example, had initiated approximately twenty cases and the Austrian Federal Chamber of Labour eight.[48]

One should treat this data with caution, however. Most of the reported cross-border cases do not fall under the category of Article 4 cross-border actions. The Article 4 model of intra-community infringement actions under the Injunctions Directive refers to cases where a qualified entity from one Member State sues in a different Member State. The two OFT cases are good examples of that. The OFT sued in Belgium (Duchesne) and the Netherlands (Best Sales) to protect British consumers against wrongdoers from different Member States. However, most of the cross-border cases listed in the 2012 Injunctions Directive report refer to situations where qualified entities sue a foreign business in *their own* Member State's courts, i.e., in the courts of the Member State of the qualified entity and affected consumers (and not in the courts of the trader's Member State), and thus form a different category of cross-border injunctions.[49] The preference for claiming for injunctive relief in domestic courts cannot be directly explained with the Injunctions Directive regime. Instead, it is linked to the fact that the Brussels I and Rome II Regulations prove beneficial for suing in domestic courts. Because the Brussels I regime allows application to domestic courts in a variety of consumer law-related instances, including the resolution of the more 'popular' disputes as identified in the 2012 Injunctions Directive report (unfair contract terms,[50] unfair commercial practices and misleading advertising[51]), intra-community infringement actions to be launched in the trader's home country do not seem to make much sense. There are various reasons for this. First, unlike in the case

---

[46] 2012 Injunctions Directive report, p. 4. Compared to the overall number of reported injunction cases under the 2012 Injunctions Directive report, 5,632, this number is still relatively small.

[47] For more details on the OFT in general and in this context in particular see Ramsay, *Consumer Law and Policy*, pp. 292–4 and 317–59.

[48] 2012 Injunctions Directive report, p. 4.

[49] *Ibid.*, pp. 4 and 6.

[50] R. Geimer, 'Art. 5 EuGVVO' in R. Geimer and R. A. Schütze (eds.), *Europäisches Zivilverfahrensrecht* (3rd edn, Munich: C. H. Beck, 2010), Article 5 EuGVVO para. 232.

[51] P. Mankowski, 'Art 5' in U. Magnus and P. Mankowski (eds.), *Brussels I Regulation* (2nd edn, Munich: Sellier, 2012), Art 5 Paras. 253–257; J. Kropholler and J. von Hein, *Europäisches Zivilprozessrecht* (9th edn, Frankfurt am Main: Verlag Recht und Wirtschaft, 2011), Article 5 EuGVO Para. 74.

of intra-community infringement actions, qualified entities can launch proceedings in their own language and thus can invest more energy and financial resources in preparing and dealing with the 'really important' issues, for example, the legal question(s) at hand. Second, qualified entities are more confident with their own legal systems, and thus are more willing to initiate proceedings. And third, because under the Rome II regime the substantive laws of the Member State where the affected consumers reside in would be applicable,[52] it makes more sense if a qualified entity from that country takes the lead role as it can be expected that it would be more familiar with the relevant laws than a foreign competent entity.

In summary of the 2012 Injunctions Directive report one can note that there is a certain positive trend in the injunctions field. In particular, cessation orders at the national level now have greater significance.[53] However, the cross-border situation looks different, although the data in the report show that qualified entities under the Injunctions Directive do make some (modest) use of it in their home country to sue foreign traders. It cannot be denied that there is a need for a more functional cross-border regime, but how can this be accomplished? In an earlier resolution

---

[52] Depending on the question in dispute, either Article 4(1) or Article 6(1) Rome II Regulation could lead to the applicability of the substantive law of the consumers' home country to protect collective interests of consumers. For the applicability of domestic substantive law via Article 4(1) Rome II Regulation in cases of unfair contract terms see, for example, the argumentation of the German Federal Court of Justice (*Bundesgerichtshof*; BGH) in its judgment in Xa ZR 19/08 (9 July 2009), Recital II.3.aa, where the BGH explains that the applicability of domestic law is 'a consequence of Article 4(1) Rome II Regulation' (translation mine). For the use of Article 6(1) Rome II Regulation in arriving at the domestic substantive laws of the consumers' home country in injunction proceedings with respect to the Unfair Commercial Practices Directive (UCPD) and the Directive on Misleading and Comparative Advertising see M. Illmer, 'Art. 6 Rome II' in P. Huber (ed.), *Rome II Regulation* (Munich: Sellier, 2011), Art. 6 Rome II para. 5, where Martin Illmer explains as follows: 'Although the material scope of Rome II's uniform conflict rule reaches further than the scope of the Directives [i.e. the UCPD and the Directive on Misleading and Comparative Advertising], it should at least cover those acts that are regarded as unfair competitive behaviour by those Directives'. See also Recital 21 Rome II Regulation, which explains that Article 6 Rome II Regulation should be understood as a clarification of Article 4 Rome II Regulation for 'matters of unfair competition' to 'protect ... consumers ... properly'. On the relationship between Articles 4 and 6 Rome II Regulation see further A. Dickinson, *The Rome II Regulation: The Law Applicable to Non-Contractual Obligations* (Oxford University Press, 2008), chapter 6, paras. 6.11–6.13 and 6.56–6.57; A. Dickinson, *The Rome II Regulation: The Law Applicable to Non-Contractual Obligations: Updating Supplement* (Oxford University Press, 2010), chapter 6, paras. 6.41 and 6.49.

[53] For national examples prior to the 1998 Injunctions Directive see Schulte-Nölke et al. (eds.), *EC Consumer Law Compendium*, pp. 386–7.

of the European Parliament (Parliament) titled 'Towards a Coherent European Approach to Collective Redress',[54] the Parliament criticised the status quo of several procedural tools in cross-border settings. With respect to cross-border injunctions, the Parliament noted that linking the injunctions mechanism of the Injunctions Directive to the regime of the CPC Regulation might show a positive effect. Thus, it mandated the Commission 'to strengthen and increase the effectiveness of existing instruments such as Directive 98/27/EC on injunctions for the protection of consumers' interests and Regulation (EC) No 2006/2004 on cooperation between national authorities responsible for the enforcement of consumer protection laws, to ensure appropriate public enforcement of consumers' rights in the EU'.[55] However, at the time of writing this book, it is not yet possible to state that these aims have been achieved.[56]

The 2012 Injunctions Directive report includes some (vaguely worded) suggestions to improve the situation. A general distinction is made between the two categories of 'non legislative measures' and 'possible changes in the legal framework', i.e., legislative measures.[57] The first group refers to actions to raise the awareness of qualified entities. The idea behind this is that not every qualified entity is properly familiar with the Injunctions Directive's model of intra-community infringement actions and how they are to be launched.[58]

The second category comprises various core legal issues. The range stretches from a possible extension of the scope of application of the Injunctions Directive to questions on the effect and enforcement of possible cessation orders. More practical obstacles such as legal costs and the duration of proceedings were also mentioned. Some of these ideas, such as financial or time-related impediments, should sound familiar, especially in the context of access to justice.

At the same time, however, the Commission has not yet found any clear answer regarding how to improve the use of injunctions, especially in

---

[54] European Parliament resolution on 'Towards a Coherent European Approach to Collective Redress', 2 February 2012, 2011/2089(INI).

[55] Ibid., para. 14.

[56] In the context of the CPC Regulation it should be noted that an extensive review project was initiated by the Commission in 2011 (see ec.europa.eu/smart-regulation/impact/planned_ia/docs/2014_sanco_001_consumer_protection_cooperation_review_en.pdf and ec.europa.eu/consumers/enforcement/index_en.htm for details). It remains to be seen if (and if so, how) the results of this review will impact on the current legal framework of the CPC Regulation. For details on the CPC Regulation see 'The Regulation on Consumer Protection Cooperation (2004)' below.

[57] 2012 Injunctions Directive report, p. 14.   [58] Ibid.

cross-border situations. Although it has stated that it 'takes note of the issues raised by stakeholders and their suggestions to address them [and that it] ... will continue monitoring the application of the Directive in the Member States',[59] the Commission was also profoundly convinced that 'there does not appear to be sufficiently strong reasons to propose amendments to the Directive at this stage'.[60] If, however, the Commission was really interested in strengthening cross-border enforcement, it would be well advised to react to the findings of the pertinent reports and studies. Otherwise, there is the justified fear that the statement that '[c]ross-border litigation ... plays, de facto, no role',[61] as concluded by Ulrike Docekal, Peter Kolba, Hans-W. Micklitz and Peter Rott in their comprehensive study on the Injunctions Directive in 2005, will become a timeless classic.

The Legal Aid Directive (2003)

The concept of providing legal aid can be considered the most genuine form of improving the traditional concept of procedural access to justice. Not only was legal aid at the centre of concern in the first wave of the Florence Project, but also various human rights doctrines have dealt with this issue.[62] Two early instruments in this respect are the 1977 European Agreement on the Transmission of Applications for Legal Aid (1977 Legal Aid Agreement)[63] and the 1980 Hague Convention on International Access to Justice (1980 Access to Justice Convention).[64] The 1977 Legal Aid Agreement focused on the application side of legal aid in cross-border settings, i.e., on the procedure for applying for legal aid (but did not regulate the issue of granting legal aid itself). In contrast, the 1980 Access to Justice Convention tried to remove legal barriers to *obtaining* legal aid in a foreign country by asking its contracting states to guarantee that '[n]ationals of any Contracting State and persons habitually resident in any Contracting State shall be entitled to legal aid for court proceedings in civil and commercial matters in each Contracting State on the same

---

[59] *Ibid.*, p. 16.   [60] *Ibid.*
[61] U. Docekal *et al.*, 'The Implementation of Directive 98/27/EC in the Member States – Summary of Results', study for Institute for European Business and Consumer Law, (2005), p. 9 (on file with the author).
[62] See 'Access to Justice in the Course of Time' in Chapter 2 above.
[63] European Agreement on the Transmission of Applications for Legal Aid, 27 January 1977.
[64] Hague Convention on International Access to Justice, 25 October 1980.

conditions as if they themselves were nationals of and habitually resident in that State'.[65] However, at the time of writing this book, neither the 1977 Legal Aid Agreement nor the 1980 Access to Justice Convention have been signed and/or ratified by all EU Member States.[66]

At the pan-EU level, it was the Tampere Council that facilitated further discussions. The Tampere Council's Presidency Conclusions expressed the wish 'to establish minimum standards ensuring an adequate level of legal aid in cross-border cases throughout the Union'.[67] The Commission answered that call, and soon after the publication of the first Commission proposal,[68] the Legal Aid Directive[69] was adopted.

The Legal Aid Directive has been applicable since 30 November 2004[70] in all Member States except Denmark and introduces a mechanism to facilitate the granting of legal aid in cross-border cases.[71] It explicitly links the provision of legal aid to the concept of procedural access to justice. Most prominently, Article 1 defines the scope and aim of the directive as follows: 'to improve access to justice in cross-border disputes by establishing minimum common rules relating to legal aid in such disputes'. To achieve this, the Legal Aid Directive asks the Member States to ensure that everybody who wants to institute cross-border legal proceedings (as defined under Article 2(1) Legal Aid Directive)[72] in civil or commercial matters (i.e., also in, but not limited to, B2C cases) has the right to

---

[65] Article 1 1980 Access to Justice Convention.

[66] See www.conventions.coe.int/Treaty/Commun/ChercheSig.asp?NT=092 &CM=8&DF=&CL=ENG and www.hcch.net/index_en.php?act=conventions. status&cid=91 for the status of the Agreement and Convention respectively.

[67] Presidency Conclusions, Tampere European Council, 15 and 16 October 1999, para. 30.

[68] Proposal for a Council Directive to improve access to justice in cross-border disputes by establishing minimum common rules relating to legal aid and other financial aspects of civil proceedings, 30 April 2002, COM(2002) 13 final.

[69] Council Directive 2003/8/EC to improve access to justice in cross-border disputes by establishing minimum common rules relating to legal aid for such disputes, 27 January 2003, OJ 2003 No. L26/41.

[70] The only exception is Article 3(2)(a) Legal Aid Directive on legal aid for pre-litigation advice which had to be implemented by the Member States by 30 May 2006.

[71] The Legal Aid Directive is based on the assumption that the financial disincentives for filing a suit are stronger in a cross-border situation as a result of '[t]he complexity of and difference between the legal systems in the Member States' (Recital 18 Legal Aid Directive).

[72] Article 2(1) Legal Aid Directive: 'For the purposes of this Directive, a cross-border dispute is one where the party applying for legal aid in the context of this Directive is domiciled or habitually resident in a Member State other than the Member State where the court is sitting or where the decision is to be enforced.'

be granted legal aid if certain conditions (as explained in the Legal Aid Directive) are met.[73]

In each Member State, 'competent authorities' exist to handle legal aid requests. These competent authorities are designated by the respective Member State as being in charge of sending and receiving legal aid applications.[74] Article 3(2) Legal Aid Directive clarifies that legal aid refers to two stages: legal aid to be enjoyed at the application stage (Articles 3(2) (a) and 8) and legal aid to be granted for the proceedings in the main subject matter (Articles 3(2)(b) and 7). With respect to the latter, Article 7 stresses that granted legal aid has to include costs that can be of particular importance in cross-border cases, such as interpretation, translation or travel costs arising in the course of the main proceedings.

The decision whether to eventually grant legal aid to the applicant is made by the competent authority of the Member State where the court with competence in the main subject matter is located.[75] In addition to this, Article 8 Legal Aid Directive states that the applicants shall already have the chance to enjoy legal aid (with respect to the support by local lawyers and the translation of necessary documents[76]) before the application is received by the aforementioned competent authority. For these cases it is for the Member State where the applicant habitually resides to provide respective legal aid.

In theory, the provisions of the Legal Aid Directive are not only applicable with respect to litigation but also with regard to mandatory or court-ordered 'extrajudicial procedures' defined by Article 10 Legal Aid Directive as those forms of non-litigation or 'non-litigative' procedures in which 'the law requires the parties to use them, or if the parties to the dispute are ordered by the court to have recourse to them'. Thus, parties

---

[73] Article 1(1) Legal Aid Directive: 'The purpose of this Directive is to improve access to justice in cross-border disputes by establishing minimum common rules relating to legal aid in such disputes.' Article 3(1) Legal Aid Directive adds: 'Natural persons involved in a dispute covered by this Directive shall be entitled to receive appropriate legal aid in order to ensure their effective access to justice in accordance with the conditions laid down in this Directive.' For the conditions that need to be fulfilled to qualify for legal aid see in particular Article 5 Legal Aid Directive. The 2012 Legal Aid Directive report explains that prior to the adoption of the Legal Aid Directive only a limited number of Member States had already offered legal aid for cross-border claims (see 2012 Legal Aid Directive report, p. 4).

[74] Article 14(1) Legal Aid Directive.   [75] Article 12 Legal Aid Directive.

[76] Pursuant to Article 13(6), likely necessary translations at the application stage may not be charged to the applicant. Member States are, however, allowed to 'lay down that the applicant must repay the costs of translation borne by the competent transmitting authority if the application for legal aid is rejected by the competent authority'.

could also possibly benefit in certain ADR cases if the general requirements for granting legal aid are fulfilled. While one imagines that this provision would be welcomed, it must be said that (as will be seen shortly) it has not yet been fully transposed into the national laws of the Member States. Moreover, *voluntary* ADR as covered by the ADR Directive and ODR Regulation does not fall under this provision. Hence, in practice, Article 10 is not of major relevance. From the viewpoint of enhanced consumer redress this is indeed regrettable.

Taking priority over the aforementioned 1977 Legal Aid Agreement and the 1980 Access to Justice Convention,[77] the Legal Aid Directive also introduces procedural rules for each stage of the application and decision processes, although some scope is left to the Member States to apply applicant-friendlier provisions[78] or to determine parameters that are not defined in detail in the directive.[79] This especially ensures that Member States already using comparable models prior to the adoption of the Legal Aid Directive can maintain their existing rules (unless they do not meet the minimum standards of the Legal Aid Directive).

Finally, it should also be noted that several important documents have been made publicly accessible. Of prime importance is the standard application form as requested by Article 16 Legal Aid Directive. This form can be found in the official languages of all Member States on the website of the European e-Justice Portal.[80] To facilitate the filing, submission and processing of the application, the standard application form is supported by another publicly accessible document – a special manual that includes information about the competent national authorities under the Legal Aid Directive.[81]

In late 2009, the European Council adopted the Stockholm Programme, a five-year (2010–2014) programme to evaluate EU legislation in the areas

---

[77] Article 20 Legal Aid Directive.   [78] Article 19 Legal Aid Directive.

[79] See, for example, Article 5 Legal Aid Directive on conditions to determine whether an applicant is worthy of enjoying legal aid in a particular case. Member States should apply 'objective factors' (Article 5 (2)) when assessing the economic situation of an applicant. However, the directive does not define any parameters for how these factors should be applied in a standardised way in the Member States. Furthermore, Article 5(3), which allows for defining national 'thresholds above which legal aid applicants are deemed partly or totally able to bear the costs of proceedings', does not really ensure certainty for consumers, who might be subject to different national thresholds depending on which Member State's court decides.

[80] The English version is available at e-justice.europa.eu/content_legal_aid_forms-157-en.do.

[81] The manual is available at ec.europa.eu/justice_home/judicialatlascivil/html/pdf/manual_la.pdf.

of justice, freedom and security.[82] The targets of the Stockholm Programme were more precisely defined by its 2010 Action Plan (Stockholm Programme Action Plan).[83] Legal Aid was put on the agenda twice in that policy paper. While the call for a 'Legislative proposal on Legal Advice and Legal Aid' refers to criminal proceedings,[84] the Stockholm Action Plan also asked for an assessment of the Legal Aid Directive.[85] The results were presented in early 2012, when the Commission delivered its report on the application of Directive 2003/8/EC to improve access to justice in cross-border disputes by establishing minimum common rules relating to legal aid for such disputes (2012 Legal Aid Directive report).[86]

The 2012 Legal Aid Directive report shows that – with regard to litigation proceedings – cross-border legal aid has been introduced in all Member States.[87] However, the situation looks different regarding extra-judicial procedures and legal aid available at the enforcement stage of judgments.[88] In both areas, national implementation is still pending in a considerable number of Member States. The somewhat vague wording of the Legal Aid Directive with only rudimentary rules for the implementation of its provisions, a general problem for the 'success' of the Legal Aid Directive, has surely been of little help in this regard.[89]

---

[82] The Stockholm Programme – An open and secure Europe serving and protecting citizens, OJ 2010 No. C115/1.

[83] See Chapter 2, note 100 above.

[84] See Stockholm Programme Action Plan, p. 14.   [85] See *ibid.*, p. 24.

[86] Report from the Commission to the European Parliament, the Council and the European Economic and Social Committee on the application of Directive 2003/8/EC to improve access to justice in cross-border disputes by establishing minimum common rules relating to legal aid for such disputes, 23 February 2012, COM(2012) 71 final. The 2012 Legal Aid Directive report presents the first comprehensive data on the implementation and practical use of the Legal Aid Directive regime. It is based on DBB Law, 'Study on the application of Council Directive 2003/8/EC of 27 January 2003 on legal aid and on the legal compliance of the national transposition, final report', report, (2011) (on file with the author).

[87] 2012 Legal Aid Directive report, pp. 4–5.   [88] *Ibid.*, p. 6.

[89] One example of an undefined term can be seen in the 'importance' factor as used by Article 6(3) Legal Aid Directive to assess the importance of a case. The 2012 Legal Aid Directive report points out that Member States interpret this term differently, with some taking the applicant's interests more strongly into consideration than others who instead focus on the general importance of the case. As the question of whether a case is of 'importance' can be decisive for the decision to grant legal aid, further clarification would be of help if one wishes to harmonise the practical accessibility of cross-border legal aid at the EU level. There has, so far, only been one case before the Court of Justice of the European Union (CJEU) with direct reference to the Legal Aid Directive: Case C-279/09, *DEB Deutsche Energiehandels- und Beratungsgesellschaft mbH* v. *Bundesrepublik Deutschland* [2010] ECR I-13849. In this case the CJEU ruled that it is left to national courts to decide whether the

Not only was vague terminology found to be a practical impediment in obtaining cross-border legal aid but also the narrow definitions of the directive. For example, the Legal Aid Directive defines the costs that should be covered by cross-border legal aid. When it comes to the costs arising in the context of applying for legal aid, Article 8 asks for relief in relation to costs 'of a local lawyer or any other person entitled by the law to give legal advice' as well as in relation to translation costs. However, the likely travel costs of the applicant, which could arise if the competent authority asks for a hearing to decide on the granting of legal aid, are not covered.[90] This lacuna, as rightly pointed out by the 2012 Legal Aid Directive report, could lead to the unwanted situation where applicants might 'be deprived of the possibility to obtain legal aid by the competent court',[91] only because they would not be able to afford their travel costs.

Another weakness of the Legal Aid Directive is that it does not contain any rules that guarantee that successful applicants will enjoy truly effective assistance from a lawyer. There are no rules on appointing a lawyer in a concrete cross-border legal aid case. Appointing lawyers is left to the discretion of the Member States and their appointing institutions. While this might not cause comparable problems in purely domestic cases, the absence of any rules in the context of the Legal Aid Directive is regrettable. In cross-border cases, both language issues and legal experience with possibly applicable foreign law are undeniably of practical relevance. Language-based communication problems between a consumer and their legal aid lawyer and/or the lawyer's insufficient knowledge of the applicable law could both have a negative impact on the true value of granted legal aid. To tackle this issue, it would be worth considering the installation of special registers or lists containing information about the

preconditions for granting legal aid in a cross-border context are fulfilled (see Recital 60 of said judgment where the CJEU states that 'it is for the national court to ascertain whether the conditions for granting legal aid constitute a limitation on the right of access to the courts which undermines the very core of that right'). The Commission interprets this positively, however, arguing that 'there has been only one case before the European Court of Justice concerning cross-border legal aid which may prove that the practical application of the Directive is satisfactory' (2012 Legal Aid Directive report, p. 14).

[90] Article 7(c) Legal Aid Directive uses the term 'applicant' in the context of travel costs. One might be tempted to interpret this in a way that would cover pre-litigation travel costs occurred at the application stage. However, the general understanding is that Article 7 refers only to cases where legal aid is already granted. For details see, e.g., European Parliament, Committee on Petitions, Notice to Members regarding petition no. 1667/2009, Ref. 445.595/REV, 11 February 2011, pp. 2–3 (with further references).

[91] 2012 Legal Aid Directive report, p. 13.

languages spoken by lawyers in the respective Member State and their knowledge of foreign laws. Member States could be asked to take these parameters into consideration when granting consumers free lawyer support in a cross-border legal aid case.[92]

Regarding the more practical side of the Legal Aid Directive, the 2012 Legal Aid Directive report refers to the Special Eurobarometer survey on civil justice published in 2010[93] (2010 Civil Justice Eurobarometer Survey), which assesses citizens' general awareness of the existence of cross-border legal aid and includes data on the actual usage of the cross-border legal aid regime. The results are far from satisfactory. With regard to citizens' awareness, the 2010 Civil Justice Eurobarometer Survey reveals that on average, only 12 per cent of EU citizens have heard of cross-border legal aid.[94] Although more positive than citizens' awareness of the European Small Claims Procedure (8 per cent on average)[95] or the European Payment Order (6 per cent on average),[96] it is nevertheless clearly not what the Commission had hoped for. One might also doubt whether the European Judicial Atlas in Civil Matters and the European e-Justice Portal (which both contain some rudimentary information on the Legal Aid Directive – and in the case of the European e-Justice Portal further the standard application form) has significantly contributed to highlighting the availability of cross-border legal aid. The lack of awareness is alarming and is further intensified by the fact that as of 2010, a considerable number of lawyers (30 per cent) had yet to obtain information about the availability of cross-border legal aid.[97]

In light of the awareness issue, it should be of no surprise that the Legal Aid Directive has not yet greatly enhanced the cross-border granting of legal aid. The 2012 Legal Aid Directive report shows that no Member State had sent more than forty (on average) legal aid applications per year to other Member States between 2005 and 2009.[98] One could even go so far as to say that the Legal Aid Directive has not shown *any* remarkably

---

[92] See *ibid.* pp. 12–13 for further suggestions.
[93] TNS Opinion & Social, 'Civil Justice', Special Eurobarometer 351, (2010), available at ec.europa.eu/public_opinion/archives/ebs/ebs_351_en.pdf.
[94] *Ibid.*, p. 50. The 2012 Legal Aid Directive report shows that the situation has slightly improved since then. Nevertheless, the numbers are still far from satisfactory. For details see 2012 Legal Aid Directive report, p. 10, where it is shown that by 2012 awareness reached 15 per cent.
[95] TNS Opinion & Social, 'Civil Justice'.   [96] *Ibid.*
[97] 2012 Legal Aid Directive report, p. 10.
[98] *Ibid.*, p. 8 (at the untitled table). (More recent data are – to the best of my knowledge – not available yet.)

positive effects in its first years. Sixteen Member States had actually sent less than an average of ten applications per year in that period.[99] Taking into account that these numbers do not exclusively refer to applications in B2C cases[100] but include any cross-border legal aid application falling under the regime of the Legal Aid Directive (i.e., to any cross-border dispute of a civil and commercial matter), the true actual relevance of the Legal Aid Directive for B2C cases is more than questionable. With that said, the conclusion of the Commission in its 2012 Legal Aid Directive report 'that the practical application of the [Legal Aid] Directive is satisfactory'[101] looks somewhat bizarre or unfortunate to say the least. The limited actual use of cross-border legal aid and the lack of citizen awareness should be reason enough for the Commission to take further steps.

The Regulation on Consumer Protection Cooperation (2004)

If one understands the procedural side of access to justice 2.0 as the quest to protect consumer interests by effectively enforcing consumer legislation, then the 2004 Regulation on Consumer Protection Cooperation (CPC Regulation)[102] is a prominent yet atypical example. Unlike other procedural mechanisms covered in this book, the CPC Regulation does not predominantly cover civil procedure law issues. The CPC Regulation is instead an example of an attempt to combat illegal business practices using (primarily) administrative enforcement (understood in this context as enforcement using administrative law devices).

With the start of the new millennium, the Commission further intensified its search for an enhanced system of European consumer protection. In Section 5 2001 Green Paper on European Union consumer protection (2001 Consumer Protection Green Paper),[103] the Commission noticed that

---

[99] *Ibid.*

[100] Concrete numbers for B2C cases are – to the best of my knowledge – not yet published. It can be assumed though that the numbers for B2C cases are lower than the total numbers.

[101] 2012 Legal Aid Directive report, p. 14.

[102] Regulation (EC) No 2006/2004 of the European Parliament and of the Council on cooperation between national authorities responsible for the enforcement of consumer protection laws, 27 October 2004, OJ 2004 No. L364/1 (as amended by Regulation (EU) No 954/2011 of the European Parliament and of the Council amending Regulation (EC) No 2006/2004 on cooperation between national authorities responsible for the enforcement of consumer protection laws, of 14 September 2011, OJ 2011 No. L259/1).

[103] Green Paper on European Union Consumer Protection, 2 October 2001, COM(2001) 531 final (2001 Consumer Protection Green Paper).

consumer confidence and a strong internal market both require 'adequate enforcement structures that ensure ... [a] consistent application'[104] of European consumer laws. However, when the 2001 Consumer Protection Green Paper was published, the 1998 Injunctions Directive was the only comprehensive enforcement regime for consumer issues at the EU level. If one wanted to enforce consumer rights more 'adequately', then additional measures were needed. Only a few months after the Member States were to have implemented the 1998 Injunctions Directive (1 January 2001) and years before the Consumer Law Compendium disclosed the first official Injunctions Directive evaluation results,[105] the 2001 Consumer Protection Green Paper had already critically commented as follows:

> The [I]njunctions Directive, while filling an important loophole and being an important tool for consumer associations is not likely to become a general-purpose tool to resolve these issues [note: the enforcement of consumer laws against 'traders acting cross-border in a fraudulent, dishonest or unfair way'].[106] The cost-benefits for a public authority of launching injunction procedures in foreign jurisdictions are never likely to be sufficiently positive for this to become a day-to-day enforcement tool.[107]

Although the possible introduction of new judicial tools was discussed at and after the Tampere Council,[108] the Commission felt that additional, alternative (mainly) non-judicial steps had to be considered. The 2001 Consumer Protection Green Paper tried to respond with the plan to introduce a cooperation platform for public authorities in collective cross-border consumer issues. To put it more precisely, the tools envisaged by the 2001 Consumer Protection Green Paper covered to a large extent various possible forms of mutual administrative cross-border assistance by public authorities.[109] With the exception of business interest representatives, who in general had not been very enthusiastic about these plans, most stakeholders welcomed the Commission's ideas as they were considered complementary methods of enforcing consumer rights in situations where some kind of enforcement deficit had been assumed to exist.[110]

The eventual result of the discussions, the CPC Regulation, was adopted three years after the publication of the 2001 Consumer Protection Green

---

[104] *Ibid.*, p. 16.   [105] See 'The Injunctions Directive (1998/2009)' above.
[106] 2001 Consumer Protection Green Paper, p. 17.   [107] *Ibid.*
[108] See, in particular, Presidency Conclusions, Tampere European Council, paragraph 30.
[109] 2001 Consumer Protection Green Paper, chapter 5.2.
[110] The responses to the 2001 Consumer Protection Green Paper are available at ec.europa. eu/consumers/enforcement/responses_gp_cons_prot_en.htm.

Paper. The CPC Regulation, which came into full effect in late December 2006,[111] introduced a cooperation network (CPC Network)[112] of public authorities (assisted by both the Commission and a group of experts from the Member States (the Committee[113])) with a primary focus on administrative enforcement and collaboration regarding cross-border consumer law issues. Under the CPC Regulation, public authorities that deal with consumer law issues under its framework are either classified as 'competent authorities' or 'single liaison offices'. While the term competent authority refers to 'any public authority established either at national, regional or local level with specific responsibilities to enforce the laws that protect consumers' interests',[114] single liaison offices have a narrower meaning and stand for 'the [i.e., the sole] public authority in each Member State designated as responsible for coordinating the application of this Regulation within that Member State'.[115] Competent authorities and single liaison offices are both registered in a joint list that is published and regularly updated in the OJ.[116] Limiting the scope of competent entities and single liaison offices to public authorities has clearly changed the regulatory landscape in some Member States such as Germany, the Netherlands and Austria, which had relied on rights enforcement by (private) consumer organisations prior to the introduction of the CPC Network. Because of the approach taken by the CPC Regulation, these Member States had to assign some public authorities with certain consumer law enforcement tasks.[117]

The activities of the CPC Network can be basically split into two groups. The first category is named 'mutual assistance' by the CPC Regulation and refers to cross-border cooperation with an external effect at either a bilateral or multilateral level. This group refers to cases in which a trader causes harm or is likely to cause harm to the collective interests of consumers in a cross-border situation by acting contrary to the rules of any

---

[111] Article 22 CPC Regulation.
[112] For comments on the CPC Network see C. Poncibò, 'Networks to Enforce European Law: The Case of the Consumer Protection Cooperation Network', *Journal of Consumer Policy*, 35 (2012), 175–95.
[113] See Articles 19 and 20 CPC Regulation for details.
[114] Article 3(c) CPC Regulation. For a definition of the term 'laws that protect consumers' interests' see Article 3(a).
[115] Article 3(d) CPC Regulation.   [116] Article 5(2) CPC Regulation.
[117] For a brief comparative overview of the situation in the Member States prior to the introduction of the CPC Regulation see M. A. Heldeweg, 'Supervisory Governance: The Case of the Dutch Consumer Authority', *Utrecht Law Review*, 2 (2006), 67–90.

EU consumer law listed in the Annex of the CPC Regulation (CPC intra-Community infringement).[118]

Simpler mutual assistance activities can be subdivided into alerts (Article 7 CPC Regulation), information requests (Article 6) and enforcement requests (Article 8). While alerts can be directly processed between competent authorities from different Member States, requests shall (pursuant to Article 12(2) CPC Regulation) be sent via the single liaison office of the transmitting Member State to the single liaison office in the receiving Member State (or – if sent to more than one Member State – to the single liaison offices in the particular Member States). The respective single liaison office in the receiving Member State(s) then forwards the request 'to the [respective] appropriate competent authority without delay'.

In case of alerts, a competent authority from one Member State contacts the competent authorities in other Member States to warn them about an occurring, or likely to occur, CPC intra-Community infringement that is causing (or would cause) damage in these other Member States. Information requests originate from a competent authority in the Member State where the illegal business activity shows (or would show) harmful effects, and are addressed to a competent authority in the Member State from which the suspect business operates. Both measures are restricted to the exchange of information.

If, however, there is evidence for the need for a competent authority to act in the Member State from which the suspect business operates for the collective benefit of consumers in another Member State, a request for enforcement measures can be issued by an applicant authority from the latter Member State to a requested authority in the first Member State pursuant to Article 8 CPC Regulation. Article 8 also constitutes an exception to the underlying rationale of the CPC Regulation to base the framework on enforcement by public authorities. Article 8(3) permits the requested authority to mandate 'a body designated in accordance with the second sentence of Article 4(2) as having a legitimate interest in the cessation or prohibition of [CPC] intra-Community infringements [most notably, this could also be a private consumer organisation] to take all necessary enforcement measures [which include possible injunction proceedings]'. However, to quote Gerrit Betlem, it would make the designated body only a 'secondary rather than a primary enforcer',[119] as the obligation to fulfil

---

[118] Article 3(b) CPC Regulation.
[119] G. Betlem, 'Public and Private Transnational Enforcement of EU Consumer Law' in W. van Boom and M. B. M. Loos (eds.), *Collective Enforcement of Consumer Law: Securing*

the request of the applicant authority would still rest with the requested competent (public) authority, should the designated body fail to reach a satisfactory solution.[120] Hence, even in this case it is the requested authority, i.e., a public authority, which remains in charge of fulfilling the enforcement request.[121] In addition to this, the applicant authority has the chance to veto the suggestion of mandating a private body with enforcement measures under certain conditions. In such a case the Commission would try to mediate between the two public authorities.

These simpler measures (i.e., alerts, information requests and enforcement requests) are complemented by large-scale multilateral mutual assistance projects conducted in more than two Member States. These projects, commonly referred to as sweeps, aim at the identification and cessation of illegal trade practices that infringe (or are likely to infringe) on consumer interests in at least three Member States. Article 9 CPC Regulation (titled '[c]oordination of market surveillance and enforcement activities') forms the basis for the sweeps and, as will be shown later, has led to a number of joint activities in the last couple of years.

As a complement to mutual assistance, Articles 16–18 CPC Regulation introduce the second big pillar of the CPC Network tasks. This group of activities refers to measures with an internal effect, i.e., cooperative administrative joint activities between competent authorities and/or single liaison offices from different Member States without a particular, concrete or imminent infringement case at hand (intra-CPC Network activities). The mechanism covered by Articles 16–18 mainly deals with the intra-CPC Network exchange of administrative information, best practice guidelines or personnel, organising joint workshops and other forms of training as well as possible administrative joint ventures with non-EU countries.

The CPC Regulation is rounded off with biennial reports to monitor the actual implementation and functioning of the CPC Network (Article 21 reports[122]). In addition, a 2011 amendment to the CPC Regulation[123]

Compliance in Europe through Private Group Action and Public Authority Intervention (Groningen: Europa Law Publishing, 2007), p. 45.

[120] Article 8(3) CPC Regulation.   [121] Article 8(4) to (6) CPC Regulation.

[122] It might be less confusing to use this term instead of biennial reports. The reports (published thus far) cover a period of two years, but are not published every two years – the second report was published three years after the first one.

[123] Regulation (EU) No 954/2011 of the European Parliament and of the Council amending Regulation (EC) No 2006/2004 on cooperation between national authorities responsible for the enforcement of consumer protection laws, 14 September 2011, OJ 2011 No. L259/1.

requested the Commission to submit an evaluation on 'the effectiveness and operational mechanisms of [the CPC] Regulation' by no later than 31 December 2014.[124] Unlike Article 21 reports, which are prepared by the Commission based on data submitted by the Member States, the evaluation 'shall be based on an *external* evaluation and extended consultation of all relevant stakeholders'[125] (emphasis added).

In July 2009, the Commission presented its first Article 21 report (2009 CPC Study report)[126]. It revealed that the CPC Network had already developed some significant results in the first two years of its existence. Several Member States, with Belgium, Hungary and France leading the way, had made extensive use of the new mechanisms.[127] More than 700 (simpler) mutual assistance activities were reported in the 2009 CPC Study report.[128] The fields of unfair commercial practices, misleading advertising and electronic commerce appear to have especially benefited from the CPC regime, with more than 100 activities in each of these fields.[129]

However, it should further be noted that the CPC Regulation was neither consistently used throughout the Member States nor with regard to the laws listed in its Annex. Ten Member States had not issued a single alert/request in the first full year of application of the regulation (2007) and six others issued no more than three.[130] The situation in the second year (2008) was not very different with nine Member States issuing no alerts/requests and five issuing no more than three.[131] And while the EU directives related to unfair commercial practices, misleading advertising and electronic commerce were extensively used for mutual assistance activities, the other directives listed in the Annex of the CPC Regulation had only very rarely (if at all) been the basis.[132] The 2009 CPC Study report thus stressed the importance of awareness-raising among the competent authorities and the need to enhance the training of officials.[133]

---

[124] Article 21a CPC Regulation.   [125] *Ibid.*
[126] Report from the Commission to the European Parliament and to the Council on the application of Regulation (EC) No 2006/2004 of the European Parliament and of the Council of 27 October 2004 on cooperation between national authorities responsible for the enforcement of consumer protection laws, 2 July 2009, COM(2009) 336 final (2009 CPC Study report).
[127] See 2009 CPC Study report, pp. 15 and 16.
[128] *Ibid.*, p. 12.   [129] *Ibid.*   [130] *Ibid.*, pp. 15 and 16.
[131] *Ibid.*, pp. 17 and 18.   [132] *Ibid.*, pp. 12 and 13.
[133] *Ibid.*, pp. 7 and 8. The Commission answered with two initiatives: the designation of special CPC Network 'trainers' and the introduction of an annual Enforcement Action Plan in cooperation with the Committee, both with the aim of offering practical guidance

With respect to the annual sweeps of Article 9 CPC Regulation the 2009 CPC Study confirmed that these multilateral activities are arguably the most striking feature of the CPC regime (in practice).[134] The first two sweeps concerned activities in the aviation (airline sweep)[135] and telecommunications sectors (mobile phone content sweep)[136] and were launched in 2007 and 2008, respectively. At the centre of the 2007 airline sweep were online airline ticket sales. The investigation of the CPC Network revealed that more than half of the scrutinised websites breached pertinent EU laws. The airline sweep led to overall positive results. More than 80 per cent of the reported websites in breach of EU legislation had been brought into compliance by early 2009,[137] prompting the then European Commissioner for Consumer Protection, Meglena Kuneva, to comment that the CPC sweeps mechanism 'has shown it has real "teeth" and can deliver'.[138]

The second sweep, the mobile phone content sweep of 2008, led to similar results. The CPC Network checked 279 'ringtone' websites, of which 58 per cent were in breach of applicable EU laws.[139] Eventually, 70 per cent of those cases were resolved favourably for consumers, either by changes made by the traders or by shutting down websites operated by wrongdoers.[140]

The 2009 CPC Study report also briefly commented on intra-CPC network activities. The message was that administrative cooperation activities had not yet shown the desired effects. Although Member State authorities had organised several CPC workshops and exchanged some experiences with respect to the application of the CPC Regulation, in general, intra-CPC network activities had not yet been widely used.

on how to use the CPC System, a special IT tool to facilitate the activities of the CPC Network (*ibid.*, pp. 9 and 10).

[134] For general information on the CPC sweeps see ec.europa.eu/consumers/enforcement/sweeps_en.print.htm.

[135] See ec.europa.eu/consumers/enforcement/sweep/index_en.htm for details.

[136] See ec.europa.eu/consumers/enforcement/sweep/mobile_phone/index_en.htm for details.

[137] European Commission, 'Airline Ticket Selling Websites – EU Enforcement Results. Questions and Answers', press release, MEMO/09/238, 14 May 2009, available at europa.eu/rapid/press-release_MEMO-09-238_en.htm.

[138] See Kuneva's comment cited in European Commission, 'Consumers: Airlines Move to Clean up Ticket Selling Websites', press release, IP/09/783, 14 May 2009, available at europa.eu/rapid/press-release_IP-09-783_en.htm.

[139] See the data in European Commission, 'EU Clean-up on Ringtone Scams. Frequently Asked Questions', press release, MEMO/09/505, 17 November 2009, available at europa.eu/rapid/press-release_MEMO-09-505_en.htm?locale=en.

[140] *Ibid.*

In 2012 the Commission issued a follow-up report, the second Article 21 report (2012 CPC Study report).[141] In the report the Commission calls the relevant period, i.e., 2009 and 2010, 'a more stable phase'[142] (because the competent authorities of most Member States had become familiar with the central IT tool, the CPC System) and provides a largely positive evaluation of the development of the CPC Network.

With respect to mutual assistance activities, the data in the 2012 CPC Study report show a decline since 2008. The Commission interprets this trend as a success. It argues that the drop might have been due to 'better prepared cases and a more rational use of the cooperation mechanism'[143] (which had also led to a faster handling of cases)[144] and/or to the fact that an amendment of the CPC System now allows for a single-track handling of cases with multiple infringement effects, whereas under the old system, parallel cases had to be filed individually.[145]

The 2012 CPC Study report also confirms the view that the annual sweeps are the key feature of the CPC framework.[146] Indeed, the Electronic Goods Sweep (2009),[147] the Online Ticket Sales Sweep (2010),[148] the Consumer Credit Sweep (2011),[149] the Digital Contents Sweep (2012)[150] and the Travel Services Sweep (2013)[151] all prove the fact that coordinated pan-EU investigations and enforcement activities have the potential to lead to positive results for consumers. In each case, compliance with EU laws had massively improved.[152]

---

[141] Report from the Commission to the European Parliament and the Council on the application of Regulation (EC) 2006/2004 of the European Parliament and of the Council of 27 October 2004 on cooperation between national authorities responsible for the enforcement of consumer protection laws, 12 March 2012, COM(2012) 100 final (2012 CPC Study report).

[142] Ibid., p. 4.   [143] Ibid., p. 8.

[144] Ibid.   [145] Ibid.

[146] The 2009 CPC Study Report calls them 'the central element' (see ibid.).

[147] See ec.europa.eu/consumers/enforcement/sweep/electronic_goods/index_en.htm for details.

[148] See ec.europa.eu/consumers/enforcement/sweep/online_ticket_sales/index_en.htm for details.

[149] See ec.europa.eu/consumers/enforcement/sweep/consumer_credits/index_en.htm for details.

[150] See ec.europa.eu/consumers/enforcement/sweep/digital_content/index_en.htm for details.

[151] See ec.europa.eu/consumers/enforcement/sweep/travel_services/index_en.htm for details.

[152] The Electronic Goods Sweep led to a compliance increase from 44 to 84 per cent (see europa.eu/rapid/press-release_IP-10-1136_en.htm); the Online Ticket Sales Sweep to an increase from 40 to 88 per cent (see europa.eu/rapid/press-release_IP-11-1094_en.htm);

One should also note, however, that several of the shortcomings identified in the 2009 CPC Study report have remained (and in some cases have intensified). For example, it is regrettable that ten Member States only issued a total of ten or fewer mutual assistance alerts/requests in the first four years of application of the CPC Regulation.[153] In addition, several formerly very active Member States, such as Belgium and Hungary, have steadily and considerably reduced their involvement over the years.[154] In the 2012 CPC Study report, the Commission thus comes to the conclusion that only 'a maximum of 9 Member States [or in other words: only one-third of the Member States] can be considered to have been using the system [of Articles 6–8 CPC Regulation] actively since the beginning'.[155]

Also, the results with regard to the intra-CPC Network activities gave no real reason for celebration. While the Commission arrived at a basically positive result, stating that the use of available funds for these activities was 'consistent',[156] it also had to concede that this consistent use had been quite 'modest'.[157] In other words, the Member States had not yet made full use of the potential of the intra-CPC Network activities.

In late 2012, a first external CPC evaluation report was published (2012 CPC Evaluation report).[158] The 2012 CPC Evaluation report presented an in-depth analysis of the CPC framework that went beyond the two Article 21 reports. In particular, it provided an interesting insight into the structure and work of the national competent authorities and single liaison offices, and by doing so it explained some of the shortcomings identified in the two Article 21 reports.

The overall findings of the 2012 CPC Evaluation report are to some extent relatively positive, calling the CPC Network 'an effective platform

---

the Consumer Credit Sweep to an increase from 30 to 77 per cent (see europa.eu/rapid/press-release_IP-12-1251_en.htm); the Digital Contents Sweep to an increase from 48 to 83 per cent (see europa.eu/rapid/press-release_IP-13-937_en.htm); and the Travel Services Sweep to an increase from 31 to 62 per cent (see http://europa.eu/rapid/press-release_IP-14-436_en.htm).

[153] 2009 CPC Study report, p. 20.   [154] *Ibid.*

[155] *Ibid.*, p. 9, where the report adds that '[t]he number of authorities that do not actively use the cooperation mechanisms established by the CPC Regulation remains significant'.

[156] *Ibid.*, p. 11.   [157] *Ibid.*

[158] Consumer Policy Evaluation Consortium (CPEC), '(External) Evaluation of the Consumer Protection Cooperation Regulation', report, (2012), available at ec.europa.eu/consumers/enforcement/docs/cpc_regulation_inception_report_revised290212_en.pdf (2012 CPC Evaluation report). A second, more comprehensive external evaluation report, i.e., the report as requested by Article 21a CPC Regulation is expected to follow by mid-2014 (information provided by Europe Direct via email on 14 February 2014 – on file with the author). The latter forms part of the CPC Regulation project initiated by the Commission in 2011 (see the references in note 56 above).

for formal cooperation'.[159] The practical importance of the mechanism was also stressed as it was found that 'the CPC Regulation framework is [now] even more needed than before given developments in technology and consumption patterns of households ... and the complexity of trader activity in aspects such as advertising, bundling of products and trading internationally have reinforced the need to provide tools to deter rogue traders and to enforce the law'.[160] However, the 2012 CPC Evaluation report further came to the conclusion that the full potential of the CPC Regulation framework had not yet been fully tapped and that its use had been 'sub-optimal'.[161] The evaluation also criticised some fundamental imperfections, for example, the lack of practical guidelines for the CPC System and problems regarding connectivity to the IT tool.[162]

While these issues are not really new and were already mentioned in the two Article 21 reports, the 2012 CPC Evaluation report presents data that could explain some shortcomings. Of particular interest are the findings with respect to the number of personnel of the single liaison offices and competent authorities in the Member States. In short it can be said that many Member States lack a sufficient number of personnel. The average number of personnel per single liaison office is 3.4[163] and the number per competent authority is only slightly higher at 4.4.[164] If one takes into consideration that most single liaison offices/competent authorities employ less than two enforcement inspectors/investigators who deal with mutual assistance issues,[165] one can understand why, for example, an increased exchange of personnel between authorities from different Member States is not very feasible in practice. Moreover, in several cases the numbers given in the report do not only refer to personnel exclusively handling CPC cases but sometimes include also mixed situations (where the respective personnel is not only in charge of CPC matters). Thus, the *actual* number of personnel in charge of CPC matters might even be lower.[166]

---

[159] 2012 CPC Evaluation report, p. 14.   [160] *Ibid.*, p. 18.

[161] See *ibid.*, p. 14 with findings regarding the mutual assistance mechanism at pp. 14 and 15.

[162] *Ibid.*, pp. 105 and 106.

[163] This number includes all five personnel categories identified by the evaluation: management, analyst/network operator, administrator, enforcement inspector/investigator and IT support (see *ibid.*, p. 108).

[164] *Ibid.*, pp. 109 and 110.   [165] *Ibid.*, pp. 108–10.

[166] See *ibid.*, p. 110, where the report explains that 'these survey results are to be taken with caution, given that many [Member States] seem to have indicated overall FTE available, rather than actual FTE specifically devoted to CPC case handling and other CPC coordination action'.

The 2012 CPC Evaluation report further illustrates practical problems with obtaining EU funding for CPC Regulation activities. Although several Member States asked for increased financial support from the Commission,[167] the evaluation showed that available funding by the Commission remained to a considerable degree untouched by the Member States.[168] One key reason for this unfortunate situation lies surely in the fact that the funding application procedures were too confusing and burdensome. Thus, to ensure that single liaison offices and competent authorities can make proper use of available monetary resources, the 2012 CPC Evaluation report asked for a simplification of the application proceedings for existing grants.[169]

The 2012 CPC Evaluation report concludes with twenty-one sectoral recommendations to improve the CPC mechanism.[170] Key suggestions include a greater involvement by the Commission in the CPC framework, an expansion of the scope of application of the CPC Regulation to include additional EU legislation and an enhancement of the cooperative mechanism by introducing minimum procedural standards and requirements for the CPC Network members when applying the regulation. While most recommendations surely make sense in the long run, the Commission – if answering the call to get more heavily involved – should, however, act in keeping with the saying 'first things first'. Before thinking about broadening the framework and asking national CPC authorities to apply minimum standards, there is the need to create an environment that is capable of meeting any likely minimum standards. In other words, if the purpose is to make full use of the CPC Network, then personnel numbers at the competent authorities and single liaison offices would have to be increased and the use of available financial resources must be facilitated. These would be prudent first steps to broaden the activities, both with respect to mutual assistance measures and intra-CPC Network activities.

When evaluating the CPC Regulation regime, one should further note a different issue of practical importance. The CPC Regulation aims at protecting collective (not directly financial) consumer interests that are harmed or likely to be harmed by traders' CPC intra-Community infringements. The CPC Regulation does not deal with specific individual

---

[167] *Ibid.*, pp. 78 and 96.
[168] *Ibid.*, pp. 17 and 105. See ec.europa.eu/consumers/tenders/information/grants/index_en.print.htm for past fundings.
[169] See 2012 CPC Evaluation report, p. 106 for details.
[170] *Ibid.*, pp. 121–3.

consumer concerns nor with compensatory consumer redress. The likely consequences of the CPC Regulation could nevertheless lead to some positive side effects for individual consumers seeking compensation. As the 2012 CPC Evaluation report rightly comments, 'the competent authority in most cases may ... attempt to form an evidence base of possible wrong doing by the trader in question'.[171] This in return could encourage individual consumers to pursue their individual interests and facilitate the procuring of evidence. Hence, it is also important to facilitate the interplay between consumer law enforcement and compliance tools to guarantee that consumer access to justice 2.0, which takes a comprehensive look at safeguarding justified consumer interests, is accomplished.

At the same time, and while the CPC Regulation could be of importance to facilitate individuals' rights enforcement, the sweeps, in particular, could, as a long-term effect, diminish the need for individual actions if wrongdoers are either forced to leave the market or become convinced to comply with the applicable rules. The practical importance of the deterrent effect of sweeps or the 'shadow of the law'[172] they would create should not be underestimated. Effective access to justice would thus, on a long-term basis, be characterised by a gradually decreasing number of court cases, or in the style of Cafaggi and Micklitz, the best laws are those that ensure a higher level of legal compliance and lower levels of litigation.[173]

The Small Claims Regulation (2007)

The prevention of unlawful behaviour by businesses with the help of injunctions was the first comprehensive European step towards improved (procedural) consumer access to justice. The 1998 Injunctions Directive, however, did not vest individual consumers with litigating powers. Launching injunction proceedings was left to designated public authorities and private bodies (qualified entities). Furthermore, the Injunctions Directive did not deal with compensatory redress. The Legal Aid Directive tried to facilitate access to the judiciary, but did not directly affect the

---

[171] *Ibid.*, p. 29.

[172] *Ibid.*, p. 20 with reference to R. H. Mnookin and L. Kornhauser, 'Bargaining in the Shadow of the Law: The Case of Divorce', *Yale Law Journal*, 88 (1979), 950–97.

[173] See F. Cafaggi and H.-W. Micklitz, 'Administrative and Judicial Enforcement in Consumer Protection: The Way Forward' in F. Cafaggi and H.-W. Micklitz (eds.), *New Frontiers of Consumer Protection: The Interplay between Private and Public Enforcement* (Antwerp: Intersentia, 2009), p. 443, where they – in a slightly different context – say that 'the best laws are those that ensure a higher level of safety and lower levels of litigation'.

trial itself. And the CPC Regulation primarily focused on administrative enforcement actions. Hence, none of these three instruments was designed to simplify the main proceedings when suing for compensation. It took the EU some time before it came up with something concrete in this respect. A year after the adoption of the 1998 Injunctions Directive, the Tampere Council intensified discussions regarding consumers' direct access to justice. It addressed several practical procedural problems consumers faced when seeking redress. One of these issues was linked to small claims, i.e., to claims of a value that many people would consider too low to launch proceedings or (because of the prevailing loser-pays principle[174]) disproportionate to the inherent financial risk of losing the case. In the section 'Better access to justice in Europe', the Tampere Council's Presidency Conclusions expressed the wish that 'special common procedural rules for simplified and accelerated cross-border litigation on small consumer ... claims'[175] should be established.

In 2002 the Commission reacted to this call with its Green Paper on a European order for payment procedure and on measures to simplify and speed up small claims litigation (Small Claims Green Paper).[176] Part III of the Small Claims Green Paper covered small claims issues. It showed that several Member States had already instituted special, simplified national procedures for low-value claims. The rules were, however, quite diverse, as was the upper limit for filing small claims in the Member States, which ranged from EUR 600 in Germany to approximately EUR 8,000 in England and Wales.[177] In addition, a study conducted as early as 1995[178] showed that the length of judicial proceedings and concerns over procedure costs, which are clearly two big disincentives for any potential claimants, are of even greater relevance in cross-border and low-value cases.[179]

---

[174] For an overview of the situation in the EU see Hodges *et al.* (eds.), *The Costs and Funding of Civil Litigation* for details, in particular pp. 114–31 (Table 1).

[175] Presidency Conclusions, Tampere European Council, para. 30. For comments on the genesis of the Small Claims Regulation see X. E. Kramer, 'The European Small Claims Procedure: Striking the Balance Between Simplicity and Fairness in European Legislation', *Zeitschrift für Europäisches Privatrecht*, 16 (2008), 355, 356–8.

[176] Green Paper on a European order for payment procedure and on measures to simplify and speed up small claims litigation, 20 December 2002, COM(2002) 746 final (Small Claims Green Paper).

[177] *Ibid.*, p. 53.

[178] H. von Freyhold *et al.* (eds.), 'Cost of Judicial Barriers for Consumers in the Single Market', report for DG SANCO, Zentrum für Europäische Rechtspolitik an der Universität Bremen, (1995), available at www.freyvial.de/Publications/egi-2.pdf.

[179] Small Claims Green Paper, pp. 59–61.

The Small Claims Green Paper was first followed by the adoption of several European instruments over the next couple of years, which addressed procedural issues other than small claims. The Legal Aid Directive was introduced in 2003, the European Enforcement Order Regulation followed in 2004[180] and in 2006 the European Order for Payment Procedure Regulation[181] dealing with uncontested claims was enacted. Regulating small claims was not off the table, though, and shortly after the adoption of the European Order for Payment Procedure Regulation, the European Small Claims Procedure Regulation (Small Claims Regulation) followed in 2007.[182]

The Small Claims Regulation has been applicable since January 2009 in all Member States except Denmark. It is not meant to replace national mechanisms, but was crafted as an alternative regime for cross-border civil and commercial cases, where the amount in dispute does not exceed EUR 2,000 (excluding possible interests, expenses and disbursements).[183] Although its scope is not limited to B2C cases, it was hoped that it could act as an effective tool for seeking fast and cheap redress, removing financial and time-related redress barriers. The Small Claims Regulation explains as follows: 'The obstacles to obtaining a fast and inexpensive judgment are exacerbated in cross-border cases. It is therefore necessary to establish a European procedure for small claims ... The objective of such a procedure should be to facilitate *access to justice*'[184] (emphasis added).

The European Small Claims Procedure (ESCP) is initiated by filling in and submitting a special form (Form A – Claim Form) to the court competent for the dispute at hand, in 'the language or one of the languages of the court' (Article 6(1) Small Claims Regulation). Pursuant to Article 4(1) Small Claims Regulation, the form can be submitted 'by post or by any other means of communication, such as fax or e-mail, acceptable to the Member State in which the procedure is commenced'.

---

[180] Regulation (EC) No 805/2004 of the European Parliament and of the Council creating a European Enforcement Order for uncontested claims, 21 April 2004, OJ 2004 No. L143/15.

[181] Regulation (EC) No 1896/2006 of the European Parliament and of the Council creating a European order for payment procedure, 12 December 2006, OJ 2006 No. L399/1.

[182] Regulation (EC) No 861/2007 of the European Parliament and of the Council of 11 July 2007 establishing a European small claims procedure.

[183] Article 2(1) Small Claims Regulation.

[184] Recital 7 Small Claims Regulation. See further www. europa.eu/legislation_summaries/consumers/protection_of_consumers/index_en.htm where the Small Claims Regulation is listed as one of the special mechanisms in the category of 'protection of consumers' economic and legal interests ... legal redress and the settlement of disputes'.

There is no obligation to be represented by a lawyer, neither when filing the claim nor during the proceedings or at the enforcement stage.[185] Instead, redress-seeking parties should enjoy (free) 'practical assistance in filling in the forms' whenever necessary.[186] All ESCP forms can be found on the website of the European e-Justice Portal.[187] In addition, Article 4(5) asks all Member States to 'ensure that the claim form is available at all courts and tribunals at which the European Small Claims Procedure can be commenced'. Once the form is submitted to the competent court, the court decides whether the claim is admissible under the Small Claims Regulation. If the answer is yes and the court then considers the submitted information to be sufficient (note: the claimant can be asked to correct or add information to make the claim 'complete'), the court will contact the defendant with a copy of the claim, a reply form (Form C – Answer Form) and any relevant additional documents.[188] Pursuant to Article 6(3), the defendant may refuse to accept the documents if they are 'not in either of the following languages: (a) the official language of the Member State addressed, or, if there are several official languages in that Member State, the official language or one of the official languages of the place where service is to be effected or to where the document is to be dispatched; or (b) a language which the addressee understands'. In such a case the claimant would have to provide a translation of the document.[189]

Pursuant to Article 5(1) Small Claims Regulation, the court procedure itself should primarily be in writing unless the court finds it necessary to conduct oral hearings. Oral hearings might also be conducted 'from a distance' with the help of video conferences or other distance communication means.[190] The ESCP is further characterised by a relatively tight procedural schedule that is hoped to lead to fast judgments.[191] Once a judgment is made, it is basically 'enforceable notwithstanding any possible appeal'[192] and without the need for any intermediate proceedings to recognise and enforce it in the Member

---

[185] Article 10 Small Claims Regulation.   [186] Article 11 Small Claims Regulation.
[187] The English versions are available at e-justice.europa.eu/content_small_claims_forms-177-en.do.
[188] Article 5(2) Small Claims Regulation.   [189] Article 6(3) Small Claims Regulation.
[190] Article 8 Small Claims Regulation: 'The court or tribunal may hold an oral hearing through video conference or other communication technology if the technical means are available.' For more on this see the later argumentation in this chapter, especially with respect to the 2013 Small Claims Regulation Proposal.
[191] See Articles 5 and 7 Small Claims Regulation for details.
[192] Article 15 Small Claims Regulation.

State of the defeated party.[193] Compared with ordinary proceedings, the ESCP is thus clearly characterised by simplified procedural rules. Norbert Reich, for example, comments on this as follows: 'The procedure is determined by the principles of "simplicity, speed and proportionality".'[194]

With the introduction of the ESCP, the Commission set itself an ambitious goal. In the Explanatory Memorandum that accompanied the 2005 Proposal for a Regulation establishing a European Small Claims Procedure[195] the Commission stressed the importance of introducing the ESCP to 'facilitate the proper functioning of the internal market'.[196] As the ESCP is characterised by simplified procedures and a mechanism based on harmonised, special forms that can be used in any competent court throughout the EU, policy makers expected that it would remove existing procedural access to justice obstacles in cross-border cases. And also some voices from within academia were convinced that the ESCP would lead to 'a clear improvement regarding the possibility of consumers to enforce their rights in front of a court'.[197]

In late 2012, ECC-Net published a study carried out independently by (and at the initiative of) a working group of four national European Consumer Centres (ECCs)[198] that provided initial insights into the practical application of the ESCP (2012 ECC-Net ESCP Study).[199] In the course of the 2012 ECC-Net ESCP Study, national ECCs contacted competent courts and judges to hear directly how the ESCP had been applied in the Member States. In addition, the ECCs included their own experiences with consumers seeking their help with regard to small claims.[200]

---

[193] Article 1 Small Claims Regulation.

[194] N. Reich, 'Cross-border Consumer Protection' in N. Reich *et al.* (eds.), *European Consumer Law* (2nd edn, Cambridge: Intersentia, 2014), p. 331.

[195] Proposal for a Regulation of the European Parliament and of the Council establishing a European Small Claims Procedure, 15 March 2005, COM(2005) 87 final (2005 Small Claims Regulation Proposal).

[196] Explanatory Memorandum accompanying the 2005 Small Claims Regulation Proposal, p. 5.

[197] M. B. M. Loos, 'Individual Private Enforcement of Consumer Rights in Civil Courts in Europe' in R. Brownsword *et al.* (eds.), *The Foundations of European Private Law* (Oxford: Hart, 2011), p. 511.

[198] The ECC Italy took the lead and was supported by the ECCs from Lithuania, Estonia and Poland.

[199] ECC-Net, 'European Small Claims Procedure Report', report, (2012), available at ec.europa.eu/consumers/ecc/docs/small_claims_210992012_en.pdf (2012 ECC-Net ESCP Study).

[200] For more details on how the study was carried out see *ibid.*, pp. 2 and 15–16.

The working group further received support from the European Judicial Network in Civil and Commercial Matters (EJN),[201] which provided the ECCs with background information on the ESCP. The results of the 2012 ECC-Net ESCP Study were alarming, but did not come as a surprise. In short, the ESCP has not yet played a significant practical role in resolving consumer complaints as originally envisaged.

First and foremost, the aim to provide possible plaintiffs with sufficient information about the mechanism, although clearly being of utmost importance, had not yet been widely achieved. National ECCs had been quite active, with 94 per cent of all ECCs having promoted the ESCP in the first four years of its applicability.[202] However, only 29 per cent of the national public authorities had taken comparable actions.[203] In addition, only slightly more than half of all Member States offered consumers practical assistance at courts pursuant to Article 11 Small Claims Regulation.[204]

What gives perhaps even greater cause for concern is the fact that four years after the launch of the ESCP, approximately half of the contacted courts and judges were not aware of its existence.[205] In addition, the 2012

---

[201] Established in 2001 the EJN originates from access to justice ideas presented at the Tampere Council, or to use EJN's own words, the EJN 'represents an original and practical response to the objectives for access to justice and judicial cooperation set by the Tampere … European Council in 1999. The EJN therefore provides valuable access to justice for persons engaged in cross-border litigation' (see ec.europa.eu/civiljustice/network/network_en.htm). While the ECCs deal with consumers and their issues directly on a daily basis, the EJN rather functions as a more general information source for interested parties, including the ECCs. In 2011 a closer cooperation between ECC and EJN was established by a joint European Parliament and Council decision (Decision No 568/2009/EC of the European Parliament and of the Council amending Council Decision 2001/470/EC establishing a European Judicial Network in civil and commercial matters, 18 June 2009, OJ 2009 No. L168/35). The EJN was asked to 'maintain relations with the European Consumer Centres Network (ECC-Net). In particular, in order to supply any general information on the working of Community and international instruments to facilitate consumer access to justice, the contact points of the Network shall be at the disposal of the members of ECC-Net' (see Article 12a(2) Council Decision 2001/470/EC establishing a European Judicial Network in civil and commercial matters inserted by Article 10 of said joint European Parliament and Council decision).

[202] 2012 ECC-Net ESCP Study, p. 31.

[203] *Ibid.*   [204] *Ibid.*, p. 20.

[205] *Ibid.*, p. 17, where one can also find the following ECC comment: 'Unfortunately there are still courts in some Member States who have never even heard about the European Small Claims procedure, and to be precise – the number of such courts is quite big. Still, the most regrettable aspect is not the fact that almost half of the courts are unaware of the procedure, but the fact that the other half – the one that is aware – is not well informed about the details and principles of the procedure itself.'

ECC-Net ESCP Study provided interesting examples of the practical problems encountered by consumers when attempting to file a small claim. In some cases the judges rejected the respective claim based on questionable arguments, such as denying the court's competence in spite of the affirmative rules of the Brussels I regime,[206] or advised the unrepresented consumer to instead use the (occasionally less favourable)[207] European Order for Payment.[208] Furthermore, in several instances the enforcement of ESCP judgments proved difficult for successful claimants.[209]

The lack of awareness on both sides, consumers and the judiciary, has obviously impeded the spread of the use of the ESCP. However, this is not the only problem encountered. The ESCP, with its relatively tight procedural schedule,[210] its basic commitment to alternative communication methods[211] and simplified enforcement mechanism free of the need for any intermediate proceedings,[212] was designed as an inexpensive and fast alternative to traditional court proceedings. The 2012 ECC-Net ESCP Study, however, proved that theory and practice are not necessarily congruent. Some of the obstacles identified in the study are well-known problems also encountered at the national level. They might, however, be even more difficult to handle in an international context. Protracted enforcement actions with respect to final judgments are good examples of such an issue,[213] especially if one takes into consideration that neither the European Judicial Atlas in Civil Matters nor the European e-Justice Portal offers much practical information on how to enforce a court ruling in the trader's Member State (at least in principle not in a language different than the official language(s) of the respective Member States).[214] Another example relates to the main proceedings. Although the ESCP should lead to fast judgments, considerably fast judgments are instead the exception, as several practical problems

---

[206] *Ibid.*, p. 22.
[207] Note: the simplified European Order for Payment Procedure can only be used for uncontested claims (see Article 1(1)(a) European Order for Payment Regulation).
[208] 2012 ECC-Net ESCP Study, p. 18.
[209] As one ECC-reported case shows, one consumer who asked the decision-making court for advice on how to proceed was told to contact ECC-Net for assistance (see *ibid.*, p. 22).
[210] See Articles 5 and 7 Small Claims Regulation.
[211] See Articles 8 and 9 Small Claims Regulation.
[212] See Article 20 Small Claims Regulation.
[213] 2012 ECC-Net ESCP Study, pp. 5 and 22.
[214] Some basic information on the national enforcement procedures in the respective Member State's official language can be found at e-justice.europa.eu/content_enforcement_of_judgments-51-en.do.

reported by some ECCs show.[215] For instance, despite the preference of the Small Claims Regulation for short, purely written proceedings, judges might still find it necessary to conduct additional, oral hearings, which would slow down the whole process, especially if both parties insist on being physically present at court in such a hearing. This issue is linked to the vague wording of Article 5(1) Small Claims Regulation, which states that the procedure shall be essentially a written one unless the court finds it necessary to hold oral hearings, but does not offer any criteria for determining such necessity. Hence, judges are relatively free in deciding whether written hearings are sufficient.

Another very important practical issue relates to the overall cost risk. At first glance, the costs that have to be taken into consideration by a consumer who wishes to launch proceedings do not seem such a big issue. As the 2012 ECC-Net ESCP Study shows, court fees to be paid for initiating an ESCP range between EUR 15 to approximately EUR 200, depending on the Member State and the amount claimed.[216] As legal representation is not required, these costs might not necessarily discourage the consumer from suing.

Court fees, however, especially in cases where the amount in dispute is quite low, might still be disproportionate to the amount in dispute.[217] In addition, the elimination of mandatory legal representation does not mean that the parties would not retain an attorney. With respect to this it should be noted that the Small Claims Regulation does not automatically exclude attorney fees from being awarded. Instead, Article 16 only states that 'the court or tribunal shall not award costs to the successful party to the extent that they were unnecessarily incurred or are disproportionate to the claim'. Because reliable evidence is lacking regarding the accuracy of both the assumption that sued traders would not choose to be represented by an attorney and that courts would necessarily find the representation by attorneys 'unnecessarily incurred' or 'disproportionate to the claim', consumers still face the risk of having to bear considerable costs if they lose.

What makes the cost risk even higher is the fact that language issues could further increase the cost risk to a level where suing would not make much sense, at least in cases where the outcome of a claim is not predictable. Article 6 Small Claims Regulation contains rules on the languages

---

[215] 2012 ECC-Net ESCP Study, p. 22.   [216] *Ibid.*, pp. 21 and 22.
[217] See *ibid.*, p. 21, where the report explains that 'it may be that the costs for translation are greater than the claim itself'.

to be used throughout the procedure. For B2C cases, in which consumers sue traders, the special jurisdiction regime of the Brussels I Regulation does to some extent mitigate the cost risk, as consumers can (in the majority of cases) sue in the courts of their home country, which means that the core documents can be submitted in their language. However, Article 6(3) Small Claims Regulation complicates matters, because a translation, to be provided by the document submitting party, is nevertheless required if the addressee refuses to accept the document because it is not in (one of) the official language(s) of his or her Member State or in a language the addressee understands. This provision might create a further, considerable financial impediment to launching a small claims proceeding.

Language-based financial issues and risks can further arise once consumers receive a judgment in their favour. As indicated above, the ESCP removes intermediary enforcement barriers because the ruling is also directly enforceable in the defendant's Member State.[218] The devil, though, is in the detail. Article 21(2) Small Claims Regulation requires the enforcement-seeking consumer to submit a copy of the judgment and a 'copy of the certificate referred to in Article 20(2)', i.e., Standard Form D, which is a standardised certificate of an ESCP judgment. Standard Form D itself is to be issued 'at no extra cost'.[219] The 'party seeking enforcement'[220] is, however, obliged to have (where necessary) the certificate translated 'into the official language of the Member State of enforcement or, if there are several official languages in that Member State, the official language or one of the official languages of court or tribunal proceedings of the place where enforcement is sought in conformity with the law of that Member State, or into another language that the Member State of enforcement has indicated it can accept'.[221] Because the number of accepted languages is usually quite limited, translating the certificate into a different language is the norm rather than the exception. In particular, in cases where the financial situation of the defendant is unclear or the execution procedure itself proves difficult, the need for the plaintiff to advance the translation costs can pose a financial risk.

These examples show that despite its ambitious goal of enhancing the rights enforcement of small claims, the ESCP shows considerable flaws and has played a considerably less significant role in the enforcement of

---

[218] Article 20(1) Small Claims Regulation.
[219] Article 20(2) Small Claims Regulation.
[220] Article 21(2) Small Claims Regulation.
[221] Article 21(2)(b) Small Claims Regulation.

small claims in its first four years than expected. At the same time, the findings of the 2012 ECC-Net ESCP Study did not let the Small Claims Regulation pass without prominent comment. When confronted with the results of the study, the then European Commissioner for Health and Consumer Policy, John Dalli, noted as follows:

> Consumers who want to take advantage of the opportunities offered by the Single Market need to be able to rely on a variety of effective and efficient means of redress. I am disappointed to see such a low level of assistance to consumers who have tried to use the European Small Claims Procedure. Today, any small amount counts and not getting proper compensation for consumers affects pockets, hurts confidence and slows down European growth.[222]

In April 2013 a further study was conducted (this time directly mandated by the Commission), the Special Eurobarometer study on the European Small Claims Procedure (2013 Eurobarometer ESCP Study).[223] The study evaluated the practical relevance of the ESCP, especially focusing on consumer awareness and its actual use. Although it took a different approach than the 2012 ECC-Net ESCP Study,[224] the 2013 Eurobarometer ESCP Study more or less confirmed the main findings of the 2012 ECC-Net ESCP Study. In addition, it added new insights by providing more representative data, i.e., data from a broader audience.

With respect to consumer awareness, the 2013 Eurobarometer ESCP Study explains that on average, only 12 per cent of consumers were aware of the existence of the ESCP.[225] With respect to the actual use of the ESCP, the 2013 Eurobarometer ESCP Study arrives at further unsatisfactory results. Although 18 per cent of the respondents reported that they had 'encountered problems where they felt they had a legitimate cause for complaint'[226] in cross-border B2C transactions and although in the vast majority of the cases the amounts at stake were less than EUR 2,000,[227] only an insignificant 1 per cent of respondents actually had used the ESCP to pursue their claims.[228]

---

[222] 2012 ECC-Net ESCP Study, p. 6.

[223] TNS Opinion & Social, 'European Small Claims Procedure', Special Eurobarometer 395, (2013), available at ec.europa.eu/public_opinion/archives/ebs/ebs_395_en.pdf.

[224] The 2013 Eurobarometer ESCP Study randomly interviewed a considerable number of citizens representing 'different social and demographic groups' (*ibid.*, p. 4) while the 2012 ECC-Net ESCP Study mainly drew upon the experience of the ECCs based on contacts with consumers as well as feedback from the judiciary (2012 ECC-Net ESCP Study, p. 2).

[225] TNS Opinion & Social, 'European Small Claims Procedure', p. 69.

[226] *Ibid.*, p. 24.   [227] *Ibid.*, p. 27.   [228] *Ibid.*, p. 69.

In light of the findings of the two studies, the Commission had no choice but to finally come forward with some more concrete ideas on how to improve the ESCP. In November 2013 it proposed an amendment to the Small Claims Regulation (and also to the European Order for Payment Procedure Regulation) (2013 Small Claims Regulation Proposal).[229]

In an accompanying press release, the Commission explained the reasons for this move as follows: 'The improved European Small Claims Procedure answers citizens' real concerns: in a recent Eurobarometer [i.e., the 2013 Eurobarometer ESCP Study], one third of the respondents said that they would be more inclined to file a claim if the procedures could be carried out ... without the need to physically go to court.'[230] In response, the 2013 Small Claims Regulation Proposal answered the issue of the 'need to physically go to the court' with a newly worded Article 8 in relation to the way oral hearings are to be held. Pursuant to Article 8 2013 Small Claims Regulation Proposal, 'oral hearing[s] shall be held through video-conference, teleconference or other appropriate distance communication technology ... where the party to be heard is domiciled in a Member State other than the Member State of the court or tribunal with jurisdiction'. The term 'shall' replaced 'may' used in Article 8 Small Claims Regulation and the 'if available' reservation to these new, alternative communication means, was deleted. The new wording of Article 8 implies that alternative means would now be given stronger preference over oral hearings with the physical presence of both parties in court.[231]

Another move towards a stronger use of alternative communication means can be found in Article 13 2013 Small Claims Regulation Proposal on the '[s]ervice of documents and other communications between the parties and the court or tribunal'. While the current Article 13(1) Small Claims Regulation asks that documents be served 'by postal

[229] Proposal for a Regulation of the European Parliament and of the Council amending Regulation (EC) No 861/2007 of the European Parliament and the Council of 11 July 2007 establishing a European Small Claims Procedure and Regulation (EC) No 1896/2006 of the European Parliament and of the Council of 12 December 2006 creating a European order for payment procedure, 19 November 2013, COM(2013) 794 final (2013 Small Claims Regulation Proposal).

[230] European Commission, 'Shopped Online and Want Your Money back? Commission Proposal on Small Claims Helps Consumers and SMEs', press release, IP/13/1095, 19 November 2013, available at europa.eu/rapid/press-release_IP-13-1095_en.htm.

[231] The parties would not be deprived, however, of their right to be heard in person in court. Article 8(2) 2013 Small Claims Regulation Proposal states as follows: 'A party shall always be entitled to appear before the court of tribunal and be heard in person if that party so requests'.

service attested by an acknowledgement of receipt', Article 13(1)[232] and (2)[233] 2013 Small Claims Regulation Proposal essentially allows for the use of 'electronic means' throughout the entire procedure. This possibility is limited, however, by the fact that the serving of documents by electronic means on a party basically requires that the receiving party accepts such electronic service (and for some documents, it is further limited by the condition that national procedural laws accept such electronic means).[234]

For B2C disputes, it is further worth noting that some additional considerations aimed to answer the cost risk issue and the lack of consumer awareness regarding the ESCP, as well as the insufficient practical assistance in using it. With respect to the first issue, Article 15a 2013 Small Claims Regulation Proposal aims to cap court fees at 10 per cent of the value of the claim (or with respect to minimum court fees – if existing – at EUR 35). One has to wait and see how Member States would implement this if the proposal were accepted, especially because the wording leaves the possibility to charge a minimum fee of EUR 35, even if that exceeds 10 per cent of the value of the claim.

Article 11 2013 Small Claims Regulation Proposal addresses issues concerning the practical assistance to be given to parties and the raising of consumers' awareness of the ESCP in slightly more detail compared with the current wording of Article 11 Small Claims Regulation. Although it should be appreciated that Article 11(1) 2013 Small Claims Regulation Proposal defines the tasks falling under 'practical assistance', Article 11(2) unfortunately misses the chance to come up with any innovative ideas regarding how to increase consumer awareness of the ESCP. Simply asking Member States to ensure that relevant information can be found in courts and on court websites without asking for any further active promotional steps is unlikely to resolve the issue. I will return to this question in the context of proper consumer information at a later stage in this book.[235]

---

[232] For documents listed in Articles 5(2) and 7(2) Small Claims Regulation, i.e., the claim form, supporting documents (if any), the answer form as well as the judgment.
[233] For all other 'written communication'.
[234] See Article 13 2013 Small Claims Regulation Proposal for details. See also Article 4(1) Small Claims Procedure which allows the use of electronic means to submit the claim form if Member States accept such practice.
[235] See Chapter 15, 'Consumer Empowerment' below.

Alternative Dispute Resolution (2008/2013)

Initial ADR trends at the EU level and the 2008 Mediation Directive

Alternative Dispute Resolution (ADR) is a popular, yet vague term. ADR does not refer to one specific alternative to litigation. Instead, the term ADR should be understood as an umbrella term referring to various different substitutes for litigation. *Black's Law Dictionary* lists some prominent ADR examples, such as arbitration or mediation.[236] It further quotes Stephen Ware, who defines ADR as 'encompassing all legally permitted processes of dispute resolution other than litigation'.[237] In addition, the dictionary stresses the practical relevance of ADR by claiming that '[a]lternative processes, especially negotiation, are used far more frequently [than litigation]'.[238] In the *New Oxford Companion to Law*, Cheryl Dolder provides another general definition of ADR: 'ADR includes a mixed bag of activities ranging from adjudication and formal, binding arbitration to informal, open-door policies, with intermediate possibilities including mediation, conciliation, and ombudsman schemes.'[239]

One could principally say that ADR stands for non-litigative means of dispute resolution, i.e., for mechanisms used to solve disputes by means other than litigation. Compared with litigation, ADR is generally believed to be a faster, more cost-effective and informal alternative,[240] which makes it especially attractive for cases that would normally (because of the low amount in dispute, time constraints or feared publicity) not be taken to courts.

---

[236] Garner, *Black's Law Dictionary*, p. 91.

[237] *Ibid.* (citing S. J. Ware, *Alternative Dispute Resolution* (St. Paul, MN: West Group, 2001), pp. 5–6).

[238] Garner, *Black's Law Dictionary*, p. 91.

[239] C. Dolder in Cane and Conaghan (eds.), *New Oxford Companion to Law*, p. 26.

[240] According to DG SANCO '[t]he advantage of ADR is that it offers more flexibility than going to court and can better meet the needs of both consumers and professionals. Compared to going to court these schemes are cheaper, quicker and more informal which means they are an attractive means for consumers seeking redress' (ec.europa.eu/consumers/redress/out_of_court/index_en.htm). For an analysis of the advantages of ADR in the context of ODR see A. Juškys and N. Ulbaitė, 'Alternative Dispute Resolution for Consumer Disputes in the European Union: Current Issues and Future Opportunities', *Issues of Business and Law*, 4 (2012), 25, 32–3; I. Benöhr, 'Consumer Dispute Resolution after the Lisbon Treaty: Collective Actions and Alternative Procedures', *Journal of Consumer Policy*, 35 (2012), 87, 99; C. Hodges, N. Creutzfeldt-Banda and I. Benöhr, 'The Hidden World of Consumer ADR – Redress and Behaviour', report for the Foundation for Law, Justice and Society, (2011), available at www.fljs.org/files/publications/Hodges-Banda-Benohr_ConsumerADR-Report.pdf. For a more differentiated analysis on the

The general phenomenon of ADR is nothing new. Simon Roberts and Michael Palmer show that non-litigative forms of dispute resolution had been used to some extent in ancient China and the Roman Empire.[241] In a more modern setting, ADR has been increasingly used in the USA, especially since the 1970s and 1980s, when the attitude towards ADR shifted from 'a hobbyhorse for a few offbeat scholars'[242] to 'attract[ing] a bandwagon following of adherents'.[243] Furthermore, in the 1970s, the Florence Project discussed European national 'alternative methods to decide legal claims' in its third access to justice wave.[244]

However, it was only in the last decade of the second millennium that ADR – in the context of B2C disputes (consumer ADR) – took on greater significance in the discussion on access to justice at the pan-EU level.[245] It was in the 1993 Consumer Access to Justice Green Paper that the Commission first clearly concerned itself with consumer ADR in Europe. The Commission identified a scattered landscape of national consumer

possible advantages of ADR for consumers see A. J. Bělohlávek, 'Autonomy in B2C Arbitration: Is the European Model of Consumer Protection Really Adequate?' *Czech (& Central European) Yearbook of Arbitration*, (2012), 17, 18, where Alexander Bělohlávek summarises as follows: 'Arbitration is not a panacea, and certainly not suitable for resolving *all* types of disputes. It has its proponents and detractors. In fact, one can hardly speak of any type (group) of dispute as being particularly suited, *a priori*, for resolution via arbitration rather than before a [general] court.' For critical comments on B2C arbitration in general see J. Dickie, *Producers and Consumers in EU E-Commerce Law* (Oxford: Hart, 2005), p. 32. See also Jeffrey Seul's illustration of the likely advantages of litigation over ADR in general in J. R. Seul, 'Litigation as a Dispute Resolution Alternative' in M. L. Moffitt and R. C. Bordone (eds.), *The Handbook of Dispute Resolution* (San Francisco, CA: Jossey-Bass, 2005), pp. 344–50.

[241] S. Roberts and M. Palmer, *Dispute Processes: ADR and the Primary Forms of Decision-Making* (Cambridge University Press, 2005), pp. 11–16.

[242] H. T. Edwards, 'Commentary: Alternative Dispute Resolution: Panacea or Anathema?', *Harvard Law Review*, 99 (1985), 668, 669.

[243] *Ibid.*

[244] See Cappelletti and Garth, 'Access to Justice', pp. 59–66.

[245] For a good overview of the development of consumer ADR in EU see in I. Benöhr, 'Alternative Dispute Resolution for Consumers in the European Union' in C. Hodges *et al.* (eds.), *Consumer ADR in Europe* (Oxford: Hart, 2012), pp. 3–5; C. Hodges, 'Current Discussions on Consumer Redress: Collective Redress and ADR', *ERA Forum*, 13 (2012), 11, 20–25. For national summaries of existing consumer ADR mechanisms in the EU see the contributions in Hodges *et al.* (eds.), *Consumer ADR in Europe*. For comments on consumer arbitration from a comparative perspective of European and North American approaches see A. J. Bělohlávek, *B2C Consumer Protection in Arbitration* (Huntington, NY: Juris, 2012); C. R. Drahozal and R. J. Friel, 'Consumer Arbitration in the European Union and the United States', *North Carolina Journal of International Law and Commercial Regulation*, 28 (2002), 357–94.

ADR tools or, to quote the 1993 Consumer Access to Justice Green Paper, 'specific out-of-court procedures for the settlement of consumer disputes'.[246] National approaches differed regarding the general availability of ADR, the designation of competent ADR bodies (i.e., the question of who is competent – a public authority or a private body) or their preferred ADR devices.[247] Overall, the 1993 Consumer Access to Justice Green Paper was quite sceptical towards the use of ADR as an alternative to litigation, commenting that 'there is ... the question as to the extent to which the guarantees of independence (or at least impartiality), which in rule-of-law states are invested in the judiciary, can be assured by the new "judges" who are increasingly being called on to settle disputes outside the framework of the courts proper'.[248] At the same time, however, it was observed that the 'trend [of ADR] ... is likely to continue'.[249]

In 1998, the Commission issued a communication on the out-of-court settlement of consumer disputes (1998 ADR Communication)[250] and a recommendation on the principles applicable to the bodies responsible for the out-of-court settlement of consumer disputes (1998 ADR Recommendation).[251] Both reacted (but with limited success) to the findings of the 1993 Consumer Access to Justice Green Paper by introducing some kind of assistance to help overcome the practical difficulties posed by the different approaches taken by the Member States towards ADR.

The main feature of the 1998 ADR Communication was the introduction of a special, standardised complaint form that consumers could use when trying to reach an out-of-court solution with traders.[252] The 1998 ADR Recommendation, on the other hand, introduced seven guiding principles for 'procedures which, no matter what they are called, lead to the settlement of a dispute through the active intervention of a third party, who proposes or imposes a solution ... [and does] not concern procedures that merely involve an attempt to bring the parties together to convince

---

[246] 1993 Consumer Access to Justice Green Paper, p. 57.

[247] *Ibid.*, pp. 57 and 58.   [248] *Ibid.*, p. 58.   [249] *Ibid.*

[250] Communication from the Commission on 'the out-of-court settlement of consumer disputes', 30 March 1998, COM(1998) 198 final (1998 ADR Communication).

[251] Commission recommendation on the principles applicable to the bodies responsible for out-of-court settlement of consumer disputes, 30 March 1998, OJ 2008 No. L115/31 (1998 ADR Recommendation).

[252] This European Claim Form for Consumers (or European Consumer Complaint Form) aimed to 'facilitate [the] communication between consumers and professionals and, should an amicable solution prove impossible, facilitate access to out-of-court procedures' (see 1998 ADR Communication, p. 2).

them to find a solution by common consent'.[253] This shows that the 1998
ADR Recommendation aimed at ADR mechanisms characterised by
a relatively strong involvement of third parties, which is, for example,
found in consumer arbitration. It was complemented by a second ADR
recommendation, a recommendation on the principles for out-of-court
bodies involved in the consensual resolution of consumer disputes (2001
ADR Recommendation).[254] The 2001 ADR Recommendation covered
ADR tools that give greater discretion to the disputing parties and limit
the decision-making or decision-proposing competences of third parties, such as mediation proceedings, and repeated some of the principles
already introduced by the 1998 ADR Recommendation.[255]

ADR was further on the agenda at the Tampere Council in 1999. The
Tampere Council continued with the policy shift from the rather reserved
attitude towards ADR expressed in the 1993 Consumer Access to Justice
Green Paper towards a greater interest in the practical use of ADR shown
by the 1998 ADR Communication and the 1998 ADR Recommendation.
Although the Presidency Conclusions only marginally referred to ADR by
asking that '[a]lternative, extra-judicial procedures should ... be created by
Member States',[256] the fact that ADR was discussed in the context of the question of how to improve access to justice in Europe showed that ADR had been
considered as a potentially important supplementary procedural device.

An important intermediate step towards a pan-EU ADR mechanism
was taken in 2002, when the Commission published its Green Paper on

---

[253] Preamble of the 1998 ADR Recommendation. The seven principles were: (1) the independence of the involved ADR body/bodies; (2) procedural transparency; (3) the adversarial principle; (4) procedural effectiveness; (5) adherence to mandatory national
consumer protection provisions (principle of legality); (6) compliance with basic procedural rights (principle of liberty); (7) and the principle of representation, i.e., the parties' right to be represented during the proceedings. For details see Chapters I to VII
1998 ADR Recommendation.

[254] Commission recommendation on the principles for out-of-court bodies involved in the
consensual resolution of consumer disputes, 4 April 2001, OJ 2001 No. L109/56 (2001
ADR Recommendation).

[255] See ibid., I.1, where the scope of the recommendation is defined as follows: 'This recommendation applies to third party bodies responsible for out-of-court consumer dispute resolution procedures that, no matter what they are called, attempt to resolve a
dispute by bringing the parties together to convince them to find a solution by common consent.' Four of the aforementioned principles are repeated by the 2001 ADR
Recommendation, slightly amended to meet the needs of user friendliness: impartiality,
transparency, effectiveness and fairness. For an interactive map of ADR tools that comply with the Commission recommendations see ec.europa.eu/consumers/redress_cons/
schemes_en.htm.

[256] Presidency Conclusions, Tampere European Council, para. 30.

alternative dispute resolution in civil and commercial law (2002 ADR Green Paper).[257] Compared with the recent Directive on alternative dispute resolution for consumer disputes (ADR Directive), which I will discuss shortly, the scope of the 2002 ADR Green Paper was both wider and narrower. It was wider because it did not focus only on B2C disputes, but on 'civil and commercial matters [in general], including ... consumer law',[258] and it was narrower, because it explicitly excluded arbitration from its scope, arguing that '[a]rbitration [was] ... closer to a quasi-judicial procedure than to an ADR as arbitrators' awards replace judicial decisions'.[259] Just like the aforementioned Presidency Conclusions of the Tampere Council, the 2002 ADR Green Paper linked ADR to access to justice ideas, arguing that ADR could be a viable supplementary option in the quest for enhanced (procedural) access to justice because ADR could help to reduce the burden on the judiciary.[260] Although the 2002 ADR Green Paper did not come forward with any concrete options in the end, it nevertheless further intensified the debate of ADR tools at the EU level, as it formulated specific questions to evaluate likely actions proposed by the Commission.[261]

What followed were two initiatives in 2004. First, a European Code of Conduct for Mediators (2004 European Code of Conduct) was adopted.[262] The 2004 European Code of Conduct contains several voluntary principles, such as the mediator's (personal and financial) independence from the parties in dispute, the mediator's impartiality as well as the principles of fairness and confidentiality of proceedings, basically following and refining the principles of the 2001 ADR Recommendation. The second 2004 initiative was the Proposal for a Directive on certain aspects of mediation in civil and commercial matters (Mediation Directive Proposal).[263] It (once again) emphasised the importance of ADR, or to

---

[257] Green paper on alternative dispute resolution in civil and commercial law, 19 April 2002, COM(2002) 196 final.

[258] *Ibid.*, p. 6.   [259] *Ibid.*

[260] *Ibid.*, pp. 7–9. For some concrete arguments why the Commission considered ADR tools as being practically important for consumers see *ibid.*, chapter 2.2.1 (titled 'Reaping the benefits of the initiatives taken in the field of consumer protection law').

[261] For a summary of the 21 questions see *ibid.*, pp. 35 and 36.

[262] The 2004 European Code of Conduct is available online at ec.europa.eu/civiljustice/adr/adr_ec_code_conduct_en.pdf (for details on the code see ec.europa.eu/civiljustice/adr/adr_ec_code_conduct_en.htm).

[263] Proposal for a Directive of the European Parliament and of the Council on certain aspects of mediation in civil and commercial matters, 22 October 2004, COM(2004) 718 final (Mediation Directive Proposal).

be more concrete in this context, the importance of mediation from the viewpoint of enhanced consumer redress.[264] The approach taken by the Mediation Directive Proposal was quite ambitious. While it limited its scope to mediation proceedings and thus excluded other forms of ADR, it tried to promote and regulate the practical use of mediation with regard to both cross-border *and* purely domestic cases. The proposal was heavily debated. In the end, it took nearly four years before the final text of the Directive on certain aspects of mediation in civil and commercial matters (Mediation Directive)[265] was adopted.

The Mediation Directive has been fully applicable since May 2011 in all Member States except Denmark. Unlike the preceding proposal, the Mediation Directive (directly) focuses only on cross-border cases.[266] The basic objective of the Mediation Directive, compared with the Mediation Directive Proposal, remained, however, unchanged. According to Article 1(1) Mediation Directive, it was designed 'to facilitate access to alternative dispute resolution and to promote the amicable settlement of disputes by encouraging the use of mediation and by ensuring a balanced relationship between mediation and judicial proceedings'.

In terms of content the Mediation Directive does not provide for much innovation. It does not directly set any qualitative standards; it only asks Member States to 'encourage, by any means which they consider appropriate, the development of, and adherence to, voluntary codes of conduct by mediators and organizations providing mediation services, as well as other effective quality control mechanisms concerning the provision of mediation services'.[267] It further fails to make the 2004 European Code of Conduct mandatory for mediation proceedings.[268]

---

[264] See the Explanatory Memorandum accompanying the Mediation Directive Proposal Explanatory Memorandum, p. 2: 'The proposed directive facilitat[es] access to dispute resolution through two types of provisions: first, provisions that aim at ensuring a sound relationship between mediation and judicial proceedings, by establishing minimum common rules in the Community on a number of key aspects of civil procedure. Secondly, by providing the necessary tools for the courts of the Member States to actively promote the use of mediation ...'.

[265] Directive 2008/52/EC of the European Parliament and of the Council on certain aspects of mediation in civil and commercial matters, 21 May 2008, OJ 2008 No. L136/3.

[266] See Article 1(2) Mediation Directive. Recital 8 Mediation Directive adds that 'nothing should prevent Member States from applying such provisions [i.e. the provisions of the Mediation Directive] also to internal mediation processes'.

[267] Article 4(1) Mediation Directive.

[268] The only reference to the European Code of Conduct is softly worded – Recital 17 Mediation Directive explains that 'Mediators should be made aware of the existence of the European Code of Conduct for Mediators which should also be made available to the general public on the Internet'.

Article 6 on the enforceability of written mediation results and Article 8 on the effect of mediation on the limitation and prescription periods more or less confirmed the status quo of mediation in many Member States. Article 6 asks the Member States to guarantee that written mediation outcomes can be made enforceable if the parties wish so. Member States have introduced (or in many cases maintained already existing) different practical solutions,[269] most notably making mediation results enforceable with the help of authentic instruments and court settlements (which, with respect to cross-border cases, are covered by Articles 57(1)[270] and 58[271] Brussels I Regulation – and with effect from 10 January 2015 by Articles 58(1)[272] and 59[273] Brussels I Regulation Recast (instead)). Article 8 Mediation Directive tries to ensure that parties do not lose the chance to sue in court or initiate arbitration due to an expiration of prescription periods during mediation proceedings. Also in this respect most Member States had already introduced pertinent legislation prior to the adoption of the Mediation Directive.

Although the Mediation Directive tried to close the gaps in cross-border ADR, it did not significantly enhance the use of ADR. In particular, two key problems remained. Mediation was and still is a relatively weak alternative mechanism, as it relies on the willingness of both parties to reach an agreement. Mediation necessarily fails if one party to the conflict refuses to cooperate. Hence, mediation is no alternative to 'stronger' ADR mechanisms in such cases. Furthermore, and perhaps even more importantly, the Mediation Directive did not oblige Member States to introduce mediation schemes. The Commission soon realised that the Mediation Directive could not be the end of the story in the quest for enhanced consumer access to justice. Additional instruments were still needed.

---

[269] ec.europa.eu/justice_home/judicialatlascivil/html/me_competentauthorities_en.jsp?countrySession=15&#statePage0.

[270] Article 57(1) Brussels I Regulation: 'A document which has been formally drawn up or registered as an authentic instrument and is enforceable in one Member State shall, in another Member State, be declared enforceable there …'

[271] Article 58 Brussels I Regulation: 'A settlement which has been approved by a court in the course of proceedings and is enforceable in the Member State in which it was concluded shall be enforceable in the State addressed under the same conditions as authentic instruments.'

[272] Article 58 (1) Brussels I Regulation Recast: 'An authentic instrument which is enforceable in the Member State of origin shall be enforceable in the other Member States without any declaration of enforceability being required.'

[273] Article 59 Brussels I Regulation Recast: 'A court settlement which is enforceable in the Member State of origin shall be enforced in the other Member States under the same conditions as authentic instruments.'

The ADR Directive (2013)

In the previous chapter, I explained that the Mediation Directive was a quite narrow attempt to regulate consumer ADR at the EU level, because it only dealt with B2C issues if they were mediated. Other prominent forms of ADR such as arbitration or consumer complaint board proceedings were beyond its scope. In addition, the Mediation Directive only 'facilitated'[274] the use of mediation, by 'encouraging the use of mediation'[275] in the Member States, but did not make the introduction of mediation bodies mandatory.

With respect to these concerns, some sectoral EU consumer laws, such as the Consumer Credit Agreements Directive in 2008,[276] or more general EU laws with particular importance also for consumers, such as the e-Commerce Directive in 2000,[277] took a different approach by referring to ADR tools regardless of their form and obliging Member States to offer out-of-court redress tools as an alternative to litigation.[278] They did so, however, only in a specific sector, within the scope of the respective directive.

What was still missing was EU legislation that comprehensively transcended both at the same time: mediation on the one hand and specific, narrow legal sectors on the other. Soon after the adoption of the Mediation Directive the Commission thus intensified its discussions on the possible introduction of a more comprehensive ADR mechanism, and took a look at the ADR experience of some Member States. In 2009 two Commission-initiated studies revealed practical problems with regard to existing comprehensive national ADR tools. A 2009 Eurobarometer study showed that in several Member States consumers were disappointed with

---

[274] Article 1(1) Mediation Directive.   [275] *Ibid.*

[276] Directive No 2008/48/EC of the European Parliament and of the Council on credit agreements for consumers, 23 April 2008, OJ 2008 No. L133/66 (Consumer Credit Agreements Directive).

[277] Directive No 2000/31/EC of the European Parliament and of the Council on certain legal aspects of information society services, in particular electronic commerce, in the Internal Market, 8 June 2000, OJ 2000 No. L178/1 (e-Commerce Directive).

[278] See Article 24 Consumer Credit Agreements Directive ('Out-of-court dispute resolution') and Article 17 E-Commerce Directive ('Out-of-court dispute settlement'). On the earlier, sectoral approach towards consumer ADR see C. Hodges, I. Benöhr and N. Creutzfeldt-Banda, 'Consumer-to-Business ADR Structures: Harnessing the Power of CADR for Dispute Resolution and Regulating Market Behaviour', report for the Foundation for Law, Justice and Society, (2012), pp. 3–4, available at www.fljs.org/files/publications/ConsumerADR-PolicyBrief.pdf.

the costs of ADR, which, although on average were relatively low,[279] were still considered as being a disincentive for using ADR.[280] A more comprehensive study, the 2009 study on the use of alternative dispute resolution in the European Union,[281] added that the main reasons consumers did not make extensive use of ADR included a 'lack of awareness which is an essential pre-requisite to access [ADR tools]';[282] a '[f]ragmentation of ADR services in larger countries';[283] 'non-compliance by business[es] with nonbinding decisions of ADR schemes and [the] refusal by business[es] to enter the procedure';[284] and – (especially) for cross-border cases – problems related to 'finding the right competent scheme'[285] as well as 'language barriers'.[286]

Two years later another study on ADR, the 2011 study on cross-border alternative dispute resolution in the European Union (2011 ADR Study) confirmed those findings.[287] Although the trend showed a steady general increase in the use of ADR,[288] the 2011 ADR Study identified a considerable gap in the practical use of consumer ADR ranging from (in total, i.e., referring to both purely domestic cases and cross-border cases) 4.73 cases per 1,000 inhabitants in Belgium to only 0.01 cases per 1,000 inhabitants in the Czech Republic in 2007.[289] Moreover, in two-thirds of the Member States, less than 1 consumer ADR case per 1,000 inhabitants was launched in 2007.[290] The national examples in the study further showed that ADR

---

[279] Civic Consulting, 'Study on the Use of Alternative Dispute Resolution in the European Union', study for DG SANCO, (2009), p. 8, where it is explained that most procedures do not cost more than EUR 50, available at ec.europa.eu/consumers/redress_cons/adr_study.pdf.

[280] TNS Qual+, 'Consumer Redress in the European Union: Consumer Experiences, Perceptions and Choices', Eurobarometer qualitative study, (2009), p. 48, available at ec.europa.eu/consumers/redress_cons/docs/cons_redress_EU_qual_study_report_en.pdf.

[281] Civic Consulting, 'Study on the Use of Alternative Dispute Resolution in the European Union'.

[282] *Ibid.*, p. 9.

[283] *Ibid.* For further comments on this issue see I. Barral-Viñals, 'Consumer Complaints and Alternative Dispute Resolution: Harmonisation of the European ADR System' in J. Devenney and K. Kenny (eds.), *The Transformation of European Private Law* (Cambridge University Press, 2013), pp. 295–315.

[284] Civic Consulting, 'Study on the Use of Alternative Dispute Resolution in the European Union', p. 9.

[285] *Ibid.*   [286] *Ibid.*

[287] Civic Consulting, 'Cross-border Alternative Dispute Resolution in the European Union', study for IMCO, (2011), pp. 48–50, available at www.europarl.europa.eu/meetdocs/2009_2014/documents/imco/dv/adr_study_/adr_study_en.pdf.

[288] See *ibid.*, p. 27 (Figure 8).   [289] *Ibid.*, p. 29 (Figure 9).   [290] *Ibid.*

was used even less in cross-border B2C cases.[291] Several stakeholders, especially consumer representatives, confirmed some earlier findings and explained that major problems in relation to cross-border ADR laid in language issues, higher levels of consumer unawareness of cross-border ADR schemes and the low-quality standard of some cross-border ADR institutions.[292]

Soon after the publication of the 2011 ADR Study, the Commission came forward with its Proposal for an ADR Directive[293] (2011 ADR Directive Proposal). Two years later the ADR Directive[294] was eventually adopted. Recital 5 ADR Directive explains the need for enhanced ADR: 'ADR ... is not running satisfactorily ... in the Union. Consumers and traders are still not aware of the existing out-of-court redress mechanisms, with only a small percentage of citizens knowing how to file a complaint ... Where ADR procedures are available, their quality levels vary considerably in the Member States.'[295] A Commission memo in early 2013 defines the rationale behind the ADR Directive as follows: 'Well-functioning ADR procedures across the EU will encourage consumers to seek solutions to the problems they encounter when buying products and services in the

---

[291] *Ibid.*, chapter 3.

[292] See, for example, BEUC, 'Alternative Dispute Resolution – European Commission's Consultation: BEUC response', position paper, X/2011/033 (2011), p. 3, available at ec.europa.eu/consumers/redress_cons/adr_responses/ca_beuc_en.pdf: 'We agree that the lack of consumer and business awareness of ADR or the gaps in the ADR coverage should be properly addressed.' BEUC adds: 'The quality ... of ADR schemes will ... serve as strong incentives for consumers to use Alternative Dispute Resolution' (*ibid.*, p. 9).

[293] Proposal for a Directive of the European Parliament and of the Council on alternative dispute resolution for consumer disputes and amending Regulation (EC) No 2006/2004 and Directive 2009/22/EC, 29 November 2011, COM(2011) 793 final. For an analysis of the proposal see M. Becklein, 'Verbesserter Zugang zum Recht für Verbraucher? der Regelungsvorschläge der EU-Kommission zur Alternativen Streitbeilegung', *Zeitschrift für das Privatrecht der Europäischen Union*, 9 (2012), 232–40. In addition, Martin Becklein comments on the ODR Regulation Proposal of the same day (Proposal for a Regulation of the European Parliament and of the Council on online dispute resolution for consumer disputes, 29 November 2011, COM(2011) 794 final) (see Becklein, 'Verbesserter Zugang zum Recht für Verbraucher? Eine Bewertung der Regelungsvorschläge der EU-Kommission zur Alternativen Streitbeilegung', 237 and 239 for details).

[294] Directive of the European Parliament and of the Council on alternative dispute resolution for consumer disputes and amending Regulation (EC) No 2006/2004 and Directive 2009/22/EC, 21 May 2013, OJ 2013 No. L165/63.

[295] The Commission had already explained this view in the Explanatory Memorandum accompanying the 2011 ADR Directive Proposal, claiming that 'the analysis of the current situation identified the following main shortcomings which hinder the effectiveness of ADR: gaps in the coverage, the lack of consumer and business awareness as well as the uneven quality of ADR procedures' (2011 ADR Directive Proposal Explanatory Memorandum, p. 2).

Single Market. This will help them save money that they can invest in a better way.'[296]

Unlike the Mediation Directive, the ADR Directive focuses only on consumer issues. However, at the same time it takes a comparatively comprehensive approach and fills several (but as will be shown later, not all) lacunae. First, it does not only deal with cross-border issues. According to Article 2(1) ADR Directive, it applies both to domestic and cross-border disputes. Second, and as its title indicates, the ADR Directive does not just cover mediation, but (nearly)[297] any form of ADR. Third, the ADR Directive does not simply encourage Member States to introduce ADR mechanisms, it makes the establishment of ADR institutions mandatory.[298] Fourth, it regulates the respective proceedings in more detail, trying to ensure that consumers can benefit from ADR not only in theory but also in practice.

These features aim to secure a seamless network of ADR in each Member State for domestic and cross-border B2C contract cases launched by one or more consumers against one or more traders. Cases in the opposite direction, i.e., cases initiated by traders against consumers, are excluded from the application of the ADR Directive.[299]

To facilitate the use of ADR, the directive imposes several obligations on the Member States to secure a certain standard within the EU. Some of these obligations, such as the principles of independence, transparency or legality of ADR, were already familiar from the 1998 and 2001 ADR Recommendations and the 2004 Code of Conduct. The big difference, however, is that now Member States *must* make sure that – within their respective territory – ADR mechanisms exist to handle B2C in accordance with these principles.[300] This move was undeniably overdue if one

---

[296] European Commission, 'A Step forward for EU Consumers: Questions & Answers on Alternative Dispute Resolution and Online Dispute Resolution', press release, MEMO/13/193, 12 March 2013, p. 1, available at europa.eu/rapid/press-release_MEMO-13-193_en.htm.

[297] For exceptions from the scope as defined by Article 2(1) ADR Directive see Article 2(2) ADR Directive.

[298] Article 5(1) ADR Directive: 'Member States shall facilitate access by consumers to ADR procedures and shall ensure that disputes covered by this Directive and which involve a trader established on their respective territories can be submitted to an ADR entity which complies with the requirements set out in this Directive.'

[299] Article 2(2)(g) ADR Directive.

[300] Article 5(1) ADR Directive stipulates that 'Member States shall ... ensure that disputes covered by this Directive and which involve a trader established on their respective territories can be submitted to an ADR entity which complies with the requirements set

wanted to guarantee that ADR entities, which engage in EU-initiated, non-litigative dispute resolution, follow a certain qualitative standard.

The ADR Directive further aims to ensure that consumers obtain fast results.[301] Under the pillar of 'effectiveness' the directive asks Member States to ensure that results of ADR proceedings are (basically) available within 90 days calculated from the date when 'the ADR entity has received the complete complaint file'.[302] Considering that – as stated also in the underlying ADR Impact Assessment of 2011 – enforcing rights is considerably time-consuming for consumers,[303] solving B2C disputes within 90 days by means of ADR would clearly be a great improvement, at least from a timeframe perspective. In addition, the effectiveness principle addresses further concerns. In addition to an improved accessibility of ADR 'irrespective of where [the parties] are',[304] one should highlight that under the ADR Directive, ADR procedures have to be offered 'free of

out in this Directive'. The binding quality criteria follow in Articles 6 to 12. The earlier Mediation Directive, on the other hand, failed to enshrine binding principles. Recital 17 Mediation Directive states that 'Mediators should be made aware of the existence of the European Code of Conduct for Mediators which should also be made available to the general public on the Internet'. Article 4(1) Mediation Directive reads as follows: 'Member States shall encourage, by any means which they consider appropriate, the development of, and adherence to, voluntary codes of conduct by mediators and organizations providing mediation service.'

[301] The ADR Directive does not, however, cover the post-decision-making stage. The question of the enforceability of the outcome of ADR is addressed only as a sideline (see Articles 7(1)(o) and 17). Nothing very innovative is found in this respect. Concrete answers are left to already existing international legislation (if relevant) or national law (see, for example, Article 9(3) ADR Directive, which says that '[w]here, in accordance with national law, ADR procedures provide that their outcome becomes binding on the trader once the consumer has accepted the proposed solution ...'). For the binding character of arbitral awards see the 1958 Convention on the Recognition and Enforcement of Foreign Arbitral Awards (New York Convention). With regard to mediation results see the previous chapter and Articles 57(1) and 58 Brussels I Regulation and Articles 58(1) and 59 Brussels I Regulation Recast.

[302] Article 8(e) ADR Directive. An exception to this 90-day-principle can be found for 'highly complex disputes'. In such cases 'the ADR entity in charge may, at its own discretion, extend the 90 calendar days' time period. The parties shall be informed of any extension of that period and of the expected length of time that will be needed for the conclusion of the dispute' (*ibid.*).

[303] Commission staff working paper, Impact Assessment accompanying the document Proposal for a Directive of the European Parliament and of the Council on Alternative Dispute Resolution for consumer disputes (Directive on consumer ADR) and Proposal for a Regulation of the European Parliament and of the Council on Online Dispute Resolution for consumer disputes (Regulation on consumer ODR), 29 November 2011, SEC(2011) 1408 final, p. 13 (with examples for average lengths of disputes in general).

[304] Article 8(a) ADR Directive.

charge or … at a nominal fee for consumers'.[305] It can be hoped that easily accessible, fast and free (or almost free) ADR would incentivise consumers to take action in cases in which they might not think it would be worthwhile to sue.

Another important provision in practice is Article 11 ADR Directive. It refers to substantive law issues and defines the minimum standard of consumer protection the respective ADR entity has to follow when actively solving a B2C dispute (as in, for example, arbitration). Article 11(1)(b) states the following:

> Member States shall ensure that in ADR procedures which aim at resolving the dispute by imposing a solution on the consumer in a situation involving a conflict of laws, where the law applicable to the sales or service contract is determined in accordance with Article 6(1) and (2) of Regulation (EC) No 593/2008, the solution imposed by the ADR entity shall not result in the consumer being deprived of the protection afforded to him by the provisions that cannot be derogated from by agreement by virtue of the law of the Member State in which he is habitually resident.

From a consumer perspective, this clarification should be welcomed. Obliging ADR entities under the ADR Directive to apply the qualitative yardstick of Article 6 Rome I Regulation has the crucial advantage that it would ensure that B2C arbitration does not lead to a scenario where consumers can obtain a relatively unbureaucratic, fast and cheap decision, which would not meet the protective substantive standards of mandatory consumer laws.[306] With Article 11, the ADR Directive clarifies that ADR schemes that 'impos[e] a solution on the consumer in a situation involving a conflict of laws'[307] must adhere to the same level of protection as courts.[308]

---

[305] Article 8(c) ADR Directive.

[306] For a comment on the importance of ensuring such a standard see M. Piers, 'Consumer Arbitration and European Private Law: A Seminal Consumer Arbitration Model Law for Europe', *European Review of Private Law*, 21 (2013), 247, 286, where Maud Piers (in an analysis conducted before the adoption of the ADR Directive) concludes as follows: '[L]egislators have adopted several protective measures of contract law that must guard the consumer from being … coerced into agreeing to disfavourable conditions or to commitments … These measures (must) apply as well to the parties engaged in consumer arbitration.' For a comment on mandatory laws in B2C arbitration prior to the adoption of the ADR Directive see J. Hörnle, *Cross-border Internet Dispute Resolution* (Cambridge University Press, 2009), p. 60.

[307] Article 11(1)(b) ADR Directive.

[308] See also the 'expertise' requirement of Article 6(a) ADR Directive which asks Member States to ensure that 'the natural persons in charge of ADR … possess the necessary

The ADR Directive can be considered a fairly encouraging attempt to enhance the alternative dispute settlement of B2C issues. On the positive side, one should note that important quality criteria are made mandatory for ADR entities falling under the regime of the directive. This surely makes ADR more attractive to consumers who are looking for an alternative to traditional litigation.[309]

Another issue that should be briefly commented on is the directive's approach towards the interplay between litigation and arbitration. Article 1 ADR Directive points out that 'the purpose of this Directive is ... to contribute to the proper functioning of the internal market by ensuring that consumers can, *on a voluntary basis*, submit complaints against traders to entities offering independent, impartial, transparent, effective, fast and fair alternative dispute resolution procedures' (emphasis added). The second sentence of Article 1 (at first sight) is somewhat confusing. It reads: 'This Directive is without prejudice to national legislation *making participation in such procedures mandatory*, provided that such legislation does not prevent the parties from exercising their right of access to the judicial system' (emphasis added). How is the Member State option of this second sentence to be understood? Taking a look at Recital 49 ADR Directive clarifies the meaning and interplay of the two sentences. It explains that 'this Directive should be without prejudice to any national rules making the participation *of traders* in such procedures mandatory ...', provided that such legislation does not prevent the parties from exercising their right of access to the judicial system' (emphasis added). This makes clear that Member States could only make the participation of the *business* party mandatory, but could not oblige consumers to use ADR instead of litigation. Consumers must still have the chance to initiate a legal proceeding in court, if they wish to do so.

Traders should not have the chance either to deprive consumers of their access to traditional courts. Pursuant to Article 10(1) ADR Directive (basically following the regime of the Unfair Contract Terms Directive

---

knowledge and skills in the field of alternative or judicial resolution of consumer disputes, as well as a general knowledge of law'.

[309] For critical comments on both the ADR Directive and the ODR Regulation see C. Meller-Hannich, A. Höland and E. Krausbeck, '"ADR" and "ODR": Kreationen der europäischen Rechtspolitik. Eine kritische Würdigung', *Zeitschrift für Europäisches Privatrecht*, 22 (2014), 8–38. The authors analyse the two instruments from a procedural access to justice perspective and arrive at the conclusion that both pose the risk of leading to a 'two-tier justice system' (translation mine) where (despite its potential to increase the number of cross-border transactions) the functionality of dispute resolution could be impaired (see *ibid.*, 38 for details).

(UCTD)),[310] 'Member States shall ensure that an agreement between a consumer and a trader to submit complaints to an ADR entity is not binding on the consumer if it was concluded before the dispute has materialised and if it has the effect of depriving the consumer of his right to bring an action before the courts for the settlement of the dispute.'

While it has to be appreciated that the ADR Directive does not force consumers into ADR, the absence of a true, practical chance for consumers to resort to ADR is regrettable. The ADR Directive makes the introduction of ADR mandatory for the Member States, but at the same time fails to give consumers the option to freely choose between litigation and ADR. Unless Member States introduce such an option pursuant to Article 1 ADR Directive, consumers can use ADR only with the traders' consent (or where courts ask the parties to use ADR prior to litigation). In other words, the mere availability of ADR cannot guarantee that consumers will really benefit from such mechanisms.

The ODR Regulation (2013)

Over the years, the volume of cross-border online B2C transactions has continuously grown. The provision of fast, unbureaucratic and effective online redress has been generally considered an important ingredient to further develop and secure the online market.[311] Various initiatives have been used to achieve online redress and have led to the introduction of an increasing number of ODR schemes.[312] However, what was missing was a legislative framework to ensure qualitative standards and the independence, impartiality and transparency of ODR schemes.

---

[310] See in particular Articles 3 and 6 UCTD and point 1(a) of its Annex. See further 'The Directive on Consumer Rights' in Chapter 9 below for some general comments on the UCTD.

[311] Recital 6 ODR Regulation explains as follows: 'The internal market is a reality for consumers in their daily lives, when they travel, make purchases and make payments. Consumers are key players in the internal market and should therefore be at its heart. The digital dimension of the internal market is becoming vital for both consumers and traders. Consumers increasingly make purchases online and an increasing number of traders sell online. Consumers and traders should feel confident in carrying out transactions online so it is essential to dismantle existing barriers and to boost consumer confidence. The availability of reliable and efficient online dispute resolution (ODR) could greatly help achieve this goal.'

[312] For examples of ODR mechanisms that already operated prior to the adoption of the ODR Regulation see P. Cortés, *Online Dispute Resolution for Consumers in the European Union* (Abingdon: Routledge, 2011), pp. xv–xvi; G.-P. Calliess and P. Zumbansen, *Rough Consensus and Running Code: A Theory of Transnational Private Law* (Oxford: Hart,

For several years, scholars had thus called for the introduction of a pan-EU ODR tool. One proponent was Pablo Cortés, who commented that '[a]ccess to justice ... should not be considered as the existing concept of the right to participate in an adversarial legal procedure in the public courts, but instead as the right to obtain redress through the most appropriate dispute resolution mechanism, which with many disputes, particularly those arising out of electronic transactions, may well be ODR'.[313] Advanced forms of trade, so it was believed, required that dispute mechanisms kept up with the times. Undeniably, ODR is a prime example of how modern technology and dispute resolution can interact.

In response to these developments and related requests, the Union legislator adopted the Regulation on online dispute resolution for consumer disputes (ODR Regulation) in temporal connection with the ADR Directive.[314] One can thus say that the introduction of a pan-EU ODR mechanism for B2C disputes was an attempt to provide a solution to the issue of procedural access to justice in modern B2C online trade.[315] Although all major stakeholder groups basically welcomed the introduction,[316] it should be noted that ODR, especially from a consumer perspective, is not a necessarily problem-free alternative to traditional litigation. Lilian Edwards and Caroline Wilson, for example, critically

2010), pp. 157–160; G.-P. Calliess, 'Online Dispute Resolution: Consumer Redress in a Global Market Place', *German Law Journal*, 7 (2006), 647, 651–654.

[313] Cortés, Online Dispute Resolution for Consumers in the European Union, p. 183..

[314] Regulation of the European Parliament and of the Council on online dispute resolution for consumer disputes and amending Regulation (EC) No 2006/2004 and Directive 2009/22/EC, 21 May 2013, OJ 2013 No. L165/1.

[315] P. Cortés, 'Developing Online Dispute Resolution for Consumers in the EU: A Proposal for the Regulation of Accredited Providers', *International Journal of Law and Information Technology*, 19 (2011), 1, 3; For comments on consumer ODR see L. K. Hofmeister, *Online Dispute Resolution bei Verbraucherverträgen: Rechtlicher Rahmen und Gestaltungsmöglichkeiten* (Baden-Baden: Nomos, 2012); P. Cortés, 'Online Dispute Resolution for Consumers – Online Dispute Resolution Methods for Settling Business to Consumer Conflict' in M. S. Abdel Wahab *et al.* (eds.), *Online Dispute Resolution: Theory and Practice* (The Hague: Eleven International Publishing, 2012), pp. 139–61. For general comments on ODR especially from a cross-border perspective see G. Kaufmann-Kohler and T. Schultz, *Online Dispute Resolution: Challenges for Contemporary Justice* (The Hague: Kluwer Law International, 2004); H. Haloush, *Online Alternative Dispute Resolution* (Saarbrücken: Verlag Dr. Müller, 2008); M. Poblet and G. Ross, 'ODR in Europe' in Abdel Wahab *et al.* (eds.), *Online Dispute Resolution*, pp. 453–69 (for European trends); for a discussion of ODR from a value-oriented justice perspective see R. Devanesan and J. Aresty, 'ODR and Justice – An Evaluation of Online Dispute Resolution's Interplay with Traditional Theories of Justice' in *ibid.*, pp. 251–93.

[316] For a summary of general views of different stakeholders on ODR see Kaufmann-Kohler and Schultz, *Online Dispute Resolution*, pp. 83–108.

analysed the potentials and risks of ODR in Europe and came to the conclusion that due process issues, in particular, could pose a threat for the success of ODR.[317]

The ODR Regulation tries to address such concerns first and foremost by introducing a standardised ODR procedure that, with respect to consumer complaints, is tightly linked to the framework of the ADR Directive and its guiding principles. Recital 18 ODR Regulation succinctly summarises the underlying mechanism of the ODR Regulation as follows:

> This Regulation aims to create an ODR platform at Union level. The ODR platform should take the form of an interactive website offering a single point of entry to consumers and traders seeking to resolve disputes out-of-court which have arisen from online transactions. ... It should allow consumers and traders to submit complaints by filling in an electronic complaint form available in all the official languages of the institutions of the Union and to attach relevant documents. It should transmit complaints to an ADR entity competent to deal with the dispute concerned. The ODR platform should offer, free of charge, an electronic case management tool which enables ADR entities to conduct the dispute resolution procedure with the parties through the ODR platform.

Although the ADR Directive and the ODR Regulation are two different legal acts, they are interconnected, as the ODR Regulation complements and is based on the regime and rules of the ADR Directive.[318] In line with the ADR Directive, the ODR Regulation can be used for settling pre-defined disputes regardless of their 'international character' – purely

---

[317] L. Edwards and C. Wilson, 'Redress and Alternative Dispute Resolution in EU Cross-Border E-Commerce Transactions', *International Review of Law Computers & Technology*, 21 (2007), 315, 321–3. For further comments on this issue see, e.g., H.-W. Micklitz and Z. Nový, 'A Proposal for a Consumer ODR Design' in G. Howells *et al.* (eds.), 'Optional Soft Law Instrument on EU Contract Law for Businesses and Consumers', study for BEUC, (2011), pp. 41–69, available at www.beuc.org/custom/2011–09955–01-E.pdf; J. Hörnle, 'Online Dispute Resolution in Business to Consumer E-commerce Transactions', *The Journal of Information, Law and Technology*, online journal, 2 (2002), available at www2.warwick.ac.uk/fac/soc/law/elj/jilt/2002_2/hornle/; J. Hörnle, 'Encouraging Online Dispute Resolution in the EU and Beyond – Keeping Costs Low or Standards High?', Queen Mary School of Law Legal Studies Research Papers, No. 122/2012 (2012), available at papers.ssrn.com/sol3/papers.cfm?abstract_id=2154214.

[318] Recital 12 ADR Directive calls the ADR Directive and ODR Regulation 'two interlinked and complementary legislative instruments'. Recital 16 ODR Regulation adds that 'This Regulation should be considered in conjunction with Directive 2013/11/EU [i.e. the ADR Directive] which requires Member States to ensure that all disputes between consumers resident and traders established in the Union which arise from the sale of goods or provisions of services can be submitted to an ADR entity'. See further the many references within the ODR Regulation to pertinent clauses of the ADR Directive.

domestic disputes fall under the applicability of the ODR Regulation.[319] At the same time the scope of the ODR Regulation is both wider and narrower than the scope of the ADR Directive. It is wider because it can be applied to B2C disputes initiated by a trader against a consumer;[320] in contrast, the ADR Directive only works in the opposite direction.[321] The regulation is narrower because it only applies in cases related to *online* sales and/or service contracts.[322]

At the heart of the European ODR regime stands the ODR platform, which is to be established by the Commission. The main purpose of the ODR platform is to facilitate online ADR by offering an easily accessible and easy-to-use entry point for redress-seeking parties in a B2C dispute. Several features are worth mentioning in this respect. First, the ODR platform shall provide a standardised scheme for both submitting and processing complaints. This includes, in particular, a standard complaint form[323] and a free-of-charge electronic case management tool, which ADR bodies can use to handle cases submitted to them.[324] Second, the ODR platform shall be accessible and usable in any of the official EU languages.[325] Third, the platform shall provide its users with practical information about ADR in general and the ODR platform in particular.[326]

To further simplify the use of the ODR platform, Member States are obliged to install at least one local 'ODR contact' point with at least two 'ODR advisors' per contact point. The task of ODR contact points and advisors is to support the parties in technical matters in relation to the ODR platform and – should the parties fail to mutually choose an ADR body to handle their case or should the concrete ODR attempt otherwise fail – inform the redress-seeking parties of alternatives to ODR on request.[327] The role of ODR contact points is without doubt of practical importance to ensure compliance with the regulatory regime of the ODR Regulation and ADR Directive and to enhance recourse to ODR. As Cortés observes, various highly developed ODR systems have been introduced so far (at the initiative of private players), but 'they have been proven not to be consumer-friendly as yet'.[328] A standardised, well-monitored and

---

[319] Recital 11 ODR Regulation: '[T]his Regulation should also apply to domestic online transactions in order to allow for a true level playing field in the area of online commerce.'

[320] See Article 2(2) ODR Regulation for details.

[321] Article 2(2)(g) ADR Directive.　　[322] Article 2 ODR Regulation.

[323] Article 5(4)(a) ODR Regulation.　　[324] Article 5(4)(d) ODR Regulation.

[325] Article 5(2) ODR Regulation.　　[326] Article 5(4)(h) ODR Regulation.

[327] See Article 7 ODR Regulation for details.

[328] Cortés, *Online Dispute Resolution for Consumers*, p. 223.

well-implemented pan-EU system would offer the chance to provide consumers with a 'real' alternative. This requires that the ODR contact points and advisors have previous ODR (or at least ADR) experience. In this respect it seems to make sense that Article 7(1) ODR Regulation encourages Member States to designate (inter alia) ECCs and national consumer organisations as ODR contact points because both already deal with general redress requests from consumers on a daily basis.[329]

One should register, however, that some questions, for example, questions on the enforceability of ODR results, remain unanswered. As the New York Convention does not explicitly refer to ODR, the absence of enforcement rules for ODR decisions is somewhat regrettable. In this respect one should note, however, that many commentators on ODR argue that the New York Convention regime could, in principle, analogously apply to binding ODR arbitration awards.[330] However, due to a lack of pertinent case law, the actual situation is not clear as yet. Cortés, for example, notes that '[t]o date, online arbitration awards have not been fully tested in the courts',[331] while Christoph Liebscher adds that '[n]o actual case has yet been presented on this issue'.[332] One must wait and see how the courts react when issues of recognition and enforceability of ODR decisions are brought before them.

---

[329] See Civic Consulting, 'Study on the Use of Alternative Dispute Resolution in the European Union', p. 62 Figure 15, where it is shown that several ECCs are already quite strongly cooperating with ADR bodies in the sense that they inform consumers about specific ways of ADR to pursue their claims by non-litigative means. For further details see 'ECC-Net: Current Activities' in Chapter 15 below.

[330] Edwards and Wilson, 'Redress and Alternative Dispute Resolution in EU Cross-Border E-Commerce Transactions', 318; Hofmeister, *Online Dispute Resolution bei Verbraucherverträgen*, p. 274; C. Liebscher, 'Article V' in R. Wolff (ed.), *New York Convention on the Recognition and Enforcement of Foreign Arbitral Awards – Commentary* (Munich: C. H. Beck, 2012), Article V Para. 408; Cortés, *Online Dispute Resolution for Consumers in the European Union*, pp. 111–12; Kaufmann-Kohler and Schultz, *Online Dispute Resolution*, pp. 216–23, where Gabrielle Kaufmann-Kohler and Thomas Schultz discuss various conditions that must be fulfilled by an ODR arbitration award to make it recognisable and enforceable under the regime of the New York Convention. But see also the doubts raised by Julia Hörnle regarding ODR arbitration prior to the adoption of the ODR Regulation in Hörnle, *Cross-border Internet Dispute Resolution*, p. 246, where she explains that with respect to 'certain types of disputes where the parties are subject to a power imbalance, … the recognition or enforcement of the award may be against public policy'.

[331] Cortés, *Online Dispute Resolution for Consumers in the European Union*, p. 112.

[332] Liebscher, 'Article V', Article V para. 408.

5

Compensatory collective redress – the next step?

The road towards the Green Paper on Consumer Collective Redress

As the previous chapters have shown, the EU has already implemented several ideas of the Florence Project to address the procedural side of access to justice. The Legal Aid Directive, for example, went straight to the heart of the concept, aiming to enable those who lack the financial means to pursue their claims in court, and by doing this covered the initial idea of access to justice embodied by the first access to justice wave. Other legal instruments, such as the Small Claims Regulation or the more recent ADR Directive and ODR Regulation, represent some of the ideas of the third access to justice wave and introduced additional, innovative means of individual dispute resolution.

The second access to justice wave of the Florence Project, the phenomenon of diffuse or collective interests, has not yet been extensively regulated at the pan-EU level, however. Certain tools have been crafted to deal with some (partial) aspects of collective interests. The Injunctions Directive, for example, was designed to bring an end to unlawful business practices that harm collective consumer interests as well as the public interest in securing compliance with the law. The possibility of combating unfair standard terms on behalf of collective consumer interests under the UCTD[1] is another example of how consumers as a group can possibly benefit from actions taken by public authorities and/or private bodies on their behalf. However, both instruments also show the shortcomings of

---

[1] For comments on the UCTD see P. Nebbia, 'Unfair Contract Terms' in C. Twigg-Flesner (ed.), *The Cambridge Companion to European Union Private Law* (Cambridge University Press, 2010), pp. 216–28; T. Wilhelmsson and C. Willett, 'Unfair Terms and Standard Form Contracts' in G. Howells *et al.* (eds.), *Handbook of Research on International Consumer Law* (Cheltenham: Edward Elgar, 2010), pp. 158–91; J. Stuyck, 'Unfair Terms' in G. Howells and R. Schulze (eds.), *Modernising and Harmonising Consumer Contract Law* (Munich: Sellier, 2009), pp. 115–44 or L. Tichý, 'Unfair Terms in Consumer Contracts' in H. Schulte-Nölke and L. Tichý (eds.), *Perspectives for European Consumer Law: Towards a Directive on Consumer Rights and Beyond* (Munich: Sellier, 2010), pp. 59–76.

existing EU legislation with respect to collective consumer interests. They deal exclusively with injunctive issues and do not allow for compensatory collective actions taken by consumers themselves or public authorities and/or private bodies on their behalf. At the time of writing this book, there still exists no legal instrument to oblige Member States to introduce a compensatory collective redress mechanism.

This does not mean that compensatory collective redress is not found in the EU. More than half of the Member States already have some kind of compensatory collective redress device(s) in place.[2] However, the approaches taken by the Member States vary – in some cases considerably. Furthermore, in many Member States the existing compensatory collective redress tools have not been extensively tested as yet, as most mechanisms were introduced quite recently: Sweden[3] introduced

---

[2] For general information on existing compensatory collective redress tools in the EU see BEUC, 'Country Survey of Collective Redress Mechanisms', survey, (2011), available at www.beuc.org/custom/2011-10006-01-E.pdf, which shows that sixteen (seventeen if one counts also the unclear status of Lithuania) out of twenty-seven Member States (Croatia was not included in the survey) had introduced compensatory collective redress tools by the end of 2011; I. Dodds-Smith and A. Brown (eds.), *The International Comparative Legal Guide to: Class & Group Actions 2014* (London: Global Limited Group, 2013); the main study and the national reports of/for Civic Consulting and Oxford Economics, 'Evaluation of the Effectiveness and Efficiency of Collective Redress Mechanisms in the European Union – Final Report Part I: Main Report', study for DG SANCO, (2008), available at ec.europa.eu/consumers/redress_cons/finalreportevaluationstudypart1-final2008-11-26.pdf; the national reports in the online portal 'Global Class Actions Exchange' available at www.globalclassactions.stanford.edu; Hodges, *The Reform of Class and Representative Actions in European Legal Systems*, pp. 10–13 (Table 1) (for an overview of compensatory collective action tools available in the EU in general as of 2008) and pp. 30–3 (Table 2) (for an overview of compensatory collective action tools available in the Nordic countries as of 2008); Stuyck et al., 'An Analysis and Evaluation of Alternative Means of Consumer Redress', pp. 270–1 (Table 1) (for an overview of compensatory collective action tools available in the EU as of 2007). Further analyses on certain national tools in the EU can be found in, for example, Wrbka et al. (eds.), *Collective Actions*; Cafaggi and Micklitz (eds.), *New Frontiers of Consumer Protection*; van Boom and Loos (eds.), *Collective Enforcement of Consumer Law*; Casper et al. (eds.), *Auf dem Weg zu einer europäischen Sammelklage?*; J. Steele and W. H. van Boom (eds.), *Mass Justice: Challenges of Representation and Distribution* (Cheltenham: Edward Elgar, 2011); J. G. Backhaus et al. (eds.), *The Law and Economics of Class Actions on Europe: Lessons from America* (Cheltenham: Edward Elgar, 2012); C. Brömmelmeyer (ed.), *Die EU-Sammelklage* (Baden-Baden: Nomos, 2013); C. Hodges and A. Stadler (eds.), *Resolving Mass Disputes* (Cheltenham: Edward Elgar, 2013); A. Nuyts and N. E. Hatzimihail (eds.), *Cross-border Class Actions: The European Way* (Munich: Sellier, 2014).

[3] P. H. Lindblom, 'Sweden', *The ANNALS of the American Academy of Political and Social Science*, 622 (2009), 231–41. For the Nordic countries in general see, e.g., K. Viitanen, 'Enforcement of Consumers' Collective Interests by Regulatory Agencies in the Nordic Countries' in van Boom and Loos (eds.), *Collective Enforcement of Consumer Law*,

a compensatory collective redress regime in 2003, The Netherlands[4] in 2005, Greece,[5] Finland[6] and Italy[7] followed in 2007 (with an Italian update in 2009), Denmark[8] reacted in 2008, Hungary in 2009,[9] Poland in 2010[10] and Malta in 2012.[11] Thus, one can basically conclude that compensatory collective redress tools are still in the early stages of development in many parts of Europe. In addition, some Member States with a longer history

pp. 83–103; K. Viitanen, 'Nordic Experience on Group Action for Compensation' in Casper *et al.* (eds.), *Auf dem Weg zu einer europäischen Sammelklage?*, pp. 219–42; P. H. Lindblom, 'Group Litigation in Scandinavia', *ERA Forum*, 10 (2009), 7–35; P. Dopffel and J. M. Scherpe, '"Grupptalan" – Die Bündelung gleichgerichteter Interessen im schwedischen Recht' in J. Basedow *et al.* (eds.), *Die Bündelung gleichgerichteter Interessen im Prozess* (Tübingen: Mohr Siebeck, 2009), pp. 429–51; A. H. Persson, 'Collective Enforcement: European Prospects in Light of the Swedish Experience' in Wrbka *et al.* (eds.), *Collective Actions*, pp. 341–63.

[4] A. Mom, *Kollektiver Rechtsschutz in den Niederlanden* (Tübingen: Mohr Siebeck, 2011); W. H. van Boom, 'Collective Settlement of Mass Claims in the Netherlands' in Casper *et al.* (eds.), *Auf dem Weg zu einer europäischen Sammelklage?*, pp. 171–92; I. Tzankova and D. Lunsingh Scheurleer, 'The Netherlands', *The ANNALS of the American Academy of Political and Social Science*, 622 (2009), 149–60; N. Frenk and K. Boele-Woelki, 'Die Verbandsklage in den Niederlanden' in Basedow *et al.* (eds.), *Die Bündelung gleichgerichteter Interessen im Prozess*, pp. 213–51.

[5] E. Alexandridou and M. Karypidou, 'Country Report Greece', report, (2009), available at ec.europa.eu/consumers/redress_cons/gr-country-report-final.pdf; A. Papathomas-Baetge, 'Die Verbandsklage im griechischen Recht' in Basedow *et al.* (eds.), *Die Bündelung gleichgerichteter Interessen im Prozess*, pp. 187–211.

[6] M. Välimäki, 'Introducing Class Actions in Finland: an Example of Law-Making Without Economic Analysis' in Backhaus *et al.* (eds.), *The Law and Economics of Class Actions on Europe*, pp. 327–41; K. Viitanen, 'Finland', *The ANNALS of the American Academy of Political and Social Science*, 622 (2009), 209–19.

[7] E. Silvestri, 'Italy', *The ANNALS of the American Academy of Political and Social Science*, 622 (2009), 138–48; A. Barba, 'Die italienische kollektive Schadensersatzklage zum Schutz der Verbraucher' in Casper *et al.* (eds.), *Auf dem Weg zu einer europäischen Sammelklage?*, pp. 243–58; R. Caponi, 'The Collective Redress Action in the Italian System', *ERA Forum*, 10 (2009), 63–9; C. Poncibò, 'Consumer Collective Redress in the European Union: The "Italian Case"' in D. Parry *et al.* (eds.), *The Yearbook of Consumer Law 2009* (Farnham: Ashgate, 2008), pp. 231–56.

[8] E. Werlauff, 'Class Actions in Denmark', *The ANNALS of the American Academy of Political and Social Science*, 622 (2009), 202–8.

[9] The Hungarian group action of 2009 was designed for antitrust law offences. Compensation for affected consumers is, however, one of the remedies allowed under its framework (for details see IMCO, 'Overview of Existing Collective Redress Schemes in EU Member States', report, (2011), pp. 25–6, available at www.europarl.europa.eu/document/activities/cont/201107/20110715ATT24242/20110715ATT24242EN.pdf).

[10] *Ibid.*, pp. 31–2. For comments on the underlying draft to the Polish mechanism and related policy considerations see M. Tulibacka, 'Poland', *The ANNALS of the American Academy of Political and Social Science*, 622 (2009), 190–200.

[11] Camilleri Preziosi Advocates, 'The Collective Proceedings Act ('CP Act')', newsletter, (2012) (on file with the author).

of such redress, for example Austria[12] and France,[13] have been re-evaluating their compensatory collective redress tools and discussing possible amendments and/or additions of new compensatory collective instruments. In France, this has recently led to the adoption of the '*loi* Hamon' (Hamon Law), which introduced a new collective redress mechanism for certain consumer and antitrust law infringements in early 2014.[14]

The variation of national rules on the one hand and the absence of compensatory collective redress devices in some national jurisdictions on the other has prompted the Commission to intensify its discussions about the possible introduction of a pan-EU compensatory collective redress tool. The field of antitrust law was the first target of compensatory collective redress. The efforts of DG COMP led to, if one limits the discussion to antitrust law issues only,[15] the publication of both a Green Paper and White Paper on damages actions for breaches of EC antitrust rules (2005 and 2008, respectively).[16] The Commission further expanded its interests to (direct)[17] consumer law. In early 2007, the EU Consumer Policy Strategy 2007–2013 was issued. It argued that the absence of a pan-EU

---

[12] G. E. Kodek, 'Collective Redress in Austria', *The ANNALS of the American Academy of Political and Social Science*, 622 (2009), 86–94.

[13] L. Usunier, 'Collective Redress and Class Actions in France' in Casper *et al.* (eds.), *Auf dem Weg zu einer europäischen Sammelklage?*, pp. 293–341; V. Magnier, 'France', *The ANNALS of the American Academy of Political and Social Science*, 622 (2009), 114–24.

[14] For details see, e.g., Freshfields Bruckhaus Deringer, 'France Adopts Class Action', newsletter, (2014), available at www.freshfields.com/uploadedFiles/SiteWide/Knowledge/Briefing%20Class%20Action_VGB.pdf; Clifford Chance, 'Introduction of Class Actions in France', newsletter, (2014), available at www.cliffordchance.com/briefings/2014/02/introduction_of_classactionsinfrance.html; Norton Rose Fulbright, 'The New "Hamon Law" Introducing French Class Actions and Its Effects on Competition and Distribution Law', newsletter, (2014), available at www.nortonrosefulbright.com/knowledge/publications/114016/the-new-hamon-law-introducing-french-class-actions-and-its-effects-on-competition-and-distribution-law; Shook Hardy & Bacon, 'France Adopts New Class Action', newsletter, (2014), available at documents.lexology.com/07791e52-c396-45c5-ba34-5a346538e913.pdf#page=1.

[15] For comments on the Collective Redress Recommendation of 2013 (that covers both antitrust *and* consumer law-related compensatory collective actions) see 'From the Green Paper on Consumer Collective Redress to the Commission's Collective Redress Recommendation' below.

[16] Green Paper on damages actions for breach of the EC antitrust rules, 19 December 2005, COM(2005) 672 final; White Paper on damages actions for breach of the EC antitrust rules, 2 April 2008, COM(2008) 165 final.

[17] It is the general understanding that the implementation of collective redress discussed in the context of antitrust law would be in the best consumer interest (for comments in this respect see the references listed in note 86 below). The discussions initiated by DG SANCO, on the other hand, deal more directly with possible infringements of consumer laws.

compensatory collective redress tool for consumers was one of '[t]he obstacles to a fully-fledged retail internal market',[18] and added that the Commission 'will also consider action on collective redress mechanisms for consumers both for infringements of consumer protection rules and for breaches of EU anti-trust rules in line with its 2005 Green Paper on private damages actions'.[19]

The Commission did not waste much time. Very soon after the publication of the 2007–2013 Consumer Policy Strategy DG SANCO called for a first broader platform to discuss further steps related to consumer compensatory collective redress. This led to the 'brainstorming event on collective [consumer] redress' in Leuven.[20] On this occasion, Meglena Kuneva (the then European Commissioner for Consumer Protection) stated that it was necessary 'to investigate the situation thoroughly with Member States, the European Parliament and stakeholders before taking any decision'.[21] It was also Kuneva who expressed later in 2007 the possibility of introducing a genuine European approach: 'To those who have come all the way to Lisbon to hear the words "class action", let me be clear from the start: there will not be any. Not in Europe, not under my watch.'[22] This did not come as much of a surprise as some prominent features of US-style class actions, such as punitive damage actions, civil jury trials, US-style contingency fees,[23] pre-trial discovery as well as opt-out, were either seldom or not at all found in the Member States. Although the Commission itself did not comment on US class actions

---

[18] EU Consumer Policy Strategy 2007–2013, p. 5.

[19] *Ibid.*, p. 11.

[20] Leuven Brainstorming Event on Collective Redress, 29 June 2007.

[21] M. Kuneva, 'Collecting Thoughts and Experiences on Corrective Redress', speech (Leuven, 29 June 2007).

[22] M. Kuneva, 'Healthy Markets Need Effective Redress', speech (Lisbon, 10 November 2007).

[23] Certain types of contingency fees, yet not in the form of US-style contingency fees, and certain types of conditional/success fees do, however, also exist in several Member States. For details see, Hodges *et al.* (eds.), *The Costs and Funding of Civil Litigation*, pp. 132–3 (Table 2); IMCO, 'Overview of Existing Collective Redress Schemes in EU Member States'. Nevertheless, the idea of introducing US-style contingency fees in the EU is strongly rejected. Stadler summarises the basic concerns as follows: 'Purely financial interests such as contingency fees may create bad incentives for representatives' (A. Stadler, 'Collective Redress Litigation – A New Challenge for Courts in Europe' in A. Bruns *et al.* (eds.), *Festschrift für Rolf Stürner zum 70. Geburtstag – Band I* (Tübingen: Mohr Siebeck, 2013), p. 1816). For further comments on US-style contingency fees (and other characteristics of US-style class actions) see 'From the Green Paper on Consumer Collective Redress to the Commission's Collective Redress Recommendation' below.

in its official documents, such proceedings were generally believed by many, including the majority of academic commentators,[24] to be incompatible with the approaches of most Member States to litigation. The key fear was that imitating the US approach could lead to unwanted side effects and to a situation contrary to the ultimate goal of enhancing the internal market.[25]

In 2007 and again in 2008, the Commission published evaluation reports on consumer compensatory collective redress available in the Member States. One of these, the study on the evaluation of the effectiveness and efficiency of collective redress mechanisms (2007 Evaluation Study) applies a useful classification of compensatory collective redress tools. A differentiation is made between the three categories of group actions, representative actions and test cases.[26] Although it should be

[24] See, e.g., J. Stuyck, 'Public and Private Enforcement in Consumer Protection: General Comparison EU-USA' in Cafaggi and Micklitz (eds.), *New Frontiers of Consumer Protection*, p. 81; A. Stadler, 'Cross-border Mass Litigation: a Particular Challenge for European Law' in Steele and van Boom (eds.), *Mass Justice*, pp. 74–75; Hodges, *Reform of Class and Representative Actions*, p. 132; R. Van den Bergh and S. Keske, 'Rechtsökonomische Aspekte der Sammelklage' in Casper *et al.* (eds.), *Auf dem Weg zu einer europäischen Sammelklage?*, p. 31; or A. Janssen, 'Auf dem Weg zu einer europäischen Sammelklage?' in *ibid.*, p. 3, who argues that class actions are based on a 'toxic cocktail' of contingency fees, punitive damages and civil jury trials. For further comments on the possible misuse of US-style class actions see, e.g., H. Beuchler, *Class Actions und Securities Class Actions in den Vereinigten Staaten von Amerika* (Baden-Baden: Nomos, 2008), pp. 187–8; A. Stadler, 'Enforcement of Private Law by Way of Collective Action in the European Union – an Overview of the Development in the European Member States' in W. Heinz and Y.-W. Kim (eds.), *Aktuelle Rechtsprobleme in Japan, Deutschland und Korea* (Konstanz: KOPS, 2009), p. 94; S. Eichholtz, *Die US-amerikanische Class Action und ihre deutsche Funktionsäquivalente* (Tübingen: Mohr Siebeck, 2002), pp. 24–8.
[25] For details on the concerns see 'From the Green Paper on Consumer Collective Redress to the Commission's Collective Redress Recommendation' below.
[26] Civic Consulting and Oxford Economics, 'Evaluation of the Effectiveness and Efficiency of Collective Redress Mechanisms in the European Union', pp. 6–7. This study was complemented by Civic Consulting, 'Study Regarding the Problems Faced by Consumers in Obtaining Redress for Infringements of Consumer Protection Legislation – Final Report Part I: Main Report', study for DG SANCO (2008), available at ec.europa.eu/consumers/redress_cons/finalreport-problemstudypart1-final.pdf. The two reports confirmed the findings of some older studies that there was ample room for improvement in consumer compensatory collective rights enforcement in Europe (see European Opinion Research Group and EOS Gallup Europe, 'Views on Business-to-consumer Cross-border Trade'; European Opinion Research Group, 'European Union Citizens and Access to Justice'; TNS Opinion & Social, 'Consumer Protection in the Internal Market'; The Gallup Organization Hungary, 'Attitudes towards Cross-border Sales and Consumer Protection').

noted that this division is not the only classification used in the debate on compensatory collective redress and that several other approaches to refer to specific forms of related devices can be found in the academic debate,[27] the categorisation of the 2007 Evaluation Study is a suitable starting point for further discussions as it refers to some basic procedural ideas of the pertinent tools.

To summarise the characteristics of the three groups with respect to consumer issues, it suffices to note the following for the purpose of this book. With the help of group actions, claims are grouped together into a single procedure launched by a group of consumers or a single claimant. This claimant can (depending on the case and the jurisdiction) either be a private body, public authority or an individual. What distinguishes group actions from representative actions is the fact that the former leads to results with a direct effect for all group members, which means that the group members can enforce their rights separately. In contrast, in representative actions, it is left to the representative to enforce the outcome. While distinguishing between group actions and representative actions can be tricky,[28] it is easier to draw a line between these two forms and test cases. Test cases lie somewhere between group and representative actions on the one hand and individual litigation on the other.[29] In this third category (just like in the cases of group and representative actions), more than one consumer's individual interests are affected. However, only a single case is selected to be litigated, while the other cases wait for a decision in the test case. If the test case is decided in favour of consumers, parallel affected consumers would – unless national procedural laws allow for a binding legal effect for similar cases[30] – try to use the likely factual convincibility of the test case for their own actions.

---

[27] For some examples see S. Wrbka, 'European Consumer Protection Law: Quo Vadis? – Thoughts on the Compensatory Collective Redress Debate' in Wrbka *et al.* (eds.), *Collective Actions*, pp. 33–7.

[28] See, for example, the Dutch group settlement model, which under the classification used by the 2007 Evaluation Study and in this book would fall under the category of group actions, whereas, e.g., the Leuven Study qualifies it as a form of representative action (see Stuyck *et al.*, 'An Analysis and Evaluation of Alternative Means of Consumer Redress', p. 261).

[29] Wrbka, 'European Consumer Protection Law: Quo Vadis?', p. 35. See *ibid.*, pp. 35–6 for a brief analysis of the advantages and disadvantages of test cases.

[30] See the comments in 'Mass Damages' below.

From the Green Paper on Consumer Collective Redress to the Commission's Collective Redress Recommendation

In late 2008 the European Commission took the next big step and presented its Green Paper on Consumer Collective Redress (Collective Redress Green Paper).[31] The Collective Redress Green Paper tried 'to assess the current state of redress mechanisms … and to provide options to close any gaps to effective redress'.[32] It presented four options aiming to facilitate consumer compensatory collective redress: taking no further action (for the moment) (option 1); improving the cooperation between the Member States (option 2);[33] mixing certain existing tools (option 3);[34] and introducing judicial pan-EU compensatory collective redress mechanisms (option 4).[35]

As expected, the Collective Redress Green Paper led to responses from a large number of affected stakeholders.[36] With the exception of businesses and business interest representatives, which to nobody's surprise largely favoured the first option[37] and strongly rejected the idea of introducing

---

[31] Green Paper on consumer collective redress, 27 November 2008, COM(2008) 794 final (Collective Redress Green Paper).

[32] *Ibid.*, paragraph 4.

[33] This second option ('improving inter-member-state cooperation') does not refer to the CPC Regulation. As shown earlier, the Consumer Protection Cooperation Regulation created a pan-EU cooperation network of public authorities to fight illegal business practices by the way of public enforcement understood as relying (primarily) on administrative law devices, but does not cover actions taken by individual consumers or compensatory actions taken on behalf of consumers. Option 2 of the Collective Redress Green Paper, on the other hand, aims to facilitate the use of cross-border compensatory collective actions by – or on behalf of – consumers with the help of a different kind of pan-EU network. The Commission mentions ECC-Net in this context. One should note that this option would not lead to the introduction of a new consumer compensatory collective redress mechanism. Instead it would try to enhance cross-border use of existing consumer compensatory collective redress devices (see *ibid.*, paras. 23–31 for details).

[34] This third option includes a variety of existing procedural devices at the EU level. It does not go into detail, however, and explain how the mentioned tools should interact (see *ibid.*, paras. 32–47).

[35] The Commission does not present any concrete ideas in this context. It merely states that option 4 should lead to 'a procedure [that] would ensure that every consumer throughout the EU would be able to obtain adequate redress in mass cases through representative actions, group actions or test cases' (*ibid.*, para. 48).

[36] For a summary of stakeholders' comments on the Green Paper on consumer collective redress see ec.europa.eu/consumers/redress_cons/response_GP_collective_redress_en.htm.

[37] See Consumer Policy Evaluation Consortium (CPEC), 'Assessment of the Economic and Social Impact of the Policy Options to Empower Consumers to Obtain Adequate Redress: First Analytical report of the Green Paper on Consumer Collective Redress', report for DG SANCO, (2009), p. 30 (on file with the author).

compensatory collective actions at a pan-EU level,[38] this fourth option found favour with all remaining stakeholder groups and was the most popular option among legal scholars, legal practitioners and European and national consumer organisations.[39]

The Collective Redress Green Paper was not the end of the story. It marked the launch of further, intense discussions at the EU level. A public hearing was held in May 2009 to discuss the responses to the Collective Redress Green Paper, and slightly amended Commission options were presented in a consultation paper in reaction to this (2009 Consultation Paper).[40] To summarise the stakeholders' positions and present refined alternatives, the rather vague options 2 and 3 of the Collective Redress Green Paper were revised and regrouped into three new options.[41] Nevertheless, and although the 2009 Consultation Paper summarised the stakeholders' positions towards compensatory collective redress, in terms of substance it offered very little in the way of innovation or novelty.

Two years later history repeated itself: the Commission once again held a public hearing,[42] issued a public consultation paper (2011 Consultation Paper)[43] and invited stakeholders to submit comments. This time, however, the Commission did not present alternative options. Neither did it propose the introduction of a pan-EU compensatory collective redress scheme. Instead, it indicated its (at least short-term) preference for a softer approach, a framework of guiding principles to be implemented by any future pan-EU compensatory collective redress mechanism. These six 'general principles to guide possible future EU initiatives on collective redress' comprised the following:

---

[38] *Ibid.*, p. 36.   [39] *Ibid.*, p. 30.

[40] The text of the 2009 Consultation Paper is available at ec.europa.eu/consumers/redress_cons/docs/consultation_paper2009.pdf.

[41] The three new options were: new option 2 ('self-regulation'); new option 3 ('non-binding setting up of collective ADR schemes and judicial collective redress schemes in combination with additional powers under the Consumer Protection Cooperation Regulation'); and new option 4 ('binding setting up of collective ADR schemes and judicial collective redress schemes with benchmarks in combination with additional powers under the Consumer Protection Cooperation Regulation') (see 2009 Consultation Paper, pp. 16–19 for details).

[42] The sessions can only be revisited as audio files available at ec.europa.eu/consumers/redress_cons/files/CR_session1.mp3; ec.europa.eu/consumers/redress_cons/files/CR_session2.mp3 and ec.europa.eu/consumers/redress_cons/files/CR_session3.mp3.

[43] Commission staff working paper public consultation: towards a coherent European approach to collective redress, 4 February 2011, SEC(2011) 173 final.

(1) the need for effectiveness and efficiency of redress;
(2) the importance of information and of the role of representative bodies;
(3) the need to take account of collective consensual resolution as a means of alternative dispute resolution;
(4) the need for strong safeguards to avoid abusive litigation;
(5) the availability of appropriate financing mechanisms, notably for citizens and small and medium-sized enterprises (SMEs); and
(6) the importance of effective enforcement across the EU.[44]

The Commission once again noted that the status and methods of compensatory collective redress (where existing) differed from Member State to Member State. It further concluded that the 'lack of a consistent approach to [compensatory] collective redress at [the] EU level may undermine the enjoyment of rights by citizens and businesses and gives rise to uneven enforcement of those rights'.[45] Relying on a mix of general principles instead of suggesting a clear, one-size-fits-all approach might thus have come as a surprise, but because of the very different pictures of collective redress in the Member States and the tough resistance from the business sector, it was the strongest measure the Commission was able to present.

Since the events in early 2011, the activities of the Commission with respect to consumer compensatory collective redress appeared to have slackened somewhat. For some time, the last official reference of the Commission to consumer collective redress was made in late 2011, when the Commission Work Programme 2012 stated that there were plans to create 'rules on collective redress [that] will set out how consumers and businesses can find effective solutions to large-scale problems'.[46] This was the only reference to collective redress in the Commission's work programme. (The subsequent Commission Work Programme 2013 did not even mention compensatory collective redress.) In reaction to the Commission's silence on this topic, the European Consumers' Organisation (BEUC), the leading pan-EU consumer representative body at the EU level, expressed concerns that the talks could peter out. In a letter to the then Commission President, José Manuel Barroso, Monique Goyens, the then Director General of BEUC, reminded him that a 'follow-up Commission Communication, expected to outline the EU's

---

[44] *Ibid.*, para. 15.   [45] *Ibid.*, para. 10.
[46] Commission Work Programme 2012 – Delivering European renewal, 15 November 2011, COM(2011) 777 final, p. 6.

next steps ... has not yet been published'[47] and added '[w]e [i.e., BEUC]
thus reiterate ... high hopes that, alongside other steps to strengthen the
Internal Market, your Commission will proceed with concrete legislative steps on collective redress'.[48] First doubts were also expressed at
the Parliament level, as shown, for example, by MEP Philippe Juvin's
question to the Commission on whether it still intended to follow up
on the issue of collective actions.[49] In a response, Viviane Reding, the
then European Commissioner for Justice, Fundamental Rights and
Citizenship, answered that 'the Commission continues its work on collective redress. It is presently considering the most appropriate course
of action to be followed'.[50] And indeed, this (temporary) silence was followed by a storm in 2013, although, as I will show briefly, in the present
context it was more like a gentle breeze.

It is not only the Commission that has dealt with compensatory collective redress in recent years. The European Parliament, for example, replied
in February 2012 to the aforementioned 2011 Consultation Paper with a
resolution titled 'Towards a Coherent European Approach to Collective
Redress' (2012 Resolution on Collective Redress).[51] It is worth taking a
slightly closer look at the 2012 Resolution on Collective Redress as it provides some interesting information on the Parliament's stance towards
compensatory collective redress.

Although the resolution does not only cover B2C situations, consumer
issues take a central role in the debate on compensatory collective redress
tools, which 'specifically but not exclusively deal ... with the infringement
of consumers' rights'.[52] In principle, the Parliament shares the opinion of
the Commission. In line with the 2011 Consultation Paper, the resolution
stresses the need for a 'common set of principles'.[53] With respect to consumer issues, the rationale behind the call for an intensified elaboration
of collective redress tools is twofold intertwined with the considerations
of the Commission. First, in the view of the Parliament, pan-EU collective

---

[47] BEUC, 'EU Action on Collective Redress', letter to Commission President José Manuel
Barroso, 25 April 2012, p. 2 (on file with the author).

[48] *Ibid.*, p. 3.

[49] A written transcript of the question is available at www.europarl.europa.eu/sides/get-
Doc.do?pubRef=-//EP//TEXT+WQ+E-2012-011593+0+DOC+XML+V0//EN.

[50] A written transcript of the answer is available at www.europarl.europa.eu/sides/getAl-
lAnswers.do?reference=E-2012-011593&language=EN.European Parliament Resolution
on 'Towards a Coherent European Approach to Collective Redress', 2 February 2012,
INI(2011) 2089.

[51] *Ibid.*, para. 15.   [52] *Ibid.*

[53] See *ibid.*, paras. 15, 19 and 20.

redress is considered to have the potential to enhance consumer (procedural) access to justice,[54] which – also according to the Parliament – is said to be currently impaired by the fact that the collective action tools used at the national levels differ widely from Member State to Member State.[55] Second, the wish to strengthen consumer access to justice is seen as a means to an end, as – again in line with the Commission – the Parliament hopes that enhanced consumer access to justice would eventually 'contribute to consumer confidence and [the] smoother functioning of the internal market'.[56]

The 2012 Resolution on Collective Redress can further be considered as a logical reaction of the Parliament to the business sector's heavy criticism of collective redress[57] and as an attempt to reinforce the arguments of business interest groups. Noting that 'efforts [have been] made by the US Supreme Court to limit frivolous litigation and abuse of the US class action system',[58] the resolution 'stresses that Europe must refrain from introducing a US-style class action system or any system which does not respect European legal traditions'.[59] The Parliament further stated that a

---

[54] See *ibid.*, para. 3, where the Parliament states that it 'recognises that national collective redress mechanisms are widely divergent, in particular in terms of scope and procedural characteristics, which may undermine the enjoyment of rights by citizens'.

[55] *Ibid.*, para. 4. See Wagner, 'Kollektiver Rechtsschutz', pp. 44–6 for critical comments on this argumentation.

[56] European Parliament Resolution on 'Towards a Coherent European Approach to Collective Redress', para. 4.

[57] See, for example, CPEC, 'Assessment of the Economic and Social Impact of the Policy Options to Empower Consumers to Obtain Adequate Redress', p. 81, where one business interest representative calls for '[s]afeguards and guidelines to avoid abuses'; *ibid.*, p. 88, where various business interest representatives refer to 'abuses in the USA'. Although the business sector often opposes compensatory collective redress because of fears of 'misuse', even the appropriate use of compensatory collective redress could lead to unwanted effects from the perspective of businesses and thus explain their general reservations against compensatory collective redress. In contrast with injunctive tools, compensatory collective redress tools would go deeper as they primarily seek (sometimes huge) compensation payments, whereas injunctions only aim to stop unlawful behaviour. As many consumers refrain from taking individual action but at the same time welcome the possibility of suing with other consumers, one could argue that businesses would indeed have more to lose than gain with the introduction of a well-working compensatory collective redress tool at the European level. Even if compensatory collective redress has the advantage of solving parallel cases in a relatively cost-effective manner in a single procedure, businesses might thus be worse off, as one can assume that not every consumer who benefits from a collective action would also be willing to take legal action alone if no collective redress scheme were available.

[58] European Parliament Resolution on 'Towards a Coherent European Approach to Collective Redress', para. 2.

[59] *Ibid.*

genuine European approach must be taken 'in order to avoid unmeritorious claims and misuse of collective redress, so as to guarantee fair court proceedings'.[60]

The 2012 Resolution on Collective Redress rejected in particular four characteristics of US-style class actions. According to the resolution, first, to avoid an uncontrolled use of collective actions, US-style contingency fees should not be used.[61] Second, the Parliament rejected opt-out tools (which are seldom found in the EU anyway[62]) arguing that their use 'is contrary to many Member States' legal orders and violates the rights of any victims who might participate in the procedure unknowingly and yet be bound by the court's decision'.[63] Third, the Parliament opposed the concept of pre-trial discovery as the 'obligation to disclose documents to the claimants ... is mostly unknown in Europe and [thus] must not form part of the horizontal framework'.[64] Finally, the resolution further

---

[60] *Ibid.*, para. 20.

[61] See *ibid.*, where it says that 'by and large, contingency fees are unknown in Europe and should not form part of the mandatory horizontal framework'. In this context see further Hodges *et al.* (eds.), *The Costs and Funding of Civil Litigation*, pp. 132–3 (Table 2), where it is explained that certain types of non-US-style contingency fees exist in several Member States.

[62] See the examples of The Netherlands, Portugal and, to a certain extent, Denmark. For comments see, for example, Stuyck *et al.*, 'An Analysis and Evaluation of Alternative Means of Consumer Redress', 291–3.

[63] European Parliament Resolution on 'Towards a Coherent European Approach to Collective Redress', para. 20, where the Parliament states that 'a collective redress system where the victims are not identified before the judgment is delivered must be rejected on the grounds that it is contrary to many Member States' legal orders and violates the rights of any victims who might participate in the procedure unknowingly and yet be bound by the court's decision'. In the same paragraph the resolution adds that 'for [an] ... action to be admissible there must be a clearly identified group, and identification of the group members must have taken place before the claim is brought'. This can prove difficult in the case of opt-out tools, where the group members do not necessarily need to be 'identified' if one understands identification as knowing the identity of each individual group member; (on this issue see R. Mulheron, *The Class Action in Common Law Legal Systems: A Comparative Perspective* (Oxford: Hart, 2004), p. 91, where Rachael Mulheron explains that 'the treatment of class numerosity and identity under ... class action regimes has been particularly flexible'. See also *ibid.*, p. 322, where Mulheron adds that '[t]he fact that individual class members cannot be listed at the outset is not fatal to the action ... Indeed, the identity of the class members may not be precisely known until they each come forward with proof of claim of the individual issues'). Although the 2012 Resolution on Collective Redress does not mention the term opt-out, it explicitly uses the term opt-in (see its para. 27, where the resolution states that 'individual victims should remain free not to pursue the opt-in collective action'). One can understand this as an additional indicator that the Parliament favours opt-in tools over opt-out alternatives.

[64] European Parliament Resolution on 'Towards a Coherent European Approach to Collective Redress', para. 20.

rejected punitive damages, explaining that any possible redress scheme 'should cover compensation only for the actual damage caused'.[65]

With respect to the current situation in the Member States one can state that under the existing national frameworks the risk of misuse of compensatory collective actions in the Member States is relatively low. The 2012 Resolution on Collective Redress refers to some pertinent studies on existing models of collective actions in the EU and stresses that 'collective redress mechanisms available within the EU have not generated disproportionate economic consequences'.[66] Still, because of the special characteristics of collective actions, especially their potential to lead to comparatively high aggregate amounts in dispute, great caution should be exercised to limit the potential risk of misuse with respect to a possible pan-EU mechanism. Blackmail settlements[67] feared by the

---

[65] *Ibid.* This last point succinctly summarises a further key rationale behind the compensatory enforcement of European consumer law. It is principally not used to punish businesses. Instead it aims to guarantee that consumers receive compensation. This of course does not mean that European consumer law does not also serve other purposes. Guaranteeing business compliance with the law is another important function of European consumer law, but this is primarily tried to be achieved with the use of injunctions or with the help of the instruments under the CPC Regulation. Put differently, unlike US punitive actions (that undeniably serve a quasi-criminal function) EU consumer law tries to achieve legal compliance by 'softer' means. Punishing legal offenders is nevertheless under certain conditions also possible in the EU but is reserved for a different legal regime. It is the task of criminal law and not consumer law to react to illegal business behaviour if it goes beyond 'simple' infringements of consumer laws and requires harsher actions. For comments from the English perspective see P. Cartwright, *Consumer Protection and the Criminal Law: Law, Theory and Policy in the UK* (Cambridge University Press, 2001). For comments on the French approach towards collective consumer protection and criminal law see Magnier, 'France'; V. Magnier and R. Alleweldt, 'Country Report France', report, (2009), available at ec.europa.eu/consumers/redress_cons/fr-country-report-final.pdf. For a discussion of punitive damages from the perspective of the interplay between punishment and compensation in general see P. O'Malley, *The Currency of Justice: Fines and Damages in Consumer Societies* (Abingdon: Routledge-Cavendish, 2009), pp. 125–9. For comments on US-style punitive damages in collective redress see, for example, F. Parisi and M. S. Cenini, 'Punitive Damages and Class Actions' in Backhaus *et al.* (eds.), *The Law and Economics of Class Actions on Europe*, pp. 131–46. On US-style punitive damages from the perspective of Member States in general see, for example, G. E. Kodek, 'Die Verbesserung des Schutzes kollektiver Interessen im Privat- und Prozessrecht' in M. Reiffenstein and B. Pirker-Hörmann (eds.), *Defizite kollektiver Rechtsdurchsetzung* (Vienna: Verlag Österreich, 2009), pp. 132–6.

[66] European Parliament Resolution on 'Towards a Coherent European Approach to Collective Redress', para. 9. For more details see in particular the findings of Civic Consulting and Oxford Economics, 'Evaluation of the Effectiveness and Efficiency of Collective Redress Mechanisms'.

[67] Blackmail settlements refer to cases in which a group of plaintiffs tries to put pressure on businesses by initiating a cost-intensive class action proceeding with wide audience

business sector, as well as fake collective actions[68], which are detrimental to consumer interests, are prominent US examples of misuse of collective redress. Although both have their origins in opt-out class actions, they could to some extent also cause harm in other forms of collective redress.[69]

appeal. Hodges defines them as follows: 'Blackmail settlements are said to occur where claims that have poor or uncertain merit are settled because it is commercially cheaper for a defendant to do so, in order to avoid the unrecoverable costs of defence, business disruption, adverse publicity and damage to shareholder value' (Hodges, *Reform of Class and Representative Actions*, p. 132 at note 5). Their main purpose is not to compensate consumers or to guarantee business compliance with legal rules but to use the power that a large group of plaintiffs can exercise on businesses (especially with the help of the media), irrespective of whether the claims are justified. Regardless of the merits of the case, sued businesses could feel forced to settle the case to avoid negative publicity caused by press reports and to keep costs as low as possible. For further comments see *ibid.*, p. 132 or Van den Bergh and Keske, 'Rechtsökonomische Aspekte der Sammelklage', p. 31.

[68] Impact-wise, fake collective actions (note: they can either take the form of fake group or fake representative actions) operate diametrically opposed to blackmail settlements and could impair consumer interests rather than business interests. Willem van Boom and Marco Loos define such actions as those 'with the hidden purpose of failing the claim, thus freeing the tortfeasor from otherwise successful individual claims' (W. van Boom and M. B. M. Loos, 'Effective Enforcement of Consumer Law in Europe: Private, Public, and Collective Mechanisms' in van Boom and Loos (eds.), *Collective Enforcement of Consumer Law*, p. 242). This phenomenon is also a bigger risk in the USA and other countries where collective actions are designed as opt-out tools because it can be assumed that an opt-out-based class covers more individual cases than collective opt-in devices. Businesses that act contrary to legal rules might want to keep their illegally gained profits as high as possible while minimising the potential financial loss caused by compensatory collective redress. This can be easily achieved by initiating a class action suit on the initiative of or in consultation with the particular wrongdoer. Closer, more invisible cooperation with the (lead) plaintiff could lead to settling the dispute at a comparatively low amount.

[69] Regarding blackmail settlements, the financial risk related to representation costs arising from litigation might in principle be a smaller threat for businesses in the EU because of the prevailing loser-pays principle (i.e., sued businesses only have to bear court costs and attorney fees if they lose the case; see Chapter 4, note 28 for a reference to the application of the loser-pays principle in the EU). Nevertheless, financial issues might still prompt businesses to settle cases as soon as possible, given the fact that in most cases it is impossible or at least very difficult to predict the court's ruling. In other words, the sword of Damocles in the form of the risk of having to bear both parties' attorney fees as well as court costs is omnipresent and the reason why blackmail settlements are also a likely threat for businesses in Europe. Test cases (with no binding effect on parallel cases) or collective opt-in tools can minimise the risk of fake collective actions, but consumers might still be dragged into such a dilemma under both. Fake test cases, even if they have no binding effect on parallel cases, might prompt consumers to settle for a comparatively low amount, convinced by the outcome of the test case. With regard to collective opt-in actions, consumers might be tempted to join the claim, misled by arguments that deprive them of the justified hope to actually receive more should they sue individually or together with others in a parallel, non-fake collective redress case.

In conclusion, one can say that the general opinion of the Parliament towards the possible introduction of a pan-EU compensatory collective redress device was quite positive, as it noted that 'injunctive relief is not sufficient when victims have suffered damage and have the right to compensation'.[70] At the same time, however, the Parliament called for caution and stressed the importance of carefully examining how best to prevent misuse.

The latest concrete development at the Commission level, the aforementioned 'gentle breeze', followed in mid-2013 when the Commission issued its Recommendation on common principles for injunctive and compensatory collective redress mechanisms in the Member States concerning violations of rights granted under Union law (Collective Redress Recommendation).[71] The Commission's Collective Redress Recommendation can be considered as (at the very least) a temporary end to the discussions on compensatory collective redress in the antitrust[72] and consumer law fields.

As stated in its title, it is only a recommendation and does not propose any binding instrument to oblige Member States to introduce collective redress tools. The political landscape and especially pressure from the business sector did not allow for more far-reaching instruments – fears over the possible misuse of mandatory compensatory collective redress were too strong.[73]

In line with the Parliament's view expressed in the 2012 Resolution on Collective Redress, the Collective Redress Recommendation tries to answer concerns regarding possible misuse by relying inter alia on some of the aforementioned ideas: a preference for opt-in tools (paragraph 21 Collective Redress Recommendation), the declared belief in the loser-pays

---

[70] European Parliament Resolution on 'Towards a Coherent European Approach to Collective Redress', para. 23.

[71] Recommendation on common principles for injunctive and compensatory collective redress mechanisms in the Member States concerning violations of rights granted under Union law, 11 June 2013, OJ 2013 No. L201/60.

[72] With respect to the enforcement discussions of antitrust rules the Commission has concurrently and additionally answered with a Proposal for a Directive on damages actions for breaches of EU Competition law (see Proposal for a Directive on certain rules governing actions for damages under national law for infringements of the competition law provisions of the Member States and of the European Union, 11 June 2013, COM(2013) 404 final). Unlike the Collective Redress Recommendation, however, it does not contain any particular rules on *collective* enforcement.

[73] In a similar vein, e.g., A. Stadler, 'The Commission's Recommendation on Common Principles of Collective Redress and Private International Law Issues', *Nederlands Internationaal Privaatrecht*, 31 (2013), 483, 483.

principle (paragraph 13) and an explicit no to punitive damages (paragraph 31). Further means of preventing a possible misuse can be seen in the reliance on representative entities (paragraph 4), the rejection of pure, i.e., US-style contingency fees (paragraph 30)[74] and the introduction of strict rules for third-party funding (paragraphs 15–16 and 32).

However, the Collective Redress Recommendation does not explicitly mandate Member States to react with any concrete measures. It does not introduce any innovative tool that would ensure that collective actions could be widely used in the EU to properly deal with the diffuse interests as expressed in the second wave of the Florence Project. Put differently and to borrow Astrid Stadler's words, the Collective Redress Recommendation would have the regrettable effect that Member States would not 'engage in fundamental reforms of their existing [if any] systems'.[75] Moreover, the Collective Redress Recommendation further fails to differentiate between different possible scenarios of multiple consumer damages, a fact that, as will be shown shortly, might also be detrimental to the success of compensatory collective redress. In the following sections I will show how suitable mechanisms to satisfy this call regarding consumer damages could, or rather should, look.

Multilayer interests

Multilayer interests – a definition

In addition to the already abundant materials published by EU institutions, there has been an incomparable number of academic contributions on compensatory collective redress.[76] It is fair to say that compensatory collective redress has been one of the most, if not the most, heavily debated procedural devices in the field of European consumer protection in the new millennium. The easiest explanation as to why collective

---

[74] Paragraph 30 Collective Redress Recommendation: 'The Member States should not permit contingency fees which risk creating such an incentive [note: This refers to paragraph 29 Collective Redress Recommendation, which says that no 'incentive to litigation that is unnecessary from the point of view of the interest of any of the parties' should be allowed]. The Member States that exceptionally allow for contingency fees should provide for appropriate national regulation of those fees in collective redress cases, taking into account in particular *the right to full compensation of the members of the claimant party*' (emphasis added).

[75] Stadler, 'The Commission's Recommendation on Common Principles of Collective Redress and Private International Law Issues', 483.

[76] For examples see the references in note 2 above.

actions are of such interest in academia is the aforementioned fact that the incomplete and diverse European landscape, with its variety of national forms of compensatory collective redress tools, provides plenty of food for academic thought.

In addition, collective actions as a compensatory tool are somehow unique, as they go beyond individual actions, show additional distinctive features and serve multiple functions. Collective actions can be seen as a tool to satisfy various groups of interest. On a different occasion, I referred to the interests addressed by collective actions as *multilayer interests* and divided them into three subgroups: individual interests, collective interests and public interests.[77] Whereas the most traditional form of litigation, individual redress, usually covers only the first of these three groups, collective actions can be used to protect all three.

One can easily identify all three categories in the field of consumer law, at least in certain cases of multiple damages. Individual consumers might have their own individual interest in getting their rights enforced when they, for example, encounter a problem with a purchased good. If that particular problem is not limited to only one product, but is further found in several other similar products (for example, serial defects in fungible goods), more than one individual consumer would have an interest in receiving compensation. One can say that in such a case collective interests in rights enforcement exist, especially if one considers that other consumers with similar problems could benefit from easier rights enforcement via shared evidence or lower individual rights enforcement costs per consumer resulting from collective enforcement. If the product in dispute further leads to some more general harm, for example, a defective product could cause health issues and thus increase the costs of medical treatment to be covered (at least partially) by the state (in those Member States where such a system exists), one could say that (in addition to individual and collective interests) a third group is affected: public interests (in the example given above, the public interest in reducing the overall costs of medical treatment and in getting reimbursed by the harm-causing trader or producer). Another example of harmed multilayer interests would be the case of mass food poisoning during a cruise trip causing individual, collective (as more than one passenger would suffer from similar symptoms) and public harm (if the public purse contributes to the health-care system).[78] A third example can be seen in malpractices by stock corporations that

---

[77] Wrbka, 'European Consumer Protection Law: Quo Vadis?', pp. 24–7.
[78] See *ibid.*, p. 25.

could, in the long run, negatively influence the company's stock market value and lead to losses for more than one shareholder (individual and collective interests). If such corporations receive financial support from the state, then the public interest (i.e., the need to keep the number of such cases at an absolute minimum) could also be affected.

A good practical example of how multilayer interests can be affected by wrongdoing can be seen in the *Deutsche Telekom* case.[79] Since the beginning of the new millennium, Frankfurt's regional court has been inundated by claims against Deutsche Telekom from close to 17,000 investors who suffered a drop in share price. They argued that certain prospectus information issued by the company in the course of the privatisation of Deutsche Telekom was misleading and other important information was missing altogether. All three aforementioned pillars were affected in this case: individual interests, as every investor who sued the company had an individual interest in obtaining individual compensation; collective interests because of the fact that similar arguments connected the individual interests, a fact that created a collective interest in easier rights enforcement and the sharing of evidence; and the public interest, as the filing of cases (nearly) led to a standstill of the judiciary in Frankfurt's regional court, which had a negative impact on the public interest, placing too high a burden on a judicial system that until then had been working well.

The *Deutsche Telekom* case was of practical importance because it prompted the German legislator to react with the introduction of a new specially crafted collective redress law (there was no German law at that time to properly address the specific problem at hand). In 2005 the Capital Markets Model Case Act (*Kapitalanleger-Musterverfahrensgesetz* or KapMuG), a special procedural combination of an opt-in based collective approach and test cases, was enacted to cope with the problem of courts being overburdened by too many parallel cases in securities litigation.[80]

As these examples show, compensatory collective redress can be used to solve issues that arise when multilayer interests are affected and cannot

---

[79] On the background of the *Deutsche Telekom* case see A. Stadler, 'A Test Case in Germany: 16 000 Private Investors vs. Deutsche Telekom', *ERA Forum*, 10 (2009), 37–50; P. Rott, 'Country Report Germany', report, (2009), available at ec.europa.eu/consumers/redress_cons/de-country-report-final.pdf and the references in the following note 80.

[80] The 2005 KapMuG was crafted as a temporary law and expired on 1 November 2012. In 2012 a revised KapMuG was enacted, which again is designed as a temporary law. One interesting new feature of the 2012 KapMuG is an opt-out based settlement negotiated in the test case procedure and approved by the relevant court in test case proceedings (see §§ 17–19 and 23 of the 2012 KapMuG). The new KapMug will expire on 1 November 2020. For details and comments on the original KapMuG see B. Hess *et al.* (eds.), *Kölner Kommentar zum KapMuG:*

be appropriately solved by traditional means. I will show shortly how the concept of multilayer interests can be used to find the most suitable collective redress device(s) for different expressions of multiple consumer damages, i.e., damages that affect more than a single individual consumer.

Multilayer interests in the debate on collective redress

Without mentioning the term explicitly, several contributors to the consumer collective redress debate have touched upon the issue of multilayer interests, mostly when weighing the advantages and disadvantages of the public versus the private enforcement of consumer laws. Roger Van den Bergh refers to the concept of multilayer interests when arguing that 'both private values and public values are served by consumer laws'.[81] In the Leuven Study, Jules Stuyck and his colleagues agree that 'collective actions for the protection of consumers' collective interests are often considered to pursue matters of public interest'.[82] Another example is provided by Luboš Tichý and Jan Balarin. They start with claiming that the most visible purpose of consumer law is to protect the individual consumer. If the same issue arises more than once, then the interests of a group of consumers could be affected. Collective actions could facilitate the enforcement of collective rights and shared interests. At the same

Kommentierung der prozessualen Vorschriften und der Anspruchsgrundlagen (Cologne: Heymanns, 2008); T. Curdt, Kollektiver Rechtsschutz unter dem Regime des KapMuG (Hamburg: Dr. Kovač, 2010); A. Halfmeier, P. Rott and E. Feess, Kollektiver Rechtsschutz im Kapitalmarktrecht: Evaluation des Kapitalanleger-Musterverfahrensgesetzes (Frankfurt: Frankfurt School Verlag, 2010); T. Kilian, Ausgewählte Probleme des Musterverfahrens nach dem KapMuG (Baden-Baden: Nomos, 2007); F. Bergmeister, Kapitalanleger-Musterverfahrensgesetz (KapMuG) (Tübingen: Mohr Siebeck, 2009); F. Reuschle, 'Das Kapitalanleger-Musterverfahrensgesetz – Eine erste Bestandsaufnahme aus Sicht der Praxis' in Casper et al. (eds.), Auf dem Weg zu einer europäischen Sammelklage?, pp. 277–92; P. Prusseit, Die Bindungswirkung des Musterentscheides nach dem KapMuG: – zu ihrem institutionellen Verständnis als Form der Interventionswirkung (Göttingen: Sierke, 2009). For details and comments on the 2012 KapMuG see A. Stadler, 'Developments in Collective Redress: What's New in the "New German KapMuG"?', European Business Law Review, 24 (2013), 731–49; T. Wiewel, 'Das neue KapMuG in Anlageberatungsfällen', Verbraucher und Recht, 28 (2013), 173–7; Clifford Chance, 'Das neue Kapitalanleger-Musterverfahrensgesetz (KapMuG)', newsletter, (2012), available at www.cliffordchance.com/briefings/2012/11/newsletter_das_neu.html.

[81] R. Van den Bergh, 'Should Consumer Protection Law Be Publicly Enforced? An Economic Perspective on EC Regulation 2006/2004 and Its Implementation in the Consumer Protection Laws of the Member States' in van Boom and Loos (eds.), Collective Enforcement of Consumer Law, p. 187.

[82] Stuyck et al., 'An Analysis and Evaluation of Alternative Means of Consumer Redress', p. 323.

time, collective actions could go further and support the public interest in effective consumer protection. Tichý and Balarin conclude that '[t]he consumer community is so significant in number and influence that consumers' concerns infiltrate the public interest in the widest sense'.[83]

The interplay between multilayer interests and collective actions can be further explained with the elaborations of DG SANCO and DG COMP. As explained earlier, DG SANCO followed DG COMP in its quest for the most suitable form of collective redress.[84] These two parallel efforts can be regarded as another example of how the concept of collective redress is linked to different layers of interests. Undeniably, not only the research work carried out by DG SANCO, but also the elaborations initiated by DG COMP aim to benefit consumers, as sound and fair competition undeniably serves (inter alia) the objective of benefiting consumers both individually and as a group. To quote DG COMP: '[A]ntitrust rules ... are enforced ... to deter anti-competitive practices forbidden by antitrust law and to protect ... consumers from these practices and any damages caused by them.'[85] The parallel debates within the Commission show how the discussion on collective actions in different legal disciplines is linked to the same underlying question of how to kill two (in actual fact three) birds with one stone. In other words, compensatory collective redress can be used to serve all three subcategories of multilayer interests: individual, collective and public interests.[86]

---

[83] L. Tichý and J. Balarin, 'Efficiency of the Protection of Collective Interests: Judicial and Administrative Enforcement in the Czech Republic' in Cafaggi and Micklitz (eds.), *New Frontiers of Consumer Protection*, p. 233. For similar comments see M. Safjan, Ł. Gorywoda and A., Jańczuk, 'Taking Collective Interest of Consumers Seriously: A View from Poland' in *ibid.*, p. 185; Stuyck *et al.*, 'An Analysis and Evaluation of Alternative Means of Consumer Redress', p. 323, where the authors explain that 'collective actions for the protection of consumers' collective interests are often considered to pursue matters of public interest'.

[84] See 'The Road towards the Green Paper on Consumer Collective Redress' above.

[85] Green Paper on damages actions for breach of the EC antitrust rules, p. 3. See also White Paper on damages actions for breach of the EC antitrust rules, p. 4, where the Commission refers to the consumers' rational disinterest in bringing individual actions as follows: 'Individual consumers, ... especially those who have suffered scattered and relatively low-value damage, are often deterred from bringing an individual action for damages by the costs, delays, uncertainties, risks and burdens involved.' See also the case law of the CJEU that explains the individual's right to sue for compensation out of antitrust offences (and by doing so, combines different interest layers) (see, for example, Case C-453/99, *Courage Ltd* v. *Crehan* [2001] ECR I-6297; and Joined Cases C-295-298/04, *Vincenzo Manfredi and Others* v. *Lloyd Adriatico Assicurazioni SpA and Others* [2006] ECR I-6619).

[86] This also explains why the concept of compensatory collective redress is approached by several authors from two different angles: competition law and consumer law. See, for

Another multilayered function of collective actions is identified by Jenny Steele and Willem van Boom.[87] They link compensatory collective actions to mass justice and argue that the latter primarily serves three functions: financial, i.e., compensating those who suffer damages; deterrence, i.e., making sure that the wrongdoing business or any other business refrains from comparable infringements; and peace.[88] The three subgoals of mass justice as ascribed to collective actions by Steele and van Boom can also be expressed with the three pillars of the multilayer interest concept. The first function, compensation, addresses issues linked to both individual and collective interests – and even public interests if the state or any other public authority suffers financial harm. The same is true of the deterrence character of compensatory collective actions – it can serve all three groups of interests – whereas the third category, the peace function, primarily deals with the relationship between the parties and thus first and foremost addresses individual and collective interests.

Also these observations help to arrive at the conclusion that compensatory collective actions aim to serve various interests (that can be grouped under the pillar of multilayer interests). Depending on which group of interests is primarily affected by legal wrongs, different forms of collective action might be the most appropriate solution when reacting to such

example, K. J. Cseres, 'Enforcement of Collective Consumer Interests: A Competition Law Perspective' in van Boom and Loos (eds.), *Collective Enforcement of Consumer Law*, pp. 131–2; Hodges, *The Reform of Class and Representative Actions in European Legal Systems*; E. Buttigieg, *Competition Law: Safeguarding the Consumer Interest: A Comparative Analysis of US Antitrust Law and EC Competition Law* (Alphen aan den Rijn: Kluwer Law International, 2009). For a different kind of interdisciplinary approach to compensatory collective redress see H. Rösler, 'The Transformation of Contractual Justice – a Historical and Comparative Account of the Impact of Consumption' in Micklitz (ed.), *The Many Concepts of Social Justice in European Private Law*, pp. 327–58.

[87] J. Steele and W. H. van Boom, 'Mass Justice and its Challenges' in Steele and van Boom (eds.), *Mass Justice*, pp. 21–4.

[88] *Ibid.*, p. 23. Steele and van Boom define this third pillar as 'encompass[ing] both an important future-regarding element in which events are left behind and the participants … can move on, and a past element in which there is a sense that a reasonable and distributively just solution has been reached' (*ibid.*). On the peace function see further E. Schilken, 'Der Zweck des Zivilprozesses und der kollektive Rechtsschutz' in C. Meller-Hannich (ed.), *Kollektiver Rechtsschutz im Zivilprozess* (Baden-Baden: Nomos, 2008), pp. 28–9. For an earlier comment on the possible interplay between individual, collective and public interests see K. Thiere, *Die Wahrung überindividueller Interessen im Zivilprozeß* (Bielefeld: Verlag Ernst und W. Gieseking, 1980). For a more recent, detailed anaylsis see N. Reich, *Individueller und kollektiver Rechtsschutz im EU-Verbraucherrecht. Von der "Nationalisierung" zur "Konstitutionalisierung" von Rechtsbehelfen* (Baden-Baden: Nomos, 2012).

situations. In the following sections I will try to explain what this means in relation to B2C disputes.

Scattered damages v. mass damages

When one looks at the pertinent policy papers, one will realise that the most common argument for why consumer compensatory collective redress is needed at the pan-EU level is closely linked to the assumed lack of consumer willingness to initiate individual actions against businesses. Unfortunately, the public debate in the field of consumer law seems to concentrate its argumentation on this issue alone. In this section I will explain why approaching the topic from different angles is necessary if one really wants to satisfy the concept of multilayer interests in the context at hand.

One key study to support the 'unwillingness to sue theory' is the 2010 Eurobarometer study on attitudes towards cross-border sales and consumer protection (2010 Cross-border Sales and Consumer Protection Study). The 2010 Cross-border Sales and Consumer Protection Study takes a detailed look at consumers' general complaint and suing behaviours in the Member States and comes to the conclusion that almost half of the consumers refrain from taking any further action after unsuccessful complaints to the trader,[89] and only very few take the matter to court.[90] This study was not the first to present detailed data on consumers' general passivity with respect to solving disputes via litigation. In addition to several national studies,[91] two pan-EU studies conducted in the 1990s dealt especially with the question of whether it is reasonably worthwhile (from a financial perspective) to pursue cross-border consumer claims. In 1995, more than a decade before the ESCP was introduced the Study on the cost of judicial barriers for consumers in the single market explained that '[t]he higher the value of the purchase the more frequent are steps to recover damages. If purchases remain below 2,000 ECU [note: the ECU was replaced by the EURO in 1999 at the rate of 1 = 1] consumers are

---

[89] On average, 46.4 per cent of respondents in the 2010 Cross-border Sales and Consumer Protection Study (see The Gallup Organization Hungary, 'Attitudes towards Cross-border Sales and Consumer Protection', p. 102).

[90] On average, 3.3 per cent of respondents, adding that a further 7.6 per cent asked a lawyer for advice (*ibid.*). In a comparable vein is the earlier discussed 2004 Access to Justice Survey, which explained that 13 per cent of respondent consumers went to court either with the support of a lawyer or alone (see Chapter 3 above).

[91] See the examples referred to in von Freyhold *et al.* (eds.), 'Cost of Judicial Barriers for Consumers in the Single Market'.

rather passiv[e] whereas this happens only rarely above this threshold'.[92] The practical importance of this conclusion becomes even more apparent if one considers that the vast majority of consumers who participated in that study, approximately 90 per cent, spent less than ECU 2,000 on the respective products.[93] Three years later, the Study on the cost of legal obstacles to the disadvantage of consumers in the single market came to a similar negative conclusion noting that 'for dispute values of 2,000 ECU, not even a cross-border first instance dispute is worth to pursue and that in most member states a dispute value of 50,000 ECU might be a reasonable value to pursue a cross-border dispute'.[94] The ESCP tried to provide an answer to these findings. However, especially in the case of particularly low and very low amounts in dispute (low- and lowest-value damages; *Bagatellschäden*) – which when occurring in parallel cases can be referred to as scattered damages (*Streuschäden*) – consumers are still considered passive, i.e., they do not usually pursue their individual claims.

In reference to this state of inaction, terms such as 'rational disinterest' (*rationales Desinteresse*)[95] or rational apathy (*rationale Apathie*)[96] can be found in the literature. Scattered damages, i.e., multiple consumer damages in which the rational disinterest remains *particularly* strong, are often commented on in this respect.[97] Although the term scattered damages

---

[92] *Ibid.*, p. 13.   [93] *Ibid.*, p. 12.

[94] von Freyhold, Vial & Partner Consultants, 'The Cost of Legal Obstacles to the Disadvantage of Consumers in the Single Market', report for DG SANCO, (1998), pp. 276–7, available at ec.europa.eu/dgs/health_consumer/library/pub/pub03.pdf.

[95] Janssen, 'Auf dem Weg zu einer europäischen Sammelklage?', p. 5.

[96] Wagner, 'Kollektiver Rechtsschutz', p. 53; Van den Bergh, 'Should Consumer Protection Law Be Publicly Enforced?', p. 183. C. Meller-Hannich, 'Einführung. Auf dem Weg zu einem effektiven und gerechten System des kollektiven Rechtsschutzes' in Meller-Hannich (ed.), *Kollektiver Rechtsschutz im Zivilprozess*, p. 14; C. Michailidou, *Prozessuale Fragen des Kollektivrechtsschutzes im europäischen Justizraum* (Baden-Baden: Nomos, 2007), p. 49.

[97] In addition to the contributions referred to in notes 95, 96 and 115, and the contributions in notes 98–102 on the mathematical determination of scattered damages see, for example, B. Cupa, 'Scattered Damages: A Comparative Law Study about the Enforcement Deficit of Low-Value Damages and the Class Action Approach', *European Review of Private Law*, 20 (2012), 504–40; G. Howells, 'Cy-près for Consumers: Ensuring Class Action Reforms Deal with "Scattered Damage"' in Steele and van Boom (eds.), *Mass Justice*, pp. 58–72; P. Kolba, '"Friedrich Müller" und Co – Praxisbeispiele zu Streuschäden' in Reiffenstein and Pirker-Hörmann (eds.), *Defizite kollektiver Rechtsdurchsetzung*, pp. 13–18; E. Kocher, 'Collective Rights and Collective Goods: Enforcement As Collective Interest' in Steele and van Boom (eds.), *Mass Justice*, pp. 127–32; H.-W. Micklitz et al., 'Gruppenklagen in den Mitgliedstaaten der Europäischen Gemeinschaft & den Vereinigten Staaten von Amerika', report, (2005), available at www.sozialministerium.at/cms/site/attachments/6/7/1/CH2247/CMS1229355722213/micklitz-stadler_gruppenklagen.pdf; Eichholtz, *Die US-amerikanische Class Action und ihre deutsche Funktionsäquivalente*, pp. 5 and 7.

remains rather vague, pertinent literature and some studies do provide certain indicators that refer to value amounts covered by that term; or in other words, where to draw the line between scattered damages and other forms of damages. Regarding scattered damages in a German context, Micklitz and Stadler arrive at an upper limit per individual damage of EUR 25.[98] In subsequent contributions (again with respect to the German market), Stadler identifies a financial threshold per affected individual of again EUR 25[99] in one instance and with reference to other commentators, she arrives at EUR 25 to EUR 200 in another.[100] With respect to the Danish situation, she identifies a threshold of EUR 270 on a third occasion.[101] Gerhard Wagner is another commentator on scattered damages. Although he does not present any concrete upper limit, he argues that (again) in Germany an amount of EUR 100 would clearly fall under the category of scattered damages, explaining that the cost risk of suing for EUR 100 by traditional means amounts to EUR 270.[102]

In addition to the two aforementioned studies from the 1990s there are several newer studies that deal with the question of financial thresholds for initiating litigation, both before and after the introduction of the ESCP. The 2004 Access to Justice Survey revealed that (with respect to problems with products and services bought domestically) 11 per cent of consumers were willing to sue if the amount in dispute was lower than EUR 100, 18 per cent if lower than EUR 200, 29 per cent if lower than EUR 500 and 47 per cent if lower than EUR 1,000.[103] In other words, the higher the amount in dispute, the more likely consumers are to overcome their

---

[98] H.-W. Micklitz and A. Stadler, *Unrechtsgewinnabschöpfung: Möglichkeiten und Perspektiven eines kollektiven Schadenersatzanspruches im UWG* (Baden-Baden: Nomos, 2003), p. 92.

[99] A. Stadler, *Bündelung von Interessen im Zivilprozess: Überlegungen zur Einführung von Verbands- und Gruppenklagen im deutschen Recht* (Heidelberg: C. F. Müller, 2004), p. 13.

[100] A. Stadler, 'Erfahrungen mit den Gewinnabschöpfungsansprüchen im deutschen Wettbewerbs- und Kartellrecht' in Reiffenstein and Pirker-Hörmann (eds.), *Defizite kollektiver Rechtsdurchsetzung*, p. 107 with further references.

[101] A. Stadler, 'Group Actions as a Remedy to Enforce Consumer Interests' in Cafaggi and Micklitz (eds.), *New Frontiers of Consumer Protection*, p. 327.

[102] See his calculation in Wagner, 'Kollektiver Rechtsschutz', p. 53 at note 53.

[103] European Opinion Research Group, 'European Union Citizens and Access to Justice', p. 28, where the study further compares the results with a Eurobarometer study conducted in 1999. The threshold stayed more or less the same. In 1999 87 per cent would have refrained from taking individual action at court if the amount at stake were below EUR 100 (compared to 89 per cent in 2004). The number of consumers willing to pursue their rights with the help of litigation for an amount below EUR 200 was the same in both years with 18 per cent overall.

rational disinterest in suing. Likewise, especially in the categories identified by Micklitz, Stadler and Wagner, i.e., the categories that would qualify as scattered damages, the rational disinterest in suing was strong.

The 2013 Eurobarometer ESCP Study (an example of a post-ESCP
Eurobarometer study) chose slightly different possible amounts in dispute
to evaluate consumers' general willingness to sue. The study also differentiated between purely domestic B2C cases and trans-border B2C transactions. It nevertheless arrived at a similar conclusion. The willingness to
sue principally rises along with the amount in dispute. In purely domestic
cases, 21 per cent of consumers were willing to sue for an amount in dispute lower than EUR 400; 41 per cent if lower than EUR 800; 48 per cent if
lower than EUR 1,200; and 54 per cent if lower than EUR 1,600.[104] Similar
financial thresholds were identified for cross-border cases. Under the condition that consumers could sue in the courts of their home country, the
willingness to sue was 20 per cent in the first category, 40 per cent in the
second, 48 per cent in the third and 53 per cent in the fourth.[105] Slightly
lower results were obtained if consumers had to sue abroad: 17 per cent in
the first category, 35 per cent in the second, 44 per cent in the third and
49 per cent in the fourth.[106] The 2013 Eurobarometer ESCP Study also
calculated the average minimum amount in dispute at which consumers
would go to court to pursue their claims in B2C cases. The average pan-
European threshold amounted to EUR 726 (for purely domestic disputes),
EUR 753 (for cross-border disputes with domestic jurisdiction) and EUR
786 (for cross-border disputes with foreign jurisdiction).[107]

These numbers give some indication of how to define scattered damages
in more detail. However, one must note that the discussion is complicated
by the fact that the threshold amount to prompt a considerable number
of consumers to individually sue differs widely among Member States.
The 2013 Eurobarometer ESCP Study identified average national thresholds between EUR 458 and 933, EUR 507 and 914 and EUR 564 and 1,070
for the three dispute categories (purely domestic disputes, cross-border
disputes with domestic jurisdiction and cross-border disputes with foreign jurisdiction).[108] Taking a closer look at the studies one can conclude
that the wide range in numbers cannot be explained by a single factor.
Varying average household income amounts among Member States can
be one factor that, to some extent, explain why consumers have different

[104] TNS Opinion & Social, 'European Small Claims Procedure', p. 44.
[105] *Ibid.*   [106] *Ibid.*
[107] *Ibid.*, pp. 46–8.   [108] *Ibid.*

perceptions of the claim amounts worth pursuing beyond initial complaints. Additional issues that can impact such perceptions include court costs, legal representation costs and other factors related to the respective judicial system. Regardless of why consumers feel that a claim is worth pursuing, the fact that the threshold amount to induce consumers to sue differs from Member State to Member State can be of importance when defining an upper cap for the category of those damages in which unwillingness is of particular significance, i.e., for the category of scattered damages. I will come back to this issue in a later chapter.

Mass damages (*Massenschäden*) are a second important category of multiple damages.[109] Unlike scattered damages, mass damages have not yet received a comparable amount of attention in the literature on consumer compensatory collective redress. Mass damages can be defined as multiple damages of a relatively high or very high individual value. In this context, one can identify two problems. First, in the case of mass damages (like in scattered damages), some rational disinterest in individual rights enforcement exists.[110] Here, however, the rational disinterest phenomenon rests on slightly different grounds. In the case of mass damages, the rational disinterest is first and foremost linked to the financial risk inherent in the prevailing loser-pays principle[111] and less so with time and 'not worth suing' concerns.[112]

Second, since in mass damages cases individuals are more likely to overcome their rational disinterest in suing, mass damages can lead to a situation where they place a too heavy burden on the judiciary. This is particularly true in cases where courts are overloaded with parallel

---

[109] In this book, the term multiple damages will be used as an umbrella term comprising both scattered damages and mass damages.

[110] Gerhard Wagner disagrees and claims that in the case of mass damages no rational disinterest in pursuing individual claims can be found at all (see Wagner, 'Kollektiver Rechtsschutz', p. 80). One should, however, not forget that the financial cost risk a claimant is exposed to can cause a rational disinterest in suing.

[111] This is especially so if the consumer does not – or because of the legal conditions in a particular Member State, cannot – enjoy financial support from legal insurances, third-party funding companies or effective state legal aid. For an overview of the situation in the EU see Hodges *et al.* (eds.), *The Costs and Funding of Civil Litigation* for details, in particular, pp. 114–31 (Table 1).

[112] Of course, consumers have to invest time to have their rights enforced in the case of mass damages, too. The possible gain is comparatively high, however, a fact that is more likely to incentivise consumers to sue than in the case of scattered damages. In general it is thus valid to say that rational disinterest is stronger in the context of scattered damages than for mass damages. The findings of the aforementioned 2004 Access to Justice Survey and the 2013 Eurobarometer ESCP Study prove this assumption.

cases that do not allow for an ordinary joinder of parties. This explains why in the case of mass damages it might not be necessarily a question of how to encourage consumers to go to court, but instead how they should file their claims. The *Deutsche Telekom* case (discussed earlier), in which the average individual damage amounted to approximately EUR 5,900,[113] is a very good example. Close to 17,000 investors overcame their rational disinterests in pursuing their individual claims, and the filing of these claims nearly led to the collapse of Frankfurt's regional court.[114]

Although an exact mathematical delimitation between the two categories might prove difficult, it is still worth dealing with scattered damages and mass damages separately because the underlying problems are, as just seen, different. In the first case it is *only* the rational disinterest of consumers that needs to be solved, whereas in the second, the further question arises of how to improve the efficiency of the courts and legal proceedings.

Some authors share the view that a classification of multiple damages into scattered and mass damages is necessary. One of them is Gerhard Wagner, who approaches the issue from the perspective of the underlying rationale behind possible redress mechanisms. He distinguishes between the principle of remediation (*Ausgleichsprinzip*) and that of deterrence (*Präventionsfunktion*) and argues that 'good legal policy must first and foremost clarify the targets pursued and possible relating alternatives of regulation. Against this background it is regrettable that the Collective Redress Green Paper does not clearly distinguish between scattered damages and mass damages, and that ... also the study on the Evaluation of the Effectiveness and Efficiency of Collective Redress Mechanisms in the European Union [i.e. the 2007 Evaluation Study] ... does not start its analysis with this differentiation'.[115] Later in his observation Wagner links the principles of remediation and deterrence to scattered damages and mass damages. He points out that 'compensation in the field of scattered damages

---

[113]   A. Kurz, 'Sturm auf die Telekom', *Financial Times Deutschland* (online), 14 May 2012 (on file with the author).

[114]   See 'Multilayer interests – a definition' above.

[115]   Wagner, 'Kollektiver Rechtsschutz', p. 50 (translation mine). For further examples of a call for a differentiation between scattered damages and mass damages see, e.g., Janssen, 'Auf dem Weg zu einer europäischen Sammelklage?', p. 3; D. Staudenmayer, 'Überlegungen der Europäischen Kommission zur kollektiven Rechtsdurchsetzung' in Casper *et al.* (eds.), *Auf dem Weg zu einer europäischen Sammelklage?*, p. 89. H.-W. Micklitz and A. Stadler, *Das Verbandsklagerecht in der Informations- und Dienstleistungsgesellschaft* (Münster-Hiltrup: Landwirtschaftsverlag, 2005).

Table 1 *Comparison of scattered damages and mass damages*

Issue	Scattered damages	Mass damages
Willingness of affected consumers to sue individually	Low to non-existent	Generally higher than in the case of scattered damages
Individual private interest in winning a collective redress case	Lower in the short run, higher in the long run (not necessarily a primarily financial interest but instead an interest in securing the legal compliance of traders; financial interest might not exist in cases where very low amounts are in dispute)	Comparatively high (these are higher the higher the amount in dispute is)
Collective private interest in winning a collective redress case	Lower in the short run, higher in the long run (not necessarily a primarily financial interest but instead an interest in business deterrence)	Comparatively high, as plaintiffs could profit from shared or more easily accessible evidence and better court efficiency (as the number of parallel cases would be reduced)
Public interest in winning a collective redress case	High (guaranteeing legal compliance)	High (making the court system more effective; guaranteeing legal compliance)
Financial risk involved in suing	Objectively rather low but subjectively high (cost-benefit analysis)	Objectively relatively high (generally, the higher the amount, the higher the cost risk, but increase is degressively proportional[a])

Table 1 (*cont.*)

Issue	Scattered damages	Mass damages
Reason(s) why a collective redress tool is needed	Consumers usually do not pursue their individual claims due to their rational disinterest in suing ('too little individual litigation' with the side effect that traders do not usually have to face compensation claims)	First and foremost: reducing the courts' burden ('too much individual litigation'); in addition: incentivising consumers to pursue claims they would not usually pursue due to their rational disinterest in suing ('too little individual litigation')
General rationale behind rights enforcement	First and foremost securing the legal compliance of traders (the rationale is stronger the lower the individual amount in dispute)	First and foremost compensation (the rationale is stronger the higher the individual amount in dispute); in addition, securing compliance of traders

a See 'Mass damages' below for details.

serves only one purpose: behaviour control'.[116] According to Wagner, remediation does not play a role in this respect. The rationale behind the possible compensation obtained in the context of scattered damage litigation is similar to the issues addressed by the Injunctions Directive: business deterrence and guaranteeing future compliance with legal rules. The

---

[116] Wagner, 'Kollektiver Rechtsschutz', p. 73. For additional comments on the deterrence potential of compensatory collective redress see R. Van den Bergh and L. Visscher, 'The Preventive Function of Collective Actions for Damages in Consumer Law', *Erasmus Law Review*, 1 (2008), 5–30.

idea of responding to scattered damages is thus very strongly intertwined with public interest concerns. Monetary individual and collective interests, the other two pillars of the multilayer interest concept, remain comparatively insignificant. In contrast, fighting mass damages (while also showing deterrent effects) primarily aims at serving the compensatory interests of the affected parties.[117] One can say that strong private individual and collective enforcement interests exist in the case of mass damages, and that they are much more pronounced than in scattered damages.

Hence, Wagner's observations confirm the view that different categories of damages ask for different solutions – the interests involved are touched upon for different reasons and to different extents. Table 1 summarises the argumentation regarding several key issues in relation to both scattered damages and mass damages. The data might help to identify suitable collective redress mechanisms in the future.

The answer(s)

General remarks

As I have just explained, because the underlying obstacles to pursuing scattered damages and mass damages differ, it is crucial to differentiate between the two categories when drafting a framework for compensatory collective redress. What is needed is a tailor-made tool, or rather (at least)[118] two tailor-made tools, which take account of the concrete features of the two damage classifications and properly balance the needs of the affected interests with possible legal solutions. In the following, I will look at how the issues described in the previous chapters could be effectively and efficiently addressed without the unjustified interference of the legal traditions of both the Member States and the EU.

Three questions, in particular, deserve closer attention in the search for a suitable procedural framework. They can be described as follows: (1) choosing between opt-in tools, opt-out tools (both of which could take the form of group actions and representative actions) and test cases; (2) choosing between group actions and representative actions (if one chooses either opt-in or opt-out); and (3) choosing between different

---

[117] Wagner, 'Kollektiver Rechtsschutz', p. 80.

[118] See 'Scattered damages' below, where I explain that – as an alternative – the solution presented in the context of scattered damages could be split into two (slightly) different tools (opt-out based on the one hand and mandatory representation on the other).

(lead) plaintiffs or representatives: public authorities, private bodies and individuals.

Scattered damages

As shown above, scattered damages refer to amounts of low and lowest value, where the rational disinterest in pursuing claims at an individual basis is particularly strong. The rational disinterest characterises such damages regardless of whether or not the cases are purely domestic or show cross-border elements. However, it is valid to say that the rational disinterest phenomenon is greater in a cross-border context, because additional issues, such as language barriers[119] or a basic scepticism of cross-border rights enforcement, might further disincentivise consumers from taking actions that go beyond making an initial complaint. In addition, one can generally conclude that the rational disinterest in pursuing claims is higher the lower the amount in dispute is, and that the deterrent effect on businesses is stronger the higher the financial threat for them. Thus, for the sake of deterrence and the restoration of legal compliance it would be of utmost importance to group as many damage claims as possible into a single action.

In the case of scattered damages, choosing between opt-in tools, opt-out tools and test cases is the easiest of the three aforementioned questions to answer. Because scattered damages are to a great extent inextricably linked with rational disinterest concerns, opt-in tools do not make much sense – in particular in those cases in which purely mathematical reflections explain that pursuing individual claims any further would not pay off for the affected individual, the rational disinterest in joining would remain strong.[120] A rational disinterest could exist even if consumers could benefit from a successful opt-in based collective action (in the sense that the potential cost risk of a collective mechanism is lower than the amount in dispute). Consumers would have to become 'active' by opting in before even getting the factual opportunity to benefit from a positive

---

[119] For a brief discussion on some ways to overcome language issues to some extent see 'Thoughts on the Future of ECC-Net' in Chapter 15 below.

[120] This case might lead to a scenario where traders do not have to fear the threat of litigation should they not positively reply to consumer complaints. Colin Scott explains this as follows: '[W]ith many smaller consumer products, there would be little prospect of a consumer pursuing a legal claim were a supplier to fail to address a complaint to the consumer's satisfaction, so the threat of legal action is likely to be fairly marginal in any calculation by businesses of their appropriate responses' (C. Scott, 'Enforcing Consumer Protection Laws' in Howells *et al.* (eds.), *Handbook of Research on International Consumer Law*, p. 541).

result from the case at hand. However, the respective amount of time required to join a proceeding would under normal circumstances very likely disincentivise consumers to opt in, especially in cases with very low individual amounts in dispute.

Just like opt-in tools test cases are, in principle, an unsuitable option.[121] A cost-benefit analysis would usually disincentivise possible plaintiffs – in the vast majority of cases suing for a considerably low amount would not stand in any acceptable relation to the efforts required by the plaintiff. Furthermore, even if the claimant launched a test case and obtained a favourable decision, other affected consumers would still face the problem of having to overcome their own rational disinterest in pursuing individual scattered damage claims. Opt-out tools are thus the only – or at least, the most effective and obvious – choice.[122]

Opt-out tools pose the risk though that not all affected consumers would have an actual chance to decide on the fate of their individual damage. For example, (depending on how opt-out devices are designed) there might be cases where consumers never find out that their claims are (or have already been) pursued with an opt-out based tool until they want to sue individually. If the judicial mechanisms cannot address such a situation, consumers might lose their opportunity to sue.[123] Thus, one could feel tempted to raise concerns about the compatibility of opt-out devices with Article 6 ECHR, which enshrines that '[i]n the determination of his civil rights and obligations [...], everyone is entitled to a fair and public hearing within a reasonable time by an independent and impartial tribunal established by law'.[124] In a resolution on the Collective Redress

---

[121] But see the explanation in the following note on the possibility of a 'combined approach'.

[122] In a similar vein Stuyck et al., 'An Analysis and Evaluation of Alternative Means of Consumer Redress', p. 290. However, one should not completely rule out test cases, as – in combination with opt-out, i.e., designed as a 'first step' to lower the objective cost risk, and in the form of enhanced test cases with semi-binding effect as outlined in the context of mass damages – they would allow for cost-saving proceedings. Of course, the basic problem, i.e., the disincentive posed by a cost-benefit analysis, would still exist.

[123] For similar concerns see Hannah Buxbaum's comment that 'the "opt out" variant used in the United States – in which a plaintiff might be part of a defined class without knowing it, and without realizing that its claim is being disposed – would be impossible' (see H. L. Buxbaum, 'Class Actions, Conflict and the Global Economy' in Bruns et al. (eds.), Festschrift für Rolf Stürner zum 70. Geburtstag, p. 1447).

[124] For comments on this see, for example, Kodek, 'Collective Redress in Austria', 89; H. Koch, 'Alternativen zum Zweiparteiensystem im Zivilprozeß', Kritische Vierteljahresschrift für Gesetzgebung und Rechtswissenschaft, (1989), 323, 337; W. Lüke, Die Beteiligung Dritter im Zivilprozess: Eine rechtsvergleichende Untersuchung zu Grundfragen der subjektiven Verfahrenskonzentration (Tübingen: Mohr Siebeck, 1993), p. 94; D. Haß, Die

Green Paper, the German Federal Council (*Bundesrat*), for example, refers to opt-out tools as being contradictory with the principle of individual rights enforcement as well as causing constitutional concerns.[125] However, this apprehension seems to be unsubstantiated in the context of scattered damages where the individual interest in rights enforcement is considerably low, if existing at all. Several judgments of the European Court of Human Rights explain that there are certain exceptions to the rule of Article 6 that each affected individual must necessarily be given the opportunity to decide on the fate of his or her claim and to the principle that the claims should not be pursued without the approval of those affected. Two examples of this are *Lithgow and Others* v. *United Kingdom*[126] and *Wendenburg and Others* v. *Germany*.[127]

Lithgow and Others v. *United Kingdom* centres around the rights of individual shareholders in a case involving the nationalisation of the British shipbuilding industry by the Aircraft and Shipbuilding Industries Act 1977. In the nationalisation proceedings, the shareholders and their interests were represented by a state-appointed representative. Direct participation of individual shareholders was excluded. The Court decided that 'the right of access to the courts ... is not absolute but may be subject to limitations'[128] and that the 'limitation on a direct right of access for every individual shareholder ... pursued a legitimate aim, namely the desire to avoid, in the context of a large-scale nationalisation measure, a multiplicity of claims and proceedings brought by individual shareholders'.[129]

In *Wendenburg and Others* v. *Germany*, the European Court of Human Rights had to decide an application by eighteen German attorneys with respect to their individual rights to be heard before the German Federal Constitutional Court. Earlier, the German Federal Constitutional Court had declared § 25 German Federal Barristers Act (*Bundesrechtsanwaltsordnung*), which granted attorneys certain exclusive rights of audience at appellate courts in several German federal states (*Länder*), to be unconstitutional. In their application to the European

---

Gruppenklage: Wege zur prozessualen Bewältigung von Massenschäden (Munich: VVF, 1996), p. 326.

[125] Resolution of the Bundesrat on the Green Paper from the Commission of the European Communities on Consumer Collective Redress, 13 February 2009, 951/08, para. 23.

[126] *Lithgow and Others* v. *United Kingdom* (1986) 8 EHRR 329.

[127] *Wendenburg and Others* v. *Germany* (2003) Eur.Ct.H.R. 71630/01.

[128] *Lithgow and Others* v. *United Kingdom*, Recital 194.

[129] *Ibid.*, Recital 197.

Court of Human Rights, Albrecht Wendenburg and seventeen of his colleagues claimed that the abolition of § 25 had deprived them of their right
to property, because most of their income had resulted from representing clients at the appellate courts. They further argued that their rights
under Article 6 ECHR were violated, as they were not given a chance to be
heard in the hearing before the German Federal Constitutional Court. It
was only the respective bar associations that were heard on their behalf.
The European Court of Human Rights confirmed the view of the German
Federal Constitutional Court regarding the compatibility of the limitation of individual rights with Article 6 and explained that 'in proceedings
involving a decision for a collective number of individuals, it is not always
required or even possible that every individual concerned is heard before
the court'.[130] In a similar vein to these two decisions of the European
Court of Human Rights are several judgments by national constitutional
courts. All these judgments emphasise that superior public and collective
interests can justify the limitation of standing to collective plaintiff bodies that represent individual interests without giving affected individuals
the right to be heard in the respective court proceeding.[131]

Several voices from academia agree with this stance. In the context of
scattered damages, Stadler, for example, links the discussion to what I
called public interests and argues that '[i]f ... a large number of consumers
have suffered only small damage due to an unlawful act [i.e., a scattered
damage], taking action against the defendant is of supra-individual or
common [public] interest and fulfils primarily a market regulatory function'.[132] For such a scenario, she defends opt-out mechanisms and argues
against possible constitutional concerns by weighing individual interests against public interests. She rightly comes to the conclusion that the
'[c]onstitutional concern against the opt-out principle does not weigh too
heavily for very small claims as individual lawsuits are no real alternative
for consumers and the common interest to react to the unlawful act of the
defendant may prevail over the individual's right to decide for him or her-
self whether to sue the wrongdoer or not'.[133] The last part of this sentence

---

[130] *Wendenburg and Others* v. *Germany*, Recital 3.
[131] Kodek, 'Collective Redress in Austria', 89, with reference to two judgments of the Austrian
Constitutional Court (*Verfassungsgerichtshof*; VfGH): judgment of 15 December 1994,
G 126/93 (= VfSlg 13,989); judgment of 11 December 1996, G 52/95 (= VfSlg 14,709).
[132] Stadler, 'Group Actions as a Remedy to Enforce Consumer Interests', p. 325. For further arguments in a similar vein see Stadler, *Bündelung von Interessen im Zivilprozess*,
p. 1; G. E. Kodek, 'Möglichkeiten zur gesetzlichen Regelung von Massenverfahren im
Zivilprozess', *ecolex*, (2005), 751, 752; Kodek, 'Collective Redress in Austria', 89.
[133] Stadler, 'Group Actions as a Remedy to Enforce Consumer Interests', p. 325.

might even be interpreted as a justification for exceptional *mandatory collective representation*, i.e., cases of collective redress in which affected individuals are not even given the chance to opt out. Such mandatory representation-style collective actions undeniably guarantee that the largest possible number of individual claims are grouped together. Using such a mechanism to respond to consumer damages would ensure that the highest possible degree of deterrence and compensation is reached. However, because it would not allow individual consumers to pursue their individual claims, mandatory representation, if used, should be used rather as an exception and be limited to those scenarios, where it could – with good reason – be ruled out that individuals would be willing to take individual actions.

There are in fact examples that show that even in opt-out sceptical Member States, certain tools that are neither opt-in nor test case devices have been implemented for suing for scattered damages. A prominent example that also touches upon consumer interests is the German *Gewinnabschöpfung* (skimming-off procedure) pursuant to § 10 German Act Against Unfair Competition (*Gesetz gegen den unlauteren Wettbewerb* (UWG)), the UWG skimming-off procedure.[134] It rests on the aforementioned idea of sacrificing individual interests for the sake of public interests in securing legal compliance from businesses. Among others,

---

[134] The UWG skimming-off procedure is crafted as a mechanism to fight practices in the field of unfair competition by allowing designated private bodies and/or public authorities to sue for an aggregate amount of damages in cases where the total amount at stake is high, but individual claims are too small for the affected consumers to make it worthwhile to sue. The mechanism of the UWG skimming-off procedure cannot really be classified as either an opt-out based tool or a mandatory representation device. Instead, it represents a *sui generis* form of collective redress tool for scattered damages (that is not based on opt-in). § 10(2) UWG reads: 'Such payments as were made by the debtor, because of the contravention, to third parties or the state shall be deducted from the profit. So far as the debtor made such payments only at a time subsequent to satisfaction of the claim pursuant to subsection (1), the competent agency of the Federation shall reimburse the debtor the profit thus paid in the sum of the recorded payments.' For comments on this type of skimming-off see H. Ofner, 'Gewinnabschöpfung und funktional ähnliche Instrumente – eine rechtsvergleichende Kurzanalyse' in Reiffenstein and Pirker-Hörmann (eds.), *Defizite kollektiver Rechtsdurchsetzung*, pp. 61–8. For the quite similarly designed *Vorteilsabschöpfung* (skimming-off in the context of an infringement of the German Act Against Restraints of Competition – GWB; GWB skimming-off procedure), see § 34a GWB. The latter, however, does not grant consumer associations standing in a skimming-off procedure (see § 34a in combination with § 33(2) GWB). For a discussion of the GWB skimming-off procedure see H. Köhler, 'Klagebefugnis der Verbraucherverbände de lege lata und de lege ferenda' in S. Augenhofer (ed.), *Verbraucherrecht im Umbruch* (Tübingen: Mohr Siebeck, 2012), pp. 65–72.

qualified consumer associations are given the opportunity to sue for an aggregate amount of scattered damages suffered by consumers due to a violation of certain provisions of the UWG.[135]

Unfortunately, though, the UWG skimming-off procedure shows some grave flaws, which make it more or less useless – Micklitz refers to it as a 'nice colourful paper tiger'.[136] One significant, practical problem with the device is that it only covers intentionally caused scattered damages.[137] This, in synergy with the fact that any amount won would have to be passed to the public purse, creates an unacceptable cost risk for consumer associations who would have to bear the cost risk without receiving anything in return.[138] To make the device more attractive in a practical sense, i.e., to convince those who are granted standing to get involved, the introduction of some kind of incentive would be clearly advantageous. Nevertheless, the UWG skimming-off procedure and some other national examples[139] are clear indicators that non-opt-in devices are realisable in practice. And since it can be assumed that they cover more scattered damages than any opt-in tool, they clearly have the potential to be a more viable tool than their opt-in counterparts.

Two further decisions are required: should one prefer group actions or representative actions and who should be given standing: public authorities, private bodies and/or private individuals?

A little earlier, I discussed two threats that opt-out tools could pose. The misuse of opt-out mechanisms could either infringe on business interests (blackmail settlements) or consumer and/or public interests

---

[135] See § 8(3)(3) UWG for details.

[136] H.-W. Micklitz, 'Collective Private Enforcement of Consumer Law: The Key Questions' in van Boom and Loos (eds.), *Collective Enforcement of Consumer Law*, p. 18. For additional critical comments see A. Stadler, 'Individueller und kollektiver Rechtsschutz im Verbraucherrecht' in H.-W. Micklitz (ed.), *Verbraucherrecht in Deutschland – Stand und Perspektiven* (Baden-Baden: Nomos, 2005), pp. 336–9.

[137] See Stadler, 'Erfahrungen mit den Gewinnabschöpfungsansprüchen', pp. 105–12; German Bundestag, 'Zwölfter Zwischenbericht der Enquete-Kommission "Internet und digitale Gesellschaft" – Verbraucherschutz', report, (2013), p. 37 (with references in note 130) (on file with the author).

[138] Stadler, 'Erfahrungen mit den Gewinnabschöpfungsansprüchen', pp. 108–9 with further references.

[139] Denmark, Portugal and The Netherlands, for example, use – to a greater or lesser extent – opt-out based models. For details see IMCO, 'Overview of Existing Collective Redress Schemes in EU Member States'. For positive comments on opt-out see R. Mulheron, 'The Case for an Opt-out Class Action for European Member States: A Legal and Empirical Analysis', *Columbia Journal of European Law*, 15 (2009), 409–53; Lindblom, 'Sweden', 240.

(fake collective actions). Certain safeguards need to be installed to prevent either one from occurring.[140] The most obvious choice is to limit the standing to certain carefully chosen public authorities and/or private bodies and to exclude individuals from the list of possible claimants in opt-out based (and, if chosen, also mandatory representation) collective actions. A look at those Member States that already have one or more collective redress mechanisms in place reveals that some Member States have traditionally relied on public authorities, while others prefer private bodies as a collective claimant. Hence, it makes sense to allow Member States to build on their experience. Instead of choosing a one-size-fits-all approach, national legislators should be given the chance to autonomously choose between certain public authorities and private bodies, or to even pick both. This would guarantee that only public authorities and private bodies that fulfil certain objective criteria, such as being independent from the influence of traders, having sufficient financial support, a sufficient number of personnel and appropriate experience or knowledge in the field of consumer law, are permitted to represent multilayer consumer interests in collective proceedings.

Relying on the decisions of national legislators to vest only experienced and well-staffed/well-equipped representative bodies with collective enforcement rights might be one way to limit possible misuse. Additional mechanisms could further contribute to the proper use of collective actions. For example, with the help of shortened initial screening procedures, courts could be allowed to single out clearly abusive claims. Furthermore, the loser-pays principle is undeniably important, as plaintiffs would have to carefully assess their chance of success in bringing a case to court. This assessment requires experience and legal knowledge and thereby closes the argumentative circle, as it can be assumed that those public authorities and/or private bodies that are designated as collective claimants by their Member States best fulfil these requirements (or could easily acquire those skills).

This leads to the question of which form is more suitable: group actions or representative actions. Because the actual difference between these two types of collective action – if understood as defined earlier[141] – primarily

---

[140] For comments on possible safeguard mechanisms to be used in collective actions see C. Hodges and R. Money-Kyrle, 'Safeguards in Collective Actions', report for the Foundation for Law, Justice and Society, 2012, available at www.fljs.org/files/publications/Collective-Actions.pdf.

[141] See 'The Road towards the Green Paper on Consumer Collective Redress' above (in particular the text at notes 26 to 30).

relates to the question of how collective action judgments are enforced, and Member States traditionally take different approaches in this respect, there is no actual need to decide at the EU level. The final decision of which category to choose should be left to the discretion of the Member States, who would be the best addressee to decide which of the two better fits into their national judicial systems.

Mass damages

Mass damages are not characterised by the same type of rational disinterest concerns as scattered damages. Factors such as the disproportionate amount of time to be invested in pursuing an individual claim or low-value amounts that would not 'convince' consumers to pursue their claims are – if they exist at all – negligible in mass damages. Nevertheless, a certain rational disinterest in pursuing individual claims exists in mass damages. Here it is, however, primarily the high cost risk that deters harmed consumers from instituting individual legal proceedings. Collective actions could to some extent help to reduce the individual cost risk because in many Member States costs increase degressively the higher the amount in dispute and the individual relative cost risk thus usually decreases if consumers have the chance to join collective actions. Put differently, the higher the total amount sued for, the lower the increase in court costs and attorney fees and most importantly, the lower the relative cost risk inherent to the loser-pays principle. This is also true in relation to individual actions and collective actions. In other words, because of the higher total amount in dispute in cases of collective actions, the respective individual (proportionate) cost risk attributable to each consumer, if they join a collective action, would be lower than in an individual proceeding.[142] Collective proceedings thus can – from a financial perspective – more easily incentivise consumers to pursue their claims.

With the help of some studies (and the *Deutsche Telekom* case), I have already explained that despite the fact that some form of rational disinterest exists in the case of mass damages, consumers are more willing to

---

[142] P. Rott, 'Kollektive Klagen von Verbraucherorganisationen in Deutschland' in Casper *et al.* (eds.), *Auf dem Weg zu einer europäischen Sammelklage?*, p. 265. Cost savings in the course of collective actions result further from the joint usability of expert witnesses' opinions or joint taking of evidence (see A. Stadler, 'Rechtspolitischer Ausblick zum kollektiven Rechtsschutz' in Meller-Hannich (ed.), *Kollektiver Rechtsschutz im Zivilprozess*, p. 114). For a general comparison of legal costs of court proceedings from an international perspective see Hodges *et al.* (eds.), *The Costs and Funding of Civil Litigation*, esp. pp. 114–31.

launch individual actions (or join collective proceedings) than in the case of scattered damages. This is due to the prospect of winning a relatively high amount; whereas in the case of scattered damages, a cost–benefit analysis would usually deter consumers from suing individually.

Several considerations need to be taken into account when choosing a suitable collective action device for mass damages. The observations above show that unlike with scattered damages, where mathematical consider-ations in combination with rational disinterest concerns ask for opt-out tools (or in some cases would even allow for mandatory representation), opt-out options are not necessarily needed to facilitate individuals' rights enforcement in the case of mass damages. The prospect of winning a rela-tively high amount would be a big enough incentive for a considerable number of consumers to pursue their claims. Further, one should not forget that Article 6 ECHR concerns remain strong. It might be nearly impossible to guarantee that all affected consumers would necessarily have an actual chance to decide on the fate of their relatively high individ-ual damage (compared with individual damages involved in the scattered damage scenario), which would be dragged into an opt-out proceeding unless they opt out. Furthermore, as most Member States have tradition-ally based their judicial systems in private law matters on the idea that initiating litigation rests on the initiative of the harmed individual, indi-vidual mass damages should only be joined in a collective action if the harmed individuals declare that they want to have their rights enforced in that way. Forcing individuals to react if they do *not* want to sue is not com-patible with this idea. All these concerns, as well as the fact that the threat of misuse is higher with opt-out tools, explain why these are not popular with most national legislators and why they are not a suitable solution for mass damages.

This leaves two possible mechanisms: opt-in tools and test cases. Opt-in based devices (in the form of both group actions and representative actions)[143] are undeniably a suitable option. They can lower the individual cost risk and reduce the number of parallel cases, i.e., they could lessen the burden for courts without the comparable concerns of opt-out tools. In addition, most Member States that have already implemented collect-ive redress at a national level have based their mechanisms on opt-in and are thus familiar with such devices.

Nevertheless, and despite the fact that the risk of misuse is lower for opt-in devices, similar anti-abusive mechanisms as discussed in the

---

[143] For a similar argument with respect to the devices discussed in the case of scattered damages see 'Scattered Damages' above (in particular text at note 141).

context of scattered damages could be introduced to reduce the still existing risk of misuse. Shortened initial screening procedures to assess the admissibility of a claim could also be used in the case of mass damages. Also the pre-selection of private bodies and public authorities to sue on behalf of consumers could be applied here. And to increase the transparency and visibility of competent public authorities and/or private bodies for redress-seeking individuals, some kind of revocable quality seal (which would be granted to qualified public authorities and/or private bodies based on state accreditation and quality evaluation) could be introduced.

The fact that the risk of misuse is considerably lower in opt-in based cases enables the granting of the right to initiate proceedings not only to public authorities and private bodies, but also to individual consumers. If it was found necessary to further reduce the risk of misuse by *private individuals*, one could, in addition to the aforementioned court screening procedures, also consider the introduction of some kind of initial supervision of or assistance for individual private plaintiffs and their attorneys by either private bodies or public authorities specialising in compensatory collective redress. These bodies/authorities could then (preferably on request) provide consumers who are interested in opting in with a feasibility assessment of the planned action as an (unbinding) advisory opinion.

An alternative option to the opt-in tool is the introduction of *enhanced* test cases. Many ordinary test-case tools face two problems: the absence of a binding effect for parallel cases (in those cases where it would be desirable from an affected consumer's point of view, i.e., if the test case led to a favourable result) and problems related to prescription periods for those cases that await a decision in the 'lead' test case. Regarding the latter, a statutory suspension of the time limitation period for similar claims should be made standard (where not existing already). To solve the first issue, a semi-lateral binding effect, i.e., binding only for the respective trader, should be considered for those cases that are decided in favour of consumers. Such a semi-lateral binding character would guarantee that consumers in parallel cases could benefit from a favourable test-case decision without being deprived of the chance to reach a better solution on an individual basis.[144]

---

[144] For an example of a semi-lateral binding effect see the Greek test-case model (for details see Alexandridou and Karypidou, 'Country Report Greece', p. 18; IMCO, 'Overview of Existing Collective Redress Schemes in EU Member States', pp. 24–5).

Further questions

Some further issues deserve closer attention in the context of compensatory collective redress. In this section, I will deal with questions regarding proper funding and some procedural issues in an international setting. However, before turning to these two, I shall answer a question the answer to which the attentive reader has surely been awaiting. Earlier, I differentiated between scattered damages, i.e., multiple damages of low and lowest individual value, and mass damages, i.e., multiple damages of higher individual value. Where then should the line be drawn between these two categories in a pan-EU framework? Providing a precise answer clearly goes beyond the scope of this book and would require an in-depth comparative analysis of the monetary disincentives to engage in collective actions in each of the twenty-eight Member States. Nevertheless, some observations are of help to get closer to an answer.

The starting point to determine the threshold between scattered damages and mass damages can be seen in a cost-benefit analysis that could single out those claims of a low and lowest value that make little or no sense to pursue individually for purely mathematical reasons. Such amounts clearly fall under the category of scattered damages. Earlier in this book, I explained that differences in household income between the Member States as well as differences with respect to court costs, attorney fees and judicial systems in general can impact on the individual cost-benefit thresholds. These observations could be used to argue for a flexible system with different thresholds in different Member States.

However, the following considerations speak against the introduction of a flexible system. It can be assumed that any pan-EU compensatory collective redress tool would very likely be crafted in a way to facilitate not only purely domestic collective redress and 'bilateral' cross-border collective redress (i.e., where claims of consumers from Member State A can be pursued against a trader from Member State B), but also to facilitate collective rights enforcement that includes affected consumers from different Member States. The suggested mechanisms for scattered damages and mass damages are based on different technical ideas that cannot be easily mixed into one and the same proceeding (opt-out tools or even mandatory representation versus opt-in devices or test cases). Thus, applying a flexible system with different thresholds between scattered damages and mass damages in different Member States would very likely complicate actual proceedings and could lead to unjustified differentiations between citizens from different Member States in the same action. Even if it were possible to mix the approaches recommended for mass damages (opt-out alone or combined with mandatory representation) and for scattered damages (opt-in and/or enhanced test cases) in the same collective action proceeding, it would be questionable whether such an approach would be acceptable because consumers would be classified into different categories determined only by the place of their habitual residence. Thus, it might make more sense to come up with a concrete, standardised amount to differentiate between scattered damages and mass damages that leads to the same dividing line in each of the twenty-eight Member States.

To facilitate the search for an amount, one should further take into account that opt-out tools and/or mandatory representation should be the exception rather than the norm, as explained with reflections on possible Article 6 ECHR concerns and the traditional ideas of the Member States to pursue private claims. One should therefore choose a lower rather than a higher threshold to differentiate between the two multiple damage categories. Based on the earlier discussed fact that the 'rational disinterest thresholds' (i.e., the question of the amount that has to be at stake to facilitate individual rights enforcement by an acceptable number of people) between the two are identified at different levels in different Member States, one would have to look for an amount commonly acceptable in all Member States using an analysis that also takes non-monetary rational disinterest issues into consideration. The ideal amount for differentiating between scattered damages and mass damages should be determined by the Member State with the lowest differentiation between these two categories. This would guarantee that traditional procedural ideas of self-determination and justified interests in actively joining collective actions are also satisfied in Member States with a lower dividing line between scattered damages and mass damages.

One contributing factor of practical importance for the success of collective redress initiated by a private body or a public authority is the financial means of collective claimants. This issue is also a popular argument for some commentators who argue against granting standing to private bodies. In their opinion, private bodies necessarily suffer from insufficient financial means, which would not make them a useful alternative to public authorities in collective redress.[145] However, looking at the situation in the Member States reveals that several countries have

---

[145] See, for example, D. R. Hensler, 'The Globalization of Class Actions: An Overview', *The ANNALS of the American Academy of Political and Social Science*, 622 (2009), 7, 23; Hodges, *Reform of Class and Representative Actions*, pp. 3 and 47; C. Hodges, 'Collectivism: Evaluating the Effectiveness of Public and Private Models for Regulating Consumer Protection' in van Boom and Loos (eds.), *Collective Enforcement of Consumer*

traditionally and successfully been relying on consumer rights enforcement by private bodies. Germany and Austria, as good examples, show how useful private bodies can be in practice. Thus, it makes much more sense to leave the decision of whether or not to mandate public authorities and/or private bodies with collective redress tasks to the individual Member States.

To minimise the cost risk for collective plaintiffs, one could first and foremost consider getting (generally)[146] rid of the loser-pays principle. However, as indicated earlier, the loser-pays principle is of practical importance because of its misuse-preventing potential, as potential plaintiffs have to 'think twice' before launching an action. Instead of removing the cost risk posed by the loser-pays principle, there are other, more suitable means of addressing financial concerns and considerations.

One appropriate means would be to ask Member States to ensure that competent private bodies and public authorities have sufficient financial support. As far as public authorities are concerned, their funding is generally guaranteed by public means. With respect to private bodies, providing (at least partial) public funding, as is already occurring for example in Germany and Austria, should be worth considering also in other Member States.

Private bodies could also be encouraged to generate extra funds to support their activities. This could be done, for example, by marketing in-depth consumer information magazines or by offering consumer interest court representation services subject to a reasonable annual membership fee. Member States could further make the accreditation of private bodies as collective claimants conditional upon signing up to mandatory legal insurance that would cover cost risks from collective actions launched by private bodies.[147]

Law, pp. 207–28; For arguments for taking a flexible approach, i.e., not to exclude private bodies from the list of possible claimants see Cafaggi and Micklitz, 'Administrative and Judicial Enforcement in Consumer Protection: The Way Forward', pp. 416–19. For the view that the reliance on public authorities as collective claimants is 'probably idealistic' see D. Fairgrieve and G. Howells, 'Collective Redress Procedures – European Debates', *International and Comparative Law Quarterly*, 52 (2009), 379, 408. For comments on this issue from the perspective of the newer Member States see A. Bakardjieva Engelbrekt, 'Public and Private Enforcement of Consumer Law in Central and Eastern Europe: Institutional Choice in the Shadow of EU Enlargement' in Cafaggi and Micklitz (eds.), *New Frontiers of Consumer Protection*, pp. 91–136.

[146] For an overview of the situation in the EU see Hodges *et al.* (eds.), *The Costs and Funding of Civil Litigation*, in particular pp. 114–31 (Table 1).

[147] On the benefits of legal insurance for compensatory collective redress see K. Purnhagen, 'United We Stand, Divided We Fall? Collective Redress in the EU from the Perspective of Insurance Law', *European Review of Private Law*, 21 (2013), 479–506.

Three further solutions are worthwhile considering. However, because all three could (at least in some Member States) create conflict with the concept of 'the winner takes all', which is still followed in several jurisdictions,[148] they should only be considered as a last resort (in combination with safeguards to prevent misuse). They should further – ideally – be limited to scattered damage cases in which there is absolutely *no* doubt that affected consumers would not launch individual proceedings (i.e., cases for which mandatory representation would be an alternative to collective actions based on opt-out tool actions). First, a pan-EU compensatory collective redress framework could introduce a comprehensive system allowing for third-party funding (such systems are currently emerging in several Member States). The suggestions made by the Collective Redress Recommendation in paragraphs 15–16 and 32 contain several ideas worth considering to prevent misuse in this case. Such means of preventing the possible misuse of third-party funding to help allay any concerns include far-reaching restrictions on remuneration for third-party funding companies and rules to reduce the possibility of influencing the claimant's litigative strategy. Second, the earlier discussed suggestion of the Collective Redress Recommendation regarding the exceptional use of 'soft'[149] forms of contingency fees (paragraphs 29–30) – where not already existing in one way or the other at the national level – could also form part of (at the very least) a 'last resort solution' if other funding methods failed. It should be noted again, however, that from the perspective of preventing possible misuse, one must make sure that US-style contingency fees are not permitted. Third, plaintiff bodies could be allowed to partially or fully retain winnings. This option could and should be linked to the condition that they use such amounts to prepare for future collective actions.

Any comprehensive regime of pan-EU consumer compensatory collective redress also faces the need to take account of questions regarding the place of jurisdiction if it is also to apply to cross-border cases. In an EU context and especially with regard to traditional, compensatory individual redress, cross-border questions are principally handled by the regime of the Brussels I Regulation.[150] Articles 15–17 Brussels I Regulation (and

---

[148] For certain exceptions see Hodges *et al.* (eds.), *The Costs and Funding of Civil Litigation*, pp. 132–3 (Table 2).

[149] See paras. 29–30 Collective Redress Recommendation for details.

[150] Council Regulation (EC) No 44/2001 on jurisdiction and the recognition and enforcement of judgments in civil and commercial matters, 22 December 2000, OJ 2001 No. L12/1.

the identically worded Articles 17–19 Brussels I Regulation Recast,[151] replacing the older version as of 10 January 2015) deal with jurisdiction in certain B2C contract disputes. Article 16(1) Brussels I Regulation/Article 18(1) Brussels I Regulation Recast gives affected consumers the chance to choose between suing in the courts of their Member State and suing in the trader's home country. This special jurisdiction provision is undeniably of practical importance because it can be assumed that most consumers would prefer to sue 'at home' due to language concerns or feelings of trust in their home country's judiciary.[152]

Unfortunately the Brussels I regime is ill-equipped to *generally* facilitate cross-border consumer compensatory collective redress. Two issues should be mentioned in this context. In the landmark decision *Shearson Lehmann Hutton Inc. v. TVB Treuhandgesellschaft für Vermögensverwaltung und Beteiligungen mbH*[153] (*Shearson Lehmann Hutton*), the Court of Justice of the European Union (CJEU)[154] ruled that the favourable jurisdiction of the consumer's home country cannot be used for claims made by representative bodies on behalf of consumers. The Advocate General explained that the pertinent provisions can be applied 'only by a consumer in relation to a contract which he himself concluded'.[155] This understanding, of course, reduces to absurdity the consumer-favourable rationale behind Article 16(1) Brussels I Regulation (Article 18(1) Brussels I Regulation Recast[156] does not change the wording), which aims to facilitate the launch of consumer claims in the likely scenario that public authorities or private bodies sue on behalf of consumers and not the consumers themselves. The rational disinterest of consumers, which would intensify if they could only sue in a foreign country, is kept within a certain limit with the help

---

[151] Regulation (EC) No 1215/2012 on jurisdiction and the recognition and enforcement of judgments in civil and commercial matters (recast), 12 December 2012, OJ 2012 No. L351/1.

[152] For comments on the question of practical problems the applicability of foreign laws can pose for the competent courts see M. Stürner, 'Effektivität des europäischen Kollisionsrechts und nationals Verfahrensrecht' in Bruns *et al.* (eds.), *Festschrift für Rolf Stürner zum 70. Geburtstag*, pp. 1084–90.

[153] Case C-89/91, *Shearson Lehmann Hutton Inc. v. TVB Treuhandgesellschaft für Vermögensverwaltung und Beteiligungen mbH* [1993] ECR I-139.

[154] It should be noted that in the context of this book the umbrella term CJEU is used when referring to judgments at the EU level.

[155] Opinion of the Advocate-General in *Shearson Lehmann Hutton*, Recital 28.

[156] It should be noted that the 2013 Proposal for a Regulation Amending the Brussels I Regulation (Recast) (Proposal for a Regulation amending Regulation (EU) No 1215/2012 on jurisdiction and the recognition and enforcement of judgments in civil and commercial matters, 26 June 2013, COM(2013) 554 final) would not change the wording.

of Article 16(1) Brussels I Regulation/Article 18(1) Brussels I Regulation Recast. However, for collective redress launched by public authorities or private bodies, the argumentation of the CJEU worsens the situation again in the mentioned cases (as defined in the pertinent judgments of the CJEU); it leads to a rational disinterest by public authorities or private bodies to file a collective actions claim in a foreign Member State. From the viewpoint of enhanced consumer access to justice, the argumentation of the CJEU sounds very unfortunate to say the least.

Admittedly, and much to the (justified) regret of several European scholars (such as Astrid Stadler,[157] Peter Rott,[158] and Jonathan Hill[159]), the Brussels I regime does not explicitly deal with the issue of cross-border compensatory collective actions brought by public authorities or private bodies on behalf of harmed consumers. However, some commentators, such as Reinhold Geimer or Jan Kropholler and Jan von Hein, have shown that there are certain scenarios where such claimants can find (and actually have found) recourse in favourable, special jurisdiction under the present Brussels I regime.[160] Nevertheless, the Brussels I regime needs to be clarified to broadly facilitate the compensatory collective enforcement of consumer rights by public authorities and private bodies. One solution might be that the CJEU itself reconsiders its interpretation of the Brussels I regime. If that turns out to be impossible, the Union legislator might want to consider aligning the wording or adding a new provision for consumer collective redress to comprehensively encompass actions taken by public authorities and/or private bodies on behalf of consumers.

Also another likely scenario could pose a headache for stakeholders. Unfortunately the Brussels I regime is not yet prepared for cases of true pan-EU collective redress to be understood as cases in which consumer claims from *different* Member States are grouped into a single

---

[157] A. Stadler, 'Die grenzüberschreitende Durchsetzbarkeit von Sammelklagen' in Casper et al. (eds.), *Auf dem Weg zu einer europäischen Sammelklage?*, p. 158.

[158] P. Rott, 'Cross-Border Collective Damage Actions in the EU' in Cafaggi and Micklitz (eds.), *New Frontiers of Consumer Protection*, p. 383.

[159] J. Hill, *Cross-border Consumer Contracts* (Oxford University Press, 2008), p. 98.

[160] Geimer, 'Art. 15 EuGVVO' in Geimer and Schütze (eds.), *Europäisches Zivilverfahrensrecht*, Article 15 EuGVVO, para. 20 (with references at notes 75 and 76); Kropholler and von Hein, *Europäisches Zivilprozessrecht*, Article 15 EuGVO, para. 12 (with references at note 48). For further examples see H. Koch, 'Internationaler Kollektiver Rechtsschutz' in Meller-Hannich (ed.), *Kollektiver Rechtsschutz im Zivilprozess*, pp. 54–5. Lisa Tortell gives examples regarding the flexible approaches by Portuguese courts towards cross-border actions taken by the Portuguese Association for Consumer Protection, DECO (see L. Tortell, 'Country Report Portugal', report, (2008), p. 10, available at ec.europa.eu/consumers/redress_cons/pt-country-report-final.pdf).

collective action claim. The special jurisdiction of Article 16(1) Brussels I Regulation/Article 18(1) Brussels I Regulation Recast, which allows consumers to sue in their Member States, could not be applied in such a case, because consumers would come from different Member States. The explicit wording of Article 16(1)Brussels I Regulation/Article 18(1) Brussels I Regulation Recast does not allow consumers to sue in a Member State that is not their home country (unless it is the trader's Member State).[161] Under the current Brussels I regime, collective actions comprising individual consumer claims from different Member States could thus, at best, be only filed in the courts of the trader's home country, and not in the home countries of affected consumers that differ from the trader's home country. Just as in the aforementioned case, it remains doubtful whether this could incentivise consumers to pursue their claims with the help of collective actions. One possible way to achieve some improvement would be to allow consumers to have their claims pursued by collective actions filed in the Member State in which the majority of affected consumers is domiciled.

---

[161] For comments on the innovative Dutch approach that gives the Amsterdam Court of Appeal the competence to declare collective settlements binding on the parties irrespective of where the consumers reside see the references in note 4 above and for further details see H. Lith, 'The Dutch Collective Settlements Act and Private International Law', report, (2010), available at ec.europa.eu/competition/consultations/2011_collective_redress/saw_annex_en.pdf; B. Allemeersch, 'Transnational Class Settlements: Lessons from Converium' in Wrbka et al. (eds.), Collective Actions, pp. 364–84; X. E. Kramer, 'Enforcing Mass Settlements in the European Judicial Area: EU Policy and the Strange Case of Dutch Collective Settlements (WCAM)' in Hodges and Stadler (eds.), Resolving Mass Disputes, pp. 63–90; I. Tzankova and D. Hensler, 'Collective Settlements in the Netherlands: Some Empirical Observations' in ibid., pp. 91–105.

6

Where do we go from here?

The procedural law devices outlined in this part of the book show that the Commission has intensified and broadened its regulation of consumer-related procedural law issues over the years. Especially in the new millennium, additional procedural mechanisms have been launched to strengthen the procedural side of consumer access to justice. All three access to justice waves identified by the Florence Project in the 1970s have, to a greater or lesser extent, been taken into account in this respect.

Nevertheless, none of the procedural law devices initiated at the EU level is without fault. This does not mean that the efforts taken so far have been in vain, but the observations in the chapters above illustrate that there is still ample room for improvement. Some issues are by nature limited to certain mechanisms, such as the earlier examples of the lack of an option for consumers to freely choose between litigation and ADR (without having to obtain the trader's consent) or missing guidelines on how to appoint suitable attorneys in cross-border legal aid cases under the Legal Aid Directive. Other issues, such as insufficient consumer awareness, insufficient awareness of other important stakeholders in the respective procedural mechanism as well as limited financial resources to successfully implement the procedural tools, pervade more than just a single mechanism. It obviously makes little sense to introduce a new mechanism without first planning for accompanying measures that are necessary to make the respective tool both visible and workable in practice, and not only on paper. The aim of enhancing the internal market with the help of new procedural devices[1] is a legitimate goal, but as Stephen Weatherill

---

[1] For the case of the ESCP see Recital 7 Small Claims Regulation where it states that '[t]he distortion of competition within the internal market due to imbalances with regard to the functioning of the procedural means afforded to creditors in different Member States entails the need for Community legislation that guarantees a level playing-field for creditors and debtors throughout the European Union' (emphasis added). In the case of the 2009 Injunctions Directive see its Recital 5, which explains that '[t]hose difficulties [i.e. the alleged lack of effectiveness of national measures] can disrupt the smooth functioning

succinctly notes: 'The problem is, in short, that the development of an integrated European market has accelerated far ahead of any notion of an integrated [well thought-out] pattern of European law enforcement.'[2]

We will have to wait and see if and how the Commission will try to remedy the existing shortcomings. In some instances, for example in the case of the ESCP, the Commission has already tried to address some of the most striking concerns (with its 2013 Small Claims Regulation Proposal). Nevertheless, more can and should be done if one really wants to enhance, to the best possible extent, the procedural side of access to justice. The mandatory introduction of comprehensive compensatory collective redress tools could add an additional, interesting new perspective in the quest for perfection. Part IV of this book will discuss further possible suggestions that could be of help. However, before turning to that issue, in Part III I will discuss the second layer of access to justice 2.0: substantive consumer law. By doing so, I will show how substantive consumer laws could provide valuable perspectives for enhancing consumer access to justice.

---

of the internal market, their consequence being that it is sufficient to move the source of an unlawful practice to another country in order to place it out of reach of all forms of enforcement' (emphasis added).

[2] Weatherill, *EU Consumer Law and Policy,* p. 293.

PART III

Substantive law – complementing access to justice 2.0

Member States may adopt or retain the most stringent provisions ... to ensure a maximum degree of protection for the consumer.

(Article 8 Unfair Contract Terms Directive)

7

Widening the scope of the value-oriented justice discussion

In Part II of this book I dealt with the traditional understanding of access to justice and explained how the Commission intensified its efforts to take stronger account of what I defined in Part I as value-oriented justice. I showed that the procedural devices covered in Part II have certain deficiencies that need to be remedied to enable them to reach their full potential. Increasing consumer confidence (and thus, in a cross-border EU context, eventually enhancing the internal market) would require more, however, than just fixing the stated defects. It warrants a proper consideration of consumer interests also from a substantive law perspective. In other words, a comprehensive, enhanced analysis of consumer access to justice – access to justice 2.0, as defined in Part I of this book – requires a more holistic approach and also needs to take account of key issues relating to substantive consumer law.

The issue of value-oriented justice as a key ingredient of access to justice 2.0 has already played an important role in the academic debate on European private law for many years. Several authors and studies have approached substantive EU laws, including substantive consumer laws, from a value-oriented justice perspective. One prominent example in this context is the social justice movement, which combines various legal, sociological and philosophical ideas.[1] The output and efforts of this

---

[1] For examples of contributions on social justice from legal academia see M. W. Hesselink, *CFR & Social Justice* (Munich: Sellier, 2008); H. Collins, 'Does Social Justice Require the Preservation of Diversity in the Private Laws of Member States of Europe?' in T. Wilhelmsson *et al.* (eds.), *Private Law and the Many Cultures of Europe* (Alphen aan den Rijn: Kluwer Law International, 2007), pp. 155–76; B. Lurger, 'The Future of European Contract Law between Freedom of Contract, Social Justice, and Market Rationality', *European Review of Contract Law*, 1 (2005), 442–68; H.-W. Micklitz, 'Social Justice and Access Justice in Private Law', EUI Working Papers, Law 2011/02 (2011), available at cadmus.eui.eu/bitstream/handle/1814/15706/LAW_2011_02.pdf?sequence=1; S. Weatherill, 'The Constitutional Competence of the EU to Deliver Social Justice', *European Review of Contract Law*, 2 (2006), 136–58; D. Kennedy, 'Thoughts on Coherence, Social Values and National Tradition in Private Law' in M. W. Hesselink (ed.), *The Politics of a European Civil Code* (The Hague: Kluwer Law International, 2006), pp. 9–31; A. Colombi Ciacchi,

movement have grown and intensified rapidly over the years, especially since the Commission announced plans to fully harmonise consumer law-related issues at the pan-EU level. It is fair to say that this movement has strongly contributed to the consolidation of the value-oriented justice debate and has introduced a strong analytical framework as a critical alternative to the conventional law and economics school (which has a smaller focus on value-oriented justice) in the discussion of the future of European private law.

One important result of the social justice school is the Social Justice Manifesto, which was published in 2004 by the Study Group on Social Justice in European Private Law (Social Justice Study Group), a group of eighteen scholars who aimed to critically analyse some of the more recent developments in the field of European contract law.[2] One of the main questions addressed by the Social Justice Manifesto concerned the direction that European contract law would and should take. The Social Justice Manifesto was an attempt to respond to the tradition of European private law and related policy-making to focus almost exclusively on issues of corrective justice and to leave questions of distributive justice aside, a phenomenon that is still to a certain extent found even in more recent times.[3]

'The Constitutionalization of European Contract Law: Judicial Convergence and Social Justice', *European Review of Contract Law*, 2 (2006), 167–80; R. Sefton-Green, 'Social Justice and European Identity in European Contract Law', *European Review of Contract Law*, 2 (2006), 275–86; J. W. Rutgers, 'An Optional Instrument and Social Dumping', *European Review of Contract Law*, 2 (2006), 199–212; J. W. Rutgers, 'An Optional Instrument and Social Dumping Revisited', *European Review of Contract Law*, 7 (2011), 350–9; H.-W. Micklitz, The Expulsion of the Concept from the Consumer Law and the Return of Social Elements in the Civil Law: A Bittersweet Polemic', *Journal of Consumer Policy*, 35 (2012), 283–96; U. Mattei and N. Fernanda, 'A "Social Dimension" in European Private Law? The Call for Setting a Progressive Agenda', *New England Law Review*, 41 (2006), 1–66; M. Meli, 'Social Justice, Constitutional Principles and Protection of the Weaker Contractual Party', *European Review of Contract Law*, 2 (2006), 159–66; T. Wilhelmsson, 'Varieties of Welfarism in European Contract Law', *European Law Journal*, 10 (2004), 712–33; T. Wilhelmsson, 'Welfare State Expectations, Privatisation and Private Law' in Wilhelmsson and Hurri (eds.), *From Dissonance to Sense*, pp. 3–36; K. Viitanen, 'The Crisis of the Welfare State, Privatisation and Consumers' Access to Justice' in *ibid.*, pp. 549–66; A. Somma, 'Social Justice and the Market in European Contract Law', *European Review of Contract Law*, 2 (2006), 181–98; or the contributions in Micklitz (ed.), *The Many Concepts of Social Justice in European Private Law*.

[2] Study Group on Social Justice in European Private Law, 'Social Justice in European Contract Law'.

[3] According to some authors this phenomenon can be also found at the level of academic research. Martijn Hesselink explains that, for example, the Draft Common Frame of Reference (DCFR) of 2009 focused primarily on corrective justice issues and was less

In response to this legislative approach, the Social Justice Manifesto emphasised the need for European private law to take stronger account of not only corrective justice, but also of distributive justice issues when debating on the future of European contract law. The Social Justice Manifesto considered such a holistic approach as the key to achieving a status of overall fairness for citizens. In the words of the Social Justice Study Group, their critique is as follows: 'As traditionally understood, the function of the European Community is to promote a free market, not to ensure that this market is corrected in the light of distributive aims. Accordingly, the European Community lacks a clear general mandate to pursue a scheme of fairness or distributive justice in its regulation of trade.'[4] Specifically regarding consumer law, the group added that 'the Commission usually presents consumer protection measures not so much as laws designed to help weaker parties but as measures for market correction, that is, to prevent distortions in competition'.[5] As the Union legislator would merely act as a market regulator,[6] ensuring fairness and distributive justice (important policies at the Member State level) would

concerned with issues of 'distributive justice' (Hesselink, *CFR & Social Justice*, p. 62 with reference to the Introduction of the DCFR). See further M. W. Hesselink, 'A Technical "CFR" or a Political Code? – An Introduction' in Hesselink (ed.), *The Politics of a European Civil Code*, pp. 3–8, where he asks for taking stronger account of distributive justice issues in this respect. In contrast to this view Horst Eidenmüller argues that the DCFR is a fairly progressive approach to take stronger account of distributive justice ideas. He explains as follows: 'The DCFR severely restricts contractual freedom and pursues distributive aims' (H. Eidenmüller, 'Party Autonomy, Distributive Justice and the Conclusion of Contracts in the DCFR', *European Review of Contract Law*, 5 (2009), 109, 109). At the same time he also states that 'it is certainly inefficient and often even impossible [though] to achieve the latter goal through private law' (*ibid.*).

[4] Study Group on Social Justice in European Private Law, 'Social Justice in European Contract Law', 660–1.

[5] *Ibid.*, 661.

[6] *Ibid.* This clash of interests between the Member States on the one hand and the European lawmakers on the other will also be prominently highlighted in my further analysis of substantive consumer law issues in the course of this book. See also *ibid.*, 673 where the Social Justice Study Group concludes as follows:

This Manifesto argues that in the construction of a European private law system, we need to ensure that the political process is geared towards the achievement of ideals of social justice. It is a mistake to conceive of this project as a simple measure of market building, because private law determines the basic rules governing the social justice of the market order. We need to recognise that the institutional processes suitable for the construction of a single market by means of negative integration are no longer appropriate as the European Union strives to achieve justice for its citizens. In particular, since the market plays an increasingly important role in securing distributive not be properly achieved. I will briefly return to the issue of social justice later in this book.[7]

Another example of a value-oriented statement on the EU's more recent efforts is Micklitz's analysis of the interaction between the Union legislator and European private law. Micklitz comments on (what he calls) the 'access justice'[8] or 'justice through access'[9] approach taken at the EU level. He explains that the main driving force behind the harmonisation of private laws at the EU level is the wish to facilitate consumer access to the B2C market.[10] In a similar vein as the aforementioned Social Justice Manifesto Micklitz concludes that this approach is different from national approaches towards consumer laws, which take strong account of ideas of social or distributive justice.[11]

Especially in light of the fact that the Commission has (as will be shown later)[12] increased its efforts to regulate more and more substantive law questions with the use of maximum harmonisation, the market regulation approach (as just discussed) has steadily reduced the actual means of the Member States to react to consumer needs and to implement national consumer protection policies.[13] The relatively radical approach by the EU has not found much favour among certain stakeholder groups. National policy makers, consumer representatives and those scholars who prominently take account of more comprehensive value-oriented justice arguments, in particular, have heavily criticised these developments. Stephen Weatherill succinctly comments on the EU's approach by stating that

> justice for the citizens of Europe, it is vital that its basic regulatory framework – the private law of contract – should embrace a scheme of social justice that secures a widespread acceptance.

[7] See Chapter 13 below.

[8] Micklitz, 'Social Justice and Access Justice in Private Law', p. 2.

[9] *Ibid.*

[10] Micklitz refers to this as follows: '[I]t is for the European Union to grant access justice to those who are excluded from the market or to those who face difficulties in making use of the market freedoms. European private law rules have to make sure that the weaker parties have and maintain access to the market – and to the European society' (*ibid.*).

[11] *Ibid.*, p. 20, where Micklitz concludes as follows: 'In what way does full harmonisation affect the dividing line between national protective concepts of justice and the EU model which puts emphasis on market behaviour and on a consumer who is circumspect and responsible? Full harmonisation takes away powers from the Member States.'

[12] For details on this issue see Chapter 8 below.

[13] Micklitz refers to this as follows: 'In what way does full harmonisation affect the dividing line between national protective concepts of justice and the EU model which puts emphasis on market behaviour and on a consumer who is circumspect and responsible? Full harmonisation takes away powers from the Member States' (Micklitz, 'Social Justice and Access Justice in Private Law', p. 20).

'[m]aximum harmonisation suppresses one important – national – source of consumer protection'.[14] In a similar vein is Brigitta Lurger's analysis of the implications of the shift from minimum to maximum harmonisation on national consumer protection regimes. She rightly shows that maximum harmonisation lowers the protective standards in several Member States and adds that 'maximum harmonization is … not only detrimental to the higher standards of protection presently in force in many Member States, but it also creates new sources of imprecision and uncertainty for the construction and application of the directives, and prevents the Member States from adapting the EC rules to the structures … used in their respective national private law systems'.[15] In this sense '[m]aximum harmonization … replaces the Member States' models of social justice or … considerably reduces their scope and practical importance'.[16] This approach towards the completion of the internal market is, according to Lurger, imbalanced as it forgets to take proper consideration of actual consumer needs. She explains the importance of taking account of justice considerations and national policy-making in private law making as follows: 'The … distributive effects of the rules of private law are important issues when it comes to the evaluation of the appropriateness of legal rules affecting the markets. Distributive and social justice is an important aspect in market law.'[17]

---

[14] S. Weatherill, 'Maximum or Minimum Harmonisation – What Kind of "Europe" Do We Want?' in K. Boele-Woelki and W. Grosheide (eds.), *The Future of European Contract Law* (Alphen aan den Rijn: Kluwer International Law, 2007), p. 145.

[15] B. Lurger, 'The "Social" Side of Contract Law and the New Principle of Regard and Fairness' in A. Hartkamp *et al.* (eds.), *Towards a European Civil Code* (4th edn, Alphen ann den Rijn: Kluwer Law International, 2011), pp. 355–6.

[16] B. Lurger, 'The Common Frame of Reference/Optional Code and the Various Understandings of Social Justice in Europe' in Wilhelmsson *et al.* (eds.), *Private Law and the Many Cultures of Europe*, p. 185. For a comment on the diverse understandings of the term social justice in the Member States see H.-W. Micklitz and F. Cafaggi, 'Introduction' in H.-W. Micklitz and F. Cafaggi (eds.), *European Private Law after the Common Frame of Reference* (Cheltenham: Edward Elgar, 2010), p. xxx, where Micklitz and Cafaggi explain that '[t]he underlying values of the DCFR … may compete with values enshrined in national legal orders, be it from the side of more social elements – more and even deeper social distributive justice towards a need oriented concept, as in the Scandinavian countries, or less social elements – not social distributive but commutative justice – as in the common law countries'.

[17] B. Lurger, 'Old and New Insights for the Protection of Consumers in European Private Law in the Wake of the Global Economic Crisis' in Brownsword *et al.* (eds.), *The Foundations of European Private Law*, p. 112. See *ibid.*, where she underlines her opposition towards the more recent trends in EU consumer law making as follows: 'Maximum harmonisation in consumer law should be stopped and, where necessary, revised.'

Lucinda Miller is another commentator in the field of value-oriented justice. In her study on the Europeanisation of contract law, Miller notes that 'the Commission is not very candid about the political or ideological underpinnings of its contract law programme. Nor does it address the programme's implications for social justice'.[18] She discusses this in light of the fact that the Commission is mainly interested in securing a well-functioning internal market by shifting from minimum to maximum contract law harmonisation and adds that the Commission's efforts in this respect do not take proper account of the value-oriented justice question. Miller concludes that '[o]ne can only lament the lack of debate from the Commission's quarters that focuses on the political values that European contract law should reflect. Contract law cannot be simply manipulated as a *technical* attempt to secure harmonization'[19] (emphasis added).

Christian Twigg-Flesner contributes to the discussion on the interplay between EU politics and law making, and comes to the conclusion 'that contract law is not value-neutral, and that attempts at Europeanisation cannot ignore the fact that a political dimension applies in determining the substance of particular model rules'.[20] He adds that the current efforts of the Commission are not sufficient, as the debate must not 'reduce contract law to a question of technicalities, and that the compromise between individualist and altruist rules needs to be discussed explicitly'.[21] Consequently, also Twigg-Flesner stresses that the current discussions on the future of European private law lack a more holistic approach that would properly consider the actual implications for all likely affected citizens, and not just the possible economic consequences for the internal market.

The same concerns, yet more concisely expressed, are voiced by Hugh Collins who criticises the lack of value-oriented debate in the field of private law by commenting as follows: 'Shockingly, we ... end up with a *technocratic* solution to a fundamental question about the future of Europe: the content of its private law rules'[22] (emphasis added). Martijn Hesselink adds: 'It is somewhat ironic that European legal scholars ...

---

[18] L. Miller, *The Emergence of EU Contract Law: Exploring Europeanization* (Oxford University Press, 2011), p. 152.

[19] *Ibid.*, p. 153.

[20] C. Twigg-Flesner, *The Europeanisation of Contract Law* (Abingdon: Routledge-Cavendish, 2008), p. 189.

[21] *Ibid.*

[22] H. Collins, *The European Civil Code: The Way Forward* (Cambridge University Press, 2008), p. 87.

seem to be more aware than European politicians of the need to repoliticize the CFR [i.e. what later was to become the CESL] process.'[23]

With respect to substantive European consumer law, one can conclude from this short excursion that taking strong and comprehensive account of value-oriented justice concepts adds important value to the overall debate on the future of European consumer law. Attempts to realise a strong internal market via legal tools can benefit from a holistic value-oriented discussion that takes account of both procedural law constructs and substantive law ideas. In this context, the concept of access to justice 2.0, which I defined in greater detail earlier and to which I will return in more detail later in this book,[24] deals with the question of how to benefit consumers to the greatest possible extent – not only from a procedural law point of view but also from a substantive law-content-based perspective. In the following chapters I will illustrate how the substantive law pillar – in particular with respect to consumer contract law – has evolved and developed over the years and will discuss some important, selected examples that are either already realised or still waiting in the pipeline.

---

[23] Hesselink, 'A Technical "CFR" or a Political Code?', p. 8.

[24] See Part IV 'Consumer Access to Justice 2.0 – A Multidimensional Framework' below.

8

Substantive consumer law making over time

Substantive consumer laws form the biggest group of the consumer acquis, which, if understood in a broader sense, can be translated as the body of EU legislation in the field of consumer law.[1] However, the term consumer acquis is usually understood in a narrower sense and only refers to eight sectoral consumer directives (seven substantive law directives and one procedural law directive), which, as will be shown shortly, have been under review in recent years.[2]

Within the group of substantive laws, the body of contract law has traditionally dominated the discussions. This is best illustrated with examples of the revision of the consumer acquis (in its narrower sense) and the plan of the Commission to introduce the Common European Sales Law (CESL), both of which (to a greater or lesser extent) focus on contract law-related issues.[3] Both pose some interesting legal and policy-related questions that are strongly linked to the value-oriented justice debate. In this Part III I will focus on these two areas, more precisely on the Directive on Consumer Rights (CRD) and the proposed CESL, because a look at them

[1] J. M. Bech Serrat, *Selling Tourism Services at a Distance: An Analysis of the EU Consumer Acquis* (Berlin: Springer, 2012), p. 5. See, in addition, Annex I 2001 Contract Law Communication for a comprehensive list of consumer acquis laws, i.e., for a list of laws that can be considered as falling under its broader definition.

[2] See Annex II Consumer Acquis Green Paper for details. Page 3 at note 3 says that: 'What is commonly referred to as the "Consumer Acquis" does not cover all consumer protection legislation in the EU.' Several directives, of which some had also been exclusively crafted for B2C cases, such as, for example, the Financial Services Directive or the Consumer Credit Directive, were left aside in this project. For related comments see Twigg-Flesner, *The Europeanisation of Contract Law*, pp. 55–61. Unless indicated otherwise I will use the term consumer acquis to refer to the consumer acquis in its narrow sense.

[3] On the interplay between these two projects see, for example, H. Schulte-Nölke, 'Scope and Role of the Horizontal Directive and its Relationship to the CFR' in Howells and Schulze (eds.), *Modernising and Harmonising Consumer Contract Law*, pp. 29–46; J. Lévayné Fazekas, 'Connection between the CFR and the Proposal for a Directive on Consumer Rights' in R. Schulze (ed.), *Common Frame of Reference and Existing EC Contract Law* (2nd edn, Munich: Sellier, 2009), pp. 309–13.

is very helpful to better understand the key arguments related to the substantive law pillar of access to justice 2.0.

The development of substantive EU laws can generally be divided into two main phases. The first, more traditional approach dates back to the mid-1980s. This movement was characterised by a scattered – or 'fragmented'[4] – approach towards consumer protection issues to respond to various, different legal situations by introducing scope-wise clearly distinguished rules at the EU level. This was done with the help of specific sectoral consumer directives based on minimum harmonisation.[5] This policy approach, i.e., the use of minimum harmonised directives, led to, inter alia, two important features at the EU level that were later the main reasons for the launch of the second phase of the development of substantive consumer laws. First, the fact that the Commission had initially chosen directives over regulations meant that the Member States were asked to implement European rules by adapting already existing national legislation or by introducing new legislation (if no comparable domestic law existed). Second, choosing minimum over maximum harmonisation enabled Member States to keep or introduce stricter (i.e., consumer-friendlier) national rules.

From a consumer's point of view, the older approach had the advantage that Member States had the chance to protect consumers to a higher degree than required by EU laws. However, from the perspective of traders and the internal market, the traditional approach showed (or rather was believed to show) certain deficiencies. The practical consequences of

---

[4] S. Cámara Lapuente and E. Terryn, 'Consumer Contract Law' in H.-W. Micklitz et al. (eds.), *Cases, Materials and Text on Consumer Law* (Oxford: Hart, 2010), p. 165. Stephen Weatherill uses the term 'wildly unsystematic' (S. Weatherill, 'The Consumer Rights Directive: How and Why a Quest for "Coherence" Has (Largely) Failed', *Common Market Law Review*, 49 (2012), 1279, 1280). James Devenney and Mal Kenny refer to this as follows: '[F]unctionalism, rather than a coherent, systemic approach, was the dominant characteristic of the body of law which emerged' (J. Devenney and M. Kenny, 'Conclusions: the Transformation of European Private Law' in Devenney and Kenny (eds.), *The Transformation of European Private Law*, p. 316). On the fragmentation in general see further J. Devenney and M. Kenny, 'The Private Law Dimension to the "State of the Union": (D)CFR/CESL Initiatives and the Europeanisation of Private Law' in *ibid.*, pp. 63–77.

[5] For general comments on this traditional European approach towards substantive private law issues see, for example, A. Johnston and H. Unberath, 'European Private Law by Directives: Approach and Challenges' in Twigg-Flesner (ed.), *The Cambridge Companion to European Union Private Law*, pp. 85–100. P. Rott, 'Verbraucherschutz im Internationalen Verfahrens- und Privatrecht' in Micklitz (ed.), *Verbraucherrecht in Deutschland*, pp. 355–95; S. Conrad, *Das Konzept der Mindestharmonisierung: Eine Analyse anhand der Verbrauchervertragsrichtlinien* (Baden-Baden: Nomos, 2004).

the need to implement directives into national law had (perhaps) been underestimated. Experience shows that different Member States reacted differently and that the consumer directives were not always implemented in exactly the same way. This was especially due to the fact that Member States had to find ways to make the prescribed rules compatible with their national consumer protection policies and to integrate them into their domestic substantive law regimes.[6] CJEU case law shows that in many instances this turned out to be technically difficult and that in some cases there was no national implementation at all.[7] In addition, and even in cases where the national implementation of the consumer directives was technically unproblematic, the minimum harmonisation approach did not fully align national rules as it gave Member States the discretion to maintain or keep consumer-friendlier standards.

By the beginning of the new millennium, the Commission had arrived at the opinion that a different approach was needed to strengthen the internal market. This second phase led to stronger attempts to defragment national laws and increased the centralisation of law making at the hands of the EU. The Commission came to the conclusion that the key to remove the two (assumed) biggest obstacles to a stronger standardisation of consumer protection at the national level, i.e., the use of directives instead of regulations and, above all, minimum instead of maximum harmonisation, was to shift the policy in the opposite direction.[8]

---

[6] For a general overview of the interplay between the policy-making interests of EU and the Member States in the European law-making process see M. Claes, 'The European Union, Its Member States and Their Citizens' in D. Leczykiewicz and S. Weatherill (eds.), *The Involvement of EU Law in Private Law Relationships* (Oxford: Hart, 2013), pp. 29–52. See further C. Twigg-Flesner, 'EU Law and Consumer Transactions without an Internal Market Dimension' in *ibid.*, pp. 317–31, with remarks on EU consumer law policy-making and its interaction with issues traditionally of strong legislative interest at the national level.

[7] For a systematic overview of some important judgments in this respect see Micklitz *et al.* (eds.), *Cases, Materials and Text on Consumer Law*. For comments on the fragmentation of national private laws as a consequence of sectoral EU law making see J. M. Smits, 'Coherence and Fragmentation in the Law of Contract' in P. Letto-Vanamo and J. M. Smits (eds.), *Coherence and Fragmentation in European Private Law* (Munich: Sellier, 2012), pp. 9–23.

[8] For comments on the shift see M. Stürner, 'Das Konzept der Vollharmonisierung – eine Einführung' in M. Stürner (ed.), *Vollharmonisierung im Europäischen Verbraucherrecht?* (Munich: Sellier, 2010), pp. 3–22; C. Twigg-Flesner, *A Cross-border-only Regulation for Consumer Transactions in the EU: A Fresh Approach to EU Consumer Law* (New York: Springer, 2012), pp. 15–17; M. B. M. Loos, 'Full Harmonisation As a Regulatory Concept and Its Consequences for the National Legal Orders. The Example of the Consumer Rights

The Commission started its new initiative by focusing primarily on the second of the two perceived internal market barriers: the issue of a

Directive' in Stürner (ed.), *Vollharmonisierung im Europäischen Verbraucherrecht*, pp. 54–5 and 87–8; M. Schmidt-Kessel, 'Der Vorschlag im Kontext der Rechtsharmonisierung in Europa' in Jud and Wendehorst (eds.), *Neuordnung des Verbraucherprivatrechts in Europa*, pp. 26–7; C. Willett and M. Morgan-Taylor, 'Recognising the Limits of Transparency in EU Consumer Law' in J. Devenney and M. Kenny (eds.), *European Consumer Protection: Theory and Practice* (Cambridge University Press, 2012), p. 143; J. Stuyck, 'Setting the Scene' in Micklitz *et al.* (eds.), *Cases, Materials and Text on Consumer Law*, pp. 20–1; H.-W. Micklitz, N. Reich and S. Weatherill, 'EU Treaty Revision and Consumer Protection', *Journal of Consumer Policy*, 27 (2004), 367–99; V. Mak, 'Review of the Consumer Acquis – Towards Maximum Harmonisation?', Tilburg Institute of Comparative and Transnational Law Working Paper, No. 2008/6 (2008), available at papers.ssrn.com/sol3/papers.cfm?abstract_id=1237011; Weatherill, *EU Consumer Law and Policy*, p. 248; Ramsay, *Consumer Law and Policy*, p. 36; W.-H. Roth, 'Kompetenzen der EG zur vollharmonisierenden Angleichung des Privatrechts' in B. Gsell and C. Herresthal (eds.), *Vollharmonisierung im Privatrecht* (Tübingen: Mohr Siebeck, 2009), pp. 13–45; N. Reich, 'Harmonisation of European Contract Law: With Special Emphasis on Consumer Law', *China-EU Law Journal*, 1 (2011), 55–94; A.-C. Mittwoch, *Vollharmonisierung und Europäisches Privatrecht. Methode, Implikationen und Durchführung* (Berlin: de Gruyter, 2013), pp. 129–33 and 138–43; C. Mayer, *Vollharmonisierung im Privatrecht – Einfluss und Wirkung auf die Konzeptionen in Österreich, in der Schweiz (über autonomes Nachvollzug) und in Deutschland* (Hamburg: Dr. Kovač, 2013). For a more recent, critical comment on the harmonisation of consumer law also with respect to domestic issues see C. Twigg-Flesner, 'Comment: the Future of EU Consumer Law – the End of Harmonisation' in Devenney and Kenny (eds.), *European Consumer Protection: Theory and Practice*, pp. 6–20, where Twigg-Flesner argues that harmonisation should focus on cross-border cases only explaining that '[t]he harmonisation model has run its course and can now be safely consigned to the scrapheap' (*ibid.*, p. 20). For a comment in contrast to this see Hans Claudius Taschner's call for an increased use of maximum harmonisation in H. C. Taschner, 'Mindestharmonisierung im Verbraucherschutzrecht' in U. Everling and W.-H. Roth (eds.), *Mindestharmonisierung im Europäischen Binnenmarkt* (Baden-Baden: Nomos, 1997), pp. 159–74 (criticised by Norbert Reich in N. Reich, 'Mindestharmonisierung im Verbraucherschutzrecht – Stellungnahme' in *ibid.*, pp. 175–9). Geraint Howells comments on the shift as follows: '[T]he notion that businesses need complete uniformity seems to be going too far. It poses unnecessary dangers for consumers if, without good reason, it is used to undermine familiar national instruments of consumer protection' (G. Howells, 'The Rise of European Consumer Law – Whither National Consumer Law?', *Sydney Law Review*, 28 (2006), 63, 71). On another occasion he also stresses the importance of the legislative leeway given to the Member States via minimum harmonisation by stating that 'Member States can act as laboratories, experimenting with practices which if successful can be integrated into EU policy' (G. Howells, 'European Consumer Law – the Minimal and Maximal Harmonisation Debate and Pro Independent Consumer Law Competence' in Grundmann and Stuyck (eds.), *An Academic Green Paper on European Private Law*, p. 76). In a similar vein is T. Wilhelmsson, 'The Ethical Pluralism of late Modern Europe and Codification of European Contract Law' in J.M. Smits (ed.), *The Need for a European Contract Law – Empirical and Legal Perspectives* (Groningen: Europa Law Publishing, 2005), pp. 123–52. Stephen Weatherill concludes his critical analysis of maximum harmonisation as follows: 'At the very least there is a perceived harmonisation deficit.[9] One of the first results was the Unfair Commercial Practices Directive (UCPD) of 2005.[10] As a fully harmonised directive, it did not allow Member States to keep or introduce consumer-friendlier national legislation for questions falling under its scope. Not only did the UCPD follow maximum harmonisation, it also embodied another more recent trend in the field of EU consumer law. Instead of limiting its scope to certain narrow commercial sectors or activities, the UCPD was designed as a 'framework' or 'horizontal' directive. Unlike most substantive consumer directives of the first phase, the UCPD is thus, in principle, broadly applicable in a number of different B2C situations.

An important and more comprehensive intermediary step in the shift in consumer law policy dates back to the early 2000s, when the 2001 Contract Law Communication, the 2003 Contract Law Action Plan and the 2004 Acquis Communication initiated a comprehensive, two-fold

strong case to be made for regarding maximum harmonization as applicable only in particular sectors and only where its use has been carefully justified in the prevailing sector-specific conditions' (Weatherill, 'Maximum or Minimum Harmonisation', p. 145). For another critique on the shift see H.-W. Micklitz, 'The Targeted Full Harmonisation Approach: Looking behind the Curtain' in Howells and Schulze (eds.), *Modernising and Harmonising Consumer Contract Law*, pp. 47–83.

[9] See, for example, the Explanatory Memorandum accompanying the Proposal for a directive of the European Parliament and of the Council concerning unfair business-to-consumer commercial practices in the Internal Market and amending directives 84/450/EEC, 97/7/EC and 98/27/EC (UCPD proposal), 18 June 2003, COM(2003) 356 final, p. 8, where the Commission claims that maximum harmonisation is needed 'to address the internal market barriers caused by [minimum harmonisation and resulting] divergent national provisions'.

[10] For comments on the UCPD see G. Howells, H.-W. Micklitz and T. Wilhelmsson, *European Fair Trading Law: The Unfair Commercial Practices Directive* (Farnham: Ashgate, 2006); H.-W. Micklitz, 'Unfair Commercial Practices and European Private Law' in Twigg-Flesner (ed.), *The Cambridge Companion to European Union Private Law*, pp. 229–42; C. van Dam and E. Budaite, 'The Statutory Frameworks and General Rules on Unfair Commercial Practices in the 25 EU Member States on the Eve of Harmonization' in C. Twigg-Flesner *et al.* (eds.), *The Yearbook of Consumer Law 2008* (Aldershot: Ashgate, 2007), pp. 107–39; R. Bragg, 'Trade Descriptions after the Unfair Commercial Practices Directive' in *ibid.*, pp. 341–5; T. Wilhelmsson, 'The Informed Consumer v the Vulnerable Consumer in European Unfair Commercial Practices Law – A Comment' in Howells *et al.*, *The Yearbook of Consumer Law 2007*, pp. 211–27; B. De Groote and K. De Vulder, 'The Unfair Commercial Practices Directive' in *ibid.*, pp. 349–79; K. Viitanen, 'The Unfair Commercial Practices Directive and Marketing Targeted at Minors' in Wilhelmsson *et al.* (eds.), *Private Law and the Many Cultures of Europe*, pp. 283–303; G. Howells, 'Unfair Commercial Practices – Future Directions' in R. Schulze and H. Schulte-Nölke (eds.), *European Private Law – Current Status and Perspectives* (Munich: Sellier, 2011), pp. 133–44. For further examples of fully harmonised directives see 'The Directive on Consumer Rights – Background and genesis' in Chapter 9 below.

discussion of consumer law issues. The key area of interest in this respect was European contract law in general, an area that – as will be shown later – had already been at the centre of interest in several research groups for a long time and eventually led to the drafting of the proposed CESL Regulation.[11] The related discussions were accompanied by a comprehensive research project that focused on the consumer acquis in its narrow sense, the Consumer Law Compendium, and eventually led to some new consumer legislation (some of which I will briefly cover in the following chapters).

In addition, the Commission began to consider the use of regulations to circumvent the necessity of implementing EU laws at the national level in a more general way – not only in the field of procedural consumer law.[12] The Proposal for a Regulation on a Common European Sales Law is the best example to show that the Commission is now also willing to use EU regulations to a greater extent to directly standardise substantive law rules.[13]

Table 2 illustrates (in a simplified way) the policy shift in the field of substantive consumer law, which has gradually occurred since the start of the new millennium.

---

[11] For details see Chapter 10 below.

[12] I have already dealt with some procedural law examples such as the Small Claims Regulation, the Regulation on Consumer Protection Cooperation and the more recent ODR Regulation in Chapter 4 of this book.

[13] In the context of the CESL Peter-Christian Müller-Graff explains that the choice of a European regulation as the legislative tool is the logical consequence of the plan of the Commission to introduce a fully standardised European sales law. A European directive, even if fully harmonised, might (according to Müller-Graff) not achieve a comparable standardisation (see P.-C. Müller-Graff, 'EU Directives as a Means of Private Law Unification' in Hartkamp *et al.* (eds.), *Towards a European Civil Code*, pp. 161–2).

Table 2 *Comparison of the 'old' v. 'new' approach in substantive EU law making*

Issue	Old approach	New approach
Regulative scope	Sectoral regulation of consumer law issues	Increased overarching regulation of consumer law issues
Level of harmonisation	Minimum harmonisation	Increased maximum (i.e., full) harmonisation
Legal mechanism	Directives	Considering the use of regulations as alternatives to directives
Implication for Member States	Chance to implement or maintain stricter (i.e., consumer-friendlier) consumer policy	No (or minimal) discretion; core consumer law issues centralised at the EU level

9

Recent trends and developments

The Directive on Consumer Rights

Background and genesis

As I explained in the previous chapter, since the mid-1980s the Union legislator has enacted numerous, mostly sectoral, substantive consumer directives. It was not uncommon for different directives to regulate similar rights and remedies, although in different ways. Put differently, in many cases the directives took an autonomous approach, which basically meant that the respective provisions were not always fully standardised. One prominent example is the withdrawal rights regime, which, in the respective directives, differed especially with regard to the length and start of withdrawal periods and the consequences of withdrawing.[1]

Approximately 20 years after the adoption of the first consumer acquis directive, the Doorstep Selling Directive, the Commission responded to this fragmentation with three communications on contract law: the 2001 Contract Law Communication, the 2003 Contract Law Action Plan and the 2004 Acquis Communication.

The 2001 Contract Law Communication initiated further discussions by referring to the underlying 'problem' of fragmentation as follows: 'In the area of contract law the Union legislator has taken a "piecemeal" approach to harmonisation. This approach combined with unforeseen market developments, could lead to inconsistencies in the application of EC law.'[2] To respond to this, the 2003 Contract Law Action Plan suggested

---

[1] See the comparison of the withdrawal rights of the Doorstep Selling Directive, the Timeshare Directive and the Distance Selling Directive in Schulte-Nölke *et al.* (eds.), *EC Consumer Law Compendium*, pp. 472–82. For further comments in these and further examples see P. Rott, 'Information Obligations and Withdrawal Rights' in Twigg-Flesner (ed.), *The Cambridge Companion to European Union Private Law*, pp. 187–200; Z. Meškić, *Europäisches Verbraucherrecht: Gemeinschaftsrechtliche Vorgaben und europäische Perspektiven* (Vienna: Manz, 2008), pp. 87–8.

[2] 2001 Contract Law Communication, para. 35.

three main measures: (1) 'to increase the coherence of the EC *acquis* in the area of contract law',[3] (2) 'to promote the elaboration of EU-wide general contract terms'[4] and (3) 'to examine further whether problems in the European contract law area may require nonsector-specific solutions such as an optional instrument'.[5] One year after this communication the Commission cemented its plans to review the consumer acquis. The 2004 Acquis Communication explained that some projects had already been planned to standardise existing rules. These actions included the '(d)evelopment of a public database of the *acquis*',[6] the '(e)stablishment of a standing working group of Member States' experts to act as a forum for information exchange and debate in the implementation of the *acquis*'[7] and the drafting of '[i]mplementation reports'[8] with respect to some of the consumer acquis directives.

To facilitate the consumer acquis discussion, a group of European scholars led by Hans Schulte-Nölke, Christian Twigg-Flesner and Martin Ebers commenced a comprehensive comparative study of the national implementations of the consumer acquis in late 2004. Six of the eight directives covered by it closely related to contract law issues: the Doorstep Selling Directive,[9] the Package Travel Directive,[10] the Unfair Contract Terms Directive,[11] the Timeshare Directive,[12] the Distance Selling Directive[13] and the Consumer Sales Directive.[14] Two primarily non-contract law-related directives completed the group: the Injunctions Directive and the Price Indication Directive.[15] One feature shared by all eight directives was that

---

[3] 2003 Contract Law Action Plan, p. 2.   [4] *Ibid.*

[5] *Ibid.*   [6] 2004 Acquis Communication, p. 4.

[7] *Ibid.*   [8] *Ibid.*

[9] Council Directive 85/577/EEC to protect the consumer in respect of contracts negotiated away from business premises, 20 December 1985, OJ 1985, No. L 372/31.

[10] Council Directive 90/314/EEC on package travel, package holidays and package tours, 13 June 1990, OJ 1990 No. L 158/59.

[11] Council Directive 93/13/EEC on unfair terms in consumer contracts, 5 April 1993, OJ 1993 No. L95/29.

[12] Directive 94/47/EC of the European Parliament and of the Council on the protection of purchasers in respect of certain aspects of contracts relating to the purchase of a right to use immovable properties on a timeshare basis, 26 October 1994, OJ 1994 No. L280/83.

[13] Directive 97/7/EC of the European Parliament and of the Council on the protection of consumers in respect of distance contracts, 20 May 1997, OJ 1997 No. L 144/19.

[14] Directive 1999/44/EC of the European Parliament and of the Council on certain aspects of the sale of consumer goods and associated guarantees, 25 May 1999, OJ 1999 No. L171/12.

[15] Directive 98/6/EC of the European Parliament and of the Council on consumer protection in the indication of the prices of products offered to consumers, 16 February 1998, OJ 1998 No. L 80/27.

they followed minimum harmonisation, i.e., all of them allowed Member States to maintain or introduce more far-reaching, consumer-friendlier national provisions.

The result of this study, the Consumer Law Compendium, was presented in 2008. Without doubt, the Consumer Law Compendium is an important collection of national implementation techniques and an important source for further consideration in the harmonisation debate. The study explained that Member States were not reluctant to make use of the chance to apply a higher level of protection in their respective jurisdictions. Although the directives led to a certain degree of standardisation, the national fragmentation resulting from diverse national consumer protection policies on the one hand and the use of different implementation techniques regarding European directives on the other became very obvious.

In early 2007 (one year before the presentation of the Consumer Law Compendium), the Commission specified its plans to revise the consumer acquis in more detail. The Green Paper on the review of the consumer acquis (Consumer Acquis Green Paper)[16] explained the assumed need for a revision with reference to the Better Regulation policy as defined by two Commission Communications in 2002.[17] In the opinion of the Commission, simpler laws would be 'more effective and be better understood'[18] and thus be 'better laws'.[19] Not only would they be 'better' than the currently existing laws, but the revision of the consumer acquis would also lead to the completion of the regulatory consumer protection framework which, according to the Commission, would eventually result in 'achiev[ing] a real consumer internal market striking the right balance between a high level of consumer protection and the competitiveness of enterprises'.[20] The argumentation of the Commission expressed in the Consumer Acquis Green Paper is thus two-tiered and principally follows

---

[16] Green Paper on the review of the consumer acquis, 8 February 2007, COM(2006) 744 final (Consumer Acquis Green Paper). For critical comments on the Consumer Acquis Green Paper see H.-W. Micklitz, 'Europäisches Verbraucherrecht – Quo Vadis? Überlegungen zum Grünbuch der Kommission zur Überprüfung des gemeinschaftlichen Besitzstandes im Verbraucherschutz vom 8.2.2007', Verbraucher und Recht, 22 (2012), 121–30.

[17] For details see Communication from the Commission – Action plan 'Simplifying and improving the regulatory environment', 5 June 2002, COM(2002) 278 final, chapter 2.2 and the accompanying Communication from the Commission – European Governance: Better lawmaking, 5 June 2002, COM(2002) 275 final. For comments and an analysis of the Better Regulation policy see Weatherill (ed.), Better Regulation and (for a summary of its main objectives) S. Weatherill, 'The Challenge of Better Regulation' in ibid., pp. 1–17.

[18] Communication from the Commission – European Governance: Better lawmaking, p. 4.

[19] Ibid.   [20] Consumer Acquis Green Paper, p. 3.

two objectives: first, a simplification of the framework of existing consumer laws to achieve 'better' laws and second, filling possible gaps by a 'completion' of the regulatory framework.

One question that remains in this context is the meaning of the somewhat ambiguous term 'simplification'. One could be tempted to assume that it stands for a simplification of the practically relevant steps consumers must take to get their rights enforced. Understood in such a way, the term would mainly relate to procedural law issues. However, when taking a look at the Consumer Acquis Green Paper and its legislative results – the Consumer Rights Directive (to be more precise: its initial draft), the new Timeshare Directive and (to some extent)[21] the more recent Proposal for a Directive on package travel and assisted travel arrangements (to distinguish it from the proposal of the 'old' Package Travel Directive I will refer to it as the 2013 Package Travel Directive Proposal)[22] – one will realise that simplification in the context of the Consumer Acquis Green Paper has a different meaning. It is associated with the quest to align and fully harmonise consumer laws as comprehensively as possible to get rid of diverse rules at both the EU level (caused by the different approaches towards similar issues taken by the directives) and the national level (caused by the different implementation approaches taken by the Member States). This approach aims to reach, as Guido Alpa explains with respect to contractual issues, 'uniformity [which would help] increase the certainty of the parties' contract conditions'.[23]

<hr/>

[21] See 'The Consumer Acquis beyond the CRD and towards the CESL' (in particular note 66) below for details.

[22] Proposal for a Directive of the European Parliament and of the Council on package travel and assisted travel arrangements, amending Regulation (EC) No 2006/2004, Directive 2011/83/EU and repealing Council Directive 90/314/EEC, 9 July 2013, COM(2013) 512 final. Its accompanying Explanatory Memorandum confirms the Commission's view that the fragmentation of national provisions causes obstacles for the well-functioning of the internal market. It explains: 'by reducing legal fragmentation ... the proposal will minimise obstacles to cross-border trade and reduce compliance costs for traders wishing to operate cross-border, and ensure a level playing-field in the travel market' (Explanatory Memorandum accompanying the 2013 Package Travel Directive Proposal, p. 6).

[23] G. Alpa, 'Harmonisation of and Codification in European Contract Law' in S. Vogenauer and S. Weatherill (eds.), The Harmonisation of European Contract Law: Implications for European Private Laws, Business and Legal Practice (Oxford: Hart, 2006), p. 169. See further G. Alpa, 'The Future of European Contract Law: Some Questions and Some Answers' in Boele-Woelki and Grosheide (eds.), The Future of European Contract Law, p. 15, where he argues that 'we should begin maximum, strict harmonisation. Only in this way can we render the provisions in the text, their interpretation, the uniformity of conduct and practices ... as homogenous as possible'.

If one replaces 'simpler laws' with 'fully harmonised laws', one arrives at the following conclusion: in the view of the Commission, fully harmonised consumer laws would be more effective and better understood. This understanding is actually in line with an argument popular with the Commission, expressed, for example, by Chapter 3.3 of the Consumer Acquis Green Paper as follows: 'Different [national] rules resulting from minimum harmonisation may have a negative impact on the internal market.'[24] In other words, the Commission is convinced that varying standards in the Member States cause a lack of consumer confidence when they engage in cross-border shopping. Admittedly, the fact that Member States are willing to go beyond the standard introduced at the EU level has some impact on consumer confidence. However, it should be noted that consumer-friendlier national rules are – from a consumer perspective – in principle to be welcomed. The problem lies rather in the fact that many consumers are afraid they will not be able to enjoy in a cross-border context the same protective standard offered by their home countries' laws for domestic transactions. Maximum harmonisation would answer this fear, but it would usually do so at the expense of higher national legislative standards. I will come back to some underlying studies and the issue of the lack of consumer confidence in cross-border trade in more detail later.[25]

Although the Consumer Acquis Green Paper did not explicitly express a preference with respect to the harmonisation level of future legislation in the consumer acquis sector, it is not difficult to see that the Commission in principle favoured maximum harmonisation from the beginning.[26] This tendency materialised in 2008 at the latest, when the Commission published its (fully harmonised)[27] Proposal for a directive on consumer rights[28] (CRD Proposal).

---

[24] Consumer Acquis Green Paper, p. 7.

[25] See 'Third Assumption: The CESL Is Clearly Needed' in Chapter 10 below for details.

[26] See Consumer Acquis Green Paper, pp. 10 and 11 for the Commission's comments on the level of harmonisation.

[27] Article 4 CRD Proposal.

[28] Proposal for a Directive of the European Parliament and of the Council on consumer rights, 8 October 2008, COM(2008) 614 final. For comments on the CRD Proposal see, e.g., H.-W. Micklitz and N. Reich, 'Crónica de una muerte anunciada: The Commission Proposal for a "Directive on Consumer Rights"', *Common Market Law Review* 46 (2009), 471–519; P. Rott and E. Terryn, 'The Proposal for a Directive on Consumer Rights: No Single Set of Rules', *Zeitschrift für Europäisches Privatrecht*, 17 (2009), 456–88; the contributions in Howells and Schulze (eds.), *Modernising and Harmonising Consumer Contract Law* (see G. Howells and R. Schulze, 'Overview of the Proposed Consumer Rights Directive' in *ibid.*, pp. 3–25 for a brief overview); M. Artz, 'Vorschlag für eine vollharmonisierte Horizontalrichtlinie zum Verbraucherrecht' in Gsell and Herresthal

While it took a comparatively broad approach, one should note that the proposal was not as broad as one could have expected. As I showed earlier, the quest for a revised consumer acquis had started as a reasonably ambitious project with eight directives. Over the years, however, the regulatory scope of the CRD project was downsized. In the end, the CRD Proposal covered only four directives, i.e., just half of the directives listed in previous consumer acquis documents and the Consumer Law Compendium: the Doorstep Selling Directive, the Unfair Contract Terms Directive, the Distance Selling Directive and the Consumer Sales Directive. Taking a look at this list, one can easily see that the CRD Proposal exclusively deals with contract law-related directives. However, even with regard to contract law, the scope of the CRD Proposal was narrower than envisaged by the Consumer Acquis Green Paper: the 1990 Package Travel Directive and the 1994 Timeshare Directive were not considered in the CRD Proposal. Plans to revise these two directives were not fully abandoned, though. Work towards a new timeshare directive was already in progress and was completed with the adoption of a new, fully harmonised Timeshare Directive in 2009.[29] The Package Travel Directive was not ignored either. In July 2013 the Commission came forward with a proposal to revise it (the 2013 Package Travel Directive Proposal), which – if adopted – would replace the 1990 Package Travel Directive.[30]

In some respects the CRD Proposal was quite far-reaching. One of the most apparent features of the proposal was the planned change from minimum to maximum harmonisation, which was in line with some other relatively recent legislation: the 2002 Financial Services Distance Contracts Directive, [31] the 2005 UCPD, the 2008 Consumer Credit

---

(eds.), *Vollharmonisierung im Privatrecht*, pp. 209–18; B. Gsell, 'Vollharmonisiertes Verbraucherkaufrecht nach dem Vorschlag für eine Horizontalrichtlinie' in *ibid.*, pp. 219–45; Loos, 'Full Harmonisation As a Regulatory Concept' in H. Eidenmüller *et al.* (eds.), *Revision des Verbraucher-acquis* (Tübingen: Mohr Siebeck, 2011); B. Jud and C. Wendehorst (eds.), *Neuordnung des Verbraucherprivatrechts in Europa / Zum Vorschlag einer Richtlinie über Rechte der Verbraucher* (Vienna: Manz, 2009). On the older minimum harmonisation approach in detail see M. Wagner, *Das Konzept der Mindestharmonisierung* (Berlin: Duncker & Humblot, 2001).

[29] Directive 2008/122/EC of the European Parliament and of the Council on the protection of consumers in respect of certain aspects of timeshare, long-term holiday product, resale and exchange contracts, 14 January 2009, OJ 2009 No. L33/10.

[30] See 'The Consumer Acquis beyond the CRD and towards the CESL' below for more comments on the 2013 Package Travel Directive Proposal.

[31] Directive 2002/65/EC of the European Parliament and of the Council concerning the distance marketing of consumer financial services and amending Council Directive 90/619/EEC and Directives 97/7/EC and 98/27/EC, 23 September 2002, OJ 2002 No. L271/16 (as

Agreements Directive and the (later) 2009 Timeshare Directive.[32] With the CRD Proposal, the Commission clearly sought to continue its policy shift towards a more centralised, comprehensive and exhaustive regulation of consumer law issues at the EU level. In this context it is worth taking a brief look at Articles 1 and 4 CRD Proposal, which reflect the 'promotion' strategy of the Commission with respect to this trend.

Article 1 CRD Proposal defines the two driving factors behind the proposal as (1) 'contribut[ing] to the proper functioning of the internal market' [via the 'simplification', i.e., maximum harmonisation, of CRD rules] and as (2) 'achiev[ing] a high level of consumer protection by approximating certain aspects of the law'. With the second of these two arguments, the Commission obviously tried to respond to critics who were sceptical about the Commission's claim that the maximum harmonisation approach could be beneficial to all consumers residing in the EU.[33] The Commission, however, forgot to mention one important fact when praising the (putatively) high level of consumer protection guaranteed by maximum harmonisation. Even if the protective level were high, it does not necessarily mean that the level would be as high as existing national standards or as beneficial for consumers as current national legislation. Various Member States (as a consequence of the older minimum harmonisation approach) used, in some instances, consumer-friendlier rules.

This is somewhat confirmed by Article 4 CRD Proposal. Article 4 elegantly describes the practical consequence of restricting the legislative powers of Member States to implement national consumer policies as follows: 'Member States *may not maintain* or introduce, in their national law, provisions diverging from those laid down in this Directive, including *more ... stringent provisions* to ensure a different level of consumer

amended by the Directive 2007/64/EC of the European Parliament and of the Council on payment services in the internal market amending Directives 97/7/EC, 2002/65/EC, 2005/60/EC and 2006/48/EC and repealing Directive 97/5/EC, 13 November 2007, OJ 2007 No. L319/1).

[32] Also the Product Liability Directive of 1985 (Council Directive 85/374/EEC on the approximation of the laws, regulations and administrative provisions of the Member States concerning liability for defective products, 25 July 1985, OJ 1985 No. L210/29) followed maximum harmonisation. Unlike the other directives listed, however, its scope is not fully limited to B2C cases.

[33] Even legal scholars who basically support the idea of maximum harmonisation have to admit that its use poses certain risks for the protective standards at the national level. Martin Schmidt-Kessel, for example, advises increased caution, noting that in the case of maximum harmonisation the 'risk of systematic collateral damages is considerably higher than in cases of minimum harmonisation' (Schmidt-Kessel, 'Der Vorschlag im Kontext der Rechtsharmonisierung in Europa', p. 28).

protection' (emphasis added). This wording, i.e., the prohibition of maintaining existing higher national standards, would not have been needed if the protective level of the CRD Proposal was as high as the standard of every single Member State. The combination of these two provisions represents an interesting strategy. On the one hand, the Commission tries to calm critics by claiming that maximum harmonisation achieves a high level of consumer protection. On the other hand, it has to admit that maximum harmonisation is not able to meet the standards of all twenty-eight national consumer law regimes. Whether this really serves consumer interests to the best possible extent is anyone's guess.

Especially in connection with the CRD Proposal's relatively broad material scope of application, the maximum harmonisation approach suggested by the proposal was heavily criticised, not only by many legal scholars[34] but also by national policy makers (as shown by Verena Cap in an interesting summary of the events in the negotiation phase of the proposal).[35] A number of chapters were strongly opposed by the Member States, especially Chapter II on general consumer information issues for a wide range of B2C sales and service contracts, Chapter IV (with a broad catalogue of general contractual consumer rights; its warranty and guarantee regimes were particuarly criticised by the Member States) and Chapter V on nontransparent and unfair contract terms. Because of the envisaged maximum harmonisation of these chapters, Member States would not have been allowed to keep their consumer-friendlier rules if the proposal was adopted in its original wording.[36] This prompted several Member States to push for the insertion of some of their national rules

---

[34] See, for example, the strongly worded criticism by Beate Gsell: 'Indeed, one can only wonder how—despite the intensive academic penetration (*Durchdringung*) of European contract law—it was possible to present a proposal of such miserable technical quality' (translation mine) (Gsell, 'Vollharmonisiertes Verbraucherkaufrecht nach dem Vorschlag für eine Horizontalrichtlinie', p. 222). For a critical analysis of the maximum harmonisation approach chosen by the CRD Proposal, see further, e.g., Howells and Schulze, 'Overview of the Proposed Consumer Rights Directive'. Howells and Schulze summarise their critique as follows: '[T]he level of the current minimum harmonisation cannot be the level of a future full harmonisation' (*ibid.*, p. 25). In a similar vein is Loos's critique of the CRD Proposal: '[I]n many areas the minimum protection level of the existing directive is simply transformed in to the maximum protection level' (Loos, 'Full Harmonisation As a Regulatory Concept', p. 79).

[35] For details on this and the following see V. Cap, 'Grundsätzliches zur Verbraucherrechte-Richtlinie: Entstehung, Anwendungsbereich, Zentralbegriffe, Harmonisierungsgrad' in P. Bydlinski and B. Lurger (eds.), *Die Richtlinie über die Rechte der Verbraucher* (Vienna: Manz, 2012), pp. 1–20.

[36] Despite the fact that several concessions were made to satisfy the national legislative interests of the Member States, the CRD did not meet full approval in the end. Spain even

on particular issues into the CRD Proposal.[37] This request (temporarily) led to the further broadening of the scope of the CRD Proposal in the Council of the European Union (Council) to appease the calls of national policy makers. Under the Belgian presidency this rather broad approach by some Member States to secure their interests was finally given up in favour of a different, narrower strategy. Instead of adding new provisions, the Member States agreed to reduce the scope of the CRD Proposal by eliminating the least acceptable provisions, i.e., Chapters II and V and the warranty and guarantee provisions of Chapter IV.[38]

In contrast to the debate in the Council, which sought to secure the retention of the legislative protective regime for the Member States, the discussions within the Parliament were first and foremost driven by the interests of business interest representatives to push for a strongly harmonised and comprehensive regulatory regime. Hence, the Parliament, in principle, tried to back the Commission and its initial proposal.[39]

The two most heavily discussed issues in the three-party negotiations were the level of harmonisation and should Chapters II, IV and V CRD Proposal be retained and incorporated in the final text (and if so, how). The consolidated position of the Member States in the Council on the one hand and the similarly strong views of the Commission and the Parliament on the other eventually led to a compromise in form of a mitigated version. Chapter V (dealing with issues covered by the UCTD)[40] as well as the warranty and guarantee provisions of Chapter IV CRD Proposal (i.e.,

voted against the final compromise solution in the Council (see *ibid.*, p. 5). For details on the vote in the Council see Council document 15492/11, 13 October 2011, p. 2.

[37] The warranty regime especially (previously regulated by the minimum harmonised Consumer Sales Directive) was inflated by distinct provisions from several Member States. For examples see Cap, 'Grundsätzliches zur Verbraucherrechte-Richtlinie', p. 4 at note 10. For further critical comments from the Member State perspective see L. Froňková, 'The New Directive on Consumer Protection: Objectives from the Perspective of the EU and the Member States' in Schulte-Nölke and Tichý (eds.), *Perspectives for European Consumer Law*, pp. 91–6; H. Beale, 'The Draft Directive on Consumer Rights and UK Consumer Law – Where Now?' in Howells and Schulze (eds.), *Modernising and Harmonising Consumer Contract Law*, pp. 289–302. For a related discussion on the final wording of the CRD see C. Amato, 'The Europeanisation of Contract Law and the Role of Comparative Law: the Case of the Directive on Consumer Rights' in Devenney and Kenny (eds.), *The Transformation of European Private Law*, pp. 45–62.

[38] Cap, 'Grundsätzliches zur Verbraucherrechte-Richtlinie', p. 5.

[39] *Ibid.*, pp. 7–8. It should be noted, however, that the Parliament version takes a more mitigated approach regarding the harmonisation level than the CRD Proposal – for details see www.europarl.europa.eu/sides/getDoc.do?pubRef=-//EP//TEXT+TA+P7-TA-2011-0116+0+DOC+XML+V0//EN.

[40] For some comments on the UCTD see already the literature cited in Chapter 5, note 1.

issues covered by the Consumer Sales Directive (CSD))[41] were basically removed from the final text. (As shown later, both the UCTD and CSD found only partial consideration in the final text of the CRD via the insertion of a new Article 8a in the UCTD and the CSD, respectively.) The material scope of the application of Chapter II CRD Proposal was more or less left unchanged. Because of pressure from the Member States, however, the final version of Chapter II deviated from the basic maximum harmonisation approach of the CRD and, via Article 5(4) CRD, allows Member States to go beyond a minimum list of mandatory pre-contractual information by maintaining or introducing additional information obligations directed at traders for contracts that do not fall under the category of distance or off-premises contracts.[42]

A brief overview of the CRD

After intense deliberations, the CRD was finally adopted on 25 October 2011.[43] Article 28(1) CRD asked the Member States to implement the directive by 13 December 2013 and to make the provisions applicable by 13 June 2014. [44]

---

[41] For some comments on the CSD see U. Magnus, 'Consumer Sales and Associated Guarantees' in Twigg-Flesner (ed.), *The Cambridge Companion to European Union Private Law*, pp. 243–56.

[42] From the perspective of those Member States that supported the trimming of the CRD regime, the adoption of the final CRD text might only be considered a stage victory though. Some issues (such as the fully harmonised catalogue of warranty rights) might return through the back door. As will be seen later, the planned introduction of a parallel alternative sales law regime for cross-border transactions, the CESL, proposed in the form of a regulation shortly before the adoption of the CRD, might (despite it being optional) lead to similar results (with respect to certain types of transactions) as the CRD Proposal had its wording not been changed. Before turning to the CESL in more detail, I should first take a look at how the CRD was eventually crafted.

[43] Compared with the amount of literature on the CRD Proposal, the number of academic contributions on the CRD is thus far relatively low. For examples of analytical comments on the CRD see, e.g., S. Grundmann, 'The EU Consumer Rights Directive: Optimizing, Creating Alternatives, or a Dead End?', *Uniform Law Review*, 118 (2013), 98–127; E. Hall, G. Howells and J. Watson, 'The Consumer Rights Directive – An Assessment of Its Contribution to the Development of European Consumer Contract Law', *European Review of Contract Law*, 8 (2012), 139–66; O. Unger, 'Die Richtlinie über die Rechte der Verbraucher – Eine systematische Einführung', *Zeitschrift für Europäisches Privatrecht*, 20 (2012), 270–304; and the contributions in Bydlinski and Lurger (eds.), *Die Richtlinie über die Rechte der Verbraucher*.

[44] For comments on the national implementation of the CRD see, e.g., the contributions in T. Brönneke and K. Tonner (eds.), *Das neue Schuldrecht: Verbraucherrechtsreform 2014* (Baden-Baden: Nomos, 2014); C. Wendehorst, 'Das neue Gesetz zur Umsetzung

Chapter I CRD defines the general scope of the directive and lists definitions of core terms used by the CRD. Chapter II contains a catalogue of mandatory consumer information for consumer contracts falling under the CRD regime[45] that are concluded neither as distance nor off-premises contracts. The Doorstep Selling Directive and the Distance Selling Directive were both repealed by the CRD. Matters formerly covered by these two directives are now (in principle)[46] standardised and regulated in Chapter III

---

der Verbraucherrechterichtlinie', *Neue Juristische Wochenschrift*, 67 (2014), 577–84; T. Halm, 'Die Umsetzung der EU-Verbraucherrechterichtlinie – Kommt ein grundlegender Umbruch im neuen Jahr?', *Verbraucher und Recht*, 29 (2014), 1–2; T. Brönneke and F. Schmidt, 'Der Anwendungsbereich der Vorschriften über die besonderen Vertriebsformen nach Umsetzung der Verbraucherrechterichtlinie', *Verbraucher und Recht*, 29 (2014), 3–9; M. Tamm, 'Informationspflichten nach dem Umsetzungsgesetz zur Verbraucherrechterichtlinie', *Verbraucher und Recht*, 29 (2014), 9–17; G. Schomburg, 'Mehr Verbraucherschutz bei Kosten für Nebenleistungen – Die Regelungen des neuen § 312a Abs. 2 bis 6 BGB', *Verbraucher und Recht*, 29 (2014), 18–23; K. Tonner, 'Die Umsetzung der Verbraucherrechterichtlinie – Auswirkungen der Vollharmonisierung', *Verbraucher und Recht*, 29 (2014), 23–7 (all on Germany); J. Stabentheiner, 'Das Verbraucherrechte-Richtlinie-Umsetzungsgesetz: Allgemeine Anmerkungen, die Änderungen des ABGB und die Neuerungen im KSchG', *Zeitschrift für Verbraucherrecht*, (2014), 68–78; J. Stabentheiner, 'Zur Umsetzung der Verbraucherrechte-Richtlinie in Österreich' in Bydlinski and Lurger (eds.), *Die Richtlinie über die Rechte der Verbraucher*, pp. 127–57; S. Wrbka, 'The Austrian Implementation of the Consumer Rights Directive – an Outline', *Hosei Kenkyu*, 81 (2014), 288–308 (all on Austria); P. Giliker, '"Copy out" and the Transposition of the Consumer Rights Directive into UK Law: Implementing a Maximum Harmonisation Directive', unpublished conference paper presented at 'DMU/Exeter Colloquium: Reshaping The Landscape Of Consumer Law And Policy', De Montfort University, 4 April 2014 (on file with the author) (on the UK).

[45] Some of the types exempted by Article 3(3) CRD are covered by other EU laws (see for example Article 3(3)(d) ('financial services'), (g) (contracts 'which fall within the scope of [the 1990 Package Travel Directive]') or (h) (contracts 'which fall within the scope of [the 2009 Timeshare Directive]')). The CRD explains the exclusions in its Recital 32 as follows: 'The existing Union legislation, inter alia, relating to consumer financial services, package travel and timeshare contains numerous rules on consumer protection. For this reason, this Directive should not apply to contracts in those areas.' Other exceptions such as the exception of contracts for the creation, acquisition or transfer of immovable property or of rights in immovable property by Article 3(3)(e) CRD or contracts for the construction of new buildings, the substantial conversion of existing buildings and for rental of accommodation for residential purposes by Article 3(3)(f) CRD are exempted from the application of the CRD because of the already existing complex national legislation in these areas (see Recital 26 CRD, which explains that such contracts 'are already subject to a number of specific requirements in national legislation').

[46] On some occasions certain contractual scenarios (that fall under the regime of Chapter III CRD) are in some respect treated slightly different than the 'ordinary' Chapter III contracts. See, e.g., the special rules for off-premises contracts that are to be performed immediately and do not involve payment obligations of more than EUR 200 (Article 7(4) CRD) or distance contracts concluded by electronic means (Article 8(2) CRD).

CRD.[47] A revised and standardised withdrawal rights regime and a list of mandatory consumer information, which basically – the mandatory information related to the withdrawal rights is the most prominent exception – follows the example of the information requirements of Article 5 CRD,[48] build the core of Chapter III.

Worth noting in the context of mandatory pre-contractual information is the absence of any concrete rule on the consequences of possible breaches of the general information requirements, i.e., with respect to information requirements under Chapter II and information requirements under Chapter III that do not relate to withdrawal rights. Article 24(1) CRD leaves this matter, in principle, to the regulatory discretion of the Member States, but at the same time guides national legislators by requiring that '[t]he penalties provided for … [are] effective, proportionate and dissuasive'.[49]

Should a trader not comply with the withdrawal information obligations for off-premises and distance contracts, additional concrete and pre-defined provisions shall apply in complement to the general national penalties to be introduced or maintained in accordance with Article 24(1). Most notably, an omission of information on the withdrawal right in relation to such contracts would extend the withdrawal period from fourteen days to a maximum of twelve months and fourteen days calculated 'from the end of the initial withdrawal period'.[50] In addition, and as explained shortly, silence on who bears the costs of returning goods would shift the obligation from the consumer to the trader pursuant to Article 14 CRD.

---

[47] For the sake of clarification Annex II CRD contains a '[c]orrelation table', which makes it easier to trace back the CRD provisions on distance and off-premises contracts to the respective provisions of the two repealed directives.

[48] The biggest technical difference between the general information requirements of Article 5 and the sector-specific information requirements of Chapter III is linked to the level of harmonisation of both regimes. While the information requirements of Chapter III in principle follow maximum harmonisation (only punctuated with some specific options in Articles 7(4) and 8(6) and minimum harmonised rules in Articles 6(7) and 9(3)), Article 5(4) allows Member States to maintain or introduce additional pre-contractual consumer information requirements in addition to the list of Article 5(1).

[49] Article 24(1) CRD.

[50] Article 10(1) CRD reads as follows: 'If the trader has not provided the consumer with the information on the right of withdrawal as required by point (h) of Article 6(1), the withdrawal period shall expire 12 months from the end of the initial withdrawal period, as determined in accordance with Article 9(2).' (Article 10(2) CRD adds that the withdrawal period expires fourteen days after the provision of the required information once the trader provides the consumer with the required information within the period extended by Article 10(1).) Put differently, the CRD thus caps the withdrawal period at a maximum of twelve months counted from the end of the initial withdrawal period,

Chapter IV (on 'other consumer rights') contains some broadly applicable, mostly fully harmonised[51] rules that (to a large extent) were now for the first time regulated at the EU level. The catalogue includes the following: certain delivery-related questions (Article 18);[52] a provision on a prohibition of charging fees for the use of means of payment (Article 19); a provision on the passing of risk for goods that are sent to the consumer (Article 20); restrictions on charges for the use of telephone lines installed by traders to facilitate contracts by consumers (with respect to concluded contracts; Article 21); and a fundamental, general rule on additional payments, i.e., on payments that exceed the remuneration for the main contractual obligation (Article 22).

i.e., the period that would have applied had the trader complied with the information requirement of Article 6(1)(h). Compared with the situation prior to the CRD, the introduction of a maximum period of one year and fourteen days is – from a consumer perspective – a step backwards. Under the repealed regime, the withdrawal periods could, in several instances, run eternally in case of unremedied failure to provide consumers with required information. On this issue see, e.g., P. Rott and E. Terryn, 'The Right of Withdrawal and Standard Terms' in Micklitz *et al.* (eds.), *Cases, Materials and Text on Consumer Law*, pp. 255–63 and the cases cited therein (in particular Case C-481/99, *Heininger* v. *Bayerische Hypo- und Vereinsbank AG* [2001] ECR I-6297, Case C-421/06, *Hamilton* v. *Volksbank Filder* [2008] ECR I-6278 on the situation in Germany prior to the enactment of the CRD and the French example illustrated in a case decided by the French Cour de Cassation in 2006: *Axa Courtage* v. *Varagne* (2006) JCP(G) 737 II 10056).

[51] Article 18(4) CRD is a notable exception. It allows Member States to go beyond the list of remedies for delivery delays.

[52] In this context it should be noted that delivery issues are one of the most important practical issues in B2C transaction. With respect to cross-border B2C trade in 2012 data presented by ECC-Net reveals that delivery problems were the most common reason for complaints, totalling 16.9 per cent of all complaints referred to ECCs (European Commission, 'The Consumer Conditions Scoreboard: Consumers at Home in the Single Market – 9th edition', p. 23 (Figure 22), available at ec.europa.eu/consumers/consumer_research/editions/docs/9th_edition_scoreboard_en.pdf). Delivery problems are also considered as being a key issue in purely domestic B2C transactions (see *ibid.*, p. 19, where it states that 29.7 per cent of respondents who concluded a domestic B2C transaction experienced delay problems, while another 8.2 per cent of respondents buying domestically reported that the purchased good did not arrive at all). Article 18 CRD only deals with the right to terminate a contract, but fails to introduce effective means to ensure that consumers actually receive ordered goods. One of the biggest issues in this respect is that traders rarely deliver the good themselves. Under normal circumstances, traders have little (if any) chance to directly influence third-party delivery services. To effectively tackle this issue, certain legal parameters could be designed to facilitate delivery services. If the first delivery attempt fails, delivery services could, for example, be obliged to attempt redelivery at the request of consumers and at a reasonable determined time. Only when consumers are not available to meet at the agreed redelivery time could delivery services be allowed to ask consumers to collect the item from a postal facility, e.g., from the local post office (if the delivery is carried out by post). Recently, discussions on how to improve delivery services have intensified, especially at a national level (for

Chapter V contains (mainly)[53] certain general mandates directed at the Member States, including provisions on the enforcement and transposition of the CRD regime into national law, information obligations in relation thereto, the earlier mentioned mandate to introduce 'effective, proportionate and dissuasive' penalties and a call for a review of the CRD by late 2016.

Unlike the Doorstep Selling Directive and the Distance Selling Directive, the two other directives covered by the CRD, the 1993 UCTD and the 1999 CSD were, contrary to the initial plans of the Commission, not repealed but only amended by two provisions in Chapter VI (on 'final provision'). Originally, and with respect to the UCTD, the CRD Proposal aimed at introducing a fully harmonised black list with absolutely prohibited contract terms[54] and a grey list with contract terms presumed to be unfair.[55] However, mainly because of pressure from the Member States via the Council, the approach eventually taken by the CRD left the UCTD and its minimum-harmonisation character principally untouched.[56] The only change to the UCTD was achieved by Article 32 CRD, which inserted a new provision, Article 8a, to address the issue of insufficient information access to national rules on unfair contract terms. Article 8a(1) UCTD asks Member States to inform the Commission about their more stringent national provisions (in case they have already made use of their legislative discretion to introduce consumer-friendlier rules pursuant to Article 8 UCTD and intend to maintain those rules or adopt more consumer-friendlier rules). This move was considered important to facilitate the exchange of information on national provisions regarding unfair contract terms among Member States, the Commission and stakeholders in B2C cross-border trade.[57]

---

details on various national approaches to this issue see N. Birger, 'Große Paketdienste wollen ihr Shop-Netz ausbauen', *Die Welt* (online), 10 November 2013, available at www.welt.de/wirtschaft/article121738270/Grosse-Paketdienste-wollen-ihr-Shop-Netz-ausbauen.html; V. Simettinger, 'Neue Lösungen für immer mehr Pakete', *ORF* (online), 11 December 2013, available at www.orf.at/stories/2207166/2207167.

[53] See the exception of the substantive provision of Article 27 CRD on inertia selling.

[54] Article 34 CRD Proposal with reference to the black list of Annex II CRD Proposal.

[55] Article 35 CRD Proposal with reference to the grey list of Point 1 of Annex III CRD Proposal. For comments on this approach see, e.g., Howells and Schulze, 'Overview of the Proposed Consumer Rights Directive', p. 22.

[56] Article 8 UCTD reads as follows: 'Member States may adopt or retain the most stringent provisions compatible with the Treaty in the area covered by this Directive, to ensure a maximum degree of protection for the consumer.'

[57] For comments on an earlier attempt to install a pan-EU database of unfair contract terms see H.-W. Micklitz and M. Radeideh, 'CLAB Europa – The European Database on Unfair Terms in Consumer Contracts', *Journal of Consumer Policy*, 28 (2005), 325–60.

In the opinion of the Commission, this should remove any uncertainty regarding foreign provisions on unfair contract terms and thus stimulate the growth of the internal market.

Article 8a(2) UCTD asks the Commission to ensure that any information received about national provisions covering unfair contract terms is made visible 'inter alia, on a dedicated website'. Article 8a(3) adds that '[t] he Commission shall forward the information … to the other Member States and the European Parliament. The Commission shall consult stakeholders on that information'. In addition to the wish to improve the information about national provisions, Article 8a can arguably be interpreted as the Commission's attempt to more closely monitor and assess the practical implementation of the directive to prepare a fully harmonised UCTD regime in the future.

With regard to the CSD, Article 33 CRD introduced a similarly worded provision by inserting the new Article 8a. Article 8a(2) and (3) CSD widely follow the wording of Article 8a(2) and (3) UCTD. As in the case of the UCTD, no further changes were made.

To a certain extent the CRD further removes some of the ambiguity of older directives. Article 16 CRD, for example, exempts certain types of off-premises and distance contracts from the withdrawal rights regime. One interesting exception with regard to distance contracts refers to the exclusion of public auctions. Although the exemption itself is nothing innovative as auctions were already excluded by Article 3(1) Distance Selling Directive, the CRD clarifies whether internet auctions fall under the category of excluded auctions and thus would not be subject to statutory withdrawal rights. Under the Distance Selling Directive regime this question was not really clear, as the directive failed to define 'auctions'.[58] Article 1(13) CRD gives an answer. According to the definition of public auctions used in that provision, the exclusion of Article 16(k) CRD refers to 'method[s] of sale where goods or services are offered by the trader to consumers, *who attend or are given the possibility to attend the auction*

---

[58] In several Member States there was discussion as to whether public auctions also refer to online auctions or only to 'traditional' auctions, i.e., to auctions that are moderated by an auctioneer and can be attended in person. For comments on this see G. Kathrein and T. Schoditsch, '§ 5b KSchG' in H. Koziol *et al.* (eds.), *Kurzkommentar zum ABGB* (4th edn, Vienna: Springer, 2014), § 5b KSchG, para. 2 (with respect to the situation in Austria); A. Hammerl, '§ 5b' in A. M. Kosesnik-Wehrle (ed.), *Konsumentenschutzgesetz (KSchG)* (3rd edn, Vienna: Manz, 2010), § 5b paras. 6–7 (on the situation in both Austria and Germany); C. Riefa, 'A Dangerous Erosion of Consumer Rights: The Absence of a Right to Withdraw from Online Auctions' in Howells and Schulze (eds.), *Modernising and Harmonising Consumer Contract Law*, pp. 178–80 (for more general comments in this respect).

in person ...' (emphasis added). Internet auctions are not covered by the exemption in Article 16(k) and are thus subject to the withdrawal right of the CRD.[59]

From a legislative–technical point of view, the final approach taken by the CRD is quite interesting. As already indicated, the CRD basically takes a maximum harmonisation approach. However, in contrast to Article 4 CRD Proposal, which anchored maximum harmonisation for the entire directive, the final wording of Article 4 CRD stipulates that 'Member States shall not maintain or introduce, in their national law, provisions diverging from those laid down in this Directive, including more or less stringent provisions to ensure a different level of consumer protection, *unless otherwise provided for in this Directive'* (emphasis added). I have already explained that Chapter II, in particular, diverges from maximum harmonisation and via its Article 5(4) allows national legislators to introduce or maintain additional pre-contractual information obligations (for contracts other than distance or off-premises contracts).[60] In addition, one can find specific 'regulatory choices' in several provisions of the CRD that round off the 'targeted full harmonisation approach'[61] and allow Member States to choose whether they would like to implement certain predefined mechanisms.[62]

The fact that the Commission was not able to anchor maximum harmonisation throughout the CRD might signal a possible important development. Unlike in some other cases of what I called the new Commission

---

[59] Article 2(u) CESL Regulation Proposal contains a similar definition. It defines public auctions as auctions where the consumer has at least 'the possibility to attend the auction in person'.

[60] For a minimum harmonisation example from a different CRD chapter see Article 6(7) CRD, which (with respect to the Article 6 regime) explains as follows: 'Member States may maintain or introduce in their national law language requirements regarding the contractual information, so as to ensure that such information is easily understood by the consumer.' See further Articles 9(3) and 18(4) CRD.

[61] On the use of the terms 'full harmonisation', 'targeted full harmonisation' and 'differentiated full harmonisation' in the context of consumer law in general and the CRD/the CRD Proposal in particular, see, e.g., B. Jud and C. Wendehorst, *'Position Paper – Vienna Conference on the Proposal for a Directive of the European Parliament and of the Council on Consumer Rights, COM(2008) 614 final'* in Jud and Wendehorst (eds.), *Neuordnung des Verbraucherprivatrechts in Europa*, p. 191 ('differentiated full harmonisation'); Loos, 'Full Harmonisation As a Regulatory Concept', p. 88 ('targeted full harmonisation'); Howells and Schulze, 'Overview of the Proposed Consumer Rights Directive', pp. 6–8 ('targeted full harmonisation'); Micklitz, 'The Targeted Full Harmonisation Approach' ('targeted full harmonisation').

[62] For the term 'regulatory choices' see Article 29(1) CRD. For examples see Articles 3(4), 5(3), 7(4) and 8(6).

approach, (such as the UCPD, the Consumer Credit Agreements Directive and the Timeshare Directive), the Commission was not successful in establishing an absolutely fully harmonised regime (in the sense of completely following maximum harmonisation) in the case of the CRD. This time the positions of the national governments and consumer interest groups were strong enough to secure the preservation of the legislative leeway for national legislators with regard to respective domestic consumer policies.

Nevertheless, maximum harmonisation basically dominates the CRD. One cannot deny that in some cases it has actually led to an improvement for consumers. One example is the length of the withdrawal period to exercise withdrawal rights granted for off-premises and distance contracts as regulated by Chapter III CRD. For both scenarios the CRD extends the withdrawal period from seven days (Article 5(1) Doorstep Selling Directive) and seven working days (Article 6(1) Distance Selling Directive), respectively, to fourteen days (Article 9(1) CRD).

However, from a consumer perspective, the maximum harmonisation approach of the CRD also led to some unfortunate consequences. One practical example refers to the cost-bearing rule with respect to the right to withdraw from distance and off-premises contracts. The related rules can be found in Articles 6(i), 6(6), 9(1) and 14 CRD. The fully harmonised Article 14 summarises the legal setting as follows: 'The consumer shall only bear the direct cost of returning the goods unless the trader has agreed to bear them or the trader failed to inform the consumer that the consumer has to bear them.'[63] In other words, it is up to the trader to decide who shall bear the direct costs of returning goods. At first sight there seems to be little difference with the Distance Selling Directive. Its Article 6 stated that '[t]he only charge that may be made to the consumer because of the exercise of his right of withdrawal is the direct cost of returning the goods'. However, one must not forget that the Distance Selling Directive was a minimum harmonisation directive. Hence, Member States were free to enact or maintain consumer-friendlier cost-bearing provisions. The shift from this (theoretically) consumer-friendly to a trader-friendlier approach becomes even more obvious with respect to the Doorstep Selling Directive, which was relatively silent on the cost issue. Article 7 of this directive only stipulated that '[i]f the consumer exercises his right

---

[63] For the latter exception see further Article 6(6) CRD: 'If the trader has not complied with the information requirements on … the costs of returning the goods as referred to in point (i) of paragraph 1, the consumer shall not bear those … costs.'

of renunciation, the legal effects of such renunciation shall be governed by national laws, particularly regarding the reimbursement of payments for goods or services provided and the return of goods received'. In other words, with respect to a withdrawal from an off-premises contract, the Doorstep Selling Directive left it to the national legislator to decide who should bear the costs of returning goods. With the introduction of the CRD this autonomous regulative power vanished.

The shift towards a business-friendlier regime shows the need for some Member States to depart from their established rules (several Member States had taken consumer-friendlier approaches in the past). The general German rule with respect to the allocation of return costs, § 357(2) of the German Civil Code (*Bürgerliches Gesetzbuch*; BGB), for example, (in its version prior to the national implementation of the CRD) read as follows: 'the ... costs of return ... may be imposed by contract on the consumer if the price of the thing ... does not exceed an amount of EUR 40 or if, where the price is higher, the consumer has at the date of the revocation not yet rendered consideration or given a part payment, unless the goods supplied do not correspond to those ordered.' This approach is obviously consumer-friendlier, but could not be maintained because Article 14 CRD rests on maximum harmonisation. The implementation of the CRD led to a revision and restructuring of § 357 BGB. The cost-related consequences are now regulated by § 357(6), which – in line with Article 14 CRD – reads as follows: 'The consumer bears the direct cost of returning the goods, if the trader informed him about this obligation in accordance with Article 246a § 1(2)(1)(2) German Introductory Act to the Civil Code (*Einführungsgesetz zum Bürgerlichen Gesetzbuch*; EGBGB). Sentence 1 [i.e., the just cited sentence] does not apply if the trader declared that he would bear the costs' (translation mine).[64]

The consumer acquis beyond the CRD and towards the CESL

At the end of the day the CRD did not cause the initially expected landslide. Although the Commission aimed to standardise as much as possible, the concessions that had to be made to the national legislators were too big to give it any real reason for celebration. The final scope, wording and chosen harmonisation level of the CRD showed that the Member States were not unconditionally willing to sacrifice their legislative interests.

---

[64] Article 246a § 1(2)(1)(2) EGBGB contains the information requirements with respect to the withdrawal right in cases of distance and off-premises contracts.

As indicated earlier, the CRD was not the only legislative outcome of the consumer acquis evaluation. At the time of writing this book, three of the four directives not included in the CRD had been either replaced or were about to be replaced. Only a couple of months before the publication of the CRD Proposal the 1998 Injunctions Directive was repealed by the 2009 Injunctions Directive (which did not lead to any substantive change of the injunctions regime, though; I have already discussed both versions in Chapter 4 of this book). Also in 2009 a new Timeshare Directive was enacted, which replaced the older 1994 version. And four years later in 2013, a new Package Travel Directive was proposed.[65]

In contrast to the CRD, the new Timeshare Directive and (to a great extent) the proposed new Package Travel Directive both follow maximum harmonisation.[66] With respect to the Timeshare Directive, Recital 3 of the new Timeshare Directive explains the rationale behind this with a familiar argument: 'In order to enhance legal certainty and fully achieve the benefits of the internal market for consumers and businesses, the relevant

---

[65] In a first plenary reading on 12 March 2014 the Parliament backed the proposal in a slightly amended version (see European Parliament legislative resolution on the proposal for a directive of the European Parliament and of the Council on package travel and assisted travel arrangements, amending Regulation (EC) No 2006/2004, Directive 2011/83/EU and repealing Council Directive 90/314/EEC, 12 March 2014, (COM(2013)0512 – C7-0215/2013 – 2013/0246(COD), available at www.europarl.europa. eu/sides/getDoc.do?pubRef=-//EP//TEXT+TA+P7-TA-2014-0222+0+DOC+XML+V0// EN&language=EN). The Parliament version is mainly based on the wording as suggested by the Internal Market and Consumer Protection Committee (IMCO), the committee responsible for the proposal at the Parliament level (for the suggested amendments by IMCO see www.europarl.europa.eu/sides/getDoc.do?type=REPORT&reference=A7-2014-0124&language=EN). For a brief summary see European Commission, 'Stress-free Holidays for 120 Million Consumers – European Parliament Backs New Rules on Package Travel', press release, MEMO/14/184, 12 March 2014, available at europa.eu/ rapid/press-release_MEMO-14-184_en.htm. See the following note for comments on the level of harmonisation.

[66] Unlike the 1990 Package Travel Directive, which (as stated in its Article 8) allowed Member States to adopt consumer-friendlier rules, the 2013 Package Travel Directive Proposal, in principle, does not grant Member States the chance to go beyond the enshrined standard. An exception to this can, however, be found in Article 12(6) 2013 Package Travel Directive Proposal. It states as follows: 'The prescription period for introducing claims under this Article shall not be shorter than one year.' The Parliament version (see note 65 above) takes a more mitigated, i.e., consumer-friendlier approach. Basically, the new Package Travel Directive (if adopted based on the wording of the Parliament version), would be based on maximum harmonisation. Article 1a of the Parliament version does, however, allow Member States to maintain or introduce consumer-friendlier provisions if explicitly allowed by the provisions of the directive (see in particular Article 11(7a) of the Parliament version in this respect; note further in this context that the minimum prescription period of Article 12(6) is extended from one to three years).

laws of the Member States need to be approximated further. Therefore, certain aspects of the marketing, sale and resale of timeshares ... should be fully harmonised.' In a similar vein, Recital 5 2013 Package Travel Directive Proposal states that '[t]he [maximum] harmonisation of certain aspects of package contracts and assisted travel arrangements is necessary for the creation of a real consumer internal market'.

It remains to be seen how the tensions between the interests of the Commission and the Parliament in fully harmonising consumer law-related issues and the interests of the national legislators (as represented in the Council) in retaining their legislative powers will be solved in the course of future legislative actions.[67] Striking the 'right' balance between centralised and decentralised interests will be crucial in this respect, because 'too much' supranational legislation could interfere with legislative interests of the Member States. Weatherill comments on this as follows: 'The Commission's development of European contract law ... [is]

---

[67] On the tensions between EU and Member State interests in drafting a pan-European contract regime see J. Ziller, 'The Legitimacy of the Codification of Contract Law in View of the Allocation of Competences between the European Union and Its Member States' in Hesselink (ed.), *The Politics of a European Civil Code*, pp. 89–113; M. W. Hesselink, 'The Politics of a European Civil Code' in *ibid.*, pp. 143–70. Loos, 'Full Harmonisation As a Regulatory Concept'; K.-H. Oehler, 'Die Umsetzung der vollharmonisierenden Richtlinie aus Sicht des innerstaatlichen Gesetzgebers' in Stürner (ed.), *Vollharmonisierung im Europäischen Verbraucherrecht?*, pp. 99–110; W. van Gerven, 'Private Law in a Federal Perspective' in Brownsword *et al.* (eds.), *The Foundations of European Private Law*, pp. 337–51; K. Lilleholt, 'European Private Law: Unification, Harmonisation or Coordination?' in *ibid.*, pp. 353–61. See further Weatherill, 'Maximum or Minimum Harmonisation', p. 145, where Weatherill explains that '"maximum harmonisation" involves a sufficiently radical redistribution of regulatory competence to call into question the very legitimacy of the EC's lawmaking pretensions'. See further Collins's comment on the difficult balance to be struck between EU and Member State policy-making in H. Collins, 'Governance Implications for the European Union of the Changing Character of Private Law' in F. Cafaggi and H. Muir-Watt (eds.), *Making European Private Law* (Cheltenham: Edward Elgar, 2008), p. 286, where he claims that 'European private law must both accommodate the requirements of a different governance system comprised of a multi-level system of rule-making ... and incorporate into its reasoning processes the modern characteristics of private law systems, which blend legal and policy discourse'. For a discussion on the recent harmonisation policies with respect to the consumer protection standard of the Rome I Regulation see B. Schinkels, '"Horizontalrichtlinie" und kollisionsrechtlicher Verbraucherschutz – zugleich ein Beitrag zum Verhältnis von Art. 3 Abs. 4 und 6 Abs. 2 Rom-I-VO' in Stürner (ed.), *Vollharmonisierung im Europäischen Verbraucherrecht?*, pp. 113–32. For comments on maximum harmonisation in the context of the DCFR see F. Zoll, 'Der Entwurf des Gemeinsamen Referenzrahmens und die Vollharmonisierung' in *ibid.*, pp. 133–41. For a comment on the possible consequences of the Lisbon Treaty for the approximation of private law see R. Streinz, 'Der Vertrag von Lissabon und die Privatrechtsangleichung' in *ibid.*, pp. 23–43.

intimately connected to the general debate about the balance that needs to be struck between, on the one hand, centralisation and uniformity in Europe and, on the other, tolerance of diversity and respect for local autonomy.'[68] Reiner Schulze frames the issue in terms of a request directed at the Commission and the Union legislator: 'In relation to national law, European private law ought ... to be treated as an autonomous subject and, at the same time, the continuance of national diversity in the dualism of supranational and national law should be respected.'[69] This matter might become very obvious with regard to one of the most recent Commission projects, the Common European Sales Law, which will be discussed in the following chapter.

[68] S. Weatherill, 'Constitutional Issues – How Much Is Best Left Unsaid?' in Vogenauer and Weatherill (eds.), *The Harmonisation of European Contract Law*, p. 103.

[69] R. Schulze, 'European Private Law: Political Foundations and Current Challenges' in Brownsword *et al.* (eds.), *The Foundations of European Private Law*, p. 306.

10

The Common European Sales Law

The genesis of the proposal on a Common European Sales Law or: the long and winding road

On 11 October 2011, shortly before the adoption of the CRD, the Commission officially published its next big project, the Proposal for a Regulation on a Common European Sales Law[1] (CESL Regulation Proposal). It is one of the latest attempts by the Commission to push for a fully standardised law to tear down the presumed internal market barriers created by the existence of diverse national laws.[2]

The CESL Regulation, if and once adopted, would introduce the CESL, an alternative sales law regime that parties to, inter alia, certain cross-

---

[1] Proposal for a Regulation of the European Parliament and of the Council on a Common European Sales Law, 11 October 2011, COM(2011) 635 final.

[2] The Commission bases the CESL Regulation Proposal on Article 114 Treaty on the Functioning of the European Union (TFEU). It is beyond the scope of this book to comment in detail on this. For a comment on basing the CESL on Article 114 TFEU see, for example, P.-C. Müller-Graff, 'Ein fakultatives europäisches Kaufrecht als Instrument der Marktordnung?' in H. Schulte-Nölke et al. (eds.), Der Entwurf für ein optionales europäisches Kaufrecht (Munich: Sellier, 2012), pp. 40–2. With respect to the fact that the CESL would (as explained further below) be an optional instrument one should further note that the CJEU (on a different occasion) explained that approximation conditions are not fulfilled where a regulation 'leaves unchanged the different national laws already in existence, [because such an instrument] cannot be regarded as aiming to approximate the laws of the Member States' (Case C-436/03, European Parliament v. Council of the European Union [2006] ECR I-3733, Recital 44). It remains to be seen how the CJEU would assess the situation in the case of the CESL. For general remarks on the competence issue in the context of European contract law see S. Weatherill, 'Competence and European Private Law' in Twigg-Flesner (ed.), The Cambridge Companion to European Union Private Law, pp. 58–9; C. Mak, 'Constitutional Aspects of a European Civil Code' in Hartkamp et al. (eds.), Towards a European Civil Code, pp. 344–6; J. W. Rutgers, 'European Competence and a European Civil Code, a Common Frame of Reference or an Optional Instrument' in ibid., pp. 311–31; S. Vogenauer and S. Weatherill, 'The European Community's Competence to Pursue the Harmonisation of Contract Law – an Empirical Contribution to the Debate' in Vogenauer and Weatherill (eds.), The Harmonisation of European Contract Law, pp. 105–48; S. Weatherill, 'Reflections on the EC's Competence to Develop a "European Contract Law"', European Review of Private

border B2C transaction contracts could agree to use. One can also say that the CESL is designed as an optional instrument (OI), which means that the parties could choose it to govern their contract (if basically falling under the scope of the CESL). To be more precise, the CESL is, as will be shown further below,[3] designed as a secondary or second-ranked sales law at the national level, or as commonly referred to in the literature, a 'second (national) regime'.[4]

Law, 13 (2005), 405–18. For collections of general comments on the CESL Regulation Proposal see, for example, Schulte-Nölke *et al.* (eds.), *Der Entwurf für ein optionales europäisches Kaufrecht*; M. Schmidt-Kessel (ed.), *Ein einheitliches europäisches Kaufrecht? Eine Analyse des Vorschlags der Kommission* (Munich: Sellier, 2012); J.-U. Hahn (ed.), *Gemeinsames Europäisches Kaufrecht: Moderner Ansatz oder praxisferne Vision?* (Munich: C.H. Beck, 2012); C. Wendehorst and B. Zöchling-Jud (eds.), *Am Vorabend eines Gemeinsamen Europäischen Kaufrechts: Zum Verordnungsentwurf der Europäischen Kommission vom 11.10.2011* (Vienna: Manz, 2012); O. Remien *et al.* (eds.), *Gemeinsames Europäisches Kaufrecht der EU? Analyse des Vorschlags der Europäischen Kommission für ein optionales Europäisches Vertragsrecht vom 11. Oktober 2011* (Munich: C.H. Beck, 2012); G. Alpa *et al.* (eds.), *The Proposed Common European Sales Law – the Lawyers' View* (Munich: Sellier, 2013); the contributions in T. Ackermann *et al.* (eds.), *Common Market Law Review* (Special Issue), 50 (2013); G. Dannemann and S. Vogenauer (eds.), *The Common European Sales Law in Context: Interactions with English and German Law* (Oxford University Press, 2013).

[3] See 'Fourth assumption: The CESL will be a bilaterally voluntary, secondary regime' below.

[4] The legal concept on which the CESL is based is not without debate and is mainly linked to the interesting discussion on whether the CESL would have to be considered as a second *intranational* or – now that Croatia has joined the EU – as a 29th *international* sales law regime (note that in the pertinent literature on this topic the term 28th regime is used instead; this is due to the fact that most of the literature on this issue stems from the time before Croatia joined the EU). Martijn Hesselink explains that one of the main reasons for the discussions can be seen in the legislative process of adapting the CESL – see M. W. Hesselink, 'How to Opt into the Common European Sales Law? Brief Comments on the Commission's Proposal for a Regulation', Centre for the Study of European Contract Law Working Paper, No. 2011–15 (2011), p. 6, available at papers.ssrn.com/sol3/papers. cfm?abstract_id=1950107 (reprinted in *European Review of Private Law*, 20 (2012), pp. 195–212). The discussion dates back to the beginning of the new millennium, before concrete plans were made regarding the introduction of the CESL as an OI. Helmut Heiss and Noemí Downes, for example, had already explained the practical importance of the decision between a 2nd and 28th/29th regime before the drafting of the CESL began – see H. Heiss and N. Downes, 'Non-Optional Elements in an Optional European Contract Law. Reflections from a Private International Law Perspective', *European Review of Private Law*, 13 (2005), 693, 700–12. Giesela Rühl adds a further concept to the discussion – the concept of a first regime. She defines it as 'a uniform law that defines its own scope of application and that will accordingly apply if the parties validly agree' (G. Rühl, 'The Common European Sales Law – 28th Regime, 2nd Regime or 1st Regime', Maastricht Faculty of Law Working Paper, No. 2012/5 (2012), p. 12, available at papers.ssrn.com/sol3/ papers.cfm?abstract_id=2025879). In practice this means that the protective regime of the Rome I Regulation could be easily circumvented by independent rules of applicability contained in the CESL itself. A similar argumentation is used by the Max Planck Institute for

Choosing the form of an OI can be considered an innovative move in the field of European consumer law.[5] Of course, it would not be the first time that the EU has opted for an OI in the area of substantive law:

Comparative and International Private Law: '[I]t seems preferable to adopt the approach considered in Art. 22(b) Rome I Regulation Proposal: the choice of the optional instrument ought to be exempted from the provisions of the Rome I Regulation ... [as t]he issue should rather be dealt with by a set of specific rules that supersede, as *leges speciales*, the Rome I Regulation' (see Max Planck Institute for Comparative and International Private Law, 'Policy Options for Progress Towards a European Contract Law – Comments on the issues raised in the Green Paper from the Commission of 1 July 2010, COM(2010) 348 final', *Rabels Zeitschrift für ausländisches und internationales Privatrecht*, 75 (2011), 371, 400–2). The Max Planck Institute for Comparative and International Private Law further refers to Recital 14 Rome I Regulation, which reads as follows: 'Should the Community adopt, in an appropriate legal instrument, rules of substantive contract law, including standard terms, such instrument may provide that the parties may choose to apply those rules.' In a similar vein is Matthias Weller's argumentation (see M. Weller, 'Art. 23 Rome I' in G.-P. Calliess (ed.), *Rome Regulations: Commentary on the European Rules of the Conflict of Laws* (Alphen aan den Rijn: Kluwer Law International, 2011), Article 23 Rome I Para. 7, where he notes that 'Recital 14 seems to indicate that a choice-of-law provision in this instrument allowing the parties to choose its rules as the applicable contract law will have priority under Article 23 [Rome I Regulation]'). For details on Recital 14 Rome I Regulation see further J. von Hein, 'Art 3 Rom I-VO' in T. Rauscher (ed.), *Europäisches Zivilprozess- und Kollisionsrecht: EuZPR / EuIPR* (Munich: Sellier, 2011), Article 3 para. 58. For comments on the legal nature of the CESL either prior to or after the publication of the CESL Regulation Proposal see M. Stürner, 'Kollisionsrecht und Optionales Instrument: Aspekte einer noch ungeklärten Beziehung', *Zeitschrift für das Privatrecht der Europäischen Union*, 8 (2011) 236–42; S. Whittaker, 'The Optional Instrument of European Contract Law and Freedom of Contract', *European Review of Contract Law*, 7 (2011), 371; H. Fleischer, 'Optionales europäisches Privatrecht (»28. Modell«)', *Rabels Zeitschrift für ausländisches und internationales Privatrecht*, 76 (2012), 235–52; W.-H. Roth, 'Stellungnahme zum "Vorschlag für eine Verordnung des Europäischen Parlaments und des Rates über ein Gemeinsames Europäisches Kaufrecht, KOM (2011) 635 endg."', opinion paper, (2011) (on file with the author); M. Fornasier, '»28.« versus »2. Regime« – Kollisionsrechtliche Aspekte eines optionalen europäischen Vertragsrechts', *Rabels Zeitschrift für ausländisches und internationales Privatrecht*, 76 (2012), 401–42; S. Wrbka, 'Consumers and the Proposal for an Optional Common European Sales Law: No Roads Lead to Rome?', Kyushu University Legal Research Bulletin, 2 (2012), pp. 9–12, available at researchbulletin.kyudai.info/?p=248; M. Lehmann, 'Dogmatische Konstruktion der Einwahl in das EU-Kaufrecht (2., 28. oder integriertes Regime) und die praktischen Folgen' in M. Gebauer (ed.), *Gemeinsames Europäisches Kaufrecht – Anwendungsbereich und kollisionsrechtliche Einbettung* (Munich: Sellier, 2013), pp. 67–88. I will briefly deal with the related, interesting question of the interplay between the CESL and the Rome I Regulation later (see 'Sixth assumption: The CESL will necessarily solve 'problems' caused by Rome I' below).

[5] In a similar vein is B. Fauvarque-Cosson, 'European Contract Law Through and Beyond Pluralism: the Case of an Optional Instrument' in L. Niglia (ed.), *Pluralism and European Private Law* (Oxford: Hart, 2013), p. 101: 'The use of an optional instrument in the field of ... sales contracts ... is innovative.'

the Community Trade Mark (CTM)[6] or the *Societas Europaea* (SE)[7] are prominent older examples.[8] However, unlike these two instruments, the CESL would require an agreement of (at least) two parties – the parties to a specific contract – and (at least in theory)[9] could not be freely chosen by just one person/entity.

Although the CESL – compared with the SE and CTM – is of rather recent origin, the political ideas behind the CESL date back to the late 1980s and mid-1990s. In 1989, several years after the 'Lando Commission' (i.e., the (academic) Commission on European Contract Law founded on the initiative of Ole Lando) had started discussions on and elaborations of European contract law principles (the Principles of European Contract Law),[10] the Parliament asked for suggestions to revise and harmonise private law rules more comprehensively at the EU level. It considered harmonisation as necessary, especially 'in branches of law which are highly important for the development of the single market, such as contract law',[11] as 'progressive harmonization of certain sectors of private law ... [was deemed to be] essential to the completion of the internal market'.[12]

---

[6] Council Regulation (EC) No 40/94 on the Community trade mark, 20 December 1993, OJ 1994 No. L11/1.

[7] Council Regulation (EC) No 1435/2003 on the Statute for a European Cooperative Society (SCE), 22 July 2003, OJ 2003 No. L207/1.

[8] For further examples see G. Low, 'A Numbers Game – The Legal Basis for an Optional Instrument in European Contract Law', Maastricht European Private Law Institute Working Paper, No. 2012/2 (2012), p. 3, available at papers.ssrn.com/sol3/papers. cfm?abstract_id=1991070. For a discussion of OIs introduced by EU laws see N. Reich, 'EU Strategies in Finding the Optimal Consumer Law Instrument', *European Review of Contract Law*, 8 (2012), 1–29.

[9] See 'Fourth assumption: The CESL will be a bilaterally voluntary, secondary regime' below for details.

[10] O. Lando and H. Beale (eds.), *Principles of European Contract Law – Parts I and II* (The Hague: Kluwer Law International, 2000); and O. Lando *et al.* (eds.), *European Contract Law – Part III* (The Hague: Kluwer Law International, 2003). For intermediary conclusions of the Lando Commission see O. Lando, 'Is Codification Needed in Europe? Principles of European Contract Law and the Relationship to Dutch Law', *European Review of Private Law*, 1 (1993), 157–70. For comments on the work of the Lando Commission and other early research groups see M. B. M. Loos and A. L. M. Keirse, 'The Optional Instrument and the Consumer Rights Directive: Alternative Ways to a New Ius Commune in Contract Law – Introduction' in A. L. M. Keirse and M. B. M. Loos, *Alternative Ways to Ius Commune – The Europeanisation of Private Law* (Cambridge: Intersentia, 2012), pp. 12–15.

[11] Resolution on action to bring into line the private law of the Member States, 26 May 1989, OJ 1989 No. C158/400, lit. E.

[12] Resolution on the harmonization of certain sectors of the private law of the Member States, 6 May 1994, OJ 1994 No. C205/518, lit. E.

For some time, though, this idea had lain rather dormant at the Commission level. It was only after the beginning of the new millennium that the Commission's 2001 Contract Law Communication expressed the wish to 'gather ... information on the need for farther-reaching EC action in the area of contract law, in particular to the extent that the case-by-case approach might not be able to solve all the problems which might arise'.[13] This was further fuelled by the Commission's idea to complement the earlier discussed elaborations on the consumer acquis with some more general principles and definitions. The 2003 Contract Law Action Plan used the term 'Common Frame of Reference' (CFR) to refer to this purpose and explained the underlying plan as follows:

> [T]he Commission will seek to increase, where necessary and possible, coherence between instruments, which are part of the EC contract law acquis, both in their drafting and in their implementation and application. Proposals will, where appropriate, take into account a *common frame of reference*, which the Commission intends to elaborate via research and with the help of all interested parties. This common frame of reference should provide for best solutions in terms of common terminology and rules, i.e., the definition of fundamental concepts and abstract terms like 'contract' or 'damage' and of the rules that apply for example in the case of non-performance of contracts[14] (emphasis added).

---

[13] 2001 Contract Law Communication, para. 10. Voices in legal academia were deeply divided on this issue. Various different views, both in favour and against a European Civil or Contract Code can be found in S. Grundmann and J. Stuyck (eds.), *An Academic Green Paper on European Private Law* (The Hague: Kluwer Law International, 2002). The collection covers contributions from the beginning of the new millennium and shows that the proponents of a pan-European instrument could not agree on the exact form and scope of a possible instrument. Various different models of a possible code were supported (see, for example, C. von Bar, 'Paving the Way forward with Principles of European Private Law' in *ibid.*, pp. 137–45; J. Basedow, 'The Case for a European Contract Law' in *ibid.*, pp. 147–57; M. W. Hesselink, 'The Politics of a European Civil Code: Who Has an Interest in What Kind of Contract Law for Europe?' in *ibid.*, pp. 181–91; O. Lando, 'Why Does Europe Need a Civil Code?' in *ibid.*, pp. 207–13; U. Mattei, 'Hard Minimal Code Now! – a Critique of "Softness" and a Plea for Responsibility in the European Debate over Codification' in *ibid.*, pp. 215–33; H.-P. Schwintowski, 'The European Civil Code: a Framework Code Only' in *ibid.*, pp. 235–48). Several other scholars disagreed (for several different reasons) with plans to introduce a detailed pan-European instrument in the near future (see, for example, H. Beale, 'Finding the Remaining Traps Instead of Unifying Contract Law' in *ibid.*, pp. 67–72; H. Collins, 'Transaction Costs and Subsidiarity in European Contract Law' in *ibid.*, pp. 269–81; N. Reich, 'Critical Comments on the Commission Communication "On European Contract Law"' in *ibid.*, pp. 283–91; R. Van den Bergh, 'Forced Harmonisation of Contract Law in Europe' in *ibid.*, pp. 249–68).

[14] 2003 Contract Law Action Plan, p. 2.

With its 2004 Acquis Communication, the Commission went into slightly greater detail and showed its preference for an OI[15] (which it had already briefly touched upon in the previous 2003 Contract Law Action Plan).[16] The Commission commented as follows: '[The 2004 Acquis Communication] intends to continue the reflection on the opportuneness of an optional instrument; … [T]he CFR would be likely to serve as the basis for the development of a possible optional instrument.'[17] Nevertheless, and despite already discussing certain parameters of a possible OI in Annex II of the 2004 Acquis Communication, no official decision regarding an OI was made at that time.

Related discussions at the academic level progressed in a comparatively faster manner. The aforementioned Lando Commission was the first significant, more relevant attempt to place the topic of European Private Law (including contract law) on a bigger European stage. Several other initiatives followed. The work of two academic groups, in particular, should be mentioned in this context:[18] the Study Group on a European Civil Code (SGECC), which followed the Lando Commission and commenced its studies in 1998[19] and the European Research Group on Existing EC Private Law (Acquis Group), which followed in 2002.[20]

The SGECC and the Acquis Group both took different yet complementary approaches in their quest to identify private law rules common to the Member States. While the SGECC concentrated on the analysis, comparison and development of national private laws, the Acquis Group focused on 'EU legislation and case-law'.[21] The approaches complemented each other and guaranteed that conclusions drawn from a legal comparison of national mechanisms could merge into a strongly based, broad

---

[15] 2004 Acquis Communication, chapters 2.1.2, 2.3 and Annex II.
[16] 2003 Contract Law Action Plan, chapter 4.1.1.
[17] 2004 Acquis Communication, pp. 2 and 5.
[18] For a comprehensive list of research groups see, e.g., Schmidt-Kessel, 'Der Vorschlag im Kontext der Rechtsharmonisierung in Europa', pp. 23–5. For brief comments on some of these working groups see B. Lurger, *Grundfragen der Vereinheitlichung des Vertragsrechts in der Europäischen Union* (Vienna: Springer, 2002), pp. 11–22 and 98–104; K. Riesenhuber, *System und Prinzipien des Europäischen Vertragsrechts* (Berlin: De Gruyter, 2003), pp. 44–51; H. Schulte-Nölke, 'Vor- und Entstehungsgeschichte des Vorschlags für ein Gemeinsames Europäisches Kaufrecht' in Schulte-Nölke *et al.* (eds.), *Der Entwurf für ein optionales europäisches Kaufrecht*, pp. 1–20; R. Zimmermann, *Die Europäisierung des Privatrechts und die Rechtsvergleichung* (Berlin: De Gruyter, 2006), pp. 45–6.
[19] For details on the work of the SGECC see www.sgecc.net.
[20] For details on the work of the Acquis Group see www.acquis-group.org.
[21] Cámara Lapuente and Terryn, 'Consumer Contract Law', p. 160.

framework. The extensive research conducted by these two and other mostly academic groups, which in the words of Roger Brownsword consisted of '[s]ome of the best private law minds in Europe',[22] surely have to be considered as an important intermediary step to the CESL.

Driven by its plan to create a CFR, the Commission decided to use the work of the SGECC and the Acquis Group for its own benefit. In 2005, the Joint Network on European Private Law (CoPECL) was founded under the EU Sixth Framework Programme for Research with funding secured from the Commission to pursue further studies.[23] Both the SGECC and the Acquis Group played key roles with respect to contract law within the CoPECL and took the lead in the quest for a CFR.

The research work of the CoPECL went slightly further than originally envisaged by the Commission and also included non-contractual issues. This might not least have been due to the fact that the SGECC and the Acquis Group had commenced their studies before the 2003 Contract Law Action Plan asked for research into a CFR that focused on contract issues and because the *concrete* scope and character of the CFR was left unclarified for several years, even after the launch of the CoPECL. Although it was clear that the CFR was meant to facilitate the growth of the internal market, for a long time it was (at least officially) undecided exactly what matters would be covered (in terms of means and scope) by such an instrument.

A major, intermediary result of the research was published in 2009 when the SGECC and the Acquis Group presented the Draft Common Frame of Reference on the Principles, Definitions and Model Rules of European Private Law (DCFR).[24] The DCFR comprised a collection of private law rules primarily (but not only) focusing on contract law. Its full title explicitly refers to the content of the DCFR, which is split into three pillars: (1) the four principles of freedom, security, justice and efficiency as the underlying principles of European Private Law in general,[25] (2) definitions of legal terms in the context of private law used at the European and Member State level[26] and (3) model rules, the largest part of the DCFR. In ten 'books', these model rules breathed life into the four DCFR

---

[22] R. Brownsword, 'The Theoretical Foundations of European Private Law: A Time to Stand and Stare' in Brownsword *et al.* (eds.), *The Foundations of European Private Law*, p. 174.

[23] For details on the work of the CoPECL see www.copecl.org.

[24] C. von Bar *et al.* (eds.), *Principles, Definitions and Model Rules of European Private Law – Draft Common Frame of Reference (DCFR) Outline Edition* (Munich: Sellier, 2009).

[25] See *ibid.*, Part 'Principles'.

[26] See the Annex of the DCFR for details.

principles and covered in a quite detailed manner common rules not only for contract law issues but also for several non-contract law issues such as non-contractual liability or unjustified enrichment.[27] The DCFR can be considered as an important milestone in the quest for the CESL. It summarises the results of extensive research carried out over a long period of time. The *Full Edition*, in particular, with more than 6,500 pages of supplementary explanations, comments and notes on the approaches taken by national legislators and references to court judgments, offers invaluable information in this respect.[28]

---

[27] See Books VI and VII respectively. See H. Beale, 'European Contract Law: the Common Frame of Reference and Beyond' in Twigg-Flesner (ed.), *The Cambridge Companion to European Union Private Law*, pp. 124–6 for some comments in this context.

[28] C. von Bar and E. Clive (eds.), *Principles, Definitions and Model Rules of European Private Law. Draft Common Frame of Reference (DCFR). Full Edition* (Munich: Sellier, 2009 and Oxford University Press, 2010). The shorter version of the DCFR, the *Outline Edition*, is also of relevance. It provides the public with a version of the full text of the DCFR (clear of detailed explanatory comments) that can be accessed freely online (ec.europa.eu/justice/policies/civil/docs/dcfr_outline_edition_en.pdf). Without doubt, the DCFR is of great relevance because it achieved the inclusion of comprehensive insights into already existing abundant literature on the academic debate on European contract law and fuelled further discussions. For examples of contributions either preceding or succeeding the publication of the DCFR see Grundmann and Stuyck (eds.), *An Academic Green Paper on European Private Law*; L. Niglia, *The Transformation of Contract in Europe* (The Hague: Kluwer Law International, 2003); Smits (ed.), *The Need for a European Contract Law*; Hesselink (ed.), *The Politics of a European Civil Code*; G.-P. Calliess, *Grenzüberschreitende Verbraucherverträge* (Tübingen: Mohr Siebeck, 2006); Vogenauer and Weatherill (eds.), *The Harmonisation of European Contract Law*; Wilhelmsson *et al.* (eds.), *Private Law and the Many Cultures of Europe*; Boele-Woelki and Grosheide (eds.), *The Future of European Contract Law*; B. Fauvarque-Cosson and D. Mazeaud (eds.), *European Contract Law – Materials for a Common Frame of Reference: Terminology, Guiding Principles, Model Rules* (Munich: Sellier, 2008); Cafaggi and Muir-Watt (eds.), *Making European Private Law*; Hesselink, *CFR & Social Justice*; Twigg-Flesner, *The Europeanisation of Contract Law*; Collins, *The European Civil Code*; Twigg-Flesner (ed.), *Common Frame of Reference and Existing EC Contract Law*; Twigg-Flesner (ed.), *The Cambridge Companion to European Union Private Law*; Stürner (ed.), *Vollharmonisierung im Europäischen Verbraucherrecht?*; Micklitz and Cafaggi (eds.), *European Private Law after the Common Frame of Reference*; Leczykiewicz and Weatherill (eds.), *The Involvement of EU Law in Private Law Relationships*; Brownsword *et al.* (eds.), *The Foundations of European Private Law*; Hartkamp *et al.* (eds.), *Towards a European Civil Code*; Schulze and Stuyck (eds.), *Towards a European Contract Law*; Schulze and Schulte-Nölke (eds.), *European Private Law*; Miller, *The Emergence of EU Contract Law*; Letto-Vanamo and Smits (eds.), *Coherence and Fragmentation in European Private Law*; Twigg-Flesner, *A Cross-border-only Regulation for Consumer Transactions in the EU*; S. Grundmann, 'The Optional European Code on the Basis of the Acquis Communitaire – Starting Point and Trends', *European Law Journal*, 10 (2004), 698–711; S. Grundmann, 'European Contract Law(s) of What Colour?', *European Review of Contract Law*, 1 (2005), 184–210; H. Beale, 'The European Commission's Common Frame of Reference Project: a Progress Report', *European Review of Contract Law*, 2 (2006), 303–14; H. Schulte-Nölke, 'EC Law on the Formation of Contract – from the Common Frame

As indicated earlier, during the elaborations and – for some time – even after the presentation of the DCFR, the future of the DCFR and the Commission's intentions regarding the envisaged CFR were not entirely clear though. Was the DCFR (the *academic* CFR) to be transformed into a *political* CFR?[29] The financial contributions by the Commission to the CFR/

of Reference to the 'Blue Button'", *European Review of Contract Law*, 3 (2007), 332–49; R. Schulze, 'Consumer Law and European Contract Law' in Howells *et al.* (eds.), *The Yearbook of Consumer Law 2007*, pp. 153–66; Heiderhoff, B., *Gemeinschaftsprivatrecht* (2nd edn, Munich: Sellier, 2007), pp. 239–50; H. Eidenmüller, 'The Common Frame of Reference for European Private Law – Policy Choices and Codification Problems', *Oxford Journal of Legal Studies*, 28 (2008), 659–708; S. Leible, 'Was tun mit dem Gemeinsamen Referenzrahmen für das Europäische Vertragsrecht? – Plädoyer für ein optionales Instrument', *Betriebs-Berater*, 63 (2008), 1469–75; U. Reifner, 'Verbraucherschutz und Neo-Liberalismus: DCFR, EU-Verbraucherrichtlinien und die Kritik Stürners', *Verbraucher und Recht*, 24 (2009), 3–11; G. Kathrein, 'Europäisches Vertragsrecht – Österreichische Haltung' in Schulze (ed.), *Common Frame of Reference and Existing EC Contract Law*, pp. 297–308; A. Somma, 'Towards a European Private Law? The Common Frame of Reference in the Conflict between EC Law and National Laws' in Micklitz and Cafaggi (eds.), *European Private Law after the Common Frame of Reference*, pp. 1–23; K. Riesenhuber, 'A Competitive Approach to EU Contract Law', *European Review of Contract Law*, 7 (2011), 115–33; W. Doralt, 'Strukturelle Schwächen in der Europäisierung des Privatrechts. Eine Prozessanalyse der jüngeren Entwicklungen', *Rabels Zeitschrift für ausländisches und internationales Privatrecht*, 75 (2011), 260–85; A. L. M. Keirse, 'European Impact on Contract Law: A Perspective on the Interlinked Contributions of Legal Scholars, Legislators and Courts to the Europeanization of Contract Law', *Utrecht Law Review*, 7 (2011), 34–51; M. Maugeri, 'Is the DCFR Ready to Be Adopted as an Optional Instrument?', *European Review of Contract Law*, 7 (2011), 219–28; M. Meli, 'The Common Frame of Reference and the Relationship between National Law and European Law', *European Review of Contract Law*, 7 (2011), 229–34.

29 For discussions on this issue and the possible fate of the DCFR see, for example, von Bar *et al.* (eds.), *Principles, Definitions and Model Rules of European Private Law – Draft Common Frame of Reference (DCFR) Outline Edition*, p. 4, where the DCFR drafters state that '[o]ne purpose of the text [i.e. of the DCFR] is to serve as a draft for drawing up a "political" Common Frame of Reference (CFR)'. See also *ibid.*, p. 7 where they go even one step further and add that 'the DCFR ought not to be regarded merely as a building block of a "political" Common Frame of Reference. The DCFR will stand on its own and retain its significance whatever happens in relation to a CFR'. Sergio Cámara Lapuente and Evelyne Terryn refer to the long uncertainty about the true concept of the CFR by commenting that 'the *legal nature* of this instrument [the CFR] has been extremely ambiguous' (Cámara Lapuente and Terryn, 'Consumer Contract Law', p. 161). For more on this 'ambiguity' see P. Giliker, 'The Draft Common Frame of Reference and European Contract Law: Moving from the "Academic" to the "Political"' in Devenney and Kenny (eds.), *The Transformation of European Private Law*, pp. 23–44; F. Möslein, 'Legal Innovation in European Contract Law: Within and beyond the (Draft) Common Frame of Reference' in Micklitz and Cafaggi (eds.), *European Private Law after the Common Frame of Reference*, p. 173; H. Muir-Watt and R. Sefton-Green, 'Fitting the Frame: An Optional Instrument, Party Choice and Mandatory/Default Rules' in *ibid.*, p. 201. For the use of the term 'academic DCFR' see, e.g., Howells and Schulze, 'Overview of the Proposed Consumer Rights Directive', p. 5; or the contributions in R.

DCFR project[30] gave some good reason to believe that the Commission had a strong interest in instrumentalising the DCFR. However, what would a version instrumentalised by the Commission be used for – and when, to what extent and in which legal form was this to be realised?

Most contributors to the debate were quite unsure about the future of the DCFR, even in the later stages of the project. In their summary of the DCFR elaborations Christian von Bar, Hugh Beale, Eric Clive and Hans Schulte-Nölke, the co-authors of the introduction to the DCFR *Outline Edition*,[31] for example, emphasised that the DCFR had been 'consciously drafted in a way that ... would allow progress to be made towards the creation of ... an optional instrument'.[32] At the same time, von Bar, Beale, Clive and Schulte-Nölke were quite modest with their expectations saying that '[i]t is still unclear whether the CFR, or parts of it, might at a later stage be used as the basis for one or more optional instruments'.[33] Reiner

Schulze *et al.* (eds.), *Der akademische Entwurf für einen Gemeinsamen Referenzrahmen* (Tübingen: Mohr Siebeck, 2008). Micklitz is another commentator who uses the term academic DCFR (see H.-W. Micklitz, 'The Visible Hand of European Regulatory Private Law. The Transformation of European Private Law from Autonomy to Functionalism in Competition and Regulation', EUI Working Papers, Law 2008/14 (2008), p. 2, available at cadmus.eui.eu/bitstream/handle/1814/8707/LAW_2008_14.pdf?sequence=1). At the same time he explains that it is also (already) a political instrument, 'as the drafters were actually working as legislators with a political mandate in mind' and adds that '[t]he collaboration between the European Commission and European academia resembles, in an ominous way, the German Professorenmodell where academia cooperates with an authoritarian executive, overriding a weak parliament' (H.-W. Micklitz, 'Introduction' in Micklitz (ed.), *The Many Concepts of Social Justice in European Private Law*, p. 24). Eric Clive uses the term 'official CFR' instead of political CFR – for his differentiation between the DCFR and the official/political CFR: see E. Clive, 'An Introduction to the Academic Draft Common Frame of Reference', *ERA Forum*, 9 (2008), 13, 14.

[30] See von Bar *et al.* (eds.), *Principles, Definitions and Model Rules of European Private Law – Draft Common Frame of Reference (DCFR) Outline Edition*, p. 55 where it states as follows: 'Before we came together with other teams in May 2005 to form the "CoPECL Network of Excellence" *under the European Commission's sixth framework programme for research, from which funds our research has since been supported*' (emphasis added).

[31] Christian von Bar, Hugh Beale and Eric Clive were members of the SGECC. Hans Schulte-Nölke was a member of the Acquis Group.

[32] von Bar *et al.* (eds.), *Principles, Definitions and Model Rules of European Private Law – Draft Common Frame of Reference (DCFR) Outline Edition*, p. 46.

[33] von Bar *et al.* (eds.), *Principles, Definitions and Model Rules of European Private Law – Draft Common Frame of Reference (DCFR) Outline Edition*, p. 46. See, in addition, Beale, 'European Contract Law', p. 129, where Beale argues that even after the publication of the DCFR 'it is hard to say' which path it would eventually take. Schulte-Nölke claims that '[i]f no framework directive is required, the optional instrument remains the one and only way forward' (H. Schulte-Nölke, 'The Way Forward in European Consumer Contract Law: Optional Instrument Instead of Further Deconstruction of National Private Laws' in Twigg-Flesner (ed.), *The Cambridge Companion to European Union Private Law*,

Schulze, a member of the Acquis Group, expressed his view as follows: '[T]he presented version of the DCFR is not yet suitable as a direct guideline for EC legislation regarding a coherent contract law'.[34]

The possible fate of the DCFR was further broadly discussed by external commentators. Jan Smits noted (in 2012) that '[t]he DCFR may have some impact …, but it is too early to say anything definitive about this at the moment'.[35] Nils Jansen praised the work of the research group for having produced an invaluable source for further discussions but at the same time claimed that 'the discourse of European private law is not mature enough … to be restated within an authoritative reference text'.[36] Horatia Muir-Watt and Ruth Sefton-Green added that '[t]he legal status of the … Common Frame of Reference is, to say the least, somewhat obscure'.[37] In a similar, rather pessimistic vein was Ewoud Hondius's observation: '[T]he outlook [for the DCFR] at present is bleak.'[38] Sergio Cámara Lapuente and Evelyne Terryn even went so far to say that the '[i]nterest in this instrument, resulting from an idea to encode private law that was on the agenda in 2001 and 2003, has gradually diminished in recent years and is no longer a priority'.[39]

In retrospect, an analysis made by Lurger in 2006 – in the midst of the CFR/DCFR elaborations – can be considered as one of the most far-sighted comments on the possible future of the CFR/DCFR. Lurger starts her observations with a reference to the 2003 Contract Law Action Plan

p. 144). For a comment on a possible framework directive see F. Zoll, 'A Need for a New Structure for European Private Law' in Brownsword *et al.* (eds.), *The Foundations of European Private Law*, pp. 555–61.

[34] R. Schulze, 'The Academic Draft of the CFR and the EC Contract Law' in Schulze (ed.), *Common Frame of Reference and Existing EC Contract Law*, p. 23.

[35] Smits, 'Coherence and Fragmentation in the Law of Contract', pp. 18–19. In a similar vein is C. Twigg-Flesner, 'The *Acquis* Principles: an Insider's Critical Reflections on the Drafting Process' in M. Andenas and C. Baasch Andersen (eds.), *Theory and Practice of Harmonisation* (Cheltenham: Edward Elgar, 2011), p. 495: 'It remains uncertain what, if anything, will become of the DCFR.'

[36] N. Jansen, 'The Authority of an Academic "Draft Common Frame of Reference"' in Micklitz and Cafaggi (eds.), *European Private Law after the Common Frame of Reference*, p. 167.

[37] Muir-Watt and Sefton-Green, 'Fitting the Frame', p. 201.

[38] E. Hondius, 'From "Toolbox" to Academic Standard: The Current and Future Status of the Draft Common Frame of Reference' in Brownsword *et al.* (eds.), *The Foundations of European Private Law*, p. 553. For arguments that the DCFR was ready to be used as a 'toolbox' see H. Beale, 'The Draft Academic Common Frame of Reference and the "Toolbox"' in Andenas and Baasch Andersen (eds.), *Theory and Practice of Harmonisation*, pp. 115–28.

[39] Cámara Lapuente and Terryn, 'Consumer Contract Law', p. 163.

and the 2004 Acquis Communication, which, as I showed earlier, were the first Commission communications to mention the possibility of introducing a pan-EU contract law in the form of an OI.[40] She explains that to defuse the OI concerns expressed by several stakeholders and external experts, the Commission, for the sake of appearance, (temporarily) removed from the official agenda the plan to introduce an OI. Lurger goes on to state that because of the absence of any alternative express views of the Commission with respect to the future of the CFR discussions, it was, however, to be expected that the Commission would eventually return to its initial idea of presenting an OI.[41]

In her analysis of the likely form and content of an OI, Lurger distinguishes between three possible scenarios and draws early, yet nevertheless in principle accurate, conclusions. Her first scenario refers to the eventually chosen path for the DCFR. Lurger explains that the Commission supported a fully harmonised OI that would basically maintain the standard of consumer protection currently found at the (average) EU level. By doing so it would pose a threat to consumers residing in Member States with consumer-friendlier regimes. This, according to Lurger, would be the consequence of two facts. First, Member States could not retain their consumer-friendlier national provisions, and second, in practice, it would solely be the traders' decision whether this 'optional code' would be used as traders were 'in a stronger negotiating position' than consumers.[42] Because of the fact that a fully harmonised regime could give traders 'an incentive to use the optional code to avoid application of a national law that exceeds the minimum protection standard prescribed by most directives',[43] this would mean that some consumers could easily be put in a worse legal position.

Lurger's second scenario draws an even more pessimistic view. With reference to the 2004 Acquis Communication, Lurger notes that the Commission's *main* goal, indeed most likely also the *only* goal, of the optional instrument … [would be the] removal of "barriers to the smooth functioning of the internal market".[44] To achieve this goal, the Commission would have to provide traders with an optional code that would stop at a lower protective level than currently offered by EU consumer laws because only in such a case would traders clearly be incentivised to opt for a new legal regime. However, in anticipation of the actual

---

[40] Lurger, 'The Common Frame of Reference', p. 179.
[41] *Ibid.*, p. 180. [42] *Ibid.*, p. 182.
[43] *Ibid.* [44] *Ibid.*, p. 183.

result of the DCFR (the proposed CESL), one can note that this scenario did not turn into reality – neither did Lurger's third scenario (which would have led to a considerably higher level of protection than currently offered by EU consumer laws).[45]

Just when academic discussions about the future of European contract law seemed to have reached new heights, events came thick and fast. In April 2010 the Commission declared its decision to instrumentalise the DCFR in the form of a European contract law when it installed the Expert Group on a Common Frame of Reference (to avoid confusion with the work on the DCFR I shall refer to it as the CESL Expert Group).[46] Taking a look at the Commission decision that underlies the introduction of the CESL Expert Group, it becomes clear that the Commission wanted the group to largely base its elaborations and the drafting of the CESL on the DCFR. Article 2 of the Commission's decision reads as follows:

> The group's task shall be to assist the Commission in the preparation of a proposal for a Common Frame of Reference in the area of European contract law, including consumer ... contract law, and in particular in:
> (a) *selecting those parts of the Draft Common Frame of Reference* which are of direct or indirect relevance to contract law; and
> (b) *restructuring, revising and supplementing the selected contents of the Draft Common Frame of Reference*, taking also into consideration other research work conducted in this area (emphasis added).

The strong connection between the DCFR and the CESL is further illustrated by the fact that a considerable number of members of the CESL Expert Group were previously actively involved in the drafting process of the DCFR, either as members of the SGECC or the Acquis Group.[47] With this move the Commission obviously wanted to ensure that the final stage in the quest for a political CFR, i.e., the drafting process of the CESL, would run as smoothly and as quickly as possible. Nevertheless, the Commission also tried to include new input by inviting some fresh faces from outside academia to the CESL Expert Group. This included two legal

---

[45] See *ibid.*, p. 184, where Lurger comments on this third scenario as follows: '[T]he nature of the optional code itself excludes such a scenario. As it will be the stronger parties who decide on the application or non-application of the optional code, they will never choose an optional code that protects their interests less than the otherwise applicable law.'

[46] Commission Decision setting up the Expert Group on a Common Frame of Reference in the area of European contract law, 26 April 2010, OJ 2010 No. L105/109.

[47] Hugh Beale, Eric Clive, Torgny Håstad, Martijn Hesselink, Irene Kull and Anna Veneziano were members of the SGECC. Luc Grynbaum, Jerzy Pisuliński and Hans Schulte-Nölke were members of the Acquis Group.

practitioners and one representative from each of the two stakeholder groups most directly affected by the possible introduction of the CESL: one business interest representative[48] and one member of the Consumer Union of Luxembourg (representing consumer interests).[49]

However, most of the CESL Expert Group members were legal scholars, which might have been why the Commission also installed a supplementary deliberative group to assist the CESL Expert Group. Unlike the CESL Expert Group, this second group, the ten-member Round Table of European key stakeholders in the area of contract law (CESL Key Stakeholders Group), consisted entirely of non-legal scholars. Thus, parallels can be drawn to the drafting process of the DCFR: to support the academic lead groups (the SGECC and the Acquis Group) with direct, practice-oriented input from stakeholders, a special stakeholder network of legal practitioners, interest representatives and public officials was set up – CFR-net.[50] In both cases the decision to install 'feedback groups' was clearly driven by the idea to strengthen both the democratic input in and output of the drafting process in an attempt to satisfy the call for transparency. This aimed to make the CESL more appealing for those most directly affected by a possible introduction.[51] However, from the viewpoint of

---

[48] The business interest representative was sent by the European Multi-channel and Online Trade Association (EMOTA).

[49] A complete list of the initial Expert Group members is available at europa.eu/rapid/press-release_IP-10-595_en.htm; an updated list is available at ec.europa.eu/transparency/regexpert/index.cfm?do=groupDetail.groupDetail&groupID=2475.

[50] Lucinda Miller explains this move of the Commission with regard to the drafting of the DCFR as follows: 'At first glance, the Commission has adopted a highly participatory model, encouraging input from a range of different stakeholders. This form of governance, one that is preceded by a round of public consultations, appears attractive owing to its seemingly democratic credentials. In the absence of a European society, the Commission seems to be finding a substitute through the public, academic and stakeholder involvement to lawmaking.' She adds that the imbalanced composition of the CFR-net group with only very limited representation of consumer interests 'considerably strips the process of any democratic appeal' (Miller, *The Emergence of EU Contract Law*, pp. 117–18). A list of members of CFR-net is available at ec.europa.eu/consumers/cons_int/safe_shop/fair_bus_pract/cont_law/cfr_net_members_en.pdf. For comments on the general role expert groups and committees play in the policy-making and legislative process of the EU see the contributions in T. Christiansen and T. Larsson (eds.), *The Role of Committees in the Policy-Process of the European Union: Legislation, Implementation and Deliberation* (Cheltenham, Edwards Elgar, 2007).

[51] For a discussion of the concepts of input and output democracy in the context of EU law making and the drafting of the CESL, in particular, see S. Wrbka, 'The Dilemma of European Consumer Representation in Deliberative Networks – the Democratic Deficit in the Context of the Drafting of the Common European Sales Law' in M. Fenwick *et al.* (eds.), *Networked Governance, Transnational Business & the Law* (Heidelberg: Springer,

consumers the attempt backfired because consumer interests were strongly underrepresented.[52] Half of the members of the CESL Key Stakeholders Group represented the interests of those business sectors that would be directly affected if the CESL became reality, while the banking and insurance industry as well as the legal profession could send two representatives each. BEUC, the European Consumer Organisation, was the only *consumer* representative in the CESL Key Stakeholders Group.[53]

2014), pp. 147–56 with further references. For comments on the democratic deficit issue and democratic legitimacy in EU law making in general see (with further references) P. Craig and G. de Búrca, *EU Law Text, Cases, and Materials* (5th edn, Oxford University Press, 2011), pp. 149–55; D. Chalmers, G. Davies and G. Monti, *European Union Law* (2nd edn: Cambridge University Press, 2010), pp. 125–36; A. Menon and S. Weatherill, 'Democratic Politics in a Globalising World: Supranationalism and Legitimacy in the European Union', LSE Law, Society and Economy Working Papers, 13/2007 (2007), available at www.lse.ac.uk/collections/law/wps/WPS13-2007MenonandWeatherill.pdf; R. Corbett, 'Democracy in the European Union' in E. Bomberg *et al.* (eds.), *The European Union: How Does It Work?* (3rd edn: Oxford University Press, 2012), pp. 141–58; R. Schütze, *European Constitutional Law* (Cambridge University Press, 2012), pp. 74–7; L. Woods and P. Watson, *Steiner & Woods EU Law* (11th edn, Oxford University Press, 2012), pp. 73–6; K. Lenaerts and P. Van Nuffel, *European Union Law* (3rd edn, London: Sweet & Maxwell, 2011), pp. 740–6; R. Michaels, 'Of Islands and the Ocean: The Two Rationalities of European Private Law' in Brownsword *et al.* (eds.), *The Foundations of European Private Law*, pp. 139–58.

[52] For related comments in the context of CFR-net see Miller, *The Emergence of EU Contract Law*, p. 119.

[53] A list of members of the CESL Key Stakeholder Group is available at ec.europa.eu/justice/contract/cesl/stakeholder-meeting/index_en.htm. The underrepresentation of consumer interests in consumer law making at the EU level is not an exception, but rather the rule. For details see Wrbka, 'The Dilemma of European Consumer Representation in Deliberative Networks', pp. 156–9, where it is shown that 70 to 80 per cent of all interest groups registered in the European Transparency Register represent mainly business interests, while groups representing consumer interests total approximately 2 per cent of all registered groups. For additional data see S. Hix and B. Høyland, *The Political System of the European Union* (3rd edn, Basingstoke: Palgrave Macmillan, 2011), p. 165; K. Karr, *Democracy and Lobbying in the European Union* (Frankfurt: Campus, 2007), p. 148 (Table 22). For an early comment on consumer representation in the EU see L. Maier, 'Institutional Consumer Representation in the European Community', *Journal of Consumer Policy*, 16 (1993), 355–74; for comments on the practical relevance of interest groups at the Parliament level see C. Neuhold and P. Settembri, 'The Role of European Parliament Committees in the EU Policy-making Process' in Christiansen and Larsson (eds.), *The Role of Committees in the Policy-Process of the European Union*, pp. 163–5. For further discussions on lobbying groups and their significance in EU policy and law making see A. R. Young, 'The European Policy Process in Comparative Perspective' in H. Wallace *et al.* (eds.), *Policy-Making in the European Union* (6th edn: Oxford University Press, 2010), pp. 45–68; H. Klüver, *Lobbying in the European Union – Interest Groups, Lobbying Coalitions, and Policy Change* (Oxford University Press, 2013); R. Watson and R. Corbett, 'How Policies Are Made' in Bomberg *et al.* (eds.), *The European Union: How*

On another occasion, I explained in detail the practical consequences that this twofold imbalance, i.e., the underrepresentation of consumer interests in both the CESL Expert Group and the CESL Key Stakeholders Group, presented for consumer interests in the drafting process of the CESL.[54] From a consumer perspective, the most unfortunate consequence in a practical sense was the fact that several justified arguments in favour of consumer interests made by BEUC during the CESL elaborations were in some cases ignored and in others not appropriately incorporated into the final text of the CESL Proposal.[55]

Because of the prior involvement of several CESL Expert Group members in the drafting of the DCFR and the extensive research conducted for its creation, the actual drafting of the CESL was relatively fast. Officially, the concrete direction in which the Commission eventually wanted to carry the CESL was still wide open. Most notably, the Green Paper on Policy Options for Progress towards a European Contract Law for Consumers and Businesses (2010 Policy Options Green Paper)[56] listed a total of seven, widely varied solutions, or 'options'. The eventually chosen option, option 4 to introduce an OI, can be considered as some kind of compromise between less far-reaching options[57] such as unbinding collections of principles and model rules on the one hand and stronger mechanisms such as the introduction of a European Contract Code or even a European Civil Code overriding existing national laws on the other.[58]

Although, on the surface, the Commission tried to avoid tying itself down to any of the options during the course of the DCFR elaborations, some Commission materials indicated that the Commission had preferred option 4 from the outset (or at least from an early stage). One example is the 2003 Contract Law Action Plan. In relation to the envisaged CFR, the plan stated that one 'objective of the common frame of reference is to

Does It Work?, pp. 122–40; I. Michalowitz, *Lobbying in der EU* (Vienna: Facultas, 2007); H.-J. Schmedes, *Wirtschafts- und Verbraucherschutzverbände im Mehrebenensystem: Lobbyingaktivitäten britischer, deutscher und europäischer Verbände* (Wiesbaden: VS Verlag, 2008); J. Greenwood, *Interest Representation in the European Union* (3rd edn, Basingstoke: Palgrave Macmillan, 2011); I. Tanasescu, *The European Commission and Interest Groups: Towards a Deliberative Interpretation of Stakeholder Involvement in EU Policy-making* (Brussels: VUBPRESS, 2009).

[54] See Wrbka, 'The Dilemma of European Consumer Representation in Deliberative Networks', pp. 159–66.

[55] *Ibid.*, pp. 163–6.

[56] Green Paper from the Commission on policy options for progress towards a European Contract Law for consumers and businesses, 1 July, 2010, COM(2010) 348 final.

[57] *Ibid.*, options 1–3   [58] *Ibid.*, options 5–7.

form the basis for further reflection on an *optional instrument in the area of European contract law*' (emphasis added).[59] I have already mentioned the 2004 Acquis Communication, which defined this idea in slightly greater detail. Another, more recent example is the 2010 Commission's Communication 'Europe 2020 – A strategy for smart, sustainable and inclusive growth'[60] (Europe 2020 Communication), which was published only a couple of months before the 2010 Policy Options Green Paper. With regard to contract law issues, the Europe 2020 Communication clarified that '[t]he Commission will propose action to tackle bottlenecks in the single market by … [m]aking it easier and less costly for businesses and consumers to conclude contracts with partners in other EU countries, notably by … making progress towards an *optional European Contract Law*'[61] (emphasis added).

Not least because of obvious proportionality concerns,[62] the Commission eventually chose option 4 of the 2010 Policy Options Green Paper over stricter approaches (i.e., approaches that would lead more easily and directly to a stronger defragmentation or 'simplification' of diverse national sales laws, as defined earlier). However, rather than legal issues, it may well have been political concerns that played the key role in choosing option 4. In the midst of the CESL elaborations, Reding explained that dealing with diverse Member States' sales law regimes did not predominantly pose a legal or economic challenge, but that the true crucial point had rather to be seen in '[t]he fact that Europe has more than 27 different legal systems for contractual transactions[, which] is … a formidable *political* challenge for Europe's single market'[63] (emphasis added). In my earlier example of the CRD, I explained that the Member States were no longer willing to comprehensively sacrifice their legislative means and interests for the sake of maximum harmonisation. Thus, the only feasible strategy that the Commission was able to follow to get close to a

---

[59] 2003 Contract Law Action Plan, p. 2.

[60] Commission's Communication 'Europe 2020 – A strategy for smart, sustainable and inclusive growth', 3 March 2010, COM(2010) 2020 final.

[61] *Ibid.*, p. 21.

[62] See, for example, the Commission's assessment of option 6 of the 2010 Policy Options Green Paper as possibly 'rais[ing] sensitive issues of subsidiarity and proportionality' (2010 Policy Options Green Paper, p. 11).

[63] V. Reding, 'The Next Steps towards a European Contract Law for Businesses and Consumers' in Schulze and Stuyck (eds.), *Towards a European Contract Law*, p. 10. See further Reinhard Zimmermann's explanation that the chosen form was the 'least intrusive solution' (R. Zimmermann, 'Codification – The Civilian Experience Reconsidered on the Eve of a Common European Sales Law', *European Review of Contract Law*, 8 (2012), 367, 397).

simplification as defined earlier[64] was to aim for an absolutely fully harmonised *optional* regime. Crafting it as an alternative second-ranked OI was surely an attempt to appease Member States by allowing them to fully maintain their primary sales laws.

In other words, from the viewpoint of the Commission, choosing option 4 was the only politically possible way to implement its plans to standardise the legal regime for cross-border B2C transaction contracts to the greatest possible extent. In the Explanatory Memorandum, which accompanied the CESL Regulation Proposal (CESL Explanatory Memorandum), the Commission defines its underlying argumentation as follows:

> Differences in contract law between Member States hinder traders and consumers who want to engage in cross-border trade within the internal market. The obstacles which stem from these differences dissuade traders, small and medium-sized enterprises (SMEs) in particular, from entering cross border trade or expanding to new Member States' markets. Consumers are hindered from accessing products offered by traders in other Member States … The need for traders to adapt to the different national contract laws that may apply in crossborder dealings makes cross-border trade more complex and costly compared to domestic trade.[65]

The CESL Explanatory Memorandum further adds the following:

> In cross-border transactions between a business and a consumer, contract law related transaction costs and legal obstacles stemming from differences between different national mandatory consumer protection rules have a significant impact. Pursuant to Article 6 … Rome I …, whenever a business directs its activities to consumers in another Member State, it has to comply with the contract law of that Member State. In cases where another applicable law has been chosen by the parties and where the mandatory consumer protection provisions of the Member State of the consumer provide a higher level of protection, these mandatory rules of the consumer's law need to be respected.[66]

I will come back to this argument later in my analysis of the CESL. At this point it is sufficient to note that the Commission considers consumer-friendlier national legislation as a highly detrimental obstacle for traders who want to trade across borders. Put differently, the Commission

---

[64] See 'The Directive on Consumer Rights' in Chapter 9 above.
[65] Explanatory Memorandum accompanying the CESL Regulation Proposal (CESL Explanatory Memorandum), p. 2.
[66] *Ibid.*

is of the opinion that the regime of Article 6 Rome I Regulation (which was introduced to protect consumers and strengthen their confidence in cross-border trade) is counterproductive. With the introduction of a standardised CESL, the Commission hopes to render Article 6 toothless (in situations covered by the CESL).[67] To put it even more bluntly, the real drive behind the CESL is the removal of diverse national consumer-protection sales law standards (that in some cases exceed EU law standards) for the sake of simplifying the traders' market access and *not* the wish to guarantee the highest possible consumer protection standards.

It did not take long for the first concrete results to be presented. The preliminary CESL draft was showcased in May 2011 – only slightly more than one year after the CESL Expert Group was formed.[68] One month later stakeholders from academia, politics and the legal profession (but not from business and consumer interest groups) came together to discuss the drafters' tentative conclusions.[69] At that time the CESL draft comprised 189 substantive provisions. Although a considerable number of external commentators recommended that the project be carefully reconsidered,[70] the Commission presented the final version – embedded in the CESL Regulation Proposal – just a few months later.

Before discussing the possible relevance of the CESL, especially its likely impact on consumer interests and cross-border trade, I should like to turn briefly to the content of the CESL Regulation Proposal in general. How is it structured? What does it contain? The following section aims to provide some answers.

The CESL Regulation Proposal in a nutshell

At the time of writing this book, the Regulation on a Common European Sales Law had not been adopted. All remarks made in the following – unless

---

[67] For details see 'Sixth Assumption: The CESL Will Necessarily Solve the 'Problems' Caused by Rome I' below.

[68] Commission Expert Group on European Contract Law, 'Feasibility Study for a Future Instrument in European Contract Law', 3 May 2011, available at http://ec.europa.eu/justice/contract/files/feasibility_study_final.pdf.

[69] The symposium (CESL draft symposium) was organised by the Centre for European Private Law of the University of Münster and the Study Centre for Consumer Law of the University of Leuven. The contributions made at the symposium are published in Schulze and Stuyck (eds.), *Towards a European Contract Law*.

[70] For examples of critical comments made at the CESL draft symposium see J. Basedow, 'European Contract Law – The Case for a Growing Optional Instrument' in *ibid.*, pp. 169–71; and H.-W. Micklitz, 'A "Certain" Future for the Optional Instrument'.

indicated otherwise – refer to and are based on the proposed text as of 11 October 2011. At the end of Part III, I shall comment on some more recent developments, especially regarding the feedback from the Parliament's Committee for Legal Affairs (JURI – the committee responsible for the proposal at Parliament level) given in September 2013. This will show how the initial plans of the Commission might develop further.

The CESL Regulation Proposal basically consists of three parts.[71] The first part, the backbone of the proposed regulation, comprises sixteen articles that contain 'administrative' rules, such as a catalogue of definitions or rules on the applicability of the CESL. The main text is followed by the centrepiece of the proposal, Annex I, the Common European Sales Law (CESL) with substantive rules for certain (primarily)[72] cross-border contracts. Although the CESL is not restricted to B2C transactions[73] (the subject of the analysis later in this book), they are undeniably an important target group of the CESL for which it introduces a considerable amount of mandatory provisions.[74] I will outline the CESL shortly.

The third and final part of the CESL Regulation Proposal is formed by a shorter annex, Annex II, the Standard Information Notice (SIN) to be used in B2C cases falling under the CESL regime. Pursuant to Article 9(1) CESL Regulation Proposal, traders who want to base a B2C cross-border contract on the CESL have the obligation to provide consumers with the SIN. I will refer to the question of the meaningfulness of the SIN later.[75]

With respect to B2C transactions Article 8(2) CESL Regulation Proposal asks for an explicit agreement on the applicability of the CESL separate from the main contract.[76] The requirement of an explicit party choice of the CESL by a separate agreement is complemented by the aforementioned obligation to provide the consumer with the SIN *before* the parties agree

[71] For a detailed commentary on the CESL Regulation Proposal see R. Schulze (ed.), *Common European Sales Law (CESL) – Commentary* (Baden-Baden: Nomos, 2012).

[72] See Article 13(a) CESL Regulation Proposal with its Member State option and the explanation of this option later in this chapter.

[73] See Article 7 CESL Regulation Proposal for details.

[74] C2B situations, on the other hand, do not fall under the CESL regime. Pursuant to the first sentence of Article 7(1) CESL Regulation Proposal the CESL requires that the '*seller* of goods or the supplier of digital content is a trader' (emphasis added). See also the definition of the term 'consumer sales contract' by Article 2(l) CESL Regulation Proposal: '"[C]onsumer sales contract" means a sales contract where the seller is a trader and the buyer is a consumer.'

[75] See 'Second assumption: The CESL will lead to improved certainty for consumers' below for details.

[76] See 'Fourth assumption: The CESL will be a bilaterally voluntary, secondary regime' below for details.

on the applicability of the CESL. If the trader fails to provide the consumer with the SIN before agreeing on the CESL's applicability, the consumer shall not be bound by such an agreement (i.e., the agreement to use the CESL) until and unless he or she, as stated in Article 9(1), 'has received the confirmation referred to in Article 8(2) accompanied by the information notice [i.e. the SIN] and has expressly consented subsequently to the use of the Common European Sales Law'.[77] This somewhat confusing wording means that the consumer has to again agree on the applicability of the CESL after receiving the SIN if he or she was not provided with the SIN prior to the initial CESL agreement. This can be understood as an attempt to increase the likelihood that the consumer is fully aware of the consequences of agreeing on the CESL. The consequence of an unremedied failure to provide the consumer with the SIN in accordance with the procedure just outlined is that the consumer can choose between the CESL and the primary sales law regime of the Member State, the law of which is chosen by the parties (with the safeguard provision of Article 6(2) Rome I Regulation) or determined by Article 6(1) Rome I Regulation. This understanding follows from the second sentence of Article 9(1) CESL Regulation Proposal, which states that the consumer would 'not be bound by the agreement [i.e., any agreement to use the CESL]' unless the listed requirements are fulfilled.

The parties' opportunity to choose the CESL for their cross-border transactions pursuant to Article 8(2) CESL Regulation Proposal (one could refer to it as an 'inter-party option') is complemented by a second option under the proposal. Article 13(a) gives Member States the option to declare the CESL applicable also for purely domestic cases (one could refer to it as a 'Member State option'). At first sight the Member State option seems dispensable, as Member States in principle have the discretion to introduce domestic legislation for cases not directly covered by EU laws (designed at their example). However, as Christiane Wendehorst rightly observes, the insertion of this provision makes sense to avoid any likely conflict with fully harmonised parallel EU laws, i.e., to avoid any likely conflict with 'the level of protection afforded by full harmonisation' of EU laws that cover CESL issues for purely domestic matters.[78]

---

[77] For detailed comments on the consequences of a 'defective' agreement on the CESL in B2C situations see C. Harvey and M. Schillig, 'Consequences of an Ineffective Agreement to Use the Common European Sales Law', *European Review of Contract Law*, 9 (2013), 143, 157–61.

[78] See C. Wendehorst, 'Article 13' in Schulze (ed.), *Common European Sales Law*, Article 13 CESL Regulation para. 3. For a similar argumentation see M. Schmidt-Kessel, 'Der

Annex I CESL Regulation Proposal, the CESL (or when put in the context of one of the provisions of its proposed wording, CESL Proposal), forms the biggest part of the regulation. Some of the CESL rules are specifically crafted for B2C situations. In this respect the CESL follows the example of the DCFR, which also differentiates between B2C and non-B2C situations (in certain instances). Unlike the DCFR, which takes a quite broad approach and includes some non-contractual issues[79] as well as some contracts not covered by the CESL,[80] the scope of the CESL is, however, exclusively limited to certain transaction contracts. And even with respect to the covered contracts, it takes a narrower approach than the DCFR because it excludes several (inter alia, DCFR-covered) issues from its scope.[81] The CESL Explanatory Memorandum explains this as follows: 'The scope [of the CESL] ... is confined to the aspects which pose real problems in cross-border transactions and does not extend to aspects which are best addressed by national laws. In respect of the material scope, the proposal contains provisions regulating the rights and obligations of the parties during the life-cycle of the contract, but it does not touch ... upon ... rules ... which are less likely to become litigious.'[82] Recital 27 CESL Regulation Proposal provides more details on these assumed 'real problems', stating that not only non-contractual issues but also certain contract-law-related issues do not fall under this term. It explains that the excluded 'issues [i.e. those issues which are not considered as 'real problems' by the CESL Explanatory Memorandum] include legal personality, the invalidity of a contract arising from lack of capacity, illegality or immorality, the determination of the language of the contract, matters of non-discrimination, representation, plurality of debtors and creditors, change of parties including assignment, set-off and merger, property law including the transfer of ownership, intellectual property law and the law of torts'. Whether these omitted issues pose fewer 'real problems' in practice is anyone's guess.[83] What is important to note, however, is the fact

Vorschlag der Kommission für ein Optionales Instrument – Einleitung' in Schmidt-Kessel (ed.), *Ein einheitliches europäisches Kaufrecht?*, p. 21.

[79]   See in particular Book V DCFR ('Benevolent intervention in another's affairs'), Book VI DCFR ('Non-contractual liability arising out of damage caused to another') and Book VII DCFR ('Unjustified enrichment').

[80]   See, for example, Book IV, Part B DCFR ('Lease of goods') and Book IV, Part C DCFR ('Services').

[81]   See, for example, Book II, Chapter 2 DCFR ('Non-discrimination') and Book II, Chapter 6 DCFR ('Representation').

[82]   CESL Explanatory Memorandum, p. 9.

[83]   For a critical comment about the exclusion of issues listed in Recital 27 CESL Regulation Proposal see S. Augenhofer, 'Aktuelle Entwicklungstendenzen im Europäischen

that the exclusion of certain issues that are also likely to be important in B2C cross-border transaction contracts elucidates that the CESL does not conclusively standardise the legal framework for cross-border cases. As I will show later in my analysis of the CESL, this must not be ignored, in particular, because it relates to one of the Commission's main arguments in favour of the CESL, namely that it would absolutely simplify the legal settings for cross-border B2C transactions.[84]

The CESL would in principle not apply to service contracts. Pursuant to Article 5 CESL Regulation Proposal, the material scope of the CESL is limited to (1) sales contracts (which in the context of the CESL only refers to goods),[85] (2) contracts for the supply of digital content[86] and (3) (as a narrow exception to the exclusion of service contracts) so-called related service contracts, a term which is defined by Article 2(m) CESL Regulation Proposal.[87]

With respect to sales contracts, being the first and biggest of the three CESL categories, it should be further noted that the definition of the term 'goods' (which is an indispensable constituent of the definition of the term 'sales contract'[88]) leads to a further reduction of the material scope of application of the CESL. Article 2(h) CESL Regulation Proposal defines goods as 'any *tangible movable* items ... exclud[ing] ... electricity and natural gas; and ... water and other types of gas unless they are put up for sale

---

Verbraucherrecht' in S. Augenhofer (ed.), *Verbraucherrecht im Umbruch* (Tübingen: Mohr Siebeck, 2012), p. 29.

[84] See 'First assumption: simplification of the legal environment for traders, reduction of business costs and lower final prices for consumers' and 'Second assumption: The CESL will lead to improved certainty for consumers' below.

[85] See Article 2(k) CESL Regulation Proposal.

[86] See Article 2(j) CESL Regulation Proposal for a definition of the term 'digital content'. For details see M. B. M. Loos *et al.*, 'The Regulation of Digital Content Contracts in the Optional Instrument of Contract Law', *European Review of Private Law*, 19 (2011), 729–58; N. Helberger *et al.*, 'Digital Content Contracts for Consumers', *Journal of Consumer Policy*, 36 (2013), 37–57; J. Pisuliński, 'The Application of the CESL to a Contract for the Supply of Digital Content (e.g. Software)' in L. Moccia (ed.), *The Making of European Private Law: Why, How, What, Who* (Munich: Sellier, 2013), pp. 205–15; C. Wendehorst, 'Article 5' in Schulze (ed.), *Common European Sales Law*, Article 5 CESL Regulation paras. 18–24.

[87] Article 2(m) CESL Regulation Proposal refers to 'any service related to goods or digital content, such as installation, maintenance, repair or any other processing, provided by the seller of the goods or the supplier of the digital content under the sales contract, the contract for the supply of digital content or a separate related service contract which was concluded at the same time as the sales contract or the contract for the supply of digital content'. For exceptions see the same article.

[88] See Article 2(k) CESL Regulation Proposal.

in a limited volume or set quantity' (emphasis added). Hence, immovable objects and intangible items are not covered by this definition – it should, however, be mentioned that the latter could fall under a different CESL category, the pillar of digital content.[89] Further exclusions from the general scope of the CESL can be found in Article 6 (on 'mixed-purpose contracts', i.e., contracts that 'include any elements other than the sale of goods, the supply of digital content and the provision of related services'[90] and 'contracts linked to a consumer credit') and – with respect to certain provisions of the CESL – in the CESL itself. These provision-related exceptions include, inter alia, the exclusion of withdrawal rights for several contractual types, such as contracts concluded by means of an automatic vending machine (Article 40(2)(a) CESL Proposal), contracts for the sale of certain print media (with the exception of subscription contracts) (Article 40(2)(g)) or contracts concluded at a public auction (Article 40(2)(h)).

The CESL itself is composed of 8 parts containing 186 articles. In addition, it includes two model documents, Appendix 1 (which contains mandatory pre-contractual information on rights of withdrawal) and Appendix 2 (which contains a withdrawal form). Both are models of documents that must be sent by traders to consumers in B2C distance and off-premises transactions in accordance with Article 17 CESL Proposal.[91]

Part I ('Introductory provisions') introduces the CESL with general principles applicable to all types of contracts that would fall under the instrument. These general principles can only be derogated from where the CESL introduces a *lex specialis*. One example of practical importance can be found in the CESL's mandatory B2C contract rules, which can be considered to override the principle of freedom of contract (at least to a certain extent[92]). Part I also contains some further fundamental rules of

---

[89] See the reference in note 86 above for details.

[90] Article 6(1) CESL Regulation Proposal.

[91] See further Article 42(2) CESL Proposal for the consequences for the withdrawal period should the trader not comply with Articles 13(1)(e) and 17 CESL Proposal. See further Articles 45(2) for consequences on bearing the direct costs of returning goods and 45(3) CESL Proposal on the diminished value of returned goods in such an event.

[92] For comments on party autonomy and its role in EU private law as well as for comments on the interplay between party autonomy and mandatory law see J. Basedow, 'Freedom of Contract in the European Union', *European Review of Private Law*, 16 (2008), 901–23; G. Wagner, 'Mandatory Contract Law: Functions and Principles in Light of the Proposal for a Directive on Consumer Rights' in A. Ogus and W. H. van Boom (eds.), *Juxtapoxing Autonomy and Paternalism in Private Law* (Oxford: Hart, 2011), pp. 9–42; W. H. van Boom and A. Ogus, 'Introducing, Defining and Balancing "Autonomy versus Paternalism"' in

the CESL, for example rules on how to interpret the CESL itself[93] or definitions of concepts used in the CESL such as 'reasonableness'[94] or 'termination of a contract'.[95]

Part II ('Making a binding contract') contains comprehensive rules on the conclusion of contracts, including rules on contractual offers and acceptances, pre-contractual information duties with additional specific obligations for traders in distance and off-premises contracts, withdrawal rights provisions for distance and off-premises contracts as well as more general defects in consent rules such as provisions on contract avoidance as a result of mistake or unfair exploitation.

Part III ('Assessing what is in the contract') is another general part in the sense that it contains provisions that basically cover all three categories of cross-border transaction contracts: sales contracts, digital content contracts and related services contracts. It contains, inter alia, extensive rules on contractual interpretation and provisions on unfair contract terms. In contrast to the respective provisions of the UCTD, the latter group is split into two lists for B2C cases: a black list with absolutely prohibited terms and a grey list of terms that are deemed unfair (based on rebuttable presumption). In addition, contract terms not covered by the two lists can in a particular case be declared unfair if they meet the general unfairness definition of Article 83 CESL Proposal.

Part IV ('Obligations and remedies of the parties to a sales contract or a contract for the supply of digital content') and Part V ('Obligations and remedies of the parties to a related service contract') split the three CESL categories into two groups with sales contracts and digital content contracts forming one group and related services contracts constituting a second. Both parts contain specific rules for the contracts of the respective group, including, for example, provisions related to remedies in case of non-performance. Supplementary, common rules on the right to sue for damages for loss resulting from non-performance (including damages for '[f]uture loss which the debtor could expect to occur')[96] can be found in the subsequent Part VI ('Damages and interest'). In addition,

---

ibid., pp. 1–8; M. E. Storme, 'Freedom of Contract: Mandatory and Non-mandatory Rules in European Contract Law', *Juridica International*, 11 (2006), 34–44; K. Kroll-Ludwigs, *Die Rolle der Parteiautonomie im europäischen Kollisionsrecht* (Tübingen: Mohr Siebeck, 2013). For further remarks on the interplay between mandatory law and party autonomy see 'Justice-related Thoughts on Mandatory Law' in Chapter 14 below.

[93] Article 4 CESL Proposal.   [94] Article 5 CESL Proposal.
[95] Article 8 CESL Proposal.   [96] Article 159(2) CESL Proposal.

this part also includes provisions on late payments and subsequent interest.[97]

Parts VII ('Restitution') and VIII ('Prescription') round off the CESL regime with some additional common provisions. The relatively short Part VII contains restitution rules for contract avoidance or termination cases, i.e., it regulates the obligation to return what has been received (or where this is not possible, to pay an equivalent amount) in such situations. Finally, Part VIII includes provisions relating to the issue of prescription, i.e., rules on the expiration of the right to enforce performance. It includes a differentiation between two different types of prescription periods (a shorter period of two years and a longer fixed period of ten or, in the case of damages related to personal injuries, thirty years),[98] determination rules regarding the end point of prescription periods and statutory as well as contractual alterations of prescription periods.

A brief analysis of the CESL Regulation Proposal

Recalling the assumptions of the Commission

The CESL is obviously a key project, if not the signature project of the Commission in the field of contract law.[99] If and once adopted, it could have far-reaching consequences for consumers and cross-border trade (under the condition that traders would be willing to use the new regime for their B2C transactions).[100] Thus, it is of practical importance to discuss certain questions raised by the CESL Regulation Proposal and to assess key Commission assumptions with respect to the CESL (if adopted based on the wording of the CESL Regulation Proposal).[101] In my brief analysis

---

[97] Part VI Sections 2 and 3 CESL Proposal.

[98] For comments on the prescription periods under the CESL Proposal see P. Møgelvang-Hansen, 'Article 179' in Schulze (ed.), *Common European Sales Law*, Article 179 CESL Regulation para. 1.

[99] In a similar vein is J. Stabentheiner, 'Der Entwurf für ein Gemeinsames Europäisches Kaufrecht – Charakteristika und rechtspolitische Aspekte', *wirtschaftsrechtliche blätter*, 26 (2012), 61, 62, where Johannes Stabentheiner calls it '*the* signature project' ('das *Prestigeobjekt*').

[100] For details see 'First assumption: simplification of the legal environment for traders, reduction of business costs and lower final prices for consumers' and 'Fourth assumption: the CESL will be a bilaterally voluntary, secondary regime' below.

[101] For comments on later suggested amendments at the Parliament stage see 'The Common European Sales Law after the CESL Regulation Proposal' below. As will be shown there, the Parliament's Legal Affairs Committee (JURI) – the committee responsible for the proposal at the Parliament level – and the Parliament itself both basically support the assumptions of the Commission.

of the CESL Regulation Proposal, I will focus on the following claims of the Commission:

1) The CESL will simplify the legal situation for traders,[102] reduce business costs[103] and as a consequence reduce the final prices paid by consumers.[104]
2) The CESL will improve the certainty of consumer rights.[105]
3) There is a clear need for the introduction of the CESL.[106]
4) The CESL will be a bilaterally voluntary, secondary regime.[107]
5) The CESL will maintain or increase the existing level of consumer protection in the EU.[108]
6) The CESL will necessarily solve the 'problems' caused by Article 6 Rome I Regulation.[109]

If all these assumptions are proven correct, then the introduction of the CESL would undeniably have the potential to strengthen consumer confidence and contribute to the growth of the internal market, which is the main justification for the CESL Regulation Proposal. Unfortunately though – and to anticipate the conclusion of the following analysis – theory and practice are not always congruent.

---

[102] CESL Explanatory Memorandum, p. 11: '[F]or traders ... [the CESL] would eliminate the need for research of different national laws'.

[103] *Ibid.*, p. 4: '[T]raders could save on the additional contract law related transaction costs and could operate in a less complex legal environment for cross-border trade on the basis of a single set of rules across the European Union.'

[104] *Ibid.*: 'Consumers would benefit from better access to offers from across the European Union at lower prices.'

[105] *Ibid.*: '[Consumers] would also enjoy more certainty about their rights when shopping cross-border on the basis of a single set of mandatory rules'.

[106] Recital 6 CESL Regulation Proposal: 'Differences in national contract laws ... constitute barriers which prevent consumers and traders from reaping the benefits of the internal market. ... [A] uniform set of contract law rules should cover the full life cycle of a contract. ... It should also include fully harmonised provisions to protect consumers.'

[107] CESL Explanatory Memorandum, p. 8: 'The Common European Sales Law will apply on a voluntary basis, upon an express agreement of the parties'; see further Article 3 CESL Regulation Proposal on the '[o]ptional nature of the Common European Sales Law'.

[108] CESL Explanatory Memorandum, p. 9: '[T]he Common European Sales Law would guarantee a high level of consumer protection by setting up its own set of mandatory rules which maintain or improve the level of protection that consumers enjoy under the existing EU consumer law.'

[109] *Ibid.*, p. 8: '[Article 6(2) Rome I Regulation] however can have no practical importance if the parties have chosen within the applicable national law the Common European Sales Law.' For the sake of clarity it should be noted that the analysis is limited to cases where the consumer would habitually reside in the EU.

First assumption: simplification of the legal environment for traders, reduction of business costs and lower final prices for consumers

One important assumption of the Commission is the claim that the CESL will necessarily simplify the legal situation for traders who wish to engage in cross-border B2C transactions and reduce the costs for both traders and consumers. In the CESL Explanatory Memorandum the Commission claims as follows: '[F]or traders … [the CESL] would eliminate the need for research of different national laws.'[110] It adds that 'traders could save on the additional contract law related transaction costs and could operate in a less complex legal environment for cross-border trade on the basis of a single set of rules across the European Union'[111] and that '[c]onsumers would benefit from better access to offers from across the European Union at lower prices'.[112]

Let me first respond to the argument that the introduction of a fully standardised optional European Sales Law, the CESL, will necessarily lead to greater legal clarity for traders who wish to conclude cross-border B2C transactions with consumers in the EU.[113] The basis for this assumption is simple: in the view of the Commission, the CESL would allow traders to use the same legal regime for any cross-border B2C transaction falling under the CESL if both parties agree on the applicability of the CESL – regardless of the Member State in which the respective consumer habitually resides. Two underlying ideas to this assumption, namely that the CESL would be a fully voluntary regime and that it could be applied without interference by private international law rules, will be discussed in later chapters. What is of interest in the present case is the question of whether the introduction of the CESL would necessarily lead to a considerable simplification of the legal setting for traders in cross-border B2C cases.

One complicating factor with respect to the related argumentation of the Commission is the fact that the CESL would add an additional sales law in each Member State and not replace existing sales laws. This would have the following consequences. As the CESL should only be an optional regime, traders would still face the need to obtain information on traditional national sales laws for two key reasons. First, the primary sales laws might be more business-friendly than the CESL. This is due to the

---

[110] CESL Explanatory Memorandum, p. 11.
[111] *Ibid.*, p. 4   [112] *Ibid.*
[113] On the question of the applicability of the CESL with respect to consumers outside the EU see the explanations and references in note 178 below.

fact that, in principle, the CESL follows a comparatively high level of protection.[114] To make an informed decision as to whether a trader would – from a legal perspective – be better off with the CESL or a primary sales law, the trader would have to obtain professional advice on both the CESL and primary sales laws. Second, it can be assumed that not every consumer would agree on the applicability of the CESL, especially in those cases where the primary sales law of the consumer's home Member State[115] contains consumer-friendlier provisions. Hence, and under the condition that the CESL would eventually turn out to be used as a second-ranked, voluntary regime not only on paper but also in practice,[116] traders would still face the need to obtain information on foreign primary sales laws. Furthermore, the fact that the CESL does not cover all possible legal questions raised by cross-border B2C transactions (I earlier explained that certain issues are left untouched) has the effect that traders need to obtain information about the different legal regulations of Member States regarding excluded legal issues. This necessity, caused by the incomplete nature of the CESL, applies regardless of whether traders would like to base their cross-border B2C transactions on the CESL.

The introduction of the CESL would thus not necessarily lead to a massive simplification of the legal situation for traders. It would further, contrary to the Commission's assumption, not necessarily help traders save money as it would not fully counteract a fragmentation of national laws, which in the words of Gerhard Wagner 'places a tax on European businesses'[117] in B2C cross-border trade. At least in the short run, expenses

---

[114] For details see 'Fifth assumption: the CESL will guarantee a high(er) standard of consumer protection without exception' below.

[115] For the purpose of this book the terms 'consumer's home country' and 'consumer's home Member State' shall refer to the Member State in which the respective consumer has his or her habitual place of residence.

[116] For more on this issue see 'Fourth assumption: the CESL will be a bilaterally voluntary, secondary regime' below.

[117] G. Wagner, 'The Virtues of Diversity in European Private Law' in Smits (ed.), *The Need for a European Contract Law*, p. 17. In a similar vein is Christian Twigg-Flesner's argumentation. He refers to the fragmentation of national sales private law systems as follows: 'This diversity has the effect of creating a non-tariff barrier to trade' (C. Twigg-Flesner, 'Introduction: Key Features of European Union Private Law' in Twigg-Flesner (ed.), *The Cambridge Companion to European Union Private Law*, p. 15). For further voices that are supportive of increased harmonisation from a financial perspective see F. Gómez, 'Some Law and Economics of Harmonizing European Private Law' in Hartkamp *et al.* (eds.), *Towards a European Civil Code*, pp. 401–26; see also comments in F. Gómez, 'The Harmonization of Contract Law through European Rules: a Law and Economics Perspective', *European Review of Contract Law*, 4 (2008), 2–30 and F. Gómez and J. J. Ganuza, 'The Economics of Harmonising Private Law Through Optional Rules' in Niglia

for external legal advice and/or the workload for internal legal counsels would actually increase, as information on an additional legal regime, i.e., the CESL regime, would be necessary to decide which legal setting would be the most suitable for a particular contract. The often-voiced argument of the Commission that businesses would spend less on legal advice[118] if the CESL were introduced thus comes to nothing.

Following on from the Commission's claim that the CESL *will* lower business costs (which would only be true if the respective trader succeeded in concluding *all* cross-border B2C contracts exclusively on the basis of the CESL)[119] the question remains whether this will also lower the final prices paid by consumers. This is linked to the question of whether businesses would be willing to pass on possible cost savings to consumers.

Whether final prices would eventually drop cannot be answered in the affirmative without reliable empirical data. To the best of my knowledge, no study to date has proven that traders in the EU would pass any likely cost savings to consumers.

One pertinent case, in which the CJEU tried to answer this issue, was *Skov* v. *Bilka*,[120] a case that dealt with the implementation of the fully harmonised Product Liability Directive (PLD).[121] Denmark decided to allow consumers to use the plaintiff-friendly strict liability regime also with respect to their contractual partner, i.e., the respective (re)seller

---

(ed.), *Pluralism and European Private Law*, pp. 177–97. For a more differentiated comment on this issue see H. Wagner, 'Economic Analysis of Cross-Border Legal Uncertainty: The Example of the European Union' in Smits (ed.), *The Need for a European Contract Law*, pp. 27–51. For critical comments on the transaction cost argument see further R. Sefton-Green, 'Choice, Certainty and Diversity: Why More Is Less', *European Review of Contract Law*, 7 (2011), 134; 138–40; W. Doralt, 'The Optional European Contract Law and Why Success or Failure May Depend on Scope Rather Than Substance', Max Planck Private Law Research Paper, No. 11/9 (2011), available at papers.ssrn.com/sol3/papers.cfm?abstract_id=1876451; R. Halson and D. Campbell, 'Harmonisation and Its Discontents: a Transaction Costs Critique of European Contract Law' in Devenney and Kenny (eds.), *The Transformation of European Private Law*, pp. 100–30.

[118] See, for example, CESL Explanatory Memorandum, pp. 2–4 and 8–10.

[119] It should be noted, however, that even in such a case a certain need to obtain legal advice on foreign laws remains. This is due to the fact that (as Recital 27 CESL Regulation Proposal explains) several legal questions that might be of importance are not covered by the CESL.

[120] Case C-402/03, *Skov Æg* v. *Bilka Lavprisvarehus A/S* [2006] ECR I-00199, Recital 28.

[121] For comments on the PLD and its national implementation see G. Howells and M. Pilgerstorfer, 'Product Liability' in Twigg-Flesner (ed.), *The Cambridge Companion to European Union Private Law*, pp. 257–72. For a historical overview of the development of product liability rules at the EU level see G. Howells, 'Product Liability: A History of Harmonization' in Hartkamp *et al.* (eds.), *Towards a European Civil Code*, pp. 889–902.

(instead of and/or in addition to the producer). This, however, was in contradiction with the fully harmonised regime of the PLD, which (primarily)[122] allowed for suing only the producer. One question the CJEU had to answer was whether the plaintiff-friendlier Danish provisions were *financially* detrimental for consumers. The CJEU answered this question in the affirmative. The main argument of the CJEU was its assumption that final prices would be higher if provisions such as the Danish provisions were maintained because traders would have to 'insure against such [strict] liability'[123] and this necessity would be factored in the final prices. In other words, according to the CJEU, prices would drop if (re)sellers did not have to insure themselves against claims resulting from product liability.[124] However, the problem is that the CJEU was not able to base its arguments on any data or other evidence. The CJEU's claim that prices would go down must thus be considered as mere speculation, as Geraint Howells and Jean-Sébastien Borghetti rightly explain. They conclude their criticism of the CJEU's decision by stating that 'nothing indicates that products were more expensive in countries which used to impose [strict] liability for defective products [also] on suppliers ... than in countries which have always channelled product liability on producers [note: as also foreseen by the PLD]'.[125] Put differently, the CJEU was unable to prove its assertion that businesses would be principally willing to pass on likely cost reductions to consumers. The fact that the end of the Danish regime meant that (re)sellers no longer had to insure against strict liability did not prove that they were willing to let consumers enjoy the cost reduction. It could just as well be argued that (re)sellers would not change their price policy for the consumers' benefit (at least not as a result from insurance cost savings) – instead they would seek to maximise their profit margin by retaining the saved amounts.

---

[122] See the exception of Article 3(3) PLD which allows for directly suing the seller instead of the producer in certain limited cases.

[123] Case C-402/03, Recital 28.

[124] For general comments on the related assumption that an increase in transaction costs leads to an increase in final prices to be paid by consumers see T. Nilssen, 'Two Kinds of Consumer Switching Costs', *The RAND Journal of Economics*, 23 (1992), 579–89; J. Sovern, 'Towards a New Model of Consumer Protection: The Problem of Inflated Transaction Costs', *William & Mary Law Review*, 47 (2006) 1635–709; S. Haupt, 'An Economic Analysis of Consumer Protection in Contract Law', *German Law Journal*, 4 (2003), 1137–64. One might be tempted to conclude that a decrease in transaction costs would, on the other hand, lower the final prices. But this, as explained in the remainder of this chapter, must not necessarily be true.

[125] G. Howells and J.-S. Borghetti, 'Product Liability' in Micklitz *et al.* (eds.), *Cases, Materials and Text on Consumer Law*, p. 452.

Hence, it can neither be expected that traders would generally face less need to obtain legal advice on applicable laws, nor can it be unconditionally stated that traders could save money. Furthermore, even if traders did save money, consumers would not necessarily financially benefit.

Second assumption: the CESL will lead to improved certainty for consumers

According to the Commission, consumers are reluctant to engage in cross-border shopping because they are confused and disincentivised by the existence of diverse national sales laws and are concerned that their substantive rights are at stake in B2C cross-border situations.[126] In the opinion of the Commission, the CESL regime would help consumers because this fully standardised sales law would resolve all doubts about their rights.[127]

---

[126] See, for example, CESL Explanatory Memorandum, p. 3. In 'Third assumption: the CESL is clearly needed' I will explain that diverse national sales laws are indeed a disincentive for consumers when shopping across borders. However, I will further show that the true obstacle in this context from a consumer perspective, i.e., the direct problem posed by diverse national sales laws, is not so much the possible uncertainty regarding which sales law is applicable, but rather the consumers' fears that their contracts would be governed by a sales law with a lower protective standard than the traditional sales law of their Member State.

[127] This assumption rests on the fact that the CESL is designed as 'a single uniform set of contract law rules with the same meaning and interpretation in all Member States' (Recital 8 CESL Regulation Proposal). The same expression is used by Article 1(1) CESL Regulation Proposal. Article 1(1) explains that the CESL is designed as 'a uniform set of contract law rules'. In this context it should not go unmentioned that – looking at how the CESL (via the CESL Regulation Proposal) would be embedded in the national legal regimes – several commentators argue that one should not consider the CESL as being a uniform law. At least it would not be a typical uniform law. Defining the term 'uniform law' in general, Franco Ferrari refers to the essential features of uniform laws (in an international context) as follows: the term refers to 'a set of identically worded legal rules that are binding on a general level in at least two jurisdictions. … [L]aw that has not been created with the intention of getting rid of the existing differences … does not constitute uniform law' (F. Ferrari, 'Uniform Law' in J. Basedow *et al.* (eds.), *The Max Planck Encyclopedia of European Private Law: Volume II* (Oxford University Press, 2012), p. 1732). The solution chosen by the Commission shows that the CESL does *not* aim to directly remove the fragmentation caused by national laws, but instead offers a second-ranked sales law regime that parties could (via explicitly opting-in) choose within the applicable national legal order over the first-ranked sales law of the respective country. For comments on this issue see Rühl, 'The Common European Sales Law' and the references in note 4 above. See also Wendehorst, 'Article 3', Article 3 CESL Regulation paras. 5–6, where she clearly differentiates between the uniform law approach and the second regime model.

The certainty argument would be correct if the CESL were to replace all existing national sales laws and to become a one-size-fits all sales regime. However, as the CESL would not cover all relevant transaction-related legal issues[128] and would add another national regime (for those matters within its scope), it is more than doubtful that it would lead to any improved certainty for consumers. It is very likely that the opposite would be the case. Consumers usually shop domestically – at least they make more purchases from domestic (re)sellers than from cross-border ones.[129] For domestic contracts the applicable sales law is the traditional, primary B2C sales law (traditional sales law) of the consumer's home Member State. Hence, consumers can be considered to be most familiar (if familiar at all) with the rules of 'their' traditional sales law. The adoption of the CESL would introduce an additional sales law at the national level, which would be only selectable for (some) B2C *cross-border* transactions (unless the Member States exercised their Member State option pursuant to Article 13a CESL Regulation Proposal and also made it applicable for purely domestic cases). Thus, the CESL would, in principle, remain quite 'foreign' to consumers. Furthermore, as the number of laws consumers could choose from for their cross-border B2C transactions (if they really had a choice)[130] would increase by one, determining the most suitable sales law would require an even better (or put differently, more comprehensively) informed decision than at present. Consumers would have to determine whether the CESL would be more beneficial in their particular case. Making the 'right' choice would – with all due respect – be undeniably almost impossible for the average consumer. Not only would the average consumer lack sufficient legal knowledge to compare selectable sales laws, but the fact that nobody can know in advance which, if any, legal problems would occur further complicates the determination of the most favourable sales law.

On top of that, the SIN (Annex II CESL Regulation Proposal), which traders have to provide to consumers before the CESL could be validly chosen to inform them about their rights, would actually complicate the situation. In reality, the SIN acts more as a Standard *Dis*information Notice. The SIN is both incomprehensible[131] and in some respects

---

[128] For details see Recital 27 CESL Regulation Proposal and the explanations in 'The CESL Regulation Proposal in a nutshell' above.

[129] For data on cross-border B2C trade see note 212 below.

[130] For details see 'Fourth assumption: the CESL will be a bilaterally voluntary, secondary regime' below.

[131] For a comment in this sense see S. Whittaker, 'The Proposed "Common European Sales Law": Legal Framework and the Agreement of Parties', *The Modern Law Review*, 75

misleading.[132] It is incomprehensive because it only focuses on certain and not always necessarily relevant aspects of the CESL. From the perspective of a consumer's limited ability to digest information, keeping information to a minimum regarding particular selected issues might be understandable.[133] However, one cannot deny the fact that in an actual case, other legal issues might be of bigger interest for consumers who would look, in vain, for related information in the SIN. The SIN is also misleading for several reasons. It would give the consumer the impression that a decision on the applicability on the CESL has already been made. The SIN starts as follows: 'The contract you are about to conclude will be governed by the Common European Sales.' The second paragraph of the SIN, which states that '[t]hese rules only apply if you mark your agreement that the contract is governed by the Common European Sales Law', obviously tries to explain to the consumer that the CESL must be chosen before it is applicable. However, because of its less prominent 'visibility' compared with the initial sentence of the SIN, this may not be of help in this respect. Consumers might think that – as a basic principle – they have no choice but to agree on the CESL. Furthermore, consumers might also get the impression that the CESL is 'better' than their traditional sales law,[134] which, as will be shown later, is not always necessarily true.

The SIN also exclusively focuses on the CESL and does not mention any other selectable sales laws. In particular, it forgets to mention the traditional sales law of the consumer's home country. One can of course argue that the task of the SIN is only to provide information about the CESL

(2012), 578, 605, where Simon Whittaker concludes his analysis of the SIN as follows: '[I]n my view, in the case of consumer contracts, the provision of information about the CESL by the trader which is specifically required by the Proposal would be insufficient to allow consumers to make a proper choice in favour of the CESL.'

[132] For a comment in this sense C. Wendehorst, 'Article 9', Article 9 CESL Regulation para. 10, where Wendehorst explains as follows: 'The SIN ... is also very dangerous for the consumer and potentially misleading: Information of the kind that the consumer has a right of withdrawal "in most cases" suggests that there is such a right even where the contract at hand falls under one of the numerous exceptions.'

[133] For an analysis of human information-processing capacities see G. A. Miller, 'The Magical Number Seven, Plus or Minus Two: Some Limits on Our Capacity for Processing Information', *Psychological Review*, 101 (1994), 343–52. See further J. Jacoby, 'Perspectives on Information Overload', *Journal of Consumer Research*, 10 (1984), 432–5. Jacob Jacoby concludes that information can lead to an overload. Thus, consumers would be 'highly selective in how much and just which information they access' (*ibid.*, 435).

[134] The second sentence of the SIN promotes the CESL as follows: '[The provisions of the CESL] have been designed to provide consumers with a high level of protection.'

and no other sales law. However, this argument does not change the fact that consumers might still find it difficult to identify the most suitable legal regime. Many consumers would surely be interested to learn about the differences between the CESL and the traditional sales law of their home country.[135] However, such information would not be contained in the SIN.

Hence, the introduction of the CESL would not make a significant contribution to the clarification of consumer rights and neither would the SIN.[136] On the contrary, consumers might be more confused than ever because the CESL would add an additional sales law and the SIN would only contain one-sided information, which could mislead consumers. Consumers would also have to spend extra time and money if they wanted to identify whether the CESL would add any value compared with traditional sales laws. Thus, consumers might experience greater levels of frustration than under the current regime and might be further disincentivised to engage in cross-border B2C trade.[137]

---

[135] See the explanations in 'Third assumption: the CESL is clearly needed' for the concerns of consumers that the protection by substantive laws in B2C cross-border transactions would be worse than in purely domestic cases.

[136] See also Karl Riesenhuber's conclusion that consumers who get the impression via the SIN that the protective standard under the CESL is necessarily as high as the traditional domestic standard might eventually be disappointed when they find out that the protection offered by the CESL could also be lower than offered by their traditional national sales law (K. Riesenhuber, 'Information über die Verwendung des Gemeinsamen Europäischen Kaufrechts – Gedanken zum Harmonisierungskonzept', Zeitung für Gemeinschaftsprivatrecht, 9 (2012), 2, 4).

[137] It should not go unmentioned that in late 2013 results were published reporting the behavioural testing of the SIN as mandated by the Directorate-General for Justice (DG JUST). The test was conducted in eight Member States and confirmed that the SIN (as proposed in the CESL Regulation Proposal) – although showing some positive effects – was in need of improvement. The report recommended several changes, most notably a revised title and introduction to raise general awareness and to make it more apparent that the CESL is an optional sales law that requires agreement from both parties before it is applicable (see The Gallup Organisation Europe et al., 'Testing of a Standardised Information Notice for Consumer on the Common European Sales Law', report for DG JUST, (2013), p. 70 (on file with the author)). Among other things, the report also commented on the possible inclusion in the SIN of a comparison of the legal provisions of the CESL and traditional sales laws, but came to the conclusion that this would make little sense. It would lead to an information overload and would not remedy the fact that most consumers do not (or only very briefly) read the SIN. Hence, there would be little value added (see ibid., p. 71). Although the conclusions of the study are in principle reasonable, some of the core issues indicated in my analysis still exist. For example, the study did not address the problem that the SIN incorrectly infers that the CESL provides consumers with the same level of protection as their traditional national laws in every single case. The recommendation to keep the SIN short (and not to include a comparison with

Third assumption: the CESL is clearly needed

Another important question concerns whether the CESL is in fact needed. To answer this question I must first answer another question: is the CESL what traders and consumers are primarily asking for to facilitate cross-border B2C trade?

As explained earlier, the Commission is of the firm belief that the different approaches of the Member States towards contract law, i.e., the fragmentation of national traditional contract laws, is the main obstacle to the growth of the internal market, and that both traders and consumers are asking for the introduction of a one-size-fits-all European sales law. With respect to cross-border B2C transactions, this assumption was especially fuelled by the Eurobarometer survey on European contract law in consumer transactions (2011 B2C Contract Survey).[138] The survey asked traders (but not consumers) about the perceived impact of several possible legal and non-legal issues on cross-border B2C trade and further asked which of them posed the biggest practical problems.

The results of the 2011 B2C Contract Survey show that traders do indeed consider contract law-related issues as a major barrier to entering the cross-border market. Two of the three most often mentioned disincentives in this regard were the '[d]ifficulty in finding out about the provisions of a foreign contract law' (ranked first with a total of 40 per cent of respondents considering this issue to have at least some practical impact) and '[t]he need to adapt and comply with different consumer protection rules in ... foreign contract laws' (ranked third with a total of 38 per cent).[139]

Although these numbers indicate that contract law issues are important for traders, they do not answer the question of whether the CESL

national laws) does not change the fact that consumers might be misled. It remains to be seen if, and if so, how the proposed SIN would be amended in the end. If the SIN is not appropriately revised, it can only be hoped that other, additional flanking measures to properly inform consumers would be taken. Active information campaigns as discussed in Part IV would be one possible means to cope with this issue.

[138] The Gallup Organization Hungary, 'European Contract Law in Consumer Transactions. Analytical Report', Flash Eurobarometer 321, (2011), available at ec.europa.eu/public_opinion/flash/fl_321_en.pdf. For a similar survey regarding B2B issues see The Gallup Organization Hungary, 'European Contract Law in Business-to-business Transactions. Analytical Report', Flash Eurobarometer 320, (2010), available at ec.europa.eu/public_opinion/flash/fl_320_en.pdf.

[139] Tax law-related issues ranked second with a rate of 39 per cent and the (primarily) non-legal issue of language differences followed in a close fourth place with 36 per cent (see The Gallup Organization Hungary, 'European Contract Law in Consumer Transactions', p. 19).

in its proposed optional form is the solution that traders actually want. The answer to this can be found in a later stage of the survey. The vast majority of respondents, an overwhelming 71.3 per cent of traders with an interest in cross-border B2C transactions, explained that they would be likely or very likely to make use of a pan-EU contract law that could be chosen for all cross-border transactions.[140] When asked about the actual form that such a regime should take, more than half (52.7 per cent) of the respondents said that they would want it to replace all existing national sales laws.[141] In comparison, only 14.6 per cent supported the idea of an *optional* contract law in the proposed form.[142] Undeniably, these numbers are not what the Commission wanted and clearly do not justify the assumption that traders with an interest in cross-border B2C transactions would necessarily extend a warm welcome to the CESL in its proposed form. In other words: it is doubtful that traders would really appreciate an optional contract law.

The Commission nevertheless celebrated the results of the 2011 B2C Contract Survey as proof for its assumption that the (optional) CESL would be of prime importance to enhance the internal market. Unfortunately, the Commission did not only misinterpret the results of the 2011 B2C Contract Survey, it also ignored a very important practical issue. An intrinsic characteristic of cross-border B2C transaction contracts, actually of any transaction contract, is the fact that they are concluded by (at least) two parties. Thus, it would have been more than advisable to take *both* sides' arguments and views into (proper) consideration when looking for a solution. Of course, discovering the reasons why traders

---

[140] *Ibid.*, p. 85 (Table 22a). For comments on the possibility of introducing a non-optional sales law (for cross-border transactions only) see Twigg-Flesner, *A Cross-border-only Regulation for Consumer Transactions in the EU*; C. Twigg-Flesner, '"Good-Bye Harmonisation by Directives, Hello Cross-Border Only Regulation?" – A Way Forward for EU Consumer Contract Law*', European Review of Contract Law*, 7 (2011), 235–56. For a strong call to pursue the introduction of a comprehensive European Contract Code see O. Lando, 'Comments and Questions Relating to the European Commission's Proposal for a Regulation on a Common European Sales Law', *European Review of Private Law*, 19 (2011), 717–28.

[141] The Gallup Organization Hungary, 'European Contract Law in Consumer Transactions', p. 91 (Table 25a).

[142] *Ibid.*; in addition to the 14.6 per cent that favoured an optional instrument for cross-border transactions only, another 22 per cent favoured an optional instrument that would be applicable to national and cross-border transactions. The proposed CESL would, however, primarily only apply to cross-border transactions (and only in the event that the respective national legislators also opt for a domestic application, cover purely national transactions (see Article 13(a) CESL Regulation Proposal)).

refrain from engaging in cross-border trade is essential to consider possible actions. However, (although the Commission briefly commented on them in the CESL Impact Assessment) it remains a mystery why it did not give *serious* consideration to consumers' wishes and needs in cross-border trade when discussing the necessity of the CESL.[143] One can also say that the drafting process lacked a broader, sociological analysis, which, to borrow Cotterrell's words, would have meant taking a look at the 'social conditions in which legal ideas are formed and used, and which … inform the regulatory demands made of them, and provide the sources of their power to regulate and control'.[144]

---

[143] The CESL Impact Assessment, which was conducted in the drafting process of the CESL Regulation Proposal, briefly touched upon consumer interests, but unfortunately used flawed logic and thus did not take proper account of consumer interests. It arrived at the conclusion that the Rome I regime would in principle be of only little help to improve consumer confidence in the cross-border B2C market. The CESL Impact Assessment tried to defend this claim with an analysis of Article 6 Rome I Regulation (for details on that provision see 'Sixth assumption: the CESL will necessarily solve the 'problems' caused by Rome I' below). It came to the conclusion that the applicability of this article was relatively limited in cross-border situations, basing its arguments on CJEU case law (see European Commission, Impact Assessment on a Common European Sales Law, 11 October 2012, SEC(2011) 1165 final, pp. 18 and 63; for a case note on the referred case law see A. A. H. van Hoek, 'CJEU – Pammer and Alpenhof – Grand Chamber 7 December 2010, joined cases 585/08 and 144/09, not yet published', *European Review of Contract Law*, 8 (2012), 93–107). The problem though is that the analysis is not completely accurate. Typical cases falling under the CESL are clearly cases that are either covered by Article 6(1)(a) or (b), i.e., cases where a targeted activities test would lead to the applicability of Article 6. Cases covered by the referred judgments would only be an exception and even in such cases (cases where the consumers are not entirely 'passive' as used by pertinent literature) the question of whether Article 6 applies can only be clarified on a case-by-case basis. However, the most important cases falling under the CESL are – if one interprets Article 6 correctly – undeniably covered by Article 6 (see, for example, Gralf-Peter Calliess's 'marketing strategy' explanations in G.-P. Calliess, 'Art. 6 Rome I' in Calliess (ed.), *Rome Regulations*, Article 6 Rome I para. 51 or Andreas Spickhoff's 'interactive website' argument in A. Spickhoff, 'Art 6 Rom I-VO' in H. G. Bamberger and H. Roth (eds.), *BGB Band 3* (3rd edn, Munich: C. H. Beck, 2012), Article 6 Rome I para. 32), and as such the argumentation of the CESL Impact Assessment is not convincing enough. In addition, a truly high-level minimum harmonisation approach to align substantive rights paired with extensive consumer and trader information (as both explained in Part IV below) and either a consumer-friendlier adjustment of the CJEU's position towards Article 6 Rome I Regulation or its legislative revision to cover cross-border B2C contracts more comprehensively would be much more effective to lead to more clarity for consumers. For a different critical comment on the CESL Impact Assessment see E. van Schagen, 'The Proposal for a Common European Sales Law: How Its Drafting Process Might Affect the Optional Instrument's Added Value for Contract Parties and Its Success' in Keirse and Loos, *Alternative Ways to Ius Commune*, pp. 85–109.

[144] R. Cotterrell, *Law's Community: Legal Theory in Sociological Perspective* (Oxford University Press, 1995), p. 3.

What information should have been derived from the results of more consumer-focused surveys on cross-border trade that already existed back then? The answer is simple: the issue of being exposed to as many as twenty-eight (at the time of publishing the proposal: twenty-seven) different national sales laws itself is *not* one of the prime concerns for consumers, at least not to a comparable extent nor in a comparable way as for traders.[145] To the best of my knowledge, no study on *consumers'* perspectives has revealed that the fragmentation of national sales laws was among the biggest concerns in cross-border B2C trade in a way that indicates the need for the CESL. The 2002 Eurobarometer study on views on business-to-consumer cross-border trade (2002 Eurobarometer B2C cross-border trade study), showed that the two biggest factors discouraging consumers from actively engaging in cross-border B2C were perceived difficulties in filing complaints and in seeking effective dispute settlement (88 per cent and 83 per cent, respectively, of respondent consumers stated that these issues were fairly or very important).[146] In contrast, difficulty in finding information on foreign consumer laws and the perceived low standard of foreign consumer laws, the two likely disincentives in the survey directly related to the fragmentation of substantive laws, fell into the bottom half of the spectrum. Although both answers scored relatively high (79 per cent and 68 per cent, respectively), one must say that they were not among the biggest concerns. In addition, as provisions of the traditional sales laws of the consumers' home countries can – as will be shown later – be consumer-friendlier than the corresponding provisions of the proposed CESL, the possible introduction of the CESL would not necessarily answer these substantive law-related consumer concerns. In principle, the Rome I Regulation might – for the great majority of cross-border B2C transactions falling under the CESL regime[147] – offer a much more suitable and direct answer to these two concerns, as it aims to guarantee that the level of protection in those cross-border B2C cases for which the CESL could

---

[145] In a similar vein is J.-J. Kuipers, 'The Legal Basis for a European Optional Instrument', *European Review of Private Law*, 19 (2011), 545, 556, where Jan Kuipers comments on the impact of diverse sales laws within (and not between) the Member States on buying behaviour and concludes that '[t]he extent to which the variety of national contract laws really discourages parties to engage in cross border trading tends to be overstated'. For general comments on the impact of regional contract laws in the EU in practice see H. L. MacQueen *et al.* (eds.), *Regional Private Laws & Codification in Europe* (Cambridge University Press, 2003).

[146] The European Opinion Research Group EEIG and EOS Gallup Europe, 'Public Opinion in Europe: Views on Business-to-Consumer Cross-border Trade', chapter II.1.1.

[147] See the explanations in note 143 above.

be typically used is kept at the same level (at the very least) as in domestic B2C transactions.

The above figures explain that neither traders nor consumers have directly asked for the introduction of the CESL. Traders, on the one hand, would prefer a regime that would totally replace the twenty-eight existing national sales laws in cross-border B2C situations. And consumer interests also would be better served by other means than the introduction of the CESL.[148] In addition to addressing various non-legal issues,[149] the priority for consumers is the fixing of procedural shortcomings and guaranteeing a truly high level of consumer protection by ensuring that the level of substantive law applicable in cross-border B2C cases is under no circumstances worse than the level of protection guaranteed in domestic B2C transactions. I will come back to these issues in Part IV of this book.

Fourth assumption: the CESL will be a bilaterally voluntary, secondary regime

In the CESL Explanatory Memorandum, the Commission states that '[t]he Common European Sales Law will be a second contract law regime within the national law of each Member State'.[150] Article 3 CESL Regulation Proposal refers to the optional character of the CESL as

---

[148] In a similar vein is Lurger's argumentation that 'the flourishing of the internal market' (translation mine) benefits only very little (if at all) from a defragmentation of (consumer) sales laws (see B. Lurger, 'Gerechtigkeitskonzepte für ein europäisches Vertragsrecht und Instrumente zu ihrer Umsetzung' in Arnold (ed.), *Grundlagen eines europäischen Vertragsrechts*, p. 137). See also her comments on the use of OIs in general and her conclusion (that she makes with reference to a Directorate-General for Internal Policies (DG IPOL) study for the Parliament) that they 'are not a success story' and that '[t]hey do not improve the legal situation and do not help the people concerned' (see B. Lurger, 'A Radical View of Pluralism? Comments on Jan Smits' in Niglia (ed.), *Pluralism and European Private Law*, p. 175 with reference to DG IPOL, 'Implementation of Optional Instruments within European Civil Law', study for the Parliament, (2012), available at www.europarl.europa.eu/RegData/etudes/etudes/join/2012/462425/IPOL-JURI_ET%282012%29462425_EN.pdf).

[149] Ewan McKendrick explains as follows: '[T]here are other more significant barriers to trade than the diversity of laws in general. Even if all legal barriers [in the form of diverse sales laws] to trade were removed ... the various non-legal barriers, such as language and culture, would remain' (E. McKendrick, 'Harmonisation of European Contract Law: The State We Are in' in Vogenauer and Weatherill (eds.), *The Harmonisation of European Contract Law*, p. 23). At the same time McKendrick confirms that certain legal barriers actually do exist. In line with the data that I have just discussed, he further explains that they are not intrinsically linked to the existence of diverse sales laws (*ibid.*).

[150] CESL Explanatory Memorandum, p. 6.

follows: 'The parties may agree that the Common European Sales Law governs their cross-border contracts for the sale of goods, for the supply of digital content and for the provision of related services within the territorial, material and personal scope as set out in Articles 4 to 7 [CESL Regulation Proposal].'[151] Article 8 CESL Regulation Proposal explains that the CESL would not be prioritised over the already existing traditional national sales law, but that it would require an express agreement to become applicable.[152] In other words, parties would have to explicitly opt in. In line with the Commission's aforementioned statement in the CESL Explanatory Memorandum, Recital 10 CESL Regulation Proposal adds that such a party agreement would 'be a choice exercised within the scope of the respective national law which is applicable'. (I will come back to this in a later chapter.)

Following the understanding of the Commission that the CESL forms an alternative *national* regime, the selection of the CESL would occur via a two-stage process. First, the parties would agree on a national law in general. Subsequently, and as a second step, the parties could choose the CESL over the primarily applicable national B2C sales law (traditional sales law) of the chosen (or otherwise determined[153]) Member State. In B2C cases, this second step, i.e., the choice of the CESL as the applicable national sales law is, pursuant to Article 8(2) CESL Regulation Proposal, to be made by an explicit, separate party choice.[154] This means that it requires

---

[151] Smits claims that the CESL's optional character is '[t]he most important aspect [of the CESL Regulation Proposal]' (J. M. Smits, 'Party Choice and the Common European Sales Law, or: How to Prevent the CESL from Becoming a Lemon on the Law Market', Maastricht European Private Law Institute Working Paper, No. 2012/13 (2012), p. 3, available at papers.ssrn.com/sol3/papers.cfm?abstract_id=2060017).

[152] With respect to B2C contracts it should further be noted that pursuant to Article 8(3) CESL Regulation Proposal the parties can choose the CESL only as a 'total package' and cannot pick only certain provisions to deviate from mandatory rules of traditional national sales laws (Article 8(3) CESL Regulation Proposal: 'In relations between a trader and a consumer the Common European Sales Law may not be chosen partially, but only in its entirety'). Wendehorst concludes as follows: 'In a consumer contract it is therefore not possible to split the applicable legal regime' (C. Wendehorst, 'Article 8' in Schulze (ed.), *Common European Sales Law*, Article 8 CESL Regulation para. 9). I will briefly return to this issue further below (see 'Fifth scenario: the parties agree on the law of the trader's home Member State and its CESL').

[153] See Article 6(1) Rome I Regulation for a determination of the general legal regime, if the parties do not agree on one. See also 'Sixth scenario: the parties agree on the CESL without reference to either Member State's legislative regime' below for an analysis of the case in which parties agree on the applicability of the CESL, but not on any general law.

[154] Christiane Wendehorst explains that referring to the CESL in the trader's standard terms is not sufficient (see C. Wendehorst, 'Article 8').

a separate party agreement to be chosen as a national law of the Member State whose general law is chosen (or otherwise determined). If the parties do not agree on the CESL, the first-ranked, traditional national sales law would be the applicable sales law. Wendehorst explains this as follows: 'The 2nd national regime model means that ... [u]nder [the] national law, parties may opt into the CESL ... by way of a separate choice.'[155] For various reasons, the particular drafting of the CESL Regulation leads to a number of interesting, and not always problem-free, consequences. I will deal with one of the issues, the issue of the relationship between the Rome I Regulation (Rome I) and the CESL, a little later. What is of greater interest at this point, is the question of how traders would and could react to the likely introduction of this new regime.

I showed in the preceding chapter that the vast majority of traders preferred the general replacement of traditional domestic sales laws with a pan-EU sales law, or at least the priority application of the CESL over traditional sales laws.[156] This might indicate that traders, if they came to the conclusion that the use of the CESL would be beneficial to their interests, would insist on the use of the CESL in cross-border B2C transactions. What would help them in this respect is the fact that the CESL contains no consumer 'safety-net' provision that would guarantee that consumers had an actual say in the decision on whether the CESL should apply in a B2C cross-border transaction.

Despite the theoretical optionality of the CESL (and leaving aside further, later-to-be-discussed Article 6 Rome I Regulation considerations), traders can thus easily turn the bilateral optionality of the CESL (i.e., the idea that both parties (traders and consumers) to a cross-border B2C transaction could jointly and freely choose the CESL to make it applicable) into a unilateral option. To circumvent unwanted traditional sales laws, traders could make the consumers' approval of the CESL a mandatory requirement for concluding a respective cross-border B2C contract and thus could very easily deprive consumers of their say in deciding on the applicable sales law. Instead of choosing between the traditional sales law and the CESL of a particular Member State, consumers would only have the chance to decide between concluding a cross-border contract based

---

[155] Wendehorst, 'Article 3' in *ibid.*, Article 3 CESL Regulation para. 7.

[156] Priority application basically means that preference would be given to the CESL over the traditional sales law at the Member State level – as is the case with respect to the United Nations Convention on the International Sale of Goods (CISG). (If the parties do not want the CISG to govern their contract – it is only applicable in B2B transactions – they have to exclude its applicability.)

on a Member State's CESL or not concluding a contract at all. According to Lurger, this is the logical consequence of the fact that '[i]n situations where one party, namely a business, is in a stronger negotiating position than the other, the first party will decide whether the optional code is chosen to apply to the contract'.[157] Jürgen Basedow comments in the same vein and succinctly describes the issue as follows: 'The choice between national [traditional] laws and the optional instrument [i.e., the CESL] will lie with businesses *exclusively*'[158] (emphasis added).

This take-it-or-leave-it approach might simply be the unfortunate result of imprecise wording in the proposal and an oversight of the Commission. However, the Commission might have also approved it to reconcile its inconsistent and self-contradictory argumentation to satisfy traders' interests in a stronger device. On the one hand, the Commission had not missed any chance to stress the presumed negative impact of diverse national sales laws and the importance of a pan-EU standardised

---

[157] Lurger, 'The Common Frame of Reference', p. 182.
[158] Basedow, 'European Contract Law', p. 169. Howells explains that the CESL 'will not be truly optional for consumers. Their choice will most likely be to contract on the basis of the Optional Instrument by pressing the "blue button" or not contract' (see G. Howells, 'European Contract Law Reform and European Consumer Law – Two Related But Distinct Regimes', *European Review of Contract Law*, 7 (2011), 173, 183). In a similar vein is Lurger's perceptive analysis of the CFR [i.e. what was to later become the proposed CESL], where she commented that '[t]he CFR and the optional code may be a wolf in sheep's clothing: They seem to hide the promotion of maximum harmonization and indirect centralization under the guise of a non-binding flexible instrument' (Lurger, 'The Common Frame of Reference', p. 185). See further Howell's and Reich's comment that the Commission would achieve 'de facto maximal harmonisation through an instrument which will not be truly optional for consumers' (G. Howells and N. Reich, 'The Current Limits of European Harmonisation in Consumer Contract Law', *ERA Forum*, 12 (2011), 39, 56–7). On the related issue of a possible CESL 'blue button' see especially H. Schulte-Nölke, 'How to Realise the "Blue Button"? – Reflections on an Optional Instrument in the Area of Contract Law' in Schulze and Schulte-Nölke (eds.), *European Private Law*, pp. 89–90. See further Schulte-Nölke's comment that traders would 'grant consumers' protection under the CESL (see H. Schulte-Nölke, 'Scope and Function of the Optional Instrument on European Contract Law' in R. Schulze and J. Stuyck (eds.), *Towards a European Contract Law* (Munich: Sellier, 2011), p. 44). In light of the fact that the CESL would – in practice – not be a bilateral OI, one has to question how Smits arrives at his conclusion that 'the fundamental choice to create an optional regime should be met with enthusiasm' (J. M. Smits, 'The Common European Sales Law (CESL) beyond Party Choice', Maastricht European Private Law Institute Working Paper, No. 2012/11 (2012), p. 4, available at papers.ssrn.com/sol3/papers.cfm?abstract_id=2039345) – or asked from a consumer's perspective: why should *they* be enthusiastic? (See further Smits, 'Party Choice and the Common European Sales Law', p. 3, where Smits refers to the optional character of the CESL as '[t]he most important aspect [of the CESL Regulation Proposal]').

instrument for the sake of the internal market. On the other hand, it could – as explained earlier[159] – propose the CESL only in the form of an OI and not in the form of a regime that would directly replace traditional sales laws in cross-border B2C situations. However, a truly optional tool, understood as a bilaterally optional tool, i.e., optional for both traders and consumers, would not have been of much help for traders who – according to the Commission – are disincentivised by diverse sales laws. True bilateral optionality would still present traders with the problem that consumers could ask for the application of traditional sales laws. The possibility for traders to decide autonomously whether to choose the CESL, i.e., the factually unilateral optionality of the CESL, could remedy this fact and attract more traders than a truly optional sales law, and all without changing the optional 'label' of the CESL. Hence, two crucial questions to be answered in the future are as follows: to what extent would traders use the CESL in practice and would they give consumers any chance to conclude a cross-border B2C transaction contract based on traditional sales laws? Put differently, how voluntary would the CESL be for consumers? If it turns out that traders could circumvent the envisaged bilateral optionality and force consumers to agree to whatever choice traders autonomously want to make, then it has to be asked whether the CESL would be truly optional. It could in fact lead to a scenario in which traditional sales laws completely lose their practical relevance in cross-border B2C trade.

Regardless of the question of whether the Commission was actually aware of this fact (and it is beyond the scope of this book to answer this question), a unilaterally optional code is clearly not what Member States and consumers would have asked for. One should (at the very least) think about including a safeguard mechanism to protect the consumers' say in deciding on the applicable sales law, not least because – as I will explain in the next section – the protective level of the CESL does not necessarily meet the standards of each of the twenty-eight traditional Member State regimes. If this does not happen, then it can only be hoped that the CJEU would take up this issue when called upon and discuss the *true* character of the CESL, especially from a proportionality perspective.[160]

---

[159] See 'The genesis of the proposal on a Common European Sales Law or: the long and winding road' above.

[160] Some voices raise concerns about the compatibility of the CESL with proportionality requirements. See, for example, H.-W. Micklitz and N. Reich, 'The Commission Proposal for a "Regulation on a Common European Sales Law (CESL) – Too Broad or Not Broad Enough?"', EUI Working Papers, Law 2012/04 (2012), pp. 9–11

Fifth assumption: the CESL will guarantee a high(er) standard of consumer protection without exception

In the CESL Explanatory Memorandum, the Commission explains that '[t]he Common European Sales Law would contain fully harmonized consumer protection rules providing for a high standard of protection throughout the whole of the European Union'.[161] Various scholars such as Reinhard Zimmermann,[162] Giesela Rühl[163] and Hans Schulte-Nölke[164] rightly agree that the general protective standard is quite high.

The devil is in the detail though. Let me recall another claim that the Commission made with respect to the CESL. In Recital 11 CESL Regulation Proposal, the Commission claims that the CESL would 'guarantee a high level of consumer protection with a view to enhancing consumer confidence in the Common European Sales Law and thus provide consumers with an incentive to enter into cross-border contracts on that

---

(available at cadmus.eui.eu/bitstream/handle/1814/20485/LAW_2012_04_ERPL_03. pdf?sequence=3) with further references to some critical comments by national legislators, in particular from the UK, Germany and Austria (see *ibid.*, pp. 7–9). For additional sceptical comments see K. Riesenhuber, 'Der Vorschlag für ein "Gemeinsames Europäisches Kaufrecht" – Kompetenz, Subsidiarität, Verhältnismäßigkeit', report for the Committee on Legal Affairs of the German Bundestag, (2012), pp. 10–13, available at papers.ssrn.com/sol3/papers.cfm?abstract_id=1998134; M. Tamm, 'Das Gemeinsame Europäische Kaufrecht als optionales Instrument – eine kritische Analyse zur Binnenmarktharmonisierungskompetenz der Kommission', *Verbraucher und Recht*, 27 (2012), 3, 10, where Marina Tamm concludes that the CESL Regulation Proposal is 'by no means proportional' (translation mine). For some general critical comments on how the CJEU's approach towards the proportionality principle has evolved see N. Reich, 'How Proportionate Is the Proportionality Principle? Some Critical Remarks on the Use and Methodology of the Proportionality Principle in the Internal Market Case Law of the ECJ' in H.-W. Micklitz and B. De Witte (eds.), *The European Court of Justice and the Autonomy of the Member States* (Cambridge: Intersentia, 2012), pp. 83–111.

[161] CESL Explanatory Memorandum, p. 4. For comments on this claim see S. Wrbka, 'The Proposal for an Optional Common European Sales Law: A Step in the Right Direction for Consumer Protection?', *EUIJ-Kyushu Review*, 1 (2011), 87, 112–14.

[162] R. Zimmermann, '*Perspektiven* des künftigen österreichischen und europäischen Zivilrechts', *Juristische Blätter*, 134 (2012), 2, 16, where Zimmermann refers to the protective standard offered by the CESL as 'remarkable' (*bemerkenswert*).

[163] Rühl, 'The Common European Sales Law', p. 7, where Rühl concludes that 'a closer look into the substantive provisions of the CESL shows that it provides for a fairly high level of consumer protection'.

[164] H. Schulte-Nölke, 'Der Blue Button kommt – Konturen einer neuen rechtlichen Infrastruktur *für* den Binnenmarkt', *Zeitschrift für Europäisches Privatrecht*, 19 (2011), 749, 755, where Schulte-Nölke comments that 'the consumer protection level recommended by the Expert Group is in total much higher than the consumer protection level of any Member State'.

basis. The rules should maintain or improve the level of protection that consumers enjoy under *Union* consumer law' (emphasis added). At first sight this slightly more detailed statement sounds convincing, as it seems that no consumer would enjoy less or weaker rights than they do at present. However, this passage reveals an important shortcoming of the CESL. It does *not* refer to the standards of national laws, which might – depending on the relevant context – still be higher.

An example from Austria can exemplify this point. The Austrian Civil Code (ABGB) contains rules governing mistakes that apply to, inter alia, sales contracts. One of the scenarios covered by § 871(1) ABGB would allow the buyer to apply these rules in the case of 'timely notification' of the mistake by a contractual party. § 871(1) explains as follows:

> If a party was mistaken with respect to the contents of a declaration given or received by him, and this mistake affects the essence or the fundamental nature of that to which the intention of the declaration was principally directed and expressed, no duties arise therefrom for the mistaken party, provided that this mistake was … timely notified to him [note: the other party, i.e., the party which did not err] (translation mine).

The CESL Proposal contains mistake rules in Article 48. Article 48(1)(b) lists four possible scenarios. The Austrian 'prompt notification rule' is not, however, included in this list. If the parties validly agreed on the CESL, an erring consumer could not benefit from the ABGB rule and would be put in a worse situation than under the Austrian traditional regime.

The fact that the standard of protection under the CESL is in several instances lower than at the national level is not only further proven by various contributions from legal academia,[165] but further confirmed directly by the Commission. In its 'Non-paper on a comparison between 27 mandatory consumer protection provisions in the Common European Sales Law proposal and national laws', the Commission analysed the standard of protection under the CESL in comparison with the traditional sales laws of the Member States. At the time of writing this book, early results had been published.[166] Although these results only concern thirteen Member States and only cover certain provisions of the CESL,

---

[165] See, for example, the article-by-article analysis of the CESL Proposal in Schulze (ed.), *Common European Sales Law* or the comprehensive discussion on the CESL Proposal from the English and German perspectives in Dannemann and Vogenauer (eds.), *The Common European Sales Law in Context* – both show that, in several instances, the protective level of the CESL might be lower than the level offered by some Member States.

[166] A summary is available at ec.europa.eu/justice/contract/files/comparative_table_-_final_version_en.pdf.

they nevertheless show that in various instances the traditional laws of Member States apply consumer-friendlier solutions.

One can thus conclude that the protective standard offered by the CESL, though generally high, is neither necessarily at the same level, let alone higher in every possible scenario. In certain cases the traditional sales law of the contract governing Member States might actually lead to better results for consumers. Rühl expresses this possibility as follows: '[W]hile it is true that the CESL exceeds – on average – the consumer protection standard offered by the member states it does not offer more protection in every single case.'[167]

From the viewpoint of consumer interests this surely is regrettable. However, as shown earlier, it is the logical consequence of the fact that every act of law making is the result of a compromise between opposing interests.[168] In the case of the CESL, and as far as it touches upon B2C issues, the balance that had to be struck concerned the interests of businesses on the one hand and consumer interests on the other, and eventually could only lead to a protective level that would be acceptable to the business sector. If one consequently takes into consideration that traders, as explained in the previous chapter, could very easily force consumers to agree on the CESL, the fact that consumers would in some instances be exposed to less protection should give reason enough to doubt that the CESL would indeed necessarily benefit consumers. It can be easily assumed that consumers could live with the introduction of the CESL if, and only if, it could absolutely guarantee that consumers in any Member State and in any contractual setting falling under the scope of application of the CESL could enjoy *at least* the same protection as offered under the respective traditional sales law, regardless of the question at hand. This means that the CESL would have to include the highest possible protection level, matching that of the traditional sales regimes of the Member States, for every one of its provisions. This would have been the only fair or just trade-off between business and consumer interests.[169] Traders could rely on a fully standardised regime for their cross-border activities, while at the same time consumer

---

[167] Rühl, 'The Common European Sales Law', p. 11.

[168] For a practical example see the explanations in the context of the drafting of the CRD in 'The Directive on Consumer Rights' in Chapter 9 above. For comments on some compromises that had to be made in the drafting process of the DCFR, the major source of the CESL, see C. von Bar, 'Die Struktur des Draft Common Frame of Reference' in R. Schulze *et al.* (eds.), *Der akademische Entwurf für einen Gemeinsamen Referenzrahmen*, pp. 35–45 (in particular his conclusions at p. 45).

[169] For a similar, yet even more critical comment see K.-H. Oehler, 'Der Vorschlag für eine Richtlinie über die Rechte der Verbraucher aus deutscher Sicht' in Jud and Wendehorst

interests would not be put at stake. Having said this, in the next section and with the help of the Rome I regime, I will discuss whether consumers in likely contractual situations might enjoy a higher level of protection (as enshrined in their home Member State's traditional sales law) if the CESL is adopted on the wording proposed by the Commission.

Sixth assumption: the CESL will necessarily solve the 'problems' caused by Rome I

EU cross-border sales contracts inevitably lead to the question of which Member State's sales law is applicable, a question that is principally regulated by the Rome I Regulation. Generally speaking, the Rome I regime rests on the idea of party autonomy, which – in the context of the Rome I Regulation – means that the parties should be basically free to agree on the law governing their contract.[170] Regarding consumer contracts, Article 6 Rome I Regulation enshrines certain well-grounded limits to this freedom. It aims to protect, as Gralf-Peter Calliess puts it, 'inexperienced' consumers[171] from the traders' power to autonomously determine the applicable legal regime to the detriment of consumers.

(eds.), *Neuordnung des Verbraucherprivatrechts in Europa*, p. 20, where Karl-Heinz Oehler discusses the issue of acceptability of fully harmonised rules from the viewpoint of consumers in the context of the CRD Proposal. He comes to the conclusion that a set of fully harmonised provisions directly serves the interests only of the *business* side and – at least from a legal perspective – would only be acceptable for consumers if it led to a considerably higher level of protection than already existing. Loos, who is basically very critical of maximum harmonisation, explains (again in the context of the CRD Proposal) that maximum harmonisation needs to ensure that the level of fully harmonised protection is 'sufficiently high' to foster consumer confidence. He further refers to CJEU case law and notes that – thus far – the CJEU does not (in principle) ask for the highest possible level of protection. Put differently, the term 'sufficiently high' would (pursuant to the CJEU) not mean that 'the highest level of consumer protection available in any of the Member States on every single point must be achieved' (Loos, 'Full Harmonisation As a Regulatory Concept', p. 76). The complicating factor in the case of the CESL, however, is that its scope is even broader than the scope of the CRD. This basically means that in the case of the CESL maximum harmonisation could do even more harm, because guaranteeing that consumers could enjoy at least the same protection as offered by the traditional sales laws of their home countries might (due to the broader scope of the CESL) be more difficult.

[170] Recital 11 Rome I Regulation explains that '[t]he parties' freedom to choose the applicable law should be one of the cornerstones of the system of conflict-of-law rules in matters of contractual obligations'.

[171] G.-P. Calliess, *Grenzüberschreitende Verbraucherverträge*, p. 93 (translation mine). For a more critical view on the rationale behind Article 6 Rome I Regulation see Z. S. Tang, *Electronic Consumer Contracts in the Conflict of Laws* (Oxford: Hart, 2009), pp. 208–13.

Before answering the question of whether the introduction of a stand-ardised CESL would render the Rome I regime practically meaningless, one should first recall the basic approach taken by the Rome I Regulation towards cross-border B2C contracts. Article 6(1) clarifies that if certain basic requirements to a cross-border B2C contract are fulfilled and the parties do not agree on any law, then the law of the consumer's home country applies. This is an exception to the rule that in the absence of a law being chosen, the law of the seller's home country applies.[172]

For contractual agreements on the governing law, Article 6(2) refers to the general rule of Article 3(1), which basically allows parties to choose the governing law. Article 6(2) Rome I Regulation does, however, also contain an important limitation that benefits consumers. It states that no party choice can 'depriv[e] the consumer of the protection afforded to him by provisions that cannot be derogated from by agreement by vir-tue of the law, which in absence of choice, would have been applicable on the basis of paragraph 1 [i.e. the law of the consumer's home coun-try]'. This provision and its 'preferential-law test'[173] to determine the more favourable law for consumers in the concrete claim at issue (*konkreter Günstigkeitsvergleich*)[174] certainly plays a key role in the context of B2C contracts, as they aim to ensure that consumers from a Member State with a higher protective standard than the standard of the chosen foreign law can rely on the protection of their home Member State's regime.

The Commission was obviously aware of the possible interference by the Rome I regime with the traders' wish to subject cross-border B2C con-tracts to the same sales law regime regardless of the buyers' residence. This is, for example, expressively stated in the CESL Explanatory Memorandum where the Commission argues that consumer-friendlier national provi-sions resulting from the Member States' discretion to introduce or main-tain a higher protective standard in the case of minimum harmonisation would be detrimental for traders who would like to trade cross-border.[175] With its plan to introduce the CESL, the Commission intended to neu-tralise the protective effects of Article 6(2) Rome I Regulation and its

---

[172] See, in particular, Article 4(1)(a) Rome I Regulation.

[173] The test is to be conducted by courts ex officio (Spickhoff, 'Art 6 Rom I-VO', Article 6 Rome I para. 32; A. Staudinger, 'Rom I-VO Art. 6' in F. Ferrari *et al.* (eds.), *Internationales Vertragsrecht* (2nd edn, Munich: C. H. Beck, 2012), Article 6 Rome I para. 73). For details on the preferential-law test see, for example, Calliess, 'Art. 6 Rome I', Article 6 Rome I paras. 68 *et seq.*; B. Heiderhoff, 'Art 6 Rom I-VO' in Rauscher (ed.), *Europäisches Zivilprozess- und Kollisionsrecht*, Article 6 paras. 51–2.

[174] Calliess, 'Art. 6 Rome I', Article 6 Rome I para. 73.

[175] CESL Explanatory Memorandum, p. 2.

preferential-law test. Introducing a fully standardised sales law would, in the opinion of the Commission, necessarily counteract Article 6(2). The Commission comments on this issue as follows:

> In cases where another applicable law has been chosen by the parties and where the mandatory consumer protection provisions of the Member State of the consumer provide a higher level of protection, these mandatory rules of the consumer's law need to be respected ... [Article 6(2) Rome I Regulation] however can have no practical importance if the parties have chosen within the applicable national law the Common European Sales Law. The reason is that the provisions of the Common European Sales Law of the country's law chosen are identical with the provisions of the Common European Sales Law of the consumer's country. Therefore the level of the mandatory consumer protection laws of the consumer's country is not higher and the consumer is not deprived of the protection of the law of his habitual residence.[176]

According to the Commission, the preferential-law test of Article 6(2) Rome I Regulation (though still being conducted) would be rendered more or less meaningless if the parties agreed on the applicability of the CESL. In the opinion of the Commission, the CESL of the consumer's home Member State would be the yardstick for sales law questions under the preferential-law test, and because its CESL is necessarily identical with the CESL of the chosen Member State, the consumer would not enjoy better protection. This argumentation is further expressed (and bluntly so) by Recital 12 CESL Regulation Proposal, which declares that Article 6(2) has 'no practical importance for the issues covered by the Common European Sales Law'. The Commission is of the firm belief that the introduction of the CESL would enable traders to escape from diverse national traditional sales laws whenever the CESL is chosen by the parties. From the viewpoint of consumer interests, this claim, if true, could have disastrous consequences for consumers if their home Member State's traditional sales law contains consumer-friendlier rules with respect to the concrete claim at issue.[177]

However, if one takes a closer look at the interplay of Article 6 Rome I Regulation and the CESL regime as proposed by the Commission, one can arrive at some interesting conclusions that could prove the Commission's

---

[176] *Ibid.*, p. 6.

[177] This is also feared by consumer representatives. BEUC claims that with the introduction of the CESL 'the Commission openly aims at preventing consumers from having access to the safety-net provided by Art 6 Rome I Regulation' (see BEUC, 'Towards a European Contract law for Consumers and Business?', position paper (2011), 13).

argument (to some extent) wrong. I would like to explain this by analysing possible contractual scenarios. For the sake of clarity I should add
that the analysis is limited to those scenarios that fulfil the basic requirements of Article 6 Rome I Regulation, i.e., to cases in which the concrete
B2C relationship falls under one of the underlying categories outlined
therein. It is further limited to cases where both the habitual residence of
the consumer and the place from which the trader's business operates are
in Member States.[178]

The possible scenarios relate to the following six situations:

1) The trader and the consumer do not agree on any applicable law.
2) The trader and the consumer agree on the law of the trader's home
   Member State[179] without agreeing on its CESL as the governing
   sales law.
3) The trader and the consumer agree on the law of the consumer's
   home Member State without agreeing on its CESL as the governing
   sales law.

---

[178] The reasons to limit the analysis to such cases are twofold. First, it can be assumed
that they are the most likely instances in which the CESL would be used. The CESL
Explanatory Memorandum, at the very least, seems to assume that such situations
would be the most likely when it argues that '[d]ifferences in contract law between
Member States hinder traders and consumers who want to engage in cross-border trade
within the internal market' (emphasis added) (CESL Explanatory Memorandum, p. 1).
Second, and more importantly, the CESL is to be applied as a sales law of a Member State.
In other words, the selection of the CESL would always have to be considered as the
selection of the CESL of a certain Member State. The wording of the CESL Regulation
Proposal leaves it in no doubt that traders operating from a non-Member State could use
the CESL for their B2C transactions with consumers from the EU. But as traders from a
non-Member State cannot agree on the CESL of their Member State (because they do not
operate from any Member States), some of the discussed six situations are not possible
in cases where a non-Member State comes into play. For an analysis of the case where
the *consumer* does not habitually reside in the EU see, e.g., H. Eidenmüller *et al.*, 'Der
Vorschlag für eine Verordnung über ein Gemeinsames Europäisches Kaufrecht: Defizite
der neuesten Textstufe des europäischen Vertragsrechts', *JuristenZeitung*, 67 (2012), 269,
274; M. Gebauer, 'Europäisches Vertragsrecht als Option – der Anwendungsbereich,
die Wahl und die Lücken des Optionalen Instruments', *Zeitschrift für das Privatrecht
der Europäischen Union*, 8 (2011), 227, 231. Both analyses do not rule out that the CESL
could be selectable also in such a case. In contrast to this see C. Wendehorst, 'Article 4' in
Schulze (ed.), *Common European Sales Law*, Article 4 CESL Regulation para. 16, where
Wendehorst argues that 'a trader in the EU/EEA cannot sell to consumers outside the
EU/EEA [using the CESL] where none of the addresses indicated by the consumer is in a
Member State'.

[179] For the purpose of this book the term 'trader's home country' and 'trader's home Member
State' shall refer to the Member State from which the trader's business operates.

4) The trader and the consumer agree on the law of the consumer's home Member State and its CESL as the governing sales law.

5) The trader and the consumer agree on the law of the trader's home Member State and its CESL as the governing sales law.

6) The trader and the consumer agree on the CESL as the governing sales law without reference to any Member State's (general) law.

Concluding from what I have just discussed, the Commission would be likely to come to the conclusions shown in Table 3.

The following analysis will explain the true legal consequences, i.e., it will identify the applicable sales law regime for each of these six scenarios.[180] Of particular interest in this respect are two questions. First, in which of these scenarios would the CESL come into play, and second, would a preferential-law test pursuant to Article 6(2) Rome I Regulation be of help for consumers if the level of protection with respect to the concrete claim at issue were better under the traditional sales law of their home Member State?

To better understand some of the following argumentations, I should once again explain that the analysis is based on the wording of the CESL Regulation Proposal, i.e., based on the version proposed by the Commission in 2011. Subsequent to this I will briefly deal with amendments suggested by the Parliament's Legal Affairs Committee (JURI). Let me now turn to the six possible scenarios mentioned above.

---

[180] It should be noted that my analysis does not cover Article 9 Rome I concerns (regarding overriding mandatory national provisions that promote public interests). Suffice to say that the actual relevance of Article 9 in the context of both, B2C transactions in general and the CESL in particular, is generally doubted. Moritz Renner deals with the interplay between Articles 6(2) and 9 Rome I Regulation and explains that the first is generally considered as *lex specialis*. He refers to several other commentators and German judgments of the BGH and concludes that while Article 9 Rome I could arguably apply to B2C transactions, such application would 'only seldom be the case' (M. Renner, 'Art. 9 Rome I' in Calliess (ed.), *Rome Regulations*, Article Rome I para. 5). For additional arguments that Article 9 is (to a limited extent) applicable in B2C cases see D. Kluth, *Die Grenzen des kollisionsrechtlichen Verbraucherschutzes* (Jena: JWV, 2009), pp. 316–19. For a view that Article 9 would in principle not apply in B2C situations see P. Stone, *EU Private International Law* (2nd edn, Cheltenham: Edward Elgar, 2010), p. 354. See also the comment by Micklitz and Reich in Micklitz and Reich, 'The Commission Proposal for a "Regulation on a Common European Sales Law (CESL)"', p. 23, where – with reference to pertinent CJEU case law – they argue that the possible scope and relevance of Article 9 Rome I Regulation for B2C issues is not of a degree which would justify a closer discussion in the context of the CESL. In a similar vein is Matthias Lehmann's analysis of the relevance of Article 9 for B2C contracts in which the consumers habitually reside in the EU (see Lehmann, 'Dogmatische Konstruktion der Einwahl in das EU-Kaufrecht',

Table 3 *Consequences of the contractual choices of the applicable law in cross-border B2C contracts according to the Commission*

Contractual agreement on an applicable law	*Consequence for Rome I application*
None	Article 6(1) Rome I Regulation → traditional sales law of the consumer's home Member State (as the CESL needs an explicit agreement)
Yes, law of the trader's home Member State without reference to its CESL	Traditional sales law of the trader's home Member State (as the CESL needs an explicit agreement), but preferential-law test pursuant to Article 6(2) Rome I Regulation with the mandatory provisions of the traditional sales law of the consumer's home Member State as yardstick for sales law-related questions
Yes, law of the consumer's home Member State without reference to its CESL	Traditional sales law of the consumer's home Member State (as the CESL needs an explicit agreement)
Yes, law of the consumer's home Member State and its CESL	Law of the consumer's home Member State and its CESL as the governing sales law
Yes, law of the trader's home Member State and its CESL	Preferential-law test pursuant to Article 6(2) Rome I Regulation with the mandatory provisions of the CESL of the consumer's home Member State as yardstick for questions falling under its regime
Yes, CESL without reference to either Member State's law	Law of the consumer's home Member State and its CESL as the governing sales law

First scenario: the parties do not agree on any applicable law

In the first scenario, the parties to a cross-border B2C contract that could principally fall under the scope of the CESL do not agree on any law to govern their contractual relationship. Article 6(1) Rome I Regulation explains that in such a case the legal regime of the consumer's home Member State would be applicable. However, the question of which of the two national sales laws (its traditional sales law or its CESL) of the said Member State would be the applicable sales law is not answered by Article 6(1). The answer is instead found in the CESL regime, which clarifies the priority issue between the two national sales law regimes. Pursuant to Article 8(2) CESL Regulation Proposal, the applicability of the CESL requires an explicit agreement between the parties.[181] If the parties – as in the present case – do not agree on the CESL, the traditional sales law of the consumer's home Member State (and not its CESL) would be the applicable sales law.

Second scenario: the parties agree on the law of the trader's home Member State without reference to its CESL

Experience shows that traders usually try to base their cross-border sales contracts on the law of their own country to avoid the applicability of foreign laws.[182] This fact is the starting point in the second scenario (and also in the fifth scenario below). The trader successfully 'convinces' the consumer to agree on the law of the trader's home Member State as the applicable law to their contract. At the same time, the parties do not explicitly agree on the CESL of the trader's home Member State (in this second scenario). As the CESL needs an explicit agreement before it can come into play, but no such agreement exists, the principally applicable sales

---

p. 82). For more comments of Article 9 (inter alia) with respect to consumer protection see F. Maultzsch, 'Rechtswahl und ius cogens im Internationalen Schuldvertragsrecht', *Rabels Zeitschrift für ausländisches und internationales Privatrecht*, 75 (2011), 60, 81–99; P. Hauser, *Eingriffsnormen in der Rom I-Verordnung* (Tübingen: Mohr Siebeck, 2012); C. M. V. Clarkson and J. Hill, *The Conflict of Laws* (4th edn: Oxford University Press, 2011), pp. 241–2; A. Köhler, *Eingriffsnormen – Der 'unfertige Teil' des europäischen IPR* (Tübingen: Mohr Siebeck, 2013).

[181] For more details on the requirements regarding the agreement on the CESL (especially also on the issue of the SIN) see 'The CESL Regulation Proposal in a nutshell' above.

[182] See, for example, the data in Vogenauer and Weatherill, 'The European Community's Competence to Pursue the Harmonisation of Contract Law', p. 121 (Table 3). In a similar vein is D. Staudenmayer, 'Der Kommissionsvorschlag für eine Verordnung zum Gemeinsamen Europäischen Kaufrecht', *Neue Juristische Wochenschrift*, 64 (2011), 3491, 3492.

law would be the traditional sales law of the trader's home Member State. Thus, also in this scenario, the CESL is of no practical relevance.

As the parties agreed on a (from a consumer's point of view) foreign law, the court would have to apply a preferential-law test pursuant to Article 6(2) Rome I Regulation. The yardstick for this test would be the law of the consumer's home Member State and, with respect to sales law issues, its traditional sales law as the primary applicable sales law. If, for example, the protection of the mandatory rules of the consumer's home Member State led to a consumer-friendlier result with respect to the concrete claim at issue, then the law of the consumer's home Member State (including its traditional sales law) would be applicable. The choice made by the parties would, of course, remain valid if the preferential-law test led to the opposite result, i.e., if the case at hand would not be decided in a way that was more beneficial for the consumer.

Third scenario: the parties agree on the law of the consumer's home Member State without reference to its CESL

Determining the applicable law (including the applicable sales law) is relatively easy in this third scenario. The parties choose the law of the consumer's home Member State, i.e., the 'law which, in the absence of choice, would have been applicable on the basis of [Article 6] paragraph 1'.[183] Hence, neither Article 6(1) (to determine a general applicable law regime in the absence of an agreement) nor the preferential-law test of Article 6(2) (to measure a foreign law against the yardstick of the consumer's home Member State's law) are required to determine the applicable general law regime.

The question of whether the traditional sales law or the CESL would be applicable is answered in a similar way as in the previous two scenarios. As the parties did not agree on the CESL, only the traditional sales law can be applicable. In the third scenario one thus arrives at the traditional sales law of the consumer's home Member State as the applicable sales law.

Fourth scenario: the parties agree on the law of the consumer's home Member State and its CESL

While in the first three scenarios the CESL is of no relevance, this fourth scenario is the first of three cases in which the CESL comes into play. In this fourth scenario, the parties agree on the applicability of the law of the consumer's home Member State and, as a second step, make an explicit

---

[183] Article 6(2) Rome I Regulation.

agreement on its CESL in accordance with Article 8 CESL Regulation Proposal.

With respect to the question of which Member State's general law is applicable, the scenario at hand does not differ from the previous scenario. The parties agree on the applicability of the consumer's home Member State – neither Article 6(1) nor the preferential-law test of Article 6(2) is required to determine the applicable general law regime.

With respect to the question of which of the two sales laws of the consumer's home Member State is applicable (its traditional law or its CESL), one has to note that the parties explicitly agree on the consumer's home Member State's CESL. Assuming that the trader also fulfils his obligations under Article 9 CESL Regulation Proposal, i.e., that the consumer is provided with the SIN, the following result occurs. The setting does not allow for a preferential-law test (because the parties did not agree on a law of country that is not the consumer's home Member State). The generally applicable law in the case at hand would thus be the consumer's home Member State law and for sales law issues its CESL.

While (from a consumer perspective) this would be unfortunate if the CESL standard were lower than the standard of the traditional sales law of the consumer's home Member State, this fourth scenario might not be of great practical relevance. Assuming that traders would want to contract with consumers from a considerable number of different Member States, maybe all twenty-seven foreign Member States, traders would (if they always agree on the consumer's home Member State's law) still be exposed to twenty-eight different national regimes (including the regime of their own home Member State for purely domestic cases) for questions not covered by the CESL. To achieve the highest possible level of standardisation, traders would rather push for the general law of their own Member State and its CESL than for the general law of a foreign Member State (including that country's CESL). In the following scenario I will deal with this very likely situation in more detail.

Fifth scenario: the parties agree on the law of the trader's home Member State and its CESL

As already mentioned, traders usually push for the law of the country from which they operate their business to govern their cross-border contracts.[184] Thus, it can be assumed that this fifth scenario would be of greater practical importance than the fourth scenario if traders want the

---

[184] See the references in note 182 above.

CESL to be the applicable sales law in a cross-border B2C transaction. Because in the case at hand the parties agree on the law (including its CESL) of a Member State other than the consumer's home Member State, courts would conduct a preferential-law test pursuant to Article 6(2) Rome I Regulation. The general law of the consumer's home Member State (or to be more precise, its mandatory rules that are of concrete interest in the respective case – for the sake of simplicity I will not explicitly mention this on other occasions where I refer to the preferential-law test) would be the general yardstick for a legal comparison, because the consumer's home Member State law would be the 'law which, in the absence of choice, would have been applicable on the basis of paragraph 1' (Article 6(2) Rome I Regulation). In this respect, there is consensus with the Commission. The crucial point, however, is the determination of the concrete yardstick for sales law issues. In other words, which of the two sales law regimes (again, for the sake of simplicity I will not explicitly refer to their mandatory rules) of the consumer's home Member State, its traditional sales law or its CESL, shall be used as the yardstick?

In the Commission's view, the situation is clear. As shown earlier, the Commission states the obvious when it claims that 'the provisions of the Common European Sales Law of the country's law chosen are identical with the provisions of the Common European Sales Law of the consumer's country'.[185] In Recital 12 CESL Regulation Proposal, the Commission adds that because there are no 'differing levels of consumer protection in the Member States … [Article 6(2) Rome I Regulation] has no practical importance for the issues covered by the Common European Sales Law'. One can conclude that the Commission is of the conviction that the CESL of the consumer's home Member State (and not its traditional sales law) would have to be taken as the yardstick for sales law-related issues in a preferential-law test.

However, Recital 12 CESL Regulation Proposal does not tell us how the Commission arrives at the assumption that the CESL of the consumer's home Member State (and not its traditional sales law, i.e., the first-ranked national sales law) would have to be taken as the yardstick. Two other passages in the CESL Regulation Proposal seem – at first sight – to offer an explanation for the Commission's assumption, but nevertheless fail in the end and for different reasons. One is Recital 10 CESL Regulation Proposal. Recital 10 explains that the CESL is to be chosen at the national level of the Member States, i.e., within their national legal orders, forming

---

[185] CESL Explanatory Memorandum, p. 6.

a part of the Member States' legal regime. It adds that '[t]he agreement to use the Common European Sales Law should therefore not amount to, and not be confused with, a choice of the applicable law within the meaning of the conflict-of-law rules and should be without prejudice to them. This Regulation will therefore not affect any of the existing conflict of law rules'. One has to interpret this explanation as an assertion by the Commission that – despite the fact that conflict of law rules would (principally) still apply – a valid selection of the CESL[186] would survive any likely preferential-law test. The only way to achieve this is to use the CESL (and not the traditional sales law) of the consumer's home Member State as the yardstick (or, alternatively, to exempt the CESL from a likely test[187]). However, as explained in a joint study of the CESL Regulation Proposal by Horst Eidenmüller, Nils Jansen, Eva-Maria Kieninger, Gerhard Wagner and Reinhard Zimmermann, the underlying chain of reasoning of the Commission, paired with the manner in which the CESL Regulation Proposal wants to achieve the result desired by the Commission, is not completely convincing but instead 'inconsistent' (*inkonsequent*).[188] And even if one said that it was convincing, one would have to note that EU law recitals have no binding legal force.[189] While they can be used for interpretative purposes (to clarify the meaning of ambiguous binding provisions), recitals themselves cannot be used as the main basis for legal argumentation. Recital 10 CESL Regulation Proposal itself therefore cannot successfully support the Commission in its argumentation.

With respect to the main body of the CESL Regulation Proposal, Article 11 is the provision that – in its first sentence – gets closest (but not close enough) to providing a possible basis for the Commission's assumption that the CESL of the consumer's home Member State should be taken as the yardstick in a preferential-law test. The relevant part of Article 11

---

[186] On the question of how to make a valid choice on the CESL see the explanations in 'The CESL Regulation Proposal in a nutshell' and 'Fourth assumption: the CESL will be a bilaterally voluntary, secondary regime' above. See further C. Wendehorst, 'Article 11' in Schulze (ed.), *Common European Sales Law*, Article 11 CESL Regulation para. 4.

[187] It should be noted, however, that exempting the CESL from a likely preferential-law test altogether is not the Commission's aim. For details see the text at notes 173 to 175 above.

[188] Eidenmüller *et al.*, 'Der Vorschlag für eine Verordnung über ein Gemeinsames Europäisches Kaufrecht', 273.

[189] Case C-134/08, *Hauptzollamt Bremen* v. *J. E. Tyson Parketthandel GmbH hanse j.* [2009] ECR I-2875, Recital 16 (with further references). For a comment on this fact in the context of the CESL Regulation Proposal see C. Wendelstein, 'Ein gestörtes Zusammenspiel zwischen Europäischem IPR und dem GEK? – Probleme der Vorschaltlösung', *Zeitschrift für das Privatrecht der Europäischen Union*, 10 (2013), 70, 77.

CESL Regulation Proposal reads as follows: 'Where the parties have validly agreed to use the Common European Sales Law for a contract [i.e., in fulfilment of the requirements of Articles 8 and 9 CESL Regulation Proposal], only the Common European Sales Law shall govern the matters addressed in its rules.' Article 11 only clarifies the more or less obvious, namely that matters falling under its scope are only to be governed by the selected CESL and not – where internal gaps exist – further by rules of the traditional sales law of the chosen Member State's legal regime. Wendehorst explains that Article 11 CESL Regulation Proposal must be read in combination with, in particular, Article 4(2) CESL Proposal. Article 4(2) CESL Proposal reads as follows: 'Issues within the scope of the Common European Sales Law but not expressly settled by it are to be settled in accordance with the objectives and principles underlying it and all its provisions, without recourse to the national law that would be applicable in the absence of an agreement to use the CESL.'[190] Article 11 CESL Regulation Proposal confirms this. However, it does not contain a conflict of law rule. Most importantly, it does not address the yardstick issue of Article 6 Rome I Regulation (nor can it be interpreted as doing so). Put differently, Article 11 CESL Regulation Proposal does not deal with the question of which sales law, the CESL or the traditional sales law of the consumer's home Member State, should be used as the yardstick in a preferential-law test should the parties agree on the CESL of a Member State other than the consumer's home Member State.

These observations show that nothing in the CESL Regulation Proposal convincingly explains why the CESL and not the traditional sales law of the consumer's home Member State should be used as the sales law yardstick in a preferential-law test. This conclusion is important and reflects the criticism of many commentators, namely that the solution presented by the CESL Regulation Proposal is unclear and problematic. Matthias Lehmann rightly and succinctly concludes that the second regime model as used by the Commission is 'extraordinarily complicated'.[191] I have already touched upon the debates on the legal nature of the proposed instrument.[192] Some brief reflections should help us to understand my further argumentation. The CESL Regulation Proposal explains that the general conflict of legal rules, i.e., the rules of the Rome I regime should

---

[190] Wendehorst, 'Article 11', Article 11 CESL Regulation para. 2.

[191] Lehmann, 'Dogmatische Konstruktion der Einwahl in das EU-Kaufrecht', p. 86 (translation mine).

[192] See 'The genesis of the proposal on a Common European Sales Law or: the long and winding road' above (in particular note 2).

not be circumvented. At the same time it does not contain any binding or clear conflict of legal rules on how a preferential-law test should be conducted. In other words, as explained earlier in this chapter, it neither contains any clear or binding rule that would replace Article 6(2) Rome I Regulation nor does it clarify which of the two national sales law regimes of the consumer's home Member State should be used as the yardstick in a preferential-law test.

In the absence of a clear regulation regarding the preferential-law test yardstick in the CESL Regulation Proposal, one thus has to look at the Rome I regime to clarify whether the traditional sales law of the consumer's home country or its CESL should be used. The answer to this can be found in the rationale behind the preferential-law test of Article 6(2) Rome I Regulation. The underlying idea behind this test is that it seeks to guarantee that consumers, if they wish to shop cross-border, are not deprived of the protective standard offered by the applicable domestic sales law of their home Member State. Put differently, Article 6 Rome I Regulation secures a certain minimum standard for consumers regardless of where they shop. Calliess accurately defines the underlying idea behind Article 6 as follows:

> Where the national legislator aims at protecting consumers from abuse of freedom of contract which may result from an inequality of bargaining power between the consumers and professionals, and therefore enacts mandatory consumer contract regulations which cannot be derogated from by agreement, *the thus created substantive consumer rights should be protected as well in an international situation*[193] (emphasis added).

Following this argumentation, there is no doubt that (unless the consumer's home Member State introduced the CESL in pursuance of the 'Member State option' of Article 13(a) CESL Regulation Proposal for purely domestic cases as either the only or primary applicable sales law) the sales law yardstick in a concrete preferential-law test would be the *traditional* sales law of the consumer's home Member State.[194]

---

[193] Calliess, 'Art. 6 Rome I', Article 6 Rome I para. 3. Bettina Heiderhoff adds that '[t]he applicability of a foreign law [in cross-border cases] is [basically] ... undesirable, as it could deprive the consumer of his or her rights in certain situations' (Heiderhoff, 'Art 6 Rom I-VO', Article 6 para. 2).

[194] For similar (possible) conclusions (yet based on slightly different considerations) see Rühl, 'The Common European Sales Law', p. 11; Eidenmüller *et al.*, 'Der Vorschlag für eine Verordnung über ein Gemeinsames Europäisches Kaufrecht', 273. In contrast to this see, however, Wendehorst, 'Article 3', Article 3 CESL Regulation para. 11 – where she (without providing convincing arguments to support her view) – claims that such an understanding 'is hardly convincing'.

In addition to the basic idea behind the preferential-law test, one should also recall that the CESL would only be introduced as a secondary national regime and not as a primary applicable sales law for cross-border cases. Nothing in the Rome I Regulation indicates that a secondary national regime would be given preference over a primary national law as the yardstick in an objective preferential-law test.

Another question of practical importance concerns whether the determined sales law yardstick in this fifth scenario, i.e., the traditional sales law of the consumer's home Member State, contains any mandatory rules in the sense of Article 6(2) Rome I Regulation. Put differently, does it contain any 'provisions that cannot be derogated from by agreement'? The answer to this is 'yes'. The traditional sales law of the consumer's home Member State's legal regime undeniably contains mandatory provisions which, taken *individually*, cannot be derogated from. Article 8(3) CESL Regulation Proposal does not change this, as it only allows the replacement of traditional mandatory provisions (within the scope of the CESL) en bloc, and not the separate replacement of individual mandatory provisions. Subjects of a preferential-law test are, however, not the total bodies of mandatory sales law provisions, but only those that are required to 'get an overall view of the level of protection ... in respect of the concrete claim at issue'.[195] Because the individual provisions of the traditional sales law of the consumer's home Member State cannot be replaced individually, they must undeniably be regarded as mandatory (as would the mandatory provisions of the CESL should the CESL eventually apply).[196]

In addition, also from a strategic perspective, it is of utmost importance to comply with the rationale behind Article 6(2) Rome I Regulation.

---

[195] Calliess, 'Art. 6 Rome I', Article 6 Rome I para. 73.

[196] With respect to questions of mandatoriness and the determination of the yardstick for a preferential-law test, Stefan Leible expressly agrees with the Commission's assumption that a preferential-law test could not be of any help to consumers. It is not entirely clear, however, what he exactly means when he (referring to the example of a B2C contract concluded between a French trader and German consumer) argues that 'even if German law were applicable, the CESL could have been chosen' (translation mine) (S. Leible, 'The Proposal for a Common European Sales Law – How Should It Function within the Existing Legal Framework', opinion paper, (2012), p. 3 (on file with the author)). Leible's argument can be interpreted in two ways. First, his argumentation could mean that the CESL should be the yardstick, because the CESL *could* have also been chosen in the case where the parties had selected the consumer's home Member State's law. This understanding is similar to that of Dirk Staudenmayer (see Staudenmayer, 'Der Kommissionsvorschlag für eine Verordnung zum Gemeinsamen Europäischen Kaufrecht', 3491–5). However, this does not prove that the parties really would have chosen it were the consumer's home Member State's law the applicable legal regime. A well-informed trader might, for example, have preferred the traditional law

As the earlier-discussed 2002 Eurobarometer B2C cross-border trade study showed, 68 per cent of consumers feared a lower protective level from foreign laws (compared with the protection of the traditional sales law of their home countries).[197] To motivate consumers to engage more actively in cross-border B2C trade, it is clearly important to guarantee that in cross-border B2C transactions consumers can enjoy at least the same protection as under the traditional sales law of their home Member State. This can (in this fifth scenario) only be guaranteed if one exercises the preferential-law test in compliance with its above-explained rationale. This could have further positive effects. It could provide a satisfying answer to the threats posed by the (in practice very likely) unilateral optionality of the CESL – it would guarantee that consumers could still enjoy (at the very least) the same protective standard offered by the traditional sales law of their home countries, if traders gave them no choice to opt for their home Member State's traditional sales law, but decided autonomously on the applicability of the CESL of their own home Member State. Furthermore, this solution would not pose much risk to traders because the CESL basically follows a relatively high level of protection. Cases in which the traditional sales law offers a higher protective standard undeniably exist (which makes it important to understand the interrelationship between the CESL regime and the Rome I Regulation in this scenario as just outlined), but they might not occur too often. Hence, consumers could eventually benefit without absolutely depriving traders of their wish for greater certainty.

of the consumer's country over its CESL, if the protective standard of that sales law were lower and thus trader friendlier than the protective level of the CESL. Similarly, a well-informed consumer might have agreed on the traditional law of his or her home Member State (and not the CESL) if that standard were higher than the CESL standard. However, the question of what they would have agreed on is not important to determine the objective yardstick for a preferential-law test. I have shown that other considerations, i.e., the rationale behind the test and the fact that the CESL is only a secondary sales law, point instead to the traditional sales law of the consumer's home Member State as the applicable yardstick. Leible could also have referred to the question of whether any of the provisions of the traditional sales law that form the basis for a preferential-law test are mandatory. As I just explained, however, it clearly contains individual 'provisions that cannot be derogated from by agreement'. Hence neither of the two possible understandings of his claim could lead to the conclusion that the CESL of the consumer's home country (and not its traditional sales law) should be the yardstick for sales law related questions.

[197] The European Opinion Research Group EEIG and EOS Gallup Europe, 'Public Opinion in Europe: Views on Business-to-Consumer Cross-border Trade', chapter II.1.1.

Sixth scenario: the parties agree on the CESL without reference
to either Member State's legislative regime

One further scenario is possible. The parties could agree on the CESL, but
forget to agree on the law of a Member State. The question which arises in
this context is whether the Rome I regime, especially Article 6(2) with its
preferential-law test, could be of relevance in this case.

Because the parties did not agree on any generally applicable law,
there is the need to refer to Article 6 Rome I Regulation, not only to
determine the Member State (and thus the legal regime) the agreed
CESL should belong to, but also to determine whose Member State's
legal regime answers those questions not covered by the CESL. Via
Article 6(1) Rome I Regulation, one would arrive at the conclusion that
the general law of the consumer's home Member State is the law that
governs the concrete contractual relationship in this scenario. This
means that the choice of the CESL in this sixth case has to be considered as the selection of the CESL of the consumer's home Member
State. At the same time, the fact that in this scenario the chosen CESL
is to be understood to form a part of the national legal regime of the
consumer's home Member State, and not of the legal regime of a foreign Member State, means that – just like in the fourth scenario – no
preferential-law test can be made. From a consumer perspective, this
might again lead to unwanted side-effects if their home Member State's
traditional sales law were more favourable. However, as shown in the
context of the previous scenario, because the most likely CESL case
would be that where the parties would explicitly agree on the CESL of
the trader's home Member State, the practical relevance of this sixth
scenario might not be that significant.

*Summarising the true consequences of the contractual choice of
the applicable law in cross-border B2C transactions*

My analysis of the actual consequences of various party agreements
on the applicable law has hopefully shown that the assumptions of the
Commission are not necessarily always correct, even if at first sight they
seem logical and convincing. In the most important scenario from a practical point of view, i.e., in the case in which the parties to a B2C contract
agree on the law of the trader's home Member State and its CESL, the
preferential-law test of Article 6(2) Rome I Regulation could still guarantee that consumers would enjoy at least the same protection as under the
traditional sales law of their home Member State.

Table 4 *Comparison of the consequences of the contractual choices of the applicable law in cross-border B2C contracts according to the Commission and in reality*

Contractual agreement on an applicable law	Consequence for Rome I application according to the Commission	Actual consequence for Rome I application
None	Article 6(1) Rome I Regulation (if requirements are fulfilled → traditional sales law of the consumer's home Member State (as the CESL needs an explicit agreement)	Article 6(1) Rome I Regulation (if requirements are fulfilled → traditional sales law of the consumer's home Member State (as the CESL needs an explicit agreement)
Yes, law of the trader's home Member State without reference to its CESL	Traditional sales law of the trader's home Member State (as the CESL needs an explicit agreement), but preferential-law test pursuant to Article 6(2) Rome I Regulation with the mandatory provisions of the traditional sales law of the consumer's home Member State as the yardstick for sales law-related questions	Traditional sales law of the trader's home Member State (as the CESL needs an explicit agreement), but preferential-law test pursuant to Article 6(2) Rome I Regulation with the mandatory provisions of the traditional sales law of the consumer's home Member State as the yardstick for sales law-related questions
Yes, law of the consumer's home Member State without reference to its CESL	Traditional sales law of the consumer's home Member State (as the CESL needs an explicit agreement)	Traditional sales law of the consumer's home Member State (as the CESL needs an explicit agreement)

Table 4 (*cont.*)

Contractual agreement on an applicable law	Consequence for Rome I application according to the Commission	Actual consequence for Rome I application
Yes, law of the consumer's home Member State and its CESL	Law of the consumer's home Member State and its CESL as the governing sales law	Law of the consumer's home Member State and its CESL as the governing sales law
Yes, law of the trader's home Member State and its CESL	Preferential-law test pursuant to Article 6(2) Rome I Regulation with the mandatory provisions of the CESL of the consumer's home Member State as the yardstick for questions falling under its regime; however, with little relevance because the CESL is the same in every Member State	Preferential-law test pursuant to Article 6(2) Rome I Regulation with the mandatory provisions of the traditional sales law of the consumer's home Member State as the yardstick for sales law-related questions
Yes, CESL without reference to any Member State	Law of the consumer's home Member State and its CESL as the governing sales law	Law of the consumer's home Member State and its CESL as the governing sales law

Table 4 summarises the findings of my analysis above and brings them face-to-face with the assumptions of the Commission with respect to the interplay between the CESL Regulation Proposal and the Rome I Regulation. It takes both the imprecise wording of the proposal as well as the rationale behind Article 6(2) Rome I Regulation into consideration.

The Common European Sales Law after the CESL Regulation Proposal

The CESL Regulation Proposal has been the subject of heated discussions in three Parliament committees. The first lot of comprehensive feedback was given by the Economic and Monetary Affairs Committee (ECON). In its opinion submitted to JURI in October 2012,[198] ECON expressed a principally positive view on the proposed CESL Regulation. In line with the Commission's justification for the CESL Regulation Proposal, ECON claimed that '[d]ifferences in contract law constitute an obstacle. ... [W]hatever can be done to eliminate it should be done'.[199] At the same time ECON asked JURI to remedy various issues it believed had not been properly incorporated in the Commission proposal. By stressing the importance that the CESL would have to ensure legal clarity, ECON, inter alia, criticised that certain important issues would still be subject to autonomous regulation by the Member States.[200] It further added that several flanking measures, such as model standard contracts, training and information sessions for legal practitioners and business representatives and explanations on the interplay with the ADR Directive and the ODR Regulation were needed to facilitate the practical use of the CESL.[201] ECON further commented on the interplay with the Rome I regime. Clearly taking a business-sided approach, it expressed concerns that the legal situation was still unresolved and recommended that measures be taken to make 'clear that the application of Article 6(2) of the Rome I Regulation does not have the effect that the consumer rights provided for in the sales law instrument [i.e., the CESL] are after all superseded by stricter national provisions'.[202]

In July 2013 the Internal Market and Consumer Protection Committee (IMCO), after heavy internal discussions,[203] submitted its opinion

---

[198] The text of ECON's opinion and the amendments to the CESL Regulation Proposal suggested by ECON (ECON amendments) can be found in JURI, 'Report on the Proposal for a Regulation on a Common European Sales Law', report, 24 September 2013, pp. 244–6 (opinion) and 246–54 (suggested amendments), available at www.europarl.europa.eu/document/activities/cont/201309/20130925ATT71873/20130925ATT71873EN.pdf.

[199] JURI, 'Report on the Proposal for a Regulation on a Common European Sales Law', p. 244.

[200] *Ibid.*, p. 245 (discussing Recital 27 CESL Regulation Proposal).

[201] See ECON amendments 3, 4 and 10 in *ibid.*, pp. 247–8 and 251.

[202] *Ibid.*, p. 245.

[203] For comments on the debate on the CESL Regulation Proposal within IMCO see C. Busch, 'From European Sales Law to Online Contract Law: The CESL in the European

and amendment suggestions to JURI. The opinion finally presented by IMCO[204] on the CESL Regulation Proposal was very critical.[205] In IMCO's view, the CESL would create more uncertainty than it would solve and would contribute very little (if anything) to adequately protect consumers in cross-border trade. In addition, IMCO also questioned the alleged positive impact on transaction costs and consumer confidence as claimed by the CESL Impact Assessment. In this context, IMCO referred to a joint evaluation with JURI and argued as follows: 'The analysis [i.e., the joint project by IMCO and JURI in response to the CESL Impact Assessment] highlights methodological failings which seriously detract from the meaningfulness of the impact assessment and call into question its value, even taking into account that there is as yet no generally accepted model for calculating transaction costs'.[206] To conclude its negative analysis of the CESL Regulation Proposal, IMCO rejected the plan to introduce an optional sales regime and recommended a return to minimum harmonisation with respect to B2C issues.[207]

JURI, essentially very supportive of the CESL Regulation Proposal,[208] answered the comments made by ECON and IMCO in late September 2013 via its Report on the Proposal for a Regulation on a Common European Sales Law (JURI CESL report). The report is based largely upon a preliminary JURI report from March 2013,[209] additional amendments

---

Parliament', *Zeitschrift für Europäisches Unternehmens- und Verbraucherrecht*, 2 (2013), 33, 35–6.

[204] For a brief explanation of the two preliminary positions that had been discussed within IMCO before the final IMCO opinion was reached see Busch, 'From European Sales Law to Online Contract Law', 36.

[205] For this and the following arguments of IMCO see JURI, 'Report on the Proposal for a Regulation on a Common European Sales Law', pp. 134–6.

[206] JURI, 'Report on the Proposal for a Regulation on a Common European Sales Law', p. 135. For some general, occasionally critical comments on the use of impact assessments in the course of EU law making see, for example, A. C. M. Meuwese, *Impact Assessment in EU Lawmaking* (Alphen aan den Rijn: Kluwer Law International, 2008); P. Andrews, 'Are Market Failure Analysis and Impact Assessment Useful?' in Weatherill (ed.), *Better Regulation*, pp. 49–81; F. Chittenden, T. Ambler and D. Xiao, 'Impact Assessment in the EU' in *ibid.*, pp. 271–86; A. C. M. Meuwese, 'Inter-institutionalising EU Impact Assessment' in *ibid.*, pp. 287–309.

[207] JURI, 'Report on the Proposal for a Regulation on a Common European Sales Law', p. 135, where IMCO argues that '[m]inimum harmonisation of aspects of performance, related services and digital contents' has positive effects for consumers.

[208] See *ibid.*, p. 128, where JURI claims that the CESL Regulation Proposal is 'a groundbreaking initiative of key importance for consumers and businesses in the internal market'.

[209] JURI, 'Draft Report on the Proposal for a Regulation on a Common European Sales Law', draft report, 6 March 2013.

suggested by JURI in May 2013[210] and a comprehensive report on the CESL Regulation Proposal published by the European Law Institute (ELI) in late 2012.[211] The latter included a draft revision of the Commission's proposal (ELI CESL Draft), which clearly influenced the JURI CESL report. Because the JURI CESL report provided the basis for the plenary discussions in the Parliament in early 2014, it is worth looking at some of its key features, especially with respect to some of my earlier comments on the CESL Regulation Proposal.

Several things are very apparent when reading the suggested amendments. In terms of structure, JURI decided to merge the CESL Regulation and its Annex I, the CESL, into a single, fully integrated instrument (for the sake of simplicity I will refer to the text recommended by JURI as the JURI CESL Draft). While this move can be considered a cosmetic correction to improve the readability of the instrument, several other developments might be of greater practical relevance.

One of the most important changes compared with the CESL Regulation Proposal is the reduced scope of its application. Pursuant to Article 1 JURI CESL Draft, the CESL 'can be used for cross-border transactions for the sale of goods, for the supply of digital content and for related services *which are conducted at a distance, in particular online,* where the parties to a contract agree to do so'. Unlike in the CESL Regulation Proposal, cross-border contracts concluded *with* the simultaneous physical presence of the parties would be excluded from the CESL regime.

Several reasons might explain why JURI reduced the scope to just distance contracts. Political considerations are, as Christoph Busch rightly argues, one important factor – it makes obvious sense to reduce its scope and thereby make it more acceptable to its opponents. From a more practical point of view, distance contracts (also in a cross-border setting), especially if concluded online,[212] are a strongly (if not the most strongly)

---

[210] JURI, 'Amendments 206–531', draft report, 3 May 2013.

[211] European Law Institute, 'Statement of the European Law Institute on the Proposal for a Regulation on a Common European Sales Law, COM(2011) 635 final', statement, (2012), available at www.europeanlawinstitute.eu/fileadmin/user_upload/p_eli/Publications/S-2-2012_Statement_on_the_Proposal_for_a_Regulation_on__a_Common_European_Sales_Law.pdf.

[212] Three studies presented to the public in the months before the publication of the JURI CESL Draft confirmed the increase in online B2C transaction contracts. The Commission's 9th Consumer Conditions Scoreboard (9th Consumer Conditions Scoreboard) as well as the 2013 Eurobarometer studies on consumer attitudes towards cross-border trade and consumer protection (2013 Eurobarometer Cross-border Protection Study) and on the European Small Claims Procedure (2013 Eurobarometer ESCP Study) all confirmed an overall increase over the years. Although the exact figures in the reports slightly differ,

growing B2C market.[213] (Also with respect to B2B transactions distance contracts play an important role.) Distance contracts thus are undeniably the most important cross-border transaction contracts for the Union legislator to regulate.

To enhance the use and usability of the CESL regime, JURI (like ECON) proposed the introduction of several flanking measures. In line with ECON, JURI stressed the need for model contract terms. These model contract terms – JURI called them 'European model contract terms'[214] – should be crafted by an expert group comprising Commission-appointed 'members representing, in particular, the interests of users'[215] of the CESL. However, it remains to be seen how the Commission would select the members in practice. The earlier-discussed compositions of the CESL Expert Group and the CESL Key Stakeholders Group cast some doubt on whether such an expert group would represent affected interests in a well-balanced way. The JURI CESL Draft further touches upon ADR and tries to promote its use in B2C contracts. It is questionable though whether the mere insertion of a provision that states that '[i]n contracts between a consumer and a trader, parties are encouraged to consider submitting disputes arising from a contract for which they have agreed to use the Common European Sales Law to an ADR entity'[216] would really lead

all three reports come to the conclusion that the online market is steadily growing. (See TNS Political & Social, 'Consumer Attitudes towards Cross-border Trade and Consumer Protection', Flash Eurobarometer 358, (2013), p. 9, available at ec.europa.eu/public_opinion/flash/fl_358_en.pdf; European Commission, 'The Consumer Conditions Scoreboard: Consumers at Home in the Single Market – 9th edition', report, (2013), p. 16, Figure 11; TNS Opinion & Social, 'European Small Claims Procedure', p. 10 for related data). All three reports also showed that there was still ample room for growth left – in particular for cross-border online B2C transactions, as only slightly more than 10 per cent of consumers had purchased from traders operating from a different Member State within the last twelve months covered by each of the three studies: 15 per cent according to the 2013 Eurobarometer Cross-border Protection Study (see TNS Political & Social, 'Consumer Attitudes towards Cross-border Trade and Consumer Protection', p. 16); and 11 per cent according to the 9th Consumer Conditions Scoreboard and the 2013 Eurobarometer ESCP Study (see European Commission, 'The Consumer Conditions Scoreboard: Consumer at Home in the Single Market – 9th edition', p. 16, Figure 11; TNS Opinion & Social, 'European Small Claims Procedure', p. 10).

[213] E. Gomez-Herrera, B. Martens and G. Turlea, 'The Drivers and Impediments for Cross-border e-Commerce in the EU', Joint Research Centre, Institute for Prospective Technological Studies, Digital Economy Working Paper, 2013/02 (2013), p. 15, available at www.alde.es/encuentros/anteriores/xvieea/trabajos/g/pdf/146.pdf.

[214] Article 186c JURI CESL.   [215] Ibid.

[216] Article 186b JURI CESL Draft. Unlike JURI, ECON further asked for the introduction of Commission-organised ADR stakeholder workshops (see ECON amendment 4 in JURI, 'Report on the Proposal for a Regulation on a Common European Sales Law', p. 248).

to an increase in the use of ADR. In addition to these two measures, JURI further recommended the introduction of a centralised, special CESL judgment database, which should facilitate the development of a common understanding of the CESL by courts in the Member States and increase the transparency of CESL-related judgments.[217]

However, the majority of amendments suggested by the JURI CESL Draft relate to Annex I CESL Regulation Proposal, i.e., the CESL itself. In most cases, the focus was put on its improvement, simplification, clarification or reconciliation with existing EU legislation. It must also be noted though that some amendments would actually worsen the situation for consumers compared with both the CESL Regulation Proposal and the existing legislation of several Member States.[218] Furthermore, when taking a more comprehensive look at the JURI CESL Draft, one must say that in principle the amendments are not able to substantially remedy most of the underlying issues, as outlined in my earlier analysis of the CESL Regulation Draft.

One matter that was (arguably) substantively changed though and thus deserves a slightly closer look is the question of the interrelationship between CESL and the Rome I regime, as the JURI CESL Draft seems to remedy the aforementioned (from the Commission's perspective) shortcomings of the CESL Regulation Draft in this case. In my analysis of the interplay between the CESL Regulation Draft and Article 6 Rome I Regulation, I explained that the wording of the former is not suitable

---

[217] Article 186a JURI CESL Draft.

[218] See, for example, the reduction of the long prescription period of ten years under Article 179(2) CESL Proposal to six years pursuant to Article 179(2) JURI CESL Draft. Another worsening of consumers' rights under the CESL can be seen in Article 119 JURI CESL Draft on the loss of the buyer's right to terminate a contract. In order not to lose the right to terminate the consumer would have to notify the trader about the non-conformity within two months from when the right arose or the consumer became aware of the non-performance. The CESL Proposal does not include a comparable provision. In both cases several traditional sales laws would be more beneficial for the consumer. For an example where the JURI CESL Draft would lead to an improvement (compared with the CESL Proposal) see Article 84(c)(a) JURI CESL Draft, which relates to reversing the statutory burden of proof to the consumer's detriment. Several Member States declare contract terms that aims to reverse the statutory burden of proof to the consumer's detriment as absolutely prohibited (as § 6(1)(11) KSchG and § 309(12) BGB show for the cases of Austria and Germany). The CESL Proposal catalogues such a term only in the grey list of its Article 85 (Article 85(a)) and not in the black list of Article 84 CESL Proposal. Under the CESL regime (as proposed by the Commission) a contract term reversing the statutory burden of proof to the consumer's detriment would thus only be *presumed* to be unfair. The JURI CESL Proposal, on the other hand, puts – in line with the national examples given above – such a clause in the black list of Article 84 (Article 84(c)(a) JURI CEL Draft).

to support the view of the Commission that if the parties to a B2C cross-border contract choose the law of a Member State (including its CESL) other than the consumer's home Member State, the preferential-law test according to Article 6(2) Rome I Regulation would use the CESL of the consumer's home Member State as the yardstick for sales law matters covered by the CESL regime. I arrived at the conclusion that – in the absence of clear (contrary) rules in either the Rome I Regulation or the CESL Regulation – the (mandatory provisions of the) traditional sales law of the consumer's home Member State would have to be taken as the yardstick for sales law-related questions in such a test.[219]

JURI, very likely having been aware of the imprecise solution taken by the CESL Regulation Draft with respect to conflict of law issues, decided to revise some critical provisions that had also been criticised by ELI in its aforementioned statement on the CESL Regulation Draft.[220] In the end JURI did not entirely follow the recommendations suggested by ELI, but instead, in principle, autonomously redrafted Recital 10 and Article 11 CESL Regulation Draft. Both new passages, Recital 10 and Article 11, try to clarify the character of the CESL as a secondary national regime and its interplay with the Rome I Regulation in more detail. Article 11(1) JURI CESL Draft especially deserves closer attention. It reads as follows:

> Where the parties have validly agreed to use the Common European Sales Law for a contract, only the Common European Sales Law shall govern the matters addressed in its rules, instead of the contract-law regime that would, in the absence of such an agreement, govern the contract within the legal order determined as the applicable law.

The chosen wording is quite interesting, as – should it be used in the form of a binding provision, i.e., embedded in an article of a possible CESL – it might clarify the situation in relation to the preferential-law test of Article 6 Rome I Regulation. Article 11(1) JURI CESL Draft does not explicitly say that the CESL of the consumer's home Member State would have to be applied as the yardstick in a preferential-law test. However, it makes it clear that – if the parties validly agree on the CESL (pursuant to Articles 8 and 9 CESL Regulation Proposal/JURI CESL Draft) – the CESL would ultimately and without exception supersede the traditional sales law of any Member State (including the consumer's home Member State). The

---

[219] See 'Fifth scenario: the parties agree on the law of the trader's home Member State and its CESL' above.

[220] See, in particular, Article 3 ELI CESL Draft (European Law Institute, 'Statement of the European Law Institute', p. 47).

newly-added phrase 'instead of the contract-law regime that would, in the absence of such an agreement, govern the contract within the legal order determined as the applicable law' explains this. It obviously refers to the primary national sales law, i.e., to the traditional sales law within the determined applicable Member State's legal regime. Article 11(1) JURI CESL Draft makes it clear that a preferential-law test pursuant to Article 6(2) Rome I Regulation could not result in the traditional sales law of the consumer's home Member State being the applicable sales law regime. This can only be achieved if the CESL of the consumer's home Member State (and not its traditional sales law) would, for matters covered by the CESL, be applied as the yardstick.[221] One can also say that as soon as the parties validly agree on the CESL, such a choice would (as an interesting consequence) turn this second regime into a first regime, which would then be used as the yardstick in a preferential-law test. Eventually this wording, if chosen, would (in the likely case that traders would successfully push for their country's law including its CESL) lead to a different conclusion than the adoption of the respective wording of the CESL Regulation Proposal (as analysed earlier in this book).[222]

It is beyond the scope of this book to answer the question of whether the solution suggested by the JURI CESL Draft is the most sophisticated way to support the Commission's wish to prevent the consumer's home Member State's traditional law being used as the yardstick in a preferential-law test. However, it must be acknowledged that Article 11(1) JURI CESL Draft would remedy the (as explained)[223]– from the Commission's perspective –insufficiently designed and unfortunate solution used in the CESL Regulation Proposal. This does not mean though that from a consumer point of view, the JURI CESL Draft solution would be appreciated. Instead the opposite is true; it would put consumers in a worse position than the CESL Regulation Proposal would in the likely fifth scenario described above, i.e. where parties agree on the law of the trader's home Member State including its CESL.

---

[221] An alternative solution (that arrives at the same result) would be to rule that the CESL does not form part of a preferential-law test. But as Recital 12 JURI CESL Draft explains, this is not what is intended. Instead, JURI (like the Commission) favours a preferential-law test that includes the CESL. (Recital 12 JURI CESL Draft notes that Article 6(2) Rome I would have 'no practical relevance to the issues covered by the Common European Sales Law, *as it would amount to a comparison between the mandatory provisions of two identical second contract-law regimes*' (emphasis added)).

[222] See 'Fifth scenario: the parties agree on the law of the trader's home Member State and its CESL' above.

[223] See *ibid.*

In February 2014 the (thus far) latest contribution to the CESL debate at the Parliament level was made. In a first plenary vote, the JURI CESL Draft received majority support in the Parliament.[224] However, at the time of writing this book, it is still too early to draw any concrete conclusions. Hans-Peter Mayer, then MEP and CESL rapporteur for IMCO, and Julia Lindemann explain that it is expected that the Council will not discuss the CESL before the second half of 2015.[225] It remains to be seen in which direction the CESL will eventually head.

---

[224] European Commission, 'Optional European Sales Law Receives Strong Backing by the European Parliament', press release, MEMO/14/137, 26 February 2014, available at europa.eu/rapid/press-release_MEMO-14-137_en.htm.

[225] H.-P. Mayer and J. Lindemann, 'Zu den aktuellen Entwicklungen um das Gemeinsame Europäische Kaufrecht auf EU-Ebene', *Zeitschrift für Europäisches Privatrecht*, 22 (2014), 1, 6.

11

Summarising comments on the defragmentation of substantive consumer laws in the context of the CRD and the CESL

In this part of the book, I have discussed several issues related to value-oriented consumer justice in the context of substantive consumer laws. I will come back to the general implications of the underlying explanations in more detail in Part IV. However, there are several points to note at this stage.

Extensive research by various study and working groups on substantive consumer laws in the EU, conducted especially in the context of the revision of the consumer acquis and the drafting of the CESL, has revealed a relatively uneven picture in the Member States.[1] The fragmentation of national approaches is deeply rooted in the different legal traditions of the Member States and their national approaches towards consumer law-related issues. The more traditional minimum harmonisation approach tried to accommodate national legislative interests, as it aimed to contribute to the growth of the internal market by reaching a certain standardisation of substantive law issues without cutting the Member States' means to introduce or maintain rules that would go beyond the EU standards.

In the course of time, EU policy makers have changed their views on how to properly address internal market needs and have gradually shifted towards more comprehensive and fully harmonised consumer law making. These attempts rested on the assumption that minimum harmonisation would not be able to positively affect the market and that the fragmentation of national substantive laws had a negative impact on market stabilisation and growth. The Commission's efforts (basically supported by the Parliament) were in practice facilitated by the aforementioned initiatives that, via a comparative analysis, researched several differences between the private law regimes of the Member States. One

---

[1] See in particular Schulte-Nölke *et al.* (eds.), *EC Consumer Law Compendium* (for the consumer acquis) and von Bar and Clive (eds.), *Principles, Definitions and Model Rules of European Private Law. Draft Common Frame of Reference (DCFR). Full Edition* (for issues covered by the CESL).

relatively comprehensive result was the Commission's CRD Proposal, which, via maximum harmonisation, tried to standardise issues previously regulated via minimum harmonisation directives and some other matters formerly unregulated at the EU level. The adopted version of the CRD, however, differed to a considerable extent from the original, fully harmonised and relatively comprehensive proposal. The defragmentation plans of the Parliament and the Commission seemed to have come to a standstill, mainly because of strong opposition from the Member States' national policy makers via the Council. The trial of strength did not lead to a clear winner. Neither primarily trader-heavy proponents of maximum harmonisation nor their opponents emerged victorious.

The Commission did not give up. The Commission's CESL Regulation Proposal continued where the Union legislator left off in the case of the CRD. It proposed another instrument that, although this time being (in theory)[2] of an optional nature, aims at a stronger defragmentation of consumer law-related issues. However, this attempt has not found unconditional approval either. Stakeholder groups expressed various concerns. Although the JURI CESL Draft tried to answer some issues, many remained and others emerged.[3] Nevertheless, in early 2014 the Parliament – in a first plenary vote – expressed its positive view on the plan to introduce the CESL. It remains to be seen, however, whether the policy makers will be able to succeed with their defragmentation plans this time.

In any event, the Commission and the Parliament still have to furnish proof that their attempts would be truly beneficial for consumer access to justice 2.0. Unless there is clear evidence that plans that consist of a mix of maximum harmonisation, defragmentation and comprehensive and broad regulation of contract and consumer law-related issues would truly enhance consumer confidence and satisfaction, one cannot say that such efforts would benefit internal market growth.[4] One might instead have to look for more appropriate alternatives. I will endeavour to identify some in Part IV.

---

[2] On this issue see Chapter 10, 'Fourth assumption: the CESL will be a bilaterally voluntary, secondary regime' above.

[3] For examples see the explanations in 'The Common European Sales Law after the CESL Regulation Proposal' in Chapter 10 above.

[4] For a similar argument against maximum harmonisation (linked to the issue of consumer confidence) see, e.g., Howells and Schulze, 'Overview of the Proposed Consumer Rights Directive', p. 8.

PART IV

Consumer access to justice 2.0 – a multidimensional framework

The association between the idea of social justice and the welfare state during the twentieth century has also tended to concentrate our ideas about social justice on issues concerning material wealth and the benefits that money can obtain. Yet social justice can be understood as a broader concept than the distribution of wealth.[1]

(Hugh Collins, 1953–)

---

[1] H. Collins, 'Does Social Justice Require the Preservation of Diversity in the Private Laws of Member States of Europe?' in T. Wilhelmsson, *et al.* (eds.), *Private Law and the Many Cultures of Europe* (Alphen aan den Rijn: Kluwer Law International, 2007), p. 161.

12

From the current state of consumer law to consumer access to justice 2.0

Recapitulating the rationale behind the Commission's efforts to regulate cross-border B2C trade

As was shown in Parts II and III of this book, over the years the EU has gradually intensified its efforts to regulate consumer law issues. By doing so, it has changed the landscape and influenced consumer protection both at the pan-EU and Member State levels. Although this has undeniably led to positive effects for consumers in some instances, this is not necessarily true in every case.[1] From the perspective of EU consumer law making, consumer protection is in principle only a means to an end. The third paragraph of the most commonly used competence article for consumer law making, Article 114 TFEU (formerly Article 95 Treaty establishing the European Community), demands that consumer laws must follow 'a high level of protection'. At the same time, Article 114(3) also refers to the first paragraph of the same article. Article 114(1) reads as follows: 'The European Parliament and the Council shall ... adopt the measures for the approximation of the provisions laid down by law, regulation or administrative action in Member States *which have as their object the establishment and functioning of the internal market*'[2] (emphasis added). Thus, the ultimate goal of EU consumer law making is the enhancement of the internal market and not necessarily the guarantee of the highest possible level of consumer protection in the Member States. One could also say that the demanded level of protection is defined as a standard that – despite its, on average, high level of consumer protection – enhances access for traders in any foreign market within the EU. From a trader perspective, more stringent rules at a national level might be counterproductive.

---

[1] For further details, see the analysis in Parts II and III above and the summary in the following chapters.

[2] See also Article 26 TFEU, to which Article 114(1) TFEU refers. Its first paragraph reads as follows: 'The Union shall adopt measures with the aim of establishing or ensuring the functioning of the internal market.'

This view is shared by several scholars who scrutinise the consequences of EU consumer laws for consumers, not only in a cross-border context but also from the perspective of protection via purely national laws. In her analysis of (inter alia, consumer) contract law developments, Lurger comments that the contract law-related actions taken at the EU level 'nurture the suspicion that the EC is seeking to intensify its market-functional approach'.[3] With respect to consumer law in general, Weatherill further adds that a 'very wide range of fields subject to pre-existing national regulation have been swept up in the net of harmonisation ... Consumer protection [for example] ... [has] become the subject of EC intervention largely in the name of the thrust to harmonise. In this way Community laws come into existence in order to integrate the market'[4] – and Micklitz asks: '[W]ho shall be protected, the market citizen and/or the weaker party?'[5] The Commission itself is, of course, of the firm belief that the related

[3] Lurger, 'The Common Frame of Reference', p. 187. See further *ibid.*, p. 197, where she concludes that with regard to the CESL elaborations 'the Commission seems to be reinforcing its focus on market-functionalism, market freedoms and freedom of contract as the predominant principles of contract law'. A similar wording is used by Reich. He explains that EU private law (especially contract law) primarily aims to 'ensur[e] an instrumental function under Internal Market aspects' (N. Reich, 'The Social, Political and Cultural Dimension of EU Private Law' in Schulze and Schulte-Nölke (eds.), *European Private Law*, p. 88).

[4] S. Weatherill, 'Harmonisation: How Much, How Little?', *European Business Law Review* 16 (2005), 533, 534. One of the most recent examples for this is given by the possible introduction of the CESL (which I extensively discussed in Part III above). In this context (and from the perspective of the business side) see, for example, Busch, 'From European Sales Law to Online Contract Law', 36, where Busch argues that 'a level playing field for businesses operating on the European consumer retail market' was needed that would offer an answer 'to the problem of "law mix" caused by the application of the law most favourable to the consumer under Article 6(2) Rome I Regulation'.

[5] H.-W. Micklitz, 'The Relationship between National and European Consumer Policy – Challenges and Perspectives' in Twigg-Flesner *et al.* (eds.), *The Yearbook of Consumer Law 2008*, p. 65. In a similar vein is Verena Lerm's conclusion in her analysis of Article 114 TFEU and the policy shift towards greater maximum harmonisation. She claims as follows: 'To achieve maximum harmonisation [the policy makers] approve of the fact that consumer protection is at the best reduced to a secondary policy target' (translation mine); see V. Lerm, 'Die Verbraucherrechte-Richtlinie im Widerspruch zur Kompetenzordnung des europäischen Primärrechts', *Zeitschrift für das Privatrecht der Europäischen Union*, 9 (2012), 166, 171. See, in addition, Alpa's observations on the future of EU consumer law. He asks for 'a [EU] consumer law that is not only inclined on the composition of economic interests among the parties in conflict, but ... above all ... founded on the protection of individual rights that, in the scale of values, can neither be deferred nor treated as equivalent to rights of an economic nature' (G. Alpa, *Competition of Legal Systems and Harmonization of European Private Law: New Paths in a Comparative Perspective* (Munich: Sellier, 2013), pp. 95–6).

legislative actions it has realised or initiated with the aim of strengthening the internal market are in the absolute best interest of consumers.[6]

In the following chapters I will summarise some of the key features of the Commission's efforts to strengthen the internal market by means of consumer legislation, which I discussed in more detail in Parts II and III of this book. This will enable the discussion to move to a more consumer interest-oriented level, to (consumer) access to justice 2.0 as outlined in Part I.

Recapitulating the situation with respect to procedural EU (consumer) laws

Unlike substantive laws, procedural laws do not directly define legal standards, rights and obligations, and can only indirectly benefit consumers by enhancing consumer rights enforcement. Nevertheless, procedural laws are (like substantive laws) of importance for consumers, as they aim to ensure business compliance with substantive rules (compliance effect) and to remedy situations that contradict substantive laws when traders cannot or do not want to comply with legal standards (compensatory effect). Both effects represent the enforcement character of procedural laws. (For the sake of simplicity I will refer to the mechanisms introduced by the laws outlined in Part II of this book as enforcement tools.)

As mentioned earlier,[7] procedural laws can, in principle, only be as good as substantive laws allow them to be. The success of procedural laws further depends on five very practically important *intrinsic* factors, which I label as awareness, skills/experience, availability, usability and effectiveness.

Awareness, first and foremost, refers to the awareness of enforcement tools of those who actually should use the mechanisms – in the present context, consumers. Awareness, however, also refers to other stakeholders involved. In the earlier example of the ESCP, I explained that both consumers *and* other important stakeholders can lack proper awareness with respect to enforcement tools.[8]

---

[6] Both procedural and substantive EU consumer laws directly refer to the ultimate goal of strengthening the internal market (for some explicit references see Article 1(1) Injunctions Directive; Recital 7 Small Claims Regulation; Article 1 CRD).

[7] See 'Access to Justice 2.0' in Chapter 2 above.

[8] See, for example, the results of the 2012 ECC-Net ESCP Study, which showed nearly every second judge who participated in the underlying study had not been aware of the existence of the ESCP – four years after the procedure had been implemented (see 2012 ECC-Net ESCP Study, p. 17).

Second, skills/experience is closely interlinked with awareness and refers to the actual, necessary ability of consumers and (where mandated to do so) third-party stakeholders (e.g., judges, attorneys, public authorities or consumer organizations) to properly engage in the respective enforcement tool.

Third, availability refers to the actual availability of a mechanism for a concrete dispute. Put differently, the question in this context is related to whether the device is available for the 'right' cases.

Fourth, usability is to be understood as relating to the involved costs or the steps that have to be taken to launch an action and to complete proceedings, or more generally speaking, to the question of *how* a mechanism works and is to be used.

Fifth and finally, compliance with the outcome of dispute resolution is also clearly important. One could refer to this factor as the effectiveness of enforcement tools. Even the most consumer-friendly decision would not satisfy consumer needs if the trader did not comply with it or if enforcement proved difficult.

Unfortunately, though, none of the enforcement tools introduced thus far at the EU level fully satisfies all five factors. I have already identified and discussed in Part II of this book the major shortcomings of some pertinent mechanisms. Table 5, in a much simplified and non-exhaustive way, summarises some of the most striking issues in this respect, dividing them into two categories. The first group refers to the issues of availability, usability and effectiveness, thus to those factors that are more 'technical' in the sense that they primarily depend on how well the respective mechanism is crafted. The second group includes issues I call awareness and skills/experience – factors that can also be improved by legislative means but are not predominantly of a technical nature.

From this table, one can conclude that some issues, especially those regarding awareness and skills/experience, run through different enforcement tools like a golden thread, as they can be found with respect to most or even all of the tools. It is also worthwhile to note that the alarmingly low level of consumer awareness is paired with a vast variation in promotional activities by private bodies and public authorities. This is well illustrated by the example of promotion activities in the context of the ESCP. The 2010 Civil Justice Eurobarometer Survey showed that on average, only 8 per cent of European consumers had heard of the ESCP. Although there has been an increase over the years, consumers' ESCP awareness is still considerably low. As the 2013 Eurobarometer ESCP Study showed, by the end of 2012 awareness had only increased slightly to an average of

Table 5 *Selected prominent flaws of the tools discussed in Part II of this book*[a]

Law/device	Availability, usability and effectiveness	Awareness and skills/ experience
Injunctions Directive	➤ Limited number of cross-border injunctions due to high costs, complexity of injunction proceedings ➤ In some cases: limited impact of cessation orders ➤ Insufficient cooperation between countries – relationship could be improved with Consumer Protection Cooperation Regulation	➤ Lack of financial resources and expertise of several qualified entities
Small Claims Regulation	➤ Insufficient support at the EU level because of the passive approach taken by the Small Claims Regulation (e.g., no provision in the Small Claims Regulation to guarantee the availability of practical information on how to enforce a judgment in a trader's Member State) ➤ Insufficient rules on speeding up proceedings ➤ Insufficient rules on language and costs ➤ Communication means not user friendly	➤ Very low consumer awareness ➤ Low awareness among the judiciary ➤ Relatively little promotion by national public authorities ➤ Insufficient support from courts

Table 5 (*cont.*)

Law/device	Availability, usability and effectiveness	Awareness and skills/ experience
Consumer Protection Cooperation Regulation	➤ Insufficient practical guidelines for the CPC System ➤ Application procedures for funding are confusing and burdensome ➤ Material scope of application could be revised	➤ Insufficient awareness of some competent authorities paired with the need to enhance the training of officials ➤ Uneven application in Member States (very active v. very passive) ➤ Low number of personnel
Legal Aid Directive	➤ Implementation deficits with regard to legal aid for extrajudicial proceedings and the enforcement stage of judgments ➤ Vague language and narrow definitions of the Legal Aid Directive and lack of support at the EU level complicates national implementation ➤ No rules for enjoying 'effective' assistance from a lawyer (language and expertise issues) ➤ Lacunae in the catalogue of covered costs	➤ Low awareness among consumers and lawyers
ADR Directive/ ODR Regulation	➤ Consumers cannot freely choose between litigation and ADR – consumers cannot seek recourse in ADR without trader consent ➤ ODR Regulation can only apply in cases related to *online* sales or service contracts	➤ ODR tools not yet well tested in the EU – lack of expertise

Table 5 (*cont.*)

Law/device	Availability, usability and effectiveness	Awareness and skills/experience
Compensatory Collective Redress	(Too early for definite statements but one can conclude the following from current discussions:) ➤ Risk of lumping scattered damages together with mass damages ➤ Questions of standing – who should principally be allowed to sue? ➤ Opt in v. opt out – or something innovative? ➤ Limited financial resources need to be overcome ➤ Questionable interplay with Brussels I (standing of public authorities and private bodies as collective claimant is not entirely clear)	(Too early for definite statements. One can conclude the following from current discussions:) ➤ Non-existence of compensatory collective redress in several Member States might complicate cross-border proceedings (lack of infrastructure and expertise) ➤ Diverse approaches taken by those Member States that already use compensatory collective redress might complicate smooth cross-border functioning

[a] For details see the explanations in the respective chapters in Part II above.

12 per cent.[9] With respect to awareness-raising activities, the 2012 ECC-Net ESCP Study explained that while 94 per cent of all ECCs had promoted the ESCP in the first four years of its applicability,[10] only 29 per cent of national public authorities had done the same.[11] One factor that might explain this gap is surely the fact that the ESCP is a prime example of a cross-border enforcement tool and is therefore closely related to

[9] TNS Opinion & Social, 'European Small Claims Procedure', p. 68.
[10] ECC-Net, 'European Small Claims Procedure Report', p. 31.
[11] *Ibid.*

matters on which most ECCs advise on a daily basis. In contrast, not all potentially involved public authorities would class the ESCP as falling under their commonly addressed issues. Regardless of the true reasons for this huge percentile difference, one should note that the results of the 2012 ECC-Net ESCP Study show that ECCs are very active in providing consumers with information regarding their rights in cross-border B2C transactions and the means to have them enforced. I will come back to this issue later.[12]

In addition to common deficiencies, Table 5 also highlights some sectoral problems. Most of the related issues are primarily of a technical nature in the sense that they would best be addressed by revising the legal parameters of the underlying respective procedural law.[13] Following the observations summarised in Table 5 one can confirm that the enforcement tools introduced by EU laws have in general not yet tapped their full potential. Corrective steps need to be taken to improve consumer confidence in cross-border rights enforcement.

Recapitulating the situation with respect to substantive EU (consumer) laws

As shown in Part III of this book, substantive EU consumer law drafting has been subject to three key developments. First, the Commission has been trying to widen the scope of regulating consumer law-related issues. Second, the Commission has been putting efforts into overcoming older, sector-specific approaches towards substantive issues by drafting and proposing more comprehensive legislation. Third, the Commission has generally shifted its attention from minimum harmonisation towards greater maximum harmonisation.[14] I will briefly comment on these developments now and more detailed explanations will follow later.[15]

The first and third trends, in particular, are not unproblematic from a consumer viewpoint, as shown, for example, by a recent analysis by Isidora Maletić regarding the interplay between Article 114 TFEU, its harmonisation

---

[12] See 'The facilitating intermediaries approach' in Chapter 15 below.

[13] The ESCP is, again, a good example. The Commission decided to remedy some of its technical issues. This move led to the 2013 Small Claims Regulation Proposal, which, although not answering all of the identified concerns, addresses some key obstacles such as the unfortunate choice of communication means and the length of proceedings. For details see 'The Small Claims Regulation (2007)' in Chapter 4 above.

[14] For details on these developments see Part III above.

[15] See further 'The substantive law pillar' in Chapter 15 below.

level with respect to consumer issues and the impact of EU legislation on national consumer protection standards. Maletić points out that Article 114(3) TFEU asks the Commission to base its consumer law proposals on a 'high level of protection', but, at the same time, Member States (unless the Union legislator adopts the respective law as a minimum harmonised law) are not allowed to 'derogate from a harmonisation norm'[16] in the field of consumer law. With this she addresses the potential risk inherent to maximum harmonisation, especially regarding the protective regimes of Member States that were already beyond the standard introduced by fully harmonised consumer laws or those that would like to go beyond it. Broadening the material scope of related (EU) legislation further magnifies this risk. I have already addressed this issue and its consequences in Part III when I discussed the gradual shift from minimum harmonisation to increased maximum harmonisation in EU consumer policy-making.

Maletić comes to the conclusion that the developments in EU consumer law policy-making pose a threat to national consumer policies and that 'Member States with a very highly developed system of consumer protection may have a particular interest in ensuring that the Commission fulfils its obligation under paragraph 3 [i.e., Article 114(3) TFEU]'.[17] In the latter statement she obviously refers to the tensions between attempts by the EU to do whatever possible to enhance the internal market and the interest of national legislators to respond to the needs and interests of consumers who habitually reside in their territories. I will also come back to this issue later.

One consequence of the older minimum harmonisation approach, arguably the key argument used by the Commission in its attempts to push for maximum harmonisation, is that several Member States decided to introduce or maintain national legislation that is more consumer-friendly

---

[16] I. Maletić, *The Law and Policy of Harmonisation in Europe's Internal Market* (Cheltenham: Edward Elgar, 2013), p. 59. For further comments on (in this respect relevant) Article 114(4) TFEU in the context of consumer law-related issues see W. Kahl, 'AEUV Art. 114' in C. Calliess and M. Ruffert (eds.), *EUV/AEUV* (4th edn, Munich: C. H. Beck, 2011), Art. 114 AUEV para. 58; H.-H. Herrnfeld, 'Artikel 114 AEUV' in J. Schwarze (ed.), *EU-Kommentar* (3rd edn, Baden-Baden: Nomos, 2012), Artikel 114 para. 96; S. Leible and M. Schröder, 'Art. 114 AUEV' in R. Streinz (ed.), *EUV/AEUV* (2nd edn, Munich: C. H. Beck, 2012), para. 90.

[17] Maletić, *The Law and Policy of Harmonisation in Europe's Internal Market*, p. 59. I have already discussed above the tension of interests between EU policies to enhance the internal market supported by the Commission and the Parliament and securing the Member States' discretion to reply to domestic consumer protection needs in the context of the CRD.

than EU legislation. One can also say that in various instances minimum harmonisation has created a two-tier regime with an absolute minimum standard introduced at the EU level and domestic adjustments to implement national consumer policies that exceed the EU-prescribed standard. Maximum harmonisation tries to answer this by installing a relatively inflexible regime that would centralise the regulation of core consumer law matters at the EU level. It is doubtful whether the recently increased efforts of the Commission to fully harmonise substantive laws to the greatest extent possible would be truly beneficial for consumers, especially in light of the fact that more consumer-friendly national standards cannot be retained. The unbalanced representation of business and consumer interests in the drafting and negotiation process of EU consumer laws[18] further intensifies the difficulties in securing a level of consumer protection that could meet the standards of all twenty-eight national regimes. In combination with maximum harmonisation, the stronger representation of business interests at the EU level paired with a broadening of the scope of consumer-related EU laws clearly poses a risk to legitimate consumer interests, which can no longer be properly served by national legislation. In addition, maximum harmonisation can be detrimental to the further development of consumer law. Member States would lose their means to introduce new concepts at the national level, and thus EU policy makers would be deprived of important trendsetters and test sites.[19] I will return to all these issues again later.[20]

Taking a more comprehensive approach for the sake of consumer access to justice

The argumentation in this book rests on the assumption that the starting point for consolidating both consumer interests and interests in properly strengthening the internal market should rest on how to improve consumer confidence in the market in general and cross-border trade in particular. As I have shown in various chapters in this book, the approaches of the Commission have primarily focused on internal market arguments, and by doing so it has not always necessarily taken proper account of consumer interests.

---

[18] For details see Wrbka, 'The Dilemma of European Consumer Representation in Deliberative Networks', pp. 156–9 (with further references); Hix and Høyland, *The Political System of the European Union*, p. 165.

[19] For details see 'The substantive law pillar' in Chapter 15 below.

[20] See *ibid.*

Furthermore, and in addition to the fact that EU consumer laws are generally not flawless themselves,[21] most concepts used so far at the EU level have been, generally speaking, relatively one-sided. That is, they predominantly focus on either procedural law issues – how to get rights enforced – or on substantive law issues – the question of which matters to regulate at the EU level and to which extent. This one-sided approach is – from a consumer perspective – clearly unfortunate as even the most sophisticated enforcement tools would not really improve consumer confidence without appropriate substantive laws to back legitimate consumer interests. Vice versa, the best possible substantive laws could not contribute to strengthening consumer confidence if no effective enforcement regime guaranteed their success. What is missing is a more holistic discussion that properly addresses both areas, i.e., an approach that takes appropriate account of consumer needs in both fields. This comprehensive approach further includes the use of certain (to be discussed later) mechanisms to facilitate consumer knowledge about such procedural and substantive means and laws. In addition, several other factors – which at first sight might not be closely related to law such as language[22] or differences in consumer behaviour and culture[23] – can also have an impact on consumer confidence in cross-border trade and could (to some extent) be addressed by law.

[21] For details see the analysis in Parts II and III above.

[22] Language barriers are of considerable significance in cross-border trade. The 2006 Consumer Protection Eurobarometer Study, for example, showed that only approximately one third of the respondent consumers were prepared to shop in a foreign language (see TNS Opinion & Social, 'Consumer Protection in the Internal Market', p. 69).

[23] Thomas Wilhelmsson comments on this as follows: 'As consumers do most of their contracting locally, one cannot presume the emergence of a Europeanized shopping culture even among those consumers who take active advantage of the internal market' (T. Wilhelmsson, 'Introduction: Harmonization and National Cultures' in Wilhelmsson et al. (eds.), Private Law and the Many Cultures of Europe, p. 15). For further comments on the interplay between culture and consumer behaviour see G. Low, 'The (Ir)Relevance of Harmonization and Legal Diversity to European Contract Law: A Perspective from Psychology', European Review of Private Law, 18 (2010), 285–305; S. Shavitt, A. Y. Lee, C. J. Torelli, 'Cross-Cultural Issues in Consumer Behavior' in M. Wanke (ed.), Social Psychology of Consumer Behavior (New York: Psychology Press, 2009), pp. 227–50. For a comment on the interplay between cultural diversity and attempts to define the average European consumer see, for example, T. Wilhelmsson, 'The Average European Consumer: a Legal Fiction?' in Wilhelmsson et al. (eds.), Private Law and the Many Cultures of Europe, pp. 243–68; on both language and culture see further Stürner, 'Das Konzept der Vollharmonisierung', p. 6, where Michael Stürner argues that non-legal issues, especially language and culture-related issues, are of higher influence on the consumer attitude towards cross-border trade than any law-related issue could be. Stürner puts his arguments on his observation that 'even a cheaper price of a good or service offered abroad would often not be enough to tempt a consumer away from his or her domestic market' (translation mine) (ibid.).

Thus, to explain the need to address the issue of how to enhance consumer confidence from a more comprehensive perspective, I introduced a broader concept in Part I of this book, which I named access to justice 2.0. The concept of access to justice 2.0 refers to the quest for a legal framework that tries to ensure that consumer interests are safeguarded to the best possible extent by identifying and implementing certain parameters. These are necessary to answer the question of how to answer consumer needs and interests in the best possible way in practice by guaranteeing a well-communicated framework of well-conceived, 'fair', substantive consumer rights on the one hand and relatively fast, uncomplicated, consumer-satisfying (and economy-boosting), easy-to-understand and easy-to-use mechanisms to enforce those rights on the other.[24]

The concept of access to justice 2.0, as introduced in Part I of this book, shows that any attempt to find a suitable mechanism necessarily touches upon value issues, as access to justice 2.0 involves a balancing of interests of stakeholders – in the present case stakeholders affected by EU consumer legislation. This led me to differentiate between 'non-valuing justice', which, simply put, refers to the judiciary and legal proceedings in a purely technical way, and 'value-oriented justice', which adds certain value considerations to both procedural and substantive laws.

The call for taking greater account of value-oriented justice in EU consumer law-making has various origins. A wide range of values matter in this context, including concerns of the democratic deficit in and lack of legitimacy of EU law-making,[25] the imbalance of represented business and consumer interests in the policy- and decision-making processes[26] as well as the often-found argument that consumers are in a weaker, at least 'less-informed', position than traders. Thus, consumer laws, if meant to

---

[24] For the sake of clarification it should be noted that this holistic approach overrides the dividing lines between procedural consumer law and substantive consumer law and takes account of consumer legislation regardless of its nature. It does not only comprise the areas selected as illustrative examples, but further includes issues that fall under consumer-related pillars not explicitly covered in this book, consumer issues that fall under, e.g., product liability law, antitrust law, financial services law or administrative law. Hence, the concept introduced should be understood as encompassing also these areas (via analogous application).

[25] For comments on these issues see Wrbka, 'The Dilemma of European Consumer Representation in Deliberative Networks' (with further references).

[26] *Ibid.*

strengthen consumer confidence, inevitably have to take proper account of value-oriented justice arguments.[27]

Against this background it does not come as much of a surprise that several consumer law commentators argue in favour of greater consideration of value-oriented justice arguments at the EU level.[28] In the next chapter I will revisit some of the arguments covered earlier in this book and subsequently answer how justice in the context of consumer access to justice 2.0 should be understood. This will facilitate an easier understanding of later arguments with respect to European consumer law.

---

[27] In his analysis of the ideal interplay between law and morals Ronald Dworkin explains that the need to consider value-oriented justice arguments generally exists in law making and explains that no community 'should ..., except in very exceptional emergency circumstances, make laws it believes unjust' (see R. Dworkin, *Justice for Hedgehogs* (Cambridge, MA: Harvard University Press, 2011), p. 401). For further comments on this issue see 'Value-oriented Justice' in Chapter 2 above.

[28] See the examples in Chapter 7 above.

13

The justice debate and consumer legislation

Expressions of justice

As explained in Part I of this book, justice in the context of (consumer) access to justice 2.0 does not only refer to non-valuing justice, i.e., the judicial system in a more technical way, but also relates to what I called value-oriented justice. Earlier I tried to define this term, a term that is not usually found in the literature. I touched upon terms such as corrective justice, distributive justice, formal justice and substantive justice. However, none of these terms alone accurately describes value-oriented justice, which merges the ideas of each of these sectoral definitions into a broader concept.

Although value-oriented justice cannot be absolutely defined, I have identified several parameters that are inherent to it. Fairness and equality are two core ingredients, and an effective judiciary, individual satisfaction and happiness are others. I also explained that value-oriented justice has to be understood as a flexible term, which is characterised by the need to balance interests in the policy-making process. The result of this can vary depending on factors such as time or the group of addressees of the respective legislation. Value-oriented, justice-based law making is further characterised by the search for the 'right' mix and interplay of different procedural and substantive laws (regardless of whether they have their origins in private or public law). If properly reflected in legislation, value-oriented justice could embody the highest possible degree of satisfaction that could be reached with the help of law.

One term that is commonly found in the justice-related literature on EU consumer law (especially in consumer contract law), arguably the most common justice expression used in this context, is social justice, a term that I briefly discussed earlier.[1] It is worthwhile mentioning this term again at this stage to see how it interacts with value-oriented justice

---

[1] See Chapter 7 above.

and how the latter, which forms an integral part of access to justice 2.0, could fit into the social justice debate.

Social justice and consumer access to justice 2.0

Value-oriented justice (as an essential part of the consumer access to justice 2.0 concept) and social justice are not necessarily interchangeable justice concepts. Whether the meaning of the relatively ambiguous term social justice gets close to or is even similar to value-oriented justice as defined in Part I is primarily linked to the way social justice is understood.

In Part III, I referred to a number of commentators on social justice. I dealt with, for example, the Social Justice Manifesto, which discusses the driving factor behind EU policy-making as follows: 'As traditionally understood, the function of the European Community is to promote a free market, not to ensure that this market is corrected in the light of distributive aims.'[2] As one can conclude from this quote and other pertinent contributions discussed earlier, a considerable number of social justice commentators ask policy makers to take greater account of both corrective *and* distributive justice ideas when drafting laws.

A closer look at the term social justice reveals that the concept cannot be understood only in such a way. Admittedly, the social justice debate usually revolves around the more conventional understanding of this term, which emphasises the significance of distributive justice. In a strongly defined way this could relate to political movements and calls for a relatively high level of state intervention in the market. Depending on the degree of such intervention, traders arguably run the risk of being unreasonably and severely limited in their actions. At the same time consumers could, in a rather extreme form of social justice, be deprived (at least to some extent) of the means to maximise private property, if social justice were characterised by the maxim of 'equal distribution' in its literal meaning.

In his study on national private law regimes, cultural diversity and the concept of social justice, Collins takes a broader approach to social justice and concludes that the term could also be understood in a different way. He explains that social justice can be basically split into two different meanings.[3] The first of his two definitions relates to 'welfare' and the

---

[2] Study Group on Social Justice in European Private Law, 'Social Justice in European Contract Law', 660–1.

[3] Collins, 'Does Social Justice Require the Preservation of Diversity in the Private Laws of Member States of Europe?', pp. 155–76.

question of a fair 'distribution of wealth'.[4] Understood this way, social justice would try to achieve a 'correct' distribution and balancing of monetary values and would reflect ideas of the aforementioned conventional social justice school of thought.

For the argumentation in this book, it is Collins's alternative definition of social justice, however, that is of relevance. Collins refers to this second group (a group that is less focused on mere monetary issues)[5] as 'well-being'.[6] This second category could be described as a state of individual happiness, satisfaction or, especially with respect to the internal market, as confidence and trust in cross-border B2C transactions. Here too a certain degree of legislative intervention exists; however, the reason for this lies less with distributive justice. Instead, the focus of state intervention rests on the attempt to remedy (especially, but not only) initial imbalances between parties, imbalances caused, for example, by information deficits or a lack of negotiating power on the side of one of the parties (usually on the consumer's side).[7] One could also say that laws in this respect try to create an atmosphere in which parties can meet on an equal footing when doing business, and that, as a safety net, proper means should exist to safeguard that consumers' legitimate legal interests are protected.

Understood in this way, law determines the rules of the game by defining the outer parameters that should allow individuals to strive for a maximisation of their individual well-being. This understanding of social

---

[4] *Ibid.*, p. 161.

[5] In a similar vein is Lurger's comment that well-being is 'not restricted to financial or material well-being' (Lurger, 'The Common Frame of Reference', p. 189).

[6] Collins, 'Does Social Justice Require the Preservation of Diversity in the Private Laws of Member States of Europe?', pp. 161–3. Bastian Schüller is another commentator who differentiates between two social justice categories. His first category relates to the 'distribution of welfare' and is similar to Collins's welfarism category. Schüller's second classification – he describes it as 'a level playing field' and 'fair results' – gets close to Collins's understanding of social justice as well-being (for details see B. Schüller, 'Social Peace Via Pragmatic Civil Rights – the Scandinavian Model of Consumer Law' in Micklitz (ed.), *The Many Concepts of Social Justice in European Private Law*, pp. 384–402).

[7] Hesselink explains this (with respect to SMEs) as follows: 'In consumer contracts SMEs are usually the stronger party' (M. W. Hesselink, 'SMEs in European Contract Law' in Boele-Woelki and Grosheide (eds.), *The Future of European Contract Law*, p. 365). For the question of asymmetric information in consumer contracts see S. I. Becher, 'Asymmetric Information in Consumer Contracts: The Challenge That Is Yet to Be Met', *American Business Law Journal*, 45 (2008), 723–74. For an interdisciplinary study of informational asymmetries in B2C situations that applies also social psychology arguments see M. W. De Hoon, 'Power Imbalances in Contracts: An Interdisciplinary Study on Effects of Intervention', TISCO Working Paper Series on Civil and Conflict Resolution Systems, No. 01/2007 (2007), available at papers.ssrn.com/sol3/papers.cfm?abstract_id=985875.

justice (like the conventional meaning of social justice) is, to some extent, restrictive, as it limits the individual's freedom to do as one pleases. At the same time, however, this second concept guarantees that each person can aim for individual well-being in a well-balanced setting. If one understands social justice as a synonym for ways to ensure individual well-being, and thus in a slightly different way than used in the more conventional social justice debate described earlier in this book,[8] then it does indeed get close to the ideas of value-oriented justice. This is because of the fact that expressions of the latter, such as happiness and satisfaction, are important contributors to the state of individual well-being.

Individual well-being, consumer confidence, access to justice 2.0 and EU consumer law making

Individual consumer well-being cannot be expressed in absolute numbers, as the reason(s) why (or why not) consumers reach such a state differ(s) on an individual basis. To enhance consumer confidence, it is, however, of undeniable importance to facilitate the ways or means for consumers to reach their individual well-being status. Such facilitation could eventually prove beneficial for the maximisation of the internal market, as it can be assumed that confident consumers would contribute to its growth.[9]

Access to justice 2.0 aims to show the way(s) to achieve a positive interconnection between individual well-being, consumer confidence and market growth with the help of consumer law making. Ideas to accomplish this rest on various factors, including data from pertinent studies, conclusions drawn from general legal experience where concrete data are lacking, and sociological and psychological analyses of consumer behaviour.

In later chapters I will argue that various parallel measures should be taken to accomplish access to justice 2.0. For the sake of simplicity I shall refer to these mechanisms in general as third-party intervention, as in each case some kind of intermediary can be identified to facilitate the endeavour. However, before discussing the suggestions, I should first deal with and respond to some counter-arguments to the not uncontested idea of third-party intervention in the B2C market.

---

[8] See Chapter 7 above.
[9] For data on the interplay between proper consumer information and consumer confidence in the cross-border B2C market see Chapter 15, note 4 below.

14

(Responses to) counter-arguments to third-party intervention

Paternalism v. liberalism

Any attempt to argue for third-party intervention in B2C situations would inevitably face some opposition, especially from the classical school of liberalism (liberalism) that claims that the B2C market would be better off without external interference. In the liberal view, the ideal market scenario would be a scenario with no or (at most) very little third-party intervention.

In contrast to this stands paternalism, whose representatives are more supportive of state intervention. Iain Ramsay, for example, refers to this school as follows: 'Paternalistic measures override individual preferences, substituting government judgements for that of the individual.'[1] He adds that '[t]hese [state] interventions are often based either on distrust of the consumer's ability to evaluate information or on the fear that individuals, even with accurate information, will act irrationally, misestimating product risks. … [Paternalism] is associated with regulation where mistakes by consumers might have costly consequences … or where consumers' short-term preferences appear to need to be overruled in favour of their long-term interests'.[2] From this definition one can see that Ramsay considers two possible scenarios where paternalism could come into play. Paternalism could be used to advise uninformed or less informed consumers to remedy the information deficit and to help them make 'rational', better-informed decisions. However, paternalism, according to Ramsay, could also go one step further. In some cases consumers will still make irrational decisions despite a high degree of information.[3] In such cases, paternalists, especially those who represent a 'harder' form of paternalism

---

[1] Ramsay, *Consumer Law and Policy*, p. 81.
[2] *Ibid.*
[3] For a claim that consumers usually tend to make irrational choices and for suggestions for traders on how to make use of that see E. Trevisan, *The Irrational Consumer: Applying Behavioural Economics to Your Business Strategy* (Farnham: Routledge, 2013).

(hard paternalism), believe that there is the need for stronger state intervention going beyond mere information activities.

One feature of paternalism is that it is, to a large extent, characterised by the use of mandatory law to rebalance the assumed power imbalance between traders and consumers. Hein Kötz refers to the use of paternalistic, mandatory law in his analysis of mandatory provisions and party autonomy. In his argumentation[4] one can find certain parallels to Collins's concepts of welfare and well-being (as described above) – although Kötz does not explicitly refer to those expressions or the term social justice. Kötz explains that the rationale behind mandatory provisions is the legislator's wish 'to protect the weaker party'.[5] 'Contractual justness' would thus replace 'contractual freedom'.[6] With the help of contractual justness, the legislators would aim to 'compensate the structural inferiority and to transform the contract into a legal relationship that is built upon cooperation, solidarity, care and fairness'.[7] According to Kötz, this in several instances justifiable rationale, which basically safeguards Collins's aforementioned idea of well-being, is not to be equated with the 'fair allocation of property'[8] (a synonym for Collins's welfare concept). Kötz explains that the latter must not be pursued with the help of contract law but instead with 'tax law and rules on transfers'.[9]

Classical liberals (liberals),[10] in particular, would criticise any use of mandatory provisions as being unnecessary to protect consumers, as they claim that the market can easily regulate itself.[11] Lucian Bebchuck and Richard Posner state that this is the result of '[t]he ... economic analysis of law ... that in a competitive market without informational asymmetries, the terms of contracts between sellers and buyers will be

---

[4] H. Kötz, *Vertragsrecht* (2nd edn, Tübingen: Mohr Siebeck, 2012), pp. 24–5.
[5] *Ibid.*, p. 24 (translation mine).   [6] *Ibid.* (translation mine).
[7] *Ibid.* (translation mine).   [8] *Ibid.*, p. 25 (translation mine).
[9] *Ibid.* (translation mine).
[10] In the context of this book the term liberals and liberalism shall refer to classical liberalism and the classical liberal school. For a critical analysis of the interplay between liberalism and value-oriented justice ideas from a US perspective see M. J. Sandel, *Liberalism and the Limits of Justice* (2nd edn: Cambridge University Press, 1998).
[11] In a similar vein is Marion Träger's observation in M. Träger, 'Party Autonomy and Social Justice in Member States and EC Regulation: Survey of Theory and Practice' in H. Collins (ed.), *Standard Terms in Europe: A Basis for and a Challenge to European Contract Law* (Alphen aan den Rijn: Kluwer Law International, 2008), p. 58, where she explains that '[f]rom the perspective of economic liberalism, there is no independent problem of material justice because the principles of freedom of contract and the equal position of the negotiating partners automatically achieve a substantively fair and equitable contract'.

optimal'.[12] According to this view, mandatory provisions are incompatible with consumers' wishes to freely negotiate, which must be preserved as 'individuals are argued to be the most able to know their own preferences [including their legal preferences] and act accordingly'.[13] I will come back to this issue shortly.[14]

Attempts to answer the concerns towards third-party intervention in consumer issues

What needs to be answered

Critics of third-party intervention in consumer matters adduce weighty arguments to the discussion. To proceed with the access to justice 2.0 concept, I would like to briefly discuss three issues in this context. I will start with comments on an attempt to overcome the critique of hard paternalism by softer paternalistic means to regulate the market. Following this, I will return to the discussion of mandatory law and the question of the interplay between mandatory provisions and party autonomy. Finally, I will deal with the liberal argument that the market could easily regulate itself and that third-party intervention would only be counterproductive.

Soft paternalism as an attempt to mediate between hard paternalism and classical liberalism

Various scholars, mainly from the USA, have tried to accommodate the differences between hard paternalism on the one hand and classical liberalism on the other by using attenuated, 'softer' paternalistic frameworks (soft paternalism). Cass Sunstein and Richard Thaler are undeniably two

---

[12] L. A. Bebchuck and R. A. Posner, 'One-Sided Contracts in Competitive Consumer Markets' in O. Ben-Shahar (ed.), *Boilerplate: The Foundation of Market Contracts* (Cambridge University Press, 2007), p. 3. For a response to their assumed informational symmetry see 'The need for alternative third-party intervention in B2C issues' below.

[13] H. Luth, *Behavioural Economics in Consumer Policy: The Economic Analysis of Standard Terms in Consumer Contracts Revisited* (Antwerp: Intersentia, 2010), p. 42. Later in her book she further explains that '[p]aternalism is regarded quite negatively from an economic perspective. Individuals can best decide for themselves, as they themselves are in the best position to know what they prefer. Governments should therefore allow individuals optimal choice, and not intervene with the options available for them' (*ibid.*, p. 68).

[14] See 'Justice-related thoughts on mandatory law' and 'The need for alternative third-party intervention in B2C issues' below.

of the most influential figures in this context. In 2003 they published their concept of 'libertarian paternalism', a prime example of soft paternalism, which tries to connect ideas of both paternalism and liberalism.[15] According to Sunstein and Thaler, this concept should 'provide ... a basis for both understanding and rethinking a number of areas of contemporary law, including those aspects that deal with ... consumer protection'.[16] Using Sunstein and Thaler's classification of human beings as Humans and Econs,[17] Daniel Kahnemann summarises the underlying idea of libertarian paternalism as follows: 'Humans, unlike Econs, need help to make good decisions, and there are informed and unintrusive ways to provide that help.'[18] Sunstein and Thaler argue that some kind of soft paternalism is needed, which would nudge people into 'directions that will make their lives better'.[19] At the same time this soft form of paternalism would avoid an unnecessary elimination of choice possibilities, as it 'alters people's behavior in a predictable way *without* forbidding any options or significantly changing their economic incentives' (emphasis added).[20] According to this view, state intervention would still be necessary to a certain degree, but unlike in the case of 'hard paternalism' where third-party intervention is regarded as totally depriving consumers of their right of

---

[15] R. H. Thaler and C. R. Sunstein, 'Libertarian Paternalism', *American Economic Review*, 93 (2003) 175–9; C. R. Sunstein and R. H. Thaler, 'Libertarian Paternalism Is Not an Oxymoron', *The University of Chicago Law Review*, 70 (2003), 1159–202.

[16] Sunstein and Thaler, 'Libertarian Paternalism Is Not an Oxymoron', 1160. A further example of an attempt to answer criticism of paternalistic legislation (that paternalism would patronise consumers) is given by Colin Camere, Samuel Issacharoff, George Loewenstein, Ted O'Donoghue and Matthew Rabin and their concept of 'asymmetric paternalism' or 'paternalism for conservatives' (C. Camerer *et al.*, 'Regulation for Conservatives: Behavioral Economics and the Case for "Asymmetric Paternalism"', *University of Pennsylvania Law Review*, 151 (2003), 1211–54). They distinguish between two groups of consumers: 'those who are boundedly rational ... and those who are fully rational' (*ibid.*, 1219). Asymmetric paternalism aims to apply two different paternalistic standards to the two groups in order to guarantee the best possible impact on individual well-being. For comments on soft paternalism from a European perspective see H. Eidenmüller, 'Liberaler Paternalismus', *JuristenZeitung*, 66 (2011), 814–21.

[17] See R. H. Thaler and C. R. Sunstein, *Nudge* (New Haven, CT: Yale University Press, 2008), p. 8, where Thaler and Sunstein explain as follows: 'To qualify as Econs, people are not required to make perfect forecasts ..., but they are required to make unbiased forecasts. ... Unlike Econs, Humans predictably err.' For further details on the two groups see *ibid.*, pp. 7–9. For a comment from the perspective of EU consumer law on this and related contributions from the USA see H.-W. Micklitz, L. A. Reisch and K. Hagen, 'An Introduction to the Special Issue on "Behavioural Economics, Consumer Policy, and Consumer Law"', *Journal of Consumer Policy*, 34 (2011), 271–6.

[18] D. Kahnemann, *Thinking, Fast and Slow* (London: Allen Lane, 2011), p. 415.

[19] Thaler and Sunstein, *Nudge*, p. 6.   [20] *Ibid.*

free decision making, it would be used as a tool to enable consumers to make a rational choice in their own best interest, minimising the possibility of irrational choices that consumers would later regret.

The concept of soft paternalism has not gone unchallenged. In the literature one can find voices that consider this concept (like hard paternalism) to be too restrictive on consumer self-determination, as any state intervention could manipulate consumers into believing that something was in their best interest despite their own legitimate preferences.[21] In other words, while soft paternalism aims to vest consumers with (what the state considers to be) an indispensable legal framework of active consumer protection and information, liberals instead welcome as little intervention as possible to guarantee genuine and uninfluenced consumer decision making.

It is not the purpose of this book to solve the disagreement between paternalists and liberals. It should be noted, however, that two important questions must be answered in the present, consumer law-focused argumentation. First, do the concepts of party autonomy and mandatory law necessarily stand in tension with each other? Second, and from the perspective of consumer satisfaction, is the (liberal) argument that the market is better off without any third-party intervention necessarily true? I will briefly deal with these two issues in the following sections.

Justice-related thoughts on mandatory law

Mandatory law is an integral part of consumer law to guarantee substantive consumer rights. Liberalism usually criticises the use of mandatory provisions for two reasons. First, liberals are convinced that the B2C market could easily regulate itself (and to the benefit of consumers). Second, liberals believe that mandatory law contradicts party autonomy, a contractual principle that societies should respect and protect.

Referring to the latter argument (I will deal with the first argument in the next chapter) and following the argumentation that mandatory law restricts contractual freedom, Lurger explains the interplay between party autonomy and fairness as follows:

> It is not self-evident where a legal system will draw the line between the conflicting principles of contractual freedom and regard and fairness.

[21] For a recent example of a critique of soft paternalism see M. D. White, *The Manipulation of Choice: Ethics and Libertarian Paternalism* (Basingstoke: Palgrave Macmillan, 2013).

The line can either be drawn more in favour of the individualistic liberal principle of contractual freedom, or more in favour of the altruistic 'social' principle of regard and fairness. The choices thus by legislatures and courts involve strong political implications for our markets, our societies and our cultures.[22]

Following this explanation, contractual freedom and party autonomy mainly embody liberal ideas, whereas mandatory laws and fairness commonly concern (social) justice-related argumentation, to which the aforementioned paternalistic school primarily relates. Just like the two concepts of liberalism and paternalism discussed earlier, party autonomy and fairness seem to be two irreconcilable ideas. Especially if one considers that mandatory provisions cannot be derogated from to the detriment of those who they aim to protect (in the case of consumer law: consumers), it is undeniably true that they limit the (stronger) party's means to push for 'weaker' legal standards. Understood in such a sense, mandatory laws and party autonomy indeed take opposite positions.

Marion Träger is another commentator who discusses the issue of party autonomy in relation to contractual fairness and puts both into context using concepts of (social) justice. In her analysis of national provisions on unfair contract terms prior to and after the implementation of the UCTD, she arrives at the conclusion that 'the conflict between the principle of freedom of contract and the idea of a substantively fair and equalised contract leads to very different solutions in the national judicial realms of contract law'.[23] Some Member States traditionally put a stronger emphasis on the principle of party autonomy, whereas others focus more on substantive contractual fairness ideas. One can also say that the differences are based on varying levels of relevance of party autonomy in the

---

[22] Lurger, 'The Common Frame of Reference', pp. 189–90. For a detailed analysis of the interplay between law, society and culture see R. Cotterrell, *Law, Culture and Society: Legal Ideas in the Mirror of Social Theory* (Farnham: Ashgate, 2006).

[23] Träger, 'Party Autonomy and Social Justice in Member States and EC Regulation', p. 58. Träger further explains that in the EU '[o]ne can find a general consensus that the idea of [formal] party autonomy does not automatically create a substantively fair and equitable contract and that legal measures are necessary to avoid the abuse of rights' and that '[t]here is a growing consciousness of an international phenomenon that the principle of party autonomy, virtually undisputed in the nineteenth century, must be restrained in favour of a fair balance of the parties' conflicting interests and in favour of the protection of the weaker party' (*ibid.*). For an additional comment on contractual fairness from the perspective of the inequality of bargaining power in B2C situations see, for example, A.-S. Vandenberghe, 'The Role of Information Deficiencies in Contract Enforcement' in Ogus and van Boom (eds.), *Juxtaposing Autonomy and Paternalism in Private Law*, pp. 62–6.

respective national legal systems.[24] Conversely, this can also be expressed as the extent of the manifestation of Member States' willingness to satisfy calls for more substantive contractual fairness, understood as appropriate 'adequacy of the price and remuneration'.[25] In this context, Träger further notes that '[t]he essential aspect of [the] discussion [over which to prioritise – party autonomy or substantive fairness] is the issue of whether the idea of substantive fairness is recognized as an independent value comparable to the principle of freedom of contract, and how the relationship of both values is considered in the respective legal systems'.[26]

However, it can be argued that party autonomy and fairness are not necessarily two opposing ideas. One can argue that fairness (addressed via mandatory provisions) actually tries to achieve *true* bilateral party autonomy. Such understanding takes greater account of the pre-contractual positions of both the trader and consumer in B2C situations, which are usually relatively imbalanced or of unequal footing. As consumers are generally believed to be at a disadvantage due to a mix of information deficits, inferior negotiating powers, a lack of legal knowledge and limited financial resources to react to unwanted legal situations, the rationale behind consumer law in general should be to remedy and further prevent market failure caused by these imbalances. This endeavour could be facilitated if the parties to a contract were able to meet on an equal footing. Hence, it is possible to argue that mandatory laws aim to facilitate the quest for material contractual freedom for both traders *and* consumers, and in such way would somehow merge the concepts of party autonomy and contractual fairness.[27] Put differently, mandatory laws do not only aim to protect consumers against legal exploitation by traders and/or from suffering harm or damage. If crafted properly, they further aim to create a legal environment in which both parties can engage in transactions with fewer legal worries than in a legal setting with no mandatory provisions. Understood in this way, one can draw parallels to the arguments of Walter Eucken and the ordoliberal school regarding party autonomy and competition law. In his posthumously published *Grundsätze der Wirtschaftspolitik*, Eucken claims as follows: 'Contractual

---

24 Träger, 'Party Autonomy and Social Justice in Member States and EC Regulation', p. 58.
25 *Ibid.*, p. 59. 26 *Ibid.*
27 See also Stefan Grundmann, who explains his view on the matter in his analysis of the ideal contract law model as follows: '[The ideal model] is characterised by an increasing, subtle and nuanced search for an optimal equilibrium between the (contractual) freedoms of *both* parties or, more generally, *all* parties concerned' (S. Grundmann, 'The Future of Contract Law', *European Review of Contract Law*, 7 (2011), 490, 527).

Freedom must not be granted for the purpose of concluding contracts that limit or remove contractual freedom.'[28] Thus, the status of ideal contractual freedom is achieved only if *both* parties to a contract can enjoy 'real'[29] party autonomy. In the case of B2C contracts this can only mean that in certain situations mandatory laws are necessary to remedy the (principally) imbalanced pre-contractual positions of traders and consumers and to create a setting where both parties can enjoy true and fair party autonomy.[30] Nevertheless, several voices still criticise mandatory rules. They state that such rules would have a negative impact on the final prices to be paid by consumers, as traders would have to take account of possible financial risks resulting from consumer-friendly legislation when calculating prices.[31] To the best of my knowledge, however, no study to date has been able to convincingly support the argument that traders would necessarily pass eventual cost savings on to consumers. Hence, not only the argument that mandatory rules necessarily counteract party autonomy, but also the argument that getting rid of mandatory rules would lead to lower final prices for consumers, still remain to be proven correct by those who oppose the use of mandatory provisions in the field of consumer law.[32]

The need for alternative third-party intervention in B2C issues

Consumer information and the negotiating powers of consumers in B2C contracts are two issues that can help explain why third-party intervention in consumer issues is needed. With regard to consumer information, Parts II and III of this book have shown that consumers suffer from a

---

[28] W. Eucken, *Grundsätze der Wirtschaftspolitik* (Tübingen: Mohr Siebeck, 1952), p. 278 (translation mine).

[29] *Ibid.* (translation mine).

[30] For the argument that the guarantee of legal standards via mandatory provisions facilitates B2C transactions, because consumers can trust that an appropriate minimum level of protection applies see G. Hager, *Strukturen des Privatrechts in Europa* (Tübingen: Mohr Siebeck, 2012), p. 15.

[31] In this sense see Kötz, *Vertragsrecht*, p. 25, where Kötz claims that it is not proven yet that the benefits for consumers resulting from mandatory rules would really outweigh the negative consequences resulting from higher prices. With respect to the CESL see O. Bar-Gill and O. Ben-Shahar, 'Regulatory Techniques in Consumer Protection: A Critique of the Common European Sales Law', New York University Law and Economics Research Papers, No. 12-12 (2012), pp. 8 and 27, available at papers.ssrn.com/sol3/papers.cfm?abstract_id=2061148.

[32] For details see 'First assumption: simplification of the legal environment for traders, reduction of business costs and lower final prices for consumers' in Chapter 10 above.

lack of legal information, be it related to procedural laws (especially to the question of how to have rights enforced), substantive laws (especially with respect to their content) or both.[33] The claim in the liberal argumentation that the absence of any mandatory laws could lead to 'a competitive [B2C] market without informational asymmetries'[34] is (unfortunately) incorrect. Looking at the current situation one has to note that the B2C market is characterised by informational asymmetries *despite* (and not because of) the existence of mandatory provisions. Removing mandatory provisions would only worsen the information asymmetry between traders and consumers, as information obligations undeniably fall under the category of mandatory laws.[35] In other words, mandatory laws are undeniably important to remedy informational asymmetries.

However, the provision of information to consumers is not without difficulties. One of the biggest problems in this respect relates to the more conventional approach of obliging traders to provide consumers with information. While it cannot be denied that this does to some degree contribute to increasing consumers' legal awareness, one must note that information provided directly by traders is usually not properly digested by consumers. Traders typically answer their legal obligation to provide consumers with pre-defined information by including such information in standard terms and conditions (standard terms). However, one of the problems in this respect is the fact that the average consumer does not usually read the legal information provided by traders, and even less so if it is included in standard terms. This phenomenon is explained by an analysis by Hanneke Luth on the interplay between consumer buying behaviour and standard terms with reference to (in absence of comprehensive European research) several studies conducted in the USA.[36] One of the studies she refers to, a study by Robert Hillman, shows that

---

[33] For an early comment on the importance of proper consumer information see S. Weatherill, 'The Role of the Informed Consumer in European Community Law and Policy', *Consumer Law Journal*, 2 (1994), 49–69.

[34] Bebchuck and Posner, 'One-Sided Contracts in Competitive Consumer Markets', p. 3.

[35] And – with respect to mandatory provisions other than mandatory information – as I explained in the previous chapter, well-crafted mandatory laws are necessary to create an environment where consumers can engage in B2C transactions without having to fear that they would be deprived of minimum rights and standards.

[36] Luth, *Behavioural Economics in Consumer Policy*, pp. 178–85 (with reference to R. A. Hillman, 'Online Consumer Standard Form Contracting Practices: A Survey and Discussion of Legal Implications' in J. K. Winn (ed.), *Consumer Protection in the Age of the 'Information Economy'* (Aldershot: Ashgate, 2006), pp. 283–311; S. I. Becher and E. Unger-Aviram, 'The Law of Standard Form Contracts: Misguided Intuitions and Suggestions for Reconstruction', *DePaul & Commercial Law Journal*, 8 (2010), 199–227;

an insignificant portion of consumers, approximately 4 per cent, try to read standard terms in online transactions 'under any circumstance',[37] whereas nearly half of the respondent consumers, 44 per cent, usually do not read them.[38] Unlike Hillman who analyses reading behaviour *reported* by consumers, Debra Stark and Jessica Choplin analyse consumers' *actual* reading behaviour. Stark and Choplin found that 95.6 per cent of consumers did not read the standard terms in the concrete case.[39] In a similar study on actual reading behaviour, Yannis Bakos, Florencia Marotta-Wurgler and David Trossen come to the conclusion that only 0.2 per cent of consumers actually access standard terms[40] and that the average time spent by consumers 'reading' standard terms amounts to just 48 seconds.[41] From Luth's comparative analysis, one can conclude that little attention is paid to the compulsory information contained in standard terms and that additional steps are needed if one really wants to improve the information level of consumers.

Standard terms also exemplify a different problem in B2C transactions. Unlike B2B transactions, B2C contracts are usually characterised by the considerably weaker negotiating powers of one of the parties (in this case, consumers)—in particular with respect to the contractual legal framework. Typical B2C contract negotiations (if existing at all), concentrate primarily on the delivery date or date of performance. The place of performance or the total price to be paid by consumers might, in some cases, also be negotiable. Other law-related questions, however, remain in principle untouched and are (in several instances) regulated by traders at will in their standard terms.[42] This fact, although being common to any kind

---

D. P. Stark and J. M. Choplin, 'A License to Deceive: Enforcing Contractual Myths Despite Consumer Psychological Realities', *NYU Journal of Law & Business*, 5 (2009), 617–744; Y. Bakos, F. Marotta-Wurgler and D. R. Trossen, 'Does Anyone Read the Fine Print? Testing a Law and Economics Approach to Standard Form Contracts', New York University Law and Economics Research Paper, No. 195 (2009), available at papers.ssrn.com/sol3/papers. cfm?abstract_id=1443256). For further explanations that the average consumer does not (or only very seldom) read standard terms see C. P. Gillette, 'Rolling Contracts as an Agency Problem', *Wisconsin Law Review*, (2004), 679–722; O. Ben-Shahar, 'The Myth of the "Opportunity to Read" in Contract Law', University of Chicago Law & Economics, John M. Olin Working Paper, No. 415 (2008), available at papers.ssrn.com/sol3/papers. cfm?abstract_id=1162922.

[37] Luth, *Behavioural Economics in Consumer Policy*, p. 179.

[38] *Ibid.*   [39] *Ibid.*, pp. 179–80.

[40] *Ibid.*, p. 179.   [41] *Ibid.*

[42] Luth refers to this as follows: 'Negotiations on less salient standard terms are ... highly doubtful' (*ibid.*, p. 188, with reference to a study by Jason Johnston (J. S. Johnston, 'The Return of Bargain: An Economic Theory of How Standard-Form Contracts Enable

of B2C contract, becomes quite visible in online B2C transactions. In such cases the technical settings do not allow for contract negotiations (and thus also not for negotiations of the standard terms). Generally speaking, consumers can only enter into an online transaction if they accept the trader's standard terms, in many instances by activating 'standard terms consent boxes' in an intermediary step towards the conclusion of the contract.[43] If a likely dispute reaches court, the provisions of the standard terms that contradict mandatory law should lose their significance.[44] However, in view of the comparatively low number of unsolved disputes that go beyond initial complaints,[45] it is more than doubtful whether the possibility that courts would overrule standard terms in breach of mandatory provisions would deter traders from using standard terms to deviate from mandatory legal provisions.[46] Without proper third-party intervention, i.e., if traders are allowed to do as they please, standard terms could undeniably get out of control. To remedy this issue at a pan-EU level, the Union legislator has already enacted various legal concepts that are supposed to provide a satisfactory solution. The Injunctions Directive, the CPC Regulation and the UCTD are prominent examples in this respect. Third-party intermediaries play an important role in this context. As already shown, their direct involvement could, however, be improved and further intensified.[47] At the same time (and although some initiatives

Cooperative Negotiation between Businesses and Consumers', *Michigan Law Review*, 104 (2006), 857–98)). For a collection of unfair standard terms used in German practice in B2C contracts see C. Woitkewtisch, 'Verbraucherschutz im AGB-Recht. Aktuelle Rechtsprechung zum Verbandsklageverfahren', *Verbraucher und Recht*, 22 (2007), 252–7.

[43] In her study on the online music download market, Ulrike Grübler explains that objecting to the seller's standard terms would usually fail due to the 'technical conditions' [translation mine] of online shopping (see U. Grübler, *Digitale Güter und Verbraucherschutz: Eine Untersuchung am Beispiel des Online-Erwerb von Musikdownloads* (Baden-Baden: Nomos, 2010), p. 88). For further comments on this issue see T. Wilcke, *Internationaler Online-Handel und Verbraucherschutz* (Baden-Baden: Nomos, 2011), p. 21 (with references at note 5).

[44] Courts have in principle the obligation to examine the possible unfairness of contract terms *ex officio* (Joined Cases C-240-244/98, *Océano Grupo Editorial* v. *Rocio Murciano Quintero* [2000] ECR I-4941, clarified by C-168/05, *Elisa María Mostaza Claro* v. *Centro Móvil Milenium SL* [2006] ECR I-10421 and Case C-243/08, *Pannon GSM Zrt.* v. *Erzsébet Sustikné Győrfi* [2009] ECR I-4713).

[45] See Chapter 3 and 'Scattered damages versus mass damages' in Chapter 5 above.

[46] Luth explains that the fact that consumers usually refrain from taking any action at all can further intensify this issue (see Luth, *Behavioural Economics in Consumer Policy*, p. 183 with reference to Becher and Unger-Aviram, 'The Law of Standard Form Contracts', 22).

[47] See the respective chapters in Part II and 'Recapitulating the Situation With Respect to Procedural EU (Consumer) Laws' in this Part IV above. For additional general comments see 'The Legislative Approach – The Procedural Law Pillar' below.

have shown certain positive effects[48]), third-party intermediaries could try to incentivise consumers to become more active. An appropriate mix of different forms of refined and/or additional third-party intervention could positively contribute to the support of consumers in this respect.

Reconciling social justice and market stimulation

As shown in the previous chapter, the call for a market free from any third-party intervention, if realised, would not resolve the issues of inadequate consumer information and imbalanced negotiating powers in B2C transactions. Hence, to ensure improved consumer confidence and to stimulate the market certain steps are needed.

Arguing for third-party intervention in consumer matters (as a contributor to consumer access to justice 2.0) might arouse indignation among liberals. However, possible concerns can be calmed if one takes a look at what third-party intervention actually means in the context of this book. Although the details will be explained in the following chapters, one can already note at this point that access to justice 2.0 aims to neither patronise consumers in their decision making nor hinder traders from engaging in the B2C market. Indeed, the contrary is the case. Access to justice 2.0 tries to show how ideas to strengthen consumer confidence, consumer well-being and the market can be reconciled.The underlying challenge is to find ways to answer consumer needs without hindering traders to offer their products to the largest possible audience. The following chapters will try to find such answers.

---

[48] See, in particular, the positive results of the sweeps under the framework of Article 9 CPC Regulation (for details see 'The Regulation on Consumer Protection Cooperation (2004)' in Chapter 4 above).

15

Consumer empowerment

A definition of consumer empowerment and general thoughts on how to achieve it

Over the last couple of years, several initiatives have explained that the full potential of the internal market is not yet fully tapped. The 2011 Evaluation of the European Consumer Centres Network (2011 ECC-Net Evaluation report) comes to the conclusion that '[t]he unrealised potential of the internal market is estimated to be in the order of EUR 194 billion'.[1] Other documents confirm that there is ample room for improvement, including the 2010 Council Recommendation on broad guidelines for the economic policies of the Member States and of the Union (in its guideline 6)[2] and the 2013 Commission's Joint Research Centre's report on the drivers and impediments for cross-border e-commerce in the EU.[3]

Strengthening consumer confidence is – without doubt – of utmost importance to boost the cross-border B2C market.[4] As the elaborations in this book have shown, the solutions presented at the EU level (or waiting

---

[1] Consumer Policy Evaluation Consortium (CPEC), 'Evaluation of the European Consumer Centres Network (ECC-Net). Final Report', report for DG SANCO, (2011), p. iii, available at ec.europa.eu/consumers/ecc/docs/final_report_cpec_en.pdf.

[2] Council Recommendation on broad guidelines for the economic policies of the Member States and of the Union, 13 July 2010, OJ 2010 No. L191/28, Guideline 6 on improving the business and consumer environment, and modernising and developing the industrial base in order to ensure the full functioning of the internal market.

[3] Gomez-Herrera, Martens and Turlea, 'The Drivers and Impediments for Cross-border e-Commerce in the EU'.

[4] For data confirming this see, for example, the findings of the 2013 Eurobarometer Cross-border Protection Study that consumer confidence in B2C trader (including cross-border B2C trade) is considerably lower if consumers lack sufficient information and legal knowledge (see TNS Political & Social, 'Consumer Attitudes towards Cross-border Trade and Consumer Protection', p. 31, where the report concludes that on average 37 per cent of consumers who were able to answer a group of specific consumer law-related questions correctly had trust in cross-border B2C online transactions, whereas the number with respect to respondents who were not able to give any correct answers dropped to, on average, 24 per cent).

in the pipeline) have not yet fully – at least not satisfactorily – addressed this issue. Consumer confidence in cross-border B2C trade is still considerably lower than with respect to domestic trade.[5]

In both consumer policy-making and legal literature one term is often used to describe attempts to raise consumer confidence: 'consumer empowerment'.[6] Although the meaning of this term might seem obvious, it is worthwhile looking further at this because it is an important ingredient in reaching consumer access to justice 2.0.

The New Oxford Companion to Law links empowerment in general to addressing the needs of the weak. It defines the term as 'entail[ing] the process of enabling persons or groups to participate more fully as rights-bearing entities within a society and state',[7] and adds that '[e]mpowerment processes must necessarily engage with the requirement of fostering individuals' and groups' agency, while simultaneously seeking to create

---

[5] *Ibid.*, p. 23, where the 2013 Eurobarometer Cross-border Protection Study shows that in late 2012 on average 59 per cent of all respondents had trust in domestic B2C online sales, whereas only 36 per cent had trust in cross-border B2C online sales.

[6] For a recent example of how the term is used in EU policy-making see European Commission, 'Empowering Consumers: A Record Year for the European Consumer Centres', press release, IP/14/162, 19 February 2014, available at europa.eu/rapid/press-release_IP-14-162_en.htm. The 2012 ECC-Net report emphasises the importance of providing consumers with proper information to strengthen consumer confidence and directly links it to the wish to enhance the internal market – on the importance of proper legal information on the level of consumer confidence see the data in note 4 above. The report frames this as follows: 'Informed and empowered consumers play a key role in strengthening competition in the internal market and stimulating growth' (European Commission, 'Help and Advice on Your Purchases Abroad – The European Consumer Centres Network 2012 Annual Report', report, (2013), p. 8, available at ec.europa.eu/consumers/ecc/docs/report_ecc-net_2012_en.pdf. At the same time the Commission comes to the conclusion that consumers' knowledge of their rights is 'worryingly low' (European Commission, 'Consumer Scoreboard Shows Where Consumer Conditions Are Best in Europe', press release, IP/12/510, available at europa.eu/rapid/press-release_IP-12-510_en.htm (with further references)). For further examples of the use of the term 'consumer empowerment' in EU policy-making and the legal literature see CPEC, 'Assessment of the Economic and Social Impact of the Policy Options to Empower Consumers to Obtain Adequate Redress'; G. Howells, 'The Potential and Limits of Consumer Empowerment by Information', *Journal of Law and Society*, 32 (2005), 349–70; J. Stuyck, 'The Notion of the Empowered and Informed Consumer in Consumer Policy and How to Protect the Vulnerable under Such a Regime' in Howells *et al.* (eds.), *The Yearbook of Consumer Law 2007*, pp. 167–86; J. Thøgersen, 'How May Consumer Policy Empower Consumers for Sustainable Lifestyles?', *Journal of Consumer Policy*, 28 (2005), 143–78; van den Meene and van Rooij, *Access to Justice and Legal Empowerment*. For an earlier comment on consumer empowerment see S. Grønmo and F. Ölander, 'Consumer Power: Enabling and Limiting Factors', *Journal of Consumer Policy*, 14 (1991), 141–69.

[7] R. Patel in Cane and Conaghan (eds.), *New Oxford Companion to Law*, p. 374.

structures which will best allow the expression of such agency. To a large degree ... empowerment is ... about participation, participatory decision-making, and democratic processes'.[8] This general definition surely summarises some basic ideas of empowerment.

In the context of consumer law, or to be more precise, with respect to consumer law in the context of the present book, empowerment is to be understood as a way to guarantee consumer access to justice 2.0. It tries to help consumers to reach a state of individual well-being and maximise their confidence in the market with the help of a proper legal framework. Worded differently, and with respect to EU consumer law, one can say that consumer empowerment refers to methods to overcome consumer distrust in or consumer frustration regarding cross-border B2C trade.

'Educating'[9] consumers, improving consumers' legal awareness, providing them with suitable rights and facilitating the possibilities to enforce them in cross-border situations are core means to empower consumers, but at the same time pose an undeniably difficult challenge. The already discussed, more conventional approach is to ask traders to provide consumers with legal information. However, the consumer information provided by traders (traders' consumer information) in B2C transactions does not completely solve the information deficit problem. I have already explained that consumers do not usually read legal information provided by traders.[10] Furthermore, in those cases where they do try to read such information there might be difficulties. Consumers might not fully understand the information or could fail to react appropriately to incorrect or incomplete information.[11]

---

[8] *Ibid.*, p. 375.

[9] For comments on educating consumers in legal matters from an international perspective see M. J. Trebilcock, 'Rethinking Consumer Protection Policy' in Rickett and Telfer (eds.), *International Perspectives on Consumers' Access to Justice*, pp. 84–5. For comments on the interplay between legal information, legal empowerment and access to justice see, e.g., M. Barendrecht, 'Legal Aid, Accessible Courts or Legal Information? Three Access to Justice Strategies Compared', TISCO Working Paper Series on Civil and Conflict Resolution Systems, No. 10/2010 (2010), available at papers.ssrn.com/sol3/papers.cfm?abstract_id=1706825.

[10] See 'The need for alternative third-party intervention in B2C issues' in Chapter 14 above for details. For comments on the limited effect of consumer information provided by traders see, in addition, G. Rühl, 'Consumer Protection in Choice of Law', *Cornell International Law Journal*, 44 (2011), 569, 578–80.

[11] Markus Artz comments on the insufficient effectiveness of traders' consumer information as follows: 'One has to ask whether the information model [used by the Commission] has not already reached its limits' (Artz, 'Vorschlag für eine vollharmonisierte Horizontalrichtlinie zum Verbraucherrecht', p. 218 (translation mine)). For a general call to support consumers additionally by other means than consumer information

Asking traders to support consumers with legal information is not the only way to address the need to empower consumers. Two other means, on which the remainder of the analysis will focus, complement this move. One can be referred to as 'consumer support', which is provided by consumer organisations, national public authorities[12] or – with respect to cross-border issues – European information centres, most prominently by ECCs. (For ease of understanding, the term consumer support can also be referred to as the 'facilitating intermediaries approach'.) In the context of the present analysis this concept comprises four pillars.

First, it can be used to describe alternative ways of providing consumers with proper legal information with the help of stakeholders (other than traders). These are usually private bodies and/or public authorities involved in consumer empowerment measures, either actively via broad information campaigns or individually by answering individual consumer questions (facilitating intermediary consumer information). Facilitating intermediary consumer information leads to two sub-questions. The first question relates to a more general information-specific question. How can information-seeking consumers properly obtain information? This is complemented by a second question: how could the information level of stakeholders involved in facilitating intermediary consumer information activities be improved? Also their knowledge level might not always be as high as it could and should be.[13]

Second, consumer support can further relate to taking actions to answer, prevent and stop incompatible business practices, and to assist consumers in dispute resolution (facilitating intermediary consumer law

(regardless of the source of information) see B. Heiderhoff, 'CESL – A Chance for True Freedom of Contract for the Consumer' in T. Drygala *et al.* (eds.), *Private Autonomy in Germany and Poland and in the Common European Sales Law* (Munich: Sellier, 2012), p. 84, where Bettina Heiderhoff explains as follows: 'Unfortunately, it has also been shown that the degree to which a consumer is able to process information and to make use of it is relatively low. Therefore, consumer protection must not be restricted to information but needs additional instruments.'

[12] These include consumer ombudsman institutions, ministries with competence in consumer issues and other national consumer support bodies. For early comments on consumer ombudsman institutions see K. Graver, 'A Study of the Consumer Ombudsman Institution in Norway with Some References to the Other Nordic Countries – I: Background and Description', *Journal of Consumer Policy*, 6 (1986), 1–23.

[13] See, for example, the issues discussed earlier regarding the qualified entities under the Injunctions Directive and competent authorities under the Consumer Protection Cooperation Regulation. The same is also true with respect to the judiciary in the context of the Small Claims Procedure, which in some countries is not yet widely known among the members of the judiciary (see Chapter 4 above for details).

enforcement support). A good example can be found in the context of standard terms. Possible actions by public authorities and/or private bodies to end the use of specific unfair contract terms for the collective benefit of consumers show that third parties can intervene for the advantage of consumers. The annual sweeps pursuant to Article 9 CPC Regulation that aim to identify and seek the cessation of certain illegal trade practices that infringe (or are likely to infringe) consumer interests (in at least three Member States) and the bi- and multilateral mutual assistance activities between Member States under Articles 6 to 8 CPC Regulation are further examples of how EU consumer legislation aims to comprehensively support consumers by ensuring legal compliance by traders. In addition, consumers can also directly benefit from facilitating intermediary consumer law enforcement support. Providing consumers with information on how to ensure that their rights are enforced in a dispute must be mentioned in this context. Another good example of direct support offered by facilitating intermediaries is the assistance of consumers to resolve disputes with traders via direct involvement of facilitating intermediaries, as will be shown later.[14]

Third, consumer support can also be understood as consumer interest representation in consumer policy and law making (facilitating intermediary consumer interest representation). Facilitating intermediaries are undeniably important in this context, as they deal with consumer concerns on a regular basis. Thus, they can provide policy and law makers with invaluable feedback from consumers.[15]

Fourth, consumer support further relates to issues that are not directly of legal concern, but which nevertheless can be approached with the help of legislation. Examples such as language differences come to mind, which – when not properly addressed – can further intensify consumer distrust in the market.[16]

The second of the two additional consumer empowerment concepts could be called the 'legislative approach'. Also this approach (like the 'facilitating intermediaries approach') includes certain third-party

[14] See 'ECC-Net: current activities' below.
[15] With regard to EU policy and law making, I briefly explained (using the example of the drafting of the CESL Regulation Proposal) how consumer representatives try to represent consumer interests in the creation process of EU consumer legislation. See 'The genesis of the proposal on a Common European Sales Law or: the long and winding road' in Chapter 10 above, in particular the text at Chapter 10, notes 48 to 55 (and the references in those notes for further details).
[16] For details see 'Taking a more comprehensive approach for the sake of consumer access to justice' in Chapter 12 above, in particular the text in notes 22 and 23.

intermediaries: national policy and law makers. These third-party intermediaries, however, (unlike the facilitating intermediaries just discussed)
have a direct influence on legislation. The legislative approach stands for a
framework of procedural and substantive consumer laws that takes both
legal and non-legal issues into appropriate consideration to create a setting that prevents (to the greatest possible extent) damage, harm and legal
exploitation by traders and to provide consumers with an effective safety
net of procedural and substantive rights in case things go wrong.[17] Such a
framework has to be understood as comprising procedural and substantive laws regardless of their origin, i.e., regardless of whether they relate
to or are based on private or public laws. With respect to substantive laws,
it should once again be mentioned though that the analysis in this book
to a large extent focuses on contractual issues (with the main emphasis
on cross-border issues and the question of how to enhance the internal
market). Nevertheless, the key points of the argumentation can *mutatis
mutandis* be applied to other areas of substantive consumer law.

Consumer empowerment in the context of access to justice 2.0 – applying an enhanced regime of consumer empowerment

Consumer empowerment as an attempt to facilitate B2C transactions

The true challenge in boosting consumer confidence and the cross-border
B2C market at the same time is to properly empower consumers without vesting them with excessive rights. Put differently, while consumer
empowerment plays a crucial role in strengthening consumer confidence,
it should not lead to a situation in which the (e.g., power, negotiating or
information) imbalance between stronger traders and weaker consumers
would be reversed, i.e., to scenarios where consumers could and would
misuse their empowered situation. I have already explained how concerns
of possible misuse play an important role in current European debates,

---

[17] Technically speaking, the aforementioned 'traders' consumer information' falls directly
under the scope of the legislative approach, as substantive laws require traders to provide
consumers with certain information. However, the legislative approach goes much further and includes the sum of core substantive and procedural rights and obligations in the
field of consumer law. The same is true of facilitating intermediaries and the environment
in which they act. They can (directly or at least indirectly) be traced back to legal provisions and thus, technically speaking, are covered by the legislative approach. However, to
stress the practical relevance of facilitating intermediaries as a 'softer' approach towards
consumer empowerment, the issue of facilitating intermediaries (like the 'traders' consumer information' approach) is discussed under a separate pillar.

for example, in discussions on how to facilitate consumer compensatory collective redress.[18] Access to justice 2.0 tries to create an environment in which traders and consumers can engage in B2C business without unwanted obstructions by either trader misbehaviour or consumer over-empowerment.

To accomplish the ambitious goal of properly empowering consumers, a two-tiered approach has to be taken.[19] It comprises both the facilitating intermediaries approach and the legislative approach outlined in the previous section. One can also say that these two approaches aim to reconcile the (at first sight) irreconcilable interests of the (conventional or classical) paternalistic and liberal schools. It must be admitted that the *arguments* brought by these two are indeed poles apart. However, reconciling the *goals* they are looking at, strengthening consumers on the one hand and serving business interests on the other, might not be impossible, as the next sections show. I will start with the first model, i.e., the facilitating intermediaries approach, before moving to the second, i.e., the legislative approach.

The facilitating intermediaries approach

General thoughts on ECC-Net as a prime example for a facilitating intermediary in cross-border B2C trade

As explained earlier, the idea of traders providing consumers with legal information, although being of undeniable importance, will not completely remedy the lack of consumer confidence in the B2C market. Another way to contribute to this endeavour is to rely (in addition) on the support of facilitating intermediaries. Using the assistance of third-party intermediaries to facilitate consumer empowerment can be realised by two means. One approach is to install a totally new mechanism. The other is to build upon existing mechanisms and refine them to a more effective level.

Choosing the first option would be necessary if existing mechanisms were so flawed that putting them on the right track would be either too time consuming or expensive to justify. Fortunately, the European situation does not fall under this category.

---

[18] For details see 'From the Green Paper on Consumer Collective Redress to the Commission's Collective Redress Recommendation' in Chapter 5 above.

[19] This two-tiered approach should be understood as complementing the earlier discussed 'traders' consumer information' approach.

In 2005, the Commission merged two consumer support institutions, the Network for the extra-judicial settlement of consumer disputes (EEJ-Net), with its focus on B2C dispute settlement, and the Euroguichet Network, the task of which was to generally advise and inform consumers, into the European Consumer Centres Network (ECC-Net). ECC-Net has one regional office (ECC) in each Member State as well as in Norway and Iceland and is co-financed by the Commission and national governments.[20] As will be seen in the following, ECC-Net has proven (even with its rather limited means) that ECC activities are (potentially) of great importance and benefit for consumers in cross-border B2C settings.

ECC-Net: current activities

Three essential categories of activity, in particular, fall under the ECC-Net pillar. All three – in one way or the other – serve consumer support ideas as outlined earlier.

Two categories aim at *directly* benefiting consumers with free-of-charge services. First, and related to what I called facilitating intermediary consumer information, ECCs are the central contact points for consumers with questions related to cross-border B2C trade. In that function, the ECCs handled approximately 48,000 information requests from consumers throughout the EU in 2013.[21] In addition to answering individual consumer questions, ECCs further provide more general information, ranging from the distribution of information brochures to maintaining information websites, public presence in the media and direct contact with consumers at public events.[22]

---

[20] The contributions by the Commission principally cover exactly 50 per cent of the respective ECC costs (insignificant exceptions prove the rule – according to the Commission via email on 10 March 2014 (on file with the author) it covered 49.9 per cent in 2011 and 49.85 per cent in 2012 of the costs of ECC Austria, and 49.5 per cent in 2011 of the costs of ECC United Kingdom). See CPEC, 'Evaluation of the European Consumer Centres Network', pp. 75–6 for further details for 2010.

[21] The overall category of 'contacts' comprises two big groups – information requests and complaints. For the concrete number of contacts and complaints handled by ECCs in 2013 see the 2013 ECC-Net infographic, available at ec.europa.eu/consumers/ecc/infographic/02_14_infograph-eccnet_2013.pdf. The total number of information requests handled can be calculated by subtracting the number of complaints from the number of overall contacts.

[22] These public events can take various forms and range from consumer information events organised by ECCs to the presence at bigger public events, such as sports events. (For some concrete examples for the latter see European Commission, 'Help and Advice on Your Purchases Abroad – The European Consumer Centres Network 2012 Annual Report', p. 3.)

Second, and related to what I called facilitating intermediary consumer law enforcement, ECCs can also contribute to resolving cross-border B2C disputes. Approximately 32,500 individual contacts fell within this category (usually referred to as the complaints category) in 2013.[23] The simplest example is providing consumers with legal advice in the case of a B2C cross-border issue (simple complaints). ECCs can also get more directly involved. They do so if they feel that direct ECC contact with traders is necessary (or at least advantageous) for consumers to reach an amicable solution with traders (complex cases).[24] In such cases, the ECC of the consumer's home country and (principally) the ECC of the trader's country work together to facilitate the consumer and trader reaching an amicable solution. If such attempts fail, consumers can receive ECC advice and assistance on how to proceed with 'stronger' redress mechanisms, which can include different forms of (other) ADR and litigation.

In its 2012 ECC-Net report, the Commission draws a relatively positive picture regarding complaints handling, especially with respect to simple complaints. The report summarises the impact of ECC-related activities as follows:

> Only partial information is available on the outcome of the complaints. In many cases, ECCs simply inform consumers about their rights, so that they can contact the trader themselves [note: this relates to simple complaints]. Consumers rarely come back to ECCs with information about the outcome of a resolved complaint. One can therefore assume that in many cases consumers come to an agreement with the trader once the ECCs had made them well aware of their rights and of what exactly they could claim or expect.[25]

At first sight, this statement does indeed sound satisfactory. However, the way in which the Commission arrives at the conclusion that in most cases of simple complaints consumers have been able to reach 'an agreement with the trader'[26] is not convincing. In the same passage the Commission explains that no comprehensive representative data were available to prove its assumption correct. The Commission argues that its positive

---

[23] For details see the 2013 ECC-Net infographic. The Commission positively comments on complaints handled via ECCs as follows: 'The ECCs ... contribute to significantly reducing the cost of litigation for consumer complaints and towards the smooth functioning of the internal market' (European Commission, 'Help and Advice on Your Purchases Abroad – The European Consumer Centres Network 2012 Annual Report', p. 6).

[24] European Commission, 'Help and Advice on Your Purchases Abroad – The European Consumer Centres Network 2012 Annual Report', p. 14.

[25] *Ibid.*   [26] *Ibid.*

conclusion primarily rests on the fact that consumers do not usually contact the respective ECC again once they have been provided with information on redress mechanisms. However, without supportive data the Commission's assumption is quite daring to say the least. It could just as well be concluded that consumers ended up frustrated over *not* reaching a solution with the respective trader and had no motivation to contact ECCs for a second time.

While the true consequences of the ECCs' handling of simple complaints remains unknown, more concrete data are available for complex cases. The 2012 ECC-Net report shows that 44.6 per cent of such cases were solved by an amicable settlement with the direct assistance of ECCs in 2012.[27] The report does not reveal how many of these settlements were fulfilled by the traders in practice, but one can justifiably argue that reaching amicable solutions in nearly half of the cases is a decent (yet not completely satisfying) result. Another 13.3 per cent of complex cases were, with the help (or at least on the advice) of ECCs, transferred to dispute resolution not directly involving ECCs.[28] However, for 42.1 per cent of the complex cases no solution was found, at least no solution directly attributable to the involvement or advice of ECCs.[29] In the future, the role of ECCs with respect to solving disputes, especially with respect to ADR/ODR, might increase and thus improve the situation, as both the ADR Directive and the ODR Regulation aim to facilitate the involvement of ECCs in ADR/ODR.[30] The true impact, of course, remains to be seen and can only be assessed when data become available.

The third category of ECC activities relates to operations that have a rather indirect effect on consumers. As the 2011 ECC-Net Evaluation report comprehensively explains, ECC-Net and ECCs provide policy makers with invaluable practical feedback on the effectiveness of consumer laws.[31] At least in theory, the experience of ECCs can also contribute to the enhancement of the legislative framework for consumer issues.[32] While

---

[27] *Ibid.*   [28] *Ibid.*

[29] The key reason for this was found in the fact that a considerable number of traders (traders in 27.8 per cent of complex cases) were unwilling to agree on any amicable solution (see *ibid.*, which also explains that 13.3 per cent of complex cases were transferred to a different (i.e. non ECC-) entity specialised in dispute resolution as a direct consequence of ECC involvement).

[30] See Articles 14(2) and 15 ADR Directive and Articles 7(1), 14(5) ODR Regulation for details.

[31] CPEC, 'Evaluation of the European Consumer Centres Network', pp. 46–51.

[32] One practical example of how ECC-Net provides the Commission with background data is the 2012 ECC-Net ESCP Study, which I discussed in Part II above. Recalling John

this structurally falls under the classification of facilitating intermediaries (I earlier referred to it as facilitating intermediary consumer interest representation), I will cover this third category later when I discuss the legislative approach towards consumer empowerment and will focus on the first two ECC tasks in the following sections.

ECC-Net: current status

In the first nine years since its merger into a unified framework, the ECCs have handled approximately 570,000 contacts (information requests and complaints).[33] The annual numbers have (in principle)[34] steadily risen over the years and peaked at slightly more than 80,000 total contacts in 2013.[35]

These numbers are surely impressive but are still considerably lower than the number of contacts handled by national consumer organisations and public authorities engaged in consumer support (mainly related to domestic consumer issues). The Austrian Consumer report 2011/2012, for example, shows that in both 2011 and 2012 the two biggest Austrian consumer support institutions, the Association for Consumer Information (*Verein für Konsumenteninformation*; VKI) and the Federal Chamber of Labour (*Kammer für Arbeiter und Angestellte*, in short: *Arbeiterkammer* or AK) served (in total) more than 400,000 consumer contacts per year.[36] In comparison, ECC Austria (*Europäisches Verbraucherzentrum Österreich*) handled 'only' approximately 3,000 contacts per year in 2011 and 2012.[37]

One explanation for this comparatively low number is surely the fact that domestic B2C markets are – especially with respect to the number

---

Dalli's somewhat surprised reactions to the findings of the 2012 ECC-Net ESCP Study that I discussed in the context of the ESCP, it will be interesting to see if, and if so, how, the Commission reacts in the near future.

[33] European Commission, 'Help and Advice on Your Purchases Abroad – The European Consumer Centres Network 2012 Annual Report', p. 8, where it states that by the end of 2012 'ECC-Net has had nearly 490,000 contacts over the past eight years'. In 2013, approximately 80,000 were added to this number (see the ECC-Net data in the 2013 ECC-Net infographic).

[34] See European Commission, 'Help and Advice on Your Purchases Abroad – The European Consumer Centres Network 2012 Annual Report', p. 11 (showing that twice – in 2009 and 2011 – there was a slight decrease).

[35] See the 2013 ECC-Net infographic.

[36] Verein für Konsumenteninformation and Kammer für Arbeiter und Angestellte für Wien, 'Bericht zur Lage der KonsumentInnen 2011/2012', report, (2013), pp. 372–375, available at www.bmask.gv.at/cms/site/attachments/4/6/7/CH2081/CMS1383664891566/bericht_zur_lage_2011__2012.pdf.

[37] *Ibid.*, p. 352.

of transactions – considerably larger than the EU cross-border B2C market. Consumers engage in domestic B2C transactions on a much more frequent basis than in cross-border B2C transactions. Hence, it can be assumed that the total number of legal issues arising from domestic B2C transactions is much higher than at a cross-border level.

Regardless of that issue, one cannot deny the fact that consumers' ECC awareness is very low. The 2011 ECC-Net Evaluation report, for example, shows that on average only 15 per cent of consumers who habitually reside in the EU have heard of ECCs.[38] Although the situation is improving – two years after this report the 2013 Eurobarometer report on consumer attitudes towards cross-border trade and consumer protection (2013 Eurobarometer Cross-border Protection Study) declared that the average consumers' ECC awareness reached 22 per cent[39] – it still has some way to go. Raising consumers' ECC awareness is thus clearly crucial to further improve the positive role ECCs can play. Arguably the most obvious way to increase consumers' ECC awareness is to ask ECCs to become more active in their self-promotion. However, under the present circumstances, this would be difficult to achieve. While there was a significant objective increase in total contacts over the years (in the period from 2009 to 2013 ECC contacts increased by 26.7 per cent[40]) the overall number of personnel (by full-time equivalents (FTE)[41]) has only slightly increased and has stayed at a relatively low level, as Table 6 illustrates.

In several instances ECCs benefit from particular support (especially administrative) provided by their national host organisations.[42] However, this support is limited, as the host organisation personnel have to

---

[38] CPEC, 'Evaluation of the European Consumer Centres Network', p. 6 (Table 1:2).

[39] TNS Political & Social, 'Consumer Attitudes towards Cross-border Trade and Consumer Protection', p. 42. Consumers' ECC awareness has thus (on average) doubled since 2006 (*ibid.*, p. 4). The 2013 Eurobarometer Cross-border Protection Study report also shows that there is a huge gap in consumers' ECC awareness in the Member States. Luxembourg had the highest number of informed consumers (49 per cent), while in Denmark and Spain only 8 per cent of consumers had heard of the ECCs (*ibid.*, p. 43).

[40] For details see the data in the 2013 ECC-Net infographic.

[41] FTEs as defined by the 2011 ECC-Net Evaluation report as 'posts estimated on basis of 220 working days [per year]' (CPEC, 'Evaluation of the European Consumer Centres Network', p. 65 (Table 3:7)).

[42] Structurally speaking, ECCs are located within 'host organisations', which can either be non-governmental organisations, governmental organisations or independent bodies. In practice ECCs and the respective host organisations work relatively closely together (depending on the ECC country). They do so by, for example, sharing infrastructures, exchanging experience and information and using promotion facilities. For a list of ECC host organisations see European Commission, 'Help and Advice on Your Purchases Abroad – The European Consumer Centres Network 2012 Annual Report', p. 10.

Table 6 *Number of personnel (in FTEs) per ECC in 2009 and 2013[a]*

ECC	2009[b]	2013[c]
Austria	7	8
Belgium	5	6
Bulgaria	5	4
Croatia	_[d]	4
Cyprus	4	4
Czech Republic	4	4
Denmark	5	6
Estonia	2	3
Finland	4	6
France	9	9
Germany	11	18
Greece	8	8[e]
Hungary	4	5
Iceland	0	1
Ireland	6	6
Italy	10	9
Latvia	4	4
Lithuania	6	6
Luxembourg	6	6
Malta	6	5
Netherlands	4	4
Norway	3	4
Poland	6	7
Portugal	4	4
Romania	6	6
Slovakia	4	3
Slovenia	4	n/a
Spain	7	7
Sweden	8	8
United Kingdom	6	7

[a] The numbers are rounded to the nearest full number.

[b] The data for 2009 are taken from CPEC, 'Evaluation of the European Consumer Centres Network', p. 65 (Table 3:7); Norwegian data for 2009 was provided by ECC Norway via email on 14 February 2014 (on file with the author). The following ECCs corrected their data for 2009 via email: ECC Czech Republic (12 February 2014), ECC Finland (28 March 2014), ECC Netherlands (28 March 2014) and ECC Sweden (19 November 2013) (all on file with the author).

Table 6 (*cont.*)

---

^c The data for 2013 were provided via email by ECC Austria (on 7 November 2013), ECC Belgium (12 February 2014), ECC Bulgaria (14 November 2013), ECC Croatia (13 November 2013), ECC Cyprus (18 November 2013), ECC Czech Republic (12 February 2014), ECC Denmark (15 November 2013), ECC Estonia (28 November 2013), ECC Finland (28 March 2014), ECC France (13 February 2014), ECC Greece (13 February 2014), ECC Hungary (31 March 2014), ECC Iceland (15 February 2014), ECC Ireland (13 November 2013), ECC Italy (14 February 2014), ECC Latvia (12 February 2014), ECC Lithuania (13 February 2014), ECC Luxembourg (27 March 2014), ECC Netherlands (28 March 2014), ECC Norway (14 February 2014), ECC Poland (19 February 2014), ECC Slovakia (4 December 2013), ECC Spain (17 February 2014), ECC Sweden (19 November 2013), ECC United Kingdom (6 December 2013) for the respective ECCs. In the cases of ECC Malta, ECC Romania and ECC Slovakia data was provided by the Commission via email on 10 March 2014 and in the case of ECC Germany by the Commission on 31 March 2014 (all on file with the author). No clear 2013 data was available for ECC Slovenia.

^d ECC Croatia started its operations with effect from 1 July 2013.

^e With effect from 1 January 2012 ECC Greece was restructured. Although the number of personnel could be kept, it should be noted that (according to information received from ECC Greece via email on 13 February 2014) all personnel are now unpaid volunteers (on file with the author).

primarily cover 'genuine' host organisation tasks. If one further takes into account that most ECC personnel are mainly involved in dealing with information requests and/or complaints,[43] it is hard to imagine how ECCs could easily intensify their self-promotion activities in a way that would rapidly increase consumers' ECC awareness (if the personnel situation is not considerably improved). I shall briefly return to this issue later.

The 2011 ECC-Net evaluation report on how to improve the impact of ECC-Net

The 2011 ECC-Net Evaluation report submitted to DG SANCO by the Consumer Policy Evaluation Consortium (CPEC), a group of several

---

[43] The way in which tasks is allocated among ECC personnel is not the same in all ECCs. In some ECCs all, or nearly all, personnel handle contacts, while in others there is a clear line between contact handlers (who usually comprise the majority of staff) and those who engage exclusively in other matters (e.g., accounting or IT).

consulting companies, is (thus far) the most comprehensive external evaluation on the work of ECC-Net and its ECCs. It gives useful insights to the value added by ECCs and the limitations of their current activities. The report also provides answers to potential concerns that strengthening the role of ECCs would not be worthwhile and would cost more than ECC-Net could contribute to the market.

In its evaluation, CPEC arrives at the conclusion that ECC-Net 'delivered direct financial benefits to consumers of at least 1.77 times its cost to the taxpayer during 2010'.[44] The 2011 ECC-Net Evaluation report also provides data that more directly relates to the issue of consumer confidence in cross-border B2C trade. The study explains that '29 per cent of the respondents ... reported an increase in confidence as a result of contacting the ECCs; while 19 per cent reported a fall in confidence'[45] and further notes that the vast majority of consumers who had contacted ECCs, 74 per cent, were basically 'satisfied with the quality of the service they receive[d] from the Network [ECC-Net]'.[46]

One can conclude three key things from these additional findings. First, ECC activities were mostly welcomed by consumers. Nearly three-quarters of consumers were basically happy with the *quality* of the service. Second, when comparing the percentage of consumers with increased confidence against those with decreased confidence, one can also say that overall, ECC activities have increased rather than decreased consumer confidence in cross-border B2C trade. Third, the quality of services, however, did not significantly influence the level of confidence in the B2C market, as slightly less than one-third of consumers reported an increase in confidence. Thus, the challenge is to find ways to further strengthen the impact of ECCs in general and on consumer confidence in particular. CPEC takes up this issue and lists six key issues that, according to the report, need to be addressed to strengthen the role of ECCs. The report states the six ECC issues as follows:

1) Limited resources spread thinly across a range of activities.
2) Lack of effective performance management tools.
3) The instability of funding. This arises in part from fiscal constraints facing many Member States. EU annual funding is also a cause of uncertainty.
4) The difficulty of satisfactorily closing cases and obtaining effective redress for consumers (which in turn presents a greater risk of

[44] CPEC, 'Evaluation of the European Consumer Centres Network', p. iii.
[45] *Ibid.*   [46] *Ibid.*

undermining the image of ECC-Net as well as consumer trust in the internal market more generally).

5) The vast majority (79 per cent) of EU citizens do not know where to get information and advice about cross-border shopping in the EU.

6) Lack of consistency in the quality of services across the Network.[47]

The 2011 ECC-Net Evaluation report also provides possible answers to these ECC issues.[48] Unfortunately, however, several of the suggested solutions seem to be half-hearted. For example, the report asks for an increase in the number of public promotion activities to be undertaken by ECCs.[49] At the same time the 2011 ECC-Net Evaluation report fails to ask for a general increase in personnel or funding.[50] The broadening of or increase in activities would, however, undeniably be facilitated by an increase in paid personnel and additional financial resources to properly cope with the increased workload.

Another ECC issue that asks for a more courageous solution relates to cross-border consumer redress. The aforementioned fourth ECC issue of the 2011 ECC-Net Evaluation report, which stresses '[t]he difficulty of satisfactorily closing cases and obtaining effective redress for consumers',[51] relates to the need for improved consumer redress to enhance consumer confidence in cross-border B2C trade. However, the report rules out any further direct involvement by ECCs in dispute resolution, arguing that this would be too expensive and not worth the legislative and administrative effort. Under the current structure and with their existing capabilities ECCs might indeed find it difficult to contribute more actively to the improvement of consumer redress. However, this should not mean that a stronger involvement is not worth considering (together with an increase in funding and the number of personnel). Taking into consideration that ECCs sit at a certain switch point for assisting consumers in their attempts to ensure that their rights are enforced, one should reconsider the role ECCs could play in the future. The examples of the ADR Directive and ODR Regulation show that ECCs can be ascribed with important roles in this respect.[52]

---

[47] *Ibid.*, p. 84.

[48] See *ibid.*, chapter 4 ('Unlocking the Potential of the Network: Recommendations for Improvement').

[49] *Ibid.*, p. 85.

[50] Instead, it suggests different *forms* of alternative, not necessarily additional, funding: it asks for 'multi annual funding' to facilitate long-term planning by the ECCs (*ibid.*, p. 84).

[51] *Ibid.*

[52] Article 14(2) ADR Directive and Article 7(1) ODR Regulation.

One should, in conclusion, note that, despite its inconsistencies, the in-depth analysis of the 2011 ECC-Net Evaluation report is important, because it basically confirms that ECC involvement could be improved and intensified. The following explanations will show ways to accomplish this.

Thoughts on the future of ECC-Net

To facilitate attempts to significantly increase consumer confidence in the internal market by strengthening the role of ECCs[53] (as a prime example of a facilitating intermediary in dealing with cross-border B2C issues), two key measures, in particular, are required. First, consumers' awareness of ECCs must be considerably and rapidly increased so that current ECC consumer support activities can beneficially reach a larger number of consumers. Second, ECCs should not only intensify their current activities, but also engage in additional tasks to positively impact on consumer confidence. Both measures undeniably warrant (or at least would be facilitated by) additional personnel and financial means. As explained in the previous chapter, an increase in external funding is required, at least initially. The responsibility to organise greater financial resources lies first with the Commission (it initiated ECC-Net and approves the designation of the local ECCs).[54] This could, for instance, be achieved to some extent by rechannelling existing funds from less sustainable projects to ECC-Net. In the long run, however, several new ECC services could be introduced to support their activities. Put differently, ECC could be encouraged to generate extra funds that have to be invested back into ECC activities and thus would reduce dependence on contributions from the Commission. (I will touch upon this issue briefly.)

---

[53] For a similar suggestion see U. Pachl, 'The Common European Sales Law – Have the Right Choices Been Made? A Consumer Policy Perspective', Maastricht European Private Law Institute Working Paper, No. 2012/6 (2012), p. 15, available at papers.ssrn.com/sol3/papers.cfm?abstract_id=2027455.

[54] ECC-Net falls under the competences of DG SANCO Unit B5 (ec.europa.eu/dgs/health_consumer/chart.pdf). See further CPEC, 'Evaluation of the European Consumer Centres Network', p. v, where it is explained that '[t]he ECCs are hosted by public bodies or non-profitmaking organisations which have been designated by the relevant competent authority in each of the participating countries and approved by the European Commission'. According to data provided by the Commission via email on 10 March 2014 the financial contributions have (at least in several instances) been increased over the years (on file with the author). However, in many cases the increase has not allowed any considerable expansion of the scope of ECC activities or the hiring of a significant number of additional personnel.

The starting point to increase the level of ECCs' positive impact on consumer confidence is (as just mentioned) the need to raise consumers' ECC
awareness. Although there has been a steady increase (from 11 per cent in
2006 to 15 per cent in 2011 and 22 per cent in 2013),[55] these numbers are
alarmingly low and measures should be further intensified to improve
the situation. The most effective way to speed up consumers' awareness-
raising would be – where not already existing – the launch of *extensive*
ECC promotional media campaigns (or in those countries where this has
already occurred, a further increase in such promotional activities), especially on TV, radio, the internet and in cinemas, newspapers, magazines
and flyers distributed to the public.

An increase in consumer awareness undeniably goes (at least in the
short- and medium-term) hand-in-hand with an increase in ECC contacts. As shown earlier, not only consumers' ECC awareness, but also the
number of complaints and information requests has steadily risen over the
years.[56] At the same time, however, this is a chance for ECCs to improve
their efficiency. The example of ECC France, which improved its information services provided on its website some years ago, illustrates that ECCs
using their own initiative can positively respond to this. In the French
example, the number of individual, direct information requests dropped
by half in 2012 compared with 2011, while ECC France registered a 40 per
cent increase in visitors to its website over the same period.[57] This shows
that properly offered public information can eventually lead to a decrease
in the workload with respect to certain activities and the chance for ECC
personnel to engage in additional tasks.

Several new projects could be launched by ECCs in attempts to improve
consumer confidence in the internal market. Put differently, widening the
range of activities to empower consumers would prove advantageous for
strengthening consumers' trust in cross-border B2C trade. I will briefly
discuss some examples in the following paragraphs and again in a later
section.

ECCs could, for instance, be encouraged to publish reasonably priced
consumer magazines that offer information that goes beyond basic, free
of charge information (as found, e.g., on ECC websites or in ECC information brochures). Such consumer magazines would very likely prod-
uce various effects. First, they could provide consumers with additional,

---

[55] See the references in notes 38 and 39 above.
[56] See 'ECC-Net: current status' above.
[57] European Commission, 'Help and Advice on Your Purchases Abroad – The European
Consumer Centres Network 2012 Annual Report', p. 14.

more detailed information on topics related to B2C cross-border trade.[58] Second, they could, if marketed properly, contribute to increasing consumers' ECC awareness and include information on how to access ECC websites and contact ECC offices. Third, ECCs would be able to generate additional financial means via such magazines, which could be invested back into other ECC activities.

Furthermore, in addition to organising basic consumer information events (as most ECCs already do), ECCs could organise reasonable fee-based seminars or workshops on cross-border B2C trade-related issues to generate extra financial means and to offer more detailed information. Depending on the design of such events, various positive effects could be achieved. First, consumers would be able to enjoy comprehensive consumer education. Via personal interactions with ECC representatives and other seminar participants, they could exchange experience and learn about their options to improve their knowledge of consumer rights and their enforcement. Second, ECCs could consider opening up such events to other stakeholders, for example, to other consumer support institutions, the judiciary or legal practitioners to remedy their – as discussed earlier – possible lack of legal awareness.[59] Similarly, ECCs could offer in-depth seminars and workshops to traders. Although traders can obtain legal information elsewhere (I will cover some prominent examples in the next section), ECC seminars and workshops that provide traders with invaluable consumer feedback could more probably, or at least more directly, help traders to find ways to properly meet consumer interests. As ECCs deal with cross-border B2C trade-related issues on a daily basis, ECC-organised trader events would not only improve the traders' knowledge of pertinent legislation, but would also facilitate their better understanding of consumer concerns. Eventually, enhanced interactions between ECCs and traders via such events would contribute to the accomplishment of

[58] In a similar vein is the 2011 ECC-Net Evaluation report. It asks for '[p]lacing greater emphasis on consumer awareness campaigns of a preventative nature relating to cross border issues … and consumer education initiatives to equip consumers with the skills and knowledge to participate in the internal market with confidence' (CPEC, 'Evaluation of the European Consumer Centres Network', p. 84).

[59] According to information provided by the ECC Finland via email on 30 March 2014, several ECCs already engage in certain awareness-raising activities with respect to various national third-party stakeholders (on file with the author). However, not all ECCs are active in this respect yet. Furthermore, ECCs (including those that are already active) could generally be encouraged to approach third-party stakeholders via reasonably priced seminars and workshops that go beyond existing activities to accomplish both awareness-raising with respect to those stakeholders and to generate additional financial means to further intensify ECC activities.

what the 2011 ECC-Net Evaluation report considers to be the ultimate objective of ECC consumer support: 'to reduce the number of "interested users" [i.e. of consumers who ask ECCs for legal information] because consumers ... are getting *satisfactory* service from traders selling cross border'[60] (emphasis added).

Yet another way to positively contribute to the growth of the internal market would be to staff ECCs with professional translators to offer certified language support at any stage of a B2C transaction, be it prior to the conclusion of a contract, in the course of contractual performance or at a complaints stage.[61] Just like the aforementioned seminars and workshops, translation services could also be offered to traders who would primarily fund such services, for example via annual subscriptions. In return, traders would be more likely to reach a greater number of consumers, as language support is the best way to overcome language barriers. In addition, because the services would be offered via ECCs, i.e., by institutions that actively engage in consumer support, it can be expected that consumer trust in such translations would be high. To facilitate the positive effects of ECC language support, traders who fund these activities free of charge for consumers could be granted special seals that they could use, for example, on their websites to show consumers that they employ ECC language support. Ultimately, it would be a win–win situation for all parties involved. ECCs would be vested with extra financial means, consumers would benefit from a wider selection of goods and services offered in their mother tongue and traders would be able to reach consumers in their language. Thus, such a move would remove, or at the very least reduce the detrimental effects of, a key (primarily) non-law-related disincentive for consumers to shop cross-border: language.[62]

---

[60] CPEC, 'Evaluation of the European Consumer Centres Network', p. 88.

[61] In the complex cases discussed earlier, ECCs already assist consumers with certain language support, mainly with respect to translating documents into English or the language(s) of the trader's home country ECC. However, the suggested language support could go further. It could also comprise language support at other stages of the transactional relationship between traders and consumers. With respect to dispute resolution, it could include broader tasks and could also be used for simple complaints, i.e., for cases where the involvement of ECCs (in issues other than those related to language) would not necessarily be needed.

[62] On the significance of language in cross-border B2C trade see Chapter 12, note 22 above. Language does, of course, play an important further role in a purely legal context, as several examples highlighted in Part II above showed. For a detailed comment on the importance of language in the context of international civil procedure law (especially regarding the situation in the EU) see P. Mankowski, 'Zur Regelung von Sprachfragen im europäischen Internationalen Zivilverfahrensrecht' in R. Geimer and R. A. Schütze

Further, language support could be directly incorporated in truly law-related issues.[63] One way to link it to legal issues would be to offer a two-stage standard term approval system offered to traders by ECCs in cooperation with competent private bodies/public authorities to fight the use of unfair contract terms. Traders could submit their standard terms to obtain both a substantive, legal compliance check with respect to the target countries (as a first step) and a certified translation into a foreign language (as a second step). Special seals could be used to inform consumers about the trustworthiness of preapproved standard terms. Such a system serves multiple interests. First, traders could make sure that their standard terms are in line with pertinent consumer legislation. Second, consumers, if they attempt to read the standard terms, would understand them more easily because they are written in a language they would be more likely to understand. Third, and this should not to be underestimated, it can be expected that consumers would place greater trust in standard terms that have been preapproved by consumer support bodies than those by trade associations and business support institutions, a further fact that would have a positive impact on consumer confidence in B2C transactions.[64]

These selected examples of possible additional ECC activities hopefully show that facilitating intermediaries can play an important role in creating a setting that facilitates cross-border B2C trade. To achieve this, the facilitating intermediaries approach applies relatively 'gentle' techniques that complement the second key pillar of consumer empowerment, the

---

(eds.), *Festschrift für Athanassios Kaissis zum 65. Geburtstag* (Munich: Sellier, 2012), pp. 607–28.

[63] It goes beyond the scope of this book to deal with the relationship between EU laws and language differences. For contributions to this debate see G. Ajani, '"A Better Coherence of EU Private Law" and Multilingualism: Two Opposing Principles?' in Schulze (ed.), *Common Frame of Reference and Existing EC Contract Law*, pp. 33–43; N. Urban, 'One Legal Language and the Maintenance of Cultural and Linguistic Diversity?', *European Review of Private Law*, 8 (2000), 51–7; G. Dannemann, S. Ferreri and M. Graziadei, 'Language and Terminology' in Twigg-Flesner (ed.), *The Cambridge Companion to European Union Private Law*, pp. 70–84; V. Heutger, 'A More Coherent European Wide Legal Language', *European Integration Online Papers*, 8 (2004), available at www.eiop.or.at/eiop/pdf/2004-002.pdf.; Mankowski, 'Zur Regelung von Sprachfragen im europäischen Internationalen Zivilverfahrensrecht'.

[64] It should not go unmentioned that standard terms compliance checks in cooperation with ECCs already occur in some instances, for example, by business support member bodies of the Enterprise Europe Network. However, it is justified to say that an enhanced institutionalised approach in combination with a comprehensive language support element and ECC quality seals would be a more effective method of raising consumer confidence.

legislative approach (i.e., the framework of proper procedural and substantive consumer laws to raise consumer confidence and facilitate B2C trade). Before turning to this second empowerment category, I would like to briefly discuss in the next section some general advantages traders could extract from proper facilitating (trader) support.

The Enterprise Europe Network (EEN)

As shown at various points in this book, the lack of information regarding consumer law is not a phenomenon limited to consumers – in various instances other stakeholders too lack sufficient knowledge. In 2013, the 9th Consumer Conditions Scoreboard, for example, explained that '[m]any retailers [were] not aware of their legal obligations towards consumers'.[65] This fact can have a negative impact on consumer access to justice 2.0, as consumers – regardless of the level of their own legal knowledge – might face problems when complaining to traders who do not possess proper legal knowledge and who are of the firm belief that their mistaken legal understanding is in fact correct.

Some recent evidence of traders' poor knowledge of pertinent consumer legislation is found in the 2013 Eurobarometer report on retailers' attitudes towards cross-border trade and consumer protection (2013 Cross-border Retailer Eurobarometer report).[66] The study evaluated traders' knowledge with respect to core consumer law-related issues, such as guarantee periods or advertising and marketing restrictions by comparing annual test results from 2009 to 2012. The data revealed in the 2013 Cross-border Retailer Eurobarometer report shows cause for alarm. Despite a small improvement over the years, traders' knowledge of pertinent legislation is still far from satisfactory. In several cases, on average, (far) less than half of the traders were able to correctly answer core consumer law-related questions.[67] Even the highest-scoring

---

[65] European Commission, 'The Consumer Conditions Scoreboard: Consumers at Home in the Single Market – 9th edition', p. 44.

[66] TNS Political & Social, 'Retailers' Attitudes towards Cross-border Trade and Consumer Protection', Flash Eurobarometer 359, (2013), available at ec.europa.eu/public_opinion/flash/fl_359_en.pdf.

[67] See, for example, the knowledge of consumer legislation in respect of guarantee issues, where there was an average increase in informed traders by 3 per cent within the testing period from on average 26 to 29 per cent (see TNS Political & Social, 'Retailers' Attitudes towards Cross-border Trade and Consumer Protection', p. 55); see further the question relating to the legal regulation of making exaggerated statements in advertisements, which was correctly answered by 32 per cent of respondent traders in 2009 and 34 per cent in 2012 (*ibid.*, p. 59).

question (is a trader allowed to 'describ[e] a product as "free" when it is only available free of charge to customers calling a premium rate phone number'?) was only correctly answered by just over two-thirds of traders (68 per cent).[68]

The 2013 Cross-border Retailer Eurobarometer report further explains that traders' knowledge of applicable consumer legislation on cross-border issues is more underdeveloped than that regarding purely domestic cases, and that many traders do not know how or where to obtain information on foreign legislation. This necessarily leads to the question of how to enhance traders' knowledge of applicable consumer legislation on cross-border transactions. One extensively discussed option with respect to cross-border B2C sales contracts, which the Commission and Parliament[69] assume would be of help, would be the introduction of the CESL, an optional sales law regime that standardises some legal issues in certain cross-border transactions. Without going into detail again, it is sufficient to note here that the CESL would not provide a complete solution to improve the situation to the desired level.[70]

A better way to overcome traders' lack of knowledge of pertinent legislation would be to offer traders easily accessible information on consumer law issues. I have already mentioned the potential of comprehensive trader seminars organised by ECCs. National chambers of commerce and comparable institutions could also intensify their activities. With respect to the latter, the Enterprise Europe Network (EEN), in particular, could play an important coordinating role.

EEN was founded in 2008 at the initiative of the Directorate-General for Enterprise and Industry (DG ENTR) and is the result of the merger of two older frameworks, the Euro Info Centre Network and Innovation Relay Centre Network. The primary aim of EEN is to facilitate business opportunities throughout the EU. Calling itself a 'one-stop shop for all your business needs'[71] EEN tries to provide businesses with support in various areas via a network of several hundred local contact points (mostly chambers of commerce and other local business support institutions)

---

[68] *Ibid.*, p. 66. The 2013 Cross-border Retailer Eurobarometer report further shows that the level of information differs strongly between the Member States. In many cases the gap in the number of informed traders between the Member State with the highest percentage of informed traders and the Member State with the lowest percentage exceeded 50 percentage points (*ibid.*, chapter III.1).

[69] For details see Chapter 10 above.

[70] See 'Fifth assumption: the CESL will guarantee a high(er) standard of consumer protection without exception' in Chapter 10 above.

[71] www.een.ec.europa.eu/about/mission.

within and outside the EU.[72] One of the services offered by EEN and its local branches is to provide traders with information on EU legislation. Although consumer laws are not the key area in this respect, providing traders with consumer law-related information falls under the competence of EEN and its contact points.[73]

Similar to the earlier discussion of the ECC-Net, EEN and its branches could undeniably make a stronger contribution to the enhancement of the internal market if they increased their efforts in *actively* advising traders on the legal situation in cross-border trade. This would clearly constitute a softer (compared with attempts to defragment national laws as discussed in Part III of this book), but nonetheless efficient and effective, alternative to tackle some key obstacles for traders to engage more actively in cross-border B2C trade.[74]

The legislative approach

The procedural law pillar

Facilitating intermediaries are of undeniable importance to improve consumer access to justice 2.0, as they aim to ensure that consumers can obtain invaluable legal information and support in B2C issues. However, this is only one approach to empower consumers and needs to be complemented by a suitable legislative framework of procedural and substantive laws to address consumers' justified legal interests and concerns.

With respect to procedural laws, I have explained that their success depends on various complementary factors. Two intrinsic issues regarding enforcement tools – I earlier defined them as awareness and skills/experience – can directly be addressed by the facilitating intermediaries approach outlined above. In contrast, the more technical factors[75] of availability, usability and effectiveness can be primarily regulated by legislative means, as they strongly interconnect with the way procedural laws are designed. In this section, I will try to express some thoughts on how to improve the overall situation with respect to these three factors in the context of consumer law.

---

[72] For details see www.een.ec.europa.eu/about/branches.

[73] Confirmed by the Commission (DG ENTR – Unit D2) via email on 4 March 2014 (on file with the author).

[74] For comments on those obstacles see 'Third assumption: the CESL is clearly needed' in Chapter 10 above.

[75] For general comments see 'Recapitulating the situation with respect to procedural EU (consumer) laws' in Chapter 12 above.

The availability of enforcement tools refers to the question of whether consumers can use existing instruments to have their rights enforced. The ADR Directive and ODR Regulation are two recent examples of attempts to improve the availability of enforcement tools. One cannot deny that both add certain value. However, as I explained in Part II of this book, they also illustrate the fact that enforcement tools often lack availability.

When it comes to the availability of consumer ADR, i.e., the *actual* possibility for consumers to start an ADR proceeding, I explained that one of the biggest practical issues relates to the actual launchability of consumer ADR. The ADR Directive asks Member States to introduce ADR mechanisms, but it fails to give consumers a true chance to choose ADR over litigation. Pursuant to the ADR Directive ADR must only be made available on a voluntary basis for both consumers *and* traders.[76] In other words, unless Member States vest consumers with the power to single-handedly choose between litigation and ADR, consumers would not have a true opportunity to launch an ADR proceeding without the trader's consent. Unfortunately, this renders the basic aim of the ADR Directive, namely to offer consumers fast and inexpensive ways to have their rights enforced, quite ineffective. A better way to answer consumer needs would be the introduction of a one-sided mandatory mechanism, which could – just like litigation – be launched by consumers *without* the trader's approval, i.e., solely based on the consumer's decision to submit the dispute to ADR[77] (under the condition that it fulfils the qualitative requirements under the ADR Directive).

Another, softer way to improve the availability of ADR would be to grant special seals (ADR seals) to traders who are willing to submit B2C disputes to independent ADR bodies (as covered by the ADR Directive). The granting could be revoked in cases where the respective trader does not comply with the outcome of ADR or if the trader refuses to have a dispute resolved by ADR. If made properly visible, for example, on the traders' websites or in the traders' business premises, ADR seals would easily indicate to consumers whether they could seek recourse in ADR should a legal issue arise.

One of the most regrettable issues with respect to ODR is the limitation of its availability under the ODR Regulation to online sales and service

---

[76] See Article 1 ADR Directive and 'The ADR Directive (2013)' in Chapter 4 above.

[77] For similar arguments from a consumer access to justice perspective see M. Barendrecht, P. Kamminga and J. H. Verdonschot, 'Priorities for the Justice System: Responding to the Most Urgent Problems of Individuals', TISCO Working Paper Series on Civil and Conflict Resolution Systems, No. 1/2008 (2008), pp. 39–40 (available at papers.ssrn.com/sol3/papers.cfm?abstract_id=1090885).

contracts. Although ODR is of undeniable importance in resolving disputes arising from online B2C transactions, it would have made sense to expand the scope to also include disputes from contracts that are not concluded online (if ODR would be able to facilitate attempts to reach a solution by non-litigative means in such cases). It is incomprehensible why the ODR Regulation was not designed to also cover such situations.

The issue of the usability of enforcement tools refers to the mechanism itself, more precisely to *how* it can be used. The example discussed earlier of the 2013 Small Claims Regulation Proposal shows the attempts of the Commission to fix several (but not all) usability shortcomings of the ESCP. Another example that touches upon the usability issue is the debate with respect to the possible introduction of a Member State obligation to install consumer compensatory collective redress mechanisms. Fears of possible misuse showed the necessity to discuss how a respective mechanism should work, i.e., how it can be used. In Part II of this book, I dealt with this issue in detail and arrived at a scenario that (to take proper account of the misuse risk without limiting the practical meaningfulness of compensatory collective redress) took a differentiated approach with tailor-made tools to sue for scattered damages and mass damages.[78]

The third technical factor of the success of enforcement tools is what I called earlier the effectiveness of devices. Put simply, effectiveness is realised if traders are willing to comply with the binding outcome of dispute resolution (regardless of whether it originates from litigation or not) without the need for consumers to take further steps. To improve the sometimes lacking effectiveness and to complement traditional means of enforcing binding dispute resolution results, certain additional measures could be taken to improve the situation. Two approaches, in particular, seem worthy of discussion. They could either be introduced as standalone mechanisms or combined in one broader approach.

The softer of the two approaches is the introduction of what one could call a compliance quality tracking system. Traders who refuse to comply with binding decisions or agreements without good reason could be put on pan-European 'non-compliance lists', which, similar to insolvency or execution registers in some Member States, could be made publicly accessible free of charge.[79] Non-compliance lists could be structured in a multi-level way, ideally ranking traders in terms of rates of non-compliance

---

[78] For details see 'The Answer(s)' in Chapter 5 above.

[79] In a similar vein are some suggestions of the 2011 ECC-Net Evaluation report. The report, inter alia, recommends the mandatory 'sharing of information and evidence about specific traders (who have breached legislation [with enforcement bodies]' (CPEC,

with binding dispute resolution results[80] (evaluated over a certain period of time). They could function as an invaluable, reliable (official)[81] source of information about the trustworthiness of traders.

Non-compliance lists could, for example, be maintained and published on ECC websites and those of other facilitating intermediaries; the websites would be regularly updated with data from courts and other dispute resolution bodies. To respond to possible name-and-shame concerns, entries in non-compliance lists could be deleted if listed traders show a change in compliance attitude, for example, if a certain period has elapsed since the most recent respective non-compliance incident has occurred without any new non-compliance incident that followed.

As traders are expected to be interested in avoiding a justified loss of reputation, it can be assumed that most traders would be likely to try their best to comply with binding dispute resolution results to avoid an entry in a non-compliance list. However, one must also bear in mind that such a system would have some gaps. Information regarding certain traders might be missing, for example, if a trader has just entered the market and has not yet been exposed to dispute resolution schemes that can provide binding results. Hence, not being listed on non-compliance lists does not automatically imply that traders are necessarily trustworthy.

'Evaluation of the European Consumer Centres Network', p. 83, where the report also emphasises the importance of the possible deterrent effects on other traders in enhancing legal compliance and strengthening consumer confidence in the market).

[80] It cannot be expected that every trader possesses sufficient legal knowledge to rightly assess the possibility of losing a case. In other words: not every case where traders are unwilling to satisfy consumer claims without binding decisions/agreements made or facilitated by third parties is worth being listed, as the legal question at hand might not be easily resolved without third-party intervention. If every binding decision and agreement (and not just non-compliance) were to be listed, this could lead to unreasonable pressure on traders to forego their rights to have B2C disputes solved (or the reaching of such results facilitated) by third parties. This explains why, in principle, entries in non-compliance lists should be limited to those cases where traders do not comply with legally binding (litigative and/or non-litigative) dispute resolution results. However, if necessary, one could also consider adding an additional category to non-compliance lists that would include (irrespective of whether traders 'freely' comply with the outcome of a case) traders who have received *multiple* binding dispute resolution decisions against them.

[81] In practice, the use of customer feedback evaluation is widely used in online B2C marketplaces. The prominent example of eBay illustrates this. Although such means can increase transparency and facilitate word-of-mouth advertising, and thus generally show positive effects, absolute reliability cannot be guaranteed. Occasionally, assessments could be unreasonably affected by subjective and skewed perceptions. Official sources, such as the proposed non-compliance lists, thus might add some important value to this kind of customer feedback. On the general importance (and also the possible risks) of private feedback mechanisms see Calliess and Zumbansen, *Rough Consensus and Running Code*, pp. 153–80.

Nevertheless, notorious non-complying traders (at least) would be listed, a fact that certainly adds some important value for consumers.

Another, yet harsher way to respond to traders' unjustified unwillingness to comply with obligations arising from the binding outcome of dispute resolution would be to vest certain competent authorities with the power to impose disciplinary sanctions. Disciplinary sanctions would – like the aforementioned non-compliance list entries, but unlike, for example, punitive damages – only be applicable if traders did not comply with binding dispute resolution results and would complement already existing traditional mechanisms of executing bodies. The sole purpose of disciplinary sanctions would be to improve traders' compliance with bindingly agreed or decided dispute resolution results or, in case this proves impossible in a certain number of subsequent cases, to aim to stop traders continuing their unlawful practices. Sanctions could (depending on the type of violation, the degree of non-compliance and the number of non-compliance actions) range from reminders and reprimands to fines and withdrawals of licence (where existing), shutting down companies and the introduction of special criminal sanctions imposed on traders via shortened proceedings. Fines resulting from disciplinary sanctions could, for example, be used to financially support the work of ECCs and other third-party intermediaries to further enhance consumer support under the facilitating intermediaries approach discussed earlier.

The substantive law pillar

Substantive consumer laws are a further important contributing factor to consumer empowerment, as they set the outer parameters for the protective level in B2C situations. Put differently, they define the substantive rights consumers have. The core issues in this respect especially revolve around the extent of the subject matter to regulate at the EU level, the level of harmonisation to be used for EU consumer laws and the interplay between the two. The issue of how EU consumer laws are generally drafted and adopted adds a further interesting factor to the discussion.

To begin with, when looking at the question of how EU consumer legislation is created, it should again be noted that the precept of the commonly used Article 114(3) TFEU that consumer legislation has to follow a 'high level of protection' does not necessarily mean that a proper consideration of consumer concerns always occurs in the drafting of consumer laws. The 2011 ECC-Net Evaluation report discussed earlier deals with concerns of consumers reported to ECCs and comes to the conclusion that it would be advisable 'to optimise the feedback of the ECCs for policy-making purposes'[82] to introduce more appropriate consumer laws. However, taking a look at some more recent legislative drafts, it is questionable whether enhanced communication alone would lead to a considerable improvement. One earlier discussed example is that of the drafting of the CESL Regulation Proposal. Because of the pressure from the business sector and the tasks as predefined by the Commission, the role that BEUC (as the main representative of consumer interests in the drafting process of the CESL) was 'allowed' to play in drafting the wording of the CESL Regulation Proposal was (from a consumer perspective) not fully satisfactory.[83] Communication itself was not the issue: BEUC actively contributed in the process and submitted detailed statements. Instead, the problem was that several of BEUC's concerns were not taken seriously and its advice (that was based on reasonable consumer interests) was to some extent disregarded.[84] These observations explain that not only the means of communication, but also the actual 'weight' of duly delivered consumer interests should be improved.

Substantive EU consumer law making faces additional dilemmas. The gradual policy shift from minimum towards greater maximum harmonisation, paired with the attempt to regulate an increasing number of subject matters at a centralised level can undeniably cause unwanted effects for national legislative policies.[85] In addition to the risk of Member States losing their means to answer the needs of 'their' consumers via national legislation that goes beyond the protective level determined by EU laws,[86] the reasonableness of a stronger reliance on maximum harmonisation is questionable on (at least) four further counts.

---

[82] CPEC, 'Evaluation of the European Consumer Centres Network', p. 87.

[83] See 'The genesis of the proposal on a Common European Sales Law or: the long and winding road' in Chapter 10 above. For examples and further details see Wrbka, 'The Dilemma of European Consumer Representation in Deliberative Networks', pp. 159–66.

[84] See the examples in Wrbka, 'The Dilemma of European Consumer Representation in Deliberative Networks'.

[85] Weatherill explains as follows: '[Maximum h]armonization policy, as an exercise in distributing competences to regulate the market between the EU and its Member States, is an intensely sensitive legal and political matter' (S. Weatherill, *Cases & Materials on EU Law* (10th edn, Oxford University Press, 2012), p. 558).

[86] In a similar vein is Thomas Wilhelmsson's following explanation: 'I have argued the case against total harmonisation. I think there are good reasons for a view according to which there should be space for national legislation and judicial activity, to cater for local needs and expectations and to preserve the required experimentalism and dynamism in the system as well as its political democratic legitimacy' (T. Wilhelmsson, 'European Consumer Law: Theses on the Task of the Member States' in Micklitz (ed.), *Verbraucherrecht in Deutschland*, p. 62). See further Weatherill, who claims that 'there

First, as Michael Stürner (with the help of several German provisions) shows, fully harmonised consumer legislation can lead to a situation where consumers fall under different levels of protection depending on the type of transaction, even if such types are quite similar to each other.[87] This surely proves detrimental to raising the level of legal simplification and certainty for consumers.

Second, the maximum harmonisation of consumer laws can (in some cases) be criticised from the perspective of the principle of proportionality, as in various instances it is questionable whether fully harmonised EU laws are the least restrictive means available to accomplish the strengthening of the internal market.[88] Approaches that involve less interference, such as a combination of the facilitating intermediaries approach and the legislative approach (as discussed in this book), would be a viable alternative to enhance the internal market (and at the same time would avoid too high a degree of interference with national legislation).

Third, maximum harmonisation can lead to legislative stagnation both at a national level and the EU level. This can be explained by the fact that under maximum harmonisation, both the national refinement of EU standards and legal competition among national systems to further develop legislative standards and to provide EU policy makers with well-tested examples become impossible. Götz Schulze refers to this situation as a state of 'fossilisation' (*Versteinerung*)[89] and stresses the importance

are reasons to be fearful that a rejection of minimum harmonisation is dangerously antagonistic to the preservation of local regulatory autonomy and space for experimentation, which are of value to the EU' (S. Weatherill, 'Minimum Harmonisation as Oxymoron? The Case of Consumer Law' in *ibid.*, p. 33). For a similar statement see further Heico Kerkmeester's conclusion that the 'diversity of preferences of citizens pleads for decentralized lawmaking' (H. Kerkmeester, 'Uniformity of European Contract Law; An Economic Study between Logic and Fact' in Smits (ed.), *The Need for a European Contract Law*, p. 86). Grundmann adds a justice perspective to this argumentation. He argues as follows: 'The more broadly the full harmonization mode is used, the more frustrated become the advantages that the national systems of law have achieved because of centuries of scholarship and practice—advantages in substantive justice and in legal certainty' (Grundmann, 'The EU Consumer Rights Directive', 126).

[87] Stürner, 'Das Konzept der Vollharmonisierung', p. 7.

[88] Stürner argues in a similar vein (see *ibid.*, pp. 6–7). Another critical comment (from the perspective of proportionality) on full harmonisation in the area of consumer law (in general) can be found in Loos, 'Full Harmonisation As a Regulatory Concept, pp. 64–5. For further examples of a proportionality critique in the context of the CESL see, e.g., the literature in Chapter 10, note 180 above.

[89] G. Schulze, 'Ökonomik der Vollharmonisierung im Gemeinschaftsprivatrecht' in Gsell and Herresthal (eds.), *Vollharmonisierung im Privatrecht* (Tübingen: Mohr Siebeck, 2009), p. 81.

of retaining legislative competition between the Member States to offer consumers the best possible legal protection.[90] Eliminating legislative competition between the Member States would counteract the obvious advantages of producing 'innovative, practically proven legal solutions, which could be adopted by later harmonisation'.[91] In other words and with respect to EU law making, maximum harmonisation would mean that national testing fields for substantive consumer laws would cease to exist in the quest to find the most suitable protective regime in the EU.[92] Thus, the further development of EU laws with the help of national innovations would become very difficult.

Fourth, and especially in connection with and in light of the aforementioned way consumer laws are made, maximum harmonisation stands for the risk of a certain race to the bottom, or – put differently – for the risk that comparatively strong national consumer protection regimes are (at least in some instances) weakened. Especially because of pressure from business interest representatives in the law-making process, it is almost impossible to reach a level of consumer protection that meets the standards of all twenty-eight Member States,[93] even in cases where the level of EU consumer protection is objectively high. In the context of the CRD, I have already explained that EU law making faces the need to make strong

---

[90] *Ibid.*, p. 80.

[91] *Ibid.* (translation mine). In a similar vein are Bernard Tilleman and Bart Du Laing, who explain that '[t]he divergence of some legal rules within the European Union can in some cases even be fruitful, as the competition between different legal solutions may lead to the optimal rule' (B. Tilleman and B. Du Laing, 'Directives on Consumer Protection as a Suitable Means of Obtaining a (More) Unified European Contract Law?' in Grundmann and Stuyck (eds.), *An Academic Green Paper on European Private Law*, p. 97).

[92] Similarly, Kathrin Kroll-Ludwigs claims that 'respecting national legal diversity is a fundamental requirement [in the quest to find the best possible solutions for consumers at the pan-EU level]' (translation mine; K. Kroll-Ludwigs, 'Ein optionales Vertragsrecht – Motor oder Hemmnis für den Binnenmarkt?', *Zeitschrift für das Privatrecht der Europäischen Union*, 9 (2012), 181, 188). The argument that there is legal competition among the Member States is not uncontested, though. While Rühl explains that 'empirical evidence shows that there is regulatory competition in contract law [also between the Member States]' (G. Rühl, 'Regulatory Competition in Contract Law: Empirical Evidence and Normative Implications', *European Review of Contract Law*, 9 (2013), 61, 89), Stefan Vogenauer argues that 'the mere coexistence of various regulatory regimes does not necessarily lead to a competitively driven lawmaking' and that '[c]laims that regulatory competition leads to … a laboratory for innovations … must … be treated with caution in the areas of contract and dispute resolution' (S. Vogenauer, 'Regulatory Competition through Choice of Contract Law and Choice of Forum in Europe: Theory and Evidence', *European Review of Private Law*, 21 (2013), 13, 77).

[93] A similar view is expressed in M. Tamm, *Verbraucherschutzrecht* (Tübingen: Mohr Siebeck, 2011), p. 241, where Tamm comments that the level of consumer protection

compromises to reconcile the opposing interests of affected stakeholders represented in the Commission, the Parliament and the Council. I have shown that the Council (as the voice of the Member States' interests) criticised the Commission's plan to completely base the CRD on maximum harmonisation – the Council was of the view that this was incompatible with the interests of some national law and policy makers that went beyond the proposed standard. On the other hand, the changes suggested by the Council were not compatible with the position of the business sector, which – as explained earlier – traditionally has a strong influence on EU policy-making. In the end, both sides had to make concessions. From the viewpoint of consumers, and although the Council was able to secure national consumer interests to some extent, the result of the three-party negotiations meant a certain weakening of consumer rights in several Member States.[94] Put generally, one can also say that EU consumer laws are based on a common denominator of involved interests, which

would be 'cemented at a lower level' (translation mine). See further *ibid.*, pp. 242–3, where she critically comments on the term 'high level of protection' as used in inter alia Article 114(3) TFEU. For critical observations in the context of the CRD Proposal see K. Trietz, 'Verbesserung des Verbraucherschutzes durch die Vollharmonisierung? – Ein Praxisbericht im deutsch-polnischen Verhältnis' in Stürner (ed.), *Vollharmonisierung im Europäischen Verbraucherrecht?*, pp. 197–208; Howells and Schulze, 'Overview of the Proposed Consumer Rights Directive', p. 25, where Howells and Schulze conclude as follows: '[T]he level of the current minimum harmonisation cannot be the level of a future full harmonisation'; Loos, 'Full Harmonisation As a Regulatory Concept', p. 77 referring to the risk of a 'race to the bottom' inherent to full harmonisation. For comments on the race to the bottom in general see further Mittwoch, *Vollharmonisierung und Europäisches Privatrecht*, pp. 138–9; C. Herresthal, 'Vertragsrecht' in K. Langenbucher (ed.), *Europäisches Privat- und Wirtschaftsrecht* (3rd edn, Baden-Baden: Nomos, 2013), pp. 84–5. For a discussion in the context of the CESL see 'Fifth assumption: the CESL will guarantee a high(er) standard of consumer protection without exception' in Chapter 10 above.

[94] For some examples see Chapter 9, note 50 and the text at Chapter 9, notes 63 and 64. The CESL is another good example of how consumer interests are not always fully satisfied. Admittedly, and as I explained in my analysis of the CESL, the CESL Proposal represents a relatively high level of protection. However, it does not necessarily meet the existing protective standards in every possible situation for which it was crafted. For several Member States this means that in certain situations consumers might *not* be as well protected as under their traditional national sales law (if, as can be expected, the protective level of the CESL is not raised). Hence, with respect to some issues and some Member States, the protective standards would be lower compared with their traditional sales regimes, should the CESL (as supported by the Parliament) become reality. In a similar vein, e.g., Grundmann, 'The EU Consumer Rights Directive', 125, where Grundmann concludes as follows: 'If already for reasons of consumer protection, full harmonization and the CESL approach are by no means superior to minimum harmonisation (quite the contrary).'

takes account of the essential claims of the stakeholders, without fully satisfying their interests.[95]

My scepticism towards maximum harmonisation does not mean, however, that I consider the research conducted in the course of the creation of laws meaningless. The contrary is in fact true. The research is clearly important to identify issues of insufficient regulation at the national level. But for the purposes of increasing consumer confidence and to strengthen the internal market, it would make more sense to answer with minimum harmonisation that follows a truly high level of protection (high-level minimum harmonisation) than with maximum harmonisation.[96] High-level minimum harmonisation could remedy insufficient national provisions, i.e., provisions that are below the standard envisaged by EU policy makers. As a result of the high level of protection it would in principle not be necessary for Member States to introduce consumer-friendlier provisions and thus could achieve an appropriate level of defragmentation. At the same time, however, high-level minimum harmonisation would avoid depriving Member States of their means to go beyond the harmonised level (in the exceptional case that they consider it necessary). It would further ensure that regulatory competition among Member States would, as Rühl frames it with reference to contract law, 'induce a race to the top … [and not] the bottom'.[97] Finally, one should not underestimate the practical importance of giving Member States the leeway to adjust their consumer laws to a higher level. Different national approaches might be the result of meeting local needs with regard to legal, economic, cultural, or language-related characteristics and might thus be necessary to satisfy the interests and needs of 'their' consumers.[98] From the viewpoint of consumer confidence building and empowering consumers with the help of substantive laws, depriving national legislators of their means to respond to those needs would only be counterproductive.

---

[95] In a similar vein is Stürner, who explains as follows: 'It is obvious that different stakeholders pursue different, sometimes opposing interests, which obviously makes it difficult to reach a reasonable compromise' (translation mine) (Stürner, 'Das Konzept der Vollharmonisierung', p. 3).

[96] For a similar argumentation in favour of high-level minimum harmonisation and against maximum harmonisation (from the perspective of consumer confidence) see Howells and Schulze, 'Overview of the Proposed Consumer Rights Directive', pp. 3–8.

[97] Rühl, 'Regulatory Competition in Contract Law', 89.

[98] In a similar vein is Loos's critique of maximum harmonisation in Loos, 'Full Harmonisation as a Regulatory Concept', p. 74, where he concludes as follows: 'Full harmonisation could … lead to a reduction in consumer protection. In this respect, minimum harmonisation may provide better results, as consumers will *at least* receive the

With respect to the CESL, one further substantive law-related issue should not go unmentioned. Some commentators argue that the CESL is needed because some, especially newer, Member States (trailing Member States) require stronger legislative 'guidance' with respect to consumer issues because their national laws are said to lag behind EU standards. With the help of the CESL those Member States would, it is hoped, be able to catch up to the legal standard(s) of the legally more advanced Member States (advanced Member States).[99] There is no evidence, however, that the CESL would actually be needed for this. While it is surely to be welcomed that trailing Member States are supported in their quest to introduce more advanced substantive laws, the commentators fail to persuasively explain why this could not be achieved by other means. EU laws that take the aforementioned high-level minimum harmonisation approach could lead to similar effects, without preventing advanced Member States from further developing legislative standards. With such an approach, the

---

protection that is offered by the directive [or EU law in general], but Member States are allowed to introduce or maintain more protective rules if they see the need for that, given the national circumstances, priorities and preferences.'

[99] See, for example, P. Varul, 'The Impact of the Harmonisation of Private Law on the Reform of Civil Law in the New Member States' in Brownsword *et al.* (eds.), *The Foundations of European Private Law*, p. 291, where Paul Varul concludes his analysis of the private law situation in the new(er) Member States as follows: '[I]t is especially the new Member States of Central and Eastern Europe who should politically support the idea of the CFR as an optional instrument.' For a comment on the possible introduction of a comprehensive, binding instrument from the Polish perspective see E. Łętowska and A. Wiewiórowska-Domagalska, 'The Common Frame of Reference – The Perspective of a New Member State', *European Review of Contract Law*, 3 (2007), 277, 293, where the authors argue as follows: 'If [a set of guidelines] is combined with a binding but flexible instrument that orders and systematises European consumer law, it may have a very positive influence on the functioning of the entire system of Polish law.' For general comments on the development of Eastern European contract laws (and their shortcomings) see N. Reich, 'Transformation of Contract Law and Civil Justice in the New EU Member Countries: The Example of the Baltic States, Hungary and Poland' in F. Cafaggi (ed.), *The Institutional Framework of European Private Law* (Oxford University Press, 2006), pp. 271–302. For general comments on the interplay between EU consumer law and the consumer laws in the newer Member States see A. Bakardjieva Engelbrekt, 'The Impact of EU Enlargement on Private Law Governance in Central and Eastern Europe: the Case of Consumer Protection' in Cafaggi and Muir-Watt (eds.), *Making European Private Law*, pp. 98–137; R. Welser (ed.), *Konsumentenschutz in Zentral- und Osteuropa* (Vienna: Manz, 2010); M. Karanikic *et al.* (eds.), *Modernising Consumer Law: The Experience of the Western Balkan* (Baden-Baden: Nomos, 2012). For a comment on recent attempts of trailing Member States to revise their private laws see E. Hondius, 'Recodification of Private Law: Central and Eastern Europe Set the Tone', *European Review of Private Law*, 21 (2013), 897–906.

legislative interests of both trailing Member States *and* advanced Member States could be satisfied.

Another, yet softer way to assist national legislators includes recommendations to implement EU model laws at the national level.[100] Such model laws, the DCFR providing a good example, would ideally be based on the findings of comparative research and could cover relatively comprehensive issues, as model laws would not pose any direct threat to existing national consumer legislation. Because of their representativeness and comprehensiveness, they could offer trailing Member States strong arguments for being followed at the national level.[101] The question remains, of course, whether model laws would be convincing enough for trailing Member States to follow.

Introducing (binding) underlying general principles (as, for example, broadly discussed and suggested by Collins) can be understood as a further potential alternative, and are worth considering. In his *The European Civil Code*, Collins comprehensively comments on differences in culture, moral values and language within the EU[102] and comes to the conclusion that instruments with detailed rules that directly (or as I explained in the case of the CESL: factually) replace national rules (at least in some

---

[100] On this possibility see Howells *et al.* (eds.), 'Optional Soft Law Instrument on EU Contract Law for Businesses and Consumers'.

[101] In a similar vein see Łętowska and Wiewiórowska-Domagalska, 'The Common Frame of Reference', 293. For a practical example for the representativeness of the DCFR see M. Grochowski, 'The Practical Potential of the DCFR Judgment of the Swedish Supreme Court (Högsta domstolen) of 3 November 2009, Case T3-08', *European Review of Contract Law*, 9 (2013), 96–104. For the argument that model laws are to a certain extent of actual relevance when revising national private laws see T. Břicháček, 'The Impact of EU Law on the Recodification of Private Law in the Czech Republic', *Zeitschrift für das Privatrecht der Europäischen Union*, 9 (2012), 160, 163, where Tomáš Břicháček claims that the DCFR occasionally was 'of inspiration' for the Czech legislator.

[102] On these differences see further Walter van Gerven's more general comment that '[i]t is important to remember the huge diversity between the legal families within the EU, which exists not only with regard to content but also, and even more so, with regard to style and mentalities' (W. van Gerven, 'Bringing (Private) Laws Closer to Each Other at the European Level' in Cafaggi (ed.), *The Institutional Framework of European Private Law*, pp. 75). For a comment on the differences of EU legal cultures from a Finnish perspective see L. Järvinen, 'Finland and the European Civil Code: A Case for Convergence?', *European Review of Private Law*, 21 (2013), 507–72. For further comments on differences in legal culture and the importance from the perspective of stronger harmonisation see, for example, R. Sefton-Green, 'Cultural Diversity and the Idea of a European Civil Code' in Hesselink (ed.), *The Politics of a European Civil Code*, pp. 71–88; J. M. Smits, 'Legal Culture as Mental Software, or: How to Overcome National Legal Culture?' in Wilhelmsson *et al.* (eds.), *Private Law and the Many Cultures of Europe*, pp. 141–51; for a strong argumentation in favour of respecting and safeguarding the legal cultures in

broader subject areas) are counterproductive. Instead, policy makers should consider the introduction of a European Civil Code composed of commonly shared principles that, at the national level, have to be followed in law making. A European Civil Code that introduces generally applicable common legal principles would, according to Collins, be a useful tool to accomplish the striking of a proper balance between EU and national interests.[103] On the one hand, it would 'breathe life into the ideal of a European Social Model and ... help to construct a sense of a European political identity which will help to unify and empower Europe'.[104] On the other hand, it would also serve justified national interests. Collins frames it as follows:

> Out of respect for cultural diversity among the peoples of Europe, however, it is important not to insist upon uniformity in private law. It is possible to obtain the necessary level of shared identity without requiring agreement on exactly the same detailed rules. A European Civil Code stated at the level of general principles would be sufficient to provide the

the EU see the contributions by Pierre Legrand. For one of his most strongly worded responses to attempts to defragment national laws – in particular in response to arguments by one of the strongest advocates of a European Civil Code, Christian von Bar – see P. Legrand, 'Antivonbar', *Journal of Comparative Law*, 1 (2006), 13–40. For another comment that advises caution see L. Kähler, 'Conflict and Compromise in the Harmonization of European Law' in Wilhelmsson *et al.* (eds.), *Private Law and the Many Cultures of Europe*, pp. 125–39. For observations from the perspective of procedural law see P. Rott, 'Effective Enforcement and Different Enforcement Cultures in Europe' in *ibid.*, pp. 305–21. For arguments that respecting legal diversity and agreeing on common fundamental principles are not necessarily two irreconcilable ideas see K. Tuori, 'Legal Culture and the General Societal Culture' in *ibid.*, pp. 21–35.

[103] On the possible use of binding general legal principles see further C. Semmelmann, 'Legal Principles in EU Law as an Expression of a European Legal Culture between Unity and Diversity', Maastricht European Private Law Institute Working Paper, No. 2012/7 (2012), p. 17 (available at papers.ssrn.com/sol3/papers.cfm?abstract_id=2049245), where Constanze Semmelmann concludes as follows: '[L]egal principles appear as alternative instruments of harmonisation ... They take diversity in a multi-layered system of governance as their starting point and, due to their open-texture, a softer form of unity as their goal.'

[104] Collins, *The European Civil Code*, p. 144. On a different occasion he adds as follows: 'This [European] civil code must be a code of principles that provide a gravitational pull towards harmonization rather than attempt through detailed rules to impose uniformity' (H. Collins, 'Why Europe Needs a Civil Code', *European Review of Private Law*, 21 (2013), 907, 921). For some of his additional comments on the importance of general legal principles for EU contract/private law see H. Collins, 'The Alchemy of Deriving General Principles of Contract Law from European Legislation: In Search of the Philosopher's Stone', *European Review of Contract Law*, 2 (2006), 213–26; H. Collins, 'The Constitutionalization of European Private Law As a Path to Social Justice?' in Micklitz (ed.), *The Many Concepts of Social Justice in European Private Law*, pp. 133–66.

common standards for the foundation of a transnational civil society and a shared European identity. Agreement on more detailed legislative proposals would always be welcome as a way of both supporting the goal of enhancing a shared identity and at the same time contributing to the internal market agenda.[105]

With respect to the issues at hand, i.e., in the context of substantive consumer and contract law making, this call could be effectively achieved by a combination of binding common legal principles and the aforementioned high-level minimum harmonisation approach regarding more concrete issues. This approach would enshrine quality standards and align national legislation at a higher standard without stopping Member States that wish to go further (in those exceptional cases that they would find it necessary to do so).

These alternative options would not only allow trailing Member States to update their national laws (the high-level minimum harmonisation approach and a European Civil Code with binding principles would even oblige them to do so), but they would also allow advanced Member States to develop (from a consumer perspective) further enhanced substantive laws. This would clearly satisfy both the call for a stronger alignment of national laws and the interests of consumers to enjoy the best possible protection.

[105] Collins, *The European Civil Code*, pp. 144–5.

16

Lessons to be drawn

The argumentation in this book has hopefully shown the need to properly approach EU consumer protection from various angles if one wants to achieve the highest possible degree of consumer satisfaction or 'well-being' (as discussed in this book). EU consumer law has steadily grown and developed over the last few decades. However, the approaches taken have been mostly one-sided and in themselves show considerable flaws.

With an increasing number of legislative efforts in recent years, EU consumer law has arrived at a crossroads. The question to be answered is which route to take. Pursuing the current course would clearly broaden the framework of procedural devices in a relatively short period of time and further centralise substantive law making in core areas. With respect to procedural laws, one has to say that the idea of introducing new, additional ways to enforce consumer rights should not be rejected per se. However, it is not so much the number of enforcement tools, but rather the way that they are designed that determines the overall success of rights enforcement. I referred to this as the factors of awareness, skills/experience, availability, usability and effectiveness. All five must be satisfied to maximise the success of rights enforcement.

With respect to substantive consumer laws, I mainly questioned whether EU policy makers with their current efforts (that focus on centralised regulation at an increasingly fully harmonised level and as comprehensively as possible) could really achieve true consumer confidence, which is essential to strengthen the internal market. In this respect, I touched upon numerous issues and explained that the related approaches taken at the EU level do not always necessarily serve this endeavour, i.e., the enhancement of consumers' trust in the internal market.

I arrived at the general conclusion that strengthening the internal market requires a different solution. The focus should be put on properly addressing consumer interests and consumer needs. I showed that consumer empowerment as a key mechanism for achieving what I defined as consumer access to justice 2.0 plays a crucial role in overcoming consumer distrust in and consumer frustration regarding cross-border B2C trade. Ensuring that consumer interests are protected in the most suitable way by both procedural and substantive law and supporting traders in their attempt to engage more actively in cross-border B2C trade are not mutually exclusive targets. Clearly, not only consumers but also traders could benefit from a mitigation of consumer disincentives with respect to cross-border B2C situations.

In the course of this book I have identified several core issues that must be taken into account when choosing an alternative approach, ideally in a combined way. The most important tasks in this respect include the guarantee of appropriate, efficient and fast consumer support (facilitating intermediaries approach) on the one hand and on the other, high-level minimum harmonised substantive provisions and standards (optionally in combination with general principles), paired with an effectual enforcement and compensation regime to guarantee legal compliance (legislative approach). In addition to these targets, EU consumer legislation should remember to also support trailing Member States, which need to 'catch up' in the field of consumer protection. This should be achieved without abolishing the competitive legislative market for national and EU policy makers via maximum harmonisation. If the Commission and the Union legislator are ready and willing to follow the advice given in this book, it can be expected that EU consumer law could really be on the right track to effectively contribute to both consumer confidence and the enhancement of the internal market.

BIBLIOGRAPHY

Abdel Wahab, M. S., Katsh, E. and Rainey, D. (eds.), *Online Dispute Resolution: Theory and Practice* (The Hague: Eleven International Publishing, 2012)

Ackermann, T., Azoulai, L., Dougan, M., Hillion, C., O'Leary, S., Roth, W.-H., Smulders, B. and Van den Bogaert, S. (eds.), *Common Market Law Review* (Special Issue), 50 (2013)

Ajani, G., "'A Better Coherence of EU Private Law" and Multilinguism: Two Opposing Principles?' in Schulze, R. (ed.), *Common Frame of Reference and Existing EC Contract Law* (2nd edn, Munich: Sellier, 2009), pp. 33–43

Alexandridou, E. and Karypidou, M., 'Country Report Greece', report (2009), available at ec.europa.eu/consumers/redress_cons/gr-country-report-final.pdf

Allemeersch, B. 'Transnational Class Settlements: Lessons from Converium' in Wrbka, S. *et al.* (eds.), *Collective Actions: Enhancing Access to Justice and Reconciling Multilayer Interests?* (Cambridge University Press, 2012), pp. 364–84

Alpa, G., *Competition of Legal Systems and Harmonization of European Private Law: New Paths in a Comparative Perspective* (Munich: Sellier, 2013)

'Harmonisation of and Codification in European Contract Law' in Vogenauer, S. and Weatherill, S. (eds.), *The Harmonisation of European Contract Law: Implications for European Private Laws, Business and Legal Practice* (Oxford: Hart, 2006), pp. 149–69

'The Future of European Contract Law: Some Questions and Some Answers' in Boele-Woelki, K. and Grosheide, W. (eds.), *The Future of European Contract Law* (Alphen aan den Rijn: Kluwer Law International, 2007), pp. 3–17

Alpa, G., Conte, G., Perfetti, U. and Graf von Westphalen, F. (eds.), *The Proposed Common European Sales Law – the Lawyers' View* (Munich: Sellier, 2013)

Amato, C., 'The Europeanisation of Contract Law and the Role of Comparative Law: the Case of the Directive on Consumer Rights' in Devenney, J. and Kenny, M. (eds.), *The Transformation of European Private Law: Harmonisation, Consolidation, Codification or Chaos?* (Cambridge University Press, 2013), pp. 45–62

American Law Institute / UNIDROIT, *Principles of Transnational Civil Procedure* (Cambridge University Press, 2006)

Andenas, M. and Baasch Andersen, C. (eds.), *Theory and Practice of Harmonisation* (Cheltenham: Edward Elgar, 2011)

Andrews, P., 'Are Market Failure Analysis and Impact Assessment Useful?' in Weatherill, S. (ed.), *Better Regulation* (Oxford: Hart, 2007), pp. 49–81

Arnold, S. (ed.), *Grundlagen eines europäischen Vertragsrechts* (Munich: Sellier, 2014)

  Vertrag und Verteilung (Tübingen: Mohr Siebeck, 2014)

  'Zum Verhältnis von Rechtsphilosophie, Rechtstheorie und europäischem Vertragsrecht' in Arnold, S. (ed.), *Grundlagen eines europäischen Vertragsrechts* (Munich: Sellier, 2014), pp. 1–18

Artz, M., 'Vorschlag für eine vollharmonisierte Horizontalrichtlinie zum Verbraucherrecht' in Gsell, B. and Herresthal, C. (eds.), *Vollharmonisierung im Privatrecht* (Tübingen: Mohr Siebeck, 2009), pp. 209–18

Audi, R. (ed.), *The Cambridge Dictionary of Philosophy* (2nd edn, Cambridge University Press, 1999)

Augenhofer, S., 'Aktuelle Entwicklungstendenzen im Europäischen Verbraucherrecht' in Augenhofer, S. (ed.), *Verbraucherrecht im Umbruch* (Tübingen: Mohr Siebeck, 2012), pp. 1–30

Augenhofer, S. (ed.), *Verbraucherrecht im Umbruch* (Tübingen: Mohr Siebeck, 2012)

Backhaus, J. G., Cassone, A. and Ramello, G. B. (eds.), *The Law and Economics of Class Actions on Europe: Lessons from America* (Cheltenham: Edward Elgar, 2012)

Bakardjieva Engelbrekt, A., 'The Impact of EU Enlargement on Private Law Governance in Central and Eastern Europe: the Case of Consumer Protection' in Cafaggi, F. and Muir-Watt, H. (eds.), *Making European Private Law* (Cheltenham: Edward Elgar, 2008), pp. 98–137

  'Public and Private Enforcement of Consumer Law in Central and Eastern Europe: Institutional Choice in the Shadow of EU Enlargement' in Cafaggi, F. and Micklitz, H.-W. (eds.), *New Frontiers of Consumer Protection: The Interplay between Private and Public Enforcement* (Antwerp: Intersentia, 2009), pp. 91–136

Bakos, Y., Marotta-Wurgler, F. and Trossen, D. R., 'Does Anyone Read the Fine Print? Testing a Law and Economics Approach to Standard Form Contracts', New York University Law and Economics Research Paper, No. 195, (2009), available at papers.ssrn.com/sol3/papers.cfm?abstract_id=1443256

Bamberger, H. G. and Roth, H. (eds.), *BGB Band 3* (3rd edn, Munich: C. H. Beck, 2012)

Bar-Gill, O. and Ben-Shahar, O., 'Regulatory Techniques in Consumer Protection: A Critique of the Common European Sales Law', New York University Law and Economics Research Papers, No. 12-12 (2012), available at papers.ssrn.com/sol3/papers.cfm?abstract_id=2061148

Barba, A., 'Die italienische kollektive Schadensersatzklage zum Schutz der Verbraucher' in Casper, M. *et al.* (eds.), *Auf dem Weg zu einer europäischen Sammelklage?* (Munich: Sellier, 2009), pp. 243–58

Barendrecht, M., 'Legal Aid, Accessible Courts or Legal Information? Three Access to Justice Strategies Compared', TISCO Working Paper Series on Civil and Conflict Resolution Systems, No. 10/2010 (2010), available at papers.ssrn.com/sol3/papers.cfm?abstract_id=1706825

Barendrecht, M., Kamminga, P. and Verdonschot, J. H., 'Priorities for the Justice System: Responding to the Most Urgent Problems of Individuals', TISCO Working Paper Series on Civil and Conflict Resolution Systems, No. 001/2008 (2008), available at papers.ssrn.com/sol3/papers.cfm?abstract_id=1090885

Barral-Viñals, I., 'Consumer Complaints and Alternative Dispute Resolution: Harmonisation of the European ADR System' in Devenney, J. and Kenny, M. (eds.), *The Transformation of European Private Law: Harmonisation, Consolidation, Codification or Chaos?* (Cambridge University Press, 2013), pp. 295–315

Basedow, J., 'European Contract Law – The Case for a Growing Optional Instrument' in Schulze, R. and Stuyck, J. (eds.), *Towards a European Contract Law* (Munich: Sellier, 2011), pp. 169–72

'Freedom of Contract in the European Union', *European Review of Private Law*, 16 (2008), 901–23

'The Case for a European Contract Law' in Grundmann, S. and Stuyck, J. (eds.), *An Academic Green Paper on European Private Law* (The Hague: Kluwer Law International, 2002), pp. 147–57

Basedow, J., Hopt, K. J., Kötz, H. and Baetge, D. (eds.), *Die Bündelung gleichgerichteter Interessen im Prozess* (Tübingen: Mohr Siebeck, 2009)

Basedow, J., Hopt, K. J., Zimmermann, R. and Stier, A. (eds.), *The Max Planck Encyclopedia of European Private Law: Volume II* (Oxford University Press, 2012)

Beale, H. 'European Contract Law: the Common Frame of Reference and Beyond' in Twigg-Flesner, C. (ed.), *The Cambridge Companion to European Union Private Law* (Cambridge University Press, 2010), pp. 116–30

'Finding the Remaining Traps Instead of Unifying Contract Law' in Grundmann, S. and Stuyck, J. (eds.), *An Academic Green Paper on European Private Law* (The Hague: Kluwer Law International, 2002), pp. 67–72

'The Draft Academic Common Frame of Reference and the "Toolbox"' in Andenas, M. and Baasch Andersen, C. (eds.), *Theory and Practice of Harmonisation* (Cheltenham: Edward Elgar, 2011), pp. 115–28

'The Draft Directive on Consumer Rights and UK Consumer Law – Where Now?' in Howells, G. and Schulze, R. (eds.), *Modernising and Harmonising Consumer Contract Law* (Munich: Sellier, 2009), pp. 289–302

'The European Commission's Common Frame of Reference Project: A Progress Report', *European Review of Contract Law*, 2 (2006), 303–14

Bebchuck, L. A. and Posner, R. A., 'One-Sided Contracts in Competitive Consumer Markets' in Ben-Shahar, O. (ed.), *Boilerplate: The Foundation of Market Contracts* (Cambridge University Press, 2007), pp. 3–11

Bech Serrat, J. M., *Selling Tourism Services at a Distance: An Analysis of the EU Consumer Acquis* (Berlin: Springer, 2012)

Becher, S. I., 'Asymmetric Information in Consumer Contracts: The Challenge That Is Yet to Be Met', *American Business Law Journal*, 45 (2008), 723–74

Becher, S. I., and Unger-Aviram, E., 'The Law of Standard Form Contracts: Misguided Intuitions and Suggestions for Reconstruction', *DePaul Business & Commercial Law Journal*, 8 (2010), 199–228

Becklein, M., 'Verbesserter Zugang zum Recht für Verbraucher? Eine Bewertung der Regelungsvorschläge der EU-Kommission zur Alternativen Streitbeilegung', *Zeitschrift für das Privatrecht der Europäischen Union*, 9 (2012), 232–40

Bělohlávek, A. J., 'Autonomy in B2C Arbitration: Is the European Model of Consumer Protection Really Adequate?' *Czech (& Central European) Yearbook of Arbitration*, (2012), 17–41

B2C Consumer Protection in Arbitration (Huntington, NY: Juris, 2012)

Ben-Shahar, O., 'The Myth of the "Opportunity to Read" in Contract Law', University of Chicago Law & Economics, John M. Olin Working Paper, No. 415 (2008), available at papers.ssrn.com/sol3/papers.cfm?abstract_id=1162922

Ben-Shahar, O. (ed.), *Boilerplate: The Foundation of Market Contracts* (Cambridge University Press, 2007)

Benöhr, I., 'Alternative Dispute Resolution for Consumers in the European Union' in Hodges, C. *et al.* (eds.), *Consumer ADR in Europe* (Oxford: Hart, 2012), pp. 1–23

'Consumer Dispute Resolution after the Lisbon Treaty: Collective Actions and Alternative Procedures', *Journal of Consumer Policy*, 35 (2012), 87–110

EU Consumer Law and Human Rights (Oxford University Press, 2013)

Bergmeister, F., *Kapitalanleger-Musterverfahrensgesetz (KapMuG)* (Tübingen: Mohr Siebeck, 2009)

Betlem, G., 'Public and Private Transnational Enforcement of EU Consumer Law' in van Boom, W. H. and Loos, M. B. M. (eds.), *Collective Enforcement of Consumer Law: Securing Compliance in Europe through Private Group Action and Public Authority Intervention* (Groningen: Europa Law Publishing, 2007), pp. 37–62

BEUC, 'Alternative Dispute Resolution – European Commission's Consultation: BEUC response', position paper, X/2011/033 (2011), available at ec.europa.eu/consumers/redress_cons/adr_responses/ca_beuc_en.pdf

'Country Survey of Collective Redress Mechanisms', survey, (2011), available at www.beuc.org/custom/2011-10006-01-E.pdf

'EU Action on Collective Redress', letter to Commission President José Manuel Barroso, (2012) (on file with the author)

'Towards a European Contract Law for Consumers and Business?', response paper (2011)

Beuchler, H., *Class Actions und Securities Class Actions in den Vereinigten Staaten von Amerika* (Baden-Baden: Nomos, 2008)

Birger, N., 'Große Paketdienste wollen ihr Shop-Netz ausbauen', *Die Welt* (online), 10 November 2013, available at www.welt.de/wirtschaft/article121738270/ Grosse-Paketdienste-wollen-ihr-Shop-Netz-ausbauen.html

Boele-Woelki, K. and Grosheide, W. (eds.), *The Future of European Contract Law* (Alphen aan den Rijn: Kluwer Law International, 2007)

Bomberg, E., Peterson, J. and Corbett, R. (eds.), *The European Union: How Does It Work?* (3rd edn, Oxford University Press, 2012)

Bragg, R., 'Trade Descriptions after the Unfair Commercial Practices Directive' in Twigg-Flesner, C. *et al.* (eds.), *The Yearbook of Consumer Law 2008* (Aldershot: Ashgate, 2007), pp. 341–5

Břicháček, T., 'The Impact of EU Law on the Recodification of Private Law in the Czech Republic', *Zeitschrift für das Privatrecht der Europäischen Union*, 9 (2012), 160–3

Brömmelmeyer, C., (ed.), *Die EU-Sammelklage* (Baden-Baden: Nomos, 2013)

Brönneke, T. and Schmidt, F., 'Der Anwendungsbereich der Vorschriften über die besonderen Vertriebsformen nach Umsetzung der Verbraucherrechterichtlinie', *Verbraucher und Recht*, 29 (2014), 3–9

Brönneke, T. and Tonner, K. (eds.), *Das neue Schuldrecht: Verbraucherrechtsreform 2014* (Baden-Baden: Nomos, 2014)

Brownsword, R., 'The Theoretical Foundations of European Private Law: A Time to Stand and Stare' in Brownsword, R. *et al.* (eds.), *The Foundations of European Private Law* (Oxford: Hart, 2011), pp. 159–74

Brownsword, R., Micklitz, H.-W., Niglia, L. and Weatherill, S. (eds.), *The Foundations of European Private Law* (Oxford: Hart, 2011)

Bruns, A., Kern, C., Münch, J., Piekenbrock, A., Stadler, A. and Tsikrikas, D. (eds.), *Festschrift für Rolf Stürner zum 70. Geburtstag – Band I* (Tübingen: Mohr Siebeck, 2013)

Busch, C. 'From European Sales Law to Online Contract Law: The CESL in the European Parliament', *Zeitschrift für Europäisches Unternehmens- und Verbraucherrecht*, 2 (2013), 33–6

Buttigieg, E., *Competition Law: Safeguarding the Consumer Interest – A Comparative Analysis of US Antitrust Law and EC Competition Law* (Alphen aan den Rijn: Kluwer Law International, 2009)

Buxbaum, H. L., 'Class Actions, Conflict and the Global Economy' in Bruns, A. *et al.* (eds.), *Festschrift für Rolf Stürner zum 70. Geburtstag – Band I* (Tübingen: Mohr Siebeck, 2013), pp. 1443–53

Bydlinski, P. and Lurger, B. (eds.), *Die Richtlinie über die Rechte der Verbraucher* (Vienna: Manz, 2012)

Cafaggi, F. 'The Great Transformation. Administrative and Judicial Enforcement in Consumer Protection: A Remedial Perspective', *Loyola Consumer Law Review*, 21 (2009), 496–539

Cafaggi, F. (ed.), *The Institutional Framework of European Private Law* (Oxford University Press, 2006)

Cafaggi, F. and Micklitz, H.-W., 'Administrative and Judicial Enforcement in Consumer Protection: The Way Forward' in Cafaggi, F. and Micklitz, H.-W. (eds.), *New Frontiers of Consumer Protection: The Interplay between Private and Public Enforcement* (Antwerp: Intersentia, 2009), pp. 401–45

Cafaggi, F. and Micklitz, H.-W. (eds.), *New Frontiers of Consumer Protection: The Interplay between Private and Public Enforcement* (Antwerp: Intersentia, 2009)

Cafaggi, F. and Muir-Watt, H. (eds.), *Making European Private Law* (Cheltenham: Edward Elgar, 2008)

Calliess, C. and Ruffert, M., *EUV/AEUV* (4th edn, Munich: C. H. Beck, 2011)

Calliess, G.-P., 'Art. 6 Rome I' in Calliess, G.-P. (ed.), *Rome Regulations: Commentary on the European Rules of the Conflict of Laws* (Alphen aan den Rijn: Kluwer Law International, 2011), Article 6 Rome I para. 51

Grenzüberschreitende Verbraucherverträge (Tübingen: Mohr Siebeck, 2006)

'Online Dispute Resolution: Consumer Redress in a Global Market Place', *German Law Journal*, 7 (2006), 647–60

Calliess, G.-P. (ed.), *Rome Regulations: Commentary on the European Rules of the Conflict of Laws* (Alphen aan den Rijn: Kluwer Law International, 2011)

Calliess, G.-P. and Zumbansen, P., *Rough Consensus and Running Code: A Theory of Transnational Private Law* (Oxford: Hart, 2010)

Cámara Lapuente, S. and Terryn, E., 'Consumer Contract Law' in Micklitz, H.-W. *et al.* (eds.), *Cases, Materials and Text on Consumer Law* (Oxford: Hart, 2010), pp. 157–238

Camerer, C., Issacharoff, S., Loewenstein, G., O'Donoghue, T. and Rabin, M., 'Regulation for Conservatives: Behavioral Economics and the Case for "Asymmetric Paternalism"', *University of Pennsylvania Law Review*, 151 (2003), 1211–54

Camilleri Preziosi Advocates, 'The Collective Proceedings Act ("CP Act")', newsletter, (2012) (on file with the author)

Cane, P. and Conaghan, J. (eds.), *The New Oxford Companion to Law* (Oxford University Press, 2008)

Cap, V., 'Grundsätzliches zur Verbraucherrechte-Richtlinie: Entstehung, Anwendungsbereich, Zentralbegriffe, Harmonisierungsgrad' in Bydlinski, P. and Lurger, B. (eds.), *Die Richtlinie über die Rechte der Verbraucher* (Vienna: Manz, 2012), pp. 1–20

Caponi, R., 'The Collective Redress Action in the Italian System', *ERA Forum*, 10 (2009), 63–9

Cappelletti, M. and Garth, B., 'Access to Justice: The Worldwide Movement to Make Rights More Effective – A General Report' in Cappelletti, M. and Garth, B. (eds.), *Access to Justice – A World Survey, Book I* (Alphen aan den Rijn: Slijthoff and Noordhoff, 1978), pp. 1–124

Cappelletti, M. and Garth, B. (eds.), *Access to Justice – A World Survey, Book I* (Alphen aan den Rijn: Slijthoff and Noordhoff, 1978)

Carr, C. L., 'The Concept of Formal Justice', *Philosophical Studies*, 39 (1981), 211–26

Cartwright, P., *Consumer Protection and the Criminal Law: Law Theory and Policy in the UK* (Cambridge University Press, 2001)

Casper, M., Janssen, A., Pohlmann, P. and Schulze, R. (eds.), *Auf dem Weg zu einer europäischen Sammelklage?* (Munich: Sellier, 2009)

Chalmers, D., Davies, G. and Monti, G., *European Union Law* (2nd edn, Cambridge University Press, 2010)

Chittenden, F., Ambler, T. and Xiao, D., 'Impact Assessment in the EU' in Weatherill, S. (ed.), *Better Regulation* (Oxford: Hart, 2007), pp. 271–86

Christiansen, T. and Larsson, T. (eds.), *The Role of Committees in the Policy-Process of the European Union: Legislation, Implementation and Deliberation* (Cheltenham: Edward Elgar, 2007)

Civic Consulting, 'Cross-border Alternative Dispute Resolution in the European Union', study for IMCO, (2011), available at www.europarl.europa.eu/meetdocs/2009_2014/documents/imco/dv/adr_study_/adr_study_en.pdf

'Study on the Use of Alternative Dispute Resolution in the European Union – Final Report Part I: Main Report', study for DG SANCO, (2009), available at ec.europa.eu/consumers/redress_cons/adr_study.pdf

'Study Regarding the Problems Faced by Consumers in Obtaining Redress for Infringements of Consumer Protection Legislation – Final Report Part I: Main Report', study for DG SANCO (2008), available at ec.europa.eu/consumers/redress_cons/finalreport-problemstudypart1-final.pdf

Civic Consulting and Oxford Economics, 'Evaluation of the Effectiveness and Efficiency of Collective Redress Mechanisms in the European Union – Final Report Part I: Main Report', study for DG SANCO, (2008), available atec.europa.eu/consumers/redress_cons/finalreportevaluationstudypart1-final2008-11-26.pdf

Claes, M., 'The European Union, its Member States and their Citizens' in Leczykiewicz, D. and Weatherill, S. (eds.), *The Involvement of EU Law in Private Law Relationships* (Oxford: Hart, 2013), pp. 29–52

Clarkson, C. M. V. and Hill, J., *The Conflict of Laws* (4th edn: Oxford University Press, 2011)

Clifford Chance, 'Das neue Kapitalanleger-Musterverfahrensgesetz (KapMuG)', newsletter, (2012), available at www.cliffordchance.com/briefings/2012/11/newsletter_das_neu.html

'Introduction of Class Actions in France', newsletter, (2014), available at www.cliffordchance.com/briefings/2014/02/introduction_of_classactionsinfrance.html

Clive, E., 'An Introduction to the Academic Draft Common Frame of Reference', *ERA Forum*, 9 (2008), 13–31

Collins, H., 'Does Social Justice Require the Preservation of Diversity in the Private Laws of Member States of Europe?' in Wilhelmsson, T. *et al.* (eds.), *Private*

Law and the Many Cultures of Europe (Alphen aan den Rijn: Kluwer Law International, 2007), pp. 155–76

'Governance Implications for the European Union of the Changing Character of Private Law' in Cafaggi, F. and Muir-Watt, H. (eds.), *Making European Private Law* (Cheltenham: Edward Elgar, 2008), pp. 269–86

'The Alchemy of Deriving General Principles of Contract Law from European Legislation: In Search of the Philosopher's Stone', *European Review of Contract Law*, 2 (2006), 213–26

'The Constitutionalization of European Private Law As a Path to Social Justice?' in Micklitz, H.-W. (ed.), *The Many Concepts of Social Justice in European Private Law* (Cheltenham: Edward Elgar, 2011), pp. 133–66

The European Civil Code: The Way Forward (Cambridge University Press, 2008)

'Transaction Costs and Subsidiarity in European Contract Law' in Grundmann, S. and Stuyck, J. (eds.), *An Academic Green Paper on European Private Law* (The Hague: Kluwer Law International, 2002), pp. 269–81

'Why Europe Needs a Civil Code', *European Review of Private Law*, 21 (2013), 907–22

Collins, H. (ed.), *Standard Terms in Europe: A Basis for and a Challenge to European Contract Law* (Alphen aan den Rijn: Kluwer Law International, 2008)

Colombi Ciacchi, A., 'The Constitutionalization of European Contract Law: Judicial Convergence and Social Justice', *European Review of Contract Law*, 2 (2006), 167–80

Conrad, S., *Das Konzept der Mindestharmonisierung: Eine Analyse anhand der Verbrauchervertragsrichtlinien* (Baden-Baden: Nomos, 2004)

Consumer Policy Evaluation Consortium (CPEC), 'Assessment of the Economic and Social Impact of the Policy Options to Empower Consumers to Obtain Adequate Redress: First Analytical Report of the Green Paper on Consumer Collective Redress', report for DG SANCO, (2009) (on file with the author)

'Evaluation of the European Consumer Centres Network (ECC-Net). Final Report', report for DG SANCO, (2011), p. iii, available at ec.europa.eu/consumers/ecc/docs/final_report_cpec_en.pdf

'(External) Evaluation of the Consumer Protection Cooperation Regulation', report, (2012), available at ec.europa.eu/consumers/enforcement/docs/cpc_regulation_inception_report_revised290212_en.pdf

Corbett, R., 'Democracy in the European Union' in E. Bomberg *et al.* (eds.), *The European Union: How Does It Work?* (3rd edn, Oxford University Press, 2012), pp. 141–58

Cortés, P., 'Developing Online Dispute Resolution for Consumers in the EU: A Proposal for the Regulation of Accredited Providers', *International Journal of Law and Information Technology*, 19 (2011), 1–28

'Online Dispute Resolution for Consumers – Online Dispute Resolution Methods for Settling Business to Consumer Conflict' in Abdel Wahab, M.

S. *et al.* (eds.), *Online Dispute Resolution: Theory and Practice* (The Hague: Eleven International Publishing, 2012), pp. 139–61

Online Dispute Resolution for Consumers in the European Union (Abingdon: Routledge, 2011)

Cotterrell, R., *Law, Culture and Society: Legal Ideas in the Mirror of Social Theory* (Farnham: Ashgate, 2006)

Law's Community: Legal Theory in Sociological Perspective (Oxford University Press, 1995)

The Sociology of Law: An Introduction (London: Butterworths, 1984)

Craig, P. and de Búrca, G., *EU Law Text, Cases, and Materials* (5th edn, Oxford University Press, 2011)

Craig, P. and de Búrca, G. (eds.), *The Evolution of EU Law* (2nd edn, Oxford University Press, 2011)

Cranston, R., *How Law Works: The Machinery and Impact of Civil Justice* (Oxford University Press, 2006)

Cseres, K. J., 'Enforcement of Collective Consumer Interests: A Competition Law Perspective' in van Boom, W. H. and Loos, M. B. M. (eds.), *Collective Enforcement of Consumer Law: Securing Compliance in Europe through Private Group Action and Public Authority Intervention* (Groningen: Europa Law Publishing, 2007), pp. 125–76

Cupa, B., 'Scattered Damages: A Comparative Law Study about the Enforcement Deficit of Low-Value Damages and the Class Action Approach', *European Review of Private Law*, 20 (2012), 504–40

Curdt, T., *Kollektiver Rechtsschutz unter dem Regime des KapMuG* (Hamburg: Dr. Kovač, 2010)

Dannemann, G., Ferreri, S. and Graziadei, M., 'Language and Terminology' in Twigg-Flesner, C. (ed.), *The Cambridge Companion to European Union Private Law* (Cambridge University Press, 2010), pp. 70–84

Dannemann, G. and Vogenauer, S. (eds.), *The Common European Sales Law in Context: Interactions with English and German Law* (Oxford University Press, 2013)

De Groote, B. and De Vulder, K., 'The Unfair Commercial Practices Directive' in Howells, G. *et al.* (eds.), *The Yearbook of Consumer Law 2007* (Aldershot: Ashgate, 2007), pp. 349–79

De Hoon, M. W., 'Power Imbalances in Contracts: An Interdisciplinary Study on Effects of Intervention', TISCO Working Paper Series on Civil and Conflict Resolution Systems, No. 01/2007 (2007), available at papers.ssrn.com/sol3/papers.cfm?abstract_id=985875

Devanesan, R. and Aresty, J., 'ODR and Justice – An Evaluation of Online Dispute Resolution's Interplay with Traditional Theories of Justice' in Abdel Wahab, M. S. *et al.* (eds.), *Online Dispute Resolution: Theory and Practice* (The Hague: Eleven International Publishing, 2012), pp. 251–93

Devenney, J. and Kenny, M., 'Conclusions: The Transformation of European Private Law' in Devenney, J. and Kenny, M. (eds.), *The Transformation of European Private Law: Harmonisation, Consolidation, Codification or Chaos?* (Cambridge University Press, 2013), pp. 316–25

'The Private Law Dimension to the "State of the Union": (D)CFR/CESL Initiatives and the Europeanisation of Private Law' in Devenney, J. and Kenny, M. (eds.), *The Transformation of European Private Law: Harmonisation, Consolidation, Codification or Chaos?* (Cambridge University Press, 2013), pp. 63–77

Devenney, J. and Kenny, M. (eds.), *European Consumer Protection: Theory and Practice* (Cambridge University Press, 2012)

The Transformation of European Private Law: Harmonisation, Consolidation, Codification or Chaos? (Cambridge University Press, 2013)

Dickie, J., *Producers and Consumers in EU E-Commerce Law* (Oxford: Hart, 2005)

Dickinson, A., *The Rome II Regulation: The Law Applicable to Non-Contractual Obligations* (Oxford University Press, 2008)

The Rome II Regulation: The Law Applicable to Non-Contractual Obligations: Updating Supplement (Oxford University Press, 2010)

Do, K. T., 'Idee der Gerechtigkeit und öffentlicher Vernunftgebrauch in einer demokratischen Gesellschaft', *Rechtstheorie*, 43 (2012), 241–9

Docekal, U., Kolba, P., Micklitz, H.-W. and Rott, P., 'The Implementation of Directive 98/27/EC in the Member States – Summary of Results', study for Institute for European Business and Consumer Law, (2005) (on file with the author)

Dodds-Smith, I. and Brown, A. (eds.), *The International Comparative Legal Guide to: Class & Group Actions 2014* (London: Global Limited Group, 2013)

Dopffel, P. and Scherpe, J. M., '"Grupptalan" – Die Bündelung gleichgerichteter Interessen im schwedischen Recht' in Basedow, J. *et al.* (eds.), *Die Bündelung gleichgerichteter Interessen im Prozess* (Tübingen: Mohr Siebeck, 2009), pp. 429–51

Doralt, W., 'Strukturelle Schwächen in der Europäisierung des Privatrechts. Eine Prozessanalyse der jüngeren Entwicklungen', *Rabels Zeitschrift für ausländisches und internationales Privatrecht*, 75 (2011), 260–85

'The Optional European Contract Law and Why Success or Failure May Depend on Scope Rather Than Substance', Max Planck Private Law Research Paper, No. 11/9 (2011), available at papers.ssrn.com/sol3/papers.cfm?abstract_id=1876451

Drahozal, C. R. and Friel, R. J., 'Consumer Arbitration in the European Union and the United States', *North Carolina Journal of International Law and Commercial Regulation*, 28 (2002), 357–94

Drygala, T., Heiderhoff, B., Staake, M. and Żmij, G. (eds.), *Private Autonomy in Germany and Poland and in the Common European Sales Law* (Munich: Sellier, 2012)

Dworkin, R., *Justice for Hedgehogs* (Cambridge, MA: Harvard University Press, 2011)

ECC-Net, 'European Small Claims Procedure Report', report, (2012), available at ec.europa.eu/consumers/ecc/docs/small_claims_210992012_en.pdf

Edwards, H. T., 'Commentary: Alternative Dispute Resolution: Panacea or Anathema?', *Harvard Law Review*, 99 (1985), 668–84

Edwards, L. and Wilson, C., 'Redress and Alternative Dispute Resolution in EU Cross-Border E-Commerce Transactions', *International Review of Law Computers & Technology*, 21 (2007), 315–33

Eichholtz, S., *Die US-amerikanische Class Action und ihre deutsche Funktionsäquivalente* (Tübingen: Mohr Siebeck, 2002)

Eidenmüller, H., 'Liberaler Paternalismus', *JuristenZeitung*, 66 (2011), 814–21
'Party Autonomy, Distributive Justice and the Conclusion of Contracts in the DCFR', *European Review of Contract Law*, 5 (2009), 109–31

Eidenmüller, H., Faust, F., Grigoleit, H. C., Janssen, N., Wagner, G. and Zimmermann, R. (eds.), *Revision des Verbraucher-acquis* (Tübingen: Mohr Siebeck, 2011)
'The Common Frame of Reference for European Private Law – Policy Choices and Codification Problems', *Oxford Journal of Legal Studies*, 28 (2008), 659–708

Eidenmüller, H., Janssen, N., Kieninger E.-M., Wagner, G. und Zimmermann, R., 'Der Vorschlag für eine Verordnung über ein Gemeinsames Europäisches Kaufrecht: Defizite der neuesten Textstufe des europäischen Vertragsrechts', *JuristenZeitung*, 67 (2012), 269–320

England, I., *Corrective & Distributive Justice* (Oxford University Press, 2009)

Eterovich, F. H., *Aristotle's Nicomachean Ethics: Commentary and Analysis* (Washington, D.C.: University of America Press, 1980)

Eucken, W., *Grundsätze der Wirtschaftspolitik* (Tübingen: Mohr Siebeck, 1952)

European Commission, 'A Step forward for EU Consumers: Questions & Answers on Alternative Dispute Resolution and Online Dispute Resolution', press release, MEMO/13/193, 12 March 2013, available at europa.eu/rapid/press-release_MEMO-13-193_en.htm
'Airline Ticket Selling Websites – EU Enforcement Results. Questions and Answers', press release, MEMO/09/238, 14 May 2009, available at europa.eu/rapid/press-release_MEMO-09-238_en.htm
'Consumer Scoreboard Shows Where Consumer Conditions Are Best in Europe', press release, IP/12/510, 29 May 2012, available at europa.eu/rapid/press-release_IP-12-510_en.htm
'Consumers: Airlines Move to Clean up Ticket Selling Websites', press release, IP/09/783, 14 May 2009, available at europa.eu/rapid/press-release_IP-09-783_en.htm
'Empowering Consumers: A Record Year for the European Consumer Centres', press release, IP/14/162, 19 February 2014, available at europa.eu/rapid/press-release_IP-14-162_en.htm
'EU Clean-up on Ringtone Scams. Frequently Asked Questions', press release, MEMO/09/505, 17 November 2009, available at europa.eu/rapid/press-release_MEMO-09-505_en.htm?locale=en

'Help and Advice on Your Purchases Abroad – The European Consumer Centres Network 2012 Annual Report', report, (2013), available at ec.europa.eu/consumers/ecc/docs/report_ecc-net_2012_en.pdf

'Optional European Sales Law Receives Strong Backing by the European Parliament', press release, MEMO/14/137, 26 February 2014, available at europa.eu/rapid/press-release_MEMO-14-137_en.htm

'Shopped Online and Want Your Money back? Commission Proposal on Small Claims Helps Consumers and SMEs', press release, IP/13/1095, 19 November 2013, available at europa.eu/rapid/press-release_IP-13-1095_en.htm

'The Consumer Conditions Scoreboard: Consumers at Home in the Single Market – 9th edition', report, (2013) available at ec.europa.eu/consumers/consumer_research/editions/docs/9th_edition_scoreboard_en.pdf

European Opinion Research Group, 'European Union Citizens and Access to Justice', Special Eurobarometer 195, (2004), available at www.medsos.gr/medsos/images/stories/PDF/eurobarometer_11-04_en.pdf

'European Union Citizens and Access to Justice – Executive Summary', summary accompanying Special Eurobarometer 195, (2004) (on file with the author)

European Opinion Research Group and EOS Gallup Europe, 'Public Opinion in Europe: Views on Business-to-consumer Cross-border Trade', Standard Eurobarometer 57.2 / Flash Eurobarometer 128, (2002), available at ec.europa.eu/public_opinion/archives/ebs/ebs_175_fl128_en.pdf

European Union Agency for Fundamental Rights, 'Access to Justice in Europe: an Overview of Challenges and Opportunities', report, (2010), available at fra.europa.eu/sites/default/files/fra_uploads/1520-report-access-to-justice_EN.pdf

Everling, U. and Roth, W.-H. (eds.), *Mindestharmonisierung im Europäischen Binnenmarkt* (Baden-Baden: Nomos, 1997)

Fairgrieve, D. and Howells, G., 'Collective Redress Procedures – European Debates', *International and Comparative Law Quarterly*, 52 (2009), 379–409

Fauvarque-Cosson, B., 'European Contract Law Through and Beyond Pluralism: The Case of an Optional Instrument' in Niglia, L. (ed.), *Pluralism and European Private Law* (Oxford: Hart, 2013), pp. 95–107

Fauvarque-Cosson, B. and Mazeaud, D. (eds.), *European Contract Law – Materials for a Common Frame of Reference: Terminology, Guiding Principles, Model Rules* (Munich: Sellier, 2008)

Fenwick, M., Van Uytsel S. and Wrbka, S. (eds.), *Networked Governance, Transnational Business & the Law* (Heidelberg: Springer, 2014)

Ferrari, F., 'Uniform Law' in J. Basedow *et al.* (eds.), *The Max Planck Encyclopedia of European Private Law: Volume II* (Oxford University Press, 2012), p. 1732

Ferrari, F., Kieninger, E.-M., Mankowski, P., Otte, K., Saenger, I., Schulze, G. and Staudinger, A. (eds.), *Internationales Vertragsrecht* (2nd edn, Munich: C. H. Beck, 2012)

Fleischacker, S., *A Short History of Distributive Justice* (Cambridge, MA: Harvard University Press, 2004)

Fleischer, H., 'Optionales europäisches Privatrecht (»28. Modell«)', *Rabels Zeitschrift für ausländisches und internationales Privatrecht*, 76 (2012), 235–52

Fornasier, M., '»28.« versus »2. Regime« – Kollisionsrechtliche Aspekte eines optionalen europäischen Vertragsrechts', *Rabels Zeitschrift für ausländisches und internationales Privatrecht*, 76 (2012), 401–42

Francioni, F., 'The Rights of Access to Justice under Customary International Law' in Francioni, F. (ed.), *Access to Justice as a Human Right* (Oxford University Press, 2007), pp. 1–55

Francioni, F. (ed.), *Access to Justice as a Human Right* (Oxford University Press, 2007)

Freeman, S., *Rawls* (Abingdon: Routledge, 2007)

Freeman, S. (ed.), *John Rawls – Collected Papers* (Cambridge, MA: Harvard University Press, 1999)

The Cambridge Companion to Rawls (Cambridge University Press, 2003)

Frenk, N. and Boele-Woelki, K., 'Die Verbandsklage in den Niederlanden' in Basedow, J. *et al.* (eds.), *Die Bündelung gleichgerichteter Interessen im Prozess* (Tübingen: Mohr Siebeck, 2009), pp. 213–51

Freshfields Bruckhaus Deringer, 'France Adopts Class Action', newsletter, (2014), available at www.freshfields.com/uploadedFiles/SiteWide/Knowledge/Briefing%20Class%20Action_VGB.pdf

Fronková, L., 'The New Directive on Consumer Protection: Objectives from the Perspective of the EU and the Member States' in Schulte-Nölke, H. and Tichý, L. (eds.), *Perspectives for European Consumer Law: Towards a Directive on Consumer Rights and beyond* (Munich: Sellier, 2010), pp. 91–6

Galanter, M., 'Afterword: Explaining Litigation', *Law & Society Review*, 9 (1975), 347–68

'Why the "Haves" Come out Ahead: Speculations on the Limits of Legal Change', *Law and Society Review*, 9 (1974), 95–160

Garner, B. A. (ed.), *Black's Law Dictionary* (9th edn, St. Paul, MN: Thomson Reuters, 2009)

Gebauer, M., 'Europäisches Vertragsrecht als Option – der Anwendungsbereich, die Wahl und die Lücken des Optionalen Instruments', *Zeitschrift für das Privatrecht der Europäischen Union*, 8 (2011), 227–36

Gebauer, M. (ed.), *Gemeinsames Europäisches Kaufrecht – Anwendungsbereich und kollisionsrechtliche Einbettung* (Munich: Sellier, 2013)

Geimer, R. 'Art. 5 EuGVVO' in Geimer, R. and Schütze, R. A. (eds.), *Europäisches Zivilverfahrensrecht* (3rd edn, Munich: C. H. Beck, 2010) Article 5 EuGVVO para. 232

Geimer, R. and Schütze, R. A. (eds.), *Europäisches Zivilverfahrensrecht* (3rd edn, Munich: C. H. Beck, 2010)

(eds.), *Festschrift für Athanassios Kaissis zum 65. Geburtstag* (Munich: Sellier, 2012)

German Bundestag, 'Zwölfter Zwischenbericht der Enquete-Kommission "Internet und digitale Gesellschaft" – Verbraucherschutz', report, (2013) (on file with the author)

Giliker, P., '"Copy out" and the Transposition of the Consumer Rights Directive into UK Law: Implementing a Maximum Harmonisation Directive', unpublished conference paper presented at 'DMU/Exeter Colloquium: Reshaping The Landscape Of Consumer Law And Policy', De Montfort University, 4 April 2014 (on file with the author)

'The Draft Common Frame of Reference and European Contract Law: Moving from the "Academic" to the "Political"' in Devenney, J. and Kenny, M. (eds.), *The Transformation of European Private Law: Harmonisation, Consolidation, Codification or Chaos?* (Cambridge University Press, 2013), pp. 23–44

Gillette, C. P., 'Rolling Contracts as an Agency Problem', *Wisconsin Law Review*, (2004), 679–722

Gómez, F., 'Some Law and Economics of Harmonizing European Private Law' in Hartkamp, A. S. *et al.* (eds.), *Towards a European Civil Code* (4th edn, Alphen ann den Rijn: Kluwer Law International, 2011), pp. 401–26

'The Harmonization of Contract Law through European Rules: A Law and Economics Perspective', *European Review of Contract Law*, 4 (2008), 2–30

Gómez, F., and Ganuza, J. J., 'The Economics of Harmonising Private Law Through Optional Rules' in Niglia, L. (ed.), *Pluralism and European Private Law* (Oxford: Hart, 2013), pp. 177–97.

Gomez-Herrera, E., Martens, B. and Turlea, G., 'The Drivers and Impediments for Cross-border e-Commerce in the EU', Joint Research Centre, Institute for Prospective Technological Studies, Digital Economy Working Paper, 2013/02 (2013), available at ftp.jrc.es/EURdoc/JRC78588.pdf

Goriely, T., 'The Government's Legal Aid Reforms' in Zuckerman, A. A. S. and Cranston, R. (eds.), *Essays on 'Access to Justice'* (Oxford: Clarendon Press, 1995), pp. 346–69

Gramatikov, M., Barendrecht, M., Laxminarayan, M., Verdonschot, J. H., Klaming, L. and van Zeeland, C., *A Handbook for Measuring the Costs and Quality of Access to Justice* (Apeldoorn: Maklu, 2010)

Graver, K., 'A Study of the Consumer Ombudsman Institution in Norway with Some References to the Other Nordic Countries – I: Background and Description', *Journal of Consumer Policy*, 6 (1986), 1–23

Greenwood, J., *Interest Representation in the European Union* (3rd edn, Basingstoke: Palgrave Macmillan, 2011)

Grochowski, M., 'The Practical Potential of the DCFR Judgment of the Swedish Supreme Court (Högsta domstolen) of 3 November 2009, Case T3-08', *European Review of Contract Law*, 9 (2013), 96–104

Grønmo, S. and Ölander, F., 'Consumer Power: Enabling and Limiting Factors', *Journal of Consumer Policy*, 14 (1991), 141–69

Grübler, U., *Digitale Güter und Verbraucherschutz: Eine Untersuchung am Beispiel des Online-Erwerb von Musikdownloads* (Baden-Baden: Nomos, 2010)

Grundmann, S., 'European Contract Law(s) of What Colour?', *European Review of Contract Law*, 1 (2005), 184–210

'The EU Consumer Rights Directive: Optimizing, Creating Alternatives, or a Dead End?', *Uniform Law Review*, 118 (2013), 98–127

'The Future of Contract Law', *European Review of Contract Law*, 7 (2011), 490–527

'The Optional European Code on the Basis of the Acquis Communitaire – Starting Point and Trends', *European Law Journal*, 10 (2004), 698–711

Grundmann, S. and Stuyck, J. (eds.), *An Academic Green Paper on European Private Law* (The Hague: Kluwer Law International, 2002)

Gsell, B., 'Vollharmonisiertes Verbraucherkaufrecht nach dem Vorschlag für eine Horizontalrichtlinie' in Gsell, B. and Herresthal, C. (eds.), *Vollharmonisierung im Privatrecht* (Tübingen: Mohr Siebeck, 2009), pp. 219–45

Gsell, B. and Herresthal, C. (eds.), *Vollharmonisierung im Privatrecht* (Tübingen: Mohr Siebeck, 2009)

Hager, G., *Strukturen des Privatrechts in Europa* (Tübingen: Mohr Siebeck, 2012)

Hahn, J.-U. (ed.), *Gemeinsames Europäisches Kaufrecht: Moderner Ansatz oder praxisferne Vision?* (Munich: C. H. Beck, 2012)

Halfmeier, A., Rott, P. and Feess, E., *Kollektiver Rechtsschutz im Kapitalmarktrecht: Evaluation des Kapitalanleger-Musterverfahrensgesetzes* (Frankfurt: Frankfurt School Verlag, 2010)

Hall, E., Howells, G. and Watson, J., 'The Consumer Rights Directive – An Assessment of Its Contribution to the Development of European Consumer Contract Law', *European Review of Contract Law*, 8 (2012), 139–66

Halm, T., 'Die Umsetzung der EU-Verbraucherrechterichtlinie – Kommt ein grundlegender Umbruch im neuen Jahr?', *Verbraucher und Recht*, 29 (2014), 1–2

Haloush, H., *Online Alternative Dispute Resolution* (Saarbrücken: Verlag Dr. Müller, 2008)

Halson, R. and Campbell, D., 'Harmonisation and its Discontents: A Transaction Costs Critique of European Contract Law' in Devenney, J. and Kenny, M. (eds.), *The Transformation of European Private Law: Harmonisation, Consolidation, Codification or Chaos?* (Cambridge University Press, 2013), pp. 100–30

Hammerl, A., '§ 5b' in Kosesnik-Wehrle, A. M. (ed.), *Konsumentenschutzgesetz (KSchG)* (3rd edn, Vienna: Manz, 2010), § 5b paras. 6–7

Hartkamp, A. S., Hesselink, M., Hondius, E., Mak, C. and du Perron, E. (eds.), *Towards a European Civil Code* (4th edn, Alphen ann den Rijn: Kluwer Law International, 2011)

Harvey, C. and Schillig, M., 'Consequences of an Ineffective Agreement to Use the Common European Sales Law', *European Review of Contract Law*, 9 (2013), 143–62

Haß, D., *Die Gruppenklage: Wege zur prozessualen Bewältigung von Massenschäden* (Munich: VVF, 1996)

Haupt, S., 'An Economic Analysis of Consumer Protection in Contract Law', *German Law Journal*, 4 (2003), 1137–64

Hauser, P., *Eingriffsnormen in der Rom I-Verordnung* (Tübingen: Mohr Siebeck, 2012)

Heiderhoff, B., 'Art 6 Rom I-VO' in Rauscher, T. (ed.), *Europäisches Zivilprozess- und Kollisionsrecht: EuZPR / EuIPR –Kommentar* (Munich: Sellier, 2011), Article 6 paras. 51–2

'CESL – A Chance for True Freedom of Contract for the Consumer' in Drygala, T. *et al.* (eds.), *Private Autonomy in Germany and Poland and in the Common European Sales Law* (Munich: Sellier, 2012), pp. 77–94

Gemeinschaftsprivatrecht (2nd edn, Munich: Sellier, 2007)

Heinz, W. and Kim, Y.-W. (eds.), *Aktuelle Rechtsprobleme in Japan, Deutschland und Korea* (Konstanz: KOPS, 2009)

Heirbaut, D. and Storme M. E., 'The Historical Evolution of European Private Law' in Twigg-Flesner, C. (ed.), *The Cambridge Companion to European Union Private Law* (Cambridge University Press, 2010), pp. 20–32

Heiss, H. and Downes, N., 'Non-Optional Elements in an Optional European Contract Law. Reflections from a Private International Law Perspective', *European Review of Private Law*, 13 (2005), 693–712

Helberger, N., Loos, M. B. M, Guibault, L., Mak, C. and Pessers, L., 'Digital Content Contracts for Consumers', *Journal of Consumer Policy*, 36 (2013), 37–57

Heldeweg, M. A., 'Supervisory Governance: The Case of the Dutch Consumer Authority', *Utrecht Law Review*, 2 (2006), 67–90

Heller A., *Beyond Justice* (Oxford: Basil Blackwell, 1987)

'Rights, Modernity, Democracy', *Cardozo Law Review*, 11 (1990), 1377–91

Hensler, D. H., 'The Globalization of Class Actions: An Overview', *The ANNALS of the American Academy of Political and Social Science*, 622 (2009), 7–29

Herresthal, C., 'Vertragsrecht' in Langenbucher, K. (ed.), *Europäisches Privat- und Wirtschaftsrecht* (3rd edn, Baden-Baden: Nomos, 2013), pp. 69–201

Herrnfeld, H.-H., 'Artikel 114 AEUV' in Schwarze, J. (ed.), *EU-Kommentar* (3rd edn, Baden-Baden: Nomos, 2012), Artikel 114 para. 96

Hess, B., Reuschle, F. and Rimmelspacher, B. (eds.), *Kölner Kommentar zum KapMuG: Kommentierung der prozessualen Vorschriften und der Anspruchsgrundlagen* (Cologne: Heymanns, 2008)

Hesselink, M. W., 'A Technical "CFR" or a Political Code? – An Introduction' in Hesselink, M. W. (ed.), *The Politics of a European Civil Code* (The Hague: Kluwer Law International, 2006), pp. 3–8

CFR & Social Justice (Munich: Sellier, 2008)

'How to Opt into the Common European Sales Law? Brief Comments on the Commission's Proposal for a Regulation', Amsterdam Law School Legal

Studies Research Paper, No. 2011–43 (2011), available at papers.ssrn.com/ sol3/papers.cfm?abstract_id=1950107 (reprinted in *European Review of Private Law*, 20 (2012), 195–212)

'SMEs in European Contract Law' in Boele-Woelki, K. and Grosheide, W. (eds.), *The Future of European Contract Law* (Alphen aan den Rijn: Kluwer Law International, 2007), pp. 349–71

'The Politics of a European Civil Code: Who Has an Interest in What Kind of Contract Law for Europe?' in Grundmann, S. and Stuyck, J. (eds.), *An Academic Green Paper on European Private Law* (The Hague: Kluwer Law International, 2002), pp. 181–91

'The Politics of a European Civil Code' in Hesselink, M.W. (ed.), *The Politics of a European Civil Code* (The Hague: Kluwer Law International, 2006), pp.143–70

Hesselink, M. W. (ed.), *The Politics of a European Civil Code* (The Hague: Kluwer Law International, 2006)

Heutger, V., 'A More Coherent European Wide Legal Language', *European Integration Online Papers*, 8 (2004), available at www.eiop.or.at/eiop/pdf/2004-002.pdf

Hill, J., *Cross-Border Consumer Contracts* (Oxford University Press, 2008)

Hillman, R. A., 'Online Consumer Standard Form Contracting Practices: A Survey and Discussion of Legal Implications' in Winn, J. K. (ed.), *Consumer Protection in the Age of the 'Information Economy'* (Aldershot: Ashgate, 2006), pp. 283–311

Hix, S. and Høyland, B., *The Political System of the European Union* (3rd edn, Basingstoke: Palgrave Macmillan, 2011)

Hodges, C., 'Collectivism: Evaluating the Effectiveness of Public and Private Models for Regulating Consumer Protection' in van Boom, W. H. and Loos, M. B. M. (eds.), *Collective Enforcement of Consumer Law: Securing Compliance in Europe through Private Group Action and Public Authority Intervention* (Groningen: Europa Law Publishing, 2007), pp. 207–28

'Current Discussions on Consumer Redress: Collective Redress and ADR', *ERA Forum*, 13 (2012), 11–33

The Reform of Class and Representative Actions in European Legal Systems: A New Framework for Collective Redress in Europe (Oxford: Hart, 2009)

Hodges, C., Benöhr, I. and Creutzfeldt-Banda, N., 'Consumer-to-Business ADR Structures: Harnessing the Power of CADR for Dispute Resolution and Regulating Market Behaviour', report for the Foundation for Law, Justice and Society, (2012), available at www.fljs.org/files/publications/ConsumerADR-PolicyBrief.pdf

Hodges, C., Benöhr, I. and Creutzfeldt-Banda, N. (eds.), *Consumer ADR in Europe* (Oxford: Hart, 2012)

Hodges, C., Creutzfeldt-Banda, N. and Benöhr, I., 'The Hidden World of Consumer ADR – Redress and Behaviour', report for the Foundation for Law, Justice and Society, (2011), available at www.fljs.org/files/publications/Hodges-Banda-Benohr_ConsumerADR-Report.pdf

Hodges C. and Money-Kyrle, R., 'Safeguards in Collective Actions', report for the Foundation for Law, Justice and Society, 2012, available at www.fljs.org/files/publications/Collective-Actions.pdf

Hodges, C. and Stadler, A. (eds.), *Resolving Mass Disputes* (Cheltenham: Edward Elgar, 2013)

Hodges, C., Vogenauer, S. and Tulibacka, M. (eds.), *The Costs and Funding of Civil Litigation: A Comparative Perspective* (Oxford: Hart, 2010)

Hofmeister, L. K., *Online Dispute Resolution bei Verbraucherverträgen: Rechtlicher Rahmen und Gestaltungsmöglichkeiten* (Baden-Baden: Nomos, 2012)

Honderich, T. (ed.), *The Oxford Companion to Philosophy* (2nd edn, Oxford University Press, 2005)

Hondius, E., 'From "Toolbox" to Academic Standard: The Current and Future Status of the Draft Common Frame of Reference' in Brownsword, R. *et al.* (eds.), *The Foundations of European Private Law* (Oxford: Hart, 2011), pp. 531–54

'Recodification of Private Law: Central and Eastern Europe Set the Tone', *European Review of Private Law*, 21 (2013), 897–906

Hörnle, J., *Cross-Border Internet Dispute Resolution* (Cambridge University Press, 2009)

'Encouraging Online Dispute Resolution in the EU and Beyond – Keeping Costs Low or Standards High?', Queen Mary School of Law Legal Studies Research Papers, No. 122/2012 (2012), available at papers.ssrn.com/sol3/papers.cfm?abstract_id=2154214

'Online Dispute Resolution in Business to Consumer E-commerce Transactions', *The Journal of Information, Law and Technology* (online journal), 2 (2002), available at www2.warwick.ac.uk/fac/soc/law/elj/jilt/2002_2/hornle/

Horwitz, A. and Wasserman, M., 'Formal Rationality, Substantive Justice, and Discrimination', *Law and Human Behavior*, 4 (1980), 103–15

Howells, G., 'Cy-près for Consumers: Ensuring Class Action Reforms Deal with "Scattered Damage"' in Steele, J. and van Boom, W. H. (eds.), *Mass Justice: Challenges of Representation and Distribution* (Cheltenham: Edward Elgar, 2011), pp. 58–72

'European Consumer Law – the Minimal and Maximal Harmonisation Debate and Pro Independent Consumer Law Competence' in Grundmann, S. and Stuyck, J. (eds.), *An Academic Green Paper on European Private Law* (The Hague: Kluwer Law International, 2002), pp. 73–80

'European Contract Law Reform and European Consumer Law – Two Related But Distinct Regimes', *European Review of Contract Law*, 7 (2011), 173–94

'Product Liability: A History of Harmonization' in Hartkamp, A. S. *et al.* (eds.), *Towards a European Civil Code* (4th edn, Alphen ann den Rijn: Kluwer Law International, 2011), pp. 889–902

'The Potential and Limits of Consumer Empowerment by Information', *Journal of Law and Society*, 32 (2005), 349–70

'The Rise of European Consumer Law – Whither National Consumer Law?', *Sydney Law Review*, 28 (2006), 63–88

'Unfair Commercial Practices – Future Directions' in Schulze, R. and Schulte-Nölke, H. (eds.), *European Private Law – Current Status and Perspectives* (Munich: Sellier, 2011), pp. 133–44

Howells, G. and Borghetti, J.-S. 'Product Liability' in Micklitz, H.-W. *et al.* (eds.), *Cases, Materials and Text on Consumer Law* (Oxford: Hart, 2010), pp. 439–98

Howells, G. and Pilgerstorfer, M., 'Product Liability' in Twigg-Flesner, C. (ed.), *The Cambridge Companion to European Union Private Law* (Cambridge University Press, 2010), pp. 257–72

Howells, G. and Reich, N., 'The Current Limits of European Harmonisation in Consumer Contract Law', *ERA Forum*, 12 (2011), 39–57

Howells, G. and Schulze, R., 'Overview of the Proposed Consumer Rights Directive' in Howells G. and Schulze, R. (eds.), *Modernising and Harmonising Consumer Contract Law* (Munich: Sellier, 2009), pp. 3–25

Howells, G. and Schulze, R. (eds.), *Modernising and Harmonising Consumer Contract Law* (Munich: Sellier, 2009)

Howells, G. and Weatherill, S., *Consumer Protection Law* (2nd edn, Aldershot: Ashgate, 2005)

Howells, G., Micklitz, H-W. and Reich, N. (eds.), 'Optional Soft Law Instrument on EU Contract Law for Businesses and Consumers', study for BEUC, (2011), available at www.beuc.org/custom/2011-09955-01-E.pdf

Howells, G., Micklitz, H.-W. and Wilhelmsson, T., *European Fair Trading Law: The Unfair Commercial Practices Directive* (Farnham: Ashgate, 2006)

Howells, G., Nordhausen, A., Parry, D. and Twigg-Flesner C. (eds.), *The Yearbook of Consumer Law 2007* (Aldershot: Ashgate, 2007)

Howells, G., Ramsay, I., Wilhelmsson, T. and Kraft, D. (eds.), *Handbook of Research on International Consumer Law* (Cheltenham: Edward Elgar, 2010)

Illmer, M., 'Art. 6 Rome II' in Huber, P. (ed.), *Rome II Regulation* (Munich: Sellier, 2011), Art. 6 Rome II para. 5

IMCO, 'Overview of Existing Collective Redress Schemes in EU Member States', report (2011), available at www.europarl.europa.eu/document/activities/cont/201107/20110715ATT24242/20110715ATT24242EN.pdf

Jacoby, J., 'Perspectives on Information Overload', *Journal of Consumer Research*, 10 (1984), 432–5

Jansen, N., 'The Authority of an Academic "Draft Common Frame of Reference"' in Micklitz, H.-W. and Cafaggi, F. (eds.), *European Private Law after the Common Frame of Reference* (Cheltenham: Edward Elgar, 2010), pp. 147–72

Janssen, A., 'Auf dem Weg zu einer europäischen Sammelklage?' in Casper, M. *et al.* (eds.), *Auf dem Weg zu einer europäischen Sammelklage?* (Munich: Sellier, 2009), pp. 3–16

Järvinen, L., 'Finland and the European Civil Code: A Case for Convergence?', *European Review of Private Law*, 21 (2013), 507–72

Johnston, A. and Unberath, H., 'European Private Law by Directives: Approach and Challenges' in Twigg-Flesner, C. (ed.), *The Cambridge Companion to European Union Private Law* (Cambridge University Press, 2010), pp. 85–100

Johnston, J. S., 'The Return of Bargain: An Economic Theory of How Standard-Form Contracts Enable Cooperative Negotiation between Businesses and Consumers', *Michigan Law Review*, 104 (2006), 857–98

Jørgensen, S., *On Justice and Law* (Aarhus University Press, 1996)

Jud, B. and Wendehorst, C., 'Position Paper – Vienna Conference on the Proposal for a Directive of the European Parliament and of the Council on Consumer Rights, COM(2008) 614 final' in Jud, B. and Wendehorst, C. (eds.), *Neuordnung des Verbraucherprivatrechts in Europa* (Vienna: Manz, 2009), pp. 189–96

Jud, B. and Wendehorst, C. (eds.), *Neuordnung des Verbraucherprivatrechts in Europa / Zum Vorschlag einer Richtlinie über Rechte der Verbraucher* (Vienna: Manz, 2009)

JURI, 'Report on the Proposal for a Regulation on a Common European Sales Law', report, 24 September 2013, available at www.europarl.europa.eu/document/activities/cont/201309/20130925ATT71873/20130925ATT71873EN.pdf

Juškys, A. and Ulbaitė, N., 'Alternative Dispute Resolution for Consumer Disputes in the European Union: Current Issues and Future Opportunities', *Issues of Business and Law*, 4 (2012), 25–34

Kahl, W., 'AEUV Art. 114' in Calliess, C. and Ruffert, M. (eds.), *EUV/AEUV* (4th edn, Munich: C. H. Beck, 2011), Art. 114 AUEV para. 58

Kähler, L., 'Conflict and Compromise in the Harmonization of European Law' in Wilhelmsson, T. *et al.* (eds.), *Private Law and the Many Cultures of Europe* (Alphen aan den Rijn: Kluwer Law International, 2007), pp. 125–39

Kahnemann, D., *Thinking, Fast and Slow* (London: Allen Lane, 2011)

Karanikic, M., Micklitz, H.-W. and Reich, N. (eds.), *Modernising Consumer Law: The Experience of the Western Balkan* (Baden-Baden: Nomos, 2012)

Karr, K., *Democracy and Lobbying in the European Union* (Frankfurt: Campus, 2007)

Kathrein, G., 'Europäisches Vertragsrecht – Österreichische Haltung' in Schulze, R. (ed.), *Common Frame of Reference and Existing EC Contract Law* (2nd edn, Munich: Sellier, 2009), pp. 297–308

Kathrein, G. and Schoditsch, T., '§ 5b KSchG' in H. Koziol *et al.* (eds.), *Kurzkommentar zum ABGB* (4th edn, Vienna: Springer, 2014), § 5b KSchG, para. 2

Kaufmann-Kohler, G. and Schultz, T., *Online Dispute Resolution: Challenges for Contemporary Justice* (The Hague: Kluwer Law International, 2004)

Keirse, A. L. M., 'European Impact on Contract Law: A Perspective on the Interlinked Contributions of Legal Scholars, Legislators and Courts to the Europeanization of Contract Law', *Utrecht Law Review*, 7 (2011), 34–51

Keirse, A. L. M. and Loos, M. B. M. (eds.), *Alternative Ways to Ius Commune – The Europeanisation of Private Law* (Cambridge: Intersentia, 2012)

Kelsen, H., *Reine Rechtslehre* (Leipzig: Franz Deuticke, 1934)

'What is Justice?' in Kelsen H. (ed.), *What Is Justice? Collected Essays* (Berkeley, CA: University of California Press, 1957), pp. 1–24

Kelsen, H. (ed.), *What Is Justice? Collected Essays* (Berkeley, CA: University of California Press, 1957)

Kennedy, D., 'Thoughts on Coherence, Social Values and National Tradition in Private Law' in Hesselink, M. W. (ed.), *The Politics of a European Civil Code* (The Hague: Kluwer Law International, 2006), pp. 9–31

Kenny, M., 'The 2003 Action Plan on European Contract Law: Is the Commission Running Wild?', *European Law Review*, 28 (2003), 538–50

Kerkmeester, H., 'Uniformity of European Contract Law; An Economic Study between Logic and Fact' in Smits, J. M. (ed.), *The Need for a European Contract Law – Empirical and Legal Perspectives* (Groningen: Europa Law Publishing, 2005), pp. 71–91

Kilian, T., *Ausgewählte Probleme des Musterverfahrens nach dem KapMuG* (Baden-Baden: Nomos, 2007)

Kluth, D., *Die Grenzen des kollisionsrechtlichen Verbraucherschutzes* (Jena: JWV, 2009)

Klüver, H., *Lobbying in the European Union – Interest Groups, Lobbying Coalitions, and Policy Change* (Oxford University Press, 2013)

Koch, H., 'Alternativen zum Zweiparteiensystem im Zivilprozeß', *Kritische Vierteljahresschrift für Gesetzgebung und Rechtswissenschaft*, (1989), 323–40

'Brauchen wir ein eigenes Verbraucherprozessrecht?' in Micklitz, H.-W. (ed.), *Verbraucherrecht in Deutschland – Stand und Perspektiven* (Baden-Baden: Nomos, 2005), pp. 345–53

'Internationaler Kollektiver Rechtsschutz' in Meller-Hannich, C. (ed.), *Kollektiver Rechtsschutz im Zivilprozess* (Baden-Baden: Nomos, 2008), pp. 53–72

Kocher, E., 'Collective Rights and Collective Goods: Enforcement as Collective Interest' in Steele, J. and van Boom, W. H. (eds.), *Mass Justice: Challenges of Representation and Distribution* (Cheltenham: Edward Elgar, 2011), pp. 118–37

Kodek, G. E., 'Collective Redress in Austria', *The ANNALS of the American Academy of Political and Social Science*, 622 (2009), 86–94

'Die Verbesserung des Schutzes kollektiver Interessen im Privat- und Prozessrecht' in Reiffenstein, M. and Pirker-Hörmann, B. (eds.), *Defizite kollektiver Rechtsdurchsetzung* (Vienna: Verlag Österreich, 2009), pp. 131–75

'Möglichkeiten zur gesetzlichen Regelung von Massenverfahren im Zivilprozess', *ecolex*, (2005), 751–4

Köhler, A., *Eingriffsnormen – Der "unfertige Teil" des europäischen IPR* (Tübingen: Mohr Siebeck, 2013)

Köhler, H., 'Klagebefugnis der Verbraucherverbände de lege lata und de lege ferenda' in Augenhofer, S. (ed.), *Verbraucherrecht im Umbruch* (Tübingen: Mohr Siebeck, 2012), pp. 63–72

Kolba, P., '"Friedrich Müller" und Co – Praxisbeispiele zu Streuschäden' in Reiffenstein, M. and Pirker-Hörmann, B. (eds.), *Defizite kollektiver Rechtsdurchsetzung* (Vienna: Verlag Österreich, 2009), pp. 13–18

Kosesnik-Wehrle, A. M. (ed.), *KSchG Kurzkommentar* (3rd edn, Vienna: Manz, 2010)

Kötz, H., *Vertragsrecht* (2nd edn, Tübingen: Mohr Siebeck, 2012)

Koziol, H., Bydlinski, P. and Bollenberger, R. (eds.), *Kurzkommentar zum ABGB* (3rd edn, Vienna: Springer, 2010)

Kramer, X. E., 'Enforcing Mass Settlements in the European Judicial Area: EU Policy and the Strange Case of Dutch Collective Settlements (WCAM)' in Hodges, C. and Stadler, A. (eds.), *Resolving Mass Disputes* (Cheltenham: Edward Elgar, 2013), pp. 63–90

'The European Small Claims Procedure: Striking the Balance Between Simplicity and Fairness in European Legislation', *Zeitschrift für Europäisches Privatrecht*, 16 (2008), 355–73

Kroll-Ludwigs, K., *Die Rolle der Parteiautonomie im europäischen Kollisionsrecht* (Tübingen: Mohr Siebeck, 2013)

'Ein optionales Vertragsrecht – Motor oder Hemmnis für den Binnenmarkt?', *Zeitschrift für das Privatrecht der Europäischen Union*, 9 (2012), 181–8

Kropholler, J. and Von Hein, J., *Europäisches Zivilprozessrecht – Kommentar zu EuGVO, Lugano-Übereinkommen 2007, EuVTVO, EuMVVO und EuGFVO* (9th edn, Frankfurt am Main: Verlag Recht und Wirtschaft, 2011)

Kuipers, J.-J., 'The Legal Basis for a European Optional Instrument', *European Review of Private Law*, 19 (2011), 545–64

Kurz, A., 'Sturm auf die Telekom', *Financial Times Deutschland* (online), 14 May 2012 (on file with the author)

Lando, O., 'Comments and Questions Relating to the European Commission's Proposal for a Regulation on a Common European Sales Law', *European Review of Private Law*, 19 (2011), 717–28

'Is Codification Needed in Europe? Principles of European Contract Law and the Relationship to Dutch Law', *European Review of Private Law*, 1 (1993), 157–70

'Why Does Europe Need a Civil Code?' in Grundmann, S. and Stuyck, J. (eds.), *An Academic Green Paper on European Private Law* (The Hague: Kluwer Law International, 2002), pp. 207–13

Lando, O. and Beale, H. (eds.), *Principles of European Contract Law – Parts I and II* (The Hague: Kluwer Law International, 2000)

Lando, O., Clive, E., Prüm, A. and Zimmermann, R. (eds.), *European Contract Law – Part III* (The Hague: Kluwer Law International, 2003)

Langenbucher, K. (ed.), *Europäisches Privat- und Wirtschaftsrecht* (3rd edn, Baden-Baden: Nomos, 2013)

Leczykiewicz, D. and Weatherill, S. (eds.), *The Involvement of EU Law in Private Law Relationships* (Oxford: Hart, 2013)

Legrand, P., 'Antivonbar', *Journal of Comparative Law*, 1 (2006), 13–40

Lehmann, M., 'Dogmatische Konstruktion der Einwahl in das EU-Kaufrecht (2., 28. oder integriertes Regime) und die praktischen Folgen' in Gebauer, M. (ed.), *Gemeinsames Europäisches Kaufrecht – Anwendungsbereich und kollisionsrechtliche Einbettung* (Munich: Sellier, 2013), pp. 67–88

Leible, S., 'The Proposal for a Common European Sales Law – How Should It Function within the Existing Legal Framework', opinion paper, (2012) (on file with the author)

'Was tun mit dem Gemeinsamen Referenzrahmen für das Europäische Vertragsrecht? – Plädoyer für ein optionales Instrument', *Betriebs-Berater*, 63 (2008), 1469–75

Leible, S. and Schröder, M., 'Art. 114 AUEV' in Streinz, R. (ed.), *EUV/AEUV* (2nd edn, Munich: C. H. Beck, 2012), para. 90

Leipold, D., 'Limiting Costs for Better Access to Justice – The German Experience' in Zuckerman, A. A. S. and Cranston, R. (eds.), *Essays on 'Access to Justice'* (Oxford: Clarendon Press, 1995), pp. 265–78

Lenaerts, K. and Van Nuffel, P., *European Union Law* (3rd edn, London: Sweet & Maxwell, 2011)

Lerm, V., 'Die Verbraucherrechte-Richtlinie im Widerspruch zur Kompetenzordnung des europäischen Primärrechts', *Zeitschrift für das Privatrecht der Europäischen Union*, 9 (2012), 166–72

Łętowska, E. and Wiewiórowska-Domagalska, A., 'The Common Frame of Reference – The Perspective of a New Member State', *European Review of Contract Law*, 3 (2007), 277–94

Letto-Vanamo, P. and Smits, J. (eds.), *Coherence and Fragmentation in European Private Law* (Munich: Sellier, 2012)

Lévayné Fazekas, J., 'Connection between the CFR and the Proposal for a Directive on Consumer Rights' in Schulze, R. (ed.), *Common Frame of Reference and Existing EC Contract Law* (2nd edn, Munich: Sellier, 2009), pp. 309–13

Liebscher, C., 'Article V' in Wolff, R. (ed.), *New York Convention on the Recognition and Enforcement of Foreign Arbitral Awards – Commentary* (Munich: C. H. Beck, 2012), Article V para. 408

Lilleholt, K., 'European Private Law: Unification, Harmonisation or Coordination?' in Brownsword, R. *et al.* (eds.), *The Foundations of European Private Law* (Oxford: Hart, 2011), pp. 353–61

Lindblom, P. H., 'Group Litigation in Scandinavia', *ERA Forum*, 10 (2009), 7–35

'Sweden', *The ANNALS of the American Academy of Political and Social Science*, 622 (2009), 231–41

Lith, H., 'The Dutch Collective Settlements Act and Private International Law', report, (2010), available at ec.europa.eu/competition/consultations/2011_collective_redress/saw_annex_en.pdf

Loos, M. B. M., 'Full Harmonisation as a Regulatory Concept and its Consequences for the National Legal Orders. The Example of the Consumer Rights Directive' in Stürner, M. (ed.), *Vollharmonisierung im Europäischen Verbraucherrecht?* (Munich: Sellier, 2010), pp. 47–98

'Individual Private Enforcement of Consumer Rights in Civil Courts in Europe' in Brownsword, R. *et al.* (eds.), *The Foundations of European Private Law* (Oxford: Hart, 2011), pp. 487–511

Loos, M. B. M. and Keirse, A. L. M., 'The Optional Instrument and the Consumer Rights Directive: Alternative Ways to a New Ius Commune in Contract Law – Introduction' in Keirse, A. L. M. and Loos, M. B. M. (eds.) *Alternative Ways to Ius Commune – The Europeanisation of Private Law* (Cambridge: Intersentia, 2012), pp. 1–20

Loos, M. B. M., Helberger, N., Guibault, L. and Mak, C., 'The Regulation of Digital Content Contracts in the Optional Instrument of Contract Law', *European Review of Private Law*, 19 (2011), 729–58

Low, G., 'A Numbers Game – The Legal Basis for an Optional Instrument in European Contract Law', Maastricht European Private Law Institute Working Paper, No. 2012/2 (2012), available at papers.ssrn.com/sol3/papers.cfm?abstract_id=1991070

'The (Ir)Relevance of Harmonization and Legal Diversity to European Contract Law: A Perspective from Psychology', *European Review of Private Law*, 18 (2010), 285–305

Lüke, W., *Die Beteiligung Dritter im Zivilprozess: Eine rechtsvergleichende Untersuchung zu Grundfragen der subjektiven Verfahrenskonzentration* (Tübingen: Mohr Siebeck, 1993)

Lurger, B., 'A Radical View of Pluralism? Comments on Jan Smits' in Niglia, L. (ed.), *Pluralism and European Private Law* (Oxford: Hart, 2013), pp. 172–6

'Gerechtigkeitskonzepte für ein europäisches Vertragsrecht und Instrumente zu ihrer Umsetzung' in Arnold, S. (ed.), *Grundlagen eines europäischen Vertragsrechts* (Munich: Sellier, 2014), pp. 101–37

Grundfragen der Vereinheitlichung des Vertragsrechts in der Europäischen Union (Vienna: Springer, 2002)

'Old and New Insights for the Protection of Consumers in European Private Law in the Wake of the Global Economic Crisis' in Brownsword, R. *et al.* (eds.), *The Foundations of European Private Law* (Oxford: Hart, 2011), pp.89–113

'The Common Frame of Reference/Optional Code and the Various Understandings of Social Justice in Europe' in Wilhelmsson, T. *et al.* (eds.), *Private Law and the Many Cultures of Europe* (Alphen aan den Rijn: Kluwer Law International, 2007), pp. 177–99

'The Future of European Contract Law between Freedom of Contract, Social Justice, and Market Rationality', *European Review of Contract Law*, 1 (2005), 442–68

'The "Social" Side of Contract Law and the New Principle of Regard and Fairness' in Hartkamp, A. S. *et al.* (eds.), *Towards a European Civil Code* (4th edn, Alphen ann den Rijn: Kluwer Law International, 2011), pp. 353–86

Lurger, B. and Augenhofer, S., *Österreichisches und Europäisches Konsumentenschutzrecht* (2nd edn, Vienna: Springer, 2008)

Luth, H., *Behavioural Economics in Consumer Policy: The Economic Analysis of Standard Terms in Consumer Contracts Revisited* (Antwerp: Intersentia, 2010)

Lyons, D., 'On Formal Justice', *Cornell Law Review*, 58 (1973), 833–61

MacQueen, H. L., Vaquer, A. and Espiau Espiau, S. (eds.), *Regional Private Laws & Codification in Europe* (Cambridge University Press, 2003)

Magnier, V., 'France', *The ANNALS of the American Academy of Political and Social Science*, 622 (2009), 114–24

Magnier, V. and Alleweldt, R., 'Country Report France', report (2009), available at ec.europa.eu/consumers/redress_cons/fr-country-report-final.pdf

Magnus, U., 'Consumer Sales and Associated Guarantees' in Twigg-Flesner, C. (ed.), *The Cambridge Companion to European Union Private Law* (Cambridge University Press, 2010), pp. 243–56

Magnus, U. and Mankowski, P. (eds.), *Brussels I Regulation* (2nd edn, Munich: Sellier, 2012)

Maier, L., 'Institutional Consumer Representation in the European Community', *Journal of Consumer Policy*, 16 (1993), 355–74

Mak, C., 'Constitutional Aspects of a European Civil Code' in Hartkamp, A. S. *et al.* (eds.), *Towards a European Civil Code* (4th edn, Alphen ann den Rijn: Kluwer Law International, 2011), pp. 333–52

Mak, V., 'Review of the Consumer Acquis – Towards Maximum Harmonisation?', Tilburg Institute of Comparative and Transnational Law Working Paper, No. 2008/6 (2008), available at papers.ssrn.com/sol3/papers.cfm?abstract_id=1237011

Maletić, I., *The Law and Policy of Harmonisation in Europe's Internal Market* (Cheltenham: Edward Elgar, 2013)

Mankowski, P., 'Art 5' in Magnus, U. and Mankowski, P. (eds.), *Brussels I Regulation* (2nd edn, Munich: Sellier, 2012), Art 5 paras. 253–7

'Zur Regelung von Sprachfragen im europäischen Internationalen Zivilverfahrensrecht' in Geimer, R. and Schütze, R. A. (eds.), *Festschrift für Athanassios Kaissis zum 65. Geburtstag* (Munich: Sellier, 2012), pp. 607–28

Mattei, U., 'Access to Justice. A Renewed Global Issue?', *Electronic Journal of Comparative Law*, 11.3 (2007), available at www.ejcl.org/113/article113-14.pdf

'Hard Minimal Code Now! – a Critique of "Softness" and a Plea for Responsibility in the European Debate over Codification' in Grundmann, S. and Stuyck, J. (eds.), *An Academic Green Paper on European Private Law* (The Hague: Kluwer Law International, 2002), pp. 215–33

Mattei, U. and Fernanda, N., 'A "Social Dimension" in European Private Law? The Call for Setting a Progressive Agenda', *New England Law Review*, 41 (2006), 1–66

Maugeri, M., 'Is the DCFR Ready to Be Adopted as an Optional Instrument?', *European Review of Contract Law*, 7 (2011), 219–28

Maultzsch, F., 'Rechtswahl und ius cogens im Internationalen Schuldvertragsrecht', *Rabels Zeitschrift für ausländisches und internationales Privatrecht*, 75 (2011), 60–101

Max Planck Institute for Comparative and International Private Law, 'Policy Options for Progress Towards a European Contract Law: Comments on the issues raised in the Green Paper from the Commission of 1 July 2010, COM(2010) 348 final', *Rabels Zeitschrift für ausländisches und internationales Privatrecht*, 75 (2011), 371–438

Mayer, C., *Vollharmonisierung im Privatrecht – Einfluss und Wirkung auf die Konzeptionen in Österreich, in der Schweiz (über autonomes Nachvollzug) und in Deutschland* (Hamburg: Dr. Kovač, 2013)

Mayer, H.-P. and Lindemann, J., 'Zu den aktuellen Entwicklungen um das Gemeinsame Europäische Kaufrecht auf EU-Ebene', *Zeitschrift für Europäisches Privatrecht*, 22 (2014), 1–7

McKendrick, E., 'Harmonisation of European Contract Law: The State We Are in' in Vogenauer, S. and Weatherill, S. (eds.), *The Harmonisation of European Contract Law: Implications for European Private Laws, Business and Legal Practice* (Oxford: Hart, 2006), pp. 5–29

Meli, M., 'Social Justice, Constitutional Principles and Protection of the Weaker Contractual Party', *European Review of Contract Law*, 2 (2006), 159–66

'The Common Frame of Reference and the Relationship between National Law and European Law', *European Review of Contract Law*, 7 (2011), 229–34

Meller-Hannich, C., 'Einführung. Auf dem Weg zu einem effektiven und gerechten System des kollektiven Rechtsschutzes' in Meller-Hannich, C. (ed.), *Kollektiver Rechtsschutz im Zivilprozess* (Baden-Baden: Nomos, 2008), pp. 13–20

Meller-Hannich, C. (ed.), *Kollektiver Rechtsschutz im Zivilprozess* (Baden-Baden: Nomos, 2008)

Meller-Hannich, C., Höland, A. and Krausbeck, E., '"ADR" and "ODR": Kreationen der europäischen Rechtspolitik. Eine kritische Würdigung', *Zeitschrift für Europäisches Privatrecht*, 22 (2014), 8–38

Menon, A. and Weatherill, S., 'Democratic Politics in a Globalising World: Supranationalism and Legitimacy in the European Union', LSE Law, Society and Economy Working Papers, 13/2007 (2007), available at www.lse.ac.uk/collections/law/wps/WPS13-2007MenonandWeatherill.pdf

Meškić, Z., *Europäisches Verbraucherrecht: Gemeinschaftsrechtliche Vorgaben und europäische Perspektiven* (Vienna: Manz, 2008)

Meuwese, A. C. M., *Impact Assessment in EU Lawmaking* (Alphen aan den Rijn: Kluwer Law International, 2008)

'Inter-institutionalising EU Impact Assessment' in Weatherill, S. (ed.), *Better Regulation* (Oxford: Hart, 2007), pp. 287–309

Michaels, R. 'Of Islands and the Ocean: The Two Rationalities of European Private Law' in Brownsword *et al.* (eds.), *The Foundations of European Private Law* (Oxford: Hart, 2011), pp. 139–58

Michailidou, C., *Prozessuale Fragen des Kollektivrechtsschutzes im europäischen Justizraum* (Baden-Baden: Nomos, 2007)

Michalowitz, I., *Lobbying in der EU* (Vienna: Facultas, 2007)

Micklitz, H.-W., 'A "Certain" Future for the Optional Instrument' in Schulze, R. and Stuyck, J. (eds.), *Towards a European Contract Law* (Munich: Sellier, 2011), pp. 181–93

'Collective Private Enforcement of Consumer Law: The Key Questions' in van Boom, W. H. and Loos, M. B. M. (eds.), *Collective Enforcement of Consumer Law: Securing Compliance in Europe through Private Group Action and Public Authority Intervention* (Groningen: Europa Law Publishing, 2007), pp. 13–33

'Cross-Border Consumer Conflicts – A French-German Experience', *Journal of Consumer Policy*, 16 (1993), 411–34

'Enforcement and Compliance: Editorial Introduction' in Brownsword, R. *et al.* (eds.), *The Foundations of European Private Law* (Oxford: Hart, 2011), pp. 415–19

'Introduction' in Micklitz, H.-W. (ed.), *The Many Concepts of Social Justice in European Private Law* (Cheltenham: Edward Elgar, 2011), pp. 3–57

'Privatisation of Access to Justice and Soft Law – Lessons from the European Community?' in Wilhelmsson, T. and Hurri, S. (eds.), *From Dissonance to Sense: Welfare State Expectations, Privatisation and Private Law* (Aldershot: Ashgate, 1999), pp. 505–48

'Social Justice and Access Justice in Private Law', EUI Working Papers, Law 2011/02 (2011), available at cadmus.eui.eu/bitstream/handle/1814/15706/LAW_2011_02.pdf?sequence=1

The Expulsion of the Concept from the Consumer Law and the Return of Social Elements in the Civil Law: A Bittersweet Polemic', *Journal of Consumer Policy*, 35 (2012), 283–96

'The Relationship between National and European Consumer Policy – Challenges and Perspectives' in Twigg-Flesner, C. *et al.* (eds.), *The Yearbook of Consumer Law 2008* (Aldershot: Ashgate, 2007), pp. 35–65

'The Targeted Full Harmonisation Approach: Looking behind the Curtain' in Howells, G. and Schulze, R. (eds.), *Modernising and Harmonising Consumer Contract Law* (Munich: Sellier, 2009), pp. 47–83

'The Visible Hand of European Regulatory Private Law. The Transformation of European Private Law from Autonomy to Functionalism in Competition and

Regulation', EUI Working Papers, Law 2008/14 (2008), available at cadmus. eui.eu/bitstream/handle/1814/8707/LAW_2008_14.pdf?sequence=1

'Unfair Commercial Practices and European Private Law' in Twigg-Flesner, C. (ed.), *The Cambridge Companion to European Union Private Law* (Cambridge University Press, 2010), pp. 229–42

Micklitz, H.-W. (ed.), *The Many Concepts of Social Justice in European Private Law* (Cheltenham: Edward Elgar, 2011)

Verbraucherrecht in Deutschland – Stand und Perspektiven (Baden-Baden: Nomos, 2005)

Micklitz, H.-W. and Cafaggi, F., 'Introduction' in Micklitz, H.-W. and Cafaggi, F. (eds.), *European Private Law after the Common Frame of Reference* (Cheltenham: Edward Elgar, 2010), pp. viii–xlvi

Micklitz, H.-W. and Cafaggi, F., (eds.), *European Private Law after the Common Frame of Reference* (Cheltenham: Edward Elgar, 2010)

Micklitz, H.-W. and De Witte, B., (eds.), *The European Court of Justice and the Autonomy of the Member States* (Cambridge: Intersentia, 2012), pp. 83–111

Micklitz, H.-W. and Nový, Z., 'A Proposal for a Consumer ODR Design' in Howells, G. *et al.* (eds.), 'Optional Soft Law Instrument on EU Contract Law for Businesses and Consumers', study for BEUC, (2011), pp. 41–69

Micklitz, H.-W. and Radeideh, M., 'CLAB Europa – The European Database on Unfair Terms in Consumer Contracts', *Journal of Consumer Policy*, 28 (2005), 325–60

Micklitz, H.-W. and Reich, N., 'Crónica de una muerte anunciada: The Commission Proposal for a "Directive on Consumer Rights"', *Common Market Law Review* 46 (2009), 471–519

'Europäisches Verbraucherrecht – Quo Vadis? Überlegungen zum Grünbuch der Kommission zur Überprüfung des gemeinschaftlichen Besitzstandes im Verbraucherschutz vom 8.2.2007', *Verbraucher und Recht*, 22 (2012), 121–30

'The Commission Proposal for a "Regulation on a Common European Sales Law (CESL)" – Too Broad or Not Broad Enough?' in Micklitz, H.-W. and Reich, N. (eds.) 'The Commission Proposal for a "Regulation on a Common European Sales Law (CESL)" – Too Broad or Not Broad Enough?', EUI Working Papers, Law 2012/04 (2012), pp. 1–38

Micklitz, H.-W. and Reich, N. (eds.) 'The Commission Proposal for a "Regulation on a Common European Sales Law (CESL)" – Too Broad or Not Broad Enough?', EUI Working Papers, Law 2012/04 (2012), available at cadmus.eui.eu/bit-stream/handle/1814/20485/LAW_2012_04_ERPL_03.pdf?sequence=3

Micklitz, H.-W. and Stadler, A., *Das Verbandsklagerecht in der Informations- und Dienstleistungsgesellschaft* (Münster-Hiltrup: Landwirtschaftsverlag, 2005)

Unrechtsgewinnabschöpfung: Möglichkeiten und Perspektiven eines kollektiven Schadenersatzanspruches im UWG (Baden-Baden: Nomos, 2003)

Micklitz, H.-W. and Weatherill, S., 'Consumer Policy in the European Community: Before and after Maastricht', *Journal of Consumer Policy*, 16 (1993), 285–321

Micklitz, H.-W., Reich, N. and Weatherill, S., 'EU Treaty Revision and Consumer Protection', *Journal of Consumer Policy*, 27 (2004), 367–99

Micklitz, H.-W., Reisch, L. A. and Hagen, K., 'An Introduction to the Special Issue on "Behavioural Economics, Consumer Policy, and Consumer Law"', *Journal of Consumer Policy*, 34 (2011), 271–6

Micklitz, H.-W., Stadler, A., Beuchler, H. and Mom, A., 'Gruppenklagen in den Mitgliedstaaten der Europäischen Gemeinschaft & den Vereinigten Staaten von Amerika', report, (2005), available at www.sozialministerium.at/cms/ site/attachments/6/7/1/CH2247/CMS1229355722213/micklitz-stadler_ gruppenklagen.pdf

Micklitz, H.-W., Stuyck, J. and Terryn, E. (eds.), *Cases, Materials and Text on Consumer Law* (Oxford: Hart, 2010)

Miller, D., *Social Justice* (Oxford University Press, 1976)

Miller, G. A., 'The Magical Number Seven, Plus or Minus Two: Some Limits on Our Capacity for Processing Information', *Psychological Review*, 101 (1994), 343–52

Miller, L., *The Emergence of EU Contract Law: Exploring Europeanization* (Oxford University Press, 2011)

Mittwoch, A.-C., *Vollharmonisierung und Europäisches Privatrecht. Methode, Implikationen und Durchführung* (Berlin: de Gruyter, 2013)

Mnookin, R. H. and Kornhauser, L., 'Bargaining in the Shadow of the Law: The Case of Divorce', *Yale Law Journal*, 88 (1979), 950–97

Moccia, L. (ed.), *The Making of European Private Law: Why, How, What, Who* (Munich: Sellier, 2013)

Moffitt, M. L. and Bordone, R. C. (eds.), *The Handbook of Dispute Resolution* (San Francisco, CA: Jossey-Bass, 2005)

Møgelvang-Hansen, P., 'Article 179' in Schulze, R. (ed.), *Common European Sales Law – Commentary* (Baden-Baden: Nomos, 2012), Article 179 CESL Regulation para. 1

Mom, A., *Kollektiver Rechtsschutz in den Niederlanden* (Tübingen: Mohr Siebeck, 2011)

Moorhead, R. and Pleasence, P. (eds.), *After Universalism: Re-engineering Access to Justice* (Oxford: Blackwell, 2003)

Möslein, F., 'Legal Innovation in European Contract Law: Within and Beyond the (Draft) Common Frame of Reference' in Micklitz, H.-W. and Cafaggi, F. (eds.), *European Private Law after the Common Frame of Reference* (Cheltenham: Edward Elgar, 2010), pp. 173–200

Muir-Watt, H. and Sefton-Green R., 'Fitting the Frame: An Optional Instrument, Party Choice and Mandatory/Default Rules' in Micklitz, H.-W. and Cafaggi, F. (eds.), *European Private Law after the Common Frame of Reference* (Cheltenham: Edward Elgar, 2010), pp. 201–19

Mulheron, R., 'The Case for an Opt-out Class Action for European Member States: A Legal and Empirical Analysis', *Columbia Journal of European Law*, 15 (2009), 409–53

The Class Action in Common Law Legal Systems: A Comparative Perspective
    (Oxford: Hart, 2004)
Müller-Graff, P.-C., 'Ein fakultatives europäisches Kaufrecht als Instrument
    der Marktordnung?' in Schulte-Nölke, H. *et al.* (eds.), *Der Entwurf für ein
    optionales europäisches Kaufrecht* (Munich: Sellier, 2012), pp. 21–45
'EU Directives as a Means of Private Law Unification' in Hartkamp, A. S. *et al.*
    (eds.), *Towards a European Civil Code* (4th edn, Alphen ann den Rijn: Kluwer
    Law International, 2011), pp. 149–83
Nebbia, P., 'Unfair Contract Terms' in Twigg-Flesner, C. (ed.), *The Cambridge
    Companion to European Union Private Law* (Cambridge University Press,
    2010), pp. 216–28
Nebbia, P. and Ashkam, T., *EU Consumer Law* (Oxford University Press, 2004)
Neuhold, C. and Settembri, P., 'The Role of European Parliament Committees in
    the EU Policy-making Process' in Christiansen, T. and Larsson, T. (eds.), *The
    Role of Committees in the Policy-Process of the European Union: Legislation,
    Implementation and Deliberation* (Cheltenham: Edward Elgar, 2007), pp.
    152–81
Niglia, L., *The Transformation of Contract in Europe* (The Hague: Kluwer Law
    International, 2003)
Niglia, L. (ed.), *Pluralism and European Private Law* (Oxford: Hart, 2013)
Nilssen, T., 'Two Kinds of Consumer Switching Costs', *The RAND Journal of
    Economics*, 23 (1992), 579–89
Norton Rose Fulbright, 'The New "Hamon Law" Introducing French Class Actions
    and Its Effects on Competition and Distribution Law', newsletter, (2014),
    available at www.nortonrosefulbright.com/knowledge/publications/114016/
    the-new-hamon-law-introducing-french-class-actions-and-its-effects-on-
    competition-and-distribution-law
Nuyts, A. and Hatzimihail, N. E. (eds.), *Cross-border Class Actions: The European
    Way* (Munich: Sellier, 2014)
O'Malley, P., *The Currency of Justice: Fines and Damages in Consumer Societies*
    (Abingdon: Routledge-Cavendish, 2009)
OECD, 'Report on the Implementation of the 2003 OECD Guidelines for Protecting
    Consumers from Fraudulent and Deceptive Commercial Practices across
    Borders', report, (2006), p. 47, available at www.oecd.org/internet/con-
    sumer/37125909.pdf
Oehler, K.-H., 'Der Vorschlag für eine Richtlinie über die Rechte der Verbraucher
    aus deutscher Sicht' in Jud, B. and Wendehorst, C. (eds.), *Neuordnung des
    Verbraucherprivatrechts in Europa* (Vienna: Manz, 2009), pp. 15–20
'Die Umsetzung der vollharmonisierenden Richtlinie aus Sicht des innerstaatli-
    chen Gesetzgebers' in Stürner, M. (ed.), *Vollharmonisierung im Europäischen
    Verbraucherrecht?* (Munich: Sellier, 2010), pp. 99–110
Offer, A., *The Challenge of Affluence* (Oxford University Press, 2006)

Ofner, H., 'Gewinnabschöpfung und funktional ähnliche Instrumente – eine rechts-vergleichende Kurzanalyse' in Reiffenstein, M. and Pirker-Hörmann, B. (eds.), *Defizite kollektiver Rechtsdurchsetzung* (Vienna: Verlag Österreich, 2009), pp. 59–92

Ogus, A., 'Better Regulation – Better Enforcement' in Weatherill, S. (ed.), *Better Regulation* (Oxford: Hart, 2007), pp. 107–22

Ogus, A. and van Boom, W. H. (eds.), *Juxtapoxing Autonomy and Paternalism in Private Law* (Oxford: Hart, 2011)

Pachl, U., 'The Common European Sales Law – Have the Right Choices Been Made? A Consumer Policy Perspective', Maastricht European Private Law Institute Working Paper, No. 2012/6 (2012), available at papers.ssrn.com/sol3/papers.cfm?abstract_id=2027455

Papathomas-Baetge, A., 'Die Verbandsklage im griechischen Recht' in Basedow, J. *et al.* (eds.), *Die Bündelung gleichgerichteter Interessen im Prozess* (Tübingen: Mohr Siebeck, 2009), pp. 187–211

Parisi, F. and Cenini, M. S., 'Punitive Damages and Class Actions' in Backhaus, J. G. *et al.* (eds.), *The Law and Economics of Class Actions on Europe: Lessons from America* (Cheltenham: Edward Elgar, 2012), pp. 131–46

Parry, D., Nordhausen, A., Howells, G. and Twigg-Flesner, C. (eds.), *The Yearbook of Consumer Law 2009* (Farnham: Ashgate, 2008)

Persson, A. H., 'Collective Enforcement: European Prospects in Light of the Swedish Experience' in Wrbka, S. *et al.* (eds.), *Collective Actions: Enhancing Access to Justice and Reconciling Multilayer Interests?* (Cambridge University Press, 2012), pp. 341–363

Piers, M., 'Consumer Arbitration and European Private Law: A Seminal Consumer Arbitration Model Law for Europe', *European Review of Private Law*, 21 (2013), 247–88

Pisuliński, J., 'The Application of the CESL to a Contract for the Supply of Digital Content (e.g. Software)' in Moccia, L. (ed.), *The Making of European Private Law: Why, How, What, Who* (Munich: Sellier, 2013), pp. 205–15

Poblet, M. and Ross, G., 'ODR in Europe' in Abdel Wahab, M. S. *et al.* (eds.), *Online Dispute Resolution: Theory and Practice* (The Hague: Eleven International Publishing, 2012), pp. 453–69

Pogge, T., *John Rawls: His Life and Theory of Justice* (Oxford University Press, 2007)

Poncibò, C., 'Consumer Collective Redress in the European Union: The "Italian Case"' in Parry, D. *et al.* (eds.), *The Yearbook of Consumer Law 2009* (Farnham: Ashgate, 2008), pp. 231–56

'Networks to Enforce European Law: The Case of the Consumer Protection Cooperation Network', *Journal of Consumer Policy*, 35 (2012), 175–95

Popper, K., *The Open Society & Its Enemies* (1st single-volume edn, Princeton University Press, 2013)

Posner, R. A., 'Rational Choice, Behavioral Economics, and the Law', *Stanford Law Review*, 50 (1998), 1551–75

Prusseit, P., *Die Bindungswirkung des Musterentscheides nach dem KapMuG: zu ihrem institutionellen Verständnis als Form der Interventionswirkung* (Göttingen: Sierke, 2009)

Purnhagen, K., 'United We Stand, Divided We Fall? Collective Redress in the EU from the Perspective of Insurance Law', *European Review of Private Law*, 21 (2013), 479–506

Quinn, M., *Justice and Egalitarianism: Formal and Substantive Equality in Some Recent Theories of Justice* (New York: Garland, 1991)

Ramsay, I., *Consumer Law and Policy* (3rd edn, Oxford: Hart, 2012)
   'Consumers Redress and Access to Justice' in Rickett, C. E. F. and Telfer, T. G. W. (eds.), *International Perspectives on Consumers' Access to Justice* (Cambridge University Press, 2003), pp. 17–45

Ratnapala, S., *Jurisprudence* (2nd edn, Cambridge University Press, 2013)

Rauscher, T. (ed.), *Europäisches Zivilprozess- und Kollisionsrecht: EuZPR / EuIPR –Kommentar* (Munich: Sellier, 2011)

Rawls, J., *A Theory of Justice* (Cambridge, MA: Harvard University Press, 1971)
   'Justice as Fairness: Political not Metaphysical', *Philosophy & Public Affairs*, 14 (1985), 223–51
   Political Liberalism (New York: Columbia University Press, 1993)

Reding, V., 'The Next Steps towards a European Contract Law for Businesses and Consumers' in Schulze, R. and Stuyck, J. (eds.), *Towards a European Contract Law* (Munich: Sellier, 2011), pp. 9–20

Reich, N., 'Critical Comments on the Commission Communication "On European Contract Law"' in Grundmann, S. and Stuyck, J. (eds.), *An Academic Green Paper on European Private Law* (The Hague: Kluwer Law International, 2002), pp. 283–91
   'Cross-border Consumer Protection' in Reich, N. *et al.* (eds.), *European Consumer Law* (2nd edn, Cambridge: Intersentia, 2014), pp. 285–337
   'EU Strategies in Finding the Optimal Consumer Law Instrument', *European Review of Contract Law*, 8 (2012), 1–29
   'Harmonisation of European Contract Law: With Special Emphasis on Consumer Law', *China-EU Law Journal*, 1 (2011), 55–94
   'How Proportionate Is the Proportionality Principle? Some Critical Remarks on the Use and Methodology of the Proportionality Principle in the Internal Market Case Law of the ECJ' in Micklitz, H.-W. and De Witte, B. (eds.), *The European Court of Justice and the Autonomy of the Member States* (Cambridge: Intersentia, 2012), pp. 83–111
   Individueller und kollektiver Rechtsschutz im EU-Verbraucherrecht. Von der "Nationalisierung" zur "Konstitutionalisierung" von Rechtsbehelfen (Baden-Baden: Nomos, 2012)

'Mindestharmonisierung im Verbraucherschutzrecht – Stellungnahme' in Everling, U. and Roth, W.-H. (eds.), *Mindestharmonisierung im Europäischen Binnenmarkt* (Baden-Baden: Nomos, 1997), pp. 175–9

'The Social, Political and Cultural Dimension of EU Private Law' in Schulze, R. and Schulte-Nölke, H. (eds.), *European Private Law – Current Status and Perspectives* (Munich: Sellier, 2011), pp. 57–88

'Transformation of Contract Law and Civil Justice in the New EU Member Countries: The Example of the Baltic States, Hungary and Poland' in Cafaggi, F. (ed.), *The Institutional Framework of European Private Law* (Oxford University Press, 2006), pp. 271–302

Reich, N. and Micklitz, H.-W., *Europäisches Verbraucherrecht* (4th edn, Baden-Baden: Nomos, 2003)

Reich, N. and Woodroffe, G. (eds.), *European Consumer Policy after Maastricht* (Dordrecht: Kluwer Academic, 2010)

Reich, N., Micklitz, H.-W., Rott, P. and Tonner, K. (eds.), *European Consumer Law* (2nd edn, Cambridge: Intersentia, 2014)

Reiffenstein, M. and Pirker-Hörmann, B. (eds.), *Defizite kollektiver Rechtsdurchsetzung* (Vienna: Verlag Österreich, 2009)

Reifner, U., 'Verbraucherschutz und Neo-Liberalismus: DCFR, EU-Verbraucherrichtlinien und die Kritik Stürners', *Verbraucher und Recht*, 24 (2009), 3–11

Remien, O., Herrler, S. and Limmer, P. (eds.), *Gemeinsames Europäisches Kaufrecht der EU? Analyse des Vorschlags der Europäischen Kommission für ein optionales Europäisches Vertragsrecht vom 11. Oktober 2011* (Munich: C. H. Beck, 2012)

Renner, M., 'Art. 9 Rome I' in Calliess, G.-P. (ed.), *Rome Regulations: Commentary on the European Rules of the Conflict of Laws* (Alphen aan den Rijn: Kluwer Law International, 2011), Article Rome I para. 5

Reuschle, F., 'Das Kapitalanleger-Musterverfahrensgesetz – Eine erste Bestandsaufnahme aus Sicht der Praxis' in Casper, M. *et al.* (eds.), *Auf dem Weg zu einer europäischen Sammelklage?* (Munich: Sellier, 2009), pp. 277–92

Rhode, D. L., *Access to Justice* (Oxford University Press, 2004)

Rickett, C. E. F. and Telfer, T. G. W., 'Consumers' Access to Justice: an Introduction' in Rickett, C. E. F. and Telfer, T. G. W. (eds.), *International Perspectives on Consumers' Access to Justice* (Cambridge University Press, 2003), pp. 1–13

Rickett, C. E. F. and Telfer, T. G. W. (eds.), *International Perspectives on Consumers' Access to Justice* (Cambridge University Press, 2003)

Riefa, C., 'A Dangerous Erosion of Consumer Rights: The Absence of a Right to Withdraw from Online Auctions' in Howells, G. and Schulze, R. (eds.), *Modernising and Harmonising Consumer Contract Law* (Munich: Sellier, 2009), pp. 177–88

Riesenhuber, K., 'A Competitive Approach to EU Contract Law', *European Review of Contract Law*, 7 (2011), 115–33

'Der Vorschlag für ein "Gemeinsames Europäisches Kaufrecht" – Kompetenz, Subsidiarität, Verhältnismäßigkeit', report for the Committee on Legal Affairs of the German Bundestag, (2012), available at papers.ssrn.com/sol3/papers.cfm?abstract_id=1998134

'Information über die Verwendung des Gemeinsamen Europäischen Kaufrechts – Gedanken zum Harmonisierungskonzept', *Zeitung für Gemeinschaftsprivatrecht*, 9 (2012), 2–6

System und Prinzipien des Europäischen Vertragsrechts (Berlin: De Gruyter, 2003)

Roberts, S. and Palmer, M., *Dispute Processes: ADR and the Primary Forms of Decision-Making* (Cambridge University Press, 2005)

Rösler, H., 'The Transformation of Contractual Justice – a Historical and Comparative Account of the Impact of Consumption' in Micklitz, H.-W. (ed.), *The Many Concepts of Social Justice in European Private Law* (Cheltenham: Edward Elgar, 2011), pp. 327–58

Ross, D., *The Nicomachean Ethics of Aristotle* (Oxford University Press, 1954)

Roth, W.-H., 'Kompetenzen der EG zur vollharmonisierenden Angleichung des Privatrechts' in Gsell, B. and Herresthal, C. (eds.), *Vollharmonisierung im Privatrecht* (Tübingen: Mohr Siebeck, 2009), pp. 13–45

'Stellungnahme zum "Vorschlag für eine Verordnung des Europäischen Parlaments und des Rates über ein Gemeinsames Europäisches Kaufrecht, KOM (2011) 635 endg."', opinion paper, 8 December 2011 (on file with the author)

Rott, P., 'Country Report Germany', report, (2009), available at ec.europa.eu/consumers/redress_cons/de-country-report-final.pdf

'Cross-border Collective Damage Actions in the EU' in Cafaggi, F. and Micklitz, H.-W. (eds.), *New Frontiers of Consumer Protection: The Interplay between Private and Public Enforcement* (Antwerp: Intersentia, 2009), pp. 379–98

'Effective Enforcement and Different Enforcement Cultures in Europe' in Wilhelmsson, T. *et al.* (eds.), *Private Law and the Many Cultures of Europe* (Alphen aan den Rijn: Kluwer Law International, 2007), pp. 305–21

'Information Obligations and Withdrawal Rights' in Twigg-Flesner, C. (ed.), *The Cambridge Companion to European Union Private Law* (Cambridge University Press, 2010), pp. 187–200

'Kollektive Klagen von Verbraucherorganisationen in Deutschland' in Casper, M. *et al.* (eds.), *Auf dem Weg zu einer europäischen Sammelklage?* (Munich: Sellier, 2009), pp. 259–76

'Verbraucherschutz im Internationalen Verfahrens- und Privatrecht' in Micklitz, H.-W. (ed.), *Verbraucherrecht in Deutschland – Stand und Perspektiven* (Baden-Baden: Nomos, 2005), pp. 355–95

Rott, P. and Terryn, E., 'The Proposal for a Directive on Consumer Rights: No Single Set of Rules', *Zeitschrift für Europäisches Privatrecht*, 17 (2009), 456–88

'The Right of Withdrawal and Standard Terms' in Micklitz, H.-W. *et al.* (eds.), *Cases, Materials and Text on Consumer Law* (Oxford: Hart, 2010), pp. 239–302

Rühl, G., 'Consumer Protection in Choice of Law', *Cornell International Law Journal*, 44 (2011), 569–601

'Regulatory Competition in Contract Law: Empirical Evidence and Normative Implications', *European Review of Contract Law*, 9 (2013), 61–89

'The Common European Sales Law – 28th Regime, 2nd Regime or 1st Regime?', Maastricht European Private Law Institute Working Paper, No. 2012/5 (2012), available at papers.ssrn.com/sol3/papers.cfm?abstract_id=2025879

Rutgers, J. W., 'An Optional Instrument and Social Dumping', *European Review of Contract Law*, 2 (2006), 199–212

'An Optional Instrument and Social Dumping Revisited', *European Review of Contract Law*, 7 (2011), 350–9

'European Competence and a European Civil Code, a Common Frame of Reference or an Optional Instrument' in Hartkamp, A. S. *et al.* (eds.), *Towards a European Civil Code* (4th edn, Alphen ann den Rijn: Kluwer Law International, 2011), pp. 311–31

Sadurski, W., 'Social Justice and Legal Justice' in Micklitz, H.-W. (ed.), *The Many Concepts of Social Justice in European Private Law* (Cheltenham: Edward Elgar, 2011), pp. 61–79

Safjan, M., Gorywoda, Ł. and Jańczuk, A., 'Taking Collective Interest of Consumers Seriously: A View from Poland' in Cafaggi, F. and Micklitz, H.-W. (eds.), *New Frontiers of Consumer Protection: The Interplay between Private and Public Enforcement* (Antwerp: Intersentia, 2009), pp. 171–206

Sandel, M. J., *Liberalism and the Limits of Justice* (2nd edn: Cambridge University Press, 1998)

Schaefer, D. L., 'Procedural Versus Substantive Justice: Rawls and Nozick', *Social Philosophy and Policy*, 24 (2007), 164–86

Schilken, E., 'Der Zweck des Zivilprozesses und der kollektive Rechtsschutz' in Meller-Hannich, C. (ed.), *Kollektiver Rechtsschutz im Zivilprozess* (Baden-Baden: Nomos, 2008), pp. 21–52

Schinkels, B., '"Horizontalrichtlinie" und kollisionsrechtlicher Verbraucherschutz – zugleich ein Beitrag zum Verhältnis von Art. 3 Abs. 4 und 6 Abs. 2 Rom-I-VO' in Stürner, M. (ed.), *Vollharmonisierung im Europäischen Verbraucherrecht?* (Munich: Sellier, 2010), pp. 113–32

Schmedes, H.-J., *Wirtschafts- und Verbraucherschutzverbände im Mehrebenensystem: Lobbyingaktivitäten britischer, deutscher und europäischer Verbände* (Wiesbaden: VS Verlag, 2008)

Schmidt-Kessel, M., 'Der Vorschlag der Kommission für ein Optionales Instrument – Einleitung' in Schmidt-Kessel, M. (ed.), *Ein einheitliches europäisches Kaufrecht?* (Munich: Sellier, 2012), pp. 1–27

'Der Vorschlag im Kontext der Rechtsharmonisierung in Europa' in Jud, B. and Wendehorst, C. (eds.), *Neuordnung des Verbraucherprivatrechts in Europa/ Zum Vorschlag einer Richtlinie über Rechte der Verbraucher* (Vienna: Manz, 2009), pp. 21–40

Schmidt-Kessel, M. (ed.), *Ein einheitliches europäisches Kaufrecht? Eine Analyse des Vorschlags der Kommission* (Munich: Sellier, 2012)

Schomburg, G., 'Mehr Verbraucherschutz bei Kosten für Nebenleistungen – Die Regelungen des neuen § 312a Abs. 2 bis 6 BGB', *Verbraucher und Recht*, 29 (2014), 18–23

Schreyögg, G. and Conrad, P. (eds.), *Managementforschung 14. Gerechtigkeit und Management* (Wiesbaden: Gabler, 2004)

Schüller, B., 'Social Peace Via Pragmatic Civil Rights – the Scandinavian Model of Consumer Law' in Micklitz, H.-W. (ed.), *The Many Concepts of Social Justice in European Private Law* (Cheltenham: Edward Elgar, 2011), pp. 384–402

Schulte-Nölke, H., 'Der Blue Button kommt – Konturen einer neuen rechtlichen Infrastruktur für den Binnenmarkt', *Zeitschrift für Europäisches Privatrecht*, 19 (2011), 749–55

'EC Law on the Formation of Contract – from the Common Frame of Reference to the "Blue Button"', *European Review of Contract Law*, 3 (2007), 332–49

'How to Realise the "Blue Button"? – Reflections on an Optional Instrument in the Area of Contract Law' in Schulze, R. and Schulte-Nölke, H. (eds.), *European Private Law – Current Status and Perspectives* (Munich: Sellier, 2011), pp. 89–104

'Scope and Function of the Optional Instrument on European Contract Law' in Schulze, R. and Stuyck, J. (eds.), *Towards a European Contract Law* (Munich: Sellier, 2011), pp. 35–45

'Scope and Role of the Horizontal Directive and Its Relationship to the CFR' in Howells, G. and Schulze, R. (eds.), *Modernising and Harmonising Consumer Contract Law* (Munich: Sellier, 2009), pp. 29–46

'The Way forward in European Consumer Contract Law: Optional Instrument Instead of Further Deconstruction of National Private Laws' in Twigg-Flesner, C. (ed.), *The Cambridge Companion to European Union Private Law* (Cambridge University Press, 2010), pp. 131–46

'Vor- und Entstehungsgeschichte des Vorschlags für ein Gemeinsames Europäisches Kaufrecht' in Schulte-Nölke, H. *et al.* (eds.), *Der Entwurf für ein optionales europäisches Kaufrecht* (Munich: Sellier, 2012), pp. 1–20

Schulte-Nölke, H. and Tichý, L. (eds.), *Perspectives for European Consumer Law: Towards a Directive on Consumer Rights and beyond* (Munich: Sellier, 2010)

Schulte-Nölke, H., Twigg-Flesner, C. and Ebers, M. (eds.), *EC Consumer Law Compendium: The Consumer Acquis and Its Transposition in the Member States* (Munich: Sellier, 2008)

Schulte-Nölke, H., Zoll, F., Janssen, N. and Schulze, R. (eds.), *Der Entwurf für ein optionales europäisches Kaufrecht* (Munich: Sellier, 2012)

Schulze, G., 'Ökonomik der Vollharmonisierung im Gemeinschaftsprivatrecht' in Gsell, B. and Herresthal, C. (eds.), *Vollharmonisierung im Privatrecht* (Tübingen: Mohr Siebeck, 2009), pp. 63–82

Schulze, R., 'Consumer Law and European Contract Law' in Howells, G. *et al.* (eds.), *The Yearbook of Consumer Law 2007* (Aldershot: Ashgate, 2007), pp. 153–66

'European Private Law: Political Foundations and Current Challenges' in Brownsword, R. *et al.* (eds.), *The Foundations of European Private Law* (Oxford: Hart, 2011), pp. 293–307

'The Academic Draft of the CFR and the EC Contract Law' in Schulze, R. (ed.), *Common Frame of Reference and Existing EC Contract Law* (2nd edn, Munich: Sellier, 2009), pp. 3–23

Schulze, R. (ed.), *Common European Sales Law (CESL) – Commentary* (Baden-Baden: Nomos, 2012)

Common Frame of Reference and Existing EC Contract Law (2nd edn, Munich: Sellier, 2009)

Schulze, R. and Schulte-Nölke, H. (eds.), *European Private Law – Current Status and Perspectives* (Munich: Sellier, 2011)

Schulze, R. and Stuyck, J. (eds.), *Towards a European Contract Law* (Munich: Sellier, 2011)

Schulze, R., von Bar, C. and Schulte-Nölke, H. (eds.), *Der akademische Entwurf für einen Gemeinsamen Referenzrahmen* (Tübingen: Mohr Siebeck, 2008)

Schütze, R., *European Constitutional Law* (Cambridge University Press, 2012)

Schwarze, J. (ed.), *EU-Kommentar* (3rd edn, Baden-Baden: Nomos, 2012)

Schwintowski, H.-P., 'The European Civil Code: a Framework Code Only' in Grundmann, S. and Stuyck, J. (eds.), *An Academic Green Paper on European Private Law* (The Hague: Kluwer Law International, 2002), pp. 235–48

Scott, C., 'Enforcing Consumer Protection Laws' in Howells, G. *et al.* (eds.), *Handbook of Research on International Consumer Law* (Cheltenham: Edward Elgar, 2010), pp. 537–62

Sefton-Green, R., 'Choice, Certainty and Diversity: Why More is Less', *European Review of Contract Law*, 7 (2011), 134–50

'Cultural Diversity and the Idea of a European Civil Code' in Hesselink, M. W. (ed.), *The Politics of a European Civil Code* (The Hague: Kluwer Law International, 2006), pp. 71–88

'Social Justice and European Identity in European Contract Law', *European Review of Contract Law*, 2 (2006), 275–86

Semmelmann, C., 'Legal Principles in EU Law as an Expression of a European Legal Culture between Unity and Diversity', Maastricht European Private Law Institute Working Paper, No. 2012/7 (2012), available at papers.ssrn.com/sol3/papers.cfm?abstract_id=2049245

Sen, A., *The Idea of Justice* (London: Penguin Books, 2010)

Seul, J. R., 'Litigation as a Dispute Resolution Alternative' in Moffitt, M. L. and Bordone, R. C. (eds.), *The Handbook of Dispute Resolution* (San Francisco, CA: Jossey-Bass, 2005), pp. 336–57

Shavitt, S., Lee, A. Y., and Torelli, C. J., 'Cross-Cultural Issues in Consumer Behavior' in Wanke, M. (ed.), *Social Psychology of Consumer Behavior* (New York: Psychology Press, 2009), pp. 227–50

Shook Hardy & Bacon, 'France Adopts New Class Action', newsletter, (2014), available at documents.lexology.com/07791e52-c396-45c5-ba34-5a346538e913. pdf#page=1

Silvestri, E., 'Italy', *The ANNALS of the American Academy of Political and Social Science*, 622 (2009), 138–48

Simettinger, V., 'Neue Lösungen für immer mehr Pakete', *ORF* (online), 11 December 2013, available at www.orf.at/stories/2207166/2207167

Simpson, J. A. and Weiner, E. S. C. (eds.), *The Oxford English Dictionary* (2nd edn, Oxford University Press, 1991)

Smits, J. M., 'Coherence and Fragmentation in the Law of Contract' in Letto-Vanamo, P. and Smits, J. (eds.), *Coherence and Fragmentation in European Private Law* (Munich: Sellier, 2012), pp. 9–23

    'Legal Culture as Mental Software, or: How to Overcome National Legal Culture?' in Wilhelmsson, T. *et al.* (eds.), *Private Law and the Many Cultures of Europe* (Alphen aan den Rijn: Kluwer Law International, 2007), pp. 141–51

    'Party Choice and the Common European Sales Law, or: How to Prevent the CESL from Becoming a Lemon on the Law Market', Maastricht European Private Law Institute Working Paper, No. 2012/13 (2012), available at papers. ssrn.com/sol3/papers.cfm?abstract_id=2060017

    'The Common European Sales Law (CESL) beyond Party Choice', Maastricht European Private Law Institute Working Paper, No. 2012/11 (2012), available at papers.ssrn.com/sol3/papers.cfm?abstract_id=2039345

Smits, J. M. (ed.), *The Need for a European Contract Law – Empirical and Legal Perspectives* (Groningen: Europa Law Publishing, 2005)

Somma, A., 'Social Justice and the Market in European Contract Law', *European Review of Contract Law*, 2 (2006), 181–98

    'Towards a European Private Law? The Common Frame of Reference in the Conflict between EC Law and National Laws' in Micklitz, H.-W. and Cafaggi, F. (eds.), *European Private Law after the Common Frame of Reference* (Cheltenham: Edward Elgar, 2010), pp. 1–23

Sovern, J., 'Towards a New Model of Consumer Protection: The Problem of Inflated Transaction Costs', *William & Mary Law Review*, 47 (2006) 1635–709

Spickhoff, A., 'Art 6 Rom I-VO' in Bamberger, H. G. and Roth, H. (eds.), *BGB Band 3* (3rd edn, Munich: C. H. Beck, 2012), Article 6 Rome I para. 32

Stabentheiner, J., 'Das Verbraucherrechte-Richtlinie-Umsetzungsgesetz: Allgemeine Anmerkungen, die Änderungen des ABGB und die Neuerungen im KSchG', *Zeitschrift für Verbraucherrecht* (2014), 68–78

Der Entwurf für ein Gemeinsames Europäisches Kaufrecht – Charakteristika und rechtspolitische Aspekte', *wirtschaftsrechtliche blätter*, 26 (2012), 61–70

'Zur Umsetzung der Verbraucherrechte-Richtlinie in Österreich' in Bydlinski, P. and Lurger, B. (eds.), *Die Richtlinie über die Rechte der Verbraucher* (Vienna: Manz, 2012), pp. 127–57

Stadler, A., 'A Test Case in Germany: 16 000 Private Investors vs. Deutsche Telekom', *ERA Forum*, 10 (2009), 37–50

Bündelung von Interessen im Zivilprozess: Überlegungen zur Einführung von Verbands- und Gruppenklagen im deutschen Recht (Heidelberg: C. F. Müller, 2004)

'Collective Redress Litigation – A New Challenge for Courts in Europe' in Bruns, A. *et al.* (eds.), *Festschrift für Rolf Stürner zum 70. Geburtstag – Band I* (Tübingen: Mohr Siebeck, 2013), pp. 1801–16

'Cross-border Mass Litigation: a Particular Challenge for European Law' in Steele, J. and van Boom, W. H. (eds.), *Mass Justice: Challenges of Representation and Distribution* (Cheltenham: Edward Elgar, 2011), pp. 73–100

'Developments in Collective Redress: What's New in the "New German KapMuG"?', *European Business Law Review*, 24 (2013), 731–49

'Die grenzüberschreitende Durchsetzbarkeit von Sammelklagen' in Casper, M. *et al.* (eds.), *Auf dem Weg zu einer europäischen Sammelklage?* (Munich: Sellier, 2009), pp. 149–68

'Enforcement of Private Law by Way of Collective Action in the European Union – an Overview of the Development in the European Member States' in Heinz, W. and Kim, Y.-W. (eds.), *Aktuelle Rechtsprobleme in Japan, Deutschland und Korea* (Konstanz: KOPS, 2009), pp. 91–104

'Erfahrungen mit den Gewinnabschöpfungsansprüchen im deutschen Wettbewerbs- und Kartellrecht' in Reiffenstein, M. and Pirker-Hörmann, B. (eds.), *Defizite kollektiver Rechtsdurchsetzung* (Vienna: Verlag Österreich, 2009), pp. 93–120

'Group Actions as a Remedy to Enforce Consumer Interests' in Cafaggi, F. and Micklitz, H.-W. (eds.), *New Frontiers of Consumer Protection: The Interplay between Private and Public Enforcement* (Antwerp: Intersentia, 2009), pp. 305–28

'Individueller und kollektiver Rechtsschutz im Verbraucherrecht' in Micklitz, H.-W. (ed.), *Verbraucherrecht in Deutschland – Stand und Perspektiven* (Baden-Baden: Nomos, 2005), pp. 319–43

'Rechtspolitischer Ausblick zum kollektiven Rechtsschutz' in Meller-Hannich, C. (ed.), *Kollektiver Rechtsschutz im Zivilprozess* (Baden-Baden: Nomos, 2008), pp. 93–125

'The Commission's Recommendation on Common Principles of Collective Redress and Private International Law Issues', *Nederlands Internationaal Privaatrecht*, 31 (2013), 483–8

Stark, D. P. and Choplin, J. M., 'A License to Deceive: Enforcing Contractual Myths Despite Consumer Psychological Realities', *NYU Journal of Law & Business*, 5 (2009), 617–744

Staudenmayer, D., 'Der Kommissionsvorschlag für eine Verordnung zum Gemeinsamen Europäischen Kaufrecht', *Neue Juristische Wochenschrift*, 64 (2011), 3491–8

'The Commission Communication on European Contract Law and Its Follow-Up' in Grundmann, S. and Stuyck, J. (eds.), *An Academic Green Paper on European Private Law* (The Hague: Kluwer Law International, 2002), pp. 37–55

'Überlegungen der Europäischen Kommission zur kollektiven Rechtsdurchsetzung' in Casper, M. *et al.* (eds.), *Auf dem Weg zu einer europäischen Sammelklage?* (Munich: Sellier, 2009), pp. 87–96

Staudinger, A. 'Rom I-VO Art. 6' in F. Ferrari *et al.* (eds.), *Internationales Vertragsrecht* (2nd edn, Munich: C. H. Beck, 2012), Article 6 Rome I para. 73

Steele, J. and van Boom, W. H., 'Mass Justice and its Challenges' in Steele, J. and van Boom, W. H. (eds.), *Mass Justice: Challenges of Representation and Distribution* (Cheltenham: Edward Elgar, 2011), pp. 1–26

Steele, J. and van Boom, W. H. (eds.), *Mass Justice: Challenges of Representation and Distribution* (Cheltenham: Edward Elgar, 2011)

Stone, P., *EU Private International Law* (2nd edn, Cheltenham: Edward Elgar, 2010)

Storme, M. E., 'Freedom of Contract: Mandatory and Non-mandatory Rules in European Contract Law', *Juridica International*, 11 (2006), 34–44

Storskrubb, E., *Civil Procedure and EU Law: A Policy Area Uncovered* (Oxford University Press, 2008)

Storskrubb, E. and Ziller, J., 'Access to Justice in European Comparative Law' in Francioni, F. (ed.), *Access to Justice as a Human Right* (Oxford University Press, 2007), pp. 177–203

Streinz, R., 'Der Vertrag von Lissabon und die Privatrechtsangleichung' in Stürner, M. (ed.), *Vollharmonisierung im Europäischen Verbraucherrecht?* (Munich: Sellier, 2010), pp. 23–43

Streinz, R. (ed.), *EUV/AEUV* (2nd edn, Munich: C. H. Beck, 2012)

Study Group on Social Justice in European Private Law, 'Social Justice in European Contract Law: a Manifesto', *European Law Journal*, 10 (2004), 653–74

Stürner, M., 'Das Konzept der Vollharmonisierung – eine Einführung' in Stürner, M. (ed.), *Vollharmonisierung im Europäischen Verbraucherrecht?* (Munich: Sellier, 2010), pp. 3–22

'Effektivität des europäischen Kollisionsrechts und nationales Verfahrensrecht' in Bruns, A. *et al.* (eds.), *Festschrift für Rolf Stürner zum 70. Geburtstag – Band I* (Tübingen: Mohr Siebeck, 2013), pp. 1071–96

'Kollisionsrecht und Optionales Instrument: Aspekte einer noch ungeklärten Beziehung', *Zeitschrift für das Privatrecht der Europäischen Union*, 8 (2011), 236–42

Stürner, M. (ed.), *Vollharmonisierung im Europäischen Verbraucherrecht?* (Munich: Sellier, 2010)

Stuyck, J., 'Public and Private Enforcement in Consumer Protection: General Comparison EU–USA' in Cafaggi, F. and Micklitz, H.-W. (eds.), *New Frontiers of Consumer Protection: The Interplay between Private and Public Enforcement* (Antwerp: Intersentia, 2009), pp. 63–90

'Setting the Scene' in Micklitz, H.-W. *et al.* (eds.), *Cases, Materials and Text on Consumer Law* (Oxford: Hart, 2010), pp. 1–69

'The Notion of the Empowered and Informed Consumer in Consumer Policy and How to Protect the Vulnerable under Such a Regime' in Howells, G. *et al.* (eds.), *The Yearbook of Consumer Law 2007* (Aldershot: Ashgate, 2007), pp. 167–86

'Unfair Terms' in Howells, G. and Schulze, R. (eds.), *Modernising and Harmonising Consumer Contract Law* (Munich: Sellier, 2009), pp. 115–44

Stuyck, J., Terryn, E., Colaert, V., Van Dyck, T., Peretz, N., Hoekx, N. and Tereszkiewicz, P., 'An Analysis and Evaluation of Alternative Means of Consumer Redress Other Than Redress Through Ordinary Judicial Proceedings', report, University of Leuven, (2007), available at www.eurofinas.org/uploads/documents/policies/OTHER%20POLICY%20ISSUES/comparative_report_en.pdf

Sunstein, C. R. and Thaler, R. H., 'Libertarian Paternalism Is Not an Oxymoron', *The University of Chicago Law Review*, 70 (2003), 1159–202

Tamm, M., 'Das Gemeinsame Europäische Kaufrecht als optionales Instrument – eine kritische Analyse zur Binnenmarktharmonisierungskompetenz der Kommission', *Verbraucher und Recht*, 27 (2012), 3–12

'Informationspflichten nach dem Umsetzungsgesetz zur Verbraucherrechterichtlinie', *Verbraucher und Recht* 29 (2014), 9–17

Verbraucherschutzrecht (Tübingen: Mohr Siebeck, 2011)

Tanasescu, I., *The European Commission and Interest Groups: Towards a Deliberative Interpretation of Stakeholder Involvement in EU Policy-making* (Brussels: VUBPRESS, 2009)

Tang, Z. S., *Electronic Consumer Contracts in the Conflict of Laws* (Oxford: Hart, 2009)

Taschner, H. C., 'Mindestharmonisierung im Verbraucherschutzrecht' in Everling, U. and Roth, W.-H. (eds.), *Mindestharmonisierung im Europäischen Binnenmarkt* (Baden-Baden: Nomos, 1997), pp. 159–74

Thaler, R. H. and Sunstein, C. R., 'Libertarian Paternalism', *American Economic Review* 93 (2003) 175–9

Nudge (New Haven, CT: Yale University Press, 2008)

The Gallup Organisation Europe, RAND Europe, Decision Technology, Gallup Institute for Advanced Behavioural Studies, 'Testing of a Standardised Information Notice for Consumer on the Common European Sales Law', report for DG JUST, (2013) (on file with the author)

The Gallup Organization Hungary, 'Attitudes towards Cross-border Sales and Consumer Protection', Flash Eurobarometer 282, (2010), available at ec.europa.eu/public_opinion/flash/fl_282_en.pdf

'European Contract Law in Business-to-business Transactions. Analytical Report', Flash Eurobarometer 320, (2010), available at ec.europa.eu/public_opinion/flash/fl_320_en.pdf

'European Contract Law in Consumer Transactions. Analytical Report', Flash Eurobarometer 321, (2011), available at ec.europa.eu/public_opinion/flash/fl_321_en.pdf

Thiere, K., *Die Wahrung überindividueller Interessen im Zivilprozeß* (Bielefeld: Verlag Ernst und W. Gieseking, 1980)

Thøgersen, J., 'How May Consumer Policy Empower Consumers for Sustainable Lifestyles?', *Journal of Consumer Policy*, 28 (2005), 143–78

Tichý, L., 'Unfair Terms in Consumer Contracts' in Schulte-Nölke, H. and Tichý, L. (eds.), *Perspectives for European Consumer Law: Towards a Directive on Consumer Rights and Beyond* (Munich: Sellier, 2010), pp. 59–76

Tichý, L. and Balarin, J., 'Efficiency of the Protection of Collective Interests: Judicial and Administrative Enforcement in the Czech Republic' in Cafaggi, F. and Micklitz, H.-W. (eds.), *New Frontiers of Consumer Protection: The Interplay between Private and Public Enforcement* (Antwerp: Intersentia, 2009), pp. 207–34

Tilleman, B. and Du Laing, B., 'Directives on Consumer Protection as a Suitable Means of Obtaining a (More) Unified European Contract Law?' in Grundmann, S. and Stuyck, J. (eds.), *An Academic Green Paper on European Private Law* (The Hague: Kluwer Law International, 2002), pp. 81–102

TNS Opinion & Social, 'Civil Justice', Special Eurobarometer 351, (2010), available at ec.europa.eu/public_opinion/archives/ebs/ebs_351_en.pdf

'Consumer Protection in the Internal Market', Special Eurobarometer 252, (2006), available at ec.europa.eu/public_opinion/archives/ebs/ebs252_en.pdf

'European Small Claims Procedure', Special Eurobarometer 395, (2013), available at ec.europa.eu/public_opinion/archives/ebs/ebs_395_en.pdf

TNS Political & Social, 'Consumer Attitudes towards Cross-border Trade and Consumer Protection', Flash Eurobarometer 358, (2013), available at ec.europa.eu/public_opinion/flash/fl_358_en.pdf

'Retailers' Attitudes towards Cross-border Trade and Consumer Protection', Flash Eurobarometer 359, (2013), available at ec.europa.eu/public_opinion/flash/fl_359_en.pdf

TNS Qual+, 'Consumer Redress in the European Union: Consumer Experiences, Perceptions and Choices', Eurobarometer qualitative

study, (2009), available at ec.europa.eu/consumers/redress_cons/docs/
cons_redress_EU_qual_study_report_en.pdf

Tonner, K., 'Die Umsetzung der Verbraucherrechterichtlinie – Auswirkungen der
Vollharmonisierung', *Verbraucher und Recht*, 29 (2014), 23–7

Tortell, L., 'Country Report Portugal', report, (2008), available at ec.europa.eu/
consumers/redress_cons/pt-country-report-final.pdf

Träger, M., 'Party Autonomy and Social Justice in Member States and EC
Regulation: Survey of Theory and Practice' in Collins, H. (ed.), *Standard
Terms in Europe: A Basis for and a Challenge to European Contract Law*
(Alphen aan den Rijn: Kluwer Law International, 2008), pp. 57–74

Trebilcock, M. J., 'Rethinking Consumer Protection Policy' in Rickett, C. E. F. and
Telfer, T. G. W. (eds.), *International Perspectives on Consumers' Access to
Justice* (Cambridge University Press, 2003), pp. 68–98

Trevisan, E., *The Irrational Consumer: Applying Behavioural Economics to Your
Business Strategy* (Farnham: Routledge, 2013)

Trietz, K., 'Verbesserung des Verbraucherschutzes durch die Vollharmonisierung? –
Ein Praxisbericht im deutsch-polnischen Verhältnis' in Stürner, M. (ed.),
Vollharmonisierung im Europäischen Verbraucherrecht? (Munich: Sellier,
2010), pp. 197–208

Tulibacka, M., 'Poland', *The ANNALS of the American Academy of Political and
Social Science*, 622 (2009), 190–200

Tuori, K., 'Legal Culture and the General Societal Culture' in Wilhelmsson, T.
et al. (eds.), *Private Law and the Many Cultures of Europe* (Alphen aan den
Rijn: Kluwer Law International, 2007), pp. 21–35

Twigg-Flesner, C., *A Cross-border-only Regulation for Consumer Transactions
in the EU: A Fresh Approach to EU Consumer Law* (New York:
Springer, 2012)

'Comment: the Future of EU Consumer Law – the End of Harmonisation' in
Devenney, J. and Kenny, M. (eds.), *European Consumer Protection: Theory
and Practice* (Cambridge University Press, 2012), pp. 6–20

'EU Law and Consumer Transactions without an Internal Market Dimension'
in Leczykiewicz, D. and Weatherill, S. (eds.), *The Involvement of EU Law in
Private Law Relationships* (Oxford: Hart, 2013), pp. 317–31

'"Good-Bye Harmonisation by Directives, Hello Cross-Border Only
Regulation?" – A Way forward for EU Consumer Contract Law', *European
Review of Contract Law*, 7 (2011), 235–56

'Introduction: Key Features of European Union Private Law' in Twigg-Flesner,
C. (ed.), *The Cambridge Companion to European Union Private Law*
(Cambridge University Press, 2010), pp. 1–19

'The Acquis Principles: An Insider's Critical Reflections on the Drafting Process'
in Andenas, M. and Baasch Andersen, C. (eds.), *Theory and Practice of
Harmonisation* (Cheltenham: Edward Elgar, 2011), pp. 474–95

The Europeanisation of Contract Law (Abingdon: Routledge-Cavendish, 2008)

Twigg-Flesner, C. (ed.), *The Cambridge Companion to European Union Private Law* (Cambridge University Press, 2010)

Twigg-Flesner, C., Parry, D., Howells, G. and Nordhausen, A. (eds.), *The Yearbook of Consumer Law 2008* (Aldershot: Ashgate, 2007)

Tzankova, I. and Gramatikov, M., 'A Critical Note on Two EU principles: A Proceduralist View on the Draft Common Frame of Reference (DCFR)' in Brownsword, R. *et al.* (eds.), *The Foundations of European Private Law* (Oxford: Hart, 2011), pp. 421–35

Tzankova, I. and Hensler, D., 'Collective Settlements in the Netherlands: Some Empirical Observations' in Hodges, C. and Stadler, A. (eds.), *Resolving Mass Disputes* (Cheltenham: Edward Elgar, 2013), pp. 91–105

Tzankova, I. and Lunsingh Scheurleer, D., 'The Netherlands', *The ANNALS of the American Academy of Political and Social Science*, 622 (2009), 149–60

Unger, O., 'Die Richtlinie über die Rechte der Verbraucher – Eine systematische Einführung', *Zeitschrift für Europäisches Privatrecht*, 20 (2012), 270–304

Urban, N., 'One Legal Language and the Maintenance of Cultural and Linguistic Diversity?', *European Review of Private Law*, 8 (2000), 51–7

Usunier, L., 'Collective Redress and Class Actions in France' in Casper, M. *et al.* (eds.), *Auf dem Weg zu einer europäischen Sammelklage?* (Munich: Sellier, 2009), pp. 293–341

Välimäki, M., 'Introducing Class Actions in Finland: an Example of Law-Making Without Economic Analysis' in Backhaus, J. G. *et al.* (eds.), *The Law and Economics of Class Actions on Europe: Lessons from America* (Cheltenham: Edward Elgar, 2012), pp. 327–41

van Boom, W. H., 'Collective Settlement of Mass Claims in the Netherlands' in Casper, M. *et al.* (eds.), *Auf dem Weg zu einer europäischen Sammelklage?* (Munich: Sellier, 2009), pp. 171–92

van Boom, W. H. and Loos, M. B. M., 'Effective Enforcement of Consumer Law in Europe; Private, Public, and Collective Mechanisms' in van Boom, W. H. and Loos, M. B. M. (eds.), *Collective Enforcement of Consumer Law: Securing Compliance in Europe through Private Group Action and Public Authority Intervention* (Groningen: Europa Law Publishing, 2007), pp. 231–54

van Boom, W. H. and Loos, M. B. M. (eds.), *Collective Enforcement of Consumer Law: Securing Compliance in Europe through Private Group Action and Public Authority Intervention* (Groningen: Europa Law Publishing, 2007)

van Boom, W. H. and Ogus, A., 'Introducing, Defining and Balancing "Autonomy versus Paternalism"' in Ogus, A. and van Boom, W. H. (eds.), *Juxtaposing Autonomy and Paternalism in Private Law* (Oxford: Hart, 2011), pp. 1–8

van Dam, C. and Budaite, E., 'The Statutory Frameworks and General Rules on Unfair Commercial Practices in the 25 EU Member States on the Eve of Harmonization' in Twigg-Flesner, C. *et al.* (eds.), *The Yearbook of Consumer Law 2008* (Aldershot: Ashgate, 2007), pp. 107–39

Van den Bergh, R., 'Forced Harmonisation of Contract Law in Europe: Not to Be Continued' in Grundmann, S. and Stuyck, J. (eds.), *An Academic Green Paper on European Private Law* (The Hague: Kluwer Law International, 2002), pp. 249–68

'Should Consumer Protection Law Be Publicly Enforced? An Economic Perspective on EC Regulation 2006/2004 and Its Implementation in the Consumer Protection Laws of the Member States' in van Boom, W.H. and Loos, M.B.M. (eds.), *Collective Enforcement of Consumer Law: Securing Compliance in Europe through Private Group Action and Public Authority Intervention* (Groningen: Europa Law Publishing, 2007), pp. 179–203

Van den Bergh, R. and Keske, S., 'Rechtsökonomische Aspekte der Sammelklage' in Casper, M. *et al.* (eds.), *Auf dem Weg zu einer europäischen Sammelklage?* (Munich: Sellier, 2009), pp. 17–40

Van den Bergh, R. and Visscher, L., 'The Preventive Function of Collective Actions for Damages in Consumer Law', *Erasmus Law Review*, 1 (2008), 5–30

van den Meene, I. and van Rooij, B., *Access to Justice and Legal Empowerment: Making the Poor Central in Legal Development Co-operation* (Leiden University Press, 2008)

van Gerven, W., 'Bringing (Private) Laws Closer to Each Other at the European Level' in Cafaggi, F. (ed.), *The Institutional Framework of European Private Law* (Oxford University Press, 2006), pp. 37–77

'Private Law in a Federal Perspective' in Brownsword, R. *et al.* (eds.), *The Foundations of European Private Law* (Oxford: Hart, 2011), pp. 337–51

van Hoek, A. A. H., 'CJEU – Pammer and Alpenhof – Grand Chamber 7 December 2010, joined cases 585/08 and 144/09, not yet published', *European Review of Contract Law*, 8 (2012), 93–107

van Parijs, P., 'Difference Principle' in Freeman, S. (ed.), *The Cambridge Companion to Rawls* (Cambridge University Press, 2003), pp. 200–40

van Schagen, E., 'The Proposal for a Common European Sales Law: How Its Drafting Process Might Affect the Optional Instrument's Added Value for Contract Parties and Its Success' in Keirse, A. L. M. and Loos, M. B. M. (eds.) *Alternative Ways to Ius Commune – The Europeanisation of Private Law* (Cambridge: Intersentia, 2012), pp. 85–109

Vandenberghe, A.-S., 'The Role of Information Deficiencies in Contract Enforcement' in Ogus, A. and van Boom, W. H. (eds.), *Juxtaposing Autonomy and Paternalism in Private Law* (Oxford: Hart, 2011), pp. 43–71

Varul, P., 'The Impact of the Harmonisation of Private Law on the Reform of Civil Law in the New Member States' in Brownsword, R. *et al.* (eds.), *The Foundations of European Private Law* (Oxford: Hart, 2011), pp. 285–92

Verein für Konsumenteninformation and Kammer für Arbeiter und Angestellte für Wien, 'Bericht zur Lage der KonsumentInnen 2011/2012', report, (2013), available at www.media.arbeiterkammer.at/PDF/VKI_AK_2011_2012.pdf

Viitanen, K., 'Enforcement of Consumers' Collective Interests by Regulatory Agencies in the Nordic Countries' in van Boom, W. H. and Loos, M. B. M. (eds.), *Collective Enforcement of Consumer Law: Securing Compliance in Europe through Private Group Action and Public Authority Intervention* (Groningen: Europa Law Publishing, 2007), pp. 83–103

'Finland', *The ANNALS of the American Academy of Political and Social Science*, 622 (2009), 209–19

'Nordic Experience on Group Action for Compensation' in Casper, M. *et al.* (eds.), *Auf dem Weg zu einer europäischen Sammelklage?* (Munich: Sellier, 2009), pp. 219–42

'The Crisis of the Welfare State, Privatisation and Consumers' Access to Justice' in Wilhelmsson, T. and Hurri, S. (eds.), *From Dissonance to Sense: Welfare State Expectations, Privatisation and Private Law* (Aldershot: Ashgate, 1999), pp. 549–66

'The Unfair Commercial Practices Directive and Marketing Targeted at Minors' in Wilhelmsson, T. *et al.* (eds.), *Private Law and the Many Cultures of Europe* (Alphen aan den Rijn: Kluwer Law International, 2007), pp. 283–303

Vogenauer, S., 'Regulatory Competition through Choice of Contract Law and Choice of Forum in Europe: Theory and Evidence', *European Review of Private Law*, 21 (2013), 13–78

Vogenauer, S. and Weatherill, S., 'The European Community's Competence to Pursue the Harmonisation of Contract Law – an Empirical Contribution to the Debate' in Vogenauer, S. and Weatherill, S. (eds.), *The Harmonisation of European Contract Law: Implications for European Private Laws, Business and Legal Practice* (Oxford: Hart, 2006), pp. 105–48

Vogenauer, S. and Weatherill, S. (eds.), *The Harmonisation of European Contract Law: Implications for European Private Laws, Business and Legal Practice* (Oxford: Hart, 2006)

von Bar, C., 'Die Struktur des Draft Common Frame of Reference' in Schulze, R., von Bar, C. and Schulte-Nölke, H. (eds.), *Der akademische Entwurf für einen Gemeinsamen Referenzrahmen* (Tübingen: Mohr Siebeck, 2008), pp. 35–45

'Paving the Way forward with Principles of European Private Law' in Grundmann, S. and Stuyck, J. (eds.), *An Academic Green Paper on European Private Law* (The Hague: Kluwer Law International, 2002), pp. 137–45

von Bar, C., and Clive, E. (eds.), *Principles, Definitions and Model Rules of European Private Law. Draft Common Frame of Reference (DCFR). Full Edition* (Munich: Sellier, 2009) and (Oxford University Press, 2010)

von Bar, C., Clive, E. and Schulte-Nölke, H. (eds.), *Principles, Definitions and Model Rules of European Private Law – Draft Common Frame of Reference (DCFR) Outline Edition* (Munich: Sellier, 2009)

von Freyhold, H., Gessner, V., Vial, E. L. and Wagner, H. (eds.), 'Cost of Judicial Barriers for Consumers in the Single Market', report for DG SANCO,

Zentrum für Europäische Rechtspolitik an der Universität Bremen, (1995), available at www.freyvial.de/Publications/egi-2.pdf

von Freyhold, Vial & Partner Consultants, 'The Cost of Legal Obstacles to the Disadvantage of Consumers in the Single Market', report for DG SANCO, (1998), pp. 276-7, available at ec.europa.eu/dgs/health_consumer/library/pub/pub03.pdf

von Hein, J., 'Art 3 Rom I-VO' in Rauscher, T. (ed.), *Europäisches Zivilprozess- und Kollisionsrecht: EuZPR / EuIPR* (Munich: Sellier, 2011), Article 3 para. 58

Wacks, R., *Philosophy of Law – A Very Short Introduction* (Oxford University Press, 2006)

Wagner, G., 'Kollektiver Rechtsschutz – Regelungsbedarf bei Massen- und Streuschäden' in Casper, M. *et al.* (eds.), *Auf dem Weg zu einer europäischen Sammelklage?* (Munich: Sellier, 2009), pp. 41–88

'Mandatory Contract Law: Functions and Principles in Light of the Proposal for a Directive on Consumer Rights' in Ogus, A. and van Boom, W. H. (eds.), *Juxtaposing Autonomy and Paternalism in Private Law* (Oxford: Hart, 2011), pp. 9–42

'The Virtues of Diversity in European Private Law' in Smits, J. M. (ed.), *The Need for a European Contract Law – Empirical and Legal Perspectives* (Groningen: Europa Law Publishing, 2005), pp. 3–24

Wagner, H., 'Economic Analysis of Cross-Border Legal Uncertainty: The Example of the European Union' in Smits, J. M. (ed.), *The Need for a European Contract Law.*, pp. 27–51

Wagner, M., *Das Konzept der Mindestharmonisierung* (Berlin: Duncker & Humblot, 2001)

Wallace, H., Pollack, M. A. and Young, A. R. (eds.), *Policy-Making in the European Union* (6th edn, Oxford University Press, 2010)

Wallacher, J., 'Ethische Perspektiven einer entwicklungsgerechten Weltwirtschaft', *Zeitschrift für Wirtschafts- und Unternehmensethik*, 4 (2003), 307–24

Wanke, M. (ed.), *Social Psychology of Consumer Behavior* (New York: Psychology Press, 2009)

Wanner, V., *Das KapMuG als allgemeine Regelung für Massenverfahren* (Baden-Baden: Nomos, 2009)

Ware, S. J., *Alternative Dispute Resolution* (St. Paul, MN: West Group, 2001)

Watson, R. and Corbett, R., 'How Policies Are Made' in Bomberg, E. *et al.* (eds.), *The European Union: How Does It Work?* (3rd edn, Oxford University Press, 2012), pp. 122–40

Weatherill, S., *Cases & Materials on EU Law* (10th edn, Oxford University Press, 2012)

'Competence and European Private Law' in Twigg-Flesner, C. (ed.), *The Cambridge Companion to European Union Private Law* (Cambridge University Press, 2010), pp. 48–69

'Constitutional Issues – How Much Is Best Left Unsaid?' in Vogenauer, S. and Weatherill, S. (eds.), *The Harmonisation of European Contract Law: Implications for European Private Laws, Business and Legal Practice* (Oxford: Hart, 2006), pp. 89–103

'Consumer Policy' in Craig, P. and de Búrca, G. (eds.), *The Evolution of EU Law* (2nd edn, Oxford University Press, 2011), pp. 837–76

EU Consumer Law and Policy (2nd edn, Cheltenham: Edward Elgar, 2013)

'Harmonisation: How Much, How Little?', *European Business Law Review*, 16 (2005), 533–45

'Maximum or Minimum Harmonisation – What Kind of "Europe" Do We Want?' in Boele-Woelki, K. and Grosheide, W. (eds.), *The Future of European Contract Law* (Alphen aan den Rijn: Kluwer Law International, 2007)

'Minimum Harmonisation as Oxymoron? The Case of Consumer Law' in Micklitz, H.-W. (ed.), *Verbraucherrecht in Deutschland – Stand und Perspektiven* (Baden-Baden: Nomos, 2005), pp. 15–36

'Reflections on the EC's Competence to Develop a "European Contract Law"', *European Review of Private Law*, 13 (2005), 405–18

'The Challenge of Better Regulation' in Weatherill, S. (ed.), *Better Regulation* (Oxford: Hart, 2007), pp. 1–17

'The Constitutional Competence of the EU to Deliver Social Justice', *European Review of Contract Law*, 2 (2006), 136–58

'The Consumer Rights Directive: How and Why a Quest for "Coherence" Has (Largely) Failed', *Common Market Law Review*, 49 (2012), 1279–317

'The Role of the Informed Consumer in European Community Law and Policy', *Consumer Law Journal*, 2 (1994), 49–69

Weatherill, S. (ed.), *Better Regulation* (Oxford: Hart, 2007)

Weinrib, E. J., *Corrective Justice* (Oxford University Press, 2012)

The Idea of Private Law (Oxford University Press, 1995)

Weiskopf, R., 'Management, Organisation und die Gespenster der Gerechtigkeit' in Schreyögg, G. and Conrad, P. (eds.), *Managementforschung 14. Gerechtigkeit und Management* (Wiesbaden: Gabler, 2004), pp. 211–51

Weller, M., 'Art. 23 Rome I' in Calliess, G.-P. (ed.), *Rome Regulations: Commentary on the European Rules of the Conflict of Laws* (Alphen aan den Rijn: Kluwer Law International, 2011), Article 23 Rome I para. 7

Welser, R. (ed.), *Konsumentenschutz in Zentral- und Osteuropa* (Vienna: Manz, 2010)

Wendehorst, C., 'Article 4' in Schulze, R. (ed.), *Common European Sales Law (CESL) – Commentary* (Baden-Baden: Nomos, 2012), Article 4 CESL Regulation para. 16

'Article 8' in Schulze, R. (ed.), *Common European Sales Law (CESL) – Commentary* (Baden-Baden: Nomos, 2012), Article 8 CESL Regulation para. 9

'Article 11' in Schulze, R. (ed.), *Common European Sales Law (CESL) – Commentary* (Baden-Baden: Nomos, 2012), Article 11 CESL Regulation para. 4

'Article 13' in Schulze, R. (ed.), *Common European Sales Law (CESL) – Commentary* (Baden-Baden: Nomos, 2012), Article 13 CESL Regulation para. 3

'Das neue Gesetz zur Umsetzung der Verbraucherrechterichtlinie', *Neue Juristische Wochenschrift*, 67 (2014), 577–84

Wendehorst, C. and Zöchling-Jud, B. (eds.), *Am Vorabend eines Gemeinsamen Europäischen Kaufrechts: Zum Verordnungsentwurf der Europäischen Kommission vom 11.10.2011* (Vienna: Manz, 2012)

Wendelstein, C., 'Ein gestörtes Zusammenspiel zwischen Europäischem IPR and dem GEK? – Probleme der Vorschaltlösung', *Zeitschrift für das Privatrecht der Europäischen Union*, 10 (2013), 70–7

Werlauff, E., 'Class Actions in Denmark', *The ANNALS of the American Academy of Political and Social Science*, 622 (2009), 202–8

White, M. D., *The Manipulation of Choice: Ethics and Libertarian Paternalism* (Basingstoke: Palgrave Macmillan, 2013)

Whittaker, S., 'The Optional Instrument of European Contract Law and Freedom of Contract', *European Review of Contract Law*, 7 (2011), 371–98

'The Proposed "Common European Sales Law": Legal Framework and the Agreement of Parties', *The Modern Law Review*, 75 (2012), 578–605

Wiewel, T., 'Das neue KapMuG in Anlageberatungsfällen', *Verbraucher und Recht*, 28 (2013), 173–7

Wilcke, T., *Internationaler Online-Handel und Verbraucherschutz* (Baden-Baden: Nomos, 2011)

Wilhelmsson, T., 'European Consumer Law: Theses on the Task of the Member States' in Micklitz, H.-W. (ed.), *Verbraucherrecht in Deutschland – Stand und Perspektiven* (Baden-Baden: Nomos, 2005), pp. 37–63

'Introduction: Harmonization and National Cultures' in Wilhelmsson, T. *et al.* (eds.), *Private Law and the Many Cultures of Europe* (Alphen aan den Rijn: Kluwer Law International, 2007), pp. 3–20

'The Average European Consumer: a Legal Fiction?' in Wilhelmsson, T. *et al.* (eds.), *Private Law and the Many Cultures of Europe* (Alphen aan den Rijn: Kluwer Law International, 2007), pp. 243–68

'The Ethical Pluralism of Late Modern Europe and Codification of European Contract Law' in Smits, J. M. (ed.), *The Need for a European Contract Law – Empirical and Legal Perspectives* (Groningen: Europa Law Publishing, 2005), pp. 123–52

'The Informed Consumer v the Vulnerable Consumer in European Unfair Commercial Practices Law – A Comment' in Howells, G. *et al.* (eds.), *The Yearbook of Consumer Law 2007* (Aldershot: Ashgate, 2007), pp. 211–27

'Varieties of Welfarism in European Contract Law', *European Law Journal*, 10 (2004), 712–33

'Welfare State Expectations, Privatisation and Private Law' in Wilhelmsson, T. and Hurri, S. (eds.), *From Dissonance to Sense: Welfare State Expectations, Privatisation and Private Law* (Aldershot: Ashgate, 1999), pp. 3–36

Wilhelmsson, T. and Hurri, S. (eds.), *From Dissonance to Sense: Welfare State Expectations, Privatisation and Private Law* (Aldershot: Ashgate, 1999)

Wilhelmsson, T., Paunio, E. and Pohjolainen, A. (eds.), *Private Law and the Many Cultures of Europe* (Alphen aan den Rijn: Kluwer Law International, 2007)

Wilhelmsson, T. and Willett, C., 'Unfair Terms and Standard Form Contracts' in Howells, G. *et al.* (eds.), *Handbook of Research on International Consumer Law* (Cheltenham: Edward Elgar, 2010), pp. 158–91

Willett C. and Morgan-Taylor, M., 'Recognising the Limits of Transparency in EU Consumer Law' in Devenney, J. and Kenny, M. (eds.), *European Consumer Protection: Theory and Practice* (Cambridge University Press, 2012), pp. 143–63

Winn, J. K. (ed.), *Consumer Protection in the Age of the 'Information Economy'* (Aldershot: Ashgate, 2006)

Woitkewtisch, C., 'Verbraucherschutz im AGB-Recht. Aktuelle Rechtsprechung zum Verbandsklageverfahren', *Verbraucher und Recht*, 22 (2007), 252–7

Wolff, R. (ed.), *New York Convention on the Recognition and Enforcement of Foreign Arbitral Awards – Commentary* (Munich: C. H. Beck, 2012)

Woods, L. and Watson, P., *Steiner & Woods EU Law* (11th edn, Oxford University Press, 2012)

Wrbka, S., 'Consumers and the Proposal for an Optional Common European Sales Law No Roads Lead to Rome?', Kyushu University Legal Research Bulletin, 2 (2012), available at researchbulletin.kyudai.info/?p=248

'European Consumer Protection Law: Quo Vadis? – Thoughts on the Compensatory Collective Redress Debate' in Wrbka, S. *et al.* (eds.), *Collective Actions: Enhancing Access to Justice and Reconciling Multilayer Interests?* (Cambridge University Press, 2012), pp. 23–56

'The Austrian Implementation of the Consumer Rights Directive – an Outline', *Hosei Kenkyu*, 81 (2014), 288–308

'The Dilemma of European Consumer Representation in Deliberative Networks – The Democratic Deficit in the Context of the Drafting of the Common European Sales Law' in Fenwick, M. *et al.* (eds.), *Networked Governance, Transnational Business & the Law* (Heidelberg: Springer, 2014), pp. 145–70

'The Proposal for an Optional Common European Sales Law: A Step in the Right Direction for Consumer Protection?', *EUIJ-Kyushu Review*, 1 (2011), 87–121

Wrbka, S., Van Uytsel, S. and Siems, M., 'Access to Justice and Collective Actions: "Florence" and Beyond' in Wrbka, S. *et al.* (eds.), *Collective Actions: Enhancing Access to Justice and Reconciling Multilayer Interests?* (Cambridge University Press, 2012), pp. 1–20

Wrbka, S., Van Uytsel, S. and Siems, M. (eds.), *Collective Actions: Enhancing Access to Justice and Reconciling Multilayer Interests?* (Cambridge University Press, 2012)

Young, A. R. 'The European Policy Process in Comparative Perspective' in Wallace, H. *et al.* (eds.), *Policy-Making in the European Union* (6th edn, Oxford University Press, 2010), pp. 45–68

Ziller, J., 'The Legitimacy of the Codification of Contract Law in View of the Allocation of Competences between the European Union and its Member States' in Hesselink, M. W. (ed.), *The Politics of a European Civil Code* (The Hague: Kluwer Law International, 2006), pp. 89–113

Zimmermann, R., 'Codification – The Civilian Experience Reconsidered on the Eve of a Common European Sales Law', *European Review of Contract Law*, 8 (2012), 367–99

  Die Europäisierung des Privatrechts und die Rechtsvergleichung (Berlin: De Gruyter, 2006)

  '*Perspektiven* des künftigen österreichischen und europäischen *Zivilrechts*', *Juristische Blätter*, 134 (2012), 2–22

Zoll, F., 'A Need for a New Structure for European Private Law' in Brownsword, R. *et al.* (eds.), *The Foundations of European Private Law* (Oxford: Hart, 2011), pp. 555–61

  'Der Entwurf des Gemeinsamen Referenzrahmens und die Vollharmonisierung' in Stürner, M. (ed.), *Vollharmonisierung im Europäischen Verbraucherrecht?* (Munich: Sellier, 2010), pp. 133–41

Zuckerman, A. A. S., 'Justice in Crisis: Comparative Dimensions of Civil Procedure' in Zuckerman, A. A. S. (ed.), *Civil Justice in Crisis, Comparative Perspectives of Civil Procedure* (Oxford University Press, 1999), pp. 3–52

Zuckerman, A. A. S. (ed.), *Civil Justice in Crisis, Comparative Perspectives of Civil Procedure* (Oxford University Press, 1999)

Zuckerman, A. A. S. and Cranston, R. (eds.), *Essays on 'Access to Justice'* (Oxford: Clarendon Press, 1995)

NAME INDEX

Alpa, Guido, 172
Aristotle, 10–13, 17
Artz, Markus, 298

Balarin, Jan, 121
Basedow, Jürgen, 232
Beale, Hugh, 199, 202
Bebchuck, Lucian, 285
Bělohlávek, Alexander, 83
Betlem, Gerrit, 63
Borghetti, Jean-Sébastien, 220
Břicháček, Tomáš, 329
Brownsword, Roger, 196
Busch, Christoph, 257
Buxbaum, Hannah, 134

Cafaggi, Fabrizio, 71, 159
Calliess, Gralf-Peter, 237, 249
Cámara Lapuente, Sergio, 200
Camere, Colin, 287
Cappelletti, Mauro, 1, 19, 20, 23, 24, 25, 29, 33
Carr, Craig, 7
Clive, Eric, 199, 202
Collins, Hugh, 160, 188, 265, 281, 282, 285, 330, 331
Cortés, Pablo, 98, 100, 101
Cotterrell, Roger, 7, 227

Dalli, John, 80
Docekal, Ulrike, 53
Dolder, Cheryl, 83
Du Laing, Bart, 326
Dworkin, Ronald, 279

Ebers, Martin, 170
Edwards, Lilian, 98
Eidenmüller, Horst, 157, 247

Englard, Izhak, 12
Eterovich, Francis, 10
Eucken, Walter, 290

Fairgrieve, Duncan, 144
Fleischacker, Samuel, 11
Francioni, Francesco, 20
Freeman, Samuel, 14

Galanter, Marc, 23
Garth, Bryant, 1, 20, 22
Geimer, Reinhold, 148
Grübler, Ulrike, 294
Grundmann, Stefan, 290, 325, 327
Grynbaum, Luc, 202

Håstad, Torgny, 202
Heiderhoff, Bettina, 238, 249
Heller, Agnes, 7
Hesselink, Martijn, 160
Hodges, Christopher, 40, 116
Höland, Armin, 96
Hondius, Ewoud, 200
Hörnle, Julia, 95
Horwitz, Allan, 6
Howells, Geraint, 165, 176, 220, 232, 327

Illmer, Martin, 51
Issacharoff, Samuel, 287

Jansen, Nils, 200, 247
Janssen, André, 107
Juvin, Phillipe, 112

Kahnemann, Daniel, 287
Kant, 8
Kaufmann-Kohler, Gabrielle, 98

Kelsen, Hans, 8–9, 10, 17
Kerkmeester, Heico, 324
Kieninger, Eva-Maria, 247
Kolba, Peter, 53
Kötz, Hein, 285, 291
Krausbeck, Elisabeth, 96
Kroll-Ludwig, Kathrin, 326
Kropholler, Jan, 148
Kull, Irene, 202
Kuneva, Meglena, 66, 106

Lando, Ole, 193, 195
Lehmann, Matthias, 248
Leible, Stefan, 250
Lerm, Verena, 268
Łętowska, Ewa, 329
Liebscher, Christoph, 101
Lindemann, Julia, 262
Loewenstein, George, 287
Loos, Marco, 116, 176, 237, 328
Lurger, Brigitta, 159, 200, 201, 202, 229, 232, 268, 288, 282
Luth, Hanneke, 286, 292, 293, 294
Lyons, David, 7

Maletić, Isidora, 274, 275
Mayer, Hans-Peter, 262
McKendrick, Ewan, 229
Meller-Hannich, Caroline, 96
Michailidou, Chrisoula, 125
Micklitz, Hans-W., 29, 53, 71, 126, 127, 138, 158, 159, 199, 241, 268
Miller, David, 8
Miller, Lucinda, 160, 203
Muir-Watt, Horatia, 200
Mulheron, Rachael, 114

O'Donoghue, Ted, 287
Oehler, Karl-Heinz, 188
Ogus, Anthony, 29

Palmer, Michael, 84
Patel, Reena, 297
Piers, Maud, 95
Pisuliński, Jerzy, 202
Plato, 8, 10
Popper, Karl, 7
Posner, Richard, 285

Quinn, Michael, 6

Rabin, Matthew, 287
Ramsay, Iain, 284
Rawls, John, 13–16, 19
Reding, Viviane, 112, 206
Reich, Norbert, 75, 232, 241, 268
Renner, Moritz, 241
Rhode, Deborah, 22
Rickett, Charles, 33
Roberts, Simon, 84
Ross, David, 10
Rott, Peter, 53, 148
Rühl, Giesela, 234, 236, 326, 328

Sadurski, Wojciech, 6
Schüller, Bastian, 282
Schulte-Nölke, Hans, 170, 199, 234
Schultz, Thomas, 98
Schulze, Götz, 325
Schulze, Reiner, 176, 189, 200, 327
Scott, Colin, 133
Sefton-Green, Ruth, 200
Semmelmann, Constanze, 331
Smits, Jan, 200, 230, 232
Stadler, Astrid, 106, 118, 126, 127, 136, 148
Staudenmayer, Dirk, 250
Steele, Jenny, 123
Storskrubb, Eva, 7
Stürner, Michael, 277, 325, 328
Stuyck, Jules, 121
Sunstein, Cass, 286, 287

Tamm, Marina, 234, 326
Telfer, Thomas, 33
Terryn, Evelyne, 200
Thaler, Richard, 286, 287
Tichý, Luboš, 121
Tilleman, Bernard, 326
Träger, Marion, 289
Twigg-Flesner, Christian, 43, 160, 165, 170, 218

van Boom, Willem, 116, 123
Van den Bergh, Roger, 121
van Gerven, Walter, 330
Varul, Paul, 329
Veneziano, Anna, 202

Vogenauer, Stefan, 326
von Bar, Christian, 199
von Hein, Jan, 148

Wagner, Gerhard, 126, 127, 128, 129, 131, 218, 247
Ware, Stephen, 83
Wasserman, Michael, 6
Weatherill, Stephen, 29, 150, 158, 165, 188, 268, 324
Weinrib, Ernest, 12

Wendehorst, Christiane, 223, 230, 231, 240, 248, 249
Wiewiórowska-Domagalska, Aneta, 329
Wilhelmsson, Thomas, 277, 324
Wilson, Caroline, 98

Ziller, Jacques, 7
Zimmermann, Reinhard, 206, 234, 247
Zuckerman, Adrian, 39

SUBJECT INDEX

access to justice, 3, 18–19, 20, 24, 26, 27, 35, 72
access, 5
Action Plan on consumer access to justice and the settlement of consumer disputes in the internal market (1996), 35
Consumer Access to Justice Green Paper (1993), 35, 84, 85
course of time, in, 19–27
EU level, 21, 25–7
Florence Access-to-Justice Project, 19–24, 102
holistic approach, 29, 278
justice, 5–18
new approach, *see* access to justice 2.0
traditional discussion, 25–7
access to justice 2.0, 27, 276–9, 278, 283
concept, 27–30
consumer confidence, and, 264, 297, 317
consumer empowerment, and, 297, 298, 302, 319
consumer interests, and, 71, 333
consumers, and, 281–3
Acquis Group, 195–6, 200, 202, 203
Common European Sales Law (CESL), and, *see* Common European Sales Law (CESL), Acquis Group
alternative dispute resolution (ADR), 25, 83–101, 320
access to justice, and, 88
ADR Communication (1998), 85–6
ADR Directive (2013), 37, 90–7
ADR Green Paper (2002), 87

ADR Recommendation (1998), 85–6
arbitration, 83, 86, 87, 89, 95, 96
availability, 320
bodies, 85
complaints, 97
consumers, and, 84
EU level, trends at, 83–9
European Code of Conduct (2004), 87
litigation, and, 150
mediation, 83, 89
Mediation Directive (2008), 88–9, 90
Mediation Directive Proposal (2004), 88
ODR, *see* online dispute resolution
Rome I Regulation, and, 95
antitrust law, 105, 117, 122
arbitration, *see* alternative dispute resolution (ADR), arbitration
awareness, 23, 65, 77, 82
alternative dispute resolution, 91
consumer, 80, 269, 270, 298
CPC Regulation, 47, 300
ECC-Net, 307
EEJ-Net, 36
enforcement tools, 269, 274
Legal Aid Directive, 59
Small Claims Regulation, 59, 82
stakeholders, other than consumers or traders, 150, 269
trader, 92, 317

better law making, 165, 171, 172, 263
business-to-consumer (B2C), 35, 79, 82, 97, 158, 225–7, 236, 293
alternative dispute resolution, and, 84, 90, 94

business-to-consumer (B2C) (*cont.*)
  CESL, and, 191, 209, 211, 212, 217,
    222, 226
  compensatory collective redress,
    and, 112
  consumer confidence, and, 282, 297
  consumer empowerment, and, 301
  Legal Aid Directive, and, 60
  mandatory rules, and, 213
  online dispute resolution, and, 98
  Small Claims Regulation, and, 80
  willingness to sue, and, 127, 128

centralisation, 188, 259
  law and policy-making, and, 164,
    175, 276, 333
  national policies, and, 324
collective damages, 106, 115, 118, 121,
    133, 134, 136, 214
  alternative approach to, 132–49
  classifying multiple, 129
  collective redress, *see* collective
    redress
  cost-benefit analysis, 143
  flexible system, 143
  inflexible system, 143
  loser-pays principle, and, 118
  mass, 128–9, 140–2, 321
  scattered, 125, 133–40, 321
  scattered versus mass, 124–32, 143
collective redress, 24
  blackmail settlements, 116, 138
  Brussels I Regulation, and, 146–9
  Collective Redress Green Paper
    (2008), 102–18
  Collective Redress
    Recommendation (2013), 117
  compensatory, 102–12, 117, 118, 151,
    302, 321
  Consultation Paper (2009), 110
  Consultation Paper (2011), 110
  contingency fees, and, 106, 114,
    118, 146
  damage classification, 132
  disincentives, 143
  domestic cases, 143
  enhanced test cases, 142

European Parliament, 112
fake actions, 116, 139
financial means, and, 144
group actions, 108, 119, 139
injunctions, and, 103
justice, enhancing, 113
legal insurance, and, 129, 146
mandatory representation, and, 137
mass damages, and, 141
mass justice, 123
multilayer interests, *see* multilayer
  interests
national frameworks, 115
non-monetary, 40, 144
opt-in, and, 117
opt-out, and, 106, 114
pre-trial discovery, and, 106, 114
punitive damages, and, 106, 115,
  118
rational disinterest, and, 125–7,
  128–9, 144
representative actions, 139
Resolution on Collective Redress
  (2012), 113–17
scattered damages, and, 124–32
state funding, and, 128, 142
test cases, 108
types of, 110, 122
US-style class actions, 106, 113
Common European Sales Law (CESL),
  190–262
  Acquis Communication (2004), and,
    166, 169, 194
  Acquis Group, and, 196, 203
  ambiguity, 232
  analysis, 215–54
  approach, 195, 232
  assumptions of European
    Commission, 215–16
  B2C and non-B2C situations, 211
  background, 190–208
  CESL Expert Group, and, 202–5,
    208, 258
  CESL Key Stakeholders Group, and,
    203, 204, 205, 206, 258
  CFR, and, 196–205
  clear need?, 225–9

Commission on European Contract
Law, and, *see* Common European
Sales Law (CESL), Lando
Commission
completeness, and, 218, 247
consumer acquis, and, 195
consumer confidence, 173, 234, 256
consumer interests, 205, 236, 237, 239
Contract Law Action Plan (2003),
and, 166, 169, 194
Contract Law Communication
(2001), and, 42, 166, 169, 194
DCFR, and, 196–205
discussions, 255
Economic and Monetary Affairs
Committee (ECON), and,
255, 257
ELI Draft, 257, 260
European Commission,
assumptions of, 216
European Parliament, and, 193, 209,
255, 257
Expert Group on a Common Frame
of Reference, and, *see* Common
European Sales Law (CESL), CESL
Expert Group, and
Explanatory Memorandum
(2011), 207
final prices, and, 219
first draft, 208
fragmentation, and, 169, 219,
225, 229
Internal Market and Consumer
Protection Committee
(IMCO), 255
JURI report, 256
Lando Commission, 193, 195
legal advice, obtaining, 221
Legal Affairs Committee (JURI),
and, 255, 256, 257, 258
legal certainty, 217, 221–4,
245–51
mandatory provisions, 250
optional instrument, as, 191, 207
overview, 208–15
parties agree on law of consumer's
member state, 244

parties agree on law of trader's
member state, 243, 245
parties do not agree on applicable
law, 243
political ideas, 193
preferential-law test, and, 238, 239,
244, 245–52, 261
protective standard, of, 234–7
Regulation Proposal, *see* Proposal
for a Regulation on a Common
European Sales Law (2011)
Rome I Regulation, and, 259, 260
secondary regime, as, 229–33
simplification, 217–21
Skov v. *Bilka*, 219
Standard Information Notice (SIN),
and, 209, 222, 224
Study Group on a European Civil
Code (SGECC), and, 195, 196,
197, 203
traders' preferences, 231
traditional laws, 217
transaction costs, and, 217, 256
voluntariness, and, 229–33
Common Frame of Reference (CFR),
194–208
consumer acquis, 28, 174
Acquis Communication (2004), and,
42, 167, 169, 170
broad sense, 162
Consumer Acquis Green Paper
(2007), 171
Consumer Law Compendium, 42–4,
48, 61, 167, 171, 174
Contract Law Action Plan (2003),
and, 42, 167, 169, 194
Contract Law Communication
(2001), and, 42, 167, 169, 194
CRD and CESL, 186–9
Directive, 169, 187
fragmentation, 169, 171, 263
harmonisation, and, 173
narrow sense, 162, 167
revision, 162, 263
standardising rules, and, 170
consumer confidence, 256, 283, 301
access to justice, and, 113

consumer confidence (*cont.*)
  access to justice 2.0, and, 264, 283,
    297, 317
  awareness, and, 313
  CESL, in, 234
  consumer information, and,
    299, 302
  cross-border B2C trade, in, 277,
    296, 311
  cross-border rights enforcement,
    in, 274
  ECC-Net, and, 312
  empowerment, and, *see* consumer
    empowerment
  EU law making, in, 283
  holistic approach to, 277
  improving, 155, 264, 276, 295
  internal market, in, 313
  legal structures, and, 61
  minimum harmonisation, and, 328,
    333, 334
  national standards, and, 173
  rights enforcement, in, 277
  value-oriented justice, and, 279
Consumer Credit Agreements
    Directive (2008), 90, 175, 185
consumer empowerment, 296, 333
  facilitating intermediaries approach,
    302–19, 334
  legislative approach, 300,
    319–32, 334
  procedural law pillar, 319–23
  substantive law pillar, 323–32
consumer protection, 326
  consumer confidence, and, 60, 234
  harmonisation, and, 159, 164, 334
  internal market, and, 40, 333
  national laws, and, 268
Consumer Protection Cooperation
    (CPC) Regulation (2004), 47, 52,
    60–72, 300
  alerts, 63
  competent authorities, 62, 68
  Consumer Protection Green Paper
    (2001), 60, 61
  CPC Evaluation report (2012), 68–70
  CPC Network, 62, 64, 65, 66, 67, 68, 70
  CPC Study report (2009), 65–6

CPC Study report (2012), 67–8
  enforcement measures requests, 63
  information requests, 63
  intra-CPC Network activities, 64, 66
  single liaison offices, 62, 68
  sweeps, 66, 67
Consumer Rights Directive (CRD)
    (2011)
  approach, 175, 184
  background and genesis, 169–78
  Consumer Sales Directive, and,
    174, 182
  Distance Selling Directive, and, 174,
    179, 182, 185
  Doorstop Selling Directive, and, 174,
    179, 182, 185, 186
  general information
    requirements, 180
  maximum harmonisation, 173, 174,
    175, 176, 178, 185
  Member States, and, 178
  minimum harmonisation, 175
  other consumer rights, and, 173,
    174, 185
  overview, 178–82
  regulatory choices, 184
  scope of application, 176
  targeted full harmonisation, 185
  Unfair Contract Terms Directive,
    and, 174, 179, 182, 183
  withdrawal rights, 180, 185
Consumer Rights Directive (CRD)
    Proposal (2008), 174–8
  Council of the European
    Union, 177
  European Commission, 173–7, 264
  European Parliament, 177, 188, 264
  harmonisation, 176
  overview, 175–6
  three-party negotiations, 177, 327
Consumer Sales Directive (1999), 178
  consumer acquis, and, 170
  CRD Proposal, and, 174
  CRD, and, 182
consumer trust
  access to justice 2.0, and, 282
  consumer empowerment, and,
    300, 333

cross-border B2C trade, in, 35,
282, 298
defragmentation of laws, and, 264
information, and, 284
internal market, in, 311, 333
judiciary, in, 147
language, and, 58, 315
legal compliance, and, 316
need for improving, 38
rights enforcement, and, 35, 38
Rome I Regulation, and, 208, 237
traders, 322, 333
translations, and, 315
unlawful practices, and, 41
consumers
access to justice, see access to
justice 2.0
CESL, see Common European Sales
Law (CESL)
confidence, see consumer
confidence
empowerment, see consumer
empowerment
information, 291, 295, 298, 299, 302
satisfaction, see satisfaction
contingency fees, see collective redress,
contingency fees
contracts, 214
cross-border, 214, 237, 257, 258
digital content, 214, 230, 257
distance, 178–80, 214, 257
off-premises, 178–80, 213
related services, 212, 214, 230
sales, 178, 212, 214, 230, 243, 318
costs, 78, 185, 256
alternative dispute resolution,
and, 83
collective enforcement, and, 119, 145
cost risk, 23, 78, 82, 140
cost-benefit analysis, 141
court, 38, 55, 128, 140, 270
cross-border legal aid, and, 58
lawyers, 21, 55, 128, 140
loser-pays principle, 23, 45, 72, 139,
140, 145
low-value claims, and, 72, 124
obstacle for pursuing claims, as, 45
preparation, 45

returning goods, of, 186
savings, 219, 291
scattered damages, see costs, low-
value claims, and
small claims, 78
transaction, 217–21
translation, 45
travel, 55, 58
Council of the European Union, 26,
57, 327
consumer access to justice, 267
cross-border transactions, 25, 51, 207,
214, 267–9
CESL, and, 211, 212, 221, 222, 234
information, and, 299
intra-community infringements,
41, 62
language, 58, 92, 315
legal environment, 54, 217
litigation difficulties, 38, 45, 225, 228
traders' legal knowledge, 318
defragmentation
consumer confidence, and, 264, 328
EU policy-making, 264
EU policy-making, and, 164, 264
fragmentation versus, 164, 169
harmonisation, and, 328
national laws, 164, 319
substantive laws, and, 164, 206, 264
deterrence, 123, 129
mass damages, and, 129
scattered damages, and, 129, 137
Directive on Consumer Rights (CRD)
(2011), see Consumer Rights
Directive (CRD) (2011)
disciplinary sanctions, 323
disputes, 35, 38, 85
alternative resolution, see alternative
dispute resolution
CPC Regulation, and, 72, 294
ECC-Net, and, 304, 305
EEJ-Net, and, 303
Florence Access-to-Justice Project,
and, 25, 102
Legal Aid Directive, and, 54, 57
Small Claims Regulation, and, 72,
82, 102

Distance Selling Directive (1997)
consumer acquis, and, 170
CRD and, 185
CRD Proposal, and, 174
repeal of, 179, 182
withdrawal rights and, 185
Doorstep Selling Directive (1985), 170
consumer acquis, and, 163, 169
CRD and, 185
CRD Proposal, 174
repeal of, 179, 182
withdrawal rights, and, 185
Draft Common Frame of Reference
(DCFR), 196–205
background, 200, 202
CESL, and, 197–200
contents, 196

ECC-Net, *see* European Consumer
Centres Network (ECC-Net)
Economic and Monetary Affairs
Committee (ECON), 255, 257
Enterprise Europe Network (EEN),
317–19
equality, 16
absolute, 9
Aristotle, and, 13
bargaining power, 249
justice, as, 6, 10, 12
Kelsen, Hans, and, 8–9
value-oriented justice, 18, 280
European Commission, 26
access to justice, and, 151, 264
Common European Sales Law, and,
see Common European Sales Law
(CESL)
consumer acquis, and, 171, 172
consumer policy-making, and, 27,
35, 36, 38, 274, 275
defragmentation, and, 169, 264
ECC-Net, and, 304, 316
harmonisation, and, 160, 167
internal market, and, 41, 60, 269, 276
market regulation approach, 158
maximum harmonisation, 158
European Consumer Centres Network
(ECC-Net)
additional tasks, 312

alternative dispute resolution, 304
benefits, 310
central contact point, as, 303
complex cases, and, 304, 305
consumer awareness, and, 306, 312
consumer confidence, and, 310
contacts, increasing, 313
cross-border redress, 304, 311
current activities, 303–6
current status, 306–9
Evaluation Report (2011), 296,
309–12
events, 314
facilitating cross-border B2C
trade, 302
facilitating intermediaries approach,
304, 305
future of, 312–17
improving impact, 309–12
information, and, 303, 313
language support, and, 316
possible additional activities,
313–16
simple complaints, and, 305
tasks, 303–6
traders, and, 299, 304
translation, and, 315
European Economic Community
(EEC), 34
European Parliament, 52, 327
collective redress, and, 111–14
CESL, 193, 209, 255, 257
consumer access to justice, 267
CRD Proposal, 177, 327
European Research Group on Existing
EC Private Law, *see* Acquis Group
Expert Group on a Common Frame
of Reference, *see* Common
European Sales Law (CESL), CESL
Expert Group

fairness, 14, 157, 214, 289–91
access to justice 2.0, and, 6, 291
consumer laws, 121, 155, 157, 158
contractual, and, 289–91
justice, as, 6
mandatory laws, and, 285, 290
party autonomy, and, 290

paternalism, and, 284–8
proceedings, 87
value-oriented justice, 18, 280
Financial Services Distance Contracts
Directive (2002), 162
Florence Access-to-Justice Project
access to justice, 24, 33, 84, 102, 150
diffuse interests, 23, 33, 102
first wave, 24, 53
legal aid, 53
procedural laws, and, 102
scope of, 19, 102
second wave, 118
substantive laws,and, 24
third wave, 84
value-oriented justice, 19, 24
waves, 20
fragmentation, 169, 228
Acquis Communication (2004), and,
169, 170
consumer acquis, 170, 263
Contract Law Action Plan (2003),
and, 169
Contract Law Communication
(2001), and, 169
harmonisation, and, 263, 264
internal market, 263
national, 171, 208, 218, 225
substantive laws, 228
full harmonisation, see maximum
harmonisation

harmonisation
better law making, and, 164, 263,
326, 332
CRD approach, 175–8
European Commission, 49, 188, 263
Full, see maximum harmonisation
high-level minimum, see minimum
harmonisation
legislative stagnation, and, 325
maximum, see maximum
harmonisation
Member States, 206
minimum, see minimum
harmonisation
national policy-making, and,
159, 325

simplification, and, 172
social justice, and, 155, 159
targeted full, 185, 328, 334
value-oriented justice, 158

illegal business practices, 41, 46, 60,
102, 300
individual well-being
consumer laws, and, 283, 298, 333
justice, and, 333
social justice, and, 282, 283
value-oriented justice, and, 280, 283
information, 34, 82, 180, 223
accurate, 284
ADR and ODR, 100
consumer, 36, 180
consumer confidence, and, 295,
301, 313
consumer empowerment, and, 299,
302, 306
CRD, and, 179, 180, 184
distance contracts, and, 180
ECC-Net, 299
exchange of, 170, 182
facilitating intermediaries approach,
and, 299, 300, 303
lack of legal, 23, 292
mandatory pre-contractual (CRD),
178, 180, 213
non-compliance, 322
obtaining, 218
off-premises contracts, and, 180,
184, 214
sector-specific requirements, 180
stakeholders, other than consumers
or traders, 317
supplying consumers, 292, 299
traders, and, 298, 301, 302, 304, 314,
318, 319, 323
Injunctions Directive, 40–53, 170
Case law, 44
cessation orders, 46
complexity of legal proceedings,
45, 46
CPC Regulation, and, 46
domestic, 41, 50
financial risk, 45
Injunctions Directive (1998), 40–4

Injunctions Directive (*cont.*)
  Injunctions Directive (2009), 44–8
  Injunctions Directive report
    (2008), 44–7
  Injunctions Directive report
    (2012), 48–52
  intra-community infringement, 43
  lack of guidance, 48
  length of legal proceedings, 45, 46
  minimum harmonisation, 41, 48
  qualified entities, 41, 42, 46, 49
  scope of application, 40, 48, 51
interests, 144
  business, 138, 276, 278, 302
  collective, 24, 33, 62, 102, 119–24,
    132, 136
  consumer, 37, 40–2, 60, 64, 70, 102,
    103, 137–9, 276, 278, 306
  diffuse, *see* interests, collective
  harmonisation, and, 276, 328, 330
  individual, 71, 108, 119, 120, 135
  interest representation, 177, 203,
    300, 306
  Member States, 327
  multilayer interests, *see* multilayer
    interests
  policy-making, and, 16, 276, 280, 327
  public, 102, 119–20, 122, 123, 136–9
internal market, 150
  barriers, 165
  CESL, and, 161, 190, 202, 216, 233, 256
  changing approaches, 263
  consumer confidence, 61, 173, 276
  defragmentation, and, 164, 319
  enhancing, 28, 37, 41, 267
  fragmentation, and, 225, 263
  harmonisation, and, 159, 175, 188,
    325, 328
  policy-making, and, 263, 267, 275
  potential, 296
  traditional approach, 163
Internal Market and Consumer
    Protection Committee (IMCO),
    255, 256

judicial system, 6, 17, 24
  access to justice, 33
  affordability, 20, 33, 58, 126
  consumer confidence, and, 128

  disinclination towards, 36
  effective, 280
  justice, and, 280
  lack of information, 23
  procedural laws, and, 17, 27
  psychological barriers, 23
  trust, in, 20, 147
justice, 5, 280
  absolute, 9
  access to, 18–27
  access to 2.0, 27–30, 281–3
  Aristotle, and, 10–13
  consumer confidence, and, 113, 155,
    278, 279, 283
  corrective, 10–13, 156, 157, 280
  distributive, 10–13, 159, 282
  formal, 7, 17, 280
  harmonisation, and, 75, 156, 159
  holistic approach to, 161
  judicial system, and, 17–25, 280
  Kelsen, Hans, and, 8–9
  key observations, 16–18
  laws, and, 17, 18, 121, 288–91
  non-valuing, 6
  Rawls, John, and, 13–16
  relative, 9
  social, *see* social justice
  societal stability, 16
  substantive, 6, 17, 24, 280
  value-oriented, *see* value-oriented
    justice
  welfare state, 265, 285
  well-being, 280, 282, 283, 285, 333

language, 3
  access to justice, 18
  alternative dispute resolution, 92
  barriers, 91, 133, 315
  cost risk, 79
  costs, and, 78
  documents, of, 74, 79
  ECC-Net, 315
  enforcement, 79
  lawyers, 59
  legal aid, and, 58
  small claims, 79
Legal Affairs Committee (JURI), 255,
    256, 257, 258
legal aid, 20–3, 25, 53, 58

access to justice, and, 20–3
cross-border, 22, 54, 57, 59, 60
directive, see Legal Aid Directive
    (2003)
European Agreement on
    Transmission of Applications of
    Legal Aid (1977), 53
Florence Access-to-Justice Project,
    and, 22, 53
Hague Convention on International
    Access to Justice (1980), 53
Tampere Council, 54
Legal Aid Directive (2003), 53–60
alternative dispute resolution, 56
application stage, 55
appointing lawyers, 58
awareness, lack of, 59
competent authorities, 55
costs, and, 55
guidelines, lack of, 150
Legal Aid Directive report
    (2012), 57–60
main proceedings, 55, 56
standard application form, 56
legal insurance, 145, 204, 220
liberalism, 284–6
mandatory law and, 288
market regulation, and, 284
party autonomy, and, 288
paternalism, and, 284–6
soft paternalism, and, 286–8
third-party intervention, and, 286–8

mandatory law, 288–91
consumer law, and, 244, 285, 288–95
criticism, 291
fairness, and, 285, 290
liberalism, and, 285, 292
party autonomy, and, 285, 289
paternalism, and, 285
preferential-law test, and, 250
Rome I Regulation, and, 239, 246,
    249, 250
maximum harmonisation, 185
approach, 175, 184
business interests, 276
CESL, and, 186, 206
consumer acquis, and, 173, 174
consumer laws, and, 275, 276, 324

consumer perspective, 185
CRD, 178, 184, 185
CRD Proposal, 174
defragmentation, 264
European Commission, and, 173, 181
full harmonisation, and, 264
inflexibility, 276
Member States, and, 158, 159,
    163, 325
minimum harmonisation, versus,
    48, 163, 263, 275, 328
Package Travel Directive proposal,
    and, 187
Policy shift, 48, 324
problems with, 159, 176, 275, 324–8
shift to, 48, 159, 164
social justice, and, 159
standard of protection, 175,
    176, 328
Timeshare Directive, new, and,
    184, 187
Mediation Directive (2008), 83–9
ADR Directive, and, 90–7
Mediation Directive Proposal
    (2004), 87
minimum harmonisation
approach, 163, 332
consumer acquis, and, 171, 173, 263
fragmentation, and, 263, 264
high-level, 328, 329, 332, 334
maximum/full harmonisation,
    versus, 48, 163, 263, 275, 328
Member States, and, 41, 164,
    185, 275
national interests, 263
shift from, 48, 274, 275
standard of protection, 238, 328
misleading advertising, 50, 65
model standard contracts (CESL), 255
multilayer interests, 118–24
collective actions, as, 122
collective redress, and, 121–4
Deutsche Telekom case, 120
enforcement of consumer laws,
    and, 121
examples of, 118–21
mass damages, and, 123–4, 140–2
mass justice, 123
scattered damages, and, 124, 133–40

non-valuing justice, 6, 16, 17, 18,
    278, 280

online dispute resolution, 25, 97, 101
    ADR, and, 99
    advisors, 100
    availability, 320
    complaints, 100
    contact point, 100
    criticism, 98
    enforceability, 101
    ODR Regulation (2013), 97–101
    platform, 100
    procedure, 99
opt-in mechanisms, 132, 143
    Collective Redress
        Recommendation (2013), 117
    mass damages, and, 141–2
    rational disinterest, and, 133
    scattered damages, and, 133–4
optional instruments, 200–2
opt-out mechanisms, 132, 143, 144
    Collective Redress
        Recommendation (2013), 146
    concerns, 134, 136
    deterrence effect, and, 133, 137
    mass damages, and, 141
    misuse, 138, 141
    scattered damages, and, 134–8

Package Travel Directive (1990),
    170, 174
    consumer acquis, and, 171, 172
    Package Travel Directive Proposal
        (2013), 172, 174, 187
party autonomy, 237, 288, 289, 290, 291
    contractual fairness, 289–91
    liberalism, and, 288–91
    mandatory law, and, 288, 289
    soft paternalism, and, 288
paternalism, 284–6
    hard, 284, 286–8
    liberalism, versus, 284–8
    soft, 286–8
policy-making
    balancing interests, 280
    better law-making, 172, 263
    consumer confidence, 297

consumer protection, 268, 275
    directives, and, 163, 164, 166, 324
    internal market, 263, 268, 275
    justice, 13, 17, 156, 280
    maximum harmonisation, 48, 275
    minimum harmonisation, 163
    procedural tools, 13
    substantive laws, 164, 263, 264, 276
    tensions, 264
Price Indication Directive (1998), 170
    consumer acquis, and, 171
procedural laws, 33, 269–74, 320
    access to justice, 17, 39
    access to justice 2.0, 27, 28, 29, 161
    availability, 270, 319
    awareness, 269, 270, 319
    broadening framework, 333
    common deficiencies, 274
    consumer empowerment, and,
        319–23
    consumer information, 292
    development, 35
    disciplinary sanctions, 323
    effectiveness, 33, 319, 321
    legislative approach, 269, 319
    non-compliance lists, 321
    sectoral problems, 274
    skills/experience, 270, 319
    technical, 270
    trader compliance, 270
    usability, 270, 319, 321
Product Liability Directive (1985), 219
proportionality, 75, 233
    CESL, 206, 325
    cost increase (collective redress), 78
Proposal for a Regulation on a
        Common European Sales Law
        (2011), 167, 190, 209, 210
    CESL Regulation Proposal, after,
        255–62
    protection, 13, 26, 171, 234
    consumer, see consumer protection
    level, 267, 325, 326

rational disinterest, 38, 125, 128, 134,
    140, 148
    amounts in dispute, and, 38,
        128, 133

collective redress, and, 127, 129,
141, 147
  costs, and, 38
  individual redress, and, 133, 140
  mass damages, and, 140–2
  overcoming, 127, 134
  scattered damages, and, 128,
  129, 133
  scattered rights, and, 125
  thresholds, 144
remediation, 129, 131
  deterrence, and, 129
  interest in, 131
  redress, and, 129
Rome I Regulation, 237–54
Round Table of European key
  stakeholders in the area of
  contract law, see Common
  European Sales Law (CESL), CESL
  Key Stakeholders Group, and

satisfaction, 17, 280, 282, 283
  consumer, 28, 264, 283, 288
  individual well-being, and, 283
  value-oriented justice, and, 27,
  280
sectoral consumer directives, 35, 163, 169
  consumer acquis, and, 162, 169
  Consumer Law Compendium, and,
  42, 48, 171
  defragmentation, 164
  fragmentation, 164
  minimum harmonisation, 163
  shift from, 162, 164
  withdrawal rights regime, 169
simplification, 25, 70
  better law making, 172
  CESL, and, 217, 218, 259
  consumer policy-making, and, 172
  harmonisation, and, 172
  internal market, 175
  substantive laws, and, 325
small claims, 77
  costs, and, 78–9
  language issues, and, 79
  national regulation of, 72
  Small Claims Green Paper (2002), 73
  Small Claims Regulation (2007), 71–82

awareness, lack of, 77
communication means, alternative,
  and, 81
cost risk, and, 78
court fees, and, 78
ECC-Net ESCP Study (2012), 77–80
enforcing judgments, 73, 74
Eurobarometer ESCP Study
  (2013), 80–1
fast judgments, and, 77
language-based risks, and, 79
oral hearings, 78, 81
practical issues, 76
procedure, 73–5
Small Claims Regulation Proposal
  (2013), new, 81, 82
social justice, 159, 281–3
  equal distribution, and, 281
  harmonisation, and, 156, 158
  law and economics, and, 156
  market stimulation, and, 295
  policy-making, and, 13, 157, 281
  Social Justice Manifesto, 156, 157,
  158, 281
  value-oriented justice, and, 155
  welfare state, and, 265, 281
  well-being, and, 282
standard terms, 102, 292–5, 300
standardisation, 245,
  see harmonisation
  directives of, 171
  level of, 263
Stockholm Programme, 57
Study Group on a European Civil Code
  (SGECC), 195, 196, 197, 203
substantive laws, 274–6
  access to justice, 18, 25, 27
  access to justice 2.0, 28, 29, 280
  binding underlying principles,
  and, 330
  consumer confidence, and, 277,
  278, 328
  consumer empowerment, and,
  323–32
  development of, 163, 274
  harmonisation, 274, 324
  high-level minimum
  harmonisation, 329

substantive laws (*cont.*)
  legislative approach, and, 323–32
  maximum harmonisation, 333
  minimum harmonisation, 263, 274
  model laws, and, 330
  national differences, in, 328
  policy-making, shift in, 263,
    274, 324
Tampere Council, 54, 61, 72, 86, 87
test cases, 107, 108, 132, 134
  collective redress, 120, 144
  enhanced, 142
  mass damages, 141, 142
  scattered damages, 133, 137
third-party funding, 118, 146
third-party intervention, 286–95
  consumer confidence, and, 288
  consumer empowerment, and, 300,
    302–19
  criticism, 286
  ECC-Net, 302
  imbalance of power, 291
  information, lack of, 291
  liberalism, and, 284–8
  mandatory law, and, 288–91
  need for, 295
  party autonomy, 288
  paternalism versus liberalism, 284
  paternalism, and, 284–8
  soft paternalism, 286–8
  types of, 283, 301
Timeshare Directive (1994), 185
  Consumer Acquis Green Paper
    (2007), 172
  consumer acquis, and, 170
  maximum harmonisation, 187
  minimum harmonisation, 174
Timeshare Directive (2009), 174,
    175, 187

traders
  clarity, 217, 218
  compliance, 41, 47, 201, 300
  EEN, and, 317, 318, 319
  ECC-Net, and, 318, 319
  interest representation, 109, 177, 203
  legal knowledge, lack of, 92, 317
  mandatory participation in ADR,
    96, 97
  rogue, 69
trust, *see* consumer trust

unfair commercial practices, 50, 65
  UCPD (2005), 166
unfair contract terms, 50, 300
  contractual freedom, and, 289
  fighting, 316
  national rules, and, 182
  UCTD, *see* Unfair Contract Terms
    Directive (UCTD) (1993)
Unfair Contract Terms Directive
  (UCTD) (1993), 97, 102, 214
  consumer acquis, and, 170
  CRD, 177, 178
  CRD Proposal, 174, 176, 182
unwillingness to sue theory, 124, 125

value-oriented justice, 6–18, 155–61
  consumer, 27, 29, 161, 278
  consumer confidence, and, 280
  consumer interest representation,
    300, 306
  law making, 280
  need for, 278
  parameters, 280
  policy-making, and, 17–25, 27, 280
  procedure, and, 17

welfare state, 22, 265
well-being, 281–3